THE THIRD REICH FROM ORIGINAL SOURCES

I KNEW HITLER

The lost testimony by a survivor from the Night of the Long Knives

KURT G. W. LUDECKE

Edited and introduced by Bob Carruthers

Pen & Sword
MILITARY

This edition published in 2013 by
Pen & Sword Military
An imprint of
Pen & Sword Books Ltd
47 Church Street
Barnsley
South Yorkshire
S70 2AS

First published in Great Britain in 2011 in digital format by
Coda Books Ltd.

Copyright © Coda Books Ltd, 2011
Published under licence by Pen & Sword Books Ltd.

ISBN 978 1 78159 223 6

A CIP catalogue record for this book is
available from the British Library

Printed and bound by CPI Group (UK) Ltd, Croydon, CR0 4YY

Pen & Sword Books Ltd incorporates the Imprints of Pen & Sword Aviation, Pen & Sword
Family History, Pen & Sword Maritime, Pen & Sword Military, Pen & Sword Discovery, Pen
& Sword Politics, Pen & Sword Atlas, Pen & Sword Archaeology, Wharncliffe Local History,
Wharncliffe True Crime, Wharncliffe Transport, Pen & Sword Select, Pen & Sword Military
Classics, Leo Cooper, The Praetorian Press, Claymore Press, Remember When, Seaforth
Publishing and Frontline Publishing

For a complete list of Pen & Sword titles please contact
PEN & SWORD BOOKS LIMITED
47 Church Street, Barnsley, South Yorkshire, S70 2AS, England
E-mail: enquiries@pen-and-sword.co.uk
Website: www.pen-and-sword.co.uk

CONTENTS

INTRODUCTION

T he book you now hold in your hands is one of the key primary sources on the early life and times of Adolf Hitler. For many years "I Knew Hitler", the memoirs of Kurt Ludecke, were discarded as the vain posturings of a get rich quick fantasist attempting to hitch his wagon to the rising star of one of the most famous politicians in Europe. Increasingly historians have come to reassess Ludecke and in the process have come to accept the voracity of much of what you are about to read here. It is now widely accepted that Ludecke is essentially an accurate, if somewhat self-aggrandising source. Until recent years, and the rehabilitation of Ludecke, scholars and general readers seeking a primary insight into the early life of Adolf Hitler have had to be content with the recollections of his boyhood friend Kubizek and his sometime business associate Reinhold Hanisch; a companion from the Vienna men's hostel. Both of these sources are generally accepted to be accurate accounts of life with Hitler. Add to this the memoirs of his war comrades and a few recent pieces which have come to light such as Alexander Moritz Frey's account of his war time experiences with Hitler and their subsequent encounters in Munich and somewhat astonishingly the main sources have all been covered. There is very little else to build upon with the result that the recent sympathetic analysis and acceptance by the wider academic community of the Ludecke memoirs gives us a highly detailed "new" and very welcome source from which to attempt to gain a better understanding of the man behind the Third Reich.

What makes Ludecke especially interesting is the fact that his memoirs were first published in 1938. At that time, although Hitler was already known as the demagogue of the far right he was not yet the monster which history now knows him to be. At the time Ludecke was writing, Hitler's most despicable deeds still lay in the future and we can therefore approach Ludecke safe in the knowledge that, although he was writing about a well-known politician, his subject had not yet achieved the universal infamy, which now attaches to his name. Ludecke is not therefore an obvious bandwagon jumper such as the now discredited Josef Greiner who simply invented much, if not all, of his sensational autobiographies. It is fitting therefore that in losing Greiner we have "found" Ludecke who is by far the more interesting character.

Kurt Ludecke was born in Berlin on 5th February 1890 less than a year later than Adolf Hitler, the man who was to become both his hero and his nemesis. Like Hitler, Ludecke was a fervent German nationalist. Also like Hitler he was something of a dilettante, but while the young Hitler lacked the funds to live the life of the Bohemian artist, Ludecke was able to used his sharp business sense to amass a personal fortune which allowed him to trot around the globe enjoying the trappings of the life of a well heeled playboy and international traveller. Following a spell in a mental institution in 1916, Ludecke had managed to have himself discharged from the army and once more headed abroad where he was able to use his verbal skills to continue to create wealth for himself. In the grim aftermath of the Great War Ludecke finally gave up his wandering ways and returned to Germany where he joined the National Socialist Workers Party in the early 1920s.

Prior to attending a rally at which Hitler was to be featured as a speaker, Ludecke had assumed that Hitler was simply just "one more fanatic" spouting rhetoric on the fringes of the Völkisch movement. However, the experience of actually hearing Hitler speak at a mass demonstration at the Konigsplatz in Munich was to prove a turning point in Ludecke's life. Awed and inspired by what he had just witnessed, Ludecke underwent a conversion of almost religious proportions. His experience was of such overwhelming intensity that Ludecke immediately decided to adopt Hitler as his heroic idol. Ludecke, in common with so many others was ecstatic in response to Hitler's amazing powers of rhetoric and as a result was so totally overwhelmed by the occurrence that he appears to have experienced a personal epiphany. Ludecke describes the momentous event in glowing terms: "His appeal to German manhood was like a call to arms, the gospel he preached a sacred truth." The next day Ludecke was privileged to gain access to the Fürher with whom he spoke for four hours and as a result of which Ludecke states that he offered himself to Hitler and the Nazi cause: "…without reservation I had given him my soul."

As a trusted senior party member, Ludecke used his social connections to raise money for the NSDAP. Soon after the Italian dictator Benito Mussolini marched on Rome and thereby seized power in Italy, Ludecke offered his services to Hitler as a National Socialist envoy to Mussolini. His attempts to raise money from Mussolini were however completely unsuccessful.

Undeterred, Ludecke turned his focus to improving Nazi public relations and did in fact manage a small coup in persuading Mussolini to send Dr. Leo Negrelli to Munich to interview Hitler on 16th October 1923 for a feature for the main Italian paper Corriere Italiano. This at least provided some much needed visibility for the Nazis in Italy, but what the party really needed, of course, was money.

Funding was always a desperate issue for The National Socialists and it should always be borne in mind that one of the original functions of the SS was to sell advertising space in the Völkischer Beöbachter. Faced with the chronic and on-going lack of funding, Ludecke embarked on a mission to appeal for funds to Henry Ford in Michigan. Wagner's children provided Ludecke's introduction to the famous industrial mogul Siegfried and Winifred Wagner, who were also staunch Hitler supporters. Despite the fact that Ford, at the time, was a vocal and highly aggressive anti-Semite even he would not contribute funds to the struggling Nazi

Party and Ludecke's star was soon on the wane.

On his return to Germany the murky world of politics soon intervened and Ludecke, as a keen and fairly high profile supporter of Ernst Roehm, increasingly found himself out of favour with Hitler who was growing increasingly distrustful of Roehm and the SA. Ludecke rapidly fell further in Hitler's estimation, twice finding himself incarcerated before eventually escaping to Switzerland and from there moving to the USA.

Ludecke finally returned to Germany in the 1950's and died peacefully at the age of 70 in 1960 at Prien am Chiemsee here in Bavaria.

Bob Carruthers
Berchtesgaden June 2011.

IN MEMORY OF

CAPTAIN ERNST ROEHM

AND

GREGOR STRASSER

AND

MANY OTHER NAZIS WHO WERE BETRAYED,

MURDERED, AND TRADUCED IN

THEIR GRAVES

ORIGINAL PREFACE

Having nothing to lose, I can afford to tell the unadorned truth as I see it, limited only by my conscience and considerations of good taste, stifling as much as I can that love of self which dominates, consciously or subconsciously, all our thinking and doing.

In the eyes of a cynic, the expression of liberal views may be what is after all the business of an exile.' Not considering myself an exile in the ordinary sense, blown across the ocean to strike root in alien soil, I have taken the liberty to write as I please.

I do not claim entire neutrality in thought, which is impossible, nor do I pretend to be free of contradictions. Only a fool does not let his judgment guide him, as it will. Goethe says: 'Nichts ist inkonsequenter als die groesste Konsequenz, weil sie umschlaegt und unnatuerliche Phaenomene zeitigt.'

The writing of this story, in a language not my own, has condemned me to re-live my life for two long years - an agony which often filled me with despair.

Though moods of maudlin self-pity, sharp self-criticism, or cynical contempt of all accepted values made it difficult sometimes to remain within the boundaries of common sense and maintain the right proportions, I have made an earnest effort throughout to be honest.

My ambition was to create a picture of the development and evolution of Hitler and the Hitler system, and at the same time reconstruct the emotions and thoughts of my former self in order to reveal for all to see the process of the progressive disillusionment of a Nazi revolutionary activist.

I wish to express my gratitude for my publishers' patience and understanding during this crucial period.

My wife has already done so much for me that the physical and moral assistance she has again given me in this work can but spur me to compensate her for what she has suffered through me.

The whole tenor of the book should convey sufficiently what I state here explicitly: there are no sour grapes drooping over my story. Looking backwards, I have long realized that even had I avoided colliding with Hitler when I did, I would have come in conflict with him sooner or later. I have the capacity to adapt myself to many things, but never would I have learned to submit myself completely to the will of the Fuehrer and his satellites, who know the forces and the whims which make worms of most men.

In view of rumours already circulating about the 'Ludecke Case,' I wish to point to a letter from Philip Bouhler, chief of Hitler's chancellery of the Party and Reich secretary of the Party, which is reproduced in the appendix. This letter, written almost a year after my escape, is conclusive evidence first, that the Supreme Court of the Party had no jurisdiction in my case, because I was Hitler's personal prisoner; and second, that the highest Party leaders and Reich ministers were inclined to settle this matter because my arrest had been unwarranted.

I have sinned, strived, suffered, and survived. I am a free man at last. The end of this book is the beginning of a new life, which is less a process of reformation and regeneration than it is the natural realization of a new self, which I hope will be better than my former self.

K. L.

Sea Spray Inn on the Dunes,
East Hampton, Long Island,
September 1937.

I

I MEET HITLER

My thirty-second year seems to me the true starting point of my story, for it was then that my scattered life became concentrated into a purpose. After years of wandering, I came back to a land that had repeatedly sent me away in disgust because it was diseased. I came back because at last I had faced the truth I had been dodging: so long as Germany was sick, there would be no happiness for me until I lent my hand to those who were trying to work out a cure. I was to flounder and make false beginnings, but before the year was out a man was to vitalize me as if he had sent a galvanic current through my body.

That man will be as important to this book as he has been, for good or evil, to the whole world.

1922

Spring in Berlin, trees in full bloom, fragrance pervading Unter den Linden, the Pariserplatz, the Tiergarten, Potsdam and its beautiful park of Sans Souci. And yet even the birds did not seem to sing so lustily as in the old days.

Everything I saw seemed sad or crazy. The sickness of the post-war period had infected all classes. For two or three years after the revolution of 1918, the Marxian element had dominated and cheapened social life. By now, however, all the better-class people who still had some means were reappearing, trying to live and forget-forget the war, forget the peace which had stripped Germany of its national self-respect. Jazz, in its manifold corrupting forms, was the national anodyne.

Inflation was growing, and the flight from the mark had begun. With the financial system unstable, all standards were collapsing. It was everybody for himself - 'apres nous le deluge.' Change and decay became visible everywhere. Everything was artificial and cheap, and now I understood the decline of our prestige abroad and the justice of those bitter complaints I had heard that German merchants were not living up to their contracts.

Many are the parallels between developments in Russia and in Germany after the crushing of the eagles. No better picture could be painted than General Krassnoff's masterful description of the Russian tragedy, From Double Eagle to Red Flag. It is a pity that no German of Krassnoff's genius and class has told the drama of his own country, a story which might aptly be titled Vom Reicksadler zum Pleitegeier.[1]

---

1 Pleitegeier: the vulture of bankruptcy.

There is only Fallada's sad little tale, Little Man, What now?

To understand the defunct German Republic and the amazing story of the Nazi triumph one must realize that the 'revolution' of November, 1918, had been no true revolution but a general breakdown and compromise on the part of all factions. When the military commanders at home surrendered to the street in the most' cowardly capitulation of all time, and generals in the field accepted the revolutionary coup as an accomplished fact, the 'new' men in Berlin who had lived in fear of the strength and loyalty of the army were astounded to find that the power was theirs; that it had, in fact, virtually been forced upon them at a time when the State machine was at dead-centre.

But the burden of power weighed heavily; the new "leaders" were actually afraid of it, for they did not know how to govern. Largely under the guidance of intellectual Jews, they were by no means genuine Red revolutionists, but petty bourgeois backed by workers of bourgeois sympathies. They were more interested in their own little social ambitions than zealous in statecraft. Being without talent for government, without ideas or ideals, instead of fighting relentlessly for the realization of their Marxian theories they did everything that might tend to encourage their enemies. Soon those irreconcilable enemies, Communists and Tories, discovered that they had little to fear, and much to gain by unscrupulous activity.

Thus the new regime found itself confronted on one hand by the 'Red Menace' and the other by internal intrigues set afoot by the old military order, which had adroitly saddled the governmental authorities with the responsibility for the armistice and the shackles of the Versailles Treaty. The Republic was soon the plaything of the moneyed interests, a tool for speculation, greed, and unsocial aims. Old groups of influence and power, who under the Empire had screened their ambitions by standing behind the militarized nobles, the Junkers, and the nominal masters of industry, now stepped brazenly into the open in partnership with Jews who even before the war had controlled vital national interests. Old parties took new names and appeared in the political arena with the same men. The Press was conscienceless, printing what it pleased without regard for either the truth or the national welfare. The war-bred apathy of the people permitted scandals to continue. And the one real and concrete power, the mighty old German Army, which under able guidance could have set this mad-house in order, had disappeared as one of the penalties of the surrender to the Allies.

During this inglorious period of transition, those parties which followed a middle course, notably the Democratic, Centrist, and Bavarian People's Party, swung the scale that was balanced by the Right and the Left. And over them all, officially, was the State, timid as a mouse.

The frustration of two direct efforts to Bolshevize Europe by raising the Red Flag in its central states was no victory for the Marxian Republicans. It was due to self-sacrificing action on the part of the 'Frei-Korps,' unofficial volunteer groups made up mainly of veterans of the old army. The collapse of the brief Soviet regime in Hungary was followed by the failure of a similar attempt in Munich, after the assassination of the Jew, Kurt Eisner, the first Republican minister of Bavaria. These were ominous defeats for Moscow, which had planned a world revolution. But the Red elements had retired only temporarily; they might spring into action again at any moment.

Abroad, Germany was under relentless pressure, in the West from the French and in the East from the Poles and the Czechs, vassals of France. And at home, adding the final touch of confusion, the mark sagged hopelessly to ever lower levels.

In this dilemma the threat of action from the Right against Berlin grew more imminent. At times the situation was so critical that the important heads of the Government more than once invited intervention by the French, in the hope of stirring up the cry of 'peril' and strengthening their hold by the dangerous expedient of 'um Schlimmeres zu verhueten' -anything to prevent the worst - a never-failing argument with the German Spiessbuerger, the petty cafe politician.

Expediency also drove the Government to seek the help of the Nationalists, who, themselves fearful of events, gladly joined forces to combat the menace of Bolshevism. The anti-militaristic Republic needed soldiers, and these the Nationalists were able to provide in the practical form of 'Frei-Korps' and 'Selbstschutz-verbaende' - Free Corps and Unions for Self-Protection.

These Frei-Korps, a peculiar post-war phenomenon, were constantly being organized by officers of the old army, with governmental sanction. They included men of all classes, but principally the middle class. Many of them were ardently patriotic, but the majority were probably men who simply could not resume civilian life after the great adventure of the war. They had neither homes nor professions to return to, no work, no hope for the future. War had become their metier, their livelihood and way of life. The Government not only tolerated them but offered them abundant activity in dealing with border disputes and the internal conflicts of the day, and in protecting property and maintaining law and order.

These Frei-Korps actually saved the Marxian Socialists from defeat at the hands of militant Communism. But they lacked programmes and political ideals, and were acting on instructions from the Government rather than on their own initiative. Their usefulness over, they were dismissed without reward or thanks.

But these were embittered and desperate men who now had nothing to lose, and large numbers of them turned against the Republic with fanatical zeal. Disobeying the dissolution order, they retained their arms, formed secret societies, and began to exercise political terrorism. An example is the notorious organization which assassinated Rathenau and Erzberger. Forces which had formerly worked for stability were now contributing to the general chaos.

A print of a painting by Hoyer entitled 'In The Beginning Was The Word'. Widely distributed in the Third Reich the painting was obviously intended to feature a clear reference to the opening of the biblical Gospel of John. This somewhat stylised image nonetheless captures the flavour of what it must have been like to hear Hitler speak.

The collapse of the poorly organized Nationalist revolt known as the Kapp-Putsch and the liquidation of the Communist rebellions gave Marxian Berlin a breathing-spell, however, and enabled it to set about the liquidation of the old Nationalist Germany, and to attempt its moral and material disarmament. The way now seemed open for foes inside and outside the country to exterminate the remaining groups of national activists.

Nationalist circles could no longer postpone a showdown with the forces working to destroy the State, and in this critical hour the national movement of 'Voelkische' or 'folkic' resistance was born.

The problem of national survival had become not only acute, but incredibly complicated. For the sake of clarifying events to come, I must detail, as briefly as possible, the various leading forces contending for supremacy.

One must remember that under the Empire the German states had enjoyed a high degree of autonomy which the new Republic was gradually curtailing. In Protestant Prussia, comprising two-thirds of the Republic, the anti-national elements-the Marxists, Pacifists, Liberals, Democrats, and Centrists-had compromised with each other until they had things fairly well under their control. But in Catholic Bavaria, the second most important state, the situation was different. After the crushing of the Red terror in Munich in 1919, a decidedly nationalistic course had been adopted, particularly by Ernst Poehner, Munich's new police-president. The Kapp-Putsch, though a failure, had nevertheless brought to Bavaria a government of the Right, headed by Doctor Gustav von Kahr, the outstanding personalities being Poechner and Doctor Wilhelm Frick, who to-day is Germany's Minister of the Interior.

Munich thus became the stronghold of patriotic resistance dedicated to a national rebirth, the stamping-ground of violent anti-Republicans and anti-Jews, many of them Prussian political activists now being sought by the Berlin police.

The Catholics, a powerful factor in the Reichstag, were organized in two political parties, the Bavarian People's Party in Bavaria, and the Centrist Party in the rest of Germany. They worked as a unit, however, with the same platform, and differed only in name. Needing their support, Protestant-Jewish Berlin made temporary concessions to Catholic Munich. Berlin's price for a hands-off policy toward Munich was the Centrist Party's help in destroying Prussia's power. This was the 'Black-Red-Gold International,' and there were those who said that it had been victorious once before. In the World War, they alleged, this inner entente had worked with outside forces for the defeat of Germany; then the fall of the German Emperor - the 'Protestant Pope' - had been Rome's price for her alliance with the international money trust.

As a result of this new alliance, the Marxian and Centrist Parties co-operated in the North, whereas in the South, the 'ultramontanes' (a sobriquet implying that political Catholic Centrists kept one ear cocked toward the Vatican beyond the Alps) drew a sharp line between the Marxists and themselves. This was logical, for it was their ambition to enlist the aid of France, of the Vatican, and of international Jewry to set up a new Austro-Bavarian Catholic state which would replace the Austro-Hungarian monarchy, whose dissolution had been so severe a loss for Rome.

At that time, the strongest of the so-called 'Unions for Self-Protection' was the well-armed 'Einwohnerwehr,' financed by the Junkers and by big industry, and protected by the Government. In the autumn of 1921, protests from France brought about the disbanding of this organization and the resignation of the Bavarian Prime Minister, Doctor von Kahr. He was replaced by Count von Lerchenfeld - a man more convenient for the Centrists.

Following the practice of similar unions which had been declared dissolved, the Einwohnerwehr soon re-formed its ranks under a new name, the 'Bund Bayern und Reich', headed by von Kahr's right-hand man, a Doctor Pittinger, who was also the confidant of Crown Prince Rupprecht of Bavaria. This time, however, the resurrected organization did not dare to bear weapons openly, for the period of armed societies, forbidden by the Treaty of Versailles but at first tolerated and supported by the German Government, had been officially pronounced at an end.

Confronted with the prospect of declining into obscurity, the leaders of the protective societies were now forced to take sides and to declare unequivocally for whom and for what they stood. The immediate problem was that of their own existence: the necessity of retaining and increasing their followers. The result was all: intensified rivalry among themselves which made the cleavage between the merely Nationalist and the folkic or racialist elements more apparent.

No master-leader rose up to unite these conflicting organizations in their one common aim - the fight against Berlin. Yet there was not room enough in Germany for them all to exist. The struggle for the survival of the fittest began to run its course through jealousies and conspiracies, in which antagonisms alternated with alliances as expediency might demand. Violence increased everywhere, fear and uncertainty were in the air, and the huge, helpless body of the German people drifted along in aimless, planless fashion, with little hope for the future.

This was the situation in Germany when I set about looking for a leader and a cause.

There was a hard apprenticeship ahead of me. I made the rounds, going from place to place, from group to group, confused, bewildered, diving now and again into the mad scramble for diversion that surrounded me, but unhappy always with a nostalgia for the proud Germany of my youth. I was looking for the German soul, or rather for the leader who would know how to reanimate it, and I was resolved not to desert again.

Among the first of many 'leaders' I encountered was an intelligent high-school teacher. His folkic, anti-Jewish organization, the 'Deutsche Werkgemeinschaft,' was of little importance, but he was adroit at taking me in. I contributed liberally until I began to suspect that some of my money was paying liquor bills.

This thirsty mentor, however, brought me into contact with other members of his group. I met the now famous 'scourge of the Jews,' Julius Streicher, then also a school-teacher.

I saw much of Streicher. Touched no doubt by the general contagion round us, we went off at an absurd little tangent of our own.

Streicher was then already fanatically intent on the Jewish problem, and there was a vast amount of reading on the subject lying more or less undigested in his immature mind. He had been analysing the Bible, with what scepticism may be imagined. But certain Old Testament seeds had sprouted in his brain. There was, for example, the wonderful principle of the fast as a means of renewing a man in body and spirit. Fasting would make us hard and fit for the struggle to save Germany.

This man was an entirely new type to me, and soon I found his enthusiasm infectious. What could we fast on?

We were in Nuremberg, and all round us in that lovely Frankenland country, cherries were hanging ripe on the trees. Why not try cherries? Jesus Christ had given cherries to his disciples, Streicher said.

Excellent! But where? Streicher knew of a place that would be ideal. So off we went.

Our regimen was to be nothing but cherries for two or three weeks, then a week of nothing but water. When that was over, we would be new beings.

I had looked forward to some idyllic spot where we could sit meditating through the long summer days in an old orchard and just eat cherries. Instead, I found myself living with Streicher in one room in a house on a village street and buying cherries from a farmer. I was footing the bills, and Streicher would absent himself for hours.

On the second day, when the whole thing had gone decidedly flat for me, I learned that Streicher had a friend in this village, And on the third day I spied him in a little restaurant tucking away a huge 'Bauern' omelet. Cherries, quite understandably, had been insufficiently sustaining fare.

There was nothing to do but laugh at ourselves. In all goodwill we parted, and I went on to Munich.

But the fasting idea had got hold of me. Several years later I was to try it again in California, this time with more resolution.

My search went on. In Munich, in an office of the 'Technische Nothilfe,' a technical organization designed for emergency service in strikes and closely linked with the Bund Bayern und Reich, I met a certain captain. I showed him and another officer the Henry Ford publications about 'The International Jew: The World's Foremost Problem,' which I had brought back from my last visit to America. The two gentlemen, who did not strike me as at all folkic or anti-Jewish, looked only politely interested. But when, as a venture, I added that I had talked at length with Mr. W. J. Cameron, the author of these famous articles, and that it might be worth while to look into the matter further, they leaped to attention. With that I left them. Smelling money now, they tried repeatedly to get in touch with me. I had been a business man too long, however, to judge the value of anything, even a political principle, by its price-tag; so I let my first impression rule me, dropped the captain, and looked elsewhere for guidance.

I found it in Berlin in the person of Count Ernst zu Reventlow, well-known editor of the Reichswart, a folkic and uncompromisingly anti-Jewish weekly. He was a former naval officer, an admirable type, tall, blue-eyed, grave of manner; a fine German and a real nobleman, of high intelligence, and wise after many years in politics.

Long talks with the Count, in Berlin and at his home in Potsdam, helped me. I was frank about myself, and he understood the problems that vexed me, having already solved some of them for himself. Accepted and guided by such a man, whose word counted for much in folkic circles, I felt less lost.

This was in the first days of July, and troubled days they were. In June the aforementioned organization had shocked the world with their assassination of

Walther Rathenau, the Jewish Minister of Foreign Affairs, not long after their killing of Reichsminister Mathias Erzberger, despised signer of the Armistice. Within a week the mark fell from fifteen hundred to six thousand to the pound. Germany groaned; desperate rumours were whispered about. With a serious crisis obviously approaching, the Right received the most serious blow it had suffered since the revolution-the proclamation of the drastic 'Laws for the Protection of the Republic.' These laws had the clarifying effect, however, of intimidating the half-hearted and the luke-warm, leaving the field to the bold and to the activists in all camps.

The final struggle for supremacy among the many would-be dictators had begun; the process of pitiless elimination of the weak was under way. It was deeds, not words, that counted now.

Reventlow suggested that I go with him to Munich, where the political situation was taking on even deeper colour. He had said that he would introduce me to General Ludendorff, and now he began to talk also of Dr. Pittinger and of one Adolf Hitler. I had heard that there was an agitator of that name; but, ill-advised by the teacher, I had not tried to meet him.

Munich was still the city of charm, but with each visit I found its political aspect more absorbing. The contrast with Berlin was marked; one was the Mecca of Marxists and Jews, the other the citadel of their enemies.

When Reventlow introduced me to Dr. Pittinger, I was warmly received into the circle of his friends. Here were Colonel Stockhausen, his chief of staff; Count von Soden, the 'chef du cabinet' of Crown Prince Rupprecht; Kahr, the ex-minister; and Poehner, the former police-president. I met many others of their group, and learned much about them, partly through Reventlow's sarcastic tongue. When they proposed appointing me liaison officer for the Bund Bayern und Reich between Bavaria and the North, I joined. But it was faute de mieux, for I could not escape a vague apprehension that somewhere, in either its personnel or its platform, the Bund was too weak for action.

The drastic new laws were threatening the sovereignty of Bavaria, and relations between Berlin and Munich were strained. Within Bavaria itself, two chief political interests were clashing: the Centrist Bavarian Peoples' Party, ready to secede from the Reich if necessary, and the Nationalist:' folkic element, opposed to any secession. The latter had used Munich, safely so far, as a base for their campaign against Berlin. The Bavarian Government, which was Centrist, was now in the quandary of choosing between surrendering its sovereignty to Berlin or risking an alliance with the folkic-Nationalists, which was also against their own interests. Finally they yielded to Berlin, making Bavaria, like the rest of Germany, a hunting-ground for Berlin police seeking the extradition of National activists.

The wave of indignation that surged through the land reached its climax in a huge mass demonstration of protest in Munich on 11 August 1922, under the sponsorship of the 'Vaeterlandische Verbaende,' which was, in effect, a holding company loosely co-ordinating all the patriotic societies, large and small, and including at that time the Nazi Party - the National Socialist German Workers' Party.

This was the greatest mass demonstration Munich had ever seen. It was one of incalculable historical importance, for on that day a little-known figure stepped into the light as a recognized public speaker of extraordinary power. This was a man who until then had literally been snubbed by the higher-ups in the patriotic societies. Now, because of his growing local importance and for the sake of a united front, he had been invited to appear as one of two speakers on a programme in which all were taking part.

Adolf Hitler was scheduled to speak last.

It needed no clairvoyance to see that here was a man who knew how to seize his opportunity. Red placards announced in huge black letters that he was to appear. Many who read them had never even heard his name. Here were inflammatory slogans: 'Versailles: Germany's Ruin ... Republic of the People or State of the Jews? ... International Solidarity: A Jewish World Swindle ... Down with the November Criminals ... The National Socialist Movement Must Conquer....'

And every one of his placards ended with the blunt phrase: 'Jews Not Admitted.'

It was a bright summer day. The Reds had tried their best to break up the Nazi columns marching through the city, comprising Storm Troopers followed by sections of the Party. Soon the assailants were in flight, bruised and beaten, and it had been demonstrated for, the first time that Nationalists as well as Reds had the right to march in formation through the streets of Munich, and that the Nazis were determined to maintain this right.

The 'Patriotic Societies' had assembled without bands and without flags. But when the Nazis marched into the Koenigsplatz with banners flying, their bands playing stirring German marches, they were greeted with tremendous cheers. An excited, expectant crowd was now filling the beautiful square to the last inch and overflowing into surrounding streets. There were well over a hundred thousand.

The first speaker, little Dr. Buckeley, harangued this mass in true political fashion. At last he relinquished the platform, and Hitler faced the multitude.

Reventlow had seen to it that we were near the speakers' stand. I was close enough to see Hitler's face, watch every change in his expression, hear every word he said.

When the man stepped forward on the platform, there was almost no applause. He stood silent for a moment. Then he began to speak, quietly and ingratiatingly at first. Before long his voice had risen to a hoarse shriek that gave an extraordinary effect of an intensity of feeling. There were many high-pitched, rasping notes - Reventlow had told me that his throat had been affected by war-gas - but despite its strident tone, his diction had a distinctly Austrian turn, softer and pleasanter than the German.

Critically I studied this slight, pale man, his brown hair parted on one side and falling again and again over his sweating brow. Threatening and beseeching, with small, pleading hands and flaming, steel-blue eyes, he had the look of a fanatic.

Presently my critical faculty was swept away. Leaning from the tribune as if he were trying to impel his inner self into the consciousness of all these thousands, he was holding the masses, and me with them, under a hypnotic spell by the sheer force of his conviction.

He urged the revival of German honour and manhood with a blast of words that seemed to cleanse. "Bavaria is now the most German land in Germany!" he shouted, to roaring applause. Then, plunging into sarcasm, he indicted the leaders in Berlin as 'November Criminals,' daring to put into words thoughts that Germans were now almost afraid to think and certainly to voice.

It was clear that Hitler was feeling the exaltation of the emotional response now surging up toward him from his thousands of hearers. His voice rising to passionate climaxes, he finished his speech with an anthem of hate against the 'Novemberlings' and a pledge of undying love for the Fatherland. "Germany must be free!" was his final defiant slogan. Then two last words that were like the sting of a lash :

"Deutschland Erwache!"

Awake, Germany! There was thunderous applause. Then the masses took a solemn oath 'to save Germany in Bavaria from Bolshevism.'

I do not know how to describe the emotions that swept over me as I heard this man. His words were like a scourge. When he spoke of the disgrace of Germany, I felt ready to spring on any enemy. His appeal to German manhood was like a call to arms, the gospel he preached a sacred truth. He seemed another Luther. I forgot everything but the man; then, glancing round, I saw that his magnetism was holding these thousands as one.

Of course I was ripe for this experience. I was a man of thirty-two, weary of disgust and disillusionment, a wanderer seeking a cause; a patriot without a channel for his patriotism, a yearner after the heroic without a hero. The intense will of the man, the passion of his sincerity seemed to flow from him into me. I experienced an exaltation that could be likened only to religious conversion.

I felt sure that no one who had heard Hitler that afternoon could doubt that he was the man of destiny, the vitalizing force in the future of Germany. The masses who had streamed into the Koenigsplatz with a stern sense of national humiliation seemed to be going forth renewed.

The bands struck up, the thousands began to move away. I knew my search was ended. I had found myself, my leader, and my cause.

Hitler evidently combined the practical and the spiritual. Counting apparently on the effect of his address in the afternoon, he had arranged for the evening a Nazi meeting in the Zirkus Krone.

This is the famous image of Hitler speaking at the Zirkus Krone in Munich in 1925. In the pages of Mein Kampf Hitler describes at length his own experience of events such as the one at which this now famous photograph was taken. Ludecke underwent a dramatic conversion of almost religious intensity on hearing Hitler speak for the first time and unconditionally pledged his life and fortune to the Nazi cause.

The term 'Nazi' had been only slightly known up to the hour of his address. Nazi-a sound of a sort that is common in Bavarian speech-is a contraction of the first word of the title of Hitler's party, the 'Nationalsozialistische Deutsche Arbeiter-Partei.' Now we were hearing these syllables wherever we went in Munich.

Reventlow and I found the Zirkus so jammed that there was scarcely room for a pin to drop. Around the platform was grouped a guard of SA-the 'Sturmabteilung,' husky fellows who looked ready to cope with any situation. I could see the need of them, for it was apparent that the Nazis, more than any others in those days, were daring to assail the Jews, the Communists, the bourgeois round-heads, denouncing what they believed evil. More Storm Troopers encircled the arena and flanked the aisle leading to the tribune. All of them wore red arm-bands bearing the now famous symbol-a black swastika in a white circle.

We were shown to seats reserved for us within a few feet of the platform. In a moment, the expectant murmur of the throng hushed, then ceased. Hitler was entering.

It took courage to risk a second address that day, but the experience of the Koenigsplatz was repeated with even greater intensity, if that was possible. Standing under his own banners, addressing his own followers, Hitler was even more outspoken, flaying the 'system' with that fury of invective of which he is a master and disclosing an extraordinary talent for conveying the most complicated matters in plastic, popular form, comprehensible to anyone.

Again his power was inescapable, gripping and swaying me as it did every one within those walls. Again I had the sensation of surrendering my being to his leadership. When he stopped speaking, his chest still heaving with emotion, there was a moment of dead silence, then a storm of cheers.

Count Reventlow introduced me to Hitler, still perspiring, dishevelled in his dirty trench-coat, his hair plastered against his brow, his face pale, his nostrils distended. Looking closely at him for a long moment, I did not need to wonder where he found the reserves of character and courage that were enabling him to forge ahead of the other leaders. Everything dwelt behind his eyes. We shook hands, and it was arranged that I was to meet him at Nazi headquarters on the following afternoon.

Then his men gathered round him, and the Count and I left. The Zirkus Krone had set the seal on my conversion.

At three the next afternoon, I stepped into the open door of what had once been a little Kaffeehaus in the Komeliusstrasse, in the poorer section of the city. This was Nazi headquarters. There was a show-window displaying Nazi literature, a large room with a reception corner barred off by a wooden rail, a counter where members paid their dues, a few tables and chairs. That was all, except for two smaller rooms beyond. Hitler took me into one of these and closed the door behind us.

At once I offered myself to him and to his cause without reservation. As frankly as I had talked to Reventlow, I told him the story of my life, dwelling especially upon years during and after the war when I had felt myself baffled at every turn.

Hitler listened closely, studying me keenly, now and then rising from his chair and pacing the floor. I was impressed again by his obvious indifference to his personal appearance; but again I saw that the whole man was concentrated in his eyes, his clear, straightforward, domineering, bright blue eyes.

When I mentioned my appointment in the Bund Bayern und Reich he frowned, but approved my suggestion that it might be wise to maintain the connection for a while, to remain vigilant and learn what was going on.

When I rose to leave, it was after seven; we had been talking for over four hours. Solemnly clasping hands, we sealed the pact.

I had given him my soul.

II

WELTBUMMLER

The soul that I surrendered to an unproved man with strangely compelling eyes now felt that it had put thirty-two years of a certain way of life definitely behind it. Those years had held a variety of experience that would cram an ordinary lifetime. My past could only be characterized as that of an adventurer. A decade later, when my enemies among the Nazis were to call me the 'Weltbummler'-globe-trotter-it was something I didn't deny and wasn't ashamed of.

I was born 5 February 1890, in Berlin, but spent my boyhood in Oranienburg, twenty miles north of the capital. There was a garden with moss-grown trees, thickets of lilac, and spacious meadows running down to the River Havel. My father was fond of walking there in the early evening after a day in his chemical plant, and as a little fellow I would trudge beside him, holding to one of his fingers while he talked about things I did not understand. He was a man of artistic tastes, of knowledge and imagination, and he kept a close eye on my education at public school in Oranienburg and later at gymnasium in Berlin. And when I was bad, which was often enough, he would cane me. Once, after one of his beatings, I rose at five the next morning and ran away from home on my bicycle. My world tour ended the second afternoon in old Pritzwalk when I plunged into the shafts of a post-wagon and picked up a gash on my head that identifies me to this day.

My life was like the life of other boys of my class; we would hang around the factory stables, play at soldiers and at games of' American Indian.' We would scalp our victim and tie him to a stake, and one day we almost set fire to him in the best tradition of Karl May, favourite author of German boys in that day. Karl May had never seen redskins, but he pictured them as eminently satisfactory fellows. Old Shatter-hand, whose repeating rifle could fire forty-eight times and wipe out an entire buffalo herd, and Winnetou, chief of the Apaches, were our heroes.

Small things float up to the surface of my memory which must have helped to set the pattern for a life, at least to shape its instinctive loyalties, its lasting antipathies.

There was the day my father found me, then a gymnasium student, puzzling in his library over the second part of Goethe's Faust. He took the book from me. "You are too young for that," he said. "Wait until you are thirty, and read it again when you are forty-five. Faust you cannot understand if you do not know that Goethe personified in Faust the struggling German soul and in Mephistopheles the tempting Jew . . . 'die Spottgeburt aus Dreck und Feuer'. . . 'der Geist der stets verneint.'"

23

And there were my friends in the gymnasium at Braunsch-weig, to which my father had transferred me after the director of the Joachimsthalsche gymnasium in Berlin had found me too intractable, too rebellious against authority, too emotional and full of life. In Braunschweig I knew two brothers, Norwin and Odal, the Freiherren von Knigge, and in the many weekends I spent at their father's baronial estate, I came to know the life of a Prussian nobleman at its best. I think it was then that, all unconsciously, I began to cherish the ideal of a traditional German culture vitalized by German blood, of a Germany preserving its racial and social integrity from any alien influence that might weaken it.

My father's death left my mother less well off, though reasonably secure, and so I struck out for myself. Three months in a Hamburg export house made me despise the career of a merchant, and I resolved to work off my compulsory army service. Volunteers were required to serve only one year, whereas conscripts had to do two or three.

A school-friend was attending the university in Munich; so I went there and the Bavarian 'Kronprinz' regiment accepted me. From my first day I had a hard time. Bavarians had little love for Berliners; I was the only one in the regiment, and they did not spare me.

In school I had always been a rebel against authority, but here I found myself under unbelievably exacting discipline. Knowing that I was a good soldier, capable and willing, I was scornful of minor regulations that seemed to me senseless. Civilian clothes were forbidden us at all times, but having become attached to a young lady who had rejected an officer of my company, I put on a dinner-jacket and took her to the theatre-and in the foyer during the intermission we ran into the officer in question.

After three days of 'Mittelarrest,' I emerged a black sheep, and a tough sergeant was put over me to see that I broke no more rules. By the time my enlistment was over, I had lost all desire for an army career and had gained a deep-rooted hatred for top-sergeants.

At nineteen, on a modest allowance, I set out for London. England, resting the might of its empire on a base of easy liberality, was a revelation to me. The English gentleman seemed rounder in knowledge, character, and outlook than his German equivalent. We had evolved a national character of our own, but it was a stiff affair. Beside one of England's world-citizens, the German was a 'schoolmaster' wherever he went-a man of irrevocable ideas, respected but not greatly liked. I felt that we had produced only one high type that could stand comparison-the German officer. In the war, he was to prove that he was a gentleman-of steel.

After studying the language for a few months, I went up to Manchester, and tried and promptly loathed the cotton business. Again three months were enough, and now I turned toward the Continent.

Hitler's piercing blue eyes were the unique feature which were most often described by those who spent time in his company. They were, by all accounts, as mesmerising as his rhetorical powers and must no doubt have played their part during the first four hour meeting with Hitler in persuading Ludecke that his future fortunes lay entwined with those of the Fürher.

Pre-war Paris spread its web of enchantment over me. I had found a modest job, but the attractions and temptations of life were so infinite that I simply had to have more money. By blindest chance I met a famous jockey, one of the kings of the turf, and he gave me a tip. I played it and won several hundred francs.

That was the beginning. I tried again, and again and again I won. Why grind away at a correspondent's desk at eight pounds a month? I gave up my job, resolved to become a cosmopolitan citizen of leisure.

The races continued to be good to me. Often I played my hunches-and they were right. A horse I backed at twenty-three to one brought me twenty-three thousand gold francs.

This was heady wine for a young fellow in his early twenties. I went to Deauville, Biarritz, Monte Carlo. Cautiously I began to play roulette. Here the initiated will smile, but they are wrong, for I won with average consistency. Then I took to baccarat and trente-et-quarante - successful at each.

When instinct prompted me, when the incandescent moment came, I would play for high stakes, and if luck was with me I would go to the maximum of six thousand francs. Once I gathered in ninety thousand gold francs in a single night, and lost sixty thousand of it the next. But I am one of the few men I ever knew who won more than he lost. Perhaps it was because, never a gambler at heart, it was easy for me to follow the wise rule of playing for a short while only.

Some of the money I invested; much of it I spent in travel -the Balearic Isles, Italy, the Dalmatian coast, Egypt, India. There was no passport nuisance in those days.

The worldly experience I gained certainly brought me no nearer to heaven, but it has helped me over many a hurdle here below. I learned to weigh values, to discriminate between the real and the unreal.

My life was one of contrasts and climaxes. I developed a genius, good or bad, for attracting curious people. Sometimes I would be plagued by a second self who stood aloof from a spurious show and asked: 'Are these your people, are these the climaxes you started out to seek?' But these moments of self-reproach were far between. Life was pleasant-far too pleasant to last.

I wore London clothes; my own chauffeur sat at the wheel of my big car; I had more money than I knew what to do with. And now I had Dolores, perhaps the one real person in my shallow world. She was the wife of another man, but we lived together.

Except for Dolores, the aimless and futile life of winning and spending would have become my routine. Every day in the year a man might kiss a countess, shake hands with a grand duke, have cocktails with an American millionaire; the only requisites were a clean face, a dinner-jacket, and some pocket-change. Repeat the formula three hundred and sixty-five days in succession and you've had a dull year.

One reason I think I was never a gambler at heart is that I can lay claim to the quality of patience-even the profound patience required of a chess-player. Chess was an obsession with me. I can still spend hour after hour over the board, unconscious of the world around me.

On an evening at the Cafe Continental, however, my concentration was broken into by the raucous cry of a newsboy. I was about to spring the decisive move in an intricate mate combination, and, I bought the boy's paper so that I could send him on his way. As I put it to one side, the headline caught my eye.

It announced the assassination of the Archduke Ferdinand in Sarajevo. "C'est la guerre," I said in thoughtless prophecy, and turned again to a matter of importance. I moved a pawn. " Check!"

The war was one of the unhappiest chapters of my life-not for its grim brutalities but for its frustrations. I wanted the war so much that I missed it altogether.

In July we motored to Heidelberg, following the lure of an international chess tourney at nearby Mannheim. There the war burst upon us. It seemed to offer the most exciting of prospects, for I had three languages and knew France like my own pocket. I applied for enlistment and received mobilization orders. Rene, my French chauffeur, was interned. I tried to persuade Dolores, an American, to leave Germany, but she refused.

I wanted the front, but was ordered instead to join an infantry regiment stationed at Lahr, in Baden. I went there by train; Dolores stayed on in Heidelberg.

Spy hysteria was gripping the nation. On the way down to Lahr, the Argus eye of doubt settled on me, for I wore London clothes and carried two conspicuously English bags. Rumours spread through the train, and I was interrogated twice by station police.

At the barracks in Lahr, I learned that the active regiment had left two days before, and I went to the Hotel zur Post. Again I drew suspicion: a military patrol ordered me to the Kommandantur, and again I was examined and released.

Stranded in a dull town, I hastened to get rid of the offending clothes by ordering a military uniform, for the 'spionitis' was growing worse. Only the night before, two German officers, a major and a captain, had been killed near Freiburg by peasants who believed them Russian agents 'carrying gold from France.'

They had stretched wires across the road, halted the car, and shot the officers without giving them a chance.

On my way back to the hotel a patrol accosted me, brought me protesting to the guard-house, and locked me up for the night. Next morning an apologetic officer in charge released me, mad clear through.

I was assigned to assist the Feldwebel, or top-sergeant of the first reserve company, with permission to go on sleeping at the inn. Less conspicuous now in my uniform, and hoping to see real service at last, I ordered a motor cycle on the advice of an old soldier. Motor cyclists were needed at the front, he said. When it finally came, it was of no avail. I was hopelessly caught in the machine.

But with my talent for getting myself into trouble, I made a serious mistake. Dolores had received only one post card from me. Conscience-smitten, I telegraphed her in English, for she knew no German, and French obviously was out of the question.

Next day I realized that the atmosphere of suspicion surrounding me had thickened again. In the evening, seeking a secluded corner of the inn, I had begun to write her a letter in English when a heavy voice exploded above me.

"Was machen Sie da? Was haben Sie hier zu suchen?"

The face peering over my shoulder looked like a cartoon of a German officer-but it was that of' Leutnant der Reserve Herr Rechtsanwalt' Stroffel. I was fed up, and slightly defiant; he made a scene. Other officers drew him away, and next day my ranking captain exonerated me. But now I had a powerful enemy, for Stroffel was a town lawyer and the judicial officer of the regiment.

Dolores arrived, wearing Paris clothes and talking eagerly in French. Apprehensively I got her upstairs. For three days I kept her out of sight, returning from barracks to take my meals with her in our rooms. On the third afternoon we had just finished lunch when a gun-butt crashed on the door. It was Stroffel, with a military escort.

It was clear that the man really thought me a spy. When snooping in closets and crawling under beds failed to produce anything incriminating, he ordered me to follow him.

My permission to live in town was now revoked. Dolores left. Several days later I was put under arrest and locked up in a cell.

I think many a young man's nerves would have broken under the strain. Mine did. I went frantic, pounding on the door of my cage, demanding a hearing. It was five days before the hearing came. The military judge seemed sympathetic.

There must have been a mistake, he said-doubtless it would be remedied.

Relieved, I went back to my cell. Soon steps approached, and the door was opened. It was Stroffel again, an official paper in his hand. Tasting every word, he read it to me. "Two weeks of 'middle arrest' for obtaining leave under false pretences"-an offence I had not committed.

I was stripped of my clothes, put into the foulest uniform to be found, and locked up in solitary confinement. Every day, for three days, one thick slice of bread and a pitcher of water. On the fourth day, a scanty meal. No reading, no smoking, no exercise.

At first I wept aloud, but presently I sat on the hard prison cot and felt, as never before, a sense of humility. For years I had lived the life of a peacock; this was my penance. In a way, it is good for a man to sit in prison for a while. He learns to think with the full power of his mind; it is, for a time at least, the ultimate in concentration.

My new humility vanished when, at the end of two weeks, I stood before Stroffel. He hoped I had learned my lesson. But I sensed a change in his attitude, and presently he gave me a letter, saying that I should have told him I had such friends as the Barons von Knigge. He wanted me to know that he bore me no ill-will.

Before my middle arrest, I had tried to communicate with friends for help in my plight, and had written to myoid school-friends, Odal and Norwin. The answer Stroffel handed me came from their aged mother, Freifrau von Knigge. It was as fine and moving a letter as I have ever received. Her two sons were already dead; one in Russia, the other in France.

When I had written my letters I had also drawn up a brief outlining the injustice done me. That brief was now going through the slow process of military law. I thought of it with satisfaction.

Next I was ordered before Major Hertel, commander of the regimental reserve, and one of Stroffel's cronies. "So you want to go to the front?" he asked, as though I had merely been away on vacation. "They tell me you have a motor cycle. I'm returning to the front in a day or two. You'd like to be my 'Ordonnanz,' wouldn't you?"

It would be both dangerous and thrilling, and I caught my breath. Then the suggestion of a sneer in his manner stopped my eager acceptance on my lips, and I asked to be allowed to think it over.

28

Besides patience, obstinacy is a quality I can lay claim to, with less likelihood of being disputed. This offer seemed plainly to be an inducement to abandon my claim for redress. Perhaps my two weeks in solitary had given me a persecution-complex. I distrusted these two men, and in the end I decided to turn the offer down. It was a mistake, of course-I knew that soon enough.

A man's nature does not change. Many years later I was to insist on vindication when vindication would have been awkward for those more powerful than I-and in doing so put my very life in jeopardy.

Three months went by in which I was the target of Stroffel's pea-shooting campaign. He could give his grudge full scope, for he was now 'Oberleutnant' of my own company. When a heaven-sent infection in my foot sent me to the hospital for an operation, I had six weeks of blessed rest and clean sheets, but in the end I went back to Stroffel.

His proddings finally got the better of my nerves. I reported sick, and then broke down in the presence of the doctor; if he couldn't have me sent somewhere, anywhere, I should either have to desert or shoot myself. He was very gentle with me. Next day they had me up for examination again. Very well, I was to be transferred. But where? To Freiburg; another soldier would accompany me. My relief was so great that I asked no questions.

In Freiburg, a street-car carried us to a large, formal-looking building surrounded by trees, inside a high wall. We entered a bare reception-room. "Wait a minute," said the soldier, and closed the door behind him.

I looked round the room. There was one window. It was barred.

My rage at having been tricked almost burst through. It was well for me that I was able to restrain it, for I was now a full-fledged patient in the psychiatric clinic of Geheimrat Professor Hoche - a civilian institution.

For a few days I ate from a wooden spoon, and someone marched at my side wherever I went. It is an odd sensation to be a sane man in an asylum and face the dilemma of determining how best to act. A sane man's first reaction would be to raise a storm-and yet I was sure that was the one thing I must avoid.

So I lived quietly among my moaning, tittering, or vacantly searching companions and did nothing at all until the day Professor Hoche came through our ward on an inspection trip. When he spoke to me in a friendly way, I looked him straight in the eye and told him I had been committed to his care by mistake. I was a soldier and an educated man, and I was sane. No doubt each of his patients told him the same thing-but I begged the privilege of speaking to him alone.

He looked at me keenly, nodded, and said: "Very well." When I was summoned to his office I did not have to plead my case, for he spoke first.

"Herr Ludecke, I have just been examining your papers. There has been a clerical error. Half our wards have been turned over to the Medical Corps as a Reserve-

Lazarett and you were intended for that section. Our present confusion sent you to the psychiatric ward. But frankly, from your papers I cannot understand why you are here at all."

He heard my story sympathetically. "Yes, yes-I know the Stroffels, they break men's spirits in misguided zeal for Germany . . . . You'd better stay here for a while and take things easy. Then we'll try to straighten out your difficulties."

Once more I found myself almost free, living in a villa in the garden among convalescent soldiers and officers. Here were men on crutches and in plaster-casts, full of straight talk about the war.

As we were allowed to enter the town whenever we pleased and were required only to sleep at the hospital, I sent for Dolores.

Freiburg was wearing the full bloom of spring; the flower-candles were bright on the gnarled old chestnut trees. We spent happy weeks together, but when spring had slipped into summer, the inevitable disquiet laid hold of me. The war was now a year old. I was still blessed with a whole body, and leading an ambiguous life far from danger. What good was a man's strength if he could not use it? If I could not get out of the regiment into some other arm of the service, I must get entirely free, so that I might live to some purpose.

"... You're right, of course," said Professor Hoche. "You've had enough idleness. All I can do is stretch a point and advise your dismissal from the service. An actual discharge can be issued only by your regiment. Are you willing to risk Stroffel again?"

Yes, I would risk him.

Dolores sailed for America, and I went back to Stroffel. He received me with a wry smile, and transferred me to a military hospital in Heidelberg as sanitary orderly.

"Can't you do better than sanitary orderly?" I asked the assignment officer, when I could get his ear. "I think we can," he said. "We'll put you down as clerk. Report to this address."

I reported and was well received. They showed me my place and the work I had to do.

"By the way," I asked, "what kind of hospital is this?" "Oh," they said, "didn't you know? It's for the insane."

Here in Heidelberg, standing in the garden of the Klinik, when the wind was right, one could hear our guns at Verdun, thundering away in one of the war's most colossal blunders. We who were inside Germany in those years were increasingly aware that mistakes were being made; that in high places there were confusion and cross-purposes, indecision and vacillation, favouritism and jealousy. This growing distrust did not contribute to the peace of mind of a man clerking in an asylum, keeping the records of men suffering from shellshock, men who trembled continually, mouths open, eyes staring, memories gone. Geheimrat Nissl, director of the Klinik, was a humane scientist of world rank. I begged him to help me to get into the aviation corps, or at least into the intelligence service, but he advised against it. My military record was bad, a formidable thing in the German Army; I had best keep quiet.

My money was still holding out, and I was living at the Hotel Victoria and faring well enough. Coal was scarce, and there was a growing shortage of food. Bootlegging of necessities began. The hated middle-men were piling up profits and sending prices soaring. While true Germans were exchanging their gold watch-chains for chains of iron, the war-profiteers - the 'Kriegsschieber' - were growing rich. It was a disgusting spectacle.

In this welter of a warring world I met a man who was to influence my future life, the man who taught me to think historically-Professor Geheimrat Alfred von Domaszewski of Heidelberg University, historian, scholar, and philosopher. From our first meeting I regarded him with a respect that ended in veneration. His was one of those rare intellects that shed light on whatever they touch.

I went steadily to his lectures and upon occasion was admitted to the circle of his friends. He would step into an old Weinstuhe and sit for hours in a corner, discoursing in the way of the ancient philosophers. Once in a while Baron Jakob von Uexkuell, a noted biologist, would accompany the professor. Over a glass of wine I sat at the feet of wisdom.

The professor was a study in human quantities. Born an Austrian, his antecedents combined the Germanic with French and Polish stock. He had elected to be German. His character had the depth of the Teutonic with the elasticity and brilliance of the French and Polish.

To the best of my recollection, Domaszewski never used the term Nordic in his discussion of peoples. That term was not in fashion then. He thought of his people as Aryan or Caucasian, Nordic being a more recent bit of nomenclature, as far as popular usage goes. But Domaszewski embodied what is understood by the Nordic character and viewpoint.

How a young mind develops a consciousness of kind would be an interesting study. My first approach, at that period or before, took such a simple form as this: Why is one tree taller, fuller, and finer than another? Why does the eagle mate with the eagle, the fox with the fox, the rat with the rat? Is the persistence of higher and lower types among humans mere chance, or is it the result of the working out of immutable basic laws?

It must be in accordance with the laws of selection and elimination, at work before my eyes. If certain formulae governed the evolution of animals and plants, would they not apply to mankind, the highest organism of all?

In nature the best as an affinity for the best, the worst attracts the worst. But men are wilful creatures, capable of thwarting nature's best intentions, to their own undoing. When good and bad mingle, or even when two widely disparate races interbreed, they produce a hybrid in which the lower qualities offset or destroy the higher inheritance, and a defective or monstrous product results. We see the law always at work among plants and animals-and men; but we are prone to ignore the vital fact that whereas in nature the unfit are ruthlessly exterminated in the struggle for existence, thus protecting the strain, in 'humanity' the defectives and undesirables are sheltered and preserved, at the expense of the fit.

It must be recognized, of course, that most of us are, in varying degree, mongrels. But there are mongrels and mongrels. The mixture of some races, bodily and psychically in harmony with each other, has brought about apparently an enrichment of the resulting stock. But in every case when races of clashing characteristics have interbred, there has been an obvious deterioration.

A pure type of any race seldom exists today. The population of Europe, for instance, is mainly a mixture of the various European races. All the nations of Europe are composed of approximately the same racial ingredients, but in various degrees of mixture. Hence, the chief difference between them is a difference in proportion of the various strains that make up their racial types. Yet that difference is decisive.

Now, what should be the best measure of any people? What better measure than their contribution to civilization; their achievements in war and peace? So it becomes worthwhile to consider the race or races that have best met this criterion. Examination shows that the Aryan, Caucasian, or Nordic strain, whichever term one prefers, has been primarily responsible for the culture of the Occident. Perhaps for the best in the Orient also; I have seen a Brahmin in Delhi with grey eyes. The caste system of India was intended to save the conquering race from absorption by the native races-but it came too late.

Before it was hopelessly diluted, the Aryan blood made India a source of culture and world enlightenment. The same could be said of Persia. Long ago it was also the Aryan character that produced Homer, Praxiteles, Pericles, Plato.

Alexander the Great was Aryan; so were Sulla, Cicero, Cresar, and the great of Rome. In the nearer centuries, Aryan stock dominated the world to its everlasting good, nurturing the Renaissance and a dozen national cultures. Nearer still, there has been a seepage from the strength of the Aryan peoples, by reason of too great liberality accorded other peoples.

My reading carried me deep into the pages of Schopenhauer, Nietzsche, and Treitschke. The discussions of Domaszewski and his friends led me also to a study of Gobineau, whose L'Essai sur l'Inegalite des Races Humaines was a cornerstone of biological thinking. He and two or three other writers of the nineteenth century already had provided the basis for a new and far-reaching political philosophy of the twentieth century. Foremost among them stood Sir Francis Galton with his

Hereditary Genius, and Houston Stewart Chamberlain, the 'renegade' Englishman, who, like Domaszewski, adopted the German viewpoint as his own and vitally influenced the 'Voelkische Bewegung' or folk-movement of latter-day Germany. Any one who would comprehend the underlying currents of this movement also may read with profit Paul Anton de Lagarde, a German despite his name, author of the Deutsche Schrijten, or German Scriptures. Later, Professor Hans F. K. Guenther compiled the studies of his forerunners, developing and popularizing the Nordic concept of life in his books, notably in his Rassenkunde des Deutschen Volkes.

This beginning of reasoning, of biological thinking, however vague at that time, aroused in me not only a latent Teutonic spirit, but a certain attachment to the people-the 'Voelkische' or folkic spirit. The inner spectacle of Germany at war helped me to comprehend the 'Volksseele'-the folk-soul. The devotion and courage, the resignation and defencelessness that I saw appealed to my own soul.

In the late autumn of 1916 with the aid of Geheimrat Nissl I finally received my military discharge. My mother was then living in reduced circumstances in Berlin; my brother, an officer in the Second Regiment of the Prussian Guard, had been wounded. He advised me not to try for active service, for my bad army record would disqualify me, but to make myself otherwise useful.

From a small beginning as broker for the sale of several hundred head of sheep, I soon found myself launched on the sort of career I had twice run away from. In a few months I was buying agent for a group of large industries and municipalities, going to Copenhagen, Amsterdam, Zurich, with the satisfaction of knowing that I was procuring needed supplies for my country-an interesting work which exempted me from further active military service and allowed me to take a deep look into the war machine and the war life of Germany. On one of my trips to Copenhagen I Was given an opportunity by the intelligence service to report on the activities of two German agents suspected of serving both sides. In the Danish capital, spies were trailing spies, and they in turn were being shadowed by super-spies, all under cover of a life of exaggerated brilliance and gaiety.

Whenever I returned to Berlin, however, I realized that it was now the gayest city of Europe. While the army faced its ring of enemies, while the people struggled through their desperate 'turnip winter,' champagne corks popped at the Adlon and the Bristol. There was scarcely any bread for the masses, but all the delicacies of the world could be had in the expensive restaurants and on the tables of the war-rich. The profiteers were drinking, dining, and dancing; plebeians with money and aristocrats with little or none were mingling in a reckless, heartless life. Nothing would have been healthier for Berlin than a lively air raid; it needed to feel the stern reality of war from the air that London and Paris knew so well.

The old German principles of sobriety and honour were even less in evidence when the war was over. Germany under the 'revolution' seemed to me a land being taken possession of by rats, everywhere emerging from their holes. I wanted to get out of a country that I could no longer recognize as mine, and so I left for Copenhagen.

There I had what seemed to me an inspiration. Why not salvage German ships lying interned in neutral ports by bringing them together under the ownership of a neutral country and under the protection of a neutral flag? A Danish-Mexican company, say, supported by German and Danish capital and flying the Mexican flag.

The Mexican minister in Copenhagen was encouraging. Danish men of affairs declared themselves ready to co-operate. Haste was the very essence of the problem: it must all be done before the signing of a peace treaty deprived us of our ships for good and all.

I went to Hamburg. The Hamburg-American line was ponderously interested in my idea. Yes, a German-and Danish-owned merchant fleet upon the seas, under the Mexican flag, would open a window on the world for Germany after four years of isolation. But Herr Ludecke took too gloomy a view. Why should we lose our ships?

I succeeded in getting the newly appointed head of the Hamburg-American line to Copenhagen to talk to the Mexican minister, who supported everything I had said. But I was defeated by the German reluctance to do anything in a hurry. There must be a technical commission to make a thorough investigation.

"No use," I said. "The treaty would be signed before we could even get started, and then you would lose your ships after all. I'm sorry."

They had thought me pessimistic. But the Treaty of Versailles took away every German ship above sixteen hundred tons, including scores of vessels in neutral ports.

Again I returned to Berlin to take stock of my situation, and again my country had changed. Marxian Socialism was spreading everywhere. The 'Kriegsschieber' had given way to the 'Revolutionsschieber,' the sly speculator taking advantage of the chaos in German life.

I had been surprised before to see Jews in Government departments. Now they were everywhere. The collapse of German life and the uncertainties of the new order were giving them their opportunity. The Jews who largely animated the Republican regime threw open the doors to their compatriots in Galicia and Poland, and Germany had uncounted thousands of strangers thrust upon her, alien in language, outlook, and spirit, the political gypsies of the world, giving real allegiance to no nation.

Jews were in high posts in the new Government. The five big 'D-banks' of the country were in Jewish hands; practically the entire theatre; a large section of the daily and periodical Press; business in every field. Jews had penetrated into the universities and the law. Germany's sources of education and thought were rapidly being brought under the domination of the Jewish influence. A population officially estimated at only six hundred thousand had gained a commanding position in wealth, in political power, and in the general conduct of affairs. . .

Inflation had begun its work of ruin. Germans would be hard put to survive in their own land.

This time I resolved to get out and stay out.

Alexander von Bismarck, an accomplished flyer, told me casually that two or three German planes had been smuggled into Holland for sale. At once I was afire with a new idea, or rather my old one, applied to planes instead of ships. We went to work. Utmost care was necessary. Inter-allied commissions had arrived to supervise the destruction of German war material, and the Republic had established a commission to co-operate. By one means or another I managed to obtain assurance that this governmental commission would look the other way should Germany's air-fleet-or a part of it-take to the air.

A certain company gave me a contract to sell whatever planes could be smuggled out. Bismarck would fly them. Two mechanics and four planes would be supplied; other planes would follow.

In June of 1919 I sailed from Amsterdam for South America, heading toward total failure.

In Rio de Janeiro, business was lagging. Buenos Aires was more promising. General Jose Francisco Uriburu, later President of the Argentine Republic, willingly granted me space at the flying field and the use of a hangar. I cabled for the four planes, the two mechanics, and Bismarck; the planes were practically sold, unseen. At length came a cable saying that they could not be shipped before November. Well before that date, a French mission arrived bringing forty planes, the whole paraphernalia of an air fleet, and an Argentine flyer who had fought in the Lafayette Escadrille and now wore the insignia of the Legion d'Honneur in his buttonhole. My prospects vanished. When Berlin cabled that my planes were ready, I answered, wishing that I could put my fury into the words: "Too late-hold them for orders."

On a ranch in Paraguay, two days' ride by horseback from the Parana, I had a lesson in applied biology. My host was of a German family of high lineage. I well remembered the nobles whom I had known at home, fastidious, arrogant, conscious of their class and their duty-the backbone of the race. Here was an old man who slouched around in ragged leather slippers, or bent for hours with a knife in hand over some steer, scraping the ticks from its sores and smearing tar over the raw flesh. Sometimes, to see the sores more clearly, he would take out his battered monocle, and I would be reminded that this cow-doctoring baron had been, in earlier days, an officer and a dandy in the Garde-Kavallerie of His Majesty the Emperor.

Gambling debts had tossed him into the oblivion of the pampas. There thirty years of cattle-raising, fatalism, and miscegenation had made him what he was. For cattle were not the only livestock that he raised on his ranch. He was the father of eleven children: seven from Indian servants, four from negroes, none from his wife.

That wife had once been a proud lady of the Imperial Court. Now, weighing two hundred and fifty pounds, she squatted for her rare bath in a crudely hewn tub that resembled a pig-trough, and waddled out after meals to relieve herself most publicly in a primitive privy.

Drinking countless rums and endless steaming mates, smoking his black cigars, the Baron would unload extraordinary local tales. Evidently there were other barons, counts, and princes who, bankrupt at home, had in this new land repaired their fortunes but lost their heritage.

My next major objective was Mexico. As the northbound ship would touch at the Panama Canal Zone, I applied for a transit visa at the American consulate in Buenos Aires and was bluntly refused. To be a German in those days was to be an outcast in Allied circles.

At the end of November, I started north by train across the pampas. Santiago refused my visa more politely; Valparaiso was equally firm. A British ship carried me to Callao - the first German passenger to be accepted by the line since the war. Only one English-speaking passenger, an American woman, was courteous to me. Several Chileans were affable enough, but took away at poker all the money I had with me - one hundred and eighty-nine English pounds. Landing without a peso in my pocket, I was saved by a chance encounter with an old school-friend from Berlin.

When the American consul in Lima turned me down, I felt that I had no choice but to strike across country for the Caribbean, avoiding the Canal Zone entirely; if I could get to Havana I would be able to ship to Vera Cruz.

My overland trip began in February 1920 from Quito, lost corner of colonial Spain, nine thousand feet above the sea. A Quicha Indian was my guide. We had two saddle-horses and two pack mules, and on my saddle-bow went my wire-haired terrier 'Jibby' who had accompanied me all the way from Germany. That trek along the Cordilleras and into Colombia had its share of thrills. I ran into chills and fever, plenty of hazards from wind and weather, none from man. But I did not get to the Caribbean. At Buenaventura I risked it after all and took ship to Balboa, and at the Panama port they interned me for lack of a visa. In the end, I think it was Jibby who got me by. On the third day another officer had appeared to hear my story. All the while I was talking, he seemed more interested in Jibby than in me, though she, for her part, appeared to be following my words most carefully.

"That little dog seems to like you a lot," he said finally.

"Go ahead, you're free. Good luck."

Havana was reluctant to receive an alemán and kept me fidgeting aboard ship all day. Finally they let me ashore, but it was a gloomy landing. I learned that the failure of a bank in Copenhagen had cost me thirty thousand marks. Now I was poor indeed. But soon I felt myself less poor, for I found Dolores. After waiting for weeks, she had been on the point of returning to New York.

We had two weeks together before my boat left for Vera Cruz. They were happy weeks, but for both of us they were charged with the realization of the subtle change in our relationship. The separation had lasted too long; we had each found out that life did, after all, go on. We still loved, but we were not in love.

Dolores went back to New York, and I to Mexico, bound, I hoped, toward fortune. .

I am not going to try to do justice here to my Mexican story, for such a fantastic adventure deserves a fuller account than I can give it here. In Germany the aeroplane company failed; in Mexico I ran into revolution. It was smouldering when I arrived. By the time it was aflame, I was a friend of General Francisco Murguia, and knew and admired President Carranza. His enemies ranked me as a 'Carranzista.'

The ill-fated train that set out from Mexico City to carry Carranza and his government to Vera Cruz had me for a passenger. Finding tunnels dynamited and his route blocked, the President took to the mountains with two hundred of his 'rurales,' leaving his gold-laden train to be looted by revolutionists. Carranza was shot in his tent, my friend Murguia by a firing-squad.

But I was neither looted nor shot, for I had made my get-away before that. On the first day of our halting progress toward Vera Cruz, I had reconnoitred the situation for myself when the Presidential train came to a dead-stop: revolutionists had sent a locomotive crashing head-on into the troop train preceding us. Certain that I was marked for death where I was, I got my bag out of the train and struck out into the country, with Jibby at my heels. A farm-house sheltered us. Eventually, after some narrow squeaks, we escaped from Mexico into Texas, by way of Laredo. My Mexican passport got me into the United States without a question.

San Antonio ... St. Louis ... Chicago ... New York ...

First impressions of America were heavy with disillusionment. Billboards . . . rubbish heaps . . . automobile graveyards . . . treeless streets.

Presently I began to be won over by the liberality of this land. Astounding, the things one could have free--cream, butter, and bread in restaurants, electric light squandered like sunlight, soap on the bathroom shelf, matches everywhere. Then a New York speakeasy, with poison at one dollar a drink! Certainly - I said to myself - America is not to be understood in a minute. I did not try. Homesickness laid hold of me, and I sailed for Germany.

My own country held no comfort. Tendencies that had been disquieting in 1919 were now intensified. Even if Germany had pleased me, I could not have stayed, for the Copenhagen bank failure had left me poor, and there was no life for me here.

An old friend advised me to try my fortune in Reval, in the new Baltic republic of Esthonia, which had broken away from the Soviets. In the first gold-rush after the Soviets opened their borders, Reval had become the base of supplies and theatre of operations for a hundred varieties of business. I needed goods to sell--but what?

The tread tyre had just come on the market. A concern in Frankfort-am-Main still had an enormous stock of treadless tyres; I opened negotiations with them, and was appointed general sales representative in the Baltic states.

Reval, or Talinn, was a picturesque city, German in its essential pattern, Russian in the gaudiness ofits frame. Almost daily, refugees arrived from Russia, crossing the border in unexplained ways, some of them living ghosts, some in rags, some with jewels concealed on their bodies. There were so many of them, their stories so tragic, that horror soon became a commonplace.

The Soviets were still political outcasts, in dire need of every conceivable product. An army of commercial adventurers- American, European, Japanese, Jewish-flocked into the already crowded city, the only open window tor the commerce of the world. There was scarcely room to stand; but for those with foreign money quarters could always be found.

The Bolsheviks were buying avidly with the Czar's gold and being victimized, paying spot-cash for carloads of rusty nails and American Army bacon too rancid for the soldiers. Granted that my tyres lacked a tread, they still were good tyres, and I sold them with a will.

As the autumn of 1920 lengthened into winter, Reval turned cruel. Snow bedded on the streets into a mass of ice; the cold bit the lungs. In this busy, money-making city, vodka and revelry ruled by night; life was desperate and reckless, full of harsh contrasts. Once I watched the owner of an island gamble it all away, village by village, farm by farm. After an evening in the Nobles Club, I would step out into the night, gaze up at the frosty stars, and then look down to see aristocrats scavenging in the streets. This was the inscrutable fate of man in a chaotic world.

Once more I was in the money, determined now to keep it. The mark, still falling, was sixty to the dollar, and I was putting my earnings into dollars and banking them in Amsterdam and Zurich. But life in Reval wore down the nerves, starved the spirit. I had made enough.

Off I went on a fitful tour. London was dismal; Paris, depressing and vulgarized now, had lost its magic. I journeyed through Switzerland to Vienna, once so beautiful, now sombre and terrible; on through Italy to Rome. Everywhere the picture was the same-Europe was gloomy, unsettled, unreal. I sailed again for America.

In New York, after a business venture which turned out a failure, a change came over me. Doubtless the sober fact that Dolores was no longer a real part of my being-a realization which left me feeling empty rather than sad-had something to do with it. At any rate I began to listen to the inner voice I had been stifling all these restless years. Go home, it said, and stay there. Whatever the future of your country may be, your own is bound up with it. As a German you can find happiness only in trying to help guide Germany's destiny.

My return led me, in the end, to Hitler.

III

THE MAKING OF A NAZI

Back in my room at the Continental after my interview with Hitler, I was soon pacing the floor in deep thought. Though my sense of spiritual elation did not lessen, the reality of the task which I had assumed was beginning to assert itself. Faith was not enough; works were ,necessary. Hitler had unfolded a practical programme which would demand the utmost of my strength and ability. I must come down out of the clouds and prepare for intelligent action.

Hitler had accepted me with definite interest; but just the same I was to-day merely one among less than a thousand inscribed members. To-morrow would I be helping him to lead, or would I be merely one of those who were led, losing my identity more and more each day as new recruits rallied under the swastika banner?

The Party was young, well-founded; nothing could prevent it from growing, and I was resolved to grow with it. The strength and will were there; I needed only knowledge and opportunity.

During the ensuing weeks I was diligent in learning the ropes, studying the inside structure of the Party, meeting people, reading pertinent literature, discharging whatever duties were given me, and publicizing the Nazi cause and the personality of Hitler wherever I could.

It was then that I began to build up my political library, buying, in addition to the usual books on economics and history, works that shed light on the special problems facing Germany. Among them were Alfred Rosenberg's The Trail of the Jew in the Change of Time and the well-known Handbook of the Jewish Question by Theodor Fritsch a greatly feared and much persecuted adversary of the Jews. His book is a widely used reference-work which reached its thirtieth edition in November 1930, endorsed by Hitler for its 'special merits as background material for the National Socialist, anti-Jewish movement.'

My reading and my talks with Reventlow revealed the extent to which other men, long before Hitler's time, had been working for the German cause by promoting folkic and anti-Jewish thought.

The emancipation of German Jews had begun in Prussia in 1812. It was, in two ways, a consequence of the French Revolution: the Revolution had hoisted 'liberalism' as a worthy banner, and in those unsettled times, when every neighbouring state needed money for defence against the Napoleonic menace, it was useful to make concessions to the people who controlled the money-the Jews.

Great Germans had declared themselves against the tendency. In 1823 Goethe, hearing that a law permitting the inter-marriage of Christians and Jews had been passed, gave himself up to passionate protest, foreseeing and predicting the gravest consequences from this new concession. Bismarck, speaking as a deputy in the Prussian Parliament in 1847, said that he was not an enemy of the Jews and was willing to grant them every privilege-except that of holding office in a Gentile state. In 1848, however, the liberalistic revolutionary movement brought the Jews a so-called emancipation, though the complete removal of all restrictions did not become a fact in law until 1869.

Throughout the nineteenth century an anti-Jewish current was latent in educated German circles, growing stronger as the consequences of Jewish emancipation became more apparent. It found expression in the definitely anti-Jewish attitude of Schopenhauer, of Richard Wagner, of Moltke, the German Field-Marshal of 1870, and of many others. But the influence of the numerous books and pamphlets dealing with the Jewish problem was not great. With the appointment, however, of the Court-Preacher Adolf Stoecker, called from Metz to Berlin by Emperor Wilhelm I, there began an anti-Marxian movement which of necessity broadened into an anti-Jewish campaign, making Stoecker virtually the apostle of German anti-Semitism.

Prominent among other anti-Jewish leaders were noblemen like Max Lieberman von Sonnenberg and Graf Ludwig zu Reventlow, the brother of Ernst. By 1893 the anti-Semitic Party in Parliament had sixteen deputies, and strong and influential economic groups, such as the 'landbund' and the 'Deutschnationale Handlungsgehilfen-Verband,' were now active in a folkie sense and in opposition to Jewry.

In German Austria, anti-Semitism developed independently of the movement in the Reich, Ritter Georg von Sehoenerer, its father and for many years its leader, was decidedly a Pan-German and therefore opposed to Rome. But another influential anti-Semite, Dr. Karl Lueger, a man of genius and later Vienna's great mayor, became his adversary, fighting his Pan-German ideas and the powerful 'Free from Rome' movement. Soon the situation in Austria was that which prevailed in the German Reich; the folkic anti-Jewish groups were wasting their strength in quarrels among themselves. Coming largely from the upper strata of society, they were weakened by their academic character and were never a serious factor in politics.

The World War led to the miserable collapse of the two Empires, and to the triumph of Marxism and the Jew. But it brought into being something else-the spirit of the front, of united comradeship, and out of this spirit, confused and scattered though it was by its division into disparate and rival groups, there was emerging a new German resurrection, a folkic rebirth coming this time from the bottom of the nation, evolving slowly but organically into a real movement of the people. Soon after the war there appeared on the scene organizations like the 'Stahlhelm,' 'Wehrwolf,' 'Jungdeutscher Orden,' 'Bund Oberland,' 'Bund Bayem und Reich,'

'Bund Viking,' 'Rossbach,' 'Reichsflagge,' and many others, all built upon a military basis and all anti-Jewish in varying degree.

In September 1922, soon after I joined the Nazis, a significant development took place: the folkic wing of the 'Deutsch-nationale Partei' broke away, and Deputies von Graefe, Wulle, and Henning founded the 'Deutschvoelkische Freiheitspartei,' which excluded Jews from membership. Another anti-Jewish organization, the 'Deutschvoelkische Schutz and Trutzbund,' created by the influential Pan-German Association, was dissolved by the hostile government. Gradually its thousands of members were to be absorbed by the Nazi Party.

This, very roughly, was the background of the anti-Jewish movement in which I now found myself an active participant. I needed to learn all I could about it, and naturally I was eager to know more about Hider personally. Today I cannot remember exactly what we who were then around him knew of his past. To us he was the 'Unknown Hero,' the yearning German-Austrian, the half-grown lad who had arrived orphaned and penniless in Vienna, carrying in his hands only a pathetic bundle but in his heart an indomitable will 'some day to be somebody.' He was the fiery youth who had come to Munich because he wanted to live among Germans, who fought with us and for us in the war, until gas temporarily blinded his eyes but gave him the inner vision that would lead us to freedom, against a hostile world.

This was my romantic picture. Before long it was part of the Hitler legend. Advertising a man is like advertising a product. When Hitler was 'discovered,' those most interested in building him up soon forgot in their enthusiasm what was truth, what was half-truth, and what was pure fabrication. At first instinctively, then deliberately as the current took him, the man himself helped to create the legend. His calculating mind early realized the drawing-power of mystery. Moreover, the facts of his un-heroic, dreaming, and frustrated youth must have embarrassed him. Scrutinizing Germans might have accused him of shiftlessness, finding the reality of his years in Vienna a trifle suspicious and of little value for the role he was to play in the future. Points noirs of the past, however harmless, when dragged into the light of day have ruined many a career.

Musing undisturbed in the quiet of his prison after the unsuccessful Beer Hall Putsch of 1923, Hitler began to write the first volume of his autobiography. Significantly, Mein Kampf tells little about his early life, and that little keeps an eye on the Hitler legend. His account of his boyhood and struggling years in Vienna is generally vague, often confusing and unconvincing, sometimes worse. This last defect was a logical outgrowth of a quality in him that some of us were soon to deplore: his Schlamperei - a sloppiness that we called 'Austrian.'

In recent years, objective historians,[1] probing the mysteries of the legend, have

---

1 Two biographies written by Germans were published in 1936:, Rudolf Olden's Hitler (Covici-Friede, New York), and Konrad Heiden's Hitler (Alfred A. Knopf, New York). Both authors are violently opposed to Adolf

begun to bring the facts of his early life to light. To-day it is possible to assemble a reasonably accurate picture of those years. I set down here what I know now-not what I knew in 1922.

Adolf Hitler, just about a year older than I, was born on 20 April 1889 in Braunau, a little Austrian town on the German border. It was a fortunate omen, he always said, to be born on the frontier between the two German countries whose reunion was regarded among young Germans as a work worthy of accomplishment by any means in their power.

His mother, Klara Poelzl, was his father's third wife, twenty-three years younger than her husband. Both parents were of peasant stock. His father, who had worked his way up from orphanhood to the post of a minor Customs official, was stern to the point of harshness, a man to be feared. He planned that his son should also enter Civil Service.

But Adolf was determined to be an artist. The thought of being tied to an office-desk, not master of his own time, filled the boy with deep aversion. Even so early, he showed a passionate wilfulness to do what he liked and to oppose what he thought wrong. The conflict ended with his father's death, in 1903, when he was fourteen, attending the Realschule in Linz, the charming capital of Upper Austria on the Danube.

Hitler himself admits that he was not successful at school, which he apparently left for good at the age of fifteen or sixteen. The next few years were empty; he must have led a rather aimless and idle life at the home of his mother, who enjoyed a small pension from the Government. She consented to his study of art. But his happy days as an art student were ended when the pictures he submitted to the Academy ·in Vienna, in 1907 and again in 1908, failed to qualify. They showed, the jury said, a talent for architecture rather than painting. His insufficient scholastic training blocked, however, entrance to the school of architecture. It was a bitter disappointment, and to it was added the sorrow of his beloved mother's death. Lonely and baffled, with only fifty crowns to his name, he went to Vienna early in 1909 to get along as best he could. He was then almost twenty.

In the Austrian capital he was barely able to exist. For the first few months he worked at odd jobs; then he was a 'decorator's man,' doing drawings or water-colours for a pittance. Sometimes he shovelled snow, and even begged in the streets. It is a matter of record that he stayed for at least three years in a men's hostel in the Twentieth District- down-and-out Bohemian, or, if you prefer, an urban vagabond. Here he came in contact with wretched souls, starving and homeless; with men of all classes in the Austrian melting-pot -noblemen, professors, tradesmen, workers;

Hitler's personality and philosophy j neither of them ever knew the man personally. Prejudice often misleads them, but their books are interesting and definitely helpful towards an understanding of Hitler and his rise to power-especially Heiden's brilliant work, a valuable contribution to the analysis of the man and his party. See also the latter's A History of National Socialism (Alfred A. Knopf, New York, 1935).

with professional tramps of many nationalities-Germans, Czechs, Poles, Magyars, Roumanians, Ruthenians, Serbs, Croats, Italians, and Jews.

Whatever Hitler may have done in these dark years, it is plain that he suffered; he himself always refers to them as years of misery and despair. It is plain also that he went on learning and observing. To deride Hitler as a former 'house-painter,' the standard belittling sobriquet flung at him by the world Press, is absurd and unfair. With equal justice one might call any American youth a waiter for the rest of his life because he earned his way through college by waiting on table. Although Hitler was not enrolled at the University, he remained an earnest student of history and life, arguing ideas and discussing politics with whoever would listen to him, and devouring newspapers and books. It was then that he learned the art of reading, which he practised constantly and discriminately, absorbing the worthwhile and rejecting the worthless.

A Roman Catholic, but never a good one, he soon ceased going to Mass and to confession.

Already at school, politics had begun to fire his imagination. Later, when he was at work on a construction job in Vienna, among the workers he came in contact for the first time with Marxian socialism. There he learned to understand those struggling 'forgotten men' whose miserable and uncertain life makes them an easy prey for agitators.

From earliest youth an instinctive nationalist, Hitler naturally soon became an anti-Marxist. In Mein Kampf he explains his rejection of Marxian internationalism because it 'denies the nation as an invention of the capitalistic classes; patriotism as an instrument of the bourgeoisie for the exploitation of the worker; the authority of the law as a means of suppressing the proletariat; the school as an institution for training both slave and slave-holder; religion as a medium for stupefying a people destined for exploitation. . . .' He rejects as well its propagating of the worship of the masses and the dictatorship of the proletariat, using the high-sounding catch-words of the French Revolution- 'Liberty, Fraternity, Equality' -without defining what liberty really is, without explaining how true equality is to be achieved among humans so different in character, outlook, and performance; or how real fraternity can be possible when one class is arrayed against the other.

Vienna in those pre-war days was not only the political and intellectual capital of Austria-Hungary but its economic centre as well. The glamour of wealth served to accentuate the bleeding poverty of the dispossessed and the unemployed. Merely by observing conditions round him and trying to analyse the forces which resulted in such disparate fortunes, Hitler learned enough to condemn the prevailing system. His practical contact with the people brought him in touch with the Jews, who even then controlled in some degree the Press and Marxian socialism in the capital. The anti-Jewish movements under Dr. Lueger and Georg von Schoenerer were still active during Hitler's Vienna period, and had considerable influence upon his future political life.

Pursuing his growing political interest, he gave some time to the study of the parliamentary system and soon learned to despise it as an instrument too easily warped by subtle influences. In brief, every experience Hitler met in Vienna, every study he undertook, helped to change him from a potential world-citizen with broad but vague sympathies to a convinced Pan-German and a fanatic anti-Jew.

Disgusted with Vienna as a conglomeration of all races and a powerful Jewish centre, he went to Munich in the spring of 1913 - and not in 1912 as he relates in his book. There he spent the happiest period of his life - the carefree months before the war.

Still earning only a meagre living as a free-lance designer and water-colourist, he could at least revel in the German atmosphere and commence the study of architecture. The whole scene in Munich helped him to expand. He wrote later that he was inspired by 'the marvellous - union of native, primitive force with the finer artistic temperament, the unique kinship between - the Hofbrauhaus and the Odeon, the Oktoberfest and· the Pynakothek.' In Munich, for the first time in his life; he felt himself really at home.

In a very real sense, he was already German when he arrived. Vienna had taught him to despise the un-German Hapsburg monarchy, the centre of the greatest social wrangle of modern time, when a dozen nationalities and a veritable motley of peoples were striving for separatism and independence in an internal warfare which had doomed Austria long before the beginning of the World War.

Feeling in his heart that he owed no allegiance to the Austrian State, in February 1914 he succeeded in being excused from the usual military service because of poor health. But when war was declared, he leaped to meet it, addressing a petition to Ludwig, King of Bavaria, for permission to serve as a volunteer. His request granted, he joined the Infantry Regiment 'List' and went to the front in October 1914.

Here again, Hitler's book is singularly silent about the facts of his war experience, an attitude which greatly helped the legend. It now is apparently established that Hitler never served in the trenches; from the beginning he acted as an orderly to the regimental staff, which usually was housed safely behind the lines with a roof overhead. Anyone who has been in the army knows that things are easier in many ways for the soldier who lives under the eye of the commander and makes himself useful to the staff of the regiment, than they are for the Frontschwein in the trenches.

But Hitler's war record is excellent. There can be no question of his personal bravery. Less than two months after he reached the front, the twenty-five-year-old Austrian volunteer was awarded the Iron Cross, Second Class. The difficult duty of a dispatch-runner often sent him across open ground under heavy fire. Wounded in October 1916, he returned to the front in March 1917, where for outstanding bravery he earned several distinctions, and finally the Iron Cross, First Class, on 4 August 1918. There are half a dozen variant accounts of how it was won; so far as I know, Hitler has never given any. The citation, though laudatory, mentions no specific exploit.

On 14 October 1918 he was gassed and temporarily blinded. The revolution breaking over Germany on 9 November found him still in hospital in Pomerania. Discharged on 13 November 1918, he went back to Munich a Staatenloser - a man without a country. The new Republic denied him German citizenship and he had lost his Austrian rights by fighting with the German army.

But Hitler was only officially homeless. All his interests and dreams were bound up with Germany's fate. He spent the winter months with the reserve battalion of his regiment in Traunstein. In March 1919 he returned to Munich, receiving his pay and food from the army until 1 April 1920. A few days after Munich was freed from the terror of the Communist regime by Bavarian and Prussian Frei-Korps, on 2 May 1919, Hitler, according to his own statement, was detailed to the 'Commission of Inquiry into the Revolutionary Incidents' with the Second Infantry Regiment in Munich. This was his first really active political employment, the birth of Hitler the politician.

After completing-a course of politico-military studies, he became instruction officer in the same regiment, with wide opportunity to speak before large gatherings and to meet people who later formed the nucleus of the Nazi Party.

Ordered to report on the activities of the 'Deutsche Arbeiter Partei,' he attended a meeting at which one of the speakers was Gottfried Feder, author of the 'Manifesto for the Abolition of the Thralldom of Interest,' the later theorist of the Party, who also drafted the Nazi programme. Hitler listened with attention, his mind stirred, his sympathy roused. After the meeting he learned that this group, which was but one of the many springing up during that unsettled time, could claim only six members. He became the seventh.

And this was the beginning-seven nobodies, penniless, lacking everything from a programme to a typewriter. Thus, out of nothing, do historical movements take their rise.

Soon Hitler forced his will upon this group, in which he was the only true activist. Taking over the propaganda function, he addressed one meeting after another, speaking to audiences of eleven, then twenty-five, then forty-seven. In December, two hundred. In January 1920, two hundred and seventy.

At last the time had come to risk a mass-meeting. Enough money had been saved to print the first pamphlet, the first placard, and the recently adopted programme-the famous Twenty-five Points. On 24 February 1920 the real birthday of the Nazi Party, in the Hofbrau Haus, festival hall and inner shrine of the whole world's beer-drinkers, known to hundreds of thousands of tourists, Hitler addressed more than a thousand people, proclaiming the Nazi programme and vehemently denouncing the Treaty of Versailles as the source of German suffering and bondage.

The complete success of that evening shaped the snowball which was eventually to become an avalanche over all Germany. But even before this, from the time its growth first became apparent, the movement drew hostile attention from two established groups; the Marxists, whose animus needs no analysis, and the Centrists, who combined monarchic, clerical, separatist, and even pro-French proclivities. Hitler's dynamic zeal in advocating the national unity of a 'Gross-Deutschland' and the annihilation of Marxism was already foreshadowing the inevitably approaching life-and-death struggle with the enemy parties.

The success of the mass-meeting meant that the first skirmish had been won. From then on, almost weekly, large halls were filled with enthusiastic crowds. On Mondays Hitler carried on a course of instruction for Party members only, and when these trained scouts were put at work, enrollment increased. That summer the 'Hakenkreuzfahne,' the swastika flag, old Nordic emblem of life and eternity, became the symbol of the Nazi movement.

The year 1921 saw the foundation of the first two local groups at Rosenheim and Landshut, not far from Munich.

But with expansion came revolt within the Party.

While Hitler, in the early summer of 1921, was spending a few days in Berlin conferring with nationalists in North Germany, the founders of the Party, irked by his growing popularity and his exigent attitude, resolved to oust him, for they saw the control of the Party slipping from their hands into his.

The teacher whose thirst I had distrusted made an attempt to use this conflict to further his own interests. With Julius Streicher's assistance, plans were laid for uniting the Nazi Party with the teacher group and depriving Hitler of his dominant position in the Munich party.

Hitler frustrated this attempt by quick and energetic action. Anton Drexler, the president, an honest, sincere, zealous, but somewhat weak man, resigned; Hitler took his place and drafted the new constitution of the Party. At a general membership meeting on 29 July 1921 the Party voted him dictatorial powers. From that time the teacher and, to a lesser degree, Streicher, were Hitler's enemies.

Responsibility to the top, authority toward the bottom, became the principle of the organization. This hierarchic order of leadership, which made and maintained Hitler as dictator of the Party, was also the key to his success and final triumph. Adopting a system of organization never before practised in German political parties, he formulated his reason for it thus: 'A movement which, at a time of the reign of the majority, in all and everything unalterably accepts the principle of leadership and the responsibility arising from it, one day, with mathematical certainty, will overcome existing conditions and emerge the victor.'

It is no exaggeration to say that the Party was saved in its greatest difficulties and times of crisis by the fact that one man alone had the final decision. This was largely, of course, because the man was Hitler. But analogies elsewhere prove that the system itself made for strength.

For one thing, this uniformly operating leadership made it impossible for saboteurs, parliamentary manipulators, or scene-shifting politicians to hide themselves behind committees presenting resolutions of so-called majorities. Thus the system prevented the effective growth of opposition groups within the organization.

On the other hand, this principle of sole leadership enabled the Nazi Party to allow its members a certain latitude. Even its best-known officers did not suffer censorship when they brought forward certain opinions provided they were presented as private opinions. But from the beginning, abuse or misuse of the Party organization for the execution of personal ideas was uncompromisingly crushed. This precedent was to prove of sweeping importance, for Hitler was to show that he understood how to identify himself with the Party to such a degree that he and the Party became one, just as he later succeeded in identifying himself with Germany so completely that Germany and he became one. Those who overlooked this tenet of Hitler's, even the highest among them, eventually had to pay the price for their forgetfulness.

The leadership principle was indeed a bold, surprising step in an era of triumphant democracy. Intelligent and necessary though it might be in abnormal times, it could become a dangerous doctrine if the dictator lacked any of the qualities necessary for supreme and single command.

That lack was not to manifest itself until many years later.

Meanwhile, the Nazis were making more enemies on the outside.

The first serious attempt to break up a Hitler meeting, on 4 November 1921, ended in a real battle and broken heads. Some seven hundred intruders, mostly Communists, were literally thrown through doors and windows into the street by only fifty Nazis. It was a memorable fight, in which, according to Hitler, two men especially distinguished themselves - Emil Maurice, later Hitler's first chauffeur and now retired to his profession of watchmaking, and Rudolf Hess, later Hitler's private secretary, and now his deputy and a Reichsminister in his cabinet.

The brawl led to the development of a specialized and highly effective 'hall-fight technique,' in which the Nazis employed every conceivable tactic for defeating even the most unequal assaults upon their meetings. This day was notable also for the formation of the 'S A,' the 'Sturm-Abteilung,' usually called, Storm Troopers.' At first their function was to protect Nazi rallies and serve as Party police, but in time they became the real political soldiers of the Party, Hitler's praetorian guard.

In December of the same year the Voelkischer Beobachter, an insignificant folkic weekly, was acquired with funds obtained from the Reichswehr by Dietrich Eckart and Captain Ernst Roehm, Hitler's staunchest supporters, of whom we shall hear more anon. Eckart, the nominal publisher, acted as editor-in-chief. Max Amann, who had been Hitler's top-sergeant in the war, was made manager of the paper and secretary of the Party, and became one of the most influential Nazis.

In this eventful year of 1921 the 'Deutsche Arbeiterpartei' changed its name. It was henceforth to be called officially the 'Nationalsozialistische Deutsche Arbeiterpartei,' more briefly, the N.S.D.A.P.- and to be known throughout the world as the Nazi Party.

By the summer of 1922 Hitler had pushed his organization so vigorously that his opponents could no longer ignore him. The old political dodge of killing a rival with silence had failed to work. By holding frequent meetings, making pyrotechnic use of his new weapon, the Voelkische Beobachter, and overcoming all difficulties by sheer will, nerve, or bluff, Hider was forcing himself and his cause upon the public consciousness.

Following the sound principle of Frederick the Great, 'attaquez-attaquez donc toujours' Hitler attacked unremittingly, forcing his enemies into the open. There was no longer any doubt who was against him, for he was being denounced and opposed with ever-increasing violence and viciousness. From now on the Jewish and clerical press made the best propaganda for the Nazi cause.

The Party had entered a new phase. From a loose group of somewhat bewildered crusaders seeking vaguely common aims, it had become a small but hardy organization with a definite purpose, an indomitable will, and a boundless faith in the Leader and the Cause.

This was the standing of the Nazis when I joined them. The Party was still very small; and though it had more self-will than most such groups, its actions and policies were still guided to some degree by the council of the previously mentioned 'Vaterlaendische Verbaende,' the union of patriotic societies.

My days had their share of excitement, filled as they were with conferences, speeches, the writing of editorials, membership drives, and money troubles. But I wanted action on a more heroic scale, and it began to look as though I would get it sooner than I expected.

By the end of August 1922 the tension between Munich and Berlin was tauter than ever. Munich's capitulation to the capital, the likelihood that Berlin police would soon begin to arrest anti-republicans even in 'sovereign Bavaria,' the financial problem of maintaining the folkic organizations in the face of an ever-increasing . inflation-all these forced the Vaterlaendische verbaende to take some sort of action.

The most important political power in the organization was Dr. Pittinger, at the head of his 'Bund Bayem und Reich.' Using his prestige to gain the backing of the combined societies, he undertook to plan a coup d'etat to seize the Bavarian

Government. The societies were to support him when he took action.

As far as one could judge from the constant secret conferences, the brave phrases, and the important air of Dr. Pittinger and his staff, great things indeed were in the offing. At last word was whispered that the coup was arranged, even to the very hour. I was ordered to relay the final instructions to co-conspirators in Berlin and other northern towns: they must mobilize at once, in readiness for drastic events when the coming crisis in Munich should bring forth a new Bavarian government.

Thrilled to the core and more than a little puffed up at being the bearer of such momentous news, which in my imagination was already foreshadowing a world event, I hurried to Berlin to meet Count Reventlow. The tall, grave Count's calm and sarcastic manner now showed nervousness and concern. We felt that history might be in the making, though we both confessed some doubt about the makers.

Excitement soon swept my doubts away as I rushed on, leaving instructions in various towns as I passed through. Reaching Stettin late at night, I roused from his bed Baron von Dewitz, leader of the Pomeranian Landbund, the largest nationalist peasant organization, and over a bottle of wine we discussed the historic hour.

Tearing along by motor through a sleepless night, I expected at every stop to hear that the great plan was accomplished. But no news came. Worried, I hastened back to Berlin to find out what had happened. Nothing had happened. The huge mass demonstration, the great human wave which was to sweep the new leaders into office on its crest, had dwindled to a ripple. Except for one small meeting in the Munich Kindl-Keller, no demonstration had been called.

Riding back to Munich in the train, angry and baffled, I saw no humour in my shattered dream of German destiny in the balance, and of myself as the German Paul Revere. But Count Reventlow, sitting across from me, seemed more amused than disappointed.

Driving directly to Pittinger's headquarters, I met the great man at the door. He was just getting into a gorgeous motor-coat and looked very haughty in his goggles-ready to speed away in his big Mercedes for his well-earned vacation in the Alps.

"Is this the coup d'etat?" I asked him, but he swept magnificently by.

Every one I met was either sheepish, disgusted, or filled with rage. Hitler's men had been the only ones ready to march, I was told. But nobody knew where Hitler was now.

Finally I found him, hiding from the police in a poorly furnished attic room. With him were only his faithful guard, Ulrich Graf, and a great police-dog. All the late newspapers were scattered about the small table and the floor. If my memory serves, this was about the 20 September 1922.

We had a long talk. The public had learned about the high plans leading to this wretched fiasco. It was a setback and a disgrace, and Hitler was beside himself.

This was no easy session, and I did not realize that now I was at last witnessing one of history's decisive moments. Hitler was at the crossroads. He had tried to work with others and had been betrayed.

When I reported my bootless journey, ending with the encounter with Pittinger, he began to rave.

"I was ready-my men were ready!" he cried, spreading his arms in a wide gesture and letting them fall despairingly to his sides. Then his eyes narrowed.

"I have learned," he said. "From now on I go my way alone. Resolutely alone. Even if not a soul follows. These cowards! I shall do it if no one else dares."

He was so wrought up that I tried to talk of other things until he should grow calmer. So I presented an idea for him to consider. What did he know, I asked, of Benito Mussolini, whose occupation of Turin with his Blackshirts was getting headlines? At the moment the parallel was no doubt a trifle galling, and he replied rather tartly that he knew only what everybody else was reading in the news reports. Then he burst out again:

"No more Pittingers, no more Fatherland societies! One party. One single party. These gentlemen-these counts and generals-they won't do anything. I shall. I alone."

Gone was Hitler's conception of himself as the advance agent, the drummer-boy. On that day of disappointment he became the Fuehrer.

I believe that this failure also altered his inner regard for the 'great' people toward whom he had previously shown a certain deference and humility. But his demeanour did not change. He had found that it worked to be naif and simple in a salon, to assume shyness. It was a useful pose, but now it covered scorn. These important people-who were they? Mediocrities! Cowards! And who was he? He was HITLER- a man endowed with triple strength: his faith in Germany's ultimate glory, his confidence in himself, and a formula for leading men.

In 1927, when he was still five years away from power, he wrote in the second volume of Mein Kampf:

'One must never forget that every really great achievement has been effected in this world not by coalitions but by the success of one single victor. Successes won by coalitions, owing to the nature of their origin, bear within themselves the seeds of future decline, possibly even to the extent of losing all that they have attained. Great and truly world-changing revolutions of a spiritual nature are conceivable and realizable only in the form of titanic struggles conducted by single forces, and never as enterprises conducted by coalitions.

'The folkic state in particular, therefore, will never be created by the compromised will of a union of folkic organizations, but only through the iron will of one single party which has forced itself to the forefront by defeating all others.'

And yet, in the face of this uncompromising declaration, Hitler's political opponents and rivals continued to cherish illusions about using him in an alliance of compromise, and to ridicule and underrate him in the prevailing short-sighted way. Doubtless they had never troubled to read his book, one of the most revealing documents ever printed. Repetitious and ill-constructed though it is, its analysis of conditions and trends is keen, and convincingly expressed. What Machiavelli was to princes, Hitler could be to every would-be dictator.

Even while the Nazi Party was in temporary eclipse through the failure of the Hitler-Ludendorff 'Beer Hall Putsch' in 1923, Hitler put into writing with surprising frankness exactly what he proposed to do. And later he did .it, bit by bit, as conditions and his growing strength allowed.

It would be foolish to say that his singleness of purpose sprang from the Pittinger episode alone; but that this was the deciding factor which started him upon his career of solitary leadership I can say with certainty. Again and again he would interrupt our discussion with some reference to the fiasco, always ending with the final dictum: 'I most work alone.'

Even on ordinary days in those times it was almost impossible to keep Hitler concentrated on one point. His quick mind would run away with the talk, or his attention would be distracted by the sudden discovery of a newspaper, and he would stop to read it avidly, or he would interrupt your carefully prepared report with a long speech as though you were an audience, emphasizing his periods with the butt of his old dog-whip.

My own little project promised to find the going rough on a day when Hitler had resolved henceforth to make his way alone. But having made it a rule always to say what I wished to say, I persisted in telling him that Count Reventlow seconded my suggestion that it might be well to find out more about Benito Mussolini. He was, I admitted, still an unproved force, working outside the law and against great odds. How useful it might be to establish contact with him no one in our ranks knew; nor did we know whether his programme really paralleled ours in any essential. But it seemed apparent that the Italian Fascist movement, like the Nazi movement, was strongly nationalist and directed against Marxism and Bolshevism, and that it might develop into an attack on the whole parliamentary system. Also, it had advanced its programme further than ours. To have an ally who was succeeding, even though the alliance were merely one of mutual sympathy, would be encouraging.

Hitler's attention was caught at last, and he heard me out. Then for a little while he thought silently, and finally asked whom I would suggest for the mission.

Taking the plunge, I suggested myself, adding that it would be a good thing to go with the backing of some well-known Nazi sympathizer, like General Ludendorff, whose name would be a passport into any political sanctum.

Hitler welcomed the idea, and told me to go ahead. I could see that his mind was already turning again toward the future, leaping over yesterday's defeat as of little importance.

Just as I was on the point of leaving, in came a man whom I recognized with surprise as the Captain who had impressed me so unfavourably a few months before: How he had discovered Hider's retreat I never knew. Curious to learn the motive behind his visit, I stayed. His business proved of the most trivial nature, and after he had gone, I candidly expressed my astonishment that Hitler tolerated such fakes. Then he said a significant thing:

"Never antagonize potential enemies. Attack them only when you can destroy them."

For my own welfare, I should have taken his advice to heart. But as later events will show, I did not.

IV

FROM LUDENDORFF TO
MUSSOLINI

To gain Hitler's consent to the use of Ludendorff's name was one thing; to get Ludendorff to lend it, another. Always rather aloof and inaccessible, he had become very cautious after the failure of the Kapp Putsch in 1920. It was certain, however, that he was keeping well informed of what was going on throughout the Reich, and though at that time he was not associated with Hitler, he must have known him. Reventlow and I decided to do our utmost to sell Hitler to the General.

It was important to present the abortive Munich coup in the light most favourable to the Party-which, indeed, simply required explaining the failure with entire candour. But more important, everything we said during the interview must contribute to Hitler's personal standing.

If we, as ambassadors, could make Ludendorff understand even a part of Hitler's sincerity and ability, if we could gain for Hitler any expectation whatsoever of the War Lord's open and active endorsement, which he had not yet seen fit to give to one of the contending groups-then truly our mission would have results far beyond the immediate project of interviewing Mussolini.

The German movement that won the backing of Ludendorff's world prestige would find its fight for recognition accelerated beyond the power of any other single influence to speed it. Hitler seemed to me to be the one leader who offered a programme which the intensely folkic veteran might fully approve.

What a combination - Ludendorff, the General, with all that name implied of caste and authority, and Hitler, the dynamic corporal, coming from the people! It stirred my imagination, and I think it touched Reventlow's as well. But though I harangued him with my most persuasive arguments, he refused to rise to my peak of enthusiasm. I was an inscribed Nazi, unshakably convinced that without fail, and to Germany's unqualified benefit, Hitler would fight his way to the top. Reventlow was older, and long familiar with the back-stage side of politics; he had seen too many political shows come and go to applaud another new one so early in its run. He liked Hitler personally, and hoped for great things from the movement; he had shown his good-will by offering it every help. Yet, so far, he had not committed himself by joining the Party.

"We will wait and see," he said, summing up in one phrase all the hopeful, sceptical wariness that public life had taught him.

As soon as Reventlow could-arrange a meeting, we went to Ludwigshoehe, outside Munich, where Ludendorff lived in seclusion in his villa, surrounded by high walls.

I had always had the greatest respect for the fine old General, whose every act, public or private, whether as military leader, gentleman or man, showed him to be possessed of the high qualities bred of the best German tradition.

Yet I knew there was probably no more sorrowful man in the land. Invincible on the battle-field, but apparently defeated in the time of 'peace' when Germany most needed fighting men, Ludendorff had retreated to this little walled-off world, where, to all appearance, the civil struggle wakened no echoes.

While we waited in his study, I found my glance held by an oil painting on the opposite wall. It showed Ludendorff with Field-Marshal von Hinderburg, monocle in hand, bending over maps spread upon a table.

As I looked at this famous picture, painted at the height of Ludendorff's career, my eyes met those of Reventlow sitting lost in thought below it, on his face the look of a man who thinks backward into the past and finds his thoughts bitter and mournful.

I lifted my eyes to the picture again, and the irony of the situation swept over me. What was I doing here? Who was I to intrude on the tragedy of this man's life?

Ludendorff was the victor of Tannenberg, by a titanic feat of arms. He became master of the German, Austrian, Bulgarian and Turkish armies. For two years he was absolute ruler from the North Sea to the Persian Gulf from the Marne to the Duna, a man possessed of more effective power than Napoleon. Selflessly and with genius he devoted his entire strength to the nation. With a Prussian education, a soldier from his youth, saturated with the idea of hierarchy, order, and discipline, accustomed to command, true to his oath, he never dreamed that his work would be sabotaged. The vile collapse of the war's end was a blow that shook his whole being.

The little men who cut the ground from under his feet said afterward that he fled. But he did not flee. He left the country from sheer rage and bitterness, to seek rest in Sweden after four years of wasted strain and effort. Writing his war memoirs and wrapping himself in silence, he turned his face away from a Germany that seemed satisfied with defeat.

Then a violent reaction took hold of him. We find him behind Bermondt and General von der Goltz in the Baltic, behind Kapp and General von Luettwitz in the Kapp-Putsch. After that, wherever true German interests brought a group together, his name was spoken, his spirit felt-but only vaguely, for his hand was seldom seen.

Before the war, as colonel and chief of the operations department of the Great General Staff, Ludendorff concerned himself little, if at all, with politics.

Consequently, when his high office during the war naturally brought him into close contact with problems of State, he was without practical experience.

Of incorruptible character and absolute veracity, with a stern sense of duty and the courage to assume responsibility, his straightforward military nature made him, ironically, a victim of the very political intrigues and parliamentarian opportunism which he detested.

He did not see the deeper significance of Germany's inner development toward the Left. Had he understood the dangerous forces at work, he would have offered the Kaiser an ultimatum in the spring of 1918, and established a dictatorship for the salvation of the Empire, while he was at the full zenith of his power and prestige, with the German people supporting him and the army his to command. Germany might not have won the war, but certainly would not have gone down in inglorious humiliation.

'Would have offered an ultimatum' is a positive statement. I make it knowingly. During this interview and others that followed, Ludendorff gradually revealed his innermost sorrow over the German defeat, and the conclusions he had reached as to the causes. Later on, when his thought had crystallized, he boldly published a summary of them:[1]

'If I had only known at the time that secret influences reaching beyond the boundary of Germany were more powerful than the Government of any nation, I should have acted differently....

'The lack of unity of purpose in both thought and deed which prevailed between statesmen and military leaders in Germany all through the war is one of the principal reasons for the ultimate debacle.'

'Today, of course, I clearly see that conditions as they prevailed at home were merely the result of a policy already inaugurated before the outbreak of the war by interests beyond the control of any government-interests whose influence veritably overshadowed the power of the nation.

'The political leadership of the Empire, consciously or unconsciously, succumbed to the influence of these interests. Germany simply was not permitted to gain victory. If I had only known then what I know now, in spite of a natural disinclination for politics, I should have interfered more energetically and earlier to save the Fatherland.'

'If I had known.'. . . His one-sided military education, the lack of certain Napoleonic qualities, too much pride and not enough intuition, but above all his ignorance of actual political conditions and world political forces-perhaps also the mentality of Hindenburg, dissuading him from any coup de force against the Emperor, however vital the need-these explain Ludendorff's tragic failure to prevent the ultimate disaster, when a bungling diplomacy and a feeble, inert home

---

1 *Appeared in the Sunday edition of the Hearst newspapers of 22 May and 29 May 1927.*

government failed to take advantage of the victories of the German army in the field.

Excellent minds in Europe have studied Ludendorff from the military side. Yet concerning the political transformation and activities of the civilian Ludendorff after the war, practically nothing is known outside Germany.

When the Empire collapsed, his entire scheme of life went with it. He believed, profoundly, that his days of usefulness and happiness were over. It is difficult to do him sufficient honour for the way he rallied, though an ageing man, and threw himself into the struggle beside young Germany for a new conception of the world.

At first he retired into himself, striving to fathom the deeper causes of the social breakdown. Recent social history was as much of a quagmire as the Masurian marshes, but eventually he won through to solid ground. Then, as a civilian, indifferent to the hatred and scorn of his enemies, he took up the fight for the liberty of his country.

He perceived now that conventional morals do not prevent men from manufacturing war, from corrupting the State, from enslaving nations. He perceived also that men with large economic interests at stake are seldom concerned over anything else, least of all the general welfare. Abandoning any idea of appealing to men of his own class, he defied society and turned toward the people, the farmers and workers. And then, because he had learned to pursue the truth to its ultimate, he challenged the Church, the Jew, and the money interests. Breaking with the past, gradually he became a revolutionary, of a different sort from those who had destroyed the Empire.

Already, here in this villa, many of the threads ran together that were being spun, wisely or unwisely, to strangle the Marxist Republic. Here it was that the Frei-Korps leaders and many others, the active agents of all interested groups, came for advice and encouragement. Some came with their hearts open, others only to use and to betray Ludendorff, as he had been betrayed before by his Kaiser and by Hindenburg.

How could Reventlow and I, waiting in his study, making our plans in the best of faith, how could we foresee that in the end he was to be betrayed again by Hitler ?

The great Feldherr entered the room. Tall and blue-eyed, massive and powerful, calm but alert and determined, he seemed a tower that defies the world.

After exchanging greetings with the Count, he welcomed me in a natural and simple manner. Seating us with a friendly gesture and a winning smile, offering cigars, he made us feel at ease.

Reventlow told him whatever he did not know about the Pittinger fiasco, reporting the reaction in Berlin. Ludendorff readily agreed that the Pittinger chapter was closed, and did not mince words over his satisfaction that these 'Romelings' had failed.

When we came to Hitler, he listened to our carefully laudatory comments with the keenest interest. Step by step, more by insinuation than, directly, we intimated how much the common welfare might be advanced if the General would give his blessing to Hitler and the Nazi cause.

His response was not evasive, but neither did he commit himself. The phrases he chose revealed a sense of humour, and I was delighted to find that the great warrior, who looked so remote and judicial, was very human after all.

But from the first it was obvious that he understood us. Agreeing that only a popular movement which offered the people a national and social programme could reclaim the farmers and workers from Marxism and succeed in building up a new Germany, Ludendorff expressed himself as warmly in sympathy with Hitler's aims. He saw clearly that while the outer liberation of Germany-the breaking of the Treaty of Versailles-would be possible only as the result of an inner rebirth, preparations abroad were necessary to create this new Germany for the Germans, free from Judah and from Rome. He also saw potential benefits from an understanding with Mussolini-or of Mussolini-and considered an overture wise, even though the Italian's future, like ours, was problematical.

"And you may use my name."

On our way back to Munich I felt a glow of pride in the success of our mission, and even Reventlow allowed himself to show a touch of satisfaction. I reported to Hitler at once. Now that my idea had the backing of Ludendorff's judgment and name, he was impatient for me to be off to Milan. Tomorrow, I promised.

At my lodgings I found a telegram from Dolores, announcing her arrival that very night. It was a tender but hopeless meeting. Impossible to convince her that my independence was gone, that Hitler and the future of Germany meant everything now.

That evening, hoping it might help her to understand, I took her to the Zirkus Krone to hear Hitler harangue a mass meeting. Exquisitely dressed, with beautiful pearls at her perfect throat, Dolores walked bewildered beside me through the crowd, led respectfully by sturdy Storm-Troopers to a box near the platform where Hitler was to speak. When he began, I kindled immediately. But Dolores, who understood not one word of German, saw only a slight figure with an absurd moustache, who waved his arms and shouted. When the arena rocked with applause, I was almost annoyed that she did not rise to her feet with the rest.

After the meeting we drove Hitler to his home. The fire-eater of the platform sat modest and exhausted in the corner of the car. It is hard for a man to be winning toward a strange lady who doesn't speak his language, especially if her lover is along-and Hitler succeeded no better than I in making a Nazi of Dolores. Worse, she definitely disliked him, and refused to understand my devotion. Her antipathy was so positive that she even warned me not to trust him, to leave him.

To make things easier for us both, I accompanied her as far as Paris. It was our final parting.

I stopped scarcely a moment in Paris; but again a trifle was to store up future trouble for me. This time it was the French francs that I acquired for our journey. After we said good-bye, they travelled innocently in my pocket to Italy, and months later, as I shall tell, they tumbled out to libel me and the Party.

Arrived in Milan, I informed myself as completely as possible about Benito Mussolini and his Blackshirts, and realized that his position was much stronger than we had supposed. Conditions here were more nearly ripe for a showdown than in Germany.

Telephoning to the Popolo d'Italia, I asked for Signor Mussolini, explaining that I had journeyed from· Munich especially to bring an important message from important people. A moment later Mussolini was on the wire, expressing his pleasure and readiness to receive me. Would I come at three that very afternoon? I was amazed and gratified at the ease with which it was arranged.

I meant to size Mussolini up, estimate his chances for success, get his opinions on crucial matters, find out whether and how we could co-operate. In this present day it is hard to believe that I had no idea what the man looked like, having never even seen his picture. I tried to visualize him. Would he wear a typical Italian face, or a Roman one? Or would he resemble Colleone, whom Verrocchio has immortalized so superbly in bronze-an expression of force, a gesture of brutality, a face conveying all the contempt for life that characterized the intelligent great carnivores of the Renaissance? He sounded like that sort of man.

I was ahead of time at the Popolo d'Italia, a thing that seldom happens. The newspaper, founded and formerly edited by the Duce, occupied an entire building of imposing size, a contrast to the headquarters of our meagre little outfit. A Blackshirt directed me to the second floor, where another conducted me to Mussolini.

Even then he had the habit of staging himself, placing his desk in the farthest corner, so that callers must approach him across the entire room.

At the desk sat a square-cut man, in a dark shabby suit and untidy shirt, with a high dome of bald forehead and powerful, almost frightening eyes. He welcomed me in a pleasant, resonant voice. I conveyed the greetings of General Ludendorff and of Adolf Hitler. Then, the preliminaries over, we sat down to talk.

My few words of Italian, however, were already exhausted. He tried some German. Laughing, we discovered that we did best in French, which we both spoke fluently.

I noticed his hands. They were small and soft, and showed how overstrung he was, for the nails were bitten not merely to the quick but almost to the moons. They shocked me slightly. He looked anything but healthy, his face sallow, his lips tired. But his strong gaze and his power of organizing his thoughts in forceful, rapid speech impressed me. And though I am German,' I rather enjoyed his slight theatricality.

In fact, the longer we talked, the more I liked him-his swing, his allures, his pose, the marvellous acting that was part and parcel of the man. Yes, I saw the Colleone through his face even then, long before he posed in martial mien under the steel helmet. I could see that this was an indomitable man; yet now he revealed such esprit and cultivation, such grace of gesture and phrase, that I completely forgot his iron core, his shabby clothes, his mutilated finger-nails.

I was very frank with him, for soon it was evident that I must begin from the beginning. Mussolini had never heard of Hitler. In fact, each of these men, now so constantly in the spotlight of world affairs, was then so obscure that a rational man in my place would have felt-politically speaking-like a hyphen connecting two zeroes. But to be a Nazi in those days required a certain fervent irrationality.

Briefly but thoroughly I sketched a picture of conditions in Germany, explaining our movement as an inevitable development working toward clearly defined results. I tried especially to emphasize the importance of Hitler and the Nazi Party as a political entity. He listened with obvious sympathy and understanding, asking many acute questions; but as a seasoned politician, he said just what he wanted to say, and no more.

He agreed that the system created at Versailles was impossible for Germany and for all concerned; that it would not hold in the long run-a viewpoint of remarkable independence in the year 1922, even though Italy had been treated shabbily at the Peace.

Then we talked about Bolshevism and Marxism, Fascism and Liberalism, and he gave me an outline of the internal drifting of Italy. When he spoke of the advance of his Blackshirts, pride gleamed in his eyes.

Touching on the issue of international finance, I found his views paralleled Hitler's. Then, pursuing the subject, I spoke of the Jews. He agreed with my facts, but was evasive about what measures they called for. While he admitted that he watched the Jews carefully, he pointed out that in Italy the Jewish question was not the problem it was in Germany. I did not know at the time that Marghareta Sarfatti, his devoted friend and biographer, was a Jewess, or that one of his early followers and an important liaison man, was a converted Jew. This man (to anticipate my story for the sake of a significant fact) ultimately married a lady from an eminent Catholic family, with the blessing of a Cardinal, and became secretary of the interior in Mussolini's cabinet. After the Matteotti scandal which almost unseated Mussolini, he was dismissed.

At last, cautiously, I ventured to sound Mussolini on a question delicate indeed-his attitude on the Tyrol, now the Alto-Adige, which, won by Italy from the Austrians, had been a rankling wound for Germans ever since, as its inhabitants were German from the soul outward.

Before my question was fully phrased, he interrupted me like lightning, accenting his words by truncheon-like strokes of his forearm.

"No discussion about that-ever!" Now the suavity was gone, the force showed through. "The Alto-Adige is Italian and must remain so. But even if it were not, military reasons alone make it imperative not to revert to the impossible old border."

Abruptly he turned to German internal affairs, mentioning Gustav Stresemann, later chancellor and foreign minister of the Republic, as a leader capable of solving Germany's problems. He had set me right about the Tyrol so thoroughly that I did not hesitate to do as much for him, putting Stresemann down as a dangerous opportunist and careerist, a selfish compromiser unacceptable to the Nazis.

There had been rumours that the King might not survive a Fascist coup. Saying that for us the form of government was of secondary importance, I raised the question of the monarchy in Italy, asking him outright what he intended. He replied in an even voice:

"That depends on the King."

Thus far, the most interesting revelation to me was the extent to which matters in Italy had developed, not merely in plan but in fact. From the definiteness with which Mussolini seemed able to answer all questions, and from his air of complete preparedness to assume the burdens of government, I was sure that an Italian crisis was imminent; the next several months or perhaps even weeks would decide the fate of his movement. It was clear that he was staking everything on one play.

"Signor Mussolini," I asked, "in case the Government does not yield, are you prepared to resort to force?"

With superb assurance, he said :

"Nous serons l'etat, parce que nous le voulons!"

We shall be the State because we will it . . . No statement so strong could be regarded as ambiguous. "That is an answer," I said, and he bowed. Our talk ended after seven in the evening. Everything had strengthened my conviction that Mussolini knew the dice had fallen, that he would have to act. I left certain that he would strike for power in a very short time. Within the month, he marched on Rome.

It was dark and very late when I stood in pyjamas on the balcony outside the window of my hotel and looked out over Lake Maggiore. The remembered lure of a station poster seen on one of my trips to Munich had prompted me to spend the night in Stresa for a last taste of the easy life that I had exchanged for politics. But I could not merge myself with the soft September night, for past and future filled my mind. Hitler ... Mussolini ... Would they save this sinking world?

Strange that a man, poised for the moment when he must act to determine the destiny of Italy, should spare four hours to talk with a stranger whose sole credentials were the name of a general, great but disgraced, and of another man totally unknown to him and still utterly powerless in what had been until recently an enemy country.

Was Mussolini apprehensive about the outcome of his plans, unwilling to spurn the smallest offer of moral support? Or was it that even today Germany stood for an almost legendary power in the Italian mind? After all, there had been a time when the appearance of one spiked helmet in the Alpine passes was enough .to throw an entire regiment into panic.

Not Hitler's name, but Ludendorff's, had impressed the Duce. In six weeks he might be in power and in need of allies. Or in six weeks he might face a firing-squad. That would be a pity; the man had an admirable personality. He had been right, of course, about the Tyrol: Italy really must hold it for reasons of defence.

How much did the Tyrol weigh in Germany's balance? Ought Hitler to jeopardize the rapprochement with Mussolini, which might even lead to an alliance, for the sake of a quarter of a million German-speaking expatriates? Surely the acceptance of Mussolini's view, a political conditio sine qua non, promised the greater benefit to Germany-even though Hitler's enemies might brand him at once as a traitor who abandoned his countrymen to a foreign power for expediency's sake.

Would those enemies prevail?

Across the midnight darkness of the lake the map of Europe loomed in my mind, weighted down by the political forces of the world of that day, forces which made any effort to free Germany seem an impossible task.

Even the most partisan optimist might despair of solving the problem by a Nazi revolution, a bold, untried, extraordinary measure which would affect and possibly antagonize the entire world.

The hugeness of the task and the absurdity of the hope swept over me. Its execution meant the liquidation of Jewry, of Rome, of liberalism with its tangled capitalistic connections; of Marxism, Bolshevism, Toryism-in short, an abrupt and complete break with the past and an assault on all existing world political forces. And all this to be consummated by a handful of obscure men in a defeated country, politically isolated, economically starved, and ruled by the diametrically opposed spirit of a capitalist plutocracy, subject to international finance, under the guise of a so-called democracy which the people were supporting!

Fantastic, that a little group of average men, without power or tradition, should think of attacking a system which, however false and inequitable, was firmly rooted in innumerable human interests and controlled by definite, concrete, intransigent factors reaching far beyond the borders of Germany. The practical obstacles were so immense that only a dreamer could believe they might be overcome.

And yet, when one analysed the problem intelligently and thought it through to the very end, was it so wholly mad?

Our great hope sprang from the fact that in the existing world outlook there was something fundamentally unwise, inorganic, and therefore weak, which during the centuries had brought about impossible, untenable conditions. If that was true, then it was equally true and far easier to believe that the creation of a new structure, a new world-outlook, organically conceived, could be carried out against all and everything, however small the initial force might be.

If the Nazi world-outlook in its simplest interpretation was, as I saw it, nothing but Nordic common sense, Nordic reasoning applied to life, then the crux of the problem was to organize a force, both mental and physical, strong enough to break all existing resistance, in order to enthrone this new reasoning, this new world-outlook, in every phase of life.

And there was Hitler. More than any one else, he had vision, faith, and the will to act. Men would follow him. It would be a long road. For the present it was better that the rank and file should not know what was before them, or understand all that was involved. Let them follow him blindly in the service of the Fatherland. Presently they should see a new Germany that would make the whole world widen its eyes in astonishment.

My imagination overflowed. The magic of the night had begun to work in me; the vastness of the struggle that a moment before had appalled me, now fascinated me. Boldness rose in me.

Now about Mussolini ... I began to plan my report.

V

WERE YOU AT COBURG?

Before my trip to Italy, I had changed my lodgings from the Hotel Continental, one of the two 'best hotels in, Munich, to a pension near the Koenigsplatz. I was not poor, for I had invested the profits of the Reval enterprise in countries whose stable currency protected me against loss through inflation; compared to most of the Party members, I was well off indeed. Simply by transferring my funds to German banks, I could have been a millionaire and very soon a billionaire-in marks. But hard cash was better, and my money stayed abroad. Following what was the general practice in those days when marks dropped lower almost hourly, I exchanged foreign credit for domestic currency only when I had to, and then for the minimum amount necessary to keep me in petty cash.

Under ordinary circumstances, my temperament would have tempted me to extravagance. But now I had little time or inclination for expensive gaiety. Working for the Party every day and most nights, active and absorbed, I continued only two indulgences: my clothes were still English-made, and whenever I was free in the evening I would dine at the Walter-spiel restaurant, renowned for its cuisine. It should have occurred to me that to be a hard-working revolutionary, yet remain well-fed and well-dressed, was in effect to lead a double life which could hardly go unremarked by our enemies and by less fortunate Nazis. One of my weak points was always to neglect my own protection.

The Nazi organization itself lived from day to day financially, with no treasury to draw on for lecture-hall rentals, printing costs, or the other thousand-and-one expenses which threatened to swamp us. The only funds we could count on were membership dues, which were small, merely a drop in the bucket. Collections at mass meetings were sometimes large, but not to be relied on. Once in a while a Nazi sympathizer would make a special contribution, and in a few cases these gifts were really substantial. But we never had money enough. Everything demanded outlays that were, compared with our exchequer, colossal. Many a time, posting the placards for some world-shaking meeting, we lacked money to pay for the paste.

Instead of receiving salaries for the work we did, most of us had to give to the Party in order to carry on. Clerks and officers, except for a very few, got no pay, and the majority of members pursued their usual occupations during the day as a livelihood. Consequently, those who gave full time to Party work were a miscellaneous crew, including only two or three who had sufficient means to support themselves. The rest were chiefly recruited from the jobless-men who would work for their meals; not the best way to build a staff, of course. We had small choice; but a better personnel could have been organized even with such material. No one in authority took the trouble. It was a loose system, and from it sprang many of the weaknesses which still characterize the Party.

For one thing, it bred jealousies. Each man, feeling that he was giving himself, wished to exercise some authority, however petty. Headquarters was a collection of little Hitlers who bowed to the big Hitler but were apt to ignore or mistrust each other. How any real progress was ever achieved by such a staff is one of the mysteries of Nazi history. Destiny must have guided us, for certainly little else did. It was every man for himself-for the Party's sake.

The Nazi aim was clear enough; the problem was how to achieve it in the shortest time with the least danger of failure, and not even Hitler, genius though he was, had a complete idea how we should proceed.

Each of our political problems brought its own solution; and each solution led to a new and greater problem, which in turn was solved partly by chance, partly by intelligent action. Each time a new step was taken, the Party advanced-and Hitler, the leader, learned as much as he taught. Probably never before in history has any other man absolutely created a party, yet been to such an extent himself the creation of that party.

This loose co-operation and uncrystallized plan of action had only one advantage: our imaginations were not stultified by the rigor mortis that always sets in when an organization has achieved its growth. If any of the subordinate officers conceived a scheme which appeared worth while, the set-up gave him every opportunity to test his idea.

My plan for interviewing Mussolini is a good illustration. Though I was without official rank in the organization, and moreover was only a new member, a mission of such great potential importance had been entrusted to me largely because it was my own idea. And as usual Hitler profited-the man had an instinct for seizing his tactical advantages.

Returning from Italy, I telephoned headquarters, and Hitler replied that he would come to see me at once at my pension -which was characteristic of our relations in that period.

At once I got down to cases, giving him a detailed report of all that Mussolini had said, how he had impressed me, what the situation seemed to be. Then, together, we began to interpret this information.

As far as I was able, I tried to convey to him my personal intuitive reaction. Hitler knew absolutely nothing about the Italian situation-the real situation, as distinct from what the papers printed. It was easy to convert him to my opinion that, within a few weeks or months, Italy might mean - Mussolini. I emphasized the fortunate similarity between Nazism and Fascism: both fervently nationalistic, anti-

Marxist, anti-Parliamentarian; in short, both dedicated to a radically new order. And I pointed out the similarity between the two leaders: both were men of the people, veterans, self-made and therefore original in their thinking; both were striking political speakers, with an appeal to the emotion and imagination of the masses. It was obvious that these facts might prove of great importance for future relations: Hitler and Mussolini would at least understand each other.

Mussolini, I said, spoke a little German and excellent French; he knew German literature, especially Goethe and Nietsche, and through them had a window on the German mind. Hitler's face hardened into aloofness for a moment; he had got the point. He was then, and still is, isolated to some degree from the minds of Europe because he knows no language other than his own, an ignorance which puts him at a disadvantage in formulating foreign policy. We advanced to a serious discussion of Mussolini and Italy.

For the first time, Hitler was really considering the ultimate possibilities of his programme in relation to the rest of Europe, and trying to see the international problem from a practical standpoint.

The natural future alliance of our new Germany, we agreed, should be England and eventually the northern European states; therefore, our logical effort-when we had the power-would be to alienate England from France. As a corollary of our organic growth, a German-English alliance was imperative. We had, however, to consider the actual political constellation. Forces currently dominant in England were, and would indefinitely remain, opposed to the Nazi Germany that we envisioned. With France holding a military trump-card, and Germany isolated politically and economically, we were in no position to bargain with England. If we had any hope of understanding among the major powers, we should find it in Italy-if Mussolini came to power.

An understanding with Mussolini would mean a flanking, menace toward France in case of conflict, and would probably create a spirit of co-operation in Austria, Hungary, and Bulgaria. In short, on Mussolini and his good-will might depend the reshaping of the European constellation for our benefit. The Tyrol, Hitler acknowledged, was not too great a price to pay for Mussolini's friendship, for if Germany's relation toward the rest of Europe were strengthened by one strong alliance, we might count on time to complete our internal reorganization without interference.

Hitler paid the closest attention when I told him of Mussolini's direct challenge to the weak Government at Rome, and how his organization of Blackshirts was taking active steps to break strikes and was waging stern warfare against the Soviet councils already entrenched in several northern cities. His eyes grew thoughtful when he heard how the Blackshirts marched into Bolshevized towns and took possession, while the garrisons kept benevolently neutral or, in some cases, even quartered the

Fascisti. Mussolini was proving how much could be achieved by sheer nerve and initiative in dealing with a vacillating government.

Discussing the repercussions the Italian struggle might have on our fight in Germany, we both felt that if for nothing else, than purely for propagandist reasons, for the psychological effect, it would be an enormous advantage to us to have an activist group in any other country succeed in overcoming Marxism and parliamentary inefficiency.

The longer we talked about Mussolini's probable importance in European affairs, the more it became apparent that the Nazi struggle for dominance was not merely an internal political question, but a foreign political problem of the gravest importance, which would become increasingly important as our programme made headway at home. This was an aspect of the Nazi future which until that time had received only the most superficial thought, a dangerous oversight on our part unless we immediately broadened our outlook to include the foreign alignment we would face when our domestic programme approached its climax.

Hitler was disturbed and pleased, both at once, by the new enlargement of our outlook which resulted from the journey to Milan. His thanks were profuse, however. For a long time, he said, he had felt that he needed an assistant who was independent, a man of the world, speaking foreign languages, with vision enough to see beyond the suburbs of Munich.

His praise would have embarrassed me, had he not followed it with a serious proposal: Would I confer in his behalf with the leaders of other German Nationalist groups, seeking to gain their moral support at least, and if possible to bring them openly into the Nazi fold?

Of course I would! It was just the sort of confidential work I wanted.

Then our conversation took a more personal turn. It was decided that I ought to sever my connection with Pittinger's 'Bund Bayem und Reich,' since Hitler had already broken with them. Until this time I had been ostensibly Pittinger's man, and Pittinger had no knowledge of my mission to Mussolini. Although I was an enrolled Nazi, I had kept my membership quiet, in accordance with Hitler's wishes.

"You haven't met Rosenberg yet?" Hitler asked me abruptly.

I replied that I knew him but slightly.

"You must know him better, get on good terms with him. He is the only man whom I always listen to. He is a thinker. His large conception of foreign policy will interest you."

Foreseeing that I should be constantly more occupied with Party matters, I asked if Hitler could suggest a good Nazi who was out of a job and willing to enter my employ. He recommended one of his most trustworthy followers, Ludwig Schmied, and promised to send him next day. Then he went home, and I to bed, happy over a job that seemed to me well done.

Ludwig Schmied proved to be a character. He was an Austrian, and a type. A volunteer in the war, he kept his uniform after the armistice, and simply transferred his allegiance to a succession of Frei-Korps, with one of which he took part in the march that overthrew the Munich Commune. Eventually he landed with the Nazis, becoming one of the first Storm Troopers. He was a splendid soldier, who understood and perfectly executed everything pertaining to soldiery-and almost nothing else.

His heart was right, there was nothing he would not try to do for me, but I soon learned he was not born for valeting. Outside the military sphere he was a typical lackadaisical Austrian, slouching about with an almost stupid expression in his spaniel-like eyes, smoking incessantly and leaving a trail of cigarette ashes behind him as he cleaned. But he was honest as gold and loyal through anything, serving with a touching devotion. And-a crowning virtue-he could cook. In fact, his cookery helped to get me into trouble-but that is a story for later on.

When I followed Hitler's advice and broke with Pittinger, openly aligning myself with the Nazi Party, I felt that I ought to make my position clear. So I had a long talk with Ernst Poehner, the former police-president of Munich, who was one of the most important anti-Berlin men in Pittinger's group. Being still a crusader, instead of simply stating my resignation I told him about the interviews with Ludendorff and Mussolini, using the former experience to convince him that the time had come for all who really desired a folkic renaissance to join forces under an active leader. That leader, I insisted, was Hitler. It might be advantageous if they would talk together.

Poehner consented, and the interview took place in Poehner's home, which was modest enough and cared for by his wife, a brave simple soul, a typical German Hausfrau.

It was interesting to watch the two men together.

Poehner was a Protestant, a man of courage, integrity, and simplicity, at that time the one man of action among all the higher functionaries in Bavaria. But his temperament, excellent for routine matters, lacked the elasticity for revolutionary acts.

With his close adviser, Dr. Wilhelm Frick, he had exercised sweeping powers from 1920 to 1921. It was alleged, but never proved or admitted, that during his term hundreds of Communists had been executed. Whatever the facts, he was one of the men most hated by Marxists and Jews. On the other hand, only his tolerance toward the Nazi Party had permitted Hitler to survive the critical early twenties. Had Poehner yielded to the clamourings of political bosses during those first years, all the troublesome folkic groups would have been exterminated.

Poehner was dark, long, and lanky, and had a ludicrous speech affliction, especially when he was excited, which made him end his sentences in an untranslatable stutter. But Hitler met him with almost awkward modesty. The decision to work

A portrait of Hitler by Heinrich Hoffmann taken at the time of the first meeting between the Führer and Ludecke.

alone evidently did not mean that Hitler was ready to spurn the help of men with prestige and power, but only that he would use everything and every one to further his individual aim. Nor can I be certain his aim included, at that time, a personal ambition for power. It may be that he would have worked wholeheartedly to advance a man of Poehner's type to the dictatorship, had such a man entered the field actively. I am sure that the vision of himself as master of Germany was not yet Hitler's motivating idea.

All through the conference Hitler sat in his cheap raincoat, wearing impossible shoes, his felt hat crushed shapeless in his hands. Talking in his softest, most winning voice, with his slurring Austrian accent, he seemed anything but the fire-eater of the platform. His mien was almost humble; but he was not dissimulating. Drawn together by their ideals and sympathies, these two men impressed each other.

An understanding was effected, though for the time being it remained a silent pact between them. Poehner would stand behind Hitler. He was not demonstrative about it, but he was won over. We left feeling that something had been gained.

The practical example of Mussolini, and Hitler's increasing confidence that his programme would be favoured at least tacitly by men like Ludendorff and Poehner, determined him to initiate the campaign of direct action which was obviously the necessary next step. Writing heroic editorials and making bristling speeches no longer sufficed. To meet the Marxists on their own ground, we had to carry the fight into the street, and use their tactic of brawling in public as a bait to win the brawny working man.

On 10 October 1922, an opportunity presented itself or rather, was manufactured by Hitler out of the slimmest materials.

A ' German Day' under the auspices of several folkic societies was arranged for that date, in Coburg. The Duke and Duchess of Coburg, who were strongly and openly nationalistic, were to be guests of honour. Hitler, whose name was already becoming known outside Munich, was invited to attend and to 'bring some company.'

He resolved that the Nazis must dominate this meeting. With superb and insolent political instinct, he seized upon the word 'company,' ordered a special train, and instead of taking the few guests he was expected to bring, set out for Coburg with about seven hundred men-a large portion of his whole party.

This was the first Nazi special train to run in Germany. Wherever it halted the sensation was terrific. Most people had never seen the swastika banner, and now they were doubly impressed, because the Laws for the Protection of the Republic were in force, with severe penalties for those who openly defied them. Our thirty-minute halt in Nuremberg, with our men shouting, our band playing martial airs, the strange 'Hakenkreuz' banners waving from the windows, created a furore. Amazed burghers and wide-eyed Jews almost fell out of the express trains passing the station, trying to decide what new menace or blessing we represented.

It was the first, most spontaneous, and best-staged escapade in Nazi annals. And the magnificent bluff of that special train, when we scarcely had money enough to hire a horse! Every man contributed to the fund, some sacrificing their last pennies. More than one had to beg a relative or sweetheart for ticket-money.

It was our first excursion outside Munich, .and we looked forward to a holiday. The long hours of train travel were whiled away in talk. I was still a comparative newcomer in the Party, not well acquainted with everyone, so I took the opportunity to study Hitler's entourage more closely.

Seven men travelled with Hitler in the same compartment-Max Amann, Hermann Esser, Dietrich Eckart, Christian Weber, Ulrich Graf, Alfred Rosenberg, and I. These men, an ill-assorted group, were a cross-section of the Party. By far the most interesting personalities among them were Eckart and the much younger Rosenberg.

Dietrich Eckart, a writer of long standing, outshone all the others with his wit and common sense. He spoke in a rumbling, blustering bass, looking positively benign with good humour; but his great, round head, powerful forehead, strong nose and chin, and piercing little eyes, indeed his whole person and carriage, revealed a dominating personality. Later I saw him in a rage when he seemed like an irate Teuton god, grim and formidable. Usually, however, when he slipped his shell-rimmed glasses up to his forehead in a characteristic gesture and peered at you, there was a depth of joviality behind his fierce front.

He was something of a genius, and to a great degree the spiritual father of Hitler and grandfather of the Nazi movement. Also, he was well-to-do, one of Hitler's first financial blessings. Born in 1868, he was older than any of us, and before we appeared on the scene in Munich, he had prepared the ground with his keen, clear-seeing weekly, Auf Gut Deutsch, which was now discontinued. He was a rabid racialist, attacking the Jews on metaphysical grounds. His Lorenzaccio is perhaps the greatest German tragedy after Goethe's Faust.

As demonstrative as Eckart was, just so calm and reserved did Rosenberg appear. A block of ice! Though a young man, he was already mature, a balanced personality, showing fine erudition and judgment in intellectual things, but little human warmth. He was predominantly Nordic in appearance, though his features were heavy and irregular. His pale lack-lustre eyes looked toward you but not at you, as though you were not there at all. His arrogant reserve and coldness were insulting, a strain on any relationship; but when he spoke he revealed himself at once as a thinker, expressing original thoughts in a fine form and with the inner assurance that marks a high intellect.

Rosenberg was three years my junior, having been born in 1893 in Reval, the old Hanseatic town where I had recouped my fortune after the war. His father, the director of a German trading-house, allowed him to study architecture in Riga. During the war the entire school was transferred to Moscow; there he continued his studies and began the cultural-historical probings which served as a foundation for his philosophical research, culminating in his epochal work, The Myth of the Twentieth Century, published in 1930 and soon put on the index by the Vatican.

Just before the German occupation he returned to Riga. Attempting to volunteer in the German Army, he was rejected. The two revolutions-Russian and German-altered all his life-plans; so he turned to politics, giving his first lecture in Reval about Marxism and the Jewish question. When the last German troops were withdrawn, he followed them to Germany, reaching Munich in the days of the Red Terror of March 1919. Officially a Russian during the war, and now a White Russian in his sympathies, he set about becoming a German citizen.

One day he walked into the midst of a street crowd which was being harangued by Soviet agitators. Overcome with memories of Russia, before he realized what he was doing he found himself replying.

"Are you crazy?" he shouted. "Do you know what it means, Bolshevism? I know. I come from Russia."

Stormed with questions and surrounded by an ever-increasing audience, he unconsciously launched into a political speech. The next day he met Dietrich Eckart, and began work at once as a collaborator on the weekly paper.

Before the year was over, the two of them met Hitler. Eckart became, as I have said, the father-protector of Hitler, placing his periodical at his disposal, and supporting him with a little money. Rosenberg, the twenty-five-year-old Baltic German, became Hitler's closest co-thinker, and more than anybody else, in his later writings, shaped the Nazi 'Weltan-schauung' -a word somewhat inadequately translated as 'world-outlook.' Who could do it better? He was then, and probably still is, the outstanding racialist and anti-clericalist in the Party, with deep-rooted convictions about the Jewish peril. Only Eckart rivalled him, though their co-operation was too close to be called rivalry.

Most of these facts, of course, I learned later. But during the long ride from Munich to Coburg, both men emerged as clear-cut personalities. Eckart, in spite of his sovereign altitude and flawless, almost too-beautiful German, which he adopted whenever his point was barbed with sarcasm, could drop into sturdy Bavarian dialect and make you feel at home with him at once, if he liked you. But Rosenberg's aloof and chilly irony frightened people away, making them feel small and uncomfortable in his presence.

Eckart I liked at once but found it difficult to be friendly with Rosenberg, not yet being inured to his razor-edged irony. I did not know then how close and fateful our relations were to become in time.

With everybody chiming in when our discussions grew heated, we forgot the

71

time, and were still in the midst of a great argument about Party policy when our train entered the environs of Coburg.

The telegraph must have flashed a warning ahead to the town. At the station we were met by a deputation from the 'German Day' committee, with a uniformed police-captain in tow. They informed us that they had made an agreement with the local trade unions, which were ruled by Marxian Socialists, that we must not enter the town in closed ranks with banners unfurled or bands playing.

When the order was presented, I was standing with Hitler and the rest. It did not occur to us that we should discuss this rebuff, much less accept it. Numbers gave us confidence. One man is helpless against five men, but ten men can resist fifty; with seven hundred, we felt able to defy all Coburg.

With characteristic vehemence, Hitler rejected the conditions, replying contemptuously to the deputation. Then, ignoring the astonished police-captain, he told Lieutenant Klintzsch, who led the Storm Troopers, to order them into line. The band struck up. With flying banners, preceded by eight stalwart Bavarians, huge roughnecks from the Chiemgau, in leather shorts, who carried alpenstocks, but kept their rubber clubs and knives hidden, we moved forward.. Hitler and the seven of us in his entourage followed the standard-bearers, and behind us moved the seven hundred men.

We swept along the platform, through the undercut and out upon the station square. There we met a great storm of insults from a crowd collected by the Reds to hoot us. Disappointed by our success in flouting the order, they hurled every sort of name at us. We were 'murderers, bandits, criminals, hoodlums.'

The S A men kept strict formation and ignored the jeers. But none of us knew the town, and when the anxious police offered to guide our column, we accepted. Guilefully they led us, not to the quarters we had arranged for in the Schuetzenhalle, but toward the Hofbrauhauskeller. Right and left as we marched, before and behind us, the crowds were gathering and becoming more threatening.

When our last man turned into the Keller, the crowd, still yelling abuse, tried to force its way in. The police locked the courtyard gates to separate us from the hostile demonstrators.

This was intolerable, and Hitler refused to be sidetracked in this way. On his order, Klintzsch commanded the S A to re-form ranks. Hitler addressed them in a few fiery words, exhorting them to prove their valour-if necessary.

The gates were opened against the protest of the now thoroughly alarmed police, and we faced the menacing thousands. With no music, but only drums beating, we marched out in the direction of the Schuetzenhalle.

The turmoil and tension reached a climax when the crowds, incited by agitators, began to throw things and to attack us bodily. Patience could endure no more; now we had to defend ourselves. We who were in the forefront with Hitler were exposed to very real danger, for cobblestones were fairly raining upon us.

Sometimes a man's muscles do his thinking. I sprang from the ranks toward a fellow who was lunging at me with his club uplifted. From behind me, my good Ludwig followed. But at the same moment, our entire column had turned on our assailants.

For nearly a quarter of an hour it was an outright battle, man to man. At first the police took no sides, striking at every one with impartial vigour. But soon, probably because they shared our enthusiastic dislike for the street rabble, most of them took our side, and before long we were masters of the field.

In the give-and-take, I did not notice whether Hitler actually joined in the fighting, but I do know that he was right in the midst of it. When the fracas was over, I would not have exchanged my own bruises for medals. I had felt now and then that the rank and file did not quite accept me. Now I was one of them. Seeing that one brawls as well in an English suit as in shoddy clothes, they forgave me my tailor.

With the street cleared, we arrived almost triumphantly at our quarters, but some of our men had been handled so brutally that they had to be sent to hospital.

It was natural that such an entrance into the town should have created the greatest excitement. Hitler's appearance in the meeting-hall that evening was greeted with undisguised curiosity by the genteel committee, who looked at him askance. The hall was full, and among the audience were the distinguished Duke and Duchess of Coburg, who later became staunch supporters of the Nazis.

I sat at the table with Eckart and Rosenberg. Again it was almost startling to see with what devotion and personal affection Hitler's immediate group regarded him in those days. Even Rosenberg, supposed to be a man without emotions, cold as the tip of a dog's nose, betrayed the warmth he felt in his heart for Hitler. All of us virtually hung on his lips as he spoke.

He walked away with the show, in a fiery speech which carried the audience off its feet. The routine addresses of the other speakers, advancing the usual patriotic appeals without much purpose, aroused little interest. No one in the hall even remembered them after Hitler flung out his defiant call for action.

After the meeting, we demonstrated what action meant. Long into the night there was fighting with the Reds, more serious than the daytime battle. Some of our men were missing; patrols which Hitler sent out to search for them had found them in horrible condition, as the result of being attacked singly by groups of our assailants. Ruthless punishment was inflicted upon the Reds wherever they appeared, and their headquarters were wrecked.

When sleep was possible at last, Hitler slept with the rest of his men, on straw.

Next morning Coburg, which had suffered for years under the Bolshevik incubus, was astonished to learn that the Reds were not invincible.

But they made one more attempt to regain the ground they had lost. By word of mouth and by handbills in which we figured as destroyers of law and order, the Reds, who themselves were simply extra-legal usurpers of Coburg's civil powers, tried to whip up the street against us. A great 'People's Demonstration' was called. Ten thousand workers would assemble on the square 'to throw the Nazis out.'

Hitler was determined to follow up his victory. One more act of contempt towards the Reds would undermine beyond repair their pretence of strength. So at noon sharp, on our way to the old Burgh, he led us through the square where the crowds were to have gathered.

But instead of ten thousand, there were only a few hundreds, for the most part meek and silent. A few newcomers, unacquainted with us, tried aggression, but were summarily put down.

It was amusing but gratifying to see the citizens of Coburg slowly begin to realize that the Marxist intimidation was at an end. Regaining courage, they began to hail us. Before long the town was alive with old Imperial flags. Police and people began to see in us the veritable saviours of the city, the long-hoped-for power which would break the Red monopoly. When we marched to the station late that evening, cheering crowds turned out for a gala occasion, while the Reds were conspicuously absent or silent.

But they remained vindictive even in defeat. At the station the train personnel, which had received threats from the Marxists, refused to run our train back to Munich. Hitler replied that if it did not start at once, he would seize every Red leader he could hunt out and, running the train with his own men, would kidnap them to Munich. The rest of the threat he left to their imaginations. Within ten minutes the train was set in motion. Next morning we were home again, stiff from a night on wooden benches in third class, but utterly happy.

Hitler and the Nazis ranked the importance of the Coburg venture so highly that to have been there became a special honour. This was officially recognized in 1932, when at the great festival on the tenth anniversary of that first victory, special badges were handed by Hitler to the men who had taken part.

It is typical of Hitler's career that the Coburg episode, which started largely as a prank, ended as one of the most important milestones in Nazi history. Indeed, its significance, in view of all its consequences, cannot be over-rated. For the first time, the authorities were openly defied; and for the first time outside Munich the Nazis carried their fight into the streets. Moreover, they came off victorious. The Storm Troopers' self-confidence increased, and their faith in their leaders was confirmed.

A new phase was beginning for Hitler's fighting men. Henceforth they were to be increasingly active. The new tactic which Coburg had inaugurated was to be continued for the next eleven years and more than any other single thing was to contribute to Hitler's eventual triumph. From then on, systematically, in cities where the Reds reigned, National Socialist Storm Troops were concentrated; flying squadrons travelled there in trucks and trains, to re-establish liberty of speech and the right of assembly for the Nationalists. Coburg had proved that nothing was to be gained for Germany by allowing the Marxists and other alien-influenced groups to monopolize the franchise, to abuse and thwart it and eventually to do away with it.

The scene of our first open conflict with the enemy became in time the first Nazi town in Germany, with a Nazi majority and a Nazi mayor. Other cities where we operated followed the same course, and gradually, through the years, Hitler became the recognized leader in many widely separated places.

The Coburg demonstration also brought an immediate and rapid increase in the ranks of the Storm Troopers. Although the entire Marxian-Jewish press raged at the brutality of Nazi rowdies who had invaded a city where they had no business, and very few of the bourgeois newspapers dared to congratulate us for at last showing the fist to the Marxists, the people, discounting the source of the condemnatory articles, began to take notice of us favourably. Many recognized that the Nazi programme well might end the corrupt bureaucracy of the Reich. In the next months, thousands of men deserted other societies or appeared from nowhere to join Hitler. His sovereignty in his own party was strengthened, and the Party grew beyond our dreams.

What seemed to others merely an insolent junket proved for us to be a decisive event.

VI

ARMS AND MEN

Hitler's intimates, as I have said, regarded him with veneration and respect. I shared their feeling, and coupled it with a deep personal affection. We were together a good deal, and out of a thousand trifling incidents, I began to piece together the puzzling fragments of his character. In spite of the simplicity, almost austerity, of his private life, his personality is by no means uncomplicated; and since Hitler is the Party, even today, his traits have large significance.

Artistic and retiring by nature, he had nevertheless thrust himself into the most violent sort of active life. There were times when he gave an impression of unhappiness, of loneliness and inward searching, so poignant that my sympathies were stirred. But in a moment, he would turn again to whatever frenzied task was next on his schedule, with the swift command of a man born for action. Outside the political field his inclinations were all toward art; yet one felt that if he had realized his early dream of becoming an architect, he would have designed great projects, not cottages.

Hitler's background and surroundings in Munich yielded important clues to his personality and his power.

In this formative period of the Nazi movement, he was surrounded chiefly by men like himself, and not by people who were rich or highly educated. The exceptions, of course, were Eckart and Rosenberg, and a few others, like Gottfried Feder, possessed of money or scholarship. Apart from these few, Hitler's associates were for the most part simple souls, a fact which had a lasting influence on his psychology. They were men from the most modest homes, like his own, men who knew nothing of the great world beyond their own towns, but were sincere, enthusiastic, loyal, looking upon Hitler as not only a genius but an inspired prophet. To understand these men was largely to understand Hitler and his power.

Night after night he sat in their little homes or in the simpler cafes of Munich, expounding his doctrines. His listeners adored him. The fact that he was one of them, not a man from above, sealed their devotion. They hung on his every word, hardly interrupting . even with a question. They were his circle of disciples, ready to do and die for him.

They felt no social embarrassment before him, because, like themselves, he was without social graces. Seeing in him the apotheosis of themselves, they were hypnotized with wonder and hope. Thousands trembled when he spoke, and yet-he was simply one of them. This in itself seemed miraculous and contributed to their unreserved acceptance of him as a saviour, a new Luther, a man embodying all their hopes for Germany and for themselves.

The fact that he was always the centre of a spellbound audience explained why for many years Hitler was unable to listen to anyone or to carry on a normal conversation. In his circle, Hitler alone talked; the others listened. There he aired his ideas and practised his speeches, thinking aloud. It gave him a firm foundation for effective speaking, but at the same time his character became set in a mould of intellectual isolation which became one of his weaknesses.

I remember distinctly how touched I was with Hitler's reception when he took me to visit the goldsmith, Gahr, one of his oldest and most devoted followers. Gahr was a man of perhaps fifty, a clean good-looking man, the true type of the old-style, honest craftsman. Modest, quiet, dignified, his whole presence revealed the narrow but sound culture of the traditional guildsman. Hitler had entrusted him with the execution of his design for a new standard, a symbol of victory which was to be presented to the Storm Troops on the first great Party Day. The goldsmith brought out the pattern; and as he discussed it with Hitler, every word, every gesture, however reserved, showed the admiration and faith that he offered the leader. It was far from humility; it was almost brotherly love, but strengthened with boundless respect.

I saw the same thing another day, when I went with Hitler to visit Oscar Koerner, a little merchant nearing his fifties, one of the founders of the Party, who had given everything to it and later was to give his life. Koerner's temperament was vivacious, quick, and eager, rather than reserved; but like Gahr, indeed like most real Germans of his station in life, he showed that he accepted Hitler as both a brother and a leader.

Hitler, on his part, seemed perfectly at home with both these types, and showed the best of humour. These were the people for whose sake he meant to rescue Germany.

I have happy memories of evenings passed with Hitler, Eckart, and the others in a Weinstube in the Barerstrasse, or in the restaurant 'Bratwurst-Gloeckle,' when Hitler's asceticism did not yet stand in the way of his accepting a glass of beer or wine. The play of humour, especially Eckart's, was contagious. Hitler liked to be amused, to laugh, and showed his utter contentment by slapping his knees. More or less by accident, I was the means of introducing an official jester into this group. The story shows me returning with a cap-and-bells when I went forth to bring back a ducal coronet. Moreover, the jester ended as one of the Party's strangest assets- and my enemy. Through my acquaintance with the widow of one of the Kaiser's sons, I met her young brother. As he was only twenty, impressionable, and one of the richest princes in Germany, I tried-for the Party's advancement and to put a plume in my own hat-to bring him into the movement. Moreover, I imagined he might take a real interest. His tutor was a wary Saxon, very suspicious, who opposed anything that might complicate his job; but nevertheless I managed to get my young Highness to two mass meetings. The effort was wasted. The fellow turned out to be an exquisite young man who suffered tortures at such intimate contact with the rough masses. Attending incognito, of course, he received such a jostling at the second meeting that he became almost ill; the close air overwhelmed him, and possibly he was frightened to learn that the lower classes could think and talk. I gave him up as a possible Nazi fighter. Nearly in tears, he fled outside to his white Mercedes, and so away forever, little dreaming that a decade later Hitler would be master of all the dukedoms in the realm. But before the young man escaped from the masses, he at least helped to make one convert for the Nazi banner. Dr. Ernst Hanfstaengl of Harvard fame, who was hearing Hitler for the first time and was enthralled by the sheer artistry of his show, saw me leaving. Taking advantage of our slight acquaintance, he edged up for an introduction and drove away with us. Finally I found myself alone with him when the Mercedes dropped us at my hotel. I stepped out, he kept pace, and up and down the street we walked, discussing Hitler. In the flush of enthusiasm, I was eloquent. His interest became less detached.

Two days later I met Hanfstaengl again in Max Amann's Nazi publishing office, where he had gone to find out more about the movement. Amann was present, and so were Hermann Esser and Christian Weber.

Weber was one of the Party's original members, and among its most effective bouncers. A former horse-trader, a typical Munich roughneck, good-hearted and naive, but of colossal nerve and strength in the Nazi cause, he was usually at Hitler's side when the air was thick and special protection was necessary. He was an immense mountain of a man, almost broader than tall, an extraordinary sight when he wore leather shorts and a Tyrolean hat sporting a dashing chamois tuft. His face was adorned by an immense Kaiser moustache and he fancied himself as a lady-killer. But his social life consisted chiefly in drinking endless seidels of beer.

Hanfstaengl, with his great, lanky height, cadaverous, lantern-jawed face and eccentric manners, amused Weber and the rest enormously. So did his wariness about joining the movement. He wished to be put on a secret list, fearing that an open avowal would expose him to the jibes of Munich society.

But I knew that the amazement of the salons would benefit us more than it could harm him: Hitler's pot-pie needed a bit of upper crust. Hanfstaengl was partner in a well-known Munich art-print publishing house, which until the war had maintained offices in New York. He was also a Harvard graduate, the son of an American mother, and had valuable connections on both sides of the Atlantic. Finally, he had money, and his position in society was secure. We could probably find special work for such a man to do.

At last Amann and I succeeded in getting him to sign, most reluctantly, on the dotted line. We put him down for one American dollar a month-not so absurd as it sounds, for at that time the dollar was worth about six thousand marks.

It was soon apparent that 'Putzi,' as we called him, would find his own special work. Fantastically enough, he became Hitler's admirer-in-chief.

Putzi's comfortable and cultivated home was unquestionably the first house of the kind to open its doors to Hitler. He seemed to feel at ease with Hanfstaengl's pretty wife and handsome children. Putzi played Wagner beautifully, and Hitler, who loved music, ranked Wagner among the demigods.

In time Hanfstaengl made himself a sort of social-secretary to Hitler, zealous in introducing him to hostesses. Hitler still had an air of shyness in the presence of those who had wealth or social authority. But his very naivety in social matters tempted the salons to lionize him. He was asked many places, and was received always with delight, though sometimes with amusement.

For instance, Putzi introduced him to the Bruckmanns, who had a fine house with good pictures and books, tasteful furniture, and excellent food. I can still see Frau Bruckmann's eyes shining as she described Hitler's truly touching dismay before an artichoke.

"But madam," he had said in his softest voice, "you must tell me how to eat this thing. I never saw one before."

In those days that naivety was sincere and genuine.

Indeed, it was a little too genuine. Hitler loved beauty and appreciated good taste, but it never occurred to him to consider himself as an object that people might examine with curious eyes. I soon gave up my futile efforts to induce him to give more heed to his person and dress, though it might have been advantageous for the leader of the Party to appear less like a refugee. He clung to his shapeless trench-coat and clumsy shoes. His hair still fell over his eyes at every vehement gesture during his speeches. He continued to eat in a hurry, some messy stuff or other, while he ran from place to place. If you succeeded in making him stand still long enough to confer on important matters, he would take out of his pocket a piece of greasy sausage and a slice of bread, and bolt them while he talked. The only improvement I was able to persuade him to, was to give up his ugly and uncomfortable hard collars for more suitable soft ones. He would never resent my suggestions, but simply ignore them.

It was a pity for the Party, eventually, that Hitler had this typical Austrian Scklamperei, this lackadaisical casualness. Aside from his many ingratiating qualities, and of course his political genius, he suffered from an all-embracing disorderliness. Naturally, this grew less with time; but in the beginning it was apparent in everything.

It showed even in his disregard for his personal safety, on which so much depended.

At one of our Monday meetings, Hitler expounded the Nazi programme with his usual mercilessness toward Party enemies, using Alfred Rosenberg's pamphlet, Character, Principles, and Aims of the Nazi Party, fresh from the press as the first printed exposition of the Nazi programme, the famous twenty-five points. The speech was of a sort to inflame not only our friends and followers, but our opponents even more.

On the way home I pointed out to Hitler that he could no longer consider himself safe from personal attack. Yet he walked through the streets sometimes alone; at the Monday meeting-place it would be easy to shoot him through the window at which he was frequently visible.

"I will live as long as I must live to do my work," he said.

I protested that Heaven protects only drunkards and fools, and laughing he said that he was doing all he reasonably could to guard himself. He was, to be sure, secretive in his movements, and made a point of never being photographed; the first picture ever to be published did not appear until about a year later. And he was never without an automatic pistol which made his hip bulge as though with some deformity. But in times as unsettled as those, and for one engaged in violent political agitation, this might have proved to be tragically inadequate.

If a man is careless of his life, however, it would be silly to ask that he should be scrupulous about lesser matters.

Hitler was always on the go but rarely on time, and we were always asking each other: 'What in hell is he doing?' All the clerical work was discharged by others, but his attitude shaped theirs; so the Party machine, none too well handled at best, more than once was in jeopardy through sheer inefficiency.

Only one thing was managed marvellously from the beginning - the propaganda, Hider's personal hobby and perhaps his strongest point. He had a matchless instinct for taking advantage of every breeze to raise a political whirlwind. No official scandal was so petty that he could not magnify it into high treason; he could ferret out the most deviously ramified corruption in high places and plaster the town with the bad news. He shone in print, and positively dazzled on the lecture platform.

By this time he had evolved a regular system for speaking.

First, if possible, he would crystallize his thoughts and perhaps shape his phrases while talking to a small group of followers. This was not always necessary, however, as his success sprang largely from the way he hammered time after time on the same few points. Audiences never tired of this repetition, any more than a Sunday-school class tires of the Holy Gospel.

But before Hitler invaded virgin territory, he was always preceded by an orator to prepare the people and warm them up to the proper pitch. He would have been dismayed and mortified for the Party's sake, and certainly disgruntled for his own, if any address of his had failed to rouse the audience. When he appeared, after this careful preparation, the response was always tremendous.

His meetings were attended by many women, who responded even more enthusiastically - and generously - than the men. Frankly, I did not fail to note that some of these devoted females were of the hysterical type, who found an emotional ecstasy in surrender to the man on the platform. He could twitch their very nerves with his forcefulness. But many of the women were as intelligently interested as the men, and without their financial aid the Party's early years would have been much more difficult. Sometime in 1922, I was present when a woman of perhaps fifty years came to the Party's office and offered all of an inheritance she had just received. And she was one of slight means.

Next to Hitler, the best political speaker at that time was Hermann Esser, a journalist and former Socialist, only about twenty-two years old, very wide awake, and ambitious, 'discovered' like Hitler by Roehm back in 1919. He had a feeling for local politics and a special flair for scandals and corruptions, which he would denounce from the tribune with righteous though happy indignation. For some time, he paved the way for Hitler's orations by raising the crowd's pulse to the proper pitch. Today he has talked himself into the position of a minister in the Bavarian Cabinet.

Life in Munich with Hitler was agreeable and exciting, but much of the time I was elsewhere, proselyting among the other folkic groups, trying to bring the leaders under Hitler's wing or to lure the sub-leaders and their men into our camp.

It was hard work.

My experience with educated and wealthy men brought many headaches and few results. It was so much easier to convince a hundred simple men of Hitler's predestination than to convert a single intellectual. The more educated the man, the greater his academic resistance to the 'impossible' and 'undignified' programme advocated by 'that uncultivated, day-dreaming radical.'

On one trip, returning from Berlin to Munich, I stopped off at Nuremberg to put the screws on my cherry-minded friend Julius Streicher, who was still commanding the Nuremberg and Franconian groups of the teacher's old association, now called by a new name. Knowing him so well, I felt sure I could convince him that Hitler's fighting party was worthier of allegiance than the teacher's futile social club.

He accompanied me to Munich, and there, in a stormy luncheon debate with the teacher present, I gained my point. Streicher promised that he and his men would secede from the parent organization and join the Nazis. Fifteen hundred men and one powerful activist gained for the Party during a single lunch-hour! I got in touch at once with Hitler. Remembering Streicher's share in his private feud with the teacher, Hitler refused at first to have anything to do with him, but after much persuasion agreed to a meeting. Peace was made between them. The conversion accomplished, Streicher and his whole group accepted Hitler's leadership. Hitler was delighted to have settled the teacher, and I thought that I had really achieved something.

But as the weeks went on, I grew discouraged over the possibility of winning other leaders to our cause before we were strong enough to treat with them on our own terms. Nor was I any more sanguine of getting important non-political men to sign up. I talked with many public personalities, such as the famous war ace, Udet, and Count Fugger, but found them all reluctant to join the movement actively or even to give it their open moral support. Though such men regarded Hitler with a sort of detached benevolence, they would not concede that the time had come for them all to rally round one leader as a crystallization point. And they feared the Socialist side of the Nazi programme.

By this time I had made myself unwelcome among my friends and acquaintances, who resented my persistent proselytizing for a cause which they neither admired nor wished to understand. But their coolness, which finally amounted to ostracism, was no hardship, because I myself became so thoroughly Nazi that I utterly disliked sharing even my private life with people who did not subscribe to Nazi ideas. I was not alone in this. Many a peaceful family circle was split into bitterly hostile groups on the Nazi question; husbands and wives, sons and parents, even brothers or sweethearts were at dagger points.

After several weeks of futile interviews, it became clear that nothing could come-except in a few rare cases-from conferences with men of position. The Nazi Party must be built up from below. I wanted to turn to some activity that would bring concrete results.

The organization was still so small that the few staff jobs were already filled, and besides, I could hardly have existed from morning to night every day in our hectic little office. My inclination, and indeed. my training, suggested some more independent work.

Could I perhaps lecture for the Party? Hitler advised against it.

"Ludecke, Sie sind zu feudal."

I was unconvinced.

"You seem too well-to-do," he insisted, "too much of a swell. You wouldn't be effective with the masses."

It was a veto. I thought then, and later proved, that it takes no great art to pound a pulpit before the populace. I had hoped at least to speak on street corners, or to warm up for the man who warmed up for Hitler.

So now, what else could I do? There were no more lions to beard at present. But the Party needed men, it needed organization, it needed disciplined strength to meet the crises into which our programme by its very nature would lead us. Strenuous times were ahead. How to prepare for them?

The Coburg experience had proved how vital the function of the Storm Troops was; yet this branch of the organization was the least developed. Something ought to be done to improve the S A.

The Storm Troops were still under the command of young Lieutenant Klintzsch, who had taken ·the men Hitler gave him, drilled them a little, and without uniforms or arms-or, to be fair, much money-had turned them into a useful corps.

But Klintzsch was only twenty-five years old, much younger than many of the troopers he commanded, and discipline suffered accordingly. Moreover, the volunteers were becoming too numerous for an inexperienced man to handle; what was needed was a strict military set-up, under a staff modelled on that of the regular army, with every unit drilled to the point of perfection, and a powerful man over them all.

Our fighting men were a target for the enemy Press. As a matter of ·fact, they were little better than gangs, and still regarded themselves more as ordinary Party members than as Storm Troopers. We needed to instil into these men a pride in their special function, perhaps even create rivalry among the various units for the honour of being Hitler's crack company.

The competitive spirit might work wonders for their morale.

I discussed the idea with Klintzsch, who agreed completely, but declared himself helpless to undertake any reforms immediately. So I decided to test the power of example. Hitler listened to my plan and told me to go ahead and form a troop, if that was what I wanted.

Ludwig and I gathered a few men, taking only well-built and able-bodied fellows who either had served in the war or had some military training. With these as a nucleus, we began regular recruiting. Soon we found that many would-be members were serving in other organizations, sometimes two or three at once, taking pride in being affiliated with this, that, and the other group simultaneously. Such overlapping of memberships meant that none of the groups possessed the actual strength their rolls indicated; nor could any of them claim the undivided loyalty of their members.

From the beginning I made it a point that no one who was serving with any other group could join my troop.

Two fine men who had been regular officers in the war were engaged as platoon leaders. For adjutant, I accepted my subaltern. Government laws and international treaties forbade the formation of the sort of troop I was developing.

Soon we had a few young students, splendid, strong fellows, among our veterans, and I began to organize a band with four drummers and four fifers.

We held drills regularly, and every Wednesday evening we assembled in a hired room at a cafe in the Schoenfeld Strasse, where I lectured on Nazi principles. Each man took the oath of allegiance on the swastika flag, pledging loyalty to Hitler and the Cause.

To have more space for our exclusive use, I leased an apartment which contained, besides living quarters for Ludwig and me, an enormous studio. At once it became a sort of armoury, the meeting-place for the men. Ludwig often had to cook for ten or twenty hungry giants. He was an excellent but very liberal cook, and without batting an eye could use the most appalling quantities of fancy groceries. As most of the men were unemployed, and of course received no pay for serving in the company, Ludwig's bounty was accepted with enthusiasm. It also provoked considerable envy among other troops, since I was the only leader who could afford to subsidize what was almost a mess-hall.

In most cases it also fell to me to buy the gear and the uniforms. Soon one whole room was reserved for tunics, army shoes, steel helmets, and so forth. Every man was completely outfitted, whereas most other troops had either no uniforms or, at best, hodge-podge makeshifts.

For headgear, we adopted the Austrian ski-cap, which, in a modified form, is now official for the S A. On our ski-caps were old army cockades. The rest of the uniform consisted of the army tunic, military breeches, puttees, and strong boots. Each man wore a leather belt, without sidearms, and of course an arm-band with the swastika, which so far had been almost the only distinguishing mark between S A men and ordinary Party members.

In the centre of our swastikas, as our company emblem, was a death's-head, a modification of which was adopted by the Schutz Staffel or SS, the Black bodyguard which Hitler later organized. They wear it now on the front of their peaked caps.

Most of our material was stored in the apartment: Not much was new, but all was in fine condition. Germany was filled with the debris of the war-uniforms, implements, even arms, which had been sold by the soldiers or stolen after the armistice from the immense army depots. It was easy to get military goods, but not to get them undamaged. I solved the problem by keeping two Jewish dealers constantly on the lookout for what we needed.

As the bearing of arms, or even the possession and concealment of them, was severely punished, usually with several years' imprisonment, it was naturally no easy task to obtain them and keep them in secret. Arms were being bootlegged, and it was an exciting business. One had to risk danger a hundred times to find a single weapon that was intact, rustless, and uniform with the rest.

By the end of December 1922, about one hundred men had enlisted under me, and some forty regular Reichswehr soldiers had pledged themselves in secret. All possessed complete uniforms, with steel helmets and field outfits. In addition, I had managed to secure and hide outside Munich, fifteen heavy Maxim guns, more than two hundred hand grenades, one hundred and seventy-five perfect rifles, and thousands of rounds of ammunition-a real arsenal.

Each Saturday and Sunday, the troop would assemble on the outskirts of Munich and drill along the country roads into the forest. The tall, evergreen woods there are dark and usually quiet, but we made them ring with crackling military commands and the roll of drums. More than once veteran officers, retired now to that peaceful country-side, would happen to come upon us in some unfrequented lane; smiling and waving their hands, they would watch us march by in splendid discipline, swift and singing, with the 'Hakenkreuz' banner flying.

When bad weather prevented outdoor drill, I was able through my connection with certain Reichswehr officers to gain the privilege of using the drill-hall of the Second Bavarian Regiment 'Kronprinz' an irregularity which later created a stir in the opposition Press.

On Party Day, scheduled for 27 January, Hitler was to dedicate the first standard to his SA. My great ambition was to appear at the presentation of the colours with my company completely equipped, perfectly drilled, and at war-strength, and to hand them over then to be sworn in by Hitler himself as 'Shock Troop Hitler Number One.'

Troop Number One would prove to Klintzsch and his subordinates that it was not impossible to give Hitler the sort of trained man-power he needed.

This idea so gripped me that I spent less time at head-quarters than wisdom would have urged, and lost touch with the Party gossips who always knew which way the wind of intrigue and rumour was blowing. Politics makes such strange bedfellows that only a rash party-member ever closes his eyes. I forgot for the moment that every office is a nest of schemers, and beyond reporting to Hitler now and then, I failed to protect my own interests at headquarters.

Looking back, I realize there was some naivety in the eager absorption with which I planned for the presentation ceremony. For instance, I searched for weeks for a giant to be the colour-bearer, and was immoderately happy when I finally found a young Goliath, a war-veteran and professional prize-fighter, more muscle than mind, but of truly impressive strength and stature. Shortly before Christmas I ordered for him a beautiful 'Hakenkreuz' banner of the heaviest silk, a special banner for my troop, and finer than any I had seen.

The troop had a jovial German Christmas, with gifts for every one and much singing and hot punch. To Hitler I gave an etching of Frederick the Great, which seemed to please him. I had intended giving him a warm blanket, because I remembered that when the nights grew cold on the trip to Coburg, he had wrapped himself in a tattered old covering which obviously had reached the retirement age. But when I offered him a new one for Christmas, he refused it, saying he could not part from the one that was his shelter all through the war. If there was an object-lesson in that for me, I saw none.

To Klintzsch I gave a few packages to distribute among his men, feeling that now we were not only friends but fellow officers. He took them readily enough and wished me a prosperous season.

But the new year - 1923 - had scarcely begun before noticed a change in the attitude of Party men toward me. What change, or what incidents gave me the impression, it would be impossible to say now; probably I noticed nothing definite. Something unpleasant was in the air . . . but the whole thing was so vague that I tried to dismiss it as an illusion.

Besides, Hitler was still my friend. He had even asked me to accompany him on an overnight trip to Landshut, where we were to be guests of the town's local group-leader.

I took along four men from my troop, beautiful specimens of German soldiery, to serve Hitler as orderlies or body-guard. When he appeared with them in the hall at Landshut, I was filled with pride.

But Klintzsch and his staff did not like it. The more the rumours about my well-drilled and well-uniformed men spread, the less I enjoyed their good-will. Yet from the beginning I had made every effort not to alienate them or to infringe upon their ground. I had given orders to my men not to mix with the regular S A groups until after the Party Day presentation, when they would no longer be my troop, but Hitler's, and had insisted that they must keep close mouths about our activities, to avoid petty jealousies. Apparently they did not. Later I heard of the dissatisfaction they aroused among other groups by reporting-of all things-Ludwig's meals!

My ban against fraternizing had raised serious suspicions among my 'friends.' My motive was innocent enough. I simply wanted our public debut to be a startling surprise. It was partly artless vainglory, partly a desire for a certain moral effect.

It never occurred to me to regard Klintzsch, his adjutant Benecke, or their coterie, as rivals, and I tried to dismiss, as absurd, rumours that they had debated whether I was building up an organization of personal followers in order to work against Hitler. My own troopers could have given them the best answer to that suspicion; there was not a man among them who had not eaten, drunk, slept, and dreamed Hitlerism. A few weeks would prove my loyalty.

Then, one night in early January, Hitler visited me in my new apartment. I took him into the studio, an immense room with skylights, comfortably furnished, one end giving into a cozy alcove, the wall of which was covered by a beautiful swastika banner.

"Schoen, das ist sehr schoen!" he exclaimed, walking around. "Exactly what I've always wanted to have. I love this place."

"I'm certain," I said, "that it won't be long before you have something far better than this."

He was amused by the dogs; my Jibby was showing herself a perfect lady and no bitch. She snapped whenever Hitler's police-dog became too inquisitive.

We sat down to a good dinner prepared and served by Ludwig, who was turkey-red with pride and excitement; his big bat ears fairly twitched, and for once there was no cigarette glued to his lip. Hitler could not help smiling; but his praise of the cookery transported bashful Ludwig to a seventh heaven.

As we were sipping our coffee, Hitler's eye fell upon some copies of the Popolo d'Italia, the London Times, and Le Temps, to which I had subscribed with the idea that they might furnish material for the Voelkischer Beobachter. Hitler's only news-organ -the V.B., as we called it-was still an undersized semi-weekly devoted almost wholly to Nazi news and propaganda. He scanned these foreign papers eagerly, although he could read nothing but German. I drew his attention to several editorials, translating as I read; but he seemed impressed chiefly by the size of The Times and the make-up of Mussolini's sheet. Quite possibly he had never seen them before.

Despite a lively discussion, I began presently to feel that Hitler was not quite as cordial as usual. He was still very friendly, and apparently frank, but there was a shadow over us. I am used to grasping a situation and meeting it openly, but when the issues are intangible I am at a loss. With Hitler I was still too much the disciple to force the issue. Moreover, I had already witnessed his tactic of arming himself with an impregnable air of aloofness when he did not like a topic, and I had no wish to butt my head against that stone wall.

He gave me only one clue, which at the time I could not follow.

Without apparent purpose and entirely aside from our conversation, he asked if I were acquainted with Oberleutnant Neumann. I replied that I knew Neumann was a friend of Captain-, and was at that time in the entourage of General Ludendorff as a sort of private secretary. Also, that I knew that he was no friend of mine, since I had expressed my distaste forcefully on an occasion when he said things I did not approve.

But this knowledge told me nothing, nor did Hitler. Our conversation turned to the Storm Troops, and again I promised him a surprise on Party Day. He questioned me about Klintzsch, and I answered that while in my opinion he was doing his best, he was not equal to his task. Hitler said that he had reached the same conclusion some time since; he had in view a splendid man whom he could not approach until he was able to offer him a salary. Then we drifted into a discussion of Party funds, which were still a serious problem. After a little further talk, he left.

I was disturbed by the overtones of the evening, but I could not believe that Hitler's confidence had been impaired by the silly gossip floating about. To worry was just to borrow trouble. Were not my time, my energy, my heart, all dedicated to Party work without any reservation? And my bank account as well? In a quiet way, I was giving money to Hitler and others, in addition to the large sums the troop was costing. The inflation had reached terrifying proportions by this time. Everybody from Reichsminister to bootblack scrambled for foreign currency. To possess valuta was to be fortunate, though it were only a single dollar bill. Klintzsch and other men, knowing from my way of life that I was less embarrassed by the crisis than most were, frequently came to me for aid and got it. Several times I gave them foreign notes, including some of the French money left over from the Paris trip.

I still remember how the last of those French notes went.

One afternoon I was in the Nazi office with Max Amann, Deitrich Eckart, and Adolf Mueller, the printer, when in stormed Hitler aflame with an idea. Scarcely pausing to acknowledge our greeting, he began dictating to Amann a stirring, exciting text to be used for placards and handbills, to be distributed at once. As always, he demanded immediate action. But Amann, shrugging his shoulders, said there was no money. Hitler raged. "Absolutely necessary-of highest importance-must be done-Do it!"

The handbill had vigour and I liked it. Acting on impulse, I took out of my pocket three hundred-franc notes and tossed them to Amann, who counted them, his eyes gleaming. Then the four of us tried our higher mathematics, and found that the French money, figured in German marks, would be ample to pay the printer.

As it turned out, this sort of ready open-handedness earned more comment than appreciation. Politicians don't believe in Santa Claus.

VII

BEHIND BARS

On 2 January the French marched into the Ruhr and occupied Essen. They had come to collect the colossal indemnity imposed on Germany by the peace which brought the 'War to End War' to a successful close. Within a few days the whole Ruhr territory, the coal-bin of Germany and the centre of its industrial life, was in enemy hands. General de Goutte, the French officer in command, declared a state of martial law, and for Germans a time of extreme humiliation and torture began.

In Bochum on 15 January demonstrating Germans were ruthlessly shot down with Maxim guns by French soldiers. Murder, rape, plunder, and insult were the order of the day. The inhabitants of the Ruhr, virtually cut off from the rest of Germany, had no recourse against the terrorism of French soldiers-white and black.

The Berlin Government answered the challenge with an order for 'passive resistance,' a needless precaution, apparently, for the inertia of the bewildered German people was threatening to confirm the Government's spineless surrender.

Hitler passionately denounced the idea of passive resistance, proclaiming that there could be no resistance except through action-and that resistance was vital to preserve the Reich from ultimate total dismemberment.

Marxism stood in the way of action? One more reason for eliminating the Marxists from politics! he cried. Scornfully he attacked the timorous measures of the chancellor, Wilhelm Cuno, calling them wilful hypocrisy, and warned that the passive attitude was equivalent to a betrayal which could result in nothing but wretched submission. He refused to join in a national 'United Front' under the Marxian leadership which in five years of power had taken no steps to prevent this catastrophe.

Times had been hard; now they were dangerous. Internal conflicts grew from day to day; antagonisms and frictions multiplied; France kept her grip on the mine-country; and those who would have taken action against the crime could not because the Government opposed them. An internal change seemed not only necessary, but imminent.

The indecisive attitude of the 'Union of Patriotic Societies' made membership more of a handicap than a help. After a mass demonstration in January against the Ruhr invasion, the Nazis withdrew.

Hitler wrote in the Voelkiscner Beohachter in that period:

'So long as a nation does not do away with the assassins within its borders, no external success can be possible. While written and spoken protests are directed against France, the real death-enemy of the German people still lurks within the walls of the nation and continues his undermining demagogy. Down with the November criminals with all their nonsense about a United Front! Let us beware of forgetting that between us and these tricksters of the nation, these corrupters of the workers, these bourgeois party criminals who are everywhere-there lie two million dead.'

In this atmosphere of political tension we approached our first large Nazi Party Day, important to us as a milestone, but still more important because we planned to make it a tremendous demonstration of popular feeling in a time of stress.

Rumours flew through the city that Hitler planned a putsch.

The atmosphere was explosive. An open conflict broke out between Hitler and the Bavarian Minister of the Interior, Dr. Schweyer, who declared a state of siege for the whole of Bavaria. Automatically this prohibited twelve mass meetings, already announced for the evening of Saturday, 27 January, at everyone of which Hitler was scheduled to speak. Every assemblage in the open was also cancelled-which meant that the great things planned for Party Day could not come off.

Hitler was in a difficult situation, but could not withdraw his arrangements. A clash between government troops and the Nazis seemed unavoidable.

Thanks to the intervention of Reichswehr Captain Ernst Roehm and General von Epp, who spoke in Hitler's behalf, he was received by General von Lossow, commander of the Reichswehr in Bavaria. Then Captain Roehm drove Hitler to see Dr. von Kahr, State commissioner of Bavaria, and police-president Nortz. At the last moment Roehm succeeded in getting police permission for the Nazi meetings and the Party Day to take place as scheduled. General von Lossow agreed to waive the ban and not to use the Reichswehr against Hitler.

This was regarded as a great triumph for Hitler, but it was really Roehm who prevented the day from being perhaps the end of Hitler's political career.

Party Day was called. Delegates were to come from all existing units in and outside Munich. The occasion was to be signalized by the first parade of the SA, which was then to receive the standard designed by Hitler-the standard with the Roman eagle. For me it was to be the tremendous occasion when I would present my troop and hand them over for incorporation in the SA.

Late on the evening of the 26th I had a short talk with Hitler at Party headquarters. He delegated me to furnish a special guard of honour at the railway station to receive the Nazis pouring into the city. I was also to maintain order among the throng at the Loewenbraukeller, where the principal meeting of the evening would be held.

Next morning I rushed about the city preparing for the big day. When everything was in order, I sent Ludwig to call for our new flagstaff, and drove home alone, happy and expectant.

The street before my house was cold and quiet. I leaped up the flights to my apartment and unlocked the door. As I burst in, two men plunged at me, seized me in their heavy grip, and forced handcuffs on my wrists. A third man, evidently in command, pronounced me under arrest.

Helpless to use my hands, but struggling violently, I dragged my captors to the studio. Only one of my subalterns was there, passively looking on. Obviously it was useless to resist, and I calmed down. But before the two 'tees released their grip, the third man snatched the ring from my finger-a gold ring with a platinum seal showing the curved Swastika and my initial inlaid in onyx.

Almost too astonished to speak, I demanded:

"What is this all about? Are you crazy? Who are you?"

"Detectives," he said. "I am Kriminal-Kommissar Rupprecht."

"Why am I arrested?"

"You will learn at Headquarters."

They began to search the apartment.

"Why did you take my ring?" And suddenly it flashed through my mind that Thad once told my subaltern of a tiny secret opening in the ring, which could contain a miniature or the lock of a loved one-or, I said jokingly, even poison. So he had been talking! He had already raised my suspicions, though I had postponed his dismissal until after Party Day to avoid difficulties.

But I realized in a moment that whatever this man might have done, he was not responsible for this arrest. Apprehensively, my mind checked over my political activities to decide just which chicken was coming home to roost.

As my first excitement died down, I was struck by an even more alarming thought. This police action was probably not against me alone, but against all prominent Nazis! No doubt the sudden permission to hold our meetings was only a ruse, and Hitler and the others were by now in custody.

There was no case against Hitler-we had done no wrong. I began to be less downhearted, supposing myself arrested in good company.

And as for me, certainly I had broken no laws. Except, of course, to collect a troop and an arsenal! The thought gave me a turn or two. The detectives opened a large office cabinet containing arm-bands and other small items of equipment, and there I saw, lying in the bottom, several hand-grenades that had been brought to me by a Reichswehr corporal and which I had not yet found time to hide. Their mere possession carried a possible prison term of several years. But the searchers seemed not to see them, and greatly relieved, I opened up everything else, to prove that my apartment concealed nothing incriminating.

Before they took me away, I wrote an order that my subaltern was to put himself and the troop under the orders of the SA until my release, which I thought would be only a matter of a day or two.

My captors drove me to police headquarters, refusing to answer my questions or to allow me to telephone Nazi head-quarters or my friends. Summarily, they shoved me into a cell, unbooked. It was ten days or so before I was permitted to get a lawyer. All that time I was held incommunicado and cross-examined each day for several days, though no charge was entered against me. Obviously I was being held for political reasons. I had the impression that they wanted to nail me down to something in order to create a case against me for high treason-I was supposed to have planned a popular uprising during the scheduled mass meetings, to overthrow the Government.

Not being allowed newspapers, I still imagined that I was only one of many who had been arrested, and did not know that Hitler and the others were perfectly free and that the Party Day had proceeded more or less as planned.

For some days I found my situation faintly interesting. But when I was transferred to another prison, I realized its gravity and vociferously demanded to be heard by a judge, my right by law within forty-eight hours after arrest.

At last a judge heard me. He told me nothing, simply asking a few purely formal questions. When it was apparent that he maintained the arrest, I expressed indignation, but, of course, that helped not at all; I was led back to the cell. All they would say was that I was held 'on suspicion' pending an investigation. What suspicion I was not told.

Being thus incommunicado, I did not know that my arrest had been front-page news all over Germany, especially in the anti-Hitler press, which was playing me up not simply as a friend and intimate of Hitler's, but as one of the chief activists and pillars of Nazism. And by one of those mental feats which only a political journalist can accomplish, the opposition was trying to identify me with an international spy of the same name as myself. My supposed namesake, I later learned, had been an agent during the war for the British Secret Service in Argentina, whence he was deported for various offences. After his arrival in Germany, in the turmoil of the new Republic, he had succeeded in entering national circles, and had even edited a nationalistic publication; he had landed, finally, as an agent of a certain foreigner. It was due to his treachery that hundreds of Germans were betrayed to the Poles.

In the end, years after my arrest, he was captured and sentenced to six years at hard labour-although by that time I felt that I had already served some of his sentence for him.

The Nazis' enemies were wilfully confusing me with this agent, of whom I had never so much as heard, in order to damage Hitler's name and the Party. Articles pointed out that the worst outcasts and traitors - typified by myself - were friends of Hitler and prominent in the Nazi Party. A story was spread that millions of French francs had been found in my apartment when I was arrested; that I was a spy in French service, and had distributed huge sums among the soldiers in the Munich garrison to win them over to Hitler. Other equally fantastic tales were hung on my name.

Behind the bars, however, I knew nothing of these calumnies, and when after two or three weeks I finally was given newspapers, my case was getting less notice. The first lawyer I retained, who did not inform me of them, and did not even mention the French-franc stories which were seriously embarrassing Hitler and the Nazis. These lies, as a matter of fact, laid the foundation for the legend that Hitler was in French pay, which kept cropping up for years and gave him grounds for a number of lawsuits against various newspapers and individuals.

All my energetic demands to be given liberty or to have a case opened got me nowhere. Instead, probably as a result of the outrageous newspaper campaign, I was subjected to a more searching investigation. By this time the police were trying their best to establish a connection between me and the famous case of Fuchs-Machhaus,[1] two men who had been arrested a few days earlier than I, on the charge of having secret relations with the head of the French Intelligence Department of the 'Second Bureau' at Mainz, in the occupied territory. Fortunately it was easy to prove that I had never met these gentlemen or anyone in their group-fortunately, I say, because it turned out that even my most unpolitical friends were being hounded for evidence by the police, who had kept me under surveillance for days before the arrest, and had noted all my comings and goings. They even searched the rooms of an English woman I knew at the Hotel Continental and questioned her for hours.

At first the new examinations revolved about the question of my Mexican passport, which I had retained because both Pittinger and Hitler urged me to do so. In those days of active post-war hatred, when it was still extremely difficult for a German citizen to get a foreign visa, a substitute nationality was useful to fall back upon. But though I was a greenhorn in politics, I was not so stupid as to leave myself open to passport trouble. I had been careful to establish my reasons for bearing two passports by talking to the chief of the political division of the Munich police, Dr. Bernreuther, a political friend of Pittinger's.

But now that I had left Pittinger for Hitler, the police brought the thing up as if it were a piece of criminal duplicity on my part. Moreover, as it is an inborn instinct for staunch Munichers to regard anyone born north of Dachau as a foreigner, I was, by either passport, an alien in their eyes. They got themselves and me into an incredible legal tangle, asking absurd questions which it was difficult to answer, so zig-zag had my journeys been.

Then there was the mystery about my money. German currency might be giddy at the moment, but French currency was leprous in their eyes-though I would have

---

1 *The true story of the Fuchs-Machhaus activities never came to light. Machhaus committed suicide shortly after my transfer to the same cell-block where he was being held, and two of his associates shot themselves when they were arrested. There is no doubt, however, that they played a part in the under-ground machinations for a Separatist movement which would have broken Bavaria from the Reich with the help of France and the Vatican.*

liked to try dropping a ten-franc note among them! They pumped me with queries: How had I earned the money? Where were my bank accounts? Why were they abroad? Why had I been giving away French francs to Nazis?

Probably no State's attorney ever before received such extraordinary and insulting notes as I directed to the chief prosecutor who had charge of this absurd investigation. Kriminal-Kommissar Rupprecht was a rather gentle old man whose good manners set him apart from the rest of the police so sharply that I mistrusted him all the more at first, though he gave every sign of friendly feeling toward me. Shortly after my note-writing began, he told me that more than once he found the prosecutor shaking his head over my latest plaguish epistle, and complaining: "This Ludecke is my most impossible case!"

Jails invariably are monotonous holes-except when a third degree breaks the-monotony. I was questioned at length, but was never mistreated. The monotony grew unbearable-yet I had to bear it. No need to dwell on the dull routine that became my life; I was to find myself, later on, inside prisons so really cruel that I looked back at this experience as at something nearly idyllic.

Now my spirits were being sustained somewhat by the thought that I was being martyred for the Cause-and not too painfully. I knew by this time that none of the other Party leaders were under arrest; so it seemed to me that I was bearing alone the brunt of our enemies' wrath. They had cornered me here, hoping to find some way to use me against the Party; my punishment was a sort of sacred trust; I must do and say nothing that might damage Hitler and the Nazis. Such reflections were almost pleasant.

It never once occurred to me that Hitler himself, even by indirection, had contributed to my plight.

After many complaints I was allowed to have books in my cell. Ludwig brought whatever volumes I requested to the jail office, but was not admitted to speak with me. I read all day. It was one of those times when even the longest books are too short. I read the Bible from Genesis to Revelation, finding the Book of Esther especially provocative of thought. I ploughed through Dietrich Eckart's works, which he had sent me with a very kind note, and gained much from them. It was interesting to find that Hitler had also learned from the same source. Many of his most essential ideas clearly had sprung from the brain of Eckart.

All this time I received no message from Hitler.

Toward the end of March, with spring in the air, I was beginning to believe that I would pass the rest of my life as an unenrolled student in the Jail-School of Cultural Reading. At last I was summoned from the cell and transferred in an ordinary police van to the court for my final hearing. It was an odd little trip, crowded in as I was among some ten or twelve other prisoners, criminals of every sort.

At police headquarters Rupprecht again treated me considerately. I had previously rebuffed his friendliness, suspecting a trick to make me talk; but this time he impressed me as genuinely kind. He told me frankly:

"Herr Ludecke, I believe I will succeed today in getting you free. I regret very much that you were dragged into this difficulty. I was against your arrest from the beginning, as there was nothing to support a true charge against you; but I had to act under orders."

Nothing about the Reichswehr recruits; nothing about the hand-grenades! I was lucky-this once. It was as I had hoped: the police preferred to close their eyes to any matter which involved the Reichswehr.

"You must be more careful in the future, since you are doing active political work in troubled times, and your good motives are not really so self-evident to your enemies - outside or inside your Party - as you think. As for the generosity that helped to get you into this situation, I can only say that it was simple-minded; no one expects or believes in such free-handedness."

He was conveying to me clearly enough that denunciations against me had come from Nazis as well as from our antagonists.

"I am not permitted to tell you what is in the record, but those whom you have so warmly defended in each of our interviews have not always done the same for you. If you will take an old-timer's advice, you will think twice before you decide what to do after you are out of here."

It was years later before I learned the whole truth and the names of the men who had been willing to put the Party in jeopardy in order to satisfy a petty grudge against me.

"From my department you are now a free man; but we must follow the regular routine. Because of your Mexican passport, I must hand you over to the foreign bureau; but I believe they will keep you only a few minutes. It is purely a formality, as you are, of course, German."

Purely a formality! So is a hanging, I reflected with some apprehension after the foreign bureau had been dragging me through a hedge for an hour or so. The head of the bureau knew all about the passport tangle, for he was personally acquainted with me through his chief. Being an extreme anti-Hitlerite, however, he tried to keep this case which reflected on the Party from fizzling out. Shutting his eyes to the obvious facts, he announced finally that he must hold me for deportation. I was an alien!

This was stretching the long arm of the law practically out of joint. Alive to my danger, I raged so loudly that at last he consented to my demands and let me report back to Rupprecht. That good man condemned this silly persecution as a cat-and-mouse game which could easily end in injury for the mouse if it were not stopped at once. My papers, which the police had seized, were still on his desk. Hastily he went through them for German identifications, and found at least a score. Thereupon I was released at last.

There had been no formal charge, no trial, nothing either legal or sensible in the whole injustice of my imprisonment. The Nazi cause had unquestionably suffered, and always thereafter my name would carry an ambiguous meaning for every German who remembered it. These things were irreparable.

I walked back with Rupprecht to his office to get my things. Thanks to a telephone message from the Kommissar, Ludwig was waiting there for me with Jibby. To the man emerging from prison, I commend the welcome of a dog; there is no canker of doubt in it.

For those first few hours it was good enough simply to be free. Even when I reached home and found the apartment almost bare-looted-I did not mind very much.

From the apartment I went on to Party headquarters, which in my enforced vacation had been moved to Schelling Strasse 39, together with the editorial offices of the V.B., which had extended its influence enormously by becoming a daily instead of semi-weekly paper.

It was apparent at once that the removal was not the only change. My first surprise came when I met Hitler descending the stairs with Dr. Hansfstaengl.

Leaving Putzi, Hitler led me back into his office, where we were joined by Rosenberg and Eckart. They asked countless questions about my experience, which any of them might have to duplicate at any time, and condoled with me in the friendliest fashion. But instead of frankly telling me the truth about the arrest, they left me still in the dark as to the influences responsible.

I still believed that our enemies had engineered the whole thing by lodging false information with the police. I knew that several S A leaders had disliked me personally, and that one Lieutenant intrigued against me; but that they would be willing to endanger the Party in order to wound me was something beyond my imagination. Nor would I have believed then, except from Hitler's own lips, that they had succeeded in infecting him with their suspicions, to the extent that he had withheld his protection when the police acted and had awaited .the result of their investigation with real anxiety.

My release was a relief to him, as much as a vindication for me.

These things it took me years to learn. And the only profit I got from the episode was an aphorism: A revolutionary must be successful or he becomes the target of supporters of his cause no less than of its enemies.

In later years, Hitler turned against men who had played a more important role and had performed greater services than I was destined ever to do. It is not ignoble for a leader to make the most ruthless sacrifices when they serve to advance or protect his all-important programme; but to make them uselessly, simply because he lacks real insight into his followers, is worse than contemptible. The future was to teach me that for all their pledges of loyalty, brotherhood, comradeship, and common endeavour, for all the lofty words uttered in every speech, very few of the chief Nazis really trusted one another; if a comrade got himself into a tight corner, either through ingenuousness or by the intrigues of others, no hand was likely to reach out to help him.

Understand, however, that I did not then realize the significance of Hitler's wait-and-see attitude. Dictated by fear and unfounded suspicion, it was damaging to me, to the Nazi cause, and above all to himself. Not until we conferred at headquarters did I realize how much my name had been smirched in the Press or to what extent the pseudo-scandal had been used to attack the Party.

My arrest had been broadcast throughout Germany and in the world Press, which, in so far as it was aware of Hitler's existence, considered him a charlatan and welcomed the chance to expose him.

The Nazis in French pay! What a story it made, with fantastic variations! A New York paper, for instance, stated that I had been shot as a spy. Everywhere some new and damning fiction appeared, largely the result of the deliberate confusion the German anti-Nazi papers had raised between myself and the other Ludecke, the spy of many aliases.

To present the facts in my case, I wrote a statement which with Hitler's consent was published in the next edition of the V.B. Unfortunately, since I was myself still ignorant of the real source of the trouble, the statement went rather wide of the facts except the one fact of my innocence: But Hitler preferred authorizing a false argument to enlightening me. The article appeared, and I set about my rehabilitation-not knowing the quicksands on which I still was standing.

Ten weeks' imprisonment would not merit so detailed an account if that had been the end of the matter. But like red threads in the weft, it kept coming up, disappearing and reappearing again, all through my political life. Even at the moment it necessitated some large changes in my plans.

Ludwig had notified the troop of my release and arranged a meeting for the next evening to celebrate the homecoming. But this would be my last meeting with the men as leader, for with all our plans gone awry, I had decided in prison that I would no longer head them in person.

In the meantime Lieutenant Klintzsch had been removed from the top command of the S A and replaced by Captain Hermann Goering. I went to him to arrange for my troop to be incorporated in the S A. This was my first encounter with the future Nazi Lohengrin, but so intent was I on my troubles that I scarcely took him in except to be aware of a vague distaste.

While we were talking, Klintzsch arrived. I asked him how my men were doing. In a rather forced way, he replied that the troop was almost intact, but that I had better make no effort to retain the leadership for myself - more or less hinting that he would know how to prevent it. Also, he advised me that it would be best not to hold a celebration with my men, adding evasively that 'other measures had been taken.'

Infuriated, I called Goering to witness that I had already turned the troop over to the organization, and said that, of course I would go to the home-coming party-but that if Klintzsch came, I would throw him out. There was a quarrel. I told him to go to the devil, and left the office.

Not until my second return to my apartment did I realize the thoroughness with which it had been looted. All the equipment for my men was gone; so were most of my personal belongings-clothing, jewellery, everything. The stolen articles had a value of several thousand gold marks.

At first I sailed into poor Ludwig, accusing him of carelessness, until I learned that these things had been 'requisitioned' and removed during his absence. Actual possession of the apartment was taken and things made so uncomfortable for Ludwig that he left.

In the evening our men assembled in the old meeting-place. When I told them that they were being transferred to the SA, despite my urging, only about thirty went over to the SA, most of them becoming members of the Hitler Shock Troop when that was established. The rest dispersed.

Of course, I had not come unscathed through my jail experience. A man's nerves will carry him through the gravest crisis, then suddenly go slack when everything is over. A rest, a respite from the worries of Munich, would be a good thing. So I gladly accepted Dietrich Eckart's invitation to go with him to the Platterhof on the Obersalzberg, in the mountains near Berchtesgaden, next to the very place where Hitler later had his cottage, Haus Wachenfeld. In those days Eckart and Hitler used to repair to this little inn when they needed a holiday.

Eckart was accompanied by his Dulcinea, thirty years younger than he. In the two days we spent together, I gained a deep insight into the old man's generous - and jealous - soul. And I found that he did not like to lose at chess. But we laughed a lot together.

He seemed to be studying me, as though to confirm an Opinion. I hoped to learn something from him about my arrest, but he never gave a hint that he knew anything special concerning it, though of course he must have. I felt that he liked me, however, and we returned to Munich in excellent spirits.

The clever old fox had more or less convinced me that it was not to my best interest to sue the State for false arrest. When we met Hitler for lunch after our arrival, he also advised me to drop the matter, in the Party's interest - and in my own, on account of my arms collection. I took the advice in good faith, thereby missing the last opportunity to clear my name completely.

Despite two days of mountain air, I still felt the prison-sag in my nerves, and suggested that I take a longer rest, with travel and perhaps make a sea voyage, before resuming work in Munich. Hitler and Eckart agreed almost too readily: it would be well from their standpoint to have the grass grow a little before I again became active in the cause. It was obvious that for the moment they would be embarrassed to have me in the public eye, although tactically that would have been the best course to take.

Looking reality straight in the face, I acknowledged that it would be more in accord with my talents, and probably more valuable to the Party, if they designated me for foreign political work, which was being almost entirely neglected.

So it was decided that during my journey I should look things over in Italy and make contacts throughout South. Central Europe, using Hitler's name and the Nazi connection as credentials. Politically and personally this was a happy expedient - for I was remorseful for having embroiled the Party and was eager to serve it in the most helpful manner while regaining my health and peace of mind.

VIII

THE JAILBIRD BECOMES AMBASSADOR

In this particular year of grace it was still the fashion to treat Hitler with levity, to deprecate his Party's activity, and to dismiss the whole Nazi programme as of negligible importance. In fact, the Nazis had little enough even of notoriety, and were ignored more often than not.

Within Germany there was a growing suspicion that it would be well to crack down soon on the loud-mouthed little agitator who kept disturbing die peace, but the possibility that he might some day out-shout every political opponent was too fantastic to merit serious thought. And outside Germany, if he was known at all, it was as merely one more ineffectual radical, no higher in stature than his soap-box made him.

Yet I now embarked earnestly, and not without some feeling of hope, on my mission as Hitler's 'ambassador' abroad. It would be difficult to convince foreign leaders that he was a coming political power worth cultivating, since I must start from scratch. I believed it could be done, however; faith is contagious. And even if no tangible results came from the tour, at least it would be something simply to have broken the ground.

First of all, I decided to spend a fortnight in idle peacefulness, away from the clamour of party strife, to renew my strength and organize my thoughts. The Mediterranean just then would be basking in the rich sunshine of late spring. So I travelled straight to Genoa and caught the first boat that sailed. It happened to be bound for Barcelona.

I shall always look back on that trip with sorrow. Barcelona may be many different places to different people-a place of ships, of bullfights, of revolutions, of a grotesque cathedral; but to me it will always be the city where I lost my most trustworthy and forgiving friend - Jibby.

The Spanish city obviously pleased her. What dog wouldn't be happy among the Spaniards, whose streets are always filled with strange debris and arresting odours?

One morning soon after our arrival, I was strolling along, reading my mail, when I came to the Paseo de Gracia, a very broad avenue where motorists step heavily on the gas. At the curb I looked back toward Jibby. The little rascal was just picking up the dirtiest, most nail-bestudded piece of wood in all the town. Scavengering was her one bad habit. Raising my finger, I scolded her for the thousandth time, and with an indulgent expression she dropped her treasure.

Jibby was well-trained otherwise. In heavy traffic I needed only to say: "Back!" and she would heel until I signalled her away again. But this day there was almost no traffic on the Paseo, so I sauntered across without calling her. Almost at the other side, I looked back from habit. Jibby was prancing along, carrying the piece of wood again. Catching my eye, she halted in the middle of the roadway and cowered, conscious of wrong-doing. At that moment a car bore down at high speed. In horror I screamed her name, and she wagged her tail for forgiveness - but already the car was over her. She was dead when I reached her.

Jibby was not a pet, she was a person. Some dogs acquire almost human intelligence, and certainly a more-than-human sympathy, when they live for years with one person. Jibby could laugh, she could cry; she knew when business troubled me, and how my love affairs were going. I was a bachelor; she was my family.

The city had no charm now. Besides, the quietude I sought was not there. Barcelona, the least Spanish and by far the richest city in Spain, is one of the world's worst hotbeds of radicalism of every sort. Unrest was in the air like a fever. The Secessionist movement was openly gaining ground, the Catalonians being sick and tired of having Barcelona abused as the heaviest taxpayer for the support of the entire nation. Intrigues festered in secret, and sometimes broke out on the streets. One night a man was shot down on the crowded Ramblas only a few yards away from me - a political murder. It was anything but an agreeable place to sojourn.

So I returned to Italy, to survey the concrete results of Fascism. It was notable how far Mussolini had already pushed his programme. In all the northern cities a dynamic new spirit was manifest among the Italians. The Bolsheviks no longer threatened the industrial centres - if indeed they ever had, for it is a moot point whether or not Mussolini over dramatized that particular danger in order to lay a stepping stone for himself. But he was also well on the way to overcoming national weaknesses that were more dangerous because they were traditional: the lethargy, the dolce far niente spirit of his amiable and wholly unmodernized countrymen. In this great social effort, the results argued well for the dictatorship.

From Italy I passed into Austria, stopping here and there, gauging everything with the eye of a Nazi.

In Vienna I got in touch with the Austrian Pan-Germanic groups and met their leader, at that time Dr. Walter Riehl, through whom I gained some curious sidelights on movements outside Germany which not only paralleled Hitler's but actually preceded it.

It surprised me to discover that as early as 1919 Rudolf Jung, a racialist deputy in Prague, had published Der Nazionale Sozialismus, which must be considered the first National Socialist hand-book, for it contained in germ-form all the main Nazi principles and had even coined the very name of the Party. Furthermore, it had put on paper, though without much practical result so far, the self-protective race consciousness of the German populations in the disjointed parts of the Austro-Hungarian empire.

The old Austrian empire had a Germanic culture, but the German people were a minority which, after the war, found itself engulfed by antagonistic majorities in the countries carved from Austria. The instinct of self-preservation led to the formation of folkic groups, which developed into the 'German National Socialist Parties' in Czechoslovakia, Austria, and Poland, as early as 1918. In 1920 they had come together at Salzburg and established an ' Interstate Bureau of the National Socialist Party of the German People,' with Dr. Riehl as chairman and headquarters in Vienna. At that conference, the pre-Hitler Nazis of Munich, represented by Anton Drexler, became members of the Interstate Bureau.

The Bureau was never politically effective, but it was at least a demonstration that the spiritual force of German race-consciousness transcended the frontiers - waiting, perhaps, for a real leader to give it direction.

These facts enabled me for the first time to look at the German Nazi movement with a broader view, from the outside .

We were, after all, not an isolated phenomenon, but an organic development of an impulse that for years had existed everywhere among the German people.

Basically, our programme was similar to that of the Interstate Bureau. But none of the other leaders possessed Hitler's ruthless driving force or was so favoured by circumstances. Now I learned that Hitler had agreed to attend a new Salzburg conference, called by Dr. Riehl for August of that year of 1923. When the parties convened, would there be a merger - or a collision? From my intimate knowledge of the mainspring which was impelling Hitler toward his destiny, I could guess the answer.

From Vienna I went on to Budapest. Hungary was now giving shelter to many German political exiles and activists. But so far, its contact with Munich was chiefly through our rivals, particularly the Pittinger group. Perhaps that could be changed.

The Hungarian aristocracy, so gracious and hospitable, received me generously, and I soon was in touch with the men most important to see. But as I had anticipated, they scarcely knew the name of Hitler. Now the tour became in earnest a mission of information and contact. Whenever and wherever it was possible to gain a useful Hungarian car, I spread the most glowingly prophetic reports of Hitler's movement, with all the ardour of a John the Baptist.

Two men in Budapest were especially receptive: Julius Goemboes and Tibor von Eckhardt, Members of Parliament who were conspicuous in political life as leaders of the Hungarian racialists, the 'Awakening Hungarians.' Both were from excellent families and definitely 'somebodies,' which made their aggressive radicalism all the more significant.

The 'Awakening Hungarians,' a party formed during the revolt against the Soviet regime of Bela Kun, in spirit and ideas closely resembled our movement, being anti-Habsburg, anti-Jewish, and anti-Bolshevik.

Goemboes, a staff officer in the Hungarian regular army during the war, had been in the forefront of politics ever since the peace. He was one of the patriots who acted against Bela Kun, and had personally blocked Emperor Karl's effort to regain the throne. In the beginning strongly against everything that was subversive, he greatly tempered his public statements in later years when he became prime minister. When I first met him on this tour, however, he was outspoken enough. The most encouraging assurance I received during the entire mission was his absolute guarantee that the group which he was slowly but steadily leading into control of the nation would never countenance a Habsburg restoration. As the Habsburgs were a Catholic dynasty, and would be able to exert strong secessionist pressure on Catholic Bavaria, this was indeed a welcome promise.

Goemboes invited me to accompany him to Balaton Foeldvar, a fashionable resort on Lake Balaton two hours from Budapest. There Tibor von Eckhardt joined us. The two of them took me under their wing, introducing me everywhere. Not a little curiosity was aroused by their friendship with 'the German.'

This charming resort was not the worst place in the world for the sort of work I had to do. Many a rich and influential Hungarian who had come there to relax was buttonholed to hear about Hitler. But they listened with sympathy and understanding, and their interest increased. By the time my visit ended, I felt that Hitler was no longer an unknown quantity to the Hungarians who counted.

My profitable Hungarian holiday closed with an incident not so much profitable as amusing.

Leaving Balaton Foeldvar by train, I quite casually joined a pretty young lady whom I had met a few days earlier. Also casually, we registered at the same hotel in Budapest. And still casually, I did not pass the night in my own room. Thereby I missed meeting the Budapest police, who were nosing like blood-hounds through my luggage during the hours I had spent on the floor above. They had somehow gained the impression that I was a certain famous Captain in disguise, wanted in Berlin on charges of high treason. By the time I finally appeared, along about dawn, they had already convinced themselves of their own stupidity. I did not dispel the mystery of where I had been 'concealed.'

That same morning I left for the Salzburg meeting called by Dr. Riehl.

Hitler was to speak, and I had an idea how his words would run. My mind still held a vivid picture of that moment in a Munich garret when he had shouted at me: "From now on I go my way alone!" How would he treat his best potential allies?

Goering was present; Rudolf Jung, author of the Handbook, had come from Prague; and, of course, the chief leaders from everywhere were there. Riehl, as chairman, made a strong effort to enlarge the scope of the Interstate Bureau. But Hitler, who knew well enough that his Party already wielded more power than all the others put together, made it clear that Munich must supplant Vienna as the centre of the movement.

The meeting ended with Riehl and Hitler at odds and only one issue settled: Hitler had shown the Nazis outside Germany that he would make his Party subordinate to none; that he and nobody else was to rule.

After the meeting he invited me to go with him to Linz, the town where he had spent most of his school years. We were together there two days. On the first day Hermann Esser, Max Amann, and Johann Singer, the Party's first and not very busy treasurer, also were present. On the second day Hitler and I had long talks alone. He showed a great interest in the work which was being done abroad, and made a special effort to bring my information about the Nazi advance up to date.

I was already aware of the major developments, having been constantly in touch with Munich through the newspapers, especially the V.B., now appearing on the stands in a new make-up, fully as large and as blatant as the issue of the Popolo d'Italia that had filled Hitler with envy when I first showed him a copy. But it was important to check the published accounts, even the Beobachter's, with Hitler's authentic information. His summary of the German internal situation was masterly. It is possible now to reproduce only the gist of it, stripped of all the vigour and colour with which he instinctively shaped his phrases.

In Bavaria the Nazis had made great strides by following the trail of national unrest. The passive resistance had already cost many gold millions, because the workers, who refused to work for the French, were being carried on a dole by the Government. Those who paid the dole and those who received it were grumbling alike. Even in this crisis the Marxists had not effected a truce with their political opponents; there was no ' united front,' as Hitler had predicted. Passive resistance was a failure.

The Marxists had set one more black mark against their name by betraying Leo Schlageter to France for his activity in sabotaging the French military occupation. Today the disgraceful story of this Nazi martyr's clumsy execution by a French rifle-squad is well known. I gathered then that Hitler's denunciations of the execution had done nothing to quiet the scandal.

Inflation had reached a disastrous point. Now the mark simply had no bottom. Germany seemed stunned, but at any moment despair might give way to revolt. The Marxist Government was steadily losing authority, and the people were looking to Munich for action and turning their backs on Berlin.

The Ruhr occupation was threatening to end Germany's statehood. As the vacillating Government was taking no steps against this danger, military resistance on the initiative of the people seemed the only alternative to extinction. The crisis

HITLER'S AIDES AND HITLER'S PROBLEMS

(Top row, left to right) Julius Streicher, the 'scourge of the Jews'; Count Ernst zu Reventlow, the 'Lone Wolf'; Rudolf Hess, Hitler's deputy. (Centre row) General Kurt von Schleicher, former Chancellor, killed in the Blood-Purge; Max Amann, Hitler's publishing partner; Baldur von Schirach, leader of the Hitler Youth. (Bottom row) General Erich Ludendorff, the war lord; Dr. Robert Ley, leader of the Labour front; the late Julius Schreck, Hitler's double and chauffeur.

loomed close ahead, and to prepare for it Hitler had made important changes in the Nazi front.

Chief among these was the reorganization of the S A, which had been begun in January with such swiftness that it was now complete. The Storm Troops were no longer a mere band of political police, but a real, military, fighting unit - armed, drilled, and competently officered.

I asked about Captain Hermann Goering, the new S A leader.

"Oh! Goering!" Hitler exclaimed, laughing and slapping his knee with satisfaction. "Splendid, a war ace with the Pour le Mérite – imagine it! Excellent propaganda! Moreover, he has money and doesn't cost me a cent. That's very important, you know."

For added strength, the Nazi SA had been allied with the 'Frei-Korps Oberland,' the 'Frei-Korps Rossbach' and the 'Reichsflagge,' and the 'Kampfbund,' under the military leadership of Colonel Kriebel. Unfortunately, and through no fault of the men, the Kampfbund had stumbled as it made its public bow.

The Reds in Munich had planned a tremendous demonstration for May Day. Hitler protested to the police, but they would not revoke the Reds' permit. When he had ordered the Kampfbund to rally with arms for a counter-demonstration, the police had declared that if he dared to use force they would retaliate ruthlessly. This time General von Lossow refused to intervene in Hider's behalf.

When the two forces gathered on May Day, groups of the Kampfbund became aggressive and were disarmed by Reichswehr troops before they retreated. Although the Nazis did succeed in disrupting the Reds' assembly, the day had yielded very bad propaganda, especially since it had been heralded as a show of power. Hitler dared not use his strength against the police-not yet. Indeed, had it not been for Roehm's renewed efforts, even this threat of defiance would have resulted in Hitler's arrest and the disbanding of the Nazi forces.

But it was clear that the national distress was near a climax which would call for heroic remedies. The growing Nazi ranks and the S A, chagrined by the May Day defeat, were tugging at the leash. The ferment had spread throughout other parties as well. Already a phrase was being whispered from man to man: " March on Berlin!
"

What chance would such a bold step have? Hitler pointed out that the Ruhr occupation had brought about a serious alienation between England and France. Europe as a whole condemned the French action; between France and Italy other factors had created hostility. If properly played up, this international chilliness could be turned to our great advantage should we move to unseat the Weimar Republic.

France certainly would seize the occasion to advance deeper into Germany; but even that misfortune would help to break down the Marxist Government, which we could try to supplant immediately with our folkic regime. If we succeeded, a temporary French advantage would not be too high a price to pay, for once in Berlin, we could launch the internal reformation which sooner or later would bring about Germany's outer liberation.

The situation boiled down to this: things seemed so bad that it was difficult to imagine them any worse. Faced with the immediate danger of losing everything, we risked more by inaction than by the most hazardous stroke. Hitler declared that he had decided to force the issue in Bavaria, and thereby to set the clock for a general coup against Berlin. Germany was a ripe apple hanging within reach; if it slipped through our fingers and smashed, we would be no hungrier than we were now.

Moreover, the whole situation was so abnormal that Hitler's chances were not limited strictly by the number of men and Maxim guns he commanded. The nation was poised for a drastic change; whoever pulled the first prop from under Berlin might very well succeed, because all Germany would spring up to topple the Government. It was chiefly a question of finding the right moment to jump-and the right people to jump with us.

Hitler said that a German Day was to take place in Nuremberg on 2 September, and there, for the first time, Ludendorff would publicly give his blessing to the Kampfbund, coming out openly on their side. I felt that in the present circumstances, with such allies, Hitler might reasonably hope to carry off a forced coup de main.

But there were misgivings at the back of my mind - I had worked with this man long enough to realize that he was no master of detail. When the moment came, he would have to act with the utmost certainty. So I asked if he had really planned every move as perfectly as was possible in advance. Did he really have the situation so well in hand that there was no danger of being premature? Above all, had he considered the fact that not only France, but also her paid allies-Poland and Czechoslovakia-might interfere by force?

"Bah! Czechs and Polacks? We'll overrun them with one corps ... why, we'll take the arms we need from them!"

That was that! The wish being father to the thought, I wanted to believe, and I believed.

When I ventured to ask whether he was not afraid of the international Jews, his face went red.

"What! I - afraid of the Jews? I shall settle that problem for good and all. Let them try to make trouble - terrorism and bombs will stop their mouths. No fear, we'll take the power and we'll use it. But if we can't do that, we'll drag all Europe with us into the abyss - at least we have that much force!"

That sent a momentary chill through my veins. But the electrifying idea that very soon, perhaps in months or even weeks, there would be action, overshadowed by any tendency I might have had to weigh the leader. To succeed with my own work, absolute trust was necessary. I must accept on faith everything that did not concern me directly.

But now Hitler's interest in the foreign aspect of the problem was awakened. With most of Europe likely to remain neutral, leaving Germany to work out its own problem, what of possible allies, he asked?

We could count on sympathy, I said, perhaps even aid, from folkic circles in nearby countries. He listened closely to my appraisal of the eventual possibilities with Hungary. But the only State which offered real hope at present, I told him, was Italy. Mussolini was firmly in the saddle, but he still had to train the horse. The Fascists were neglecting nothing to stabilize their power, and on the whole Italy supported them; yet some internal opposition lingered, which could be neatly offset by a foreign concord.

Italy as the solitary Fascist State would be like a ship struggling against the adverse tides of all Europe. A Fascist Germany could only be of help. There were no conflicting interests which would militate against such a friendship. To the contrary, our common problems under existing conditions ought to create a mutual sympathy, even an active alliance.

For instance, the Catholic Church, which loomed large in the internal politics of each country, would interpose no bars between us, since Hitler and Mussolini were alike at odds with the Pope. Such questions as democracy and communism Hitler intended to deal with, when the time came, as brusquely as the Duce had. On the whole, it seemed that our programme could clash over one problem only: the Tyrol. Therefore, I suggested, it was imperative that Hitler spread the word throughout Italy that Nazi Pan-Germany would not look longingly on the Tyrol. As for the delicate matter of the 'Anschluss' - the union of Austria with Germany - his wisest policy would be to evade any flat declaration of his plans in that direction.

If we acted along these lines, I saw no reason to believe that Mussolini would not feel a benevolent, however silent, sympathy with our plans. Of course he could not be expected to commit himself until we acted in Germany. His status had changed since our last talk together; then he was only a radical politician, now he was prime minister. As a statesman, he would measure us by no yardstick except our usefulness to Italy, and that postulated a stronger Germany than the weakling Marxist State. But if we could prove our strength, probably he would go a long way with us.

"Good, good!" Hitler broke in before I could finish. "I believe you are right - and that your most valuable work lies ahead of you in Italy. You know now how things stand with us. Will you go to Rome at once?"

He was alive now with the idea of preparing that friendliest nation for coming events in Germany. After some discussion, we decided that my new mission would have a fivefold purpose:

To interest Mussolini, so that in case of conflict with France when the split came between Munich and Berlin, Italy would stand on the flank of France, if not as our ally, at least as a benevolent neutral.

To declare our disinterest in the Tyrol, and to minimize the Austrian question; stressing, however, our opposition to the throne-snatching Habsburgs, Italy's enemy for generations back.

To swing the Press into sympathy with us, correcting the present system by which Italy received all its German news from Berlin agencies which naturally shaped public opinion in favour of our enemies.

To do whatever was possible to counteract the influence of the Berlin Government, using every opportunity to foster our plans and further our prestige.

And finally, if possible, to get money.

That night we decided to celebrate the new venture in advance. Linz was only a little town, but it was German, which is to say that it boasted the usual quota of beer-gardens and restaurants. To the largest and gaudiest we made our way.

Nowadays, when his least grimace is likely to be immortalized by the photo-lens, Hitler has frozen his features into a series of false-faces, some smiling, others frowning, this one benign, the next one grim. Even among his intimates he often assumes something of a poker face. Every politician, of course, must at times distort his face in the baby-kissing pucker or the Pro Bono Publico scowl, but Hitler has to a great degree escaped this nuisance, since he today enjoys the enviable power of being able to ignore the electorate. Nevertheless I scan the rotogravures in vain for a glimpse of his old-time open countenance.

On this night in Linz, he was still enough of a nobody to be himself. His face was vividly expressive. Each shade of feeling or thought was instantly reflected there, an entertaining study because his mind is kaleidoscopic. He loves nothing so much as to pour out his knowledge and opinions into a friendly ear. In later years, as my detachment grew, he sometimes secretly amused me with his Chautauqua airs; but I remember other times when his words came close to poetry. His mind is certainly furnished with more ideas about more subjects than most political men can claim, and in private speech he often is gifted with beauty of language. Even at this period he was referring nearly everything, from art to zoology, to his all-absorbing task - a trait which frequently lent unexpected sparkle to his conversation.

The big restaurant to which he led me enclosed what seemed like acres of Linz within its walls of abominably painted panels and gilt plaster. We had scarcely sat down before his architect's eye focused on the decorations of the room.

"Baroque," he explained needlessly, pointing at the bulbous cupids and fruity garlands. "Bad baroque. Has it ever occurred to you that there's no such thing as merely poor baroque? The style has no middle quality; when it is not perfect, it's impossible. And, of course, the very spirit of the style, its lush intimacy, makes it dangerous to splash baroque elements over a hall of such dimensions. One might as well gild a barn. But heavens, what a magnificent place this would be for a rally!

Why, in this one room alone, I could swing all Linz !"

So it went, all that evening. He was in a gay mood.

Next afternoon Hitler revealed still another side of his character. It was our last day together, and he asked me to go with him to the Poestlingberg, which is indeed a sight worth seeing. Out of the plain it rises abruptly, a towering peak surveying the country-side, an isolated height reaching skyward above the fields and woods.

When we reached the crest, a thrilling view unrolled below us. The Danube made a great loop into the distance and back again; and as far as eye could reach, the farms and villages lay upon the flat lowland-modest, placid and peaceful, the broad, pleasant face of ancient Germania.

We sat for a while in silence. Hitler gazed over the vast landscape with love in his eyes; this was the scene he had known in his childhood. Evidently some inner vision coloured his thoughts. At last he spoke, softly:

"Long ago there was no Poestlingberg here; all was level. No heights, no valleys, but only the unbroken earth, washed smooth by the primal tides as they flowed and ebbed over the world. Then the fires burst up from the earth's centre; the ice marched down from the poles; and the earthquakes convulsed like birth-pangs, shaping the face of the land. And after long cycles of cataclysmic change, some titanic force, elemental yet governed by supreme laws, thrust up this peak from the plane; some irresistible underground movement carved it out of the deepest bedrock and lifted it high here to dominate everything. . . . Who knows what set this force in motion? The crucial strain could have come from the heavy overload of some distant mountain range. Or perhaps the natural outlet of the fire deep in the earth's core was choked, until its pent-up energy blew this mountain sky-high like a stopper from a flask. Who knows? We believe these things are ruled by law; but the law itself partly eludes us. A pity, for the processes of Nature may symbolize mankind's little life...."

I had turned toward Hitler with astonishment. His ambitions were no secret from me, and now I suspected him of deliberately drawing the grandiose parallel at which his soliloquy hinted. But I was wrong. It was the land itself, the story of the grassy rocks about us, which filled his inner vision. He was just a smallish man sitting there in a neat, cheap, blue-serge suit, his head bare, his eyes shining - and I realized that he was peering backward through the mists of Time, and not forward into his own future.

For the moment he had utterly forgotten himself. When he picked up his discourse again, the poetic mood was gone; instead of hearing about the Creation, I heard the legends of all the landmarks within eyesight.

"How do you remember all this?"

The question recalled Hitler to himself.

"You forget that I went to school here, that I love this mountain and the fields below and all the things that grow here."

The floodgates of his memory opened. With that broad view spread out below, he spoke of his boyhood in the little town of Linz. I saw him through his own eyes, as he searched out the significance of those early years. He told me of the dreams which had impelled him to fight his way up from poverty and nothingness; he spoke without sentimentality, as though he had reasoned the matter through and had no doubt how the story would end. Here and there his mind flashed, catching up threads of logic and desire which his words knotted into a net for the future.

Finally he said, in a voice vibrant with intensity and with a hard gleam in his eyes: "Day after day, night after night, for four years I have been animated and dominated by the burning desire to act. Now, at last, the hour of action is near! "

I experienced something like a second conversion. The sincerity of his conviction redoubled my loyalty. In the face of every difficulty this man would lead us forward, because in his soul he believed that circumstance had laid upon his shoulders the burden of Germany's salvation. No selfish ambition showed in his dream. Pride, yes; but pride balanced by the humility with which he accepted his task. He burned for power-because power alone can transmute ideas into action. He wanted money, because money paves the road to power. He hoped to hold the masses in the hollow of his hand, but only to remould them along stronger, nobler lines. For himself, he desired just one thing: a reborn Fatherland, where he could share the new life with the people of his race, proudly and in peace.

The selfless grandeur of his vision held me spellbound. He meant all that he said, and I knew it. Though I had already sensed some of his petty human weaknesses, I believed in his power to achieve-and I believed that here was a man honest clear through, uncompromising, incorruptible, who would march unswerving toward a goal that was good. Now I knew that the Poestlingberg truly symbolized his exalted destiny. He stood with his head in the clouds, his feet firmly braced on his native earth, his heart in the future.

As we went down the mountain-side, I felt that I would see him next time, either victorious or in prison - or perhaps read some morning in Rome that he had lost his life for his ideals. Germany was in an agony of readjustment; the equilibrium was delicate; one strong man could swing the balance, if he were willing to stake his life on the move-and stake it wisely. Of all the men in Germany, Hitler the dreamer, the visionary, was most ready.

When we took leave of each other that night, I still felt the glow of self-sacrifice which his words had kindled. We said an affectionate farewell.

Just as I turned away, emotionalized almost beyond speech, Hitler flung after me a final injunction so brutally practical that I jumped.

"Fetzen Sie aus Mussolini heraus, was Sie koennen!"

"Rip out of Mussolini whatever you can! '

Oh, the feet of clay!

With credentials signed by Hitler, certifying that I was his agent and Press representative of the Party, I returned first to Budapest. Hitler had agreed that it was advisable to let our friends know that the situation in Germany was approaching a showdown, and to prepare them for violent developments in the near future, without revealing any details.

Hungary, which held a strategic geographical position, was just as eager to break the chains of the Trianon Treaty that had taken away two-thirds of her territory as we were to break the fetters of Versailles. Although the Hungarians were divided in their politics, at least they showed a united front against their enemies and refused to accept the treaty of enslavement as final. In every restaurant, in every train, in every public place, wherever one went, one met the words Nem - Nem - Soka! No - No - Never!

The Hungarians knew well enough that they could never act single-handed, but must wait until the Germans took the initiative. Once our march on Berlin was accomplished, an uprising in Hungary would help us; it would keep at least parts of the Jugoslavian, Czechoslovakian, and Rumanian armies at bay in case of conflict, accelerate results in Austria, and possibly force Italy to side with Hungary against Jugoslavia. In return, when we had the situation in hand in Germany, we could aid in bringing Goemboes to power.

Satisfied with the assurances received in Budapest, I travelled via Venice to Milan at the end of August. Mussolini was expected there next day, his first return since his rise to power; the occasion was the opening of the motor races in nearby Monza, where the speed-thirsty dictator would officiate.

His brother Arnaldo, who had succeeded to the editorship of the Popolo d'Italia, told me that Mussolini would visit the paper next afternoon at three, and advised me to be present if I wished to speak with him.

I was there early, wondering if Mussolini the dictator would receive me with the cordial frankness and freedom of Mussolini the revolutionary.

Punctually he arrived with his entourage. As he mounted the steps, it was at once apparent that his dress was immaculate. Later I noticed his clean, well-kept hands - no more chewed finger-nails. He was the picture of health, tanned and electric with energy.

I stepped forward and bowed. To my relief he recognized me instantly, spoke cordially, this time in fairly good German, and continued to chat while he read the credentials from Hitler[1] which I tendered to him. He was gracious, but there was no escaping the fact that this was the prime minister; his very inflection was more reserved than formerly.

---

1 *Reproduced in this book.*

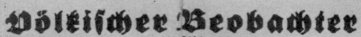

CREDENTIALS

MUNICH, August 21, 1923.

Herr Kurt Ludecke, born February 5, 1980, in Berlin, is hereby charged with the representation of the National-Socialist German Worker's Party in the Kingdom of Italy.

We ask that Herr Ludecke be recognized in this capacity and be accorded assistance at all times. These credentials are valid from the present until December 31, 1923.

(Signed) ADOLF HITLER

Chairman of the National-Socialist German Worker's Party

Faint pencilled inscription by Goering in Innsbruck: "Ludecke acts on my behalf. Assist."

wConveying most respectful greetings from Hitler, I said that I would appreciate a longer talk, and he suggested that I return to Rome on his train that night.

The return journey was a triumph for Mussolini. His private coach was attached to the regular train, and all along the way, through the whole night, it was met by cheering multitudes at each station. Naturally my imagination saw Hitler travelling between Munich and Berlin in similar fashion.

Past four in the morning came word that Mussolini would see me; his Excellency had been so busy and the hour was so advanced that he would be able to give me only a moment.· I was able to tell him, however, that the situation between Munich and Berlin was tense; that the nationalist spirit had almost reached the boiling point; that Berlin had lost all authority and Germany might soon have to face very serious decisions; that I was not in Italy to admire the Raphaels or the scenery, but to increase Italy's sympathy for Hitler and its understanding of the German problem.

Mussolini was courteous, but it was obvious that he would not commit himself in any way. It would have been tactless and stupid of me to try to say more; so I merely expressed the hope that in Rome he would provide an opportunity to discuss matters. He nodded pleasantly, and dismissed me.

Early next day, still yawning after too short a sleep, I rubbed my eyes wide open to capture every glimpse of familiar Rome. I hailed a cab just to ramble about. Each turning of the road meant something. At this spot, Sulla single-handed had confronted a rebellious populace; at that spot Dolores and I had walked together in the moonlight; along this very avenue a carriage-driver, wheeling me home from some gala, declaimed Dante for my benefit while his weary nag clopped out a sedate rhythm.

Nothing had changed, on the surface, in Mussolini's Rome. We bustle in and out the gates, I reflected, but Rome remains unalterable. Centuries ago the walls of these palaces and hovels were tinged with the same mellow ochre; the fountains were as murmurous; the Roman nights as wonderful. Old Tiber's yellow flood flows now as it flowed for Romulus; the ancient ghosts in the ruins pay no heed to us mortals who inherit the remnants of their glory. Yet now this is our day here; and who can tell if our own ghosts may not return to haunt the Piazza di Spagna or the Ulpia, deeming them pleasanter places than anything the hereafter will offer?

Alas, I had little enough of pleasure this trip. From the moment I unpacked my bags, I was busy laying out a campaign, making my arrival known where it would do most good, preparing interviews. The first thing of all was to change the tone of the newspapers, which so far reflected Berlin's hostile attitude. That meant unremitting work.

A day or so later there came good news to spur me on. The German Day in Nuremberg had been a tremendous success. Ludendorff had taken part publicly with Hitler, and more than sixty thousand men of the Kampfbund had marched before them. Altogether, things seemed to be coming our way.

In Spain, too, since my recent visit, the spotlight was focusing more closely on a 'strong man.'

Through sleepless nights, King Alfonso had been looking with envy towards Italy, where Mussolini already had established his regimented order. So when Don Miguel Primo de Rivera, the military commander of the seething province of Catalonia, declared a dictatorial government in September 1923 the King hastily legalized his coup d'etat. Parliament was dissolved, trial by jury and right of free speech suspended, the trains began to run on time, and nobody dared to strike - in short, another dictatorship was born.

This was a development which-provided it were not reversed-might be of great importance for us in Germany. France still figured as a most serious problem in Hitler's plans; but with a Fascist Italy on her flank and a Fascist pro-German Spain at her back, she would think twice before turning her full power against us.

Encouraged, I tried for another talk with Mussolini. Instead, his secretary of foreign affairs, at that time Baron Russo, received me, saying that we might speak freely together, and he would convey my information to the Duce.

Baron Russo listened with interest, but as I had expected, no help or special commitment was offered. Mussolini, being legally Prime Minister of Italy, in friendly relations with the Government in Berlin, could not officially take notice of the representative of a party opposing that Government. I could only hope that my words would really be relayed to the Duce, and that their seed would germinate.

For the moment, the Press was more accessible.

Hitler's name gave me greater authority now than it had a few months earlier, for already there were vague rumours abroad concerning his possible importance. Playing him up deliberately, I formed such good connections with the larger papers that within a month the colour of the news changed. New attention was turned upon the German situation. Throughout Italy, interviews and articles appeared, giving the Fascists a picture of the crisis different from that which Berlin had painted.

My relations with the Idea Nazionale and other pro-Fascist newspapers were excellent. The editors of the Corriere d'Italia, at that time the semi-official organ of the Government, extended special courtesies. Following my suggestion, they sent an accredited correspondent to Munich, a Dott, Leo Negrelli, who had already seen service in Budapest. Travelling with my letters of introduction, he gained front-page interviews with Hitler and Ludendorff. The Party in Munich gave him royal treatment which was not wasted.

I also succeeded in making valuable connections with correspondents from other countries, who reported my activities in Rome to their home Press, which created further propaganda for the Nazis-or, in a few cases, against us. Not everyone liked the work I was doing.

The Avanti, the Socialist organ in Milan, at that time still going strong, was so aroused by the news I inspired that it honoured me with a front-page article, 'Il Signore Ludecke - L'Anima Damnata di Hitler,' complaining vehemently that such propaganda against a recognized Government ought not to be tolerated in Italy. If a Socialist German had dared to talk as Ludecke talked, they protested, he would at once have been escorted to the border by carabinieri. I basked in this back-handed compliment.

On 25 September Cuno resigned as Chancellor of Germany, and Gustav Stresemann, arch-enemy of our ideas, succeeded him. With the stroke of a pen he ended the passive resistance, leaving Germany without even that poor bulwark against the rapacity of France. Stresemann was enjoying the most favourable world Press of any German politician since the war; so I concentrated on weakening his position, in Italy at any rate.

'As much as is in me,' wrote St. Paul to the Gentiles, 'I am ready to preach the gospel to you that are in Rome.' Taking that as a motto, I became bold indeed in dealing with Hitler's enemies. For example, the pro-Fascist journal, L'Epoca, in the issue of 25 October 1923 gave nearly its whole front page to one of my interviews, under the headline 'Il Governo di Berlino Accusato di Tradimento dal Rappresentante di Hitler - Intervista de L'Epoca col. sig. Ludecke.'

The accusation of treason against Berlin was in truth audacious enough; but it created the furore I intended, and gave me an opportunity to incorporate a concise statement of the Nazi credo and programme, by virtue of which, I affirmed, Hitler would cure Germany's sickness.

Parenthetically, I notice now how strangely it falls on the ear to hear various Italian papers characterized as PTO or anti-Fascist. State censorship, oiled by a good portion of the State budget, has long since made it as absurd to speak of an anti-Fascist paper in Italy, as of an anti-Fascist Mussolini. The Duce, in addition to holding eight out of the ten Cabinet positions today, has also seated his spectre in every editorial chair from the Alps to Sicily. But the power of the Press is something to be attacked cautiously; though the work of subjugation is absolutely necessary under a dictatorship, it takes time. When I exercised my right of free speech, I was simply sharing in the common liberty; there was no general censorship yet. Consequently it was possible to salt the interviews with observations which would not be likely to pass today in any paper in Italy.

With my outspoken opinions in print, all coupled with Hitler's name, it was natural that important Fascists should show a greater interest in our cause. As Hitler's spokesman, I was kept busy all the time by Press work, personal meetings, and the reports which had to be sent to Munich, with clippings. Rosenberg and Eckart knew how to handle their end, reprinting my stuff with a great fanfare in the Voelkischer Beobachter. More than an echo of all this reached Berlin, where the anti-Nazi Press retaliated with fulminations against Herr Hitler's 'Ambassador,' never failing to use the quotes. .

There was no time for Roman social life, which is like nothing else in the world-a curious set of wheels-within-wheels; papal, royal, Fascist, and international coteries, all revolving in separate circles, each clique a cog in the most fascinating social machine on earth, yet one never asking the other to tea. I could not even find time to visit St. Peter's, and barely managed to squeeze in a night with a Russian lady.

The work did have its rewards, of course. Hitler's name became one to be reckoned with. When Mussolini issued invitations for his first reception to the King - a social and political sensation which rocked Rome - there was a great scramble for cards by all the important foreigners. Many of them were disappointed, but I, as representative of the Nazi Party, a party which still had nothing more tangible than a future to recommend it, was asked in my official capacity to be among those who gathered that night in the Palazzo Venezia to see how a Dictator would greet his King.

The autumn sun burnishes Rome's patina to a richer beauty. The spirit that was alive in the city added to its charm. Everywhere else in Europe I had found the people blighted with weariness, depression, and mistrust, behind a false mask of desperate gaiety. But Italy was like a nation whose youth had been renewed.

This new spirit, even so early as 1923, one year after Mussolini's rise to power, was impressive to anyone who remembered pre-Fascist days, when Italy was a poorly organized nation, without energy or objective, in grave danger of dissolution from within and oppression from without.

Now, instead of decay and debility, a new Renaissance in twentieth-century terms seemed imminent, thanks to the self-willed regime which had imposed its strict discipline upon the people. The change was almost a miracle. Inspired by the dynamic personality of Mussolini, the Italians seemed filled with enthusiasm and a joyful will-to-power. The old men, whose futile carpings had achieved nothing, no longer carped - because they dared not. And the young men, the fresh, vital youths through whom the Italy of to-morrow would blossom, had given themselves over 'with complete faith to the Duce, who knew how to value them, to mould them, and to use them.

Young men were everywhere, with picks and shovels, with rifles-a light in their eyes, their arms uplifted in brawny salutes, their lungs bursting with 'Vivas' for the leader who thundered his message of national glory over the land. Young women, too, were beginning to leave their shuttered homes, to live in the sunlight and take their part.

It did not appear incongruous that the anthem of this reborn country should have as a refrain the lyrical words: 'Youth, springtime of beauty. . . .'

If this is a dictatorship, I thought to myself, then the sooner in Germany, the better for us!

IX

HITLER STRIKES AND FAILS

In Germany, developments had run their course during my months in Italy. The political situation had shifted so rapidly, on so many fronts, that it would be tiresome to trace here all the devious changes. However, the struggle which was leading up to Hitler's denouement did present, in its larger outlines, several aspects of peculiar interest, important to this story.

The loss of Memel and the complete let-down of the Berlin Government after its abandonment of the 'passive resistance' in the Ruhr threw the entire nation into a turmoil of indignation. From day to day, forces in the political field aligned and realigned themselves, some to defend Berlin, but most to attack it. The capital was ringed round with enemies.

In Bavaria the Government was in the hands of the Bavarian People's Party, whose plans for the restoration of the Wittelsbach dynasty were forcing them to face the serious opposition of Berlin-an estrangement which could only please the Hitler-Ludendorff group of folkic Nationalists. Hitler knew that his party did not yet possess strength enough to effect a nationwide coup alone or even in combination with its immediate allies. His hope-and his plan-was to steer the steam-roller when Bavaria pooled all its power for an assault on the Marxist Government. How to achieve such a coalition, under his own command, would depend on circumstances; and the first necessity was the growing breach between Munich and Berlin.

In northern Germany, the Deutsch-Voelkische Freiheits Partei-the German Folkic Liberty Party-was making progress paralleling that of the Nazis. Though this movement did not have an actual Nazi programme, it was radically anti-Berlin on a folkic basis. In the Rhineland, in Thuringia and Saxony, the ferment of revolution was at work. The Ruhr was ready for anything, however desperate, that might alter its abject misery.

Captain Ernst Roehm had resigned as Reichswehr officer and had openly joined Hitler. Since 1920, Roehm had been a most practical ally, diverting considerable Reichswehr funds to the Nazis, with the consent of his superior, General van Epp. Germany had begun to re-arm the very day the disarmament pact was signed, and Roehm had access to secret appropriations made by the Government to support the so-called 'Black Reichswehr'-the illegally armed troops. Now Roehm, who was already a master in 'Waffenschiebungen,' or arms-bootlegging, practically became master of ordnance for the Nazis. Their arsenals bulged.

It was also due to Roehm's work that on 25 September Hitler was handed the sovereign political leadership of the Kampfbund, whose principles were at the same time publicly accepted by the 'Deutsche Hochschulring,' a college association of more than one hundred thousand students.

Both Munich and Berlin saw a danger signal in such a gain of influence for Hitler. In his new role as chief of the best-organized activists in Germany, he attacked the shameful capitulation to the Ruhr invasion even more boldly, calling Chancellor Stresemann a traitor in the Beohachter's largest type.

Hitler inaugurated a series of fourteen Nazi mass-meetings to emphasize his defiance. The Bavarian Government answered by declaring a state of siege, which automatically forbade the scheduled meetings, and appointed von Kahr 'General Staatskommissar,' with dictatorial powers.

Kahr published a programme to restore the authority of the State for the sake of order and peace, cancelled throughout Bavaria the 'Laws for the Protection of the Republic, and stopped the orders for the arrest of leading activists such as Captain Ehrhardt, Heiss, and Rossbach.

A few days later Captain Heiss, leader of the 'Reichsflagge,' broke with Hitler. The Reichsflagge split into two groups, one following Heiss and the other, under Roehm, remaining with the Kampfbund as 'Reichskriegsfiagge.'

With Munich and Berlin in hostility towards each other, the situation everywhere in Germany approached chaos. Characteristic of the prevailing confusion was the foolhardiness of Major Buchrucker in Kuestrin, who tried to seize the town's fortress with a group of the Black Reichswehr and was arrested.

Nazi group reinforcing him escaped and fled to Bavaria.

By the middle of October, Socialist-Communist coalition governments had been organized in Saxony and Thuringia. Zeigner, the new minister-president of Saxony, was openly preparing a platform for Bolshevism.

In Aachen, separatists proclaimed a 'Rhineland Republic' with the help of France, which recognized it officially on 25 October. But the population revolted, real battles were fought, and the Red separatists retreated to the Palatinate, where they set up an autonomous government on 5 November under the protection of the French General de Metz.

Thoroughly alarmed, the war ministry in Berlin sent Reichswehr troops to re-establish the State's authority. Nationalist and Communist disturbances occurred throughout the country. Relations between Paris and Berlin became sharper every day, with France arrogantly and brutally demanding Germany's unconditional submission.

The President, Fritz Ebert, had already transferred his executive duties to the Minister of War, General-Oberst von Seeckt, now commander-in-chief of the army with supreme power throughout the Reich-provided he knew how to use it.

A Government decree declared the Deutsch-Voelkische Freiheits Partei dissolved.

The same fate threatened the Nazis and their other allies; it looked now as if they would all be driven underground.

The more violently the Kampfbund fought the Government, the harsher grew Berlin's retaliation against Hitler's camp. The 'States Tribunal,' the juridical body created to carry out the arbitrary 'Laws for the Protection of the Republic,' summoned prominent men like Dietrich Eckart, Hermann Esser, Captain Weiss, and finally Hitler himself to appear before the court in Leipzig. Of course they did not go, and violent protests on their behalf were made to the Bavarian Government by the Kampfbund: protection must be extended to patriots or the Kampfbund would take the job of protecting them into its own hands.

The currency inflation had now reached nightmare proportions. In early November the mark soared to astronomical figures, the pound bringing officially twenty-five trillion marks and unofficially thirty-five trillions.

In those hectic weeks, Hitler concentrated his attacks on the folly of imagining there could be compromise with France, for France was determined to ruin Germany. Again and again he urged revolt against the impossible obligations of the Versailles Treaty, never failing now to emphasize the need for an understanding with England and Italy.

All the forces opposed to Bolshevism, all those who resented the national humiliation and sensed the national danger, were opening their eyes to Hitler's potential value as leader of a real resistance.

The Nazi movement and the Kampfbund were growing at feverish tempo. A certain percentage of the newcomers, of course, were camp-followers and opportunists. Many people of wealth and social position suddenly discovered their patriotic hearts and made common cause with us, in the belief that Hitler might, after all, come out on top and share the spoils with them. Many others gave money to the movement without actually joining it. Nazis and Kampfbund members were giving to the limit, sometimes literally sacrificing their last million marks for the cause.

Financing the Kampfbund was a difficult problem. To understand how difficult, one must remember the insane gyrations German currency was taking. The country was in a state of financial epilepsy, both ludicrous and ghastly.

To illustrate:

Suppose a clerk has just received his pay, so many hundreds of millions of marks. Knowing that by to-morrow it might decrease in value by several hundred per cent, he stands wondering what to buy, what tangible form to give his marks before they are worthless. He might as well toss them in the gutter as deposit them in the bank. What about another pair of shoes? But the price is preposterous - 170,000,000 marks. He hesitates; he has worked hard for his money, he really doesn't need shoes- and that's too much for them anyway.

A few hours later he decides that perhaps shoes would be best after all. Already his closet is cluttered with too much soap, too many neckties, too much shoe polish. Going back to the shop, he learns that the price has jumped to 325,000,000 marks. Yet the money in his pocket has not increased. Someone or something has cheated him of half his wages before he can spend a single note, and in the pitiful confusion of his heart he calls on God to damn the bankers and the Government.

And so it went with everything. The people, buying frantically in their flight from the mark, dared not retain currency for an hour. That explains the false prosperity which kept industry humming during the inflation years. There was little unemployed labour at a time when England already had millions out of work. Owners of buildings and homes, not knowing what else to do with their marks, would order perhaps a new annex or general repairs-anything to get some value out of the tumbling currency.

Many unfortunates, especially old folk and country folk, never learned to keep abreast of the plummeting mark. Bewildered, used to counting by the Pfennig instead of astronomically, they lost everything before they realized that the savings of a frugal lifetime could turn into worthless paper overnight.

Those who lived on pensions or who thought themselves secure in the possession of bonds or life insurance were made destitute. Securities that had been bought with thousands of gold marks were paid of in paper that would not purchase matches enough to burn them. Bank accounts dwindled to zero-or to figures followed by nine zeros, which meant no more. I received notice from a bank where I had borrowed on war loan certificates valued at eight thousand gold marks, that they had closed out my account because it was no longer worth keeping on the books.

It was months before small shopkeepers realized that they must use adding machines to protect themselves against overwhelming losses. Even large hotels like the Adlon in Berlin were slow to learn that only a steeply sliding rate of exchange, revised upward every hour, could protect them from bankruptcy when they accepted foreign money. For a long time a foreigner with foreign coin could live like a grand seigneur on next to nothing a week.

When prices were boosted, every transaction became an exasperating nuisance. To pay for a luncheon, a trillion marks had to change hands, perhaps by the basketful. The largest letter-envelope was too small to carry all the stamps required; they were pasted on separate sheets attached to the letter.

Thousands of visitors came from everywhere, invading Germany with their sound 'valuta,' to fatten on the distress of the nation. Some came only to satisfy personal needs-to buy a furpiece, a jewel, or a motor car. Others came down like vultures to snatch anything that had speculative value. Among them were many Jews-but Jews or no Jews, they were all birds of prey, picking the carcass of German thrift.

Houses, whole blocks of buildings, beautiful estates for which the owners asked quadrillions of marks, went into the hands of foreigners from Amsterdam, London, and New York, for a few hundred dollars. Debtors inside and outside Germany rushed to pay their debts with marks that were literally valueless. A whole nation suffered from the greatest swindle in history.

Under such hardships, the country rocked with panic. Out of such despair, any sort of violence might develop. A government cannot with impunity allow some obscure influence to wipe out the employer's payroll, rob the shopkeeper's till, rifle the housewife's tea-pot hoard, and cheat the earners and savers until the whole nation is mortgaged. International finance is mysterious, but money is something the common man understands and needs. Touch his money, and he may submit for a while; but sooner or later he strikes back.

In Germany the forces of rebellion needed only one strong man who knew his purpose to unite them in an irresistible uprising. Eyes of friends and foes alike were centred on Munich.

The Beohachter's campaign of invective became so defiant that Berlin could no longer pretend to ignore it. When at last Hitler published an article which almost openly called the Reichswehr to revolt, the War Ministry, now the executive power in the Reich, demanded that the Beohachter be silenced.

Von Kahr refused, on the ground that suppression of the paper would outrage the public, perhaps to the point of rebellion. Confusing events now followed each other swiftly. Only one thing was clear: the conflict between Berlin and Munich.

The War Ministry answered von Kahr by ordering General von Lossow, the commander of the 7th Reichswehr Division in Bavaria, to stop the Beohachter's press by force of arms. As a civil power, Bavaria was autonomous; but the military authority, operating from Berlin, was a long arm of the Government which reached across every state border. By law it had been given supreme power during this emergency.

General von Lossow, after consulting with Kahr, declined to carry out the War Ministry's orders. Berlin at once sent him orders of dismissal, designating General Freiherr van Kress to replace him. Kahr would not recognize General von Kress. Lossow retained command of the 7th Division, and its men were hastily sworn in to the Bavarian Government, thus cancelling their oath to the Republic and making them subject to Bavaria as a sovereign state.

A more extreme act in defiance of the Constitution was hardly possible. Von Lossow was liable to court martial, von Kahr to arrest for high treason. Having taken a step so audacious neither could withdraw.

Developments so far were grist to the Nazi mill. Nothing could serve the interests of the Nazis so well as an irreparable breach between the Berlin Government which they hated and the Munich Government which they hoped to use.

At first, Kahr did not say he was speaking for the Reich. His public proclamation, addressed to the Bavarian people, not to all Germany, emphasized only Bavarian issues and made Lossow's troops the servants of Bavarian interests alone.

But, to escape the stigma of having staged plain military mutiny and treason, Kahr had to justify his procedure by seeming to have at heart the welfare of the entire Reich. Therefore he privately assured the Kampfbund that he would march upon Berlin to solve the national German problem. Lossow also said he was ready for the coup d'etat, provided there was 'a fifty-one per cent chance for success.'

This was, however, an empty pledge, by which Kahr intended to dupe the rival factions into supporting his plans. He even conferred with groups in North Germany regarding a national dictatorship, after flatly refusing to deal any further with the Reich Government. Everyone was convinced by such manoeuvres that the 'march on Berlin' was merely a question of days. The various groups which hoped to participate oiled their rifles.

At a mass meeting, Hitler boldly proclaimed: "The German problem will be solved only when the swastika waves from the Reichstag in Berlin. There is no going backward, only forward."

Of course Hitler knew well· enough that a dictatorship by von Kahr would be supported by the Bavarian People's Party; only insofar as it served to check the influence of the Nazi Party; therefore Kahr's courtship of the Kampfbund was no more than a political expedient. , Outwardly the leaders were co-operating, but now it was really a game of one man trying to outwit the other.

Both Lossow and Seisser, the commander of the Bavarian State police, declared that delay was no longer necessary. Yet they waited. Hitler gained the impression that they were impatient to have the coup accomplished, but did not themselves wish to take the initiative, expecting that of him.

The political pot was ready to boil over. Berlin had lost the last remnant of its authority. When will Munich act? was the universal question throughout Germany. With feverish impatience everybody looked to the day which would bring liberations and economic recovery-or final dissolution. The cry for action became clamourous.

Kahr and Hitler could not hold back their followers much longer. Captain Ehrhardt, who had thrown in his lot with Kahr, was ordered to mobilize men on the northern border of Bavaria. This was tantamount to an armed threat against Berlin. Completing the rupture, Kahr declared Bavaria absolutely independent of the Reich, militarily, financially, and in taxation.

Now surely the march on Berlin would be ordered. But still Kahr hung back, though his situation was untenable from any standpoint. Finally, pressed by Ludendorff, he announced that he was ready and anxious to act - but that everything must be delayed just a little longer until he could bring in certain other groups in northern Germany.

The truth was that this little 'dictator was in a quandary what to dictate.

There is no doubt that Kahr, advocate of the 'King,' had never really intended marching on Berlin, but only to use Lossow, Seisser, Pittinger, and others on that side, as well as the Kampfbund and Hitler, for the restoration of the Wittelsbach monarchy. But now the situation was beyond him. He found himself swept forward in the whirlwind of national passion. Every day it became less possible to localize the planned coup d'etat in Bavaria. His principals used the strongest pressure to force a decision, and at last he decided to act.

Indeed, having kindled a forest fire to roast one Wittelsbach chestnut, Kahr had to hurry. A few days more, and all his hopes would turn to ashes in the general conflagration.

At this juncture, Hitler received secret information that Kahr intended to, proclaim the Bavarian monarchy on 12 November.

There was no longer any choice for Hitler. He must forestall this coup or else abandon his own plans for bringing a new National Government to an undivided Germany. If his movement was to survive, he must at any cost frustrate the proclamation of the monarchy. Action was the only course. The decision was critical-one hour too soon, one hour too late, and the work of years would be undone. Yet now that Kahr had taken his stance, it was imperative for Hitler to step ahead of him and launch his arrow first.

Kahr's plan was to prepare the ground for the Wittelsbach restoration by speaking before a meeting which would include the elite of all the Nationalists inside and outside Munich. He called such a meeting. The date was announced as 8 November.

On that night, Hitler resolved, he would leap into action himself.

From information I received in Rome on the morning of 8 November, I realized that any hour might bring the climax.

Nervous and restless, late that evening I went to the office of the Corriere d'Italia. Negrelli, their Munich correspondent, had sent in no unusual news. I returned to my hotel-but not to sleep. No man can live his life for the realization of one dream alone, and then endure with composure the moment when that dream must become iron reality. Add uncertainty to the other emotions, and the strain is as cruel as anything can be.

Decisive things were happening - but what, what, what? At three in the morning, unable to endure it for a moment longer, I dressed and rushed again to the Corriere d'Italia. A friendly editor who was especially interested in Munich because of our work together told me that nothing of real moment had been reported. But he advised me to wait with him; some telegrams which had just arrived were being read at that moment.

While we were talking, the first faint pallor of dawn began to lighten the sky outside his window. The night had passed-and I was still in the dark! Only men who have watched beside child-beds can match the suspense I knew.

At last another editor came into the room waving a dispatch and shouting its message:

"Colpo d'Estato a Monaco!"

Coup d'etat at Munich!

The telegram was deciphered in my presence, but contained only the tantalizing report that Hitler, acting with Ludendorff, had proclaimed a national revolution. I stayed on at the newspaper office, reading the Munich messages as they came. They said nothing new except that Kahr, Lossow, and Seisser had joined the revolution, and that all Munich had turned out in a jamboree of joy.

Now the suspense was unbearable, and I resolved to leave at once for Munich.

Returning to my hotel, I found reporters waiting. Overnight I had become a man of new importance. I accepted an invitation to go see Virginio Gayda, then the influential editor of the Messagero, but to-day, as editor of the Giornale d'Italia, virtually Mussolini's mouthpiece. I gave him a jubilant interview on condition that it would not be published until he received confirmation that the march on Berlin was well under way.

When I again returned to the hotel, two strangers presented themselves as secret police and very politely asked if I would be good enough to answer a few questions at police headquarters. There a higher official informed me that my interpreter had been arrested as a 'suspicious' Socialist. What could I tell them about him?

It was preposterous. He was a dear old man, educated and intelligent-a German who spoke and wrote Italian beautifully. I had found him living in the greatest distress, camping in a crude hut in the courtyard of some old building.

He was certainly a Socialist of a mild sort, but I told the police official I was sure the old man was simply a harmless old intellectual. Nevertheless they held him, probably for deportation. I left a hundred lire for the poor fellow, but never found out what became of him.

During this interrogation, however, I was asked to identify myself. A clerk carried my credentials out of the room, returning with them fifteen minutes later, when I was politely allowed to leave. I was sure that they were photostated, and I still suspect that my unfortunate interpreter had been seized simply as a pretext for looking at my own papers and correspondence. Was it only a casual incident of police routine,or had some one-the German embassy, perhaps-suddenly taken a more intense: interest in Hitler's emissary because of the events in Munich?

After a brief interview with Baron Russo, the Secretary of Foreign Affairs, I rushed to the station to catch the midday express which would connect at Verona with the Innsbruck-Munich express.

The noon editions in Rome still carried big headlines about the successful revolution, with the added news that the Crown Prince of Bavaria had joined the revolutionists. Everything looked rosy, and yet my heart held a premonition of evil.

The dispatches hadn't quite the right ring.

Only to be there! I had told Hitler that it would break my heart to be out of Germany when things started going, that I wanted to be with them in the front line in Munich, and he had said laughing: "You can fIy here when it begins."

Evening came, and then the night, but sleep was still impossible. Now my doubts and fears were serious, for the evening papers, instead of bringing fuller information, merely stated that communications were interrupted. That was ominous. If the revolution had succeeded, the wires would be humming with news, for Hitler knew better than anyone the value of the Press.

I recalled the warnings I had spoken in Linz, when I asked him earnestly to be wary about trusting Kahr and the Pittinger crowd. Had they perhaps tricked him after all?

Long past midnight, when we stopped at Bologna, I heard the cry of 'Extra! Extra!' Almost paralysed with apprehension, I leaned from the window to buy a newspaper. In letters as black as mourning-I can never forget their impact upon my eye-it blazoned the tragic news: LUDENDORFF ARRESTATO! My knees sagged. Then I gleaned a straw of hope: the report was dated from Berlin. Perhaps our enemies were falsifying the news.

At last the train reached Verona, there to be hitched on to the Innsbruck-Munich express. A passenger .entered, carrying the Corriere delta Sera. Almost beside myself, I snatched the paper from his hand-and in its headlines was disaster.

A correspondent had succeeded in telephoning, from the border town of Kufstein, the first detailed story of the putsch. Hitler's group had been on the verge of success, and then had totally collapsed. No explanation of the breakdown was offered, just the bare fact. The Nazis were defeated and in flight; Ludendorff was under arrest; and there were rumours that he and Hitler had been shot.

Too horrible to believe, yet believe I must. Useless to cling to the idea that these were lies from Berlin. Skimpy though the article was, it cleaved too close to the dreadful possibilities to be all fiction. We had known there would be no middle ground between triumph and utter failure, and knowing this, we took our chance. The chance had betrayed us. Denial was futile, for if anything had gone wrong, then everything was lost. My hand shook as I returned the newspaper whose cold-blooded paragraph pronounced Finis for our movement.

I had to get the facts, the entire tragic story. It would be bitter, for the whole pattern of my future had been ripped apart. Each sharp little detail of how, why, when, where, would twist in my mind like a knife; but that pain would be almost a luxury compared to the leaden ache of this half-knowledge.

In Munich they will tell me everything, was my first thought. But reason came to the rescue, warning me that no Nazi could go there now. It would be foolhardy and futile. Government agents would certainly seize me at the border because of my work in Rome. For my own safety, and for the sake of keeping a free hand in case I could help my comrades, it would be Wiser to remain in Italy until a reliable report reached me. Then, if the damage to the Party proved not to be irreparable, I could launch a new attack from this vantage-point beyond the long arm of Berlin.

A forlorn hope, that last - but the only hope. So I changed trains for Milan, which I had left nine weeks before in such high spirits. After telegraphing my address to friends in Vienna, I shut myself into a hotel-room for two days, and gave myself up to despair, admitting no one.

On the 12th the newspapers definitely announced Hitler's arrest. This blow might mean the end of the Party forever, an immense gain in power and prestige for the opposition, and general demoralization of the Nationalist patriots. It might mean Hitler's death if he were tried and found guilty of treason. It might mean, perhaps, the end of Germany-so much had hung on the fate of the Leader that tragic night.

Slowly I began to realize also that everyone connected with Hitler was in a precarious personal situation. My own position was not much more enviable than his. If I were barred from Germany, where could I turn? The Italian mission had cost a great deal of money, all of it my own. Ever since I had gone into politics, my purse had been open, and now I was near the end of my resources. Only a small sum and a few bonds remained. It had not worried me, for when Hitler should come to power his success would assure me a future. At the worst well, no need to speculate any more; the worst had come.

Finally, after two days of mental torture, word came from Vienna that refugee Nazi leaders were gathering in Salzburg. A second telegram, from Hanfstaengl, asked me to join them there, and to stop en route at Innsbruck to visit Goering, who was lying wounded in the hospital.

Any sort of action was welcome, even if it were nothing more cheerful than the funereal duty of catching a train to attend an inquest, which the Salzburg gathering promised to be.

At Innsbruck, Goering's wife met me, and together we drove to the hospital.

There, for the first time, I gained first-hand information about the events of the night of 8 November, which had risen to an exciting climax at midnight only to sink into abysmal and baffling defeat on the morning of the 9th.

X

THE 'BEER HALL PUTSCH'

Did History wear the mask of Tragedy or Comedy on that night of 8 November 1923? Goering's report, and others which I was to receive in Salzburg and later in Munich, gave me a clear picture of the actual happenings before and during the putsch.

A hostile world Press gave the story a great play. Hitler's heroic attempt to keep Germany intact in the crucial hour was ridiculed as the clownish act of a house-painter with a Charlie Chaplin moustache; his failure became immortalized as the 'Beer Hall Putsch.' Journalism shot all its barbs of scorn into the Nazis.

Rejecting the published accounts, I made my own careful and thorough investigation of the facts. My knowledge is based on first-hand information gained from detailed conversations with the immediate and chief actors of the drama. Goering sketched for me a fairly clear and full outline, which was soon filled in with detail supplied by Rossbach, Hanfstaengl, Esser, and others. Still later I was able to add the final touches during talks with Rosenberg, Roehm, Amann, Poehner, and Hitler himself.

It took months to assemble the whole story, but I shall tell it here as it finally shaped itself in my mind.

The National Socialist German Workers' Party came into existence as a passionate and instinctive rebellion against the tremendous spiritual and political corruption of the times, and had its source in the inner aversion of hundreds of thousands of decent German citizens to the world-outlook and State-concept of that day. Adolf Hitler's message of rebirth touched the deepest feelings of these ordinary people, dispelling their sense of inferiority and giving them a new faith, a new purpose, the promise of new life.

This inner rebirth implied the will to fight for a new state which would realize the future they envisioned. National Socialism by its very character was bound to undertake the liberating deed.

The first effort towards this deliverance, which millions were already awaiting came on 8 November. It was brutally crushed.

On Hitler's side were glowing patriotism, enthusiasm, faith, and the courage to act-Young Germany; on the other side, cold sobriety, self-interest, slipperiness, and hypocrisy-the desperate attempt of a dying generation to stay in power. The practised calculations of the latter were to prevail-for yet a while.

The Burgerbraukeller lies in the outer part of Munich, beyond the River Isar.

The eventful evening of the struggle found it the scene of a great mass meeting. Dr. Gustav von Kahr was to have the platform.

Everybody who was anybody was there-well-known Nationalists and Rightist politicians from all parts of Germany; high dignitaries, officers, and civilians with great names. Almost the entire Bavarian Cabinet attended. Hitler was merely one of the many special guests.

Nothing had been overlooked that would advertise this evening as a political rally of the highest importance. The open breach between Munich and Berlin had created unequalled excitement, and the big hall was filled to the last inch. No doubt some faint rumour of Kahr's purpose had reached others besides Hitler.

All eyes were Kahr when he rose on the tribune to speak. Could he really be a dictator, a second Bismarck-this swarthy, little man, square head stooped between awkward shoulders, an old-fashioned double-breasted morning-coat reaching almost to his knees, who had revealed thus far more the mentality of a cunning peasant than the breadth of a statesman?

No-he was no dictator; he was the State Commissioner with dictatorial powers, conferred on him out of political necessity by the Bavarian People's Party because of their fear of Hitler.

Speaking slowly, his small dark eyes wandering nervously from the audience to his notes, he obviously was feeling none too comfortable in his role.

Dead silence reigned in the hall. Everyone was keyed up with curiosity, on the qui vive to hear a decisive pronouncement.

None ever came.

Hitler was standing with Rosenberg near the entrance, looking not at Kahr, but at a watch in his hand. With unbearable precision, the minute-hand advanced.

8.27-8.28-8.29-Eight-thirty!

The door was flung open; steel-helmeted men burst through, pushing Maxim guns into the hall. Other steel helmets appeared menacingly at every window. Hitler snapped the watch back into his pocket, seized his revolver, and elbowed his way forward through the crowd behind his heavily armed body-guard.

The hall was thrown into the wildest commotion. Only a few of the audience realized the significance of this extraordinary disturbance. Within a few seconds no one could be heard above the uproar.

Kahr, too shaken to speak even if he could have been heard, stared aghast as Hitler jumped up on a table and fired two shots into the ceiling, demanding quiet. In an instant, the stillness was absolute; one could even hear Hitler breathing hard.

Then he leaped to the tribune, gesturing Kahr aside, and shouted to the audience:

"The National Revolution has begun. Six hundred armed men are covering the hall!" though in reality there were only sixty. "No one may leave. The barracks of the Reichswehr and of the police are occupied; the Reichswehr and the police have joined the Hakenkreuz flag. The Bavarian Government is deposed. The Reich Government is deposed. The new Reich Government-Hitler-Ludendorff-Poehner-Hoch!"

It was not true, but it worked.

While the minister-president and the other ministers were taken into custody by Shock Troopers, Hitler beckoned Kahr, Seisser, and Lossow to follow him into a nearby room. There he and Poehner implored them to join the revolution. The rescue of Bavaria alone was too small a goal, Hitler told them. Bavaria must be preserved as part of the Reich and used as a spring-board for the national revolution. Kahr and Poehner should control Bavaria with dictatorial powers-but for this purpose alone. He himself would head the Reich Government; Ludendorff would take over the Reichswehr, with Lossow as War Minister and Seisser as Minister of Police.

The trio were trapped. Not knowing how things really stood, they hesitated and tried to gain time. Hitler, now almost beside himself with excitement, drew his gun, saying that he had four bullets left: three for them and one for himself-if they refused to support him.

At this moment Ludendorff entered with Dr. Max von Scheubner-Richter, political" advisor to the Kampfbund. But alas, the General had left off his uniform and his medals! When Scheubner-Richter had called at Ludendorff's home that evening to tell him for the first time what was under way and to summon him in the name of Germany, the great soldier simply took up his hat and hastened to Munich in the morning coat he happened to be wearing.

Had Napoleon, returning from Elba, tried to rally his veterans in a morning-coat, the history of Europe might have been different.

Nevertheless, Ludendorff's entrance ended the impasse.

"Your Excellency's wishes are my orders," said von Lossow. Next Seisser agreed to serve. Then Kahr, unable to hesitate any longer, also accepted, and they all returned to the hall, where Goering had been talking against time to the dumbfounded crowd. Hitler replaced him. Repeating that the Government of the November criminals in Berlin was now deposed, and announcing the names and offices of the new Government heads, he finished his short speech with:

"Tomorrow Germany will see a National Government or us dead!"

Then Ludendorff spoke with earnest emotion, accepting his part in the new Government 'of his own volition.'

Von Kahr, visibly moved, shook Hitler's hand though looking reproachfully into his eyes, and announced that he would 'act as Statthalter of the Wittelsbach monarchy destroyed five years ago by impious hands.'

Von Lossow followed, declaring himself ready to reorganize the army; and Seisser ended the speeches by promising that he would rebuild the police for the new order. Poebner, not a man of many words, merely beamed.

All the speeches were interrupted with roars of applause.

But there had been one little incident which probably set in motion the machinery for Hitler's undoing. At the moment when Hitler jumped on the table, General von Lossow's adjutant, using the authority of his full uniform, duped the Nazi guards at the door and slipped unobserved out of the hall.

The Kampfbund had gathered that evening in another hall, unaware that what was ostensibly just another meeting was really a mobilization. When eight-thirty came, Captain Roehm informed the ranks that the national revolution had begun. Delirious with joy at the prospect of action, the men left for the posts assigned them.

Roehm, with his Reichskriegsflagge, took possession of the War Ministry, only half a block from the Ludwigsstrasse, the chief avenue of Munich. The main body of the S A and the Oberland marched through a cheering town to the Burgerbraukeller, where the Kampfbund established headquarters.

So far, all had been as orderly as a revolution can be; but now confusion began to raise obstacles. Rossbach, under orders to occupy government buildings, met with resistance. The police parried his demands by pretending that, since they all were united now under the new Government, surrender was not necessary. At that, Rossbach's men encamped in the streets with machine-guns mounted. Only the coolness of the commanders prevented bloodshed.

Meanwhile Rossbach succeeded in winning over the cadets, and with him at their head the whole 'Infantrieschule' paraded in full regalia through the streets. Crowds surged about them in an uproar of rejoicing.

All through the night, new groups of the Kampfbund kept arriving from all directions, from other cities, from the country and the mountains, proudly bearing arms taken out of hiding. In the early morning hours, some even came riding into the city on horseback. Finally, puffing with pride, a band of earnest valiants clattered down the streets with two cannon, one drawn by steeds, the other by men.

To prevent possible leaks, Hider had kept his plans secret from all except those who were indispensable for the execution of his coup at the Burgerbraukeller meeting. Even the Shock Troops (among whom, incidentally, were a number of my former men) received their orders only at the very last minute. The general alarm, with specific instructions for the whole Kampfbund, was not given until eight-thirty. Then motor-cyclists in pre-planned relays carried the word from point to point.

Among other things, the general plan called for the occupation of the engineers' barracks, where some three hundred Oberland men had expected to receive their arms. But they found the doors closed against them: the regular commander of the engineers, a Nazi sympathizer, had been replaced that morning by an officer who refused to yield.

Now Hitler made a crucial error. After all, the arming of a few hundred men was a minor matter at such a moment. Solidarity and unity were more important, and above all action-but in another direction. Hitler should have known that Kahr, Lossow, and Seisser would not be reliable, for they had pledged allegiance at the point of a gun.

Colonel Kriebel, commander of the Kampfbund, had already sent a competent officer to adjust matters at the engineers' barracks. Obviously this was not Hitler's business; his place was at the nerve-centre of the putsch. Yet Hitler-originator and only co-ordinator of the whole plot-left the vital post of supreme command and ran off on the same trifling errand. And while he was failing to settle the matter, he failed at the same time to keep his new 'colleagues' under his thumb.

With the leader no longer in evidence, the other members of the new 'Government' remained in conference for a while. Kahr announced that the proper authorities had been informed of the change in government, and asked Poehner to give the news to the Press. That was as far as their concerted statesmanship managed to go. Then these gentlemen - Ludendorff, Poehner, Kahr, Seisser, and Lossow-took leave of each other.

Ludendorff drove to the War Ministry. Lossow went to the Stadtkommandantur. Kahr and Seisser drifted off, God knows where. And Poehner, the new Bavarian Minister-President, went home to bed.

History shows no revolutions which have been won between the sheets-and this one was not to be the exception.

When Captain Roehm tried to get in touch with General von Lossow in the Stadtkommandantur, he was not admitted, and became suspicious. Not so Ludendorff. When one of his officers intimated that all might not be above-board in Lossow's direction, the great Feldherr frowned and made a characteristic reply:

"A German General does not break his word!"

An hour before midnight Hitler appeared at the War Ministry and embraced Captain Roehm.

"This is the happiest and most wonderful day of my life," he said, glowing, apparently all unaware of signs of impending disaster. "Now we shall see better times-we will all work, day and night, towards our great goal-to rescue Germany from her misery and disgrace."

As the night wore on, Ludendorff and Kriebel, waiting at the War Ministry, began to have misgivings, and sent several officers in turn to Lossow to find out what was going on. They did not return; each of them had been arrested on the spot. Then, at dawn, Poehner was roused from his bed to inform himself of the situation. Accompanied by Major Huehnlein, he went to police headquarters, and they also were arrested.

Finally, in the early morning, Ludendorff and Kriebel joined Hitler at the Burgerbraukeller. Still no news from Kahr, Lossow, or Seisser. Hitler and Ludendorffat last were realizing that something had gone amiss.

Lossow's adjutant, when he slipped out of the hall at the beginning of the coup, had rushed to the Stadtkommandantur with the news. There steps were taken to strike back at Hitler at once. When Lossow reached the Stadtkommandantur he was virtually held prisoner, and General van Danner, who was merely commander of the garrison, forced Lossow, commander of the whole division, to execute the orders by which it was planned to crush the putsch.

All Hitler's enemies had worked feverishly to forestall developments contrary to their interests and aims, which were monarchical and clerical. As was to be expected, Cardinal van Faulhaber played an especially active role that night. Crown Prince Rupprecht, informed at the earliest moment, from his castle in Berchtesgaden issued a strong appeal to the Bavarian officer-corps not to join the 'rebels,' reminding his officers of their oath to the Wittelsbachs.

Kahr and Seisser had been on the side of the Nazis as late as one o'clock in the morning, but about that time Pittinger, who violently condemned Hitler, informed them of Lossow's predicament and of the stern attitude of the 'King.' Bewildered at the crazy turn of events, twice twisted within one short night, and finding the Bavarian Reichswehr Division, the main weapon of the new 'Government,' snatched from their hands, Kahr and Seisser broke their new allegiance and returned to the old.

General von Lossow, who had in truth been not entirely loath to yield to the pressure on him, joined Kahr and Seisser at the infantry barracks on Oberwiesenfeld. Here the three, recovering from their first startled surrender to the putsch, began to direct its suppression. Orders were broadcast from the radio station near by, commanding the garrisons outside Munich to send troops at top-speed to the capital.

Morning found the Landespolizei or state police still with Hitler and Ludendorff. The morning papers lauded the national revolution enthusiastically, hailing the turn of events and Hitler's proclamation as though the new order had come to stay. The offices of the Marxian Muenchener Post were demolished; the political bosses of the Marxian parties were placed under arrest and ordered shot. No one outside the immediate entourage of Hitler and Ludendorff knew how seriously the situation was now going against them. Even Hitler and two thousand S A men who had received rifles from a secret depot were unaware that the firing-pins, ordinarily removed to prevent misuse of the weapons, had not been replaced; in an encounter they would have been completely worthless.

After eight in the morning, Reichswehr troops from outside Munich began to march into the city in answer to the radio summons. Together with the Landespolizei, which Seisser now had in hand again, they took up strategic positions. Field artillery and Maxim guns were brought into position on the Ludwigsstrasse. Several battalions of Reichswehr surrounded the War Ministry to retake it from Roehm.

Many of these outside troops had left their garrisons hailing the revolution, and learned only now that they were to be used instead to crush it.

It became known that Ludendorff's arrest had been ordered. Groups of civilians gathered in indignation, realizing that the wind had shifted. Confusion and fear seized the town which a few hours earlier had been the scene of celebration.

The council in the Burgerbraukeller had become gloomier and gloomier. A hundred plans were discussed and discarded -among them, the desperate coup of storming the Reichswehr barracks before they could be re-enforced. It would have been madness, for the Kampfbund was no match for regular troops with armoured cars, light artillery, gas, and all the paraphernalia of war.

Finally Ludendorff's advice prevailed, and it was decided to march into Munich. Counting on a huge popular demonstration in their favour, they hoped that with tens of thousands of burghers marching behind them through the heart of the city the Reichswehr and police would refuse to fire. The situation might be carried, after all, by the strength of the almost unanimous sympathy and enthusiasm of the people for the 'national revolution.' Streicher, Esser, and other speakers were sent out to whip up the populace to a favourable response.

In the hour before noon on 9 November, about seven thousand men of the Kampfbund, in files eight abreast, their rifles slung across their backs to proclaim their peaceful intention, marched over the Isar bridge into the inner city, followed by thousand of Nazis and their sympathizers.

Dense cordons of police on the other side of the river were quickly disarmed; some of them even threw away their rifles as they saw Ludendorff and Hitler approach. An ever-increasing number of cheering people joined the procession, which wound its way unmolested to the Marienplatz, where most of Munich's citizens had already assembled.

From here a veritable human flood poured down the street towards the Odeonsplatz. Ahead was the Ludwigsstrasse, blocked by Reichswehr. The flood advanced. In its front rank marched Hitler, Ludendorff, and other leaders, directly behind Streicher and a colour-bearer with the Hakenkreuz banner. Steadily they went on in the face of the waiting troops.

Suddenly, only a few yards away, Landespolizei-the Bavarian State police-rushed forward from their place of concealment behind the Feldhemhalle, levelled their carbines, and took aim.

The officer in command ordered his platoon to fire on the Nazis. He repeated the order twice, then tore a rifle from the hands of a reluctant soldier. Streicher screamed:

"Ludendorff-don't shoot your General! Hitler and Ludendorff . . .!" It was too late. A volley rent the air, killing fourteen men in the Nazi ranks.

Ludendorff, erect and unhurt, marched straight ahead and was arrested. Hitler, who had been at Ludendorff's side, walking arm-in-arm with Scheubner-Richter, was dragged to the ground with a dislocated shoulder when the Doctor crumpled under the hail of lead. Hitler's bodyguard threw himself on his master, covering him with his body and instinctively thinking, as he later told me: 'Ulrich Graf, jetzt hat's dich doch erwischt!' He received eleven bullets. Beside him Kurt Neubauer, Ludendorff's faithful valet, who had sprung in front of the General to protect him, lay dead with the upper part of his head ripped away.

At sound of the firing, the crowds in the rear wavered and halted. Then panic seized the street. In a desperate scramble for safety, everyone fled.

The revolution was finished.

Roehm, still holding out in the War Ministry, decided that to resist in such a hopeless trap would be to murder his loyal men, two of whom had already been shot. He surrendered and was at once arrested.

Ludendorff was released a few hours later, after pledging his word to hold himself at the disposal of the authorities. Hitler had been helped to his car and had escaped into the mountains.

When the pain in his shoulder grew unbearable and the petrol was all but gone, he remembered that they were near Uffing, where Hanfstaengl had a country house. By chance Erna Hanfstaengl, Putzi's sister, was at home to admit him. A persistent rumour says that she saved Hitler from suicide in this bitter hour. When, years later, I asked him about it, he answered with great simplicity: "No, that is not true; she did not save me from suicide. Naturally my spirits were very low-the mere presence of a woman may have kept me from the thought of ending my life."

It was there, on 2 November, that Hitler was arrested.

With its leaders either arrested, in hiding, or in flight, the Kampfbund dispersed; to continue armed resistance would have been utter folly.

The cabinet ministers and those opponents who had been imprisoned were released. By a fortunate miracle, none of them, not even those scheduled for death, had been shot. The execution of Socialist town-councillors and Marxist leaders would have made Rider's situation desperate indeed.

Martial law was declared throughout Bavaria. The Nazi Party and the Kampfbund were dissolved by State decree, and all their property was seized. Every Nazi activity was ruthlessly put down; prison terms up to fifteen years threatened anyone who dared to continue the movement. Persons found bearing weapons risked being shot at sight. The Voelkischer Beohachter was banned. In short, every means and method of aiding the Nazi cause was suppressed. Now it had really been driven underground.

The Government buildings were surrounded with barbed wire, and soldiers patrolled the streets in the face of a furious, cursing population.

So ended the 'Beer Hall Putsch '-eventually to find its anti-climax in a trial which astonished the world.

The 'Beer Hall Putsch' is indeed one of the most contradictory events in history. The preliminary manoeuvres were handled with consummate intelligence and even brilliance; the hour of action was distinguished by naivety and carelessness passing belief.

The situation leading up to it must be briefly reviewed.

The Hitler-Ludendorff group was not strong enough to undertake a revolution against Berlin and the Bavarian authorities simultaneously. Hitler knew he must wait until he could manoeuvre the Bavarian Government-controlled by the Kahr-Lossow-Pittinger group with the aim of establishing the monarchy under Crown Prince Rupprecht-into such a predicament that common interest would force them to march on Berlin together. In his turn, Kahr, knowing Hider's value as an agitator, counted on using him to a certain point, then crushing him. There was no faith between them, yet for the time being they were inter-dependent.

Realizing this, Hitler had deliberately led the Bavarian Government in the direction most useful to him, pitching up the situation in masterly fashion. Attacking the Berlin Government on every issue, he forced Berlin to take action against him. This could be done only through the Bavarian Government, and Kahr naturally refused to move against Hitler, for the obvious reason that to do so would be to give his own plans a setback.

This defiance of Berlin resulted in the open conflict between Bavaria and the Reich which Hitler had desired. And now began a race between Kahr and Hitler for the upper hand. Secretly Kahr brought his plan for the establishment of a Bavarian monarchy to the point of action. And Hitler, learning how near the crisis was, made his secret plan to act first. .

Hitler's putsch was at least as well prepared as Kahr's plot. Arrangements had been made in detail with the Bavarian Reichswehr and the State police. Berlin circles had been informed; organizations in the North stood ready for action on the 9 November. When Hitler struck, thousands would follow.

It would be a master stroke. Munich was virtually in his hands, Bavaria at his fingertips, Berlin almost within reach. In the beginning, all went well. In the end, everything was lost.

The truth is that an abiding conflict within Hitler's own character made him inadequate for the role he assumed. He is masterly in tactics, inept in executive detail.

After the Kahr-Lossow-Seisser trio had publicly joined the national revolution, they should have been kept under close surveillance and not permitted to go about at will. Under no circumstances should they have been allowed to come under the influence of agencies opposed to the revolution, or to confer with enemies of Hitler and Ludendorff.

Every minute was precious. Hitler should not have wasted a second before entrenching himself. The radio station and the postal and telegraph buildings should have been seized at' once, to flash vital orders all over the country. Strict instructions should have been issued for the Bavarian Reichswehr and the police to be sworn in that very night to the new Government. Without delay the whole garrison of Munich should have been informed that the revolution was accomplished, and forced to pledge themselves to the new Government in the presence of Kahr, Lossow, and Crown Prince Rupprecht, who should have been taken into 'protective custody'- with honeyed words, of course. Cardinal Faulhaber-a most precious hostage-should also have been very politely 'protected,' to keep him from putting his finger in the pie.

Of course, wisdom after the event is the easiest sort of statesmanship. These precautions, however, were not only fully possible under the circumstances, but were indeed absolutely imperative for success. In such a situation, it was essential to plan with utmost care and to act with greatest thoroughness. Boldness alone was not enough.

With the Munich garrison, the main force of the Bavarian division, firmly controlled by the new Government; with the garrisons in other cities properly instructed; with the chief opponents on the Bavarian chessboard safely checkmated, all of Bavaria would have been in the hands of Hitler and Ludendorff as a great spearhead for their thrust at Berlin.

It is quite possible that General Ludendorff, who still enjoyed tremendous prestige throughout the Reich, would have met no serious resistance in leading a national force against the capital. The Reichswehr was not likely to support its Marxian masters against the victor of Tannenberg.

It is also quite possible, considering the well-founded and widespread discontent of the people, that a general popular uprising might have swept Hitler into Berlin on a wave of national enthusiasm.

Who can say what would have happened then?

The new 'National Government' would not have been a purely National Socialist Government; Kahr's crowd, though unwilling allies, would still have been indispensable. The Nazis could not at first have exercised the unifying force of the Fascists under Mussolini, who, appointed by the King, had the support of the army.

It is futile to argue whether Ludendorff and Hitler, once in Berlin, could have succeeded in steering the German ship safely through the hurricane. It is certain, however, that if they had gone so far and then had failed, it would have been the end of Germany. One truth emerges: Germany was not yet ripe for a Nazi regime, and the world political constellation was definitely favourable. Hitler's failure at that time really saved the German people from the irreparable calamity that certainly would have followed a half-success.

Twelve years later, on 9 November 1935, after the remains of the sixteen slain Hitlerites had been laid to rest with royal pomp, as martyrs to the cause, in two temples on the Koenigsplatz, Hitler told his old comrades in a private gathering that his decision to attempt the march on Berlin had been the gravest of his life: he had acted to save Germany from a plot which would have divided her and which he would describe in detail in his memoirs.

"But fate meant well with us," said the Fuehrer. "It did not permit success of the action which, even if it had temporarily succeeded, must have failed in the end, because of the inner faults of the movement and its inadequate organization and spiritual foundations. We know that today. We acted strongly and courageously, but Providence acted wisely."[1]

Indeed, Hitler's blunder, though at first it seemed to have defeated him forever, leaving him helpless and hopeless, in a strange paradox ultimately turned events to his greatest advantage. His defeat became the foundation for his later triumph.

For the debacle of the putsch, however, he alone was responsible. The coup was planned without consulting Ludendorff, called in only at the last moment to lend his name. The General's mentality, his psychology, should have been well known to Hitler. The severest reproach one can level against Ludendorff is that in an historical moment he appeared in the wrong coat.

Through lack of foresight, Hitler failed when by sheer daring he had drawn success within his grasp. Yet even his grotesque collapse prevented the secession of Bavaria which would have disrupted the Reich. And while he was still in prison, a laughing-stock for all the world, with apparently every thread of his life's work unravelled, there was that in his nature which impelled him to shake off his despair and begin again to weave a new pattern for Germany

Hitler still believed in his destiny.

1 *New York Times, 10 November 1935*

XI

SALZBURG

During the stop-over at Innsbruck, while Captain Hermann Goering was telling me his move-by-move story of the putsch, I had a chance to size up the man himself. The captain was to provide me with an interesting though disappointing study.

If Hitler was to recover lost ground and advance to greater power than before, he must with increasing frequency assign places of importance to men within the ranks or to newcomers. His judgment in this matter was of vital concern to everyone. To me it was especially important, inasmuch as I represented the Nazis abroad and would continue to do so if the Party survived. My work might succeed or fail according to the character of the men Hitler chose to enlarge the circle of his immediate assistants.

The original inner circle, with which I could now identify myself in point of service, was truly an odd collection of personalities: Rosenberg the reticent, Eckart the expansive, and a motley comprising the rest of us, each with traits and talents so individual that we sometimes clashed, yet all as harmonious as angels on at least two themes--our personal devotion to Hitler, and our readiness to sacrifice everything for the principles of the Nazi programme.

In the dark moment after the Munich fiasco, it would have been easy to believe that we had sacrificed everything. But there is a happy resilience in the human spirit, and my mind was beginning to look forward and upward again. If faith and effort could build a stronger structure out of the wreckage of our plans, then surely we would see the day when this defeat would appear, in retrospect, as nothing more than a temporary setback. And when that day came, what sort of men would represent us before Germany and the world?

Would they be worthy of Hitler's trust? Would they be loyal without being yes-men? Would their convictions be sincere, or only stiffened by the starch of self-interest? Most important of all, would they personify to some extent the ideals we were trying to advance?

It troubled my conscience a little that I had helped the Party to capture Hanfstaengl. It is true he knew how to make the much-harried Hitler smile, a useful function; but while Hitler smiled, the onlookers cast sidelong glances at each other.

Goering had served with us even less time than Hanfstaengl, some ten months all told, and I had met him only once before leaving Munich. Yet from the first he had held a position of real influence; so my curiosity regarding him was keen.

At Innsbruck I learned-from his own lips and at great length-that the eminent captain had received a light bullet wound during the demonstration on 9 November when sixteen Nazis were killed. He was discharged from the hospital the day after my arrival, however, and rejoined his wife at the hotel, where the three of us passed the time together.

Frau Goering, born Baroness Karin von Fock of the Swedish nobility, was a charming woman, quiet and sympathetic, who walked with a particularly handsome and free carriage. Goering showed without reserve that he adored her. I imagine he felt in his heart that she was far superior to himself. So did I. On this first meeting, and always thereafter, I was impressed by the way she, a foreigner, stood at his side through every trial of the Party, spending her fortune on it and on him. During the Innsbruck visit, she was still somewhat overwrought from having personally engineered her husband's escape into Austria. Her health, always delicate, never fully recovered from that strain, and in 1931 she died.

As Goering could not easily travel to Salzburg on account of his wound, he asked me to represent him at the meeting, writing his authorization on the credentials which Hitler had signed. I pocketed the document which coupled the name of a man I now distrusted to a name I revered. With a real sense of relief I left for Salzburg.

By telegraph I had arranged for Hanfstaengl to meet my train at Salzburg. I found the town buried under an early snowstorm; the station, so crowded in summer, was deserted. Hanfstaengl finally appeared. He said he was certain that detectives would be crossing the border to seize us both at any moment. Therefore, he told me, he had hidden himself away in a little country inn on the outskirts of the town, where he now took me to share his double room.

It was about eleven in the evening. The inn had no electric light and no heating system; there was not even a fire in our room. It was almost impossible to suppress my amusement when he finally undressed and we both lay in bed, figures from the pen of Wilhelm Busch. Putzi, his knobby knees drawn up to his chin, sat tangled in a huddle beside me, trying to keep warm under typical peasant quilts too short for him. The candles threw a flickering, dim light on his grotesque features, his eyes burned with excitement, and altogether he looked like something to frighten bats away.

We talked nearly the whole night through. Putzi has an artistic mind and his story of the defeat in Munich was a triumph of vivid interpretation.

"What good is it now to have a receipt and a mortgage on the office furniture?" he wailed.

He also unburdened himself about the personal problem Hitler was to him. For instance, he could not be persuaded to dine properly, but still preferred the picnicky food that could be gobbled anywhere. The only improvement Putzi had been able

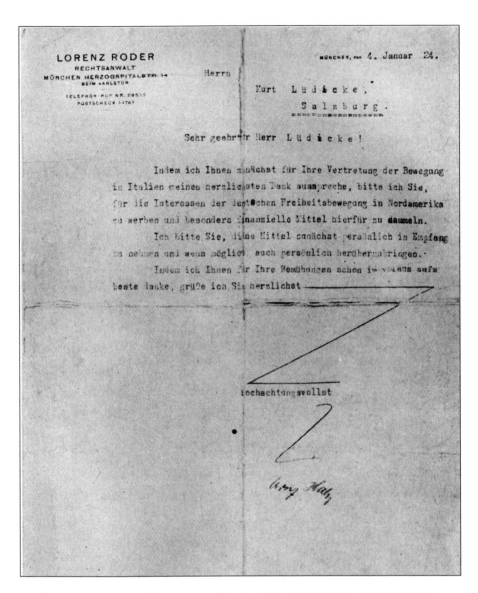

HITLER'S LETTER, SIGNED IN PRISON, ON THE LETTERHEAD OF HIS LAWYER

Much esteemed Herr Ludecke,

First expressing my heartiest thanks for your representation of the movement in Italy, I ask you to solicit in the interests of the German Liberty Movement in North America and especially to assemble financial means for it.

I ask you to receive these means personally, and, if possible, to bring them over in person.

Thanking you in advance for your efforts, I greet you most heartily.

(Signed) ADOLF HITLER

to make was to drag him to a dentist-and I acknowledged that to be a real triumph.

Putzi's gossip, mostly trivial, held one gratifying bit for me. Hitler had slapped his knees with satisfaction over the success of my Italian Press campaign, exclaiming: "I told you that he could do it!"

Next day I met the other Nazis gathered in Salzburg. There were Hermann Esser and Gerhard Rossbach, the daring, gay-hearted Frei-Korps leader, who had established his fame fighting in the Baltic in 1919; the calm, composed Lieutenant-Captain Hoffmann, a splendid naval officer who formerly had served in the Ehrhardt Brigade and now was chief of staff for Goering. It was Hoffmann, much more than Goering, who had achieved the reorganization of the SA on a military basis, showing himself a very able man and a tireless worker. He, Rossbach, and I became great friends.

Our situation was certainly cheerless. No one had any money or any way to get it. With very little left, I had to be careful, but did what I could.

We tried our best to keep in touch with Munich and to reorganize from Salzburg. Under the circumstances, we realized it would be difficult indeed to convince outsiders that our cause was by no means lost; that there was still a future for us so long as the problems which had called us together remained unsolved; that now, more than ever, we were resolved to pursue our aims. To be truthful, it was pretty difficult to convince ourselves. But we set about printing pamphlets and handbills, which were carried by night over the border and secretly distributed in Bavaria to lift the morale of Hitler's followers. Our tactics were to blame von Kahr, Lossow, and Seisser for the debacle, accusing them of bad faith and worse intentions.

This was not only plausible but true. Kahr, the practised hypocrite, had not hesitated to make peace with the Berlin Government, politely assuring Commander-in-Chief von Seeckt, who offered to lend him Reichswehr re-enforcements, that he had "the Bavarian situation well in hand."

Indeed, too well in hand, from the Nazi viewpoint. The Party was dissolved, and we could hope for little financial support from our former members. In the last few months the organization had grown large, with hundreds of employees, now suddenly thrown on the street or arrested, leaving their families destitute. One of our problems was to succour them.

"If we only had our hands on the money you seized in Munich!" I mourned aloud-for the Salzburg refugees had told me that on the night of the putsch, several business-like raids had bagged more than enough to meet our present needs. When the revolution collapsed, the authorities had recovered the notes, still tied in neat bundles.

We discussed wild projects for solving the money question. One man especially excelled in daring imagination. He first proposed counterfeiting on a large scale, which the others seriously pondered until we agreed that such a plan needed too much capital to operate. Then he declared himself ready with his men to execute a series of hold-ups which would yield enough to refinance the Party.

Finally we dropped all this fantastic planning as useless. But it is significant. Then and afterwards, many Nazi activists would stop at nothing, even criminal offences, to help the cause and Hitler. This was true of not only the real Nazis who were body and soul with the cause, but also of those who pretended allegiance for selfish reasons. If ever the Jesuitic principle 'the end justifies the means' was applied with brutality and without scruple, it was during the Nazi struggle for power-especially by those for whom the end was identical with personal interests.

It is only fair, however, to point out that in those days of oppression it was not possible to act as a good Nazi, or indeed as a good German, without violating a long list of absurd laws and conventions. Today, of course, the shoe is on the other foot.

At last our emergency council got in touch with Alfred Rosenberg, who had been designated by Hitler to lead the Party during his imprisonment. Rosenberg was in hiding in Munich, changing his quarters almost every night because the police were searching for him. He could do little to direct us. Therefore, acting chiefly on our own initiative, we arranged a Nazi conference, to take place in Vienna during the first part of December, between ourselves and the Austrian and Czech Nazi leaders.

One night I went in his company to the Hotel Europaischer Hof to see Admiral von Hintze, the last minister of foreign affairs before the fall of the Empire. The main topic of our conversation was, of course, the Beer Hall Putsch. The admiral had been there, sitting in the front row near Poehner, within a few yards of the tribune.

One of my first questions was whether he could remember how General Ludendorff had been dressed. I knew already that he had worn mufti, but I was interested to hear the diplomat's reaction.

"He did not wear his uniform-unfortunately," Hintze said. Then his tone became contemptuous. "Hitler too-dressed in a morning coat, that most difficult of all garments to wear, let alone a badly cut morning-coat, and let alone a man with as bad a figure as Hitler, with his short legs and long torso. When I saw him jump on the table in that ridiculous costume, I thought, 'Armes Kellnerlein!'"

'Poor little waiter!' It made me boil inwardly, for I knew this admiral with the supercilious and haughty mien whose father had been a grocer in a little Brandenburger town. His remark may have been justified by appearances, but certainly not by reality. Indeed, I often wonder if Hitler's utterly mediocre appearance was not one of his greatest assets, leading his enemies continually to underestimate him.

When the date for our conference arrived, Putzi and I went together to -Vienna. Esser had already gone, but Hoffman and Rossbach had to stay behind, since we had been unable to raise ticket-money.

Our conference next day only confirmed the disastrous state of affairs facing the

Nationalsozialistische Partei Großdeutschlands
Zwischenstaatliche Kanzlei
Wien, 6. Bezirk, Matrosengasse 9
Fernsprecher Nr. 75-61   Postsparkassenkonto 147.7

V O L L M A C H T und L E G I T I M A T I O N .

Herr Kurt Georg Luedecke, geboren am 5. Februar 1890 zu
Berlin, wird hiedurch mit der Vertretung der National-Sozia-
listischen Partei Gross-Deutschlands in den Vereinigten Staa-
ten von Nord- Amerika betraut.

Herr Luedecke ist ermächtigt, für die National-Sozialisti-
sche Partei Gross- Deutschlands Geldsammlungen einzuleiten
und Spenden in jeder Höhe entgegenzunehmen. Ebenso können Geld-
beträge an das Konto "Germaniaspende " Wiener Bankverein
überwiesen werden.   Zweigstelle

Wir bitten, Herrn Luedecke in dieser Eigenschaft anzuerken-
nen und ihm auf seiner Propagandareise jederzeit Unterstützung
mit Rat und Tat zu gewähren.

Eigenhändige Unterschrift
unseres Vertreters:

K. Luedecke

Credentials for the United States, signed in Vienna, 15 December, 1923, by Austrian and Czech Nazi leaders, two of whom, R. Jung and Hans Knirsch, were members of the Parliament in Prague. They authorize the author to represent the National-Socialist Party for Greater Germany and to collect funds for it.

Nazis. It was difficult to lay any plan for reconstruction because that meant money, and obviously it would be next to impossible to raise funds for a lost cause; which the public believed ours to be.

Jung and Knirsch, Nazi deputies from Prague, were splendid, contributing all their party could spare. But they had problems of their own, and though their generosity warmed our hearts and lifted our spirits, it scarcely altered our financial status.

nthusiastically seconded. I was
to raise money in the United
roe which laid mountainous

ic which identified me as the
ossdeutschlands' in the United
Party. Reluctantly I accepted
personal funds, and I had very
ent that we must explore every

ighten our gloom. The Ring
ony with the drab and poverty-
sepulchral places, haunted by
d them with laughter and life.

d, Dr. Philipp von Langenhan,
nething of the pre-war spirit.
manners, an excellent causeur,
ad aided the Nazis in Bohemia-

t Sacher's, the almost legendary
dezvous of Austro-Hungarian
w people of note who remained
f the monarchy, more than one
thout being asked to pay, until
se republican days, Frau Sacher
hiskies and smoking her black

cigars, she cursed the Republic and got away with it. Governments were to her no different from people; she liked them or disliked them, and there was no appeal from her judgment. It was a privilege to be asked into her own apartment, the walls of which were covered with signed pictures of emperors, kings, dukes, and plain citizens whom her good-will had raised to a sort of private peerage.

1 Reproduced in this book

145

I was taken up to the private suite of a member of one of the richest and oldest families of the fallen Habsburg empire. We had a long talk, for it had been intimated that the Prince might be able to help our cause.

After sounding me out, he disclosed an astounding project. I can speak of it now without breaking his confidence, for later developments brought the whole scheme to light.

The Prince proposed nothing less than the distribution, on a vast scale, of counterfeit French notes in denominations of a hundred and a thousand francs. Every problem had been solved in advance, except that of putting the notes into circulation through trustworthy agents. Would I become one of them--on a commission large enough to solve the immediate desperate situation of the Nazi treasury?

I was assured that high personages were involved in Germany as well as Hungary.

Pressing further, I learned that the counterfeits were to be made in the Hungarian Military Topographical Institute, a branch of the War Ministry at Budapest. As for my personal risk, the Prince promised that if the scheme miscarried, I would be immune to punishment in Germany and Hungary, since the plotters, had. semi-official endorsement .

A little thought convinced me that this stupendous plot was more than a money-making scheme. Obviously its two-fold purpose was to wreck French currency and to provide enough forged notes to finance revisionist propaganda against France and the Little Entente states. And of course undue risks were involved. Anything ceases to be a secret when more than one person knows about it. Having recently experienced an arrest on trumped-up suspicions, I had no desire to bring a true charge down upon my head, especially when the plan seemed to me too ambitious to succeed.

Politely I said that I would think the matter over. The Prince understood my refusal.

The plan went ahead, by the way. Sometime at the end of 1925 or 1926, I forget just which, two of the agents were arrested in Brussels. Then the French Government stepped in, and the affair became the greatest political scandal in Hungary's political history. To placate France, the Prince and the Budapest chief of police were sentenced to four years' imprisonment. They served only a few months, however, and those as pleasantly as possible, for Goemboes, who was Minister of War at that time, saw to it that the Prince was properly exonerated on the grounds that he had 'assumed responsibility before the courts in order to protect the country from serious harm.'

Another encounter in Vienna lives in my memory as something even more extraordinary. Some one introduced me to a well-known author of anti-Jewish books, and I spent a whole evening with him. His name was somewhat known through his books, but I for my part had never heard of him; so I found myself quite unprepared for the strange discussion which ensued.

He was a peculiar and pathetic personality, a full-blooded Jew who was an apostate from his people and his religion; who uncompromisingly attacked the Jew and the Jewish spirit in his speeches and writings, yet could not enter into the Gentile world with which he strove to ally himself. Whether the attitude which turned his life into a tragedy sprang from his mind or his emotions, I cannot say. This was the first time I had talked at length with an intellectual and erudite Jew about the German-Jewish problem, and though even among Gentiles I was now discovering a widespread doubt of the Nazi programme, I was amazed to find that he still passionately endorsed it.

He did not consider himself a Jew, either spiritually or physically, in spite of his two Jewish parents. Convinced that he was the result of a phenomenon which biologists call 'mutation,' he presented himself as a Gentile. Seriously believing that he looked very much like Houston Stewart Chamberlain, the declared scientific enemy of the Jewish people, he produced as proof one of his pamphlets which showed their pictures facing each other. Looking at his eyes and fair hair, I had to agree that the photographs bore a striking resemblance. Never before had I considered the Jewish problem from the standpoint of the individual Jew who finds much to condemn in his own people and dares to say so. He was an extreme case; yet some of his findings were sound. Discovering that his people were resentful of criticism, he had turned his coat -without finding it any warmer. My mind reverted at once to the two famous apostates, Spinoza and Uriel de Acosta, who were excommunicated from the synagogues, and I reflected that there is no more sorrowful destiny than that which over¬takes those who alienate their own people without making friends elsewhere.

He sought to convince me that he could be a valuable ally in the Nazi struggle. Intuition and reason told me to remain reserved. But it was distressing to witness the despair of this exhausted and high-strung man, who beyond question was sincere. Ostracized on one side and rejected on the other, he was indeed an outcast. The tragic overtones of our interview made a deep impression on me, and at the earliest moment I spoke about him at length with Rosenberg. Needless to say, there was no place for him in the Party.

As soon as I had settled my business in Vienna, I returned to Salzburg for a final meeting with the Nazis. Eagerly we weighed the latest news. My companions were concentrated chiefly on the dispatches from Munich, I on the reaction of the world Press to the putsch, especially American, English, French, and Italian comments. Only now did I fully realize to what extent Hitler's cause had been damaged by ridicule. Irreparable, it seemed to me; but to the other refugees, whose political life had .seldom carried them beyond the boundaries of Bavaria except as fugitives, this difficulty seemed a minor matter, and they continued to believe with insistent eagerness that I could accomplish something abroad.

Preparing for my journey, I dared not hope to accomplish anything. The world had known little about Hitler until it learned of his failure; then it had laughed him into disgrace.

The last news I had about my imprisoned leader was that he was so deep in shame and despair that only the visit of a staunch friend, Frau Bechstein, had dissuaded him from taking his own life in his cell.

Hitler had been informed of our conference in Vienna and of the credentials I had received for my mission in America. In prison he managed to sign for me a letter which was brought to me by his lawyer. Incidentally, that document, reproduced in this book with a translation, has specific historic interest. Hitler has repeatedly and emphatically denied ever having solicited-let alone accepted-money from abroad. His own letter gives him the lie.

Bearing little except these credentials, I sailed from Cherbourg and crossed a gloomy sea on my way to New York.

XII

ANTI-SEMITISM: MODEL T

An afternoon in January 1924 saw me in New York with Siegfried and Winifred Wagner in their suite at the old Waldorf. They were preparing for a tour on which Siegfried was booked to conduct his father's music in the principal cities of America.

His father's music . . .!

If Nazism were a religion, then we would need to search no further than Richard Wagner's vast operatic creations to find our liturgical music. It is Nordic to the last flute-note. And not simply because the great cycle deals with Teuton gods and heroes, let me hasten to add.

One side of Wagner's genius did achieve the civilized apotheosis of primitive northern myths, shaping them into a poetic text which is in itself a noble work, deeply symbolic. But to a far greater degree, the language of his music itself, the sheer tonal revelation of his inherited racial consciousness, is Nordic. If Brunnhilde were called Rebekah, if Wotan were Quetzlcoatl, and Siegfried were Patrick or Wladyslaus or Hiawatha, the impact of the music would be the same. It is shot through with one spirit, inimitable and unmistakable, which can only be called the Nordic spirit.

Therefore it seemed propitious that Hitler's errand in America should have led me so soon into the pleasant company of the great Wagner's own son and daughter-in-law Surely a good augury! Gradually optimism began to rise in me again.

They were here on a mission not very different from mine. Bayreuth, their home and their father's shrine, had suffered during the war. The Festspielhaus had remained empty; no foreigners could make the famous pilgrimage, and Germans were too busy with the grim exigencies of life and death. Even after the peace, Bayreuth remained a haunted town. Music needs patronage, and Wagner was unfortunately in disrepute among wealthy foreigners because he was German. The fact that he had died a generation before 1914 did not soften the reaction. At the height of the anti-German hysteria, his operas were either shelved in enemy countries, or at best performed in indifferent translations while mobs demonstrated against the treason of playing German music at all. In America, the Lohengrin wedding march ·was shunned like the influenza, while countless war-brides marched altarwards to the syrupy strains of meaningless substitutes.

It was to repair this damage that the young Wagners had come to the United States. Already there was a sheepish suspicion in Allied countries that it had been a little far-fetched to regard Isolde's love-death as enemy propaganda. But prejudice dies slowly. Bayreuth had not regained its pre-war popularity as the very root and flower of Wagnerian opera. By performing his father's music, Siegfried hoped to reawaken interest in the annual Bayreuth festival; and naturally the concert fees would be useful, too.

So here I sat, talking with the man for whose nursing the incomparable 'Siegfried Idyll' had been composed-and we scarcely mentioned music! An inscrutable Providence often creates strange necessities in our lives. We were discussing money. More particularly, we were speaking of the chance of interesting Henry Ford (to Europeans the incarnation of money in its alluring bulk) in the Nazi movement. Winifred Wagner, though she had been born of English parents and was a German only by adoption, was an enthusiastic admirer of Hitler; and being a very active woman who managed her husband's business affairs, she now took a hand in mine.

During my hurried visit to America in 1921, I had found time for several talks with W. J. Cameron, the editor of Henry Ford's Dearhorn Independent. That publication was now embarked on an anti-Jewish campaign, and Cameron was writing and publishing a series of explosive articles. Nothing so outspoken had previously appeared in print in the United States. There was of course widespread debate about the merits of the campaign. For the first time in post-Civil War history, Jewry was being anatomized as a malignant growth on the body of the nation, and factions pro and con blew a gale of words towards Detroit. Ford personally became the very centre of this storm of praise and abuse.

Naturally I was pro-Ford, and I tried to reassure myself that his convictions would make him actively pro-Hitler. Although so far he had advocated no corrective programme, his attitude towards the Jewish question seemed to me enlightened enough to promise us co-operation.

Cameron, the capable journalist who had so successfully phrased Ford's inarticulate racial uneasiness, had been very receptive when we met. He was naturally eager for outside assistance, and I knew that another meeting with him could be arranged easily. But I was here this time to beg a favour, not to give help. The problem was to reach headquarters-which in the Ford Empire means Henry himself. I had to speak with him in person, alone, and to induce him to back the Nazi Party in return for its guarantee of a practical application of his views.

First of all, then, how to gain Ford's ear?

Discussing various manoeuvres, the Wagners and I finally decided to pin our hopes on Mrs. Ford's hospitable inclination toward celebrities. How much we could count on the musician's name meaning something special, was debatable. In the case of Mr. Ford, it would perhaps have been better to present my case through some hillbilly fiddler, as his musical tastes were intensely folksy. But his wife and son would surely be eager to meet the Wagners, if only for the relief of hearing tidings of the world outside Detroit. I have sometimes thought that the strikes which occur in Detroit are a form of protest against not injustices, but boredom. Detroit may have its agreeable seasons; I have never seen them. From the time I first stepped out of the station and looked about at the February grimness and industrial grime of the city, it and its suburbs have stuck in my memory as the least delightful scene to which my travels ever carried me. It reminded me of the Ruhr, which Germans value but avoid. However, all this is by the way.

Together, the Wagners and I left for Detroit. Our plan hinged on whether Mrs. Ford would invite them to be her guests. If this happened, the rest of the plot was obvious-a word in Mr. Ford's presence, a hint, a request . . .

Human nature did not fail us. The invitation was waiting for my friends when we checked into the Statler. After spending the afternoon with the Fords at their Dearborn home, they drove to the concert together. I joined Frau Wagner there in her box. Her charming smile told me she had been successful. I was to see Henry Ford, the multi-millionaire. With one rasp of his pen he could solve the Nazis' money problem. More than that, if he showed sound vision and good-will, he could lend us sufficient prestige to push the programme ahead like a battering-ram. All through the world, wherever there was a road, the name of Ford was known and respected.

Fired by the heroic themes which were springing (albeit somewhat indifferently) from Siegfried's baton, my mind saw the dawning of the gods-without remembering their ultimate Twilight 1 When I returned to the hotel, I was still making supplications to Wotan, and I dreamed of the Rheingold. Next morning Mr. Leibold, Ford's secretary, called at nine, and drove me out to Dearborn to meet the man who was already a modem myth in his own right.

At that time, Ford liked to circulate among his men to keep tab on his Empire, and seldom received visitors in his office. Liebold had scarcely left me there, however, when Ford entered with an alert step and welcomed me. The Dearborn Independent in the flesh! His clear, bright eyes and his strong face, almost free from wrinkles, did not betray his more than sixty years. Neither did his face give much information as to how he had already piled up a fortune equal to what one of his workmen might earn in forty thousand lifetimes of steady work.

I thanked him for his kindness in giving me his time, and explained that since my message was of a delicate and confidential nature, it would be easier if we talked privately. Just then Liebold returned, and Ford offered to show me the laboratory. After walking through it for a while, he took me into a vacant room and shut the door.

Ford seated himself in an arm-chair, hoisted one foot to the desk, clasped his hands over his knee, and looked at me quizzically. His grey eyes were friendly but keen. His lean, graceful figure and well-shaped head showed character and race. He spoke with a firm, pleasant voice. I was impressed by his naturalness and simplicity; but his entire presence wore that mantle of aloofness which shelters men of wealth and power.

According to reports, which I could now easily credit, here was a man with a hard-set personality, who chose his own ideas and clung to them, who could be at once a radical pioneer and an obstinate Conservative. I pulled myself together. How could I impress this man with the merits of my case enough, to divert a fraction of his fortune to Hitler's use? After all, the motive behind my visit was not calculated to endear me at the outset. It is no advantage to begin relations with a stranger by asking him for money-and still less advantageous when the request involves so much besides. Ford was engaged in a campaign tangent to our own, which was favourable. But no man in the public eye can endow an insurgent revolutionary movement as casually as he would contribute to the Bide-A-Wee Home for Homeless Animals; there being a profound difference of opinion about what constitutes human welfare, donations in that direction may backfire.

Equally disconcerting was the limited time of this conference. However, the line of attack was clear-cut; if Henry Ford was to be persuaded to support Hitler, he must be convinced first that Hitler could give a broadly effective demonstration of the racial theories which Cameron's work was merely stating in abstract.

Bravely I launched forth, and talked with the most emphatic eloquence at my command. Either he would understand or he would not. Hope and fear played tag through the playground of my nerves.

Ford's interests ranged from petty antiquarianism to titanic social projects, from his cherished McGuffey Readers to his revolutionary wage-scale for industrial workers; but it was said in some quarters that while his mind went all the way between these two extremes, it ran on a single track. His anti-Jewish campaign might be conclusive disproof of this, or again it might be just one more sign of his nostalgia for the peaceful horse-and-buggy days which he had done so much to destroy. 'History as written is the bunk!' he is alleged to have said at some time. But I believed the Nazis were offering him a chance to make history himself, and if his views were sincere, it would be worth every penny it cost him. On the other hand, I knew the inside story of his Peace Ship expedition, when he sent the Oscar 11 across the Atlantic-a futile ark, bearing good tidings to no one but the jokesmiths. It would be natural for him to shun a second international venture. I was none too sure of my ground.

First, I briefly outlined the character of the Nazi movement in its relation to the German situation, emphasizing that Germany was the theatre in which a drama of supreme importance was destined to open. Hitler's ultimate rise to power was inevitable, I said; and when he had the power, whether soon or late, his first act would be to inaugurate the social programme for which the Dearborn Independent's articles provided such suggestive material. It was necessary that the Nazi movement be speeded up, not only for Germany's sake, but for the world's. Between 1914 and 1918, the white world had been wasting itself in what was virtually a civil war, with the dreadful result that white solidarity was destroyed. It must be re-established at any cost. Nothing could be expected of the politicians then in control of the Governments, since they by no means represented the real people. Individual initiative by high-minded and courageous men was imperative. Hitler, I declared, was such a man; in spite of temporary defeat and defamation, Hitler and the Nazis whom he swayed were ready to tackle this most difficult of all questions and solve it-ruthlessly if need be, but without compromise. Men must be men in this decisive hour of the race; and if white men everywhere stood together, victory would crown their efforts.

Ford listened keenly. He was hearing for the first time things which he could not learn from American newspapers, which, as the Dearborn Independent alleged, were controlled by Jews. But it would be untrue to say that his response was enthusiastic. Occasionally he nodded; once in a while he interjected a curt remark: "I know ... yes, the Jews, these cunning Jews..." All my own best cunning was quite inadequate to pry something less non-committal out of him.

I mentioned our admiration for the salutary work he was doing with Mr. Cameron, stressing the idea that Munich and Dearborn shared the same 'Weltanschauung,' and that two of the four volumes of his weekly articles which were already translated into German had been received with enthusiasm. All that stood between us and an immediate application within Germany of the views which he and Hitler held in common was-money. The Nazis were the only important active group in the world with a positive programme for establishing a new, non-Judaized order; but at this hour of oppression and dereliction, they were rendered helpless for lack of money. Would it not be farsighted for him to . . .?

If I had been trying to sell Mr. Ford a wooden 'nutmeg, he couldn't have shown less interest in the proposition. With consummate Yankee skill, he lifted the discussion back to the idealistic plane to avoid the financial question. I admired his adroitness, but I had not come five thousand miles to trade compliments. As much as I dared, I twisted my phrases into dollar marks, and only stopped pressing him when he moved as though to leave the room.

Ford was deeply interested in what I had to tell, but he was not at all interested in what I had to ask. So much was obvious already. But as long as he was willing to listen, there was still a chance to prod him into active sympathy, or at least to talk him into considering the question further, instead of dismissing it peremptorily.

I renewed my efforts. Referring again to Ford's own gospel according to Cameron, I paraphrased as much as I could recall of a passage which I give here in part: 'This office (of the Dearhorn Independent) holds thousands of written assurances from newspapermen all over the land, and from all parts of the world, testifying to the truth of our statements, that organizations had been proposed, for various purposes; that strong organizations had offered themselves as vehicles for the carrying out of any plan the Dearhorn Independent might propose. But that all such undertakings had been avoided, our belief being that simply to state the truth, and let it work its own right will, was sufficient . . .

'The Jewish question will be solved, and its solution will begin in the United States. But that does not mean that it will come as the result of a popular movement. Great changes do not occur that way.'

Praising the tone and content of Cameron's work, I permitted myself to disagree with his conclusion. I pointed out that the Nazis, who had long studied the subject, were convinced that only a popular movement, inspired and guided by a belligerent leader, could unseat the Jews from their position. I declared that in the United States the time was not ripe; such a movement could be launched successfully only in a country which, while still virile in its instincts, was suffering physically and morally under humiliation and suppression. I argued that in this world struggle for new concepts of life and state, Germany-because of her geographic position, her historic past, and the terrific pressure of her present plight-was predestined to become the torch-bearer of liberation.

Because of these same conditions, and certain imponderables which I tried to explain, Hitler sooner or later would emerge on top. But much misery and unnecessary sacrifice would be spared us, and the long painful process brought rapidly to a climax, if now, in our distress, we could claim some material co-operation from our far-flung moral alliances. With Hitler's far-sighted leadership supported by clear-seeing men of wealth within the great white nations, we could much sooner bulwark white solidarity against the onslaught of the undermen throughout the world, and begin to rebuild Nordic preeminence.

Encouraged by Ford's continued attention, I enlarged on the fact that Hitler's success or failure was by no means only a German issue. It was a world issue, with the future of America involved as much as any nation's, and coming developments would prove this statement.

To bring home this point to the great industrialist, I quoted again from the articles which had been issued under his imprimatur:

'Fifty years ago,' Cameron had written, 'international banking, which was mostly in control of the Jews, was on top of business. . . . Then came that new thing, Industry . . . As industry gathered strength and power, it became a powerful money magnet, drawing the wealth of the world in its train, not however, merely for the sake of possessing the money, but of making it work. The war came, in which the former broker-masters of the world had undoubtedly their large part. . . . And now the two forces, Industry and Finance, are in a struggle to see whether Finance is again to become the master, or Creative Industry. This is one of the elements which is bringing the Jewish Question to the bar of public opinion.'

Diplomatically I conveyed that whoever helped us now would not fare badly from a business standpoint. If Ford lent us his concrete support-which was all we needed to grasp control of Germany-a binding agreement could be arranged whereby large concessions would be guaranteed there, and possibly elsewhere, from the moment of Hitler's rise to power. Pointing to the probability that a Nazi regime in Germany might lead to a change also in the Russian situation, with the re-opening of that vast market, I emphasized the tremendous rewards his initiative would bring, not only by advancing his business interests, but also by furthering his grandiose social policies throughout the world. Since 1918, the United States had really held the balance of the world in its hands, though without making intelligent use of this power. Now, if ever, was the moment to risk a forward step, to cross the threshold with Hitler into a future which would change the face of this earth.

It became apparent, as I scanned Ford's face for hints of his reaction, that he either had no idea of the complex necessity of such a programme, or else was afraid of its very complexity. Machines he could master easily, but the cogs and springs of human life were different. I am sure that when this campaign was first launched, Ford did not dream of the possible consequences. Like that gesture of unsurpassed futility, the Peace Ship, this venture too had been undertaken with a certain naivety. He was bewildered, and somewhat offended, by the intractability of the public.

At the time of this interview, he knew already that he had put his finger into a hornet's nest. Experience was teaching him that it is one thing to see through the Jewish game, but another thing to talk about it. The weight of obloquy heaped on him could not make him hold his head less high; but the Jews' spontaneous boycott of his products, tightening every time he opened his mouth, pinched him in the ledgers, where even a multi-millionaire is vulnerable. Disappointed and alarmed by the results of his Dearborn crusade, he was doubly wary about playing Croesus to a similar movement abroad, especially when the Nazis promised to employ drastic acts instead of feeble editorials. He became immediately very wary when I pressed toward my goal with frank requests for money. The more I mentioned the word, the more Henry Ford cooled down from idealist to business man.

Only to-day, when in writing this scene I am obliged to re-live it, can I view my desperate earnestness throughout this interview with the detached amusement that I am sure Ford must then have felt.

At last, with utter finality, he said:

"Well, that you talk over with Cameron."

Talk it over with the Man in the Moon!

Ford led me next to Cameron's office and introduced us, unaware that we had met already. Then he left us alone, while I went through the empty form of renewing my petition.

I had several subsequent conferences with Cameron, whom I found to be a very able man, strongly imaginative, but not given to action. Diligent research and colourful reporting were his forte; initiative he lacked. Clearly he would not try to sway Ford, for whom he showed a respect that was nothing short of veneration. I was certain of this. He simply wasn't the type, and moreover, I knew from personal experience how fruitless the effort probably would be.

It was useless to spend more time in Detroit; so I threw my discouragement into a suitcase along with my soiled shirts and left for Washington. But how I needed now a fraction of the optimism which so far-against all reason-had buoyed up my heart! Ended was the pipe-dream of hurrying back to Munich with the promise of a million-dollar loan. Ended was the vision of Hitler's happy face when he heard the good news, ended my project of diverting a tithe of the sum to organize a foreign political bureau for the Party, with myself in charge.

And how I regretted having to tell the Wagners that our strategy had led to nothing! Theirs had been no idle interest, but a sincere desire to speed Hitler's advance. They had done what they could, as had I, and we had failed. It would be sad news to Siegfried, who fully subscribed to his father's written opinion that the Jew is 'the plastic demon of decay.' By virtue of race and parentage, the young Wagners were natural Hitlerites, and they had hoped, almost as ardently as myself, that the Dearborn Independent's loud declaration of concern over the Jewish problem would be bolstered by a cheque for Hitler. But there was no appeal from this adverse decision.

What a resounding syllable is a rich man's No!

There was no comfort or profit in cuddling the lost hope. As the train neared Washington, I said to myself: 'If the giant turned out to be one-eyed, then go after the pigmies! It will take a lot of talking to collect your million a dollar at a time, but get to it. America is full of money-and full of Germans. Try the Germans.'

I did. And even today I burn with resentment when I think of the experience. Concerning this protracted misadventure, conscience is for once lenient; I don't blame myself. Had the sirens themselves sung my cause, results would have been just as negative. The eloquence I wasted might easily have raised a fund to rescue moths from the sun; but Hitler and the Nazis rated nothing better than a perpetually empty collection plate. I was howled down in derision each time I spoke of him as a coming world power. It is a grim satisfaction now to remark that simply as fortune-telling, my talks were worth the money I asked-and didn't get.

The first venture into the midst of my transplanted countrymen came in Washington. A German society invited me to address a meeting, at which the allotment of welfare funds would be discussed.

Funds from German-American circles at that time were mostly distributed through the Left parties in Germany, who headed the welfare commissions as one phase of their control of the public life. These sums were not very large at best; but not one penny of them ever reached the Nazis, many of whom, after the Munich defeat, were in sore straits as individuals. I tried to give a fair picture of the true situation. These people, who knew next to nothing about the Nazis, listened with round eyes when I pleaded the tragedy of Hitler's setback, which temporarily had thrown so many of his followers into distress. At first it seemed as though I had won my case; I began to hope that this prosperous group of German-Americans would divert at least a few hundred dollars to the Nazi poor.

Then a typical cartoon 'Dutchman,' apparently a successful 'Plattdeutscher' grocer and one of the influential leaders of the colony, rose to rebut me. He attacked the Nazis historically, religiously, racially, politically, socially, ethically, and personally, reserving his best and last efforts for me.

I could see, while he spoke, how feeling changed and turned against me. When he had finished, only one man dared to oppose him, speaking in favour of the Nazi movement-but to no avail. I abandoned the money question and tried to turn the tide once more, to undo at least the anti-Hitler sentiment which had been created; but the opposition by this time was so strong that they almost threw me out of the hall.

In Pittsburgh, Cleveland, Chicago, Milwaukee, St. Louis, and other cities, experiences were just as disheartening. It was a hopeless business to interest people in a movement which had become the butt of the Press. Also, while a considerable minority of my expatriate countrymen shared the Nazi outlook, a majority misunderstood and condemned it. In other words, I discovered that the situation abroad was simply the home situation in little, and no more rewarding from a financial standpoint.

Of course I succeeded in interesting a few people a great deal, but most of these had no money to spare. It was as if the Nazi struggle could enlist none but the dispossessed.

In all New York there was only one well-known and wealthy German-American who showed active sympathy. 'He brought me into contact with other men of his class, in the hope of persuading them to organize a pro-Hitler committee. But his influence could not override Hitler's disrepute. If the men didn't laugh in my face, they laughed behind my back; and they laughed loudest of all when I declared that ten years would prove them poor prophets.

My nearest approach to success, really too trifling to be dignified by that description, was with the 'Barbarossa-Bund,' a New York society which no longer exists. I addressed the members several times. My first appearance was hard sailing indeed. A storm of personal denunciation swamped me, until I managed to get the drift of the charge which was hurled against me. I was-after all that time-still the other Ludecke, the sinister figure of the French spy stories! Even when I explained that my die-hard double would scarcely dare to appear under the name Ludecke, and certainly wouldn't present himself as a Hitlerite, they remained suspicious.

Not until the worthy gentlemen had written a letter of inquiry to Herr von Kursell, Ludendorff's spokesman, and had received his reply sponsoring me, did they give me a fair chance to speak. Afterwards, perhaps in expiation, they for a time sent a few dollars each month to the address in Munich.

And that was the nearest I came to raising funds. It was also my last effort in America. For one reason or another-indifference, caution, poverty, prejudice, or plain selfishness-the people who had been approached had declined almost to a man. On occasions when they said no with special emphasis, I wondered bitterly if the fault lay in me, if my powers of persuasion were having a reverse effect. But when my spirits sank to their lowest, the bedrock of hard fact would give me a new foothold, and I would console myself with the truth: the message I was trying to bring to these complacent people was so radical, so forward-looking, so far-reaching, so vast in its implications, that it either frightened them or left them numb with lack of understanding.

Just about the time when it became obvious that the little men were not going to be of much use, the big man in Dearborn stepped out of the picture for good. Before leaving Detroit I had, at Cameron's suggestion, prepared a memorandum which succinctly outlined the proposition. Now came a telegram just as succinct, Ford's final answer through his subordinate:

'The proposal will probably not be entertained-Cameron.'

Probably not! It was no longer news to me.

Meanwhile, to salvage whatever I could, I made every effort to cement relations with men who might prove useful later on. One name in particular intrigued me-that of a man who was very much in the public eye because of his quasi-political activity in the religious and racial fields. It was difficult to tell from the newspapers just what medicine he meant to give this ailing world, but the general opinion was that it would be an unpalatable dose. Therefore, thought I, there may be something in it! In any event his organization, constantly growing in spite of the deadly ridicule and contumely heaped upon it, was a potent ferment in the American melting-pot, and worth examining.

His headquarters were in Washington, so there I returned once more. I can confess now that I felt somewhat as one might feel on the way to one's first Walpurgis Night. For my quarry was the Imperial Wizard of the Invisible Empire-and I am a practical man, not given to abracadabra.

The publicity man of the Ku Klux Klan was easily accessible, and through him the Imperial Wizard granted an interview. I hardly knew what to expect, but I felt a moment of flatness when he received me in an ordinary suit instead of his spectacular Inquisition costume. It was an expensive suit, however. The Invisible Empire was verging on over-population, boasting five million Knights, none of whom was permitted to write his membership cheque in invisible ink.

With such a flood of money pouring in, any man of genius might have been able to anticipate, in America, the work Hitler eventually did in Germany, But neither the 'publicity man' nor the 'Imperial Wizard' impressed me as possessing the requisite genius, or even the qualities of leadership. They simply seemed to me to be making a good thing, while it lasted, out of the idea of combining a masquerade party with a lynching party, and their greatest concern was to keep the Invisible Empire from becoming all too visible in its crudity, naivety, and viciousness.

Nevertheless, the Ku Klux Klan was an interesting study. I did not need much political knowledge to know that it would come to nothing in spite of its appeal to the anti-Negro, anti-Jewish, and anti-Catholic sentiment by which many Americans, particularly in the Southern states, could be pricked into action. First, its organization as a 'secret society' -without any secrets which were not shared by thousands -made it too inefficient an instrument to achieve its own aims. It is impossible to hold discipline in any larger body of any secret society. Whereas secret organizations are very useful to push open ones and do their dirty work for them, no secret society as such can gain political control in any country; and when its most secretive act is to burn a giant kerosene cross on a prominent hilltop, then it ceases to be alarming except to students of human nature. Second, the whole structure of the K.K.K. sooner or later would lead to a general break-up. A society which gets the majority of its members by selling its ideals like commodities is doomed from the beginning. The K.K.K. salesmen received 20 per cent of the initiation fee of every new member, and another 20 per cent of what he paid for his regalia. So, of course, it was natural that many if not most agents didn't care a hang what kind of members they got; what interested them was the commission.

The system worked very well for a while, from the financial viewpoint. The Wizard sold more muslin than Sears-Roebuck, and a large percentage of America's manhood decked itself in cotton robes. For a while, too, it seemed likely that the Klan might really become a political power. It enlisted members in Congress, among those politicians who always know which way the wind is blowing and don't care how badly it smells. It monopolized the editorial pages, receiving every now and then a favourable comment. By talking big and acting violently, it frightened the established parties into serious opposition. Throughout America there were mingled fear and hope that the Klan would prevail. Since it didn't, one may judge that the fear outweighed the hope. Under different leaders, and differently organized, the outcome would have been otherwise.

Until I came to love America, and therefore to know it better, I could not understand how such a show-me nation could subscribe in such numbers to the fantastic ritual and absurd quackery of the Klan. A fraction of the Klan programme (insofar as it was ever clearly formulated) was surely worthy of adherence; but its preponderant mummery would have insured a much more speedy demise in any other country. I believe now that the Klan was symptomatic of that peculiar spiritual diet-deficiency from which the democratic United States suffer. Without the romantic background of a monarchy, lacking even the nimbus of a popular army, the crowd turns with a sort of hunger to the solemn hocus-pocus of Shrines, Empires, Grottoes, Brotherhoods, Sisterhoods, and Grand Lodges. Symbolism satisfies a deep instinct in human nature; and when ordinary life is stripped bare of symbolism, then the first comer can exploit the people if he speaks in parables and dresses in outlandish robes. America is the only country where fat, successful men are willing to parade Main Street in fancy costumes, gaudy with red satin and gold braid, carrying scimitars and wearing turbans. The English, it is true, love pageantry; but theirs is performed by paid servants of the State, which is different. In America your grocer or banker or pastor is likely to pay annual dues for the privilege. After my first amazed glimpse of a procession of Shriners, I could only smile when the Babbitts joked about the German goose-step or called the Nazi swastika a boy-scout emblem.

The contact which I established with the white-robed K.K.K. never had any practical results, for obvious reasons. There was some correspondence back and forth for a while. If the Wizard could not contribute to the Nazis, I decided, then perhaps the Nazis could contribute to him. It would be something to have five million men organized in America far a purpose parallel to our own, regardless of whether they actually entered the political arena or remained merely a side-show. One of the K.K.K.'s last letters to me ran thus:

'Be not alarmed concerning the Knights overlooking the Jewish world-power. The battle of the Klan with its present strategy contemplates different phases and you can be assured that nothing is "diverting" the organization from its original programme. Recently at Kansas City, Dr. Evans defined a legitimate and yet intense Americanism and Nationalism, which was most enthusiastically received by the organization and those outside of the organization who are " instinctively" inclined to sympathy with the principles of the Klan.'

Somehow, in spite of the enthusiasm which he reported, the Klan's Empire became more and more invisible during the next three years, until even the Press stopped trying to re-materialize it. The pother about colour and creed subsided beneath the surface again; America returned to its accustomed habit of burying its head in the sand whenever certain ugly questions reared their horrid miens; and I concluded that the Wizards and Kleagles had simply guided their followers into a blind alley. There was some talk among the Knights concerning the fortune which the Wizard must have made in his heyday; then there was less talk, and finally no talk at all. The Klan, which could have changed American life under different leadership, was consigned to the newspaper morgues.

But during this visit in Washington, I had two other experiences which taught me something.

First, there was my connection with a rather mysterious person, an Englishman addressed variously as 'captain' and 'doctor.' I met him in the flat of an unusually intelligent and scholarly woman who had been employed by Ford's Dearborn Independent to collect material for articles.

Though there was great secrecy about the Englishman, I was given to understand that he was a man of importance, connected with the British Secret Service. This was probably true at that time, because I found him at the British consulate-general, where he had an office under another name than the one I knew him by. In fact it was he who procured for me the visa with which I returned to England.

Our conversation was vividly interesting, since the captain had been very busy in America during the war and could talk arrestingly of the behind-the-scenes manoeuvres which had turned the tide against Germany. He also recited for me the detailed story of how Leon Trotsky had been seized from a Norwegian steamer by the British navy and interned in a Canadian prison camp near Halifax, from which, after an inexplicable release, he continued his journey to Russia to help Lenin establish Bolshevism.

The captain promised to show me the photostat of a million-dollar cheque from a New York Jewish banking firm, which he said was found on Trotsky at the arrest. As a Nazi, it didn't take me two seconds to arrange this information to my own satisfaction: Jewish Bankers and Race subsidizing Trotsky, Trotsky letting loose Communism, Communism launching itself against Germany's resistance - and, if Germany fell, the end of the Gentile world. But I must anticipate right here by saying that I did not see the photostat then, and have never seen it, though again and again, when we met in later years, I asked the captain to produce it. The experience helped to teach me that in these days of high-pressure propaganda, it is possible to create considerable smoke with no fire at all.

The second lesson in my American education was of a different sort. It taught me that a fatal fire can flame with no smoke at all. But to speak plainly, without metaphor, it showed me that the German people during the war were kept in almost total ignorance of decisive world events, their knowledge of which might have brought the war to a vastly different ending.

I had fallen in love with the city of Washington. The Easter season was in full bloom, complete with cherry blossoms. The pleasant avenues of maple and elm were gay with high-school graduates making their pilgrimage from all over America, and the whole atmosphere of the capital was festively youthful and new-world. The failure of my mission left me with a deplorable amount of spare time, but I

161

kept from moping by spending most of my free hours exploring the public shrines. The Corcoran Gallery. The glorious Lincoln Memorial, whose graven tablets left me bewildered: I could not decide which people Lincoln meant when he said "Of the people, by the people, for the people." The clean square shaft of the Washington Monument. The Pan-American Building, that harbinger of dissolution. The Capitol, freighted with memories of the days when America was Nordic Protestant-primitively so, as Statuary Hall showed, but none the less Nordic Protestant. And then-the Library of Congress.

The Library was a revelation, in many ways. It is one of the few great libraries in any part of the world where books are made readily available, instead of being jealously hoarded. In Paris, the Bibliotheque is more closely guarded than the Mint. In London the British Museum keeps its volumes listed in clumsy ledgers, apparently to discourage students. But in Washington, any comer can find practically anything he wishes to read, and read it undisturbed. I revelled in the privilege.

Giving way to an old desire, I went one afternoon to the section where newspapers are preserved, and asked for copies of the Washington papers on several challenging dates: August 1914; December 1917, when the Russian menace became undeniable; November 1918.

It was a paper of the last date which shed new light for me on the events of the period. It happened to be an extra edition of the Washington Times, a Hearst paper. Across the full front page, in letters three inches high, was blazoned the head-line: GERMANY SURRENDERS. At each end of the head-line a American flag waved bleakly in black ink. Below was a brief column of news:

London-Germany has agreed to the Armistice terms laid down by the Allies. It is understood the terms are virtually the same as those which were signed by Austria, providing for the occupation of a large number of towns by the Allies, demobilization of the enemy armies, and turning over a large part of the army and navy equipment ... practically an unconditional surrender to the United States and associate powers.

'Signature of an armistice does not mean signature of the final peace terms. These will be decided at a conference, probably at The Hague.

'But the agreement of the Kaiser's chiefs to the armistice conditions of the Allies means the stripping of the enemy of such a great part of his military power that he will be virtually at the mercy of the Allies, and will have to accept their dictates as to peace agreements.'

There was nothing extraordinary in those three paragraph. After such a war, such an armistice was no more predatory than Germany should expect. But the date at the top of the page made the news seem strange almost to incredibility. It was 7 November! Until this moment I had believed that the Armistice came on the 11th. Germans had not heard of it until then. And only now, by turning to the next issue of the Times, did I learn that on the afternoon of the 7th, all America had left its job, its classroom, its kitchen, its plough, to join in a whirl of joy, celebrating the end of the war. The news was false, as it happened; yet spontaneously the people of America had turned out with horns and confetti, to dance in the streets and to embrace one another-less in triumph than in simple thankfulness that the slaughter was over.

'Where were our editors at that moment? Why did we not hear the news? 'Who kept from the German public the fact that America had committed itself to a peace by popular acclamation? America had in fact surrendered-not to the Germans, but to the horrors of cruel warfare, to the futility of wasteful death: No government, not even the 'Wilson Government, would have dared to press hostilities after such a national demonstration. But while the United States hailed the Armistice, we in my country, who knew of no Armistice, turned weary eyes toward our leaders, waiting for revolution to end everything. And end everything the revolution did.

We could have kept on to a fair peace had we known the news which was being shouted from the house-tops throughout the rest of the world. 'But the agreement of the Kaiser's chiefs means the stripping of the enemy of such a great part of his military power that he will be virtually at the mercy of the allies and will have to accept their dictates as to peace agreements.' Who made such a suicidal submission-or more pointedly, I asked myself, who forced the Kaiser and his chiefs to make it? Who but the political leeches that had grown fat by sucking the substance out of the German nation! The Berlin Government-the Marxists, the very men who were still in power!

Occupation, demobilization, indemnities-already six years of humiliation and hardship, with how many more years to come before the end? And what would the end be? I could not guess. Only one thing was certain: Germany's house would not be set in order until Hider swept the traitors out of their easy-chairs. That might be late-or never. For what power had the leader now-imprisoned, impoverished, the butt of ridicule, a victim of the very system he was sworn to abolish!

That issue of the Washington Times had more news for me, albeit six years late. Except for the Armistice announcement the pages were filled with routine reports prepared before the great news arrived. It was a moment of war-time history crystallized, a fragment of the American memory fixed through the years; simply by reading a column here, a paragraph there, I could see the world as it must have been seen by millions on that dramatic day. But not quite the same, because hindsight now showed so much of the news in a blinding light.

And the Kaiser, the forgotten man of Doorn. It startled me to have him suddenly brought to mind by a crude cartoon. Germany itself seldom remembered the Emperor, and the good people of the enemy countries had forgotten how they yelled to have him hauled through the triumphant capitals in an iron cage. But here he was before me, just as Hearst's portion of the American public had seen him in 1918:

The cartoon showed Wilson as a stern schoolmaster, of the little-red-brick rather than the Princeton sort. Before him trembles Wilhelm, an abashed schoolboy, conscious' of his guilt in drawing a map of the world on the blackboard, over the inscription: 'It belongs to me-Kaiser Bill.' On the schoolmaster's desk is a book labelled Democracy; in his hand an upraised yardstick, Justice. He is beckoning grimly to the Kaiser. Out of the room, weeping, slink the Kaiser's gang, already licked: Austria, Bulgaria 'I'm glad it's over!') and Turkey ('He struck me in the Dardanelles!'). The drawing was crude, the whole conception on the moronic side; but no doubt it was effective in those latter months of the war hysteria.

Years later, when I was to be aware of the blatancy of certain Nazi propaganda, I remembered this cartoon. For one of the strangest characteristics of the propaganda of hate is this: it can be launched only with cunning subtlety, but once public judgment has been debased, no puerile cat-call is too obvious for the people to echo.

The whole four-page extra which was crumbling between my fingers seemed to smell of decay, of death, as if it had been dug up from a tomb.

During this unprofitable American begging-tour, the country and the people had awakened a real affection in me. Under other circumstances it would have been the happiest of visits. But I was not here on a personal mission; so reluctantly I acknowledged defeat, and began the homeward trip, empty-handed.

From now on the journey became a series of miniature copies of the previous months-matched pearls in the string of perfect failures.

In New York I saw the Wagners again. They entered a restaurant, chatting brightly with two wealthy Jewish ladies who were known as patrons of the arts. Siegfried and his wife averted their eyes, I turned my glance away, and we did not speak, because obviously this was not the moment to pick up our discourse where we had left off.

In London, as in New York and Washington, all my interviews were sterile. The motto of the men who received me was 'My time is your time '-but time wasn't money. The only real profit from my efforts was the personal contacts I effected among men whose co-operation in the future could help the Nazis.

One of these new allies was W. A. Peters, the secretary of 'The Britons,' an anti-Jewish organization whose slogan was 'Britain for the Britons.' Another was the Rt. Hon. Lord Sydenham of Combe, a former Governor of Bombay, the author of a sensational pamphlet, The Jewish World Problem.

Through Lord Sydenham I met the Duke of Northumberland, and was invited to weekend at Albury Park, his country seat. Northumberland was a leading shareholder in the Morning Post, the most important Tory paper, anti-German by tradition. Though he listened courteously to my expose of the German situation, it was at once apparent that he was too aloof and faraway from the real demands of our time to take a practical interest in the German world struggle. Just as great financiers and push-cart pedlars everywhere show the same character-patterns, so do the higher nobility of all nations. In exact ratio to their nobility they are insulated from common problems. Moreover, since the last German world struggle had been viewed by the Tories as a direct threat against England, it may have been still - bit too early to expect enthusiasm from his Grace. He and his lady tendered me excellent meals, charming dinner conversation, pleasant walks in the gardens, and nothing more.

In Paris I first looked up a venerable friend, Maitre Urbain Gohier, a fearless fighter and the well-known editor of the now defunct anti-Jewish weekly La Vieille France. I went to him not for money, which seldom passed through his hands, but for spiritual replenishment.

Gohier, then already nearing seventy, was a tragic figure, but somehow splendid in his misfortune. I found him in a little attic apartment on the Boulevard du Palais, sitting hunched in an arm-chair, a worn blanket wrapped over his thin knees, a velvet cap on his finely chiselled bald skull, writing his brilliant notes by the dim light of an oil lamp. Conversing with him was an experience above the ordinary run. His sensibilities were acute, and his words flowed freely and clearly. The lucidity of his mind, the beauty of his flawless French, the force of his arguments, were inspiring. But his bitterness and irony, his searing pessimism, were saddening and discouraging.

"En France," he said, "tout est perdu; et si grande est la lachete de nos hommes, je ne voyais de salut pour l'Europe et pour la race blanche que dans une entente raiyonnee de la France et de l'Allemagne...."

Gohier, convinced of the ruin of France in a biological sense, had resigned himself unwillingly to the belief that no resurrection was possible so long as France pursued her present African policy. He was one of the few Frenchmen who recognized that only an international system of nationalisms, a 'White Alliance,' could solve the racial problem. But his was a voice in the wilderness; his impassioned pleas for racial solidarity awakened as little response as had my own efforts in Hitler's behalf, and we commiserated together. Years later he sent me a copy of La Nouvelle Aurore, his last publication, with his last editorial of all marked. Headed' Paroles d'un Francais,' it ended with these words :

Solitaire, j'ai survecu, fidele implacablement a la mission 'de l'ecrivain qui est de proclamer sa verite, de centroler les pouvoirs politiques, de resister aux tyrannies sociales, de traquer les scelerats et de bafouer les histrions, de briser les fetiches et de renverser les idoles, de precher par l'exemple le mepris des hochets et des sportules, d'eveiller la conscience et la raison du peuple, de purifier les coeurs et de susciter des volontes. En voici le dernier temoignage.

For me this noble soul wrote some lines which I hold in great esteem.

Je suis bien content d'avoir de vos nouvelles. Je me demanderais souvent ce que vous etiez devenu; je craignais que votre belle figure de guerrier n'eut ete gatee dans le tourbiIlon de business et de dollars....

Je connais votre force et votre courage; il ne me reste qu'a faire des voeux ardents pour votre succes. J'ai trente ans de trop pour combattre aupres de vous. Je ne me compte pas, avec mes soixante-dix ans, n'ayant plus qu'un souffle de vie, sans cartouches, et juge 'compromettant' par mes tristes concitoyens. Je n'ose vous donner une collaboration qui serait pessimiste, done decourageante, done mauvaise. Mais je serai toujours la pour les informations dont vous aurez besoin. Dans ce monde de rnensonge, de fourberie et de venalite, vous savez que moi, du moins, je suis sur.

Bien cordialement

URBAIN GOHIER

And so his career closed, apparently barren of achievement. But it would be sad indeed if one had to believe that such a distinguished lifetime of truth-seeking and truth-telling could end without leaving some afterglow of enlightenment in the public mind.

My talks with Gohier had filled me with gladness and gloom at the same time- and in this uncertain state of mind I made my final effort to gain some concrete good for the Nazi Party. I tackled the White Russians. Divided among themselves, they at least were united in hatred of the Soviet regime, which Hitler also opposed in theory. If he came to power, his opposition might be effective. A single Imperial jewel, sold over the counter, could bring enough money to set things going again in Germany. And even failing such largesse (for by now experience had taught me the frailty of political charity) there were other ways in which the Royal refugees could be useful.

Boris Brasol, then the Grand Duke Cyril's representative in the United States, had given me letters of introduction to Cyril and other Russians. With these letters I soon found myself amidst the Paris colony. At a little restaurant, 7 Rue Pauquet, which was run by the Cossack Colonel Narichkine and the handsome princess who was his wife, many former

Czarist generals and anti-Soviet plotters foregathered. Not all of them, however. The remnants of the Czar's Court, scattered throughout Europe, were split into two factions, the Cyril group and the group which adhered to the Grand Duke Nicolai Nicolaievitch, former commander-in-chief of the Russian armies. These two factions feuded with each other relentlessly. Naturally the Nazis were most in sympathy with Cyril, who was orientated toward Germany, rather than with Nicholas, whose attitude was pro-French. It was mainly the Cyril group which frequented Narichline's restaurant. Some of them were old friends, familiar from the days of my Reval venture.

The Grand Duke himself was not in Paris. So I hurried south to Nice, where he lived in the Chateau Fabron. I presented my letters to the chamberlain, receiving in the time prescribed by Court etiquette a summons to the Chateau. With all due formality, I was introduced to the Grand Duke Cyril and his wife.

It was not difficult to discover that the Grand Duchess, an intelligent and ambitious woman, the sister of Queen Marie of Roumania, ruled over her husband. So I cast my nets mainly toward her. I hinted that through her kinship with the Spanish Court, she might be able to interest Primo de Rivera in fostering Hitler's plans. It was not an impossible hope, since Spain was a long-time friend of Germany. Other hopes also were worth testing, which concerned Roumania, where Marie was still a potent political figure, and the neighbouring countries. I based my appeal on the obvious desirability of bringing Hitler's programme to fruition and thereby establishing a strong anti-Soviet State at Russia's front door.

However, their somewhat Imperial Highnesses' reaction to each discreet suggestion was so stiff-necked that I abandoned hope long before they had a chance definitely to refuse, and dropped the matter. From then on the conference continued in a manner which was quite polite but utterly meaningless. I did not even ask for money, as it was obvious that every rouble they had rescued from the Red Terror was desperately needed to keep up their high position. Politics had become for these landless lords and ladies merely a pastime, not a matter of life or death.

But for me it was a very vital matter. This journey across two continents had not been planned as a pleasure tour. I dreaded the thought of returning to Munich with empty hands, but now the last arrow in my quiver was spent. No-not the last one! Why shouldn't I try again the good fortune which had blessed me during former days in Monte Carlo?

True enough, I possessed little with which to tempt fortune. But I scraped together the last money I had with me, sold a gold cigarette-case, took a third-class ticket for the short ride to Monaco, and with just two thousand francs, faced the green cloth.

I did not strike it once. In five coups, in less than ten minutes, the money was gone. I had to borrow some to get home to Germany.

XIII

HITLER IN PRISON

In February 1924, when Henry Ford blinked his grey eyes at me and framed a tactful refusal to share the white man's burden with the Nazis, I could hear the Fates snickering.

Had I been in Munich on the 26th of that same month I might have heard them laugh out loud over a very private practical joke-though none of the human actors involved found much reason to smile.

The occasion was the greatest political trial in German history. The liberty of ten men was at stake. Hitler, Ludendorff, and their companions of the Beer Hall Putsch had been brought to the bar on charges of high treason. As the world knows, they were let off lightly. But the point of the jest, the irony of fate, is this: by triumphing over this adversity, Hitler was doomed to betray his own ideals. How this was so, was not at once apparent. Hitler himself may not see the point to this day.

The trial was not quite the sort that is personified by the familiar figure of Justice, blindfolded, holding the scales. Though meanwhile the normal civil power had regained supreme authority throughout the Reich, the court found it convenient to exclude whatever evidence would incriminate Kahr, Lossow, and Seisser, who, sacrificed on the political altar, had surrendered their dictatorial positions to a regular government. This pretty trio, called as witnesses, offered, in fact, some of the prosecution's most damaging testimony concerning the 'treason.' Yet their undeniable complicity was a great advantage for the defendants, who could have charged them with the seditious attempt to separate Bavaria from the Reich-a silent threat which forced the court to be very lenient. The only government official accused of complicity was Poehner's friend, Dr. Wilhelm Frick, then head of the political division of the Munich police administration. It is significant to note that the secret director of this judicial comedy was Guertner, then Bavarian minister of justice, but today Reichsminister of Justice in Hitler's cabinet.

All the delicate issues of the trial were heard behind closed doors, with public and Press excluded. It was less easy to exclude the truth. The trial was, in reality, little more than a grandstand play to appease Berlin, with the silent understanding that the culprits would not be penalized too heavily if they consented to abide by the rules of politics thereafter.

Only ten of the chief Nazi activists were brought to the dock. Goering, Rossbach, and Esser had fled the country-I had seen all three of them in Austria. Dietrich Eckart, dying, had been hastily cast out of prison a few weeks before the trial. One day more and the State would have had to bear the unenviable stigma of having 'martyrized' him, for he expired within twenty-four hours of his release. Of the remaining ten defendants, Ludendorff was the only one found 'not guilty' in the verdict, rendered on I April. Hitler, Kriebel, Poehner, and Dr. Weber were sentenced to five years' fortress-detention, with the proviso that after serving six months they might be set free on probation for good behaviour. Frick, Roehm, Brueckner, and two other prisoners were condemned to lesser terms, but their sentences were suspended or parole was granted within a short time.

'Fortress-detention,' a punishment reserved for political offenders, has no parallel in English-speaking countries and needs explanation. A fortress is, of course, just what the name implies-a military stronghold where the normal life of the garrison lightens the monotony for the few prisoners committed to the somewhat casual care of the soldiers; sometimes they may even move freely by day within the city limits.

Landsberg, to which Hitler was sent, was an obsolete fortress under a civilian administration, with regular warders in charge; but confinement there, as in an active fortress, was not dishonouring, and involved no other hardship than the loss of liberty.

All in all, these ten men who had tried to wreck the State were treated gently. This was partly, as has been pointed out, because the court was embarrassed by the complicity of Kahr's crowd, and to hush that, it was necessary to soft-pedal all the proceedings. But Hitler's eloquence in justifying the putsch was almost equally responsible for the tenderness with which he and his men were treated.

Hitler was canny enough to realize that the dock is as good a soap-box as any other, and that a prisoner on trial may profit by the conspicuousness of that dangerously exposed position. With the greatest aplomb, he appeared before the court not as defendant but as accuser. Before Germany and the world, addressing himself more to the Press reporters than to the court, he made what was perhaps his most impressive public appearance. Far from paying the full penalty for his grotesque defeat, he rose to new heights of self-justification and took on greater stature in the eyes of the world.

First of all, Hitler assumed sole responsibility for the putsch. It was a clever move, clothing him in the garments of heroism without requiring him to run much risk. The truth would have been served better had he simply acknowledged responsibility for the failure of the putsch. But his gesture had its effect upon the audience. His shrewdness and no doubt his genuine sense of righteousness did the rest. Through sheer force of words and emotion, he turned his disgrace into a triumph, so complete that even the prosecutor's indictment became a remarkable testimonial to his honourable motives!

There had been only one incident to blur the picture-a touch of jealous spleen on the part of General von Lossow, called as a witness. As one of the trio of Bavarian officials involved in the putsch, but shielded by the court, Lossow was in a delicate situation. Not indicted himself, he must have realized that the charge of treason, though not levelled at him, had sullied him in the eyes of all present. Each new chisel-stroke on the statue of Hitler the Hero obviously pinked the Lossow pride. On the witness stand the doughty general suddenly grew purple with rage, stabbed the floor with his scabbard, and roared:

"But there are two Hitlers!"

Then he stamped out of the court.

This sour moment was soon buried, however, under the emotion aroused by Hitler's closing address. It was a long, passionate harangue, a medley of old refrains and of startling new personal avowals, marred by a few of those rhetorical immaturities with which he habitually interlards his speeches.

He would pass from youthful naivety to dramatic eloquence: "What I had before me, from the first day, was an ambition a thousand times greater than that of merely becoming a government minister. I do not consider it worthy of a great man that his name should be recorded in history merely as having been a minister. I wished to be the destroyer of Marxism. I shall achieve this task, and once I have done so the title of minister will be, for me, only an absurdity. When stood for the first time before Richard Wagner's grave, my heart filled with pride at the thought that there lay a man who had forbidden that his tombstone should bear the inscription: 'Here lies His Excellency Privy Counsellor and Music Director Baron Richard von Wagner.' Not out of modesty did I wish to be the drummer. That is the highest post; the others are little things. . . .

"We face punishment because the attempt 'failed.' The deed of November eighth did not fail. It would have failed if a mother had come to me afterwards and said, 'Herr Hitler, you have my son on your conscience.' But I can assure you, no mother came to me .... Of the young men who fell, it will some day be said, 'These, too, died for the liberation of the Fatherland' . . . I believe that the time will arrive when the masses which to-day stand with our flags in the streets will join forces with those who fired on us on November ninth. I believe that blood will not always divide us. Some day the hour will come when the Reichswehr will stand on our side, officers and men. The following which we have built is growing more rapidly from day to day, from hour to hour....

"Pronounce us a thousand times guilty-but history, the goddess of a higher truth and of a better law, will tear down the judgment of this court: for she will find us innocent."

The court, however, could not laugh off certain mundane laws as easily as might the goddess of history, and was constrained to find Hitler guilty. He was sentenced with the gentle qualifications which politics recommended, and on April Fools' Day he returned under guard to the old fortress at Landsberg to begin his five-year term.

How does the 'leadership principle' operate within an activist group when the supreme leader is deprived of his freedom of action?

In theory, the situation which now faced the Nazis could be handled smoothly through deputies in the hierarchy. Apparently, as it worked out in practice, the theory failed to take into account the human element. Or - for who knows Hitler's mind? - the very essence of the theory, in so far as it applied to such a contingency as this, may have been distilled from a perfect foreknowledge of how the rats will play when the cat's away. It is news to no one to say that Hitler's leadership survived the period of his imprisonment; but it may be news to tell how his subordinates improved the golden hours during which they were left to their own devices.

Suspicion, jealousy, and intrigue were already in full flower when I reached Munich in May-having re-entered my own country without difficulty. Disgusting bickerings and violent squabbles were souring the sweet fellowship of the folkic knighthood. The various groups quarrelled internally and with each other. There was definitely bad blood between the blue-eyed crusaders. Nor were their antagonisms private scandals-enemies clawed each other in public, regardless both of the spectacle they were giving the shocked onlookers and of the damage they were doing themselves. And of all these contending folkic parties, the Nazis could least afford an open schism, because they were already under a severe handicap from the official dissolution of the Party. Indeed, only under a new name[1] had they dared reorganize at all, and the most serious problems confronted them.

But from the moment of my arrival, my eager questions concerning the Party brought only depressing answers. The man on the street-my cabby, my porter, the hotel clerk-spoke sourly of the Nazis, as if they had disappointed him. I tried at once to find Rosenberg, who as Hitler's designated spokesman would be able to explain this strange turn of affairs. Failing to locate him, I went to the Eher Verlag, the publishing office of the reorganized Party. There I found Max Amann, Herman Esser, Julius Streicher, and a few others who long since have fallen into oblivion. Hanfstaengl, who had ventured to creep back to Munich after the beginning of the trial, was there too, a sort of super-presence, like a ghost haunting a ruined building.

The loud 'Hello' which greeted my entrance rapidly diminuendoed as I reported the penny-pinching instinct that prevailed throughout America. A silence of disappointment followed my recital.

"But if I had succeeded in getting funds abroad, who would disburse the money here? There seems to be some dissension among us. What is wrong in Nazi circles?"

Now a storm of words made the air murky. To my great concern, I heard that the old Nazi nucleus had split. Alfred Rosenberg was Hitler's deputy and-the appointed leader of the Party during his imprisonment-yet these men spoke of him with hatred and contempt. One could see all their resentment of his intellectuality, his reserve,

---

1 *Grossdeutsche Volksgemeinschaft,' of brief duration.*

his cold unfellowship, boiling to the surface. But they had rationalized this dislike. It was for 'the good of the Party' that they were ranged against him. Calling him a traitor, they claimed that he was partly Jewish, and that as a Balt of un-German origin he had spied for France during the war. I had to listen to many such spiteful stories, most of them so palpably groundless that it was difficult for me to keep my face straight or my tongue still. But I managed, as I wished to know what really lay behind all this dangerous nonsense.

Self-interest was the answer.

These were ambitious men, hypnotized by their dreams of personal power, their schemes for advancing themselves through the Party. Because the Party offered them the means of succeeding, they were eager for its success; but they were even more solicitous for their own success-and stupidly so. They were in too great a hurry to get somewhere. Their impatient little minds could not grasp the folly of ripping the Party machine apart to fashion roller-skates for themselves.

Uselessly I tried to point out that success could come to us only through an orderly, well-balanced advance of the whole Nazi movement. Their reply was that since a period of semi-quiescence had been imposed on us, as far as organization work was concerned, we could best spend our time doing some Party house-cleaning. What if the dust we raised did antagonize the public? They, the men of action within our ranks, would at least get rid of the whey-faced thinkers who hampered the movement; and later on, when Hitler returned to guide them, he would find the whole group moving as one muscle, no longer inhibited by the nervous intellectuality of men like Rosenberg.

These things I learned during my first day in Munich. The situation disturbed me deeply. My impassioned lectures in America had not been empty rhetoric, but a sincere declaration of faith in Nazi unity and Nazi destiny. It seemed to me now that I had been asking for money under false pretences, for surely this sort of spiteful backbiting was not the heroic struggle for which I had tried to gain support. After months of strenuous work propagandizing my fellow spirits as patriots who would gladly lay down their very lives for Germany, it was a come¬down to find them so ignobly engaged.

Up to this time Rosenberg and I had never achieved real cordiality in our relations, because he was a person who took a good deal of knowing, and I had been usually out of the country. Though I had long since ceased to feel rebuffed by his naturally frigid manner, I had never sought his company, in spite of my admiration for him as a thinker and a co-worker. Now, however, thoroughly alarmed by the split within the Party, I excused myself from further mud-slinging with the detractors of Rosenberg.

My reason for refusing to cast my lot with them was two-fold. First, I wanted a chance really to judge the situation, with full knowledge of the facts which had created it. Second, there lurked in my mind a strong suspicion that Rosenberg, far more than his detractors, was maintaining the ideals to which I had supposed the Party and all good Nazis were committed. The more objectively I weighed the issues, the less I could forgive the men who had engineered this explosion.

A third consideration also counted, albeit at that time I could truly disclaim it as an important motive in my decisions. If the Party split was definite and irreparable, then it was important to place myself on the stronger side if my own career was to continue. Important, yes-but as it turned out, I could not make the necessary compromises with my temperament when it became clear that the stronger side was the side I detested. The instinct of self-preservation failed to overcome certain inborn and perhaps romantic standards by which I habitually judged my actions. In this controversy, I deliberately chose the weaker side, believing it the better one, and hoped against hope that our good motives would offset the opposition's numerical strength.

Rosenberg was not at home, and for several hours I paced the street before his lodgings. He did not return until past two in the morning, having been detained at a secret meeting. Though he no longer lived in hiding, the official ban on Nazi activities made it wise for him to attend to Hitler's business at odd hours, and surreptitiously.

In judging him for the apparently indecisive role he was now playing in the Party crisis, though he was nominally Hitler's deputy, it must be remembered that he was a marked man. He had been detained in jail for six weeks on the charge of treason and eventually released for lack of conclusive evidence.

Rosenberg's interest in the American mission did not evaporate when he learned that it had failed. He wished to know why and to what extent the Americans had remained cold to Hitler's message, and whether they had withheld moral support as well as money. I was pleased to find a Nazi taking an intelligent interest in the foreign problem; but things of greater moment were in order, so I came directly to the point.

What was wrong within the Party?

For the first time in our long relationship Rosenberg spoke with such heat that all his iciness was melted. The personal attacks on himself he dismissed with a contemptuous phrase. But when he spoke of the peril into which the entire programme was being plunged by the dangerous jealousies of his rivals, he abandoned all reserve.

"How can they be so blind?" he cried. "They attack me because I represent Hitler, whom they dare not attack, helpless though he is. If they eliminate me, they move one step nearer the top. But they forget that they too represent Hitler, and that even he merely represents something larger than any of us-a moral duty, a German destiny of which we are only the humble servants!"

In his opinion, our personal aims as individuals were utterly unimportant beside the great common aim of realizing the Nazi ideals. Those ideals were largely his own philosophy, and first formulated by him-yet he declared that to advance them, he would willingly withdraw from the active fight, if his conscience could consent to such an easy way out.

"But my heart is with the movement," he said, "and I cannot see it taken over by opportunists whose purpose is to use Germany, rather than to serve her. As long as I can, I intend to stand out against their attempts to pervert the function of our Party."

We talked frankly for a long time. When I left at breakfast-time my mind was made up. I would stand by Rosenberg, if Party quarrels went so far that it became necessary to choose sides. Or rather, not sides, but levels, for it was clear that he stood for the higher aims of the Nazi movement, the aims which were ethically justified, noble in purpose and worthy of adherence. His enemies, on the other hand, embodied the materialistic means by which those aims had to be achieved in this materialistic world, and had at best only slight claim to respect-absolutely none if they defeated their usefulness by wrenching their blind force free from Rosenberg's guiding spirit. Indeed, if their effort succeeded, they might become a serious danger to the Nazi movement, and to all Germany-if not to the world as well.

I shared Rosenberg's horror in contemplating the infant Frankenstein which we had fathered, and resolved that to the limits of my power I would work to re-establish within the Party the balance which it had lost. The prospect that the inner circle of Hitler's aides might really come to a lasting separation, with the lower elements triumphing and the Party becoming a sort of monster, brawny and brutal and soulless, filled me with dread.

In this crisis, instinctively I turned toward Hitler for a clarification of the issues. He was allowed to have visitors at Landsberg, but it took a week or so of red-tape to get a visiting permit. I applied at once, and passed the days of waiting by making a closer scrutiny of the Munich imbroglio. Each side was trying to drum up allies. Though my sympathy was already pledged to Rosenberg and also to Gregor Strasser, I listened to the other group, also, to gather information about their plans. Believing me still on the fence, they wheedled and flattered me to get me to jump their way.

Hitler was the one man with power to set things straight; yet he never so much as lifted his little finger or spoke one word. At first I imagined he must be ignorant of conditions, because of his isolation. Not until Hitler and I talked together for a full hour did I realize the error of this supposition, and how much he had deliberately fostered, or at least tolerated, the Party division.

This conversation with Hitler came a few days later. For me, the occasion was nearly as memorable as our first talk together, because it too marked a milestone: it was the first time I appraised him with wide-open eyes, judging him with my mind instead of my heart. I felt that I had the right to do so. In 1922, when he admitted me to the inner ranks of the little Nazi Party, I could offer him nothing in exchange except my lostness, my deep unrest, my willingness to help hew a path in the direction he pointed out. He gained an eager disciple, while I gained a cause my heart could love and serve.

But things were different by 1924. Experience had come to me, experience not always palatable, for though prison, bankruptcy, and danger, insecurity at home and abuse abroad, may be good lessons, they are not pleasant. I had spent good spiritual coin for my political long pants, and I meant to wear them like a man. I no longer asked to be led by the hand, or feared being stood in the corner for asking questions out of turn. On the other hand, I had no desire to caper ahead of the Nazi procession. All I wanted was to get intelligent marching orders from Hitler, and to follow where he guided-but he must not shirk the responsibility of guidance. If he failed to insist on his leadership, or if it seemed possible that he was leading us up a blind alley or down a wrong road, then by virtue of the very lessons he had taught me, I was bound to question his reasons.

So, bewildered by the Party's discord, I travelled down to Landsberg to ask the Fuehrer how the danger could best be dispelled. Instead of finding a solution, I added new doubts and difficulties to the problem. For I learned that Hitler, always a contradictory character, was going through a new change; he was shifting, so to speak, from the true north of idealism to the magnetic north of realism. But because the process was not yet complete, it was hard to put my finger on the deviation, and though it troubled me, it was simply as a passing thing.

True, during the time we were together, I felt that his halo had lost a little of its brightness; but it was easy to believe that it was merely tarnished by the prison air. The change was subtly altering him, but it was not to conquer him easily or soon. Its full results would not appear until later.

However, all this is ahead of my story.

An hour by train brought me to the ancient fortress of Landsberg, a charming little city, dreaming in baroque on the River Lech. After a short walk through the pleasant country-side I saw large modern buildings surrounded by stone walls, which looked more like a sanatorium than a fortress prison. The little hills which it crowned were bowered in flowers and trees. A charming landscape for a picnic or a painting, but .not prison-like. The whole atmosphere of the place, even when I reached the gates, was inviting. A genial guard took me in tow, chatting pleasantly about Herr Hitler as he led me toward the wing where the 'prisoner of honour' was housed. It seemed as if man, stone, and nature had mellowed with warmth and respect for the famous malefactor.

Somewhere beyond the window of the waiting-room, the warder told me, lay an open-air gymnasium for the prisoners. While I was peering out for a glimpse of them, the door behind me opened. I turned. There stood Hitler.

He was wearing leather shorts and a Tyrolean jacket, his shirt open at the throat.

His cheeks glowed with healthy red, and his eyes shone; the fire-eater had not been quenched by his time-serving. On the contrary, he looked better physically, and seemed happier than I had ever seen .him. Landsberg had done him a world of good!

He greeted me with the hearty air of a host receiving a guest. Gone from his manner was the nervous intensity which formerly had been his most unpleasant characteristic. Although he appeared calmer and more certain of himself.

A warder accompanied him, a jolly fellow with friendly eyes. When we sat down at the table to talk, the keeper sat also, to comply with the rules; but he chose a chair almost out of ear-shot and kept beaming indulgently on his favourite prisoner, looking more Santa Claus than Cerberus.

Hitler's mode of durance vile was so obviously the poetic ideal, so contrary to my own prison-life, that I was somewhat taken aback. Phrases of sympathy were scarcely in order as a prologue for this interview; so I began by congratulating him on his triumphant good health.

"Yes, I couldn't be feeling better," he laughed, showing his old sense of humour. "This is the first good rest I've ever enjoyed."

He told me of his large sunny, comfortable room. The guards, he said, treated him with every possible consideration, and every day he received a sheaf of heartening letters from faithful friends.

"No doubt this is the first time you ever led a regular life," I said.

This picture he sketched of a typical prison day did not strike me as being particularly confining. The prisoners arose at six, breakfasted at seven, and walked in the garden from eight until ten. Lunch with his fellow-prisoners (some additional twenty members of the unsuccessful coup), with Hitler presiding, sounded more like a social affair. In the afternoon one prisoner served tea to the others in their cells. Before and after the six o'clock supper, which was also served in their cells, they were again free to exercise in the garden for an hour or so. Lights-out sounded at ten for all prisoners except Hitler. He was permitted to read or work until midnight or longer. Considering the hectic tempo of the life he had been leading, this sojourn in prison was exactly what Hitler needed. It gave him time to rest, to think, and to plan.

But I was not spending the week-end at Landsberg. Time pressed, and I tried to switch him into more serious channels. I have spoken before of his genius for dismissing topics which he does not wish to discuss. Time after time during this talk he availed himself of it, ending further conversation as effectively as though he had suddenly darkened a room where deaf-mutes were talking on their fingers. I noticed that he barred, in particular, any reminder of the putsch, and any question concerning his policy toward the Party schism.

The putsch was water under the bridge, an unprofitable subject except in so far as it provided a lesson in Party procedure for the future. Also, Hitler was plainly embarrassed, as I was, by the memory of our intimate meeting on the Poestlingberg, when we had mutually vowed so many things which never came to pass. Gladly I eschewed the subject as too delicate. But the lesson it taught was another matter, which Hitler himself took up.

"From now on," he said, "we must follow a new line ,of action. It is best to attempt no large reorganization until I am freed, which may be a matter of months rather than of years."

I must have looked at him somewhat incredulously.

" Oh, yes," he continued, "I am not going to stay here much longer. When I resume active work it will be necessary to pursue a new policy. Instead of working to achieve power by an armed coup, we shall have to hold our noses and enter the Reichstag against the Catholic and Marxist deputies. If out-voting them takes longer than out-shooting them, at least the results will be guaranteed by their own Constitution! Any lawful process is slow. But already, as you know, we have thirty-two Reichstag deputies under this new programme, and are the second largest Party in the Bavarian Landtag-diet. Sooner or later we shall have a majority - and after that, Germany. I am convinced this is our best line of action, now that conditions in the country have changed so radically."

I was not a little surprised to hear the Fuehrer talking this way. Only a few weeks earlier he had voiced through Esser and Streicher his violent opposition to any participation in the May elections, and had raged when Party members had entered as candidates despite his ban. I could not then see into Hitler's mind. Twelve years of hindsight, however, are better than one flash of clairvoyance.

Leaving Hitler for the moment still seated across the table in Landsberg, let me try to set forth his attitude at that time as I understand it now.

The unexpected success in the elections undoubtedly had swayed him. Probably more important was the fact that conditions had indeed altered. Most immediate and far-reaching, of the changes was the end of the inflation, which stopped just short of final chaos a few days after the putsch. Germany's new coin, the gold Renten mark, proved to be stable; but the bankers, instead of winning public thanks for terminating the financial madness, became more than ever the target of abuse. It was a common saying that if the money-masters could stop the inflation practically overnight, they must have been responsible for it originally, and certainly were guilty of having permitted it to go on so long.

Whereas the worthless paper money had been something to pass along to the next victim as fast as possible, the good, new, gold money was scarce and valuable. Those who could lay hands on it held on, and not enough currency entered circulation to fill the arteries of commerce. Banks officially charged interest of 12 or 15 per cent, private loans being even more exorbitant. Fury against the bankers was proportionate.

On the other hand, the sudden stabilization ended the general panic, and with it the illusory solidarity of the people. The Haves and the Have-nots, renouncing the loose union into which their common plight had forced them, now resumed their habitual antagonism. Thus, while the anti-capitalist sentiment which Hitler had orchestrated was intensified in some quarters, better economic conditions were robbing the tune of its mass appeal, and he could no longer count on wooing the mob with it. As for the desperate remedies by which he had proposed to cure the other national ills, it was best for a while to advocate less violent measures. As long as the crisis had remained desperate, a great part of the nation had endorsed direct action; but now that the danger appeared less imminent, he would find only scattered support.

Moreover, on account of his absence from the platform and the Party's dissolution through official decree, there could be no hope of renewing the struggle along the old lines. Though Hitler's well-publicized forensics at the court trial had repaired most of the damage, Nazi prestige had suffered after the putsch, the National Socialist German Workers' Party remained under a legal ban. Technically it was dead as a door-nail, beyond resurrection.

The situation was less discouraging than it sounds, however. Max Amann had kept his private publishing concern when the Nazi offices were dismantled by the police. There a Party headquarters had been set up again. No need to organize a new staff; the old staff would serve well enough. And the former members, as many as could be reached since our Party records had been destroyed, would no doubt renew their allegiance when they learned that the old Party programme was to be renovated, whitewashed, and used over again.

Hitler had scarcely reached Landsberg before the Party, using these subterfuges, began to creep back into the political arena, which was still damp with the blood of sixteen Nazi dead. But having failed to storm the barricades, the Party was altering its tactics and was commencing to tunnel into the voting booths. The sixteen martyrs might come in handy later on; but the general setback which accompanied martyrdom was too great a risk to run again. Peaceful means were more expedient.

As a first move, Gregor Strasser and Rosenberg formed an alliance with Albrecht von Graefe, leader of the northern German Folkic Liberty Party, of which Count Reventlow was the most prominent member. The Nazi Party being dissolved, this combination was needed to permit Nazis to participate in the coming Reichstag elections. Before the merger, the Protestant North had proceeded separately under Graefe for aims similar to Hitler's in the Catholic South, and neither leader had been exactly triumphant. Uniting, and absorbing a number of smaller folkic groups, they worked together under the new name of 'Nationalsozialistische Deutsche Freiheits Bewegung,' and appeared before the public as a legal body with a regular political platform, represented by candidates for election, who courted the enfranchised citizens for votes. The case was not unlike that in Die Meistersinger, where the hero, having once failed to wed the maid, decides to win her according to the rules.

Before my return from America the reorganized Nazis had already been tested in their first election campaign, meeting with such unforeseen success that the wisdom of the new procedure was apparent-as a political step to power, that is. The election was held on 4 May. The middle class and the peasantry, still smarting from the inflation and the Ruhr invasion, and much impressed by the Hitler-Ludendorff trial, cast nearly two million votes (out of a total vote of over 29 million) for the new group, which elected 32 representatives out of 472, among them Ludendorff, Roehm, Frick, and Graefe. Nazis thereupon took seats in the Reichstag among the Communists, Socialists, Jews, and Catholics, not to deliberate solemnly with these colleagues concerning the welfare of the Weimar Republic, but to undermine it from within.

This new departure in Nazi procedure, this radical change from violent anti-parliamentarianism to practical participation, deserves such long mention because it truly marked the turning-point for the Party. From then on our way lay sharply up-and down. It was the beginning from which rose the whole present Nazi power in Germany. But it also revealed Hitler as a leader who could shift overnight if his personal interests seemed to demand it. He first definitely opposed participation in the elections, not so much because he feared for the Nazi principles and foresaw possible corruption of Nazi deputies, but because he feared for his own position as the supreme leader of the Party. His own status as an Austrian precluded his entering the Reichstag elections. Any Nazi deputy enjoying immunity and financial independence[2] might threaten Hitler's authority if he were not complete master of the Party machine which appointed the candidates and assured their election. So long as he was in prison, he could not exercise, let alone maintain, sole authority over a party which was in process of reorganization and reorientation, exposed to new influences under altered conditions.

That was why Hitler did not desire the success of the new combination. He knew too well how quickly the world forgets, and that it would be next to impossible for him to resume his old supreme leadership if his absence were to last too long, while other leaders were successfully rebuilding a new party. Hence, as it was obvious that Esser and Streicher would have little or nothing to say in the new combination, Hitler found in them willing and effective tools for sabotaging the reconstruction work until his release.

A new course? Yes, the legal course via the parliament. Under the circumstances, it really seemed the only feasible way to power. The May election had shown its

---

2 *The income of a deputy, including a first-class ticket for German railways all over the Reich, made him practically independent of the Party treasury.*

possibilities. Very well then, let it proceed-but only with Hitler at the helm of a new National Socialist Workers' Party, rebuilt by him under his sole and supreme leadership.

Needless to say, I was not seer enough to foresee the distant results of the new trend when Hitler and I discussed the situation at Landsberg. Nor was I daring enough to voice the serious apprehensions half-awakened by the obvious change in Hitler himself. Every sign warned me that he was still true to his old character in at least one trait, the most unfortunate one of all, which in time served to insulate him from those very colleagues whose counsel he most needed.

Hitler was determined to dominate. He domineered shrilly, violently, and usually with success. Browbeaten as a child, under-privileged as a youth, he had to raise his voice against the world to lift himself above the mob; and once the process was begun, it fed upon itself, until he was complete master of the rhetoric of abuse. His public speeches owed their impassioned power less to intellectual content than to the strident force of the invective with which he clothed his phrases. But neither the Jews nor the Versailles Treaty nor any of his political bugbears had ever called forth his supreme denunciation; that was reserved for friends and Party members who had lapsed from grace. I had never been the object of this unpleasantness, but I had seen him throw the full diapason of his wrath into the ears of someone who had thwarted him or had prodded him into anger. So I steered clear of all controversy during my talk at Landsberg.

I reported the failure of the American mission, but he was not cast down by that. Indeed, he was so confident of final victory that my own misgivings were dispelled, for his mood was contagious. Just as his anger could blast a listener, so could his good-humour persuade. The voice which eventually talked the German nation into surrendering its liberties easily talked me into forgetting the purpose of my visit, and in the end I found myself back at the gates of the fortress without having mentioned the precarious state of the Party. He gave me an inscribed photograph, the first ever made of him as a political leader. After promising to call again soon, I returned to Munich, lulled into thinking that affairs might not be so bad after all.

But things in Munich went from bad to worse. Some drastic solution was necessary. Conferences which followed between Hitler, Rosenberg, myself, and others did not move the leader to make a decision which would end the impossible hostility among his followers. Just as sympathetically as he listened to one side he listened to the other. Both factions continued to speak in his name, and the voice of authority was not heard.

To suppose that Hitler, behind prison walls, may have been to some extent ignorant of conditions outside is to be unjust to his political genius. A more reasonable supposition is that which I have already indicated: he was deliberately fostering the schism in order to keep the whip-hand over the Party. Trusting nobody but himself, he may well have feared to lose control if he delegated more power to one group than to the other. Two factions bickering together would retard Party progress, which was unfortunate; but one faction triumphant could destroy him- and whether for Germany's sake or for his own, Hitler was governed by a colossal will to survive and advance.

Naturally, Hitler's equivocation, which to most of us was incomprehensible and distasteful, was especially awkward for Ludendorff, who since the Reichstag election had made every effort to hold the various groups together under the new name, the National Socialist German Liberty movement. As Hitler doubtless desired, this combination of rival elements which might have been welded into an effective instrument failed to achieve real unity. Many of the activists, especially among the Nazis, did not understand and did not wish to accept the change from an uncompromising strong-arm policy to a quibbling system of parliamentary tactics. Hitherto the legitimate channels to power had been spurned and condemned by the Nazis, who saw how leaders on every side were corrupted by the limitations, as well as the rewards, of the vote system. Already they were justly complaining that they had been tricked in their first electoral campaign. Out of the thirty-two folkic deputies, only twelve were avowed Nazis, whereas an overwhelming majority of the folkic votes had been cast by Nazis.

Moreover, religious questions deepened the rift between the groups. Hitler, no matter how vehemently he had denounced political clericalism, had always carefully distinguished between the temporal and spiritual spheres, and had never attacked the Catholic faith. But now the Protestant North Germans who had entered the movement with Graefe were driving the alliance into a fight against the Catholic Church. In as much as Munich and South Germany generally, the stronghold of folkic instinct, were Catholic, the result was a regional split, widened by the fact that the majority of Graefe's followers belonged to the more educated bourgeois class, and were therefore suspicious of the radical socialist programme of the Nazis. The fact that a minority preferred Hitler's programme only intensified the antagonisms, which now occupied their spokesmen's attention to the exclusion of more important things. The leaders of the Northern groups were in most cases bourgeois parliamentarians who had deserted the nationalist Party. They were frightened by the growing anti-capitalist sentiment, which they denounced as leading toward ' National Bolshevism.' Their denunciation proved a boomerang, for soon all their social-minded followers went over .to the Nazis, who resented the Bolshevik label but welcomed the recruits.

In short, dissensions throughout the folkic movement had reached such bitterness that the movement was paralysed. Some co-ordinating authority had to be established-with or without the consent of Hitler. Otherwise, things would drift until his release; or they might go to pieces entirely before that time, for no one knew when Hitler would be free again. His parole depended on the generosity-or stupidity-of his enemies.

When I went to Hitler again for a decision on this situation, he sidestepped the issue entirely, as he had done already with Rosenberg and Gregor Strasser. He neither did nor said anything which could clarify the issue. Though he was fully informed about the danger, he remained stubbornly evasive. After several such fruitless conferences, we were forced to acknowledge that Hitler was prepared to risk everything rather than delegate a portion of his personal authority while he remained confined. .

Hitler habitually rationalizes his choices. It is likely that, being faced with a distasteful choice in this case, he arrived at the lofty conclusion that there was no choice-that being the one man entrusted by destiny with the salvation of Germany he had no moral right to shift his responsibility to deputy saviours. But whatever the motive, the practical effect of his vacillation was obvious. Instead of bringing order out of the confusion, he deliberately increased it, and among his followers none was able to rise up to challenge or usurp his power.

As time went on, Hitler's shilly-shally became more and more apparent, as did his unmistakable preference for the demagogues Esser and Streicher, who could be counted on to tear down whatever influence Ludendorff or Graefe, Rosenberg or Strasser managed to build up. Esser's continual abuse of Rosenberg grew more outrageous with each attack. Rosenberg seriously thought of forcing the issue by taking the matter into court. However, in the interest of the Party, he was reluctant to take this step. In the long run it would have served the Party and his own interest better if he had acted at that time, using all means to free the Party of unworthy elements. A strong attitude, taken publicly, would have forced Hitler to declare his own attitude unequivocally. In opposing men of the calibre of Esser and Streicher, it was suicidal to handle affairs with kid gloves, for they always wore brass knuckles.

It was typical of Esser's ethics that, finding himself in a tight place where he was condemned from many sides, he once threatened publication of compromising Party material in a well-known Jewish paper.

Unfortunately, these intrigues and vicious calumnies were known to our enemies, who looked with gusto at the spectacle of brotherly assassination which raged not only among the Nazis, but among all the folkic groups. It goes without saying that they exploited this state of affairs to the limit in order to damage the cause.

As for Streicher and Amann, it is only fair to say that their attitude was dictated not by petty, selfish ambition, but by fanatic devotion to Hitler, whom both regarded as the only true prophet. This fervent conviction and their limitations of experience, made them unbearable fellows at times and created very unpleasant situations. Yet Amann's position as holder of the money-bag and as Hitler's most intimate confidant in financial matters was unassailable, just as Streicher's importance as unchallenged leader of the Nazi stronghold in Nuremberg and Franken, second only to Munich and Lower-Bavaria, was such that he could not be ousted. Amann's energy, initiative, and grit were priceless qualities in dangerous times, and he deserves great credit for keeping the Party's finances in order under most harassing difficulties. And despite Streicher's shortcomings, he deserved Hitler's esteem for conquering and holding his domain for the Fuehrer at the sacrifice of his own comfort and security. No Nazi in responsible position suffered so many jail sentences and so much personal persecution as did Streicher in Nuremberg, which indeed was infested by Jews. However stupid Hitler's toleration of Streicher's psychopathic zeal may seem, however cruel and inexcusable Streicher's hatred and brutal treatment of the Jews, it must not be forgotten that the Jews themselves did much to provoke his wrath. .

During these days of strife, I saw Rosenberg almost daily, and I also came into close contact with Gregor Strasser and Captain Ernst Roehm, who were unswervingly loyal to the ideals which Hitler had proclaimed up to this time. For me, these men and Dr. Frick now composed the positive and constructive element of the Party. Two of them I should like to endow, however feebly with life in these pages; they live as vividly in my mind as they must live in Hitler's conscience. They are dead men now, murdered three years ago as I write.

Gregor Strasser's background shows some similarity to Hitler's. Three years younger than the Fuehrer, he was born in a Catholic-Bavarian district, south of the Danube. His father, like Hitler's was a petty official. A war volunteer like Hitler, Gregor Strasser was promoted to a lieutenancy, and decorated for valour with the Iron Cross, First Class. After the war he fought under General von Epp, the present Governor of Bavaria, against the Munich Soviet Republic in May 1919. He married in 1920 and set up his own business as an apothecary in Landshut. There he organized the war veterans of the town into the well-armed' Batallion Landshut.' Late in 1920 he heard of Hitler and cast in his lot with him. Hitler appointed Strasser S A leader and district leader of the Nazi Party for Lower-Bavaria. At the time of the Beer Hall Putsch he was in Munich, holding his men in readiness to fight. Arrested for that, he was later released as a result of his election to the Bavarian Landtag. He was the first Nazi to make a speech in a German parliament.

The first time I saw much of Strasser was in May of that same year, when he was still a young man. He seemed most genuine and of almost touching simplicity and modesty. I remember riding with him in a train from Munich to Nuremberg one day in 1924. He was an odd sight, this big man in his home-made breeches, black woollen stockings, and heavy shoes, with a little Tyrolean hat perched like a plate atop his head, completely out of harmony with his broad and massive features. But at the same time he impressed me with his calm strength, his pithy humour, and robust health, suggesting at once something oaken and powerful. His was a strong personality which developed rapidly. I was surprised at the power of his speech, when a few weeks later, for the first time, I heard him addressing a meeting in a voice like the roar of a lion. Yet he never lost that Bavarian 'Gemuet-lichkeit,' blended with the coarseness of a bear.

But next to Hitler, the man most impressive to me at that time was Captain Roehm, whose life reads like a novel. Part of it he wrote himself, in his 'Story of a Rebel'-Die Geschichte eines Hochverraeters, unobtainable in Nazi Germany today.

'On 23 July 1906 I became a soldier.' This day seemed to him to mark the birth of his conscious life; apparently the date of his physical birth, 28 November 1887 was unimportant, I consider the world, consciously, from a one-sided viewpoint, that of a soldier,' is another of his characteristic utterances.

The son of a railway official, he went into the war a lieutenant and emerged a captain, after distinguishing himself in the fighting line and as a staff officer. In 1919 he was almost arrested when he joined Franz von Epp's then illegal Frei-Korps. With von Epp, he marched against Red Munich, and in March 1920 he aided in the suppression of the Communist insurrection in the Ruhr. He often jeopardized his military position by his participation in extra-legal activities, but continued to hold his post until he resigned in the summer of 1923.

The folkic and in fact the whole Nationalist movement after the November revolution of 1918 is inconceivable without Roehm, without his practical and successful activity in organizing and doing things. He was a brilliant leader of men, an excellent officer, fearless and straightforward. His massive, round head, battle-scarred and patched, looked like something hammered from rock. He was the living image of war itself, in contrast to his polished manner and exceptional and instinctive courtesy. That, with his naturalness, diplomatic tact, and savoir faire distinguished him from leading Nazis, then and afterwards, who for the most part were boorish and arrogant, or were bullies. For all his one-sided military mind, he was a passionate politician, having, for a soldier, a rare intelligence and understanding for politics. I liked his keen, open gaze and his firm handclasp.

One of Hitler's first backers, Roehm was of decisive importance to the Party, finding money, arms, and men at the most critical times. Without him, the Fuehrer could never have dared the Beer Hall Putsch, could never have reached the Chancellorship.

Still on parole for his part in the putsch, Roehm had received from Hitler full authority to reorganize the scattered remnants of the Kampfbund, an absolute carte blanche to carry out on his own responsibility this most delicate of tasks. Starting over again from the beginning, he recruited new troops from the dispersed ranks, and gradually whipped them into a new semi-military organization called the 'Frontbann.' Aside from the political difficulties he encountered, it was uphill work to regain the confidence of men who had our disastrous defeat fresh in mind. Roehm could not be everywhere at once; so he asked me to work for him as I travelled through Germany.[3] My part was to persuade the men and the groups with whom I came in contact that the Nazi fight had not collapsed but was still going on.

Armed with papers to show that I spoke for the men in authority, I carried the message to one city after another, even into Berlin. It was a journey filled with secret meetings, with conspiracies, promises, and new hopes. Wherever I could, I got in touch with the old group leaders, endeavouring to rouse their enthusiasm anew, and to bind their allegiance again to the Nazis. Many of the men with whom I conferred were veritable condottieri, such as Captain von Heydebreck and Edmund Heines. Almost without exception they resumed Roehm's work eagerly, only too glad to be busy again at the secret military work without which they found life wearisome.

This end of the movement, handled with Roehm's usual thoroughness, began to prosper. Within the political section, however, difficulties continued to multiply. The break-up of the Party seemed imminent. The situation tempted disloyal, ambitious men or folkic cranks to try to bring the Party under their own control, or to take their followers with them into other parties. Contrasts of a theoretical and tactical nature became more and more apparent, dividing even the loyalists into ineffectual minorities. There seemed no possible solution for these troubles other than quick and definite action to centralize the authority again. Hitler still held the authority, but had steadily refused to take a clear stand or to say which one of the quarrelling groups really represented his authority.

The only course left for us was to face him with an accomplished fact. From then until now, that has been the only way to deal with him. And even in those days it was an unpleasant course.

While Roehm, Rosenberg, and Strasser shared my opinion that there was little time to lose, none of them was ready· to take the first step in defiance of Hitler's indecision. Since my own work had been chiefly in the foreign field, my name carried no weight among the general Party following, and it was impossible for me to act personally in this crisis. But I could try to bring others to act in a ' palace plot.'

Sure of Roehm's co-operation, I finally succeeded in convincing Rosenberg and Strasser that we must act as a group. Strasser, with Rosenberg assenting, agreed to take over the authority while Hitler was in prison. At a meeting in Munich, Strasser and Rosenberg declared our intention in unmistakable terms to the most important men of the interested groups, among whom were Dr. Frick, Dr. Glaser, Dr. Buttmann, who led the Nazi bloc in the Bavarian Congress, and Captain Wilhelm Weiss, Ludendorff's chief spokesman. The meeting endorsed the idea in principle, leaving its execution up to Strasser. Unfortunately, he allowed the session to close without announcing definite procedure to force the issue.

But neither of the men on whom the plan depended, was quite courageous

_____

3 *His carte-tie-visite, on which was inscribed a message authorizing me to speak in his behalf, is reproduced in the Appendix.*

enough actually to carry the plan to a point from which there could be no retreat. The obvious first step, a good housecleaning and airing of Party head¬quarters right there in Munich, was never taken. Strasser, not yet the lion that he later became, deferred to Rosenberg, and Rosenberg was no match for the situation. The same scruples that set him above his enemies made him impotent to deal with them. Never so much a man of action as a man of thought, he now showed himself a Hamlet, procrastinating while he weighed the issues. But the man to be removed was not the sort of man who could be thought out of the Party; he had to be kicked out, and when he felt the boot, he would retaliate with public howls, which Rosenberg dreaded. So nothing was done.

Nor was anything ever done. Hitler, however selfish his motive, was probably not guilty of poor judgment when he refused to trust his powers to subordinates. It almost seemed as if he alone were fitted by temperament to wield real power, to risk positive action, to face difficulties. Rosenberg, far his superior intellectually, was timid in the face of such a situation as this; and so no amendment was made in the Party's affairs. They simply went from bad to worse. And Hitler spoke no word to set them straight.

Two Hitlers. . . .

Heresy, I would have called the accusation six months before; but now I began to feel that Lossow had really pressed close to the truth. By an ironic quirk of justice it was the best in the Fuehrer which withered after the trial, while the less worthy traits flourished.

Naturally, I did not comprehend the change at that time as easily as I phrase it now. Sympathy for Hitler's plight, loyalty to his cause, and the long-time habit of trusting his motives, all counted heavily in the scales even while I was first daring to weigh him. Still I could not quite escape the conviction that Hitler assayed lighter than fine metal should. It was as though the acid test of the last few months had revealed unsuspected dross in the sterling Leader. I could see it-but I would not see it. And whether I would or would not, eventually I had to.

XIV

CHRISTMAS STORY

In the course of the summer, an international anti-Jewish congress was held in Paris and I went to it as the German delegate. Organized by a former Austrian diplomat, Georg de Pottere, it drew delegates from the principal European countries but none from the United States. The main meeting was presided over by a priest of the Catholic Church, and was held in the rectory. Thus did the Roman Catholic Church have the distinction of sponsoring the first international anti-Jewish gathering in history.

Urbain Gohier, the pre-eminent French anti-Jew, was not even invited, for as a Protestant he did not see eye to eye with the said priest's solution of the Jewish question. When I called on him, he remarked about it sarcastically, and showed me the priest's French edition of the famous Protocols of Zion, which the good priest concluded with an affirmation that the only salvation from Judah was a return to the bosom of the Church. To hasten this outcome, the dignitary was fighting the Jews and the Freemasons by editing the Revue Internationale des Societes Secretes.

This meeting had been called to organize a White Internationale to co-operate in fighting world Bolshevism, Free-masonry, and Jewry. Nothing came of it except a second conference at Easter 1925, in Salzburg, which I attended with Rosenberg. Nothing whatsoever came of the second meeting.

However, the Paris trip yielded at least one concrete result-the publication of a much-discussed booklet, Deux Jours Chez Ludendorff, by Pierre Dominique, the nom de plume of a well known contributor to various French newspapers, who at that time was Right rather than Left, in contrast to his later activities. I was introduced to him by a recommended and trustworthy person, but I did not know until later that he was really a Dr. Luechini and that he was a psychiatrist by profession. Had I known, I should have been extremely cautious, for I cannot get rid of a certain suspicion against psychiatrists: they seem to believe everybody crazy but themselves.

The booklet gave, in dialogue form, a generally fair and intelligent interpretation of the German situation, with particular emphasis on the Nazi movement, and a summary of what German developments after a Nazi victory would mean for France. The name of Ludendorff was used in the title because of its publicity value, whereas the book really dealt at considerable length with Nazism and with Hitler as a political leader. The first study of the subject to appear anywhere outside Germany, it was the product of a close collaboration between Dominique and me.

Whatever aspect of my work was to blame I cannot say, but something happened that cut short my stay in France. It was after I had returned to Paris from London, where Tibor von Eckhardt and I had gone straight from the Congress to work for the cause.

One afternoon I went as usual to buy papers at a kiosk not far from my hotel.

Scanning the headlines, I had suddenly the feeling of being watched. Raising my eyes casually, I caught the gaze of what looked like a typical French detective, standing on the other side of the kiosk.

To make sure, I tucked the papers under one arm and, lightly swinging my stick, sauntered down the rue St. Honore. Crossing the rue Cambon, I saw my man following me slowly.

I went into a bistro for a drink, to decide what I was going to do with my shadow. When I emerged from the bar with a plan in mind, he was idling behind a car. Jumping into a passing taxi, I drove to the Place de la Concorde, back along the rue de Rivoli, and stopped at the Hotel Meurice, which I had picked because it had two exits.

The friend who lived there was not in. So I took a cup of tea alone, tried a telephone connection-always a hateful undertaking in Paris-wrote a petit bleu, and, when it was getting dark, ventured out again, choosing the exit to the colonnades on the rue de Rivoli, confident that I had lost my 'tec. It gave me a little shock to discover him behind a pillar, talking to a chauffeur, with his eyes on me. So I walked a few blocks, now deeply disturbed. Wheeling suddenly round, I almost collided with the pest, but he passed me with the most unconcerned expression in the world.

Jumping again into a taxi, I set off towards the Champs-Elysees, hoping to lose myself in the heavy before-dinner traffic. But no! In a traffic stop at the Rond Point, just at the moment when the avenue was lighted as by a magic wand, another antique red taxi edged up slowly almost abreast of my old hack. Inside it was the little French 'tec, huddled behind a newspaper. Now our chauffeurs began to talk to each other. I couldn't hear what they said, but my suspicion was soon confirmed. I told my driver to hurry, and while he was weaving through a never-ending stream of cars, I observed him swinging his door now and again, as though he were indicating his position.

Convinced by now that my pursuer was a plain-clothes man from the Surete, and that the fool apparently still believed I had not noticed him, I made up my mind to shake him at least temporarily. Later in the evening I was to have an interesting meeting with some French Fascists and White Russians, and I didn't intend to miss it.

Circling the Etoile, we raced down the beautiful Avenue du-Bois-de-Boulogne, which ends at the Porte Dauphine, one of the entrances to the Bois. Here, at this wide opening, I ordered the driver to turn and go back the way he had come. I wanted definite proof that the bull was following me: he would have to turn right under my eyes.

He turned.

On both sides of the Champs-Elysees between the Rond Point and the Place de la Concorde, there are restaurants and music-halls scattered among the trees of a lovely park. This would be a good place to get rid of the fly. Here it would take him quite a while to get in touch with headquarters for new orders, and I would gain an advantage of at least twenty-five or thirty minutes.

The driver pulled up short on my order, and I stepped out.

I paid the fare with an eye on my friend, whose taxi had stopped with a shrieking of brakes some thirty yards behind me. On the sidewalk between us stood a French agent de police, cape over shoulder and white baton in hand. First I took a few steps away, then turned and walked right up to the stocky little man, who was now within a few yards of the policeman. I grasped the fellow by the arm. He began an indignant protest, but I told him to shut up and called to the officer.

"This man," I said, "has been pestering me for three hours, following my every step. He's either from the Surete or a 'louche personage.' Please inquire into his identity. I'm all right-here's my passport."

But the guardian of the peace shrugged his shoulders-evidently these people have a way of signalling each other-and said to me, like a real diplomat: "Cher monsieur, what would you have me do? You say one thing, and this gentleman another. You say yourself that he hasn't openly molested you, and he even denies even having noticed you. I don't see what I can do in this matter."

But I had gained my breathing-spell. Hailing another taxi, I said to the little one: "If you must glue your nose to my behind, please don't do it so obviously." As I taxied away, I saw him walking rather meekly down the street.

Certain that I had been watched for the past two or three days, I hurried to my hotel to prepare myself for the inevitable little visit next morning. They usually knock at your door between six and seven.

Not that I had any secret documents revealing sinister plans. But there were a few papers, addresses, and letters, for example the protocol of the international anti-Semitic meeting, which if found might provoke embarrassing questions, and it seemed wise to secrete them elsewhere. I called the valet who served Tibor ven Eckhardt and told him to have a bottle of 'cognac fine' at hand and to be ready at my summons early next morning to serve breakfast for three. Less than half an hour after my encounter with the detective I was riding through the streets again, unmolested this time, with my papers safe in a brief-case.

I had a frugal but animated dinner with my interesting friends, seeking and giving information, and debating matters of mutual interest. Among them I vaguely recall General Koutiepoff, who later assumed the leadership of the White Russians and then disappeared mysteriously in broad daylight from a street in Paris, an alleged victim of Moscow's OGPU. There were also a Japanese colonel and another Russian general, the latter a delegate from the famous Ataman Semenoff, who was married to a Mongolian princess and at that time was still a protégé of Japan and the White Russian hope in the Far East.

From there I drove to the Bar des Artistes to meet a lovely American friend, a dancer who moved her shapely limbs through a special number in one of the music-halls. She was all excited when I told her my little story, and only too willing to hide my brief-case in her swanky cabriolet, which carried us within two blocks of my hotel. I stepped out alone; she was to follow later.

As I had expected, the hotel was being watched again; another 'tec slouched in a doorway across the street. But my apartment had not been disturbed, and I resolved to let the morrow take care of its own worries, and not to forgo the agreeable night in prospect.

But it seemed wise to be most circumspect. In the cold, grey dawn there was a discreet exit from my room. Perhaps an hour later, when I was sleeping very soundly, a none too gentle knock made me bounce in my bed. The awakening was cruel, and it took me a while to gather my senses. Then repeated knocking brought me to my feet, wide awake now. The anticipated scene had been thoroughly rehearsed in my mind, and I was determined not to let my good humour desert me.

"La Silrete? Enchante! But come in, mes chers messieurs, you are welcome-sit down, I beg of you. I am at your orders."

My two French 'tecs - there are always two when they get you out of bed at impossible hours - looked at each other in amazement. They were just as short and stocky as my little one of the day before, except that one was considerably rounder than the other and wore an almost human expression on his coarse features. He seemed especially astonished by the warmth of my welcome. "Il est fou-fou-fou!" he said three or four times.

"Cher monsieur," I said gently, "I am not crazy-I am fatigued, extremely fatigued, but I assure you I am not crazy. I was expecting you, that's all."

And I called Jean, the valet. Over a cognac and a hot coffee sitting comfortably round a shaky table, I told them of my yesterday's adventure with their colleague. Within fifteen minutes we were friends. 'Fatty' was especially impressed. "C'est epatant-epatant-epatant!" he repeated, gulping cognacs and helping himself to ham and eggs with utmost gusto. The whole scene was so amusing that for the time I forgot my exhaustion and the ordeal ahead. Finally, the other one said, with apologies, that they were required to search the room and take me to the prefecture for questioning.

"I understand-go ahead while I take my bath and dress."

It was past nine o'clock when we arrived at that huge, forbidding, grey old structure, the Prefecture of Police. I knew by then that these two really didn't know much except that I was apparently regarded as politically suspicious. But I had time to slip a fifty-franc note into Fatty's hand, and he assured me that in less than an hour I would sleep again. 'I hope in my own bed,' I thought gloomily, feeling increasingly depressed as we walked down endless grim corridors.

At last I was placed on a bench in an anteroom, and Fatty opened an inner door to report my arrival. He would be back in just a moment, he said. I had to wait more than an hour before I was called in.

The usual routine. Questions... Who? What? Why? I got through that all right. Then came a few queries more embarrassing-about my carte d'identite and the Mexican passport of some years ago, and so forth. But I was apparently explaining even the Mexican adventure to the satisfaction of my inquisitor, a typical, dry, old French official, long-faced and thin, completely bald but adorned with a luxurious beard. Now and then, as if amused, he would blink at me over his pince-nez, which were perched askew on the end of his nose and would jump whenever he curled his nostrils. As I talked, I watched them in fascination, expecting any moment to see them leap clear, but they never did.

My spirits were reviving. Fatty, sitting at the end of the desk, was still regarding me with eyes of indulgent amazement, and presently I couldn't resist breaking off one of my explanations with an aside to him in the words he was so obviously thinking: 'Epatant-epatant-epatant!' That ended the examination. My good Frenchman rose.

"Merci, monsieur, that's enough. I'm satisfied. There are just a few formalities-it won't be long now. Be good enough to wait outside."

I made my best bow and trundled my tired frame to the door, closing it very slowly behind me in the hope of catching a word or two. What I heard was: 'Un type extraordinaire. Il est fou . . . fou . . . fou!'

'Good Lord!' I thought, going hot and cold all over, 'for heaven's sake, not that-anything but that!' - for I was seeing a vision of the Psychiatrische Klinik of Freiburg in 1915. I collapsed on my bench in a moment of sheer panic. Had I overplayed my good humour-had I been too epatant? But I had ample time to get myself in hand again, for the 'won't be long now' was long enough. At last Fatty emerged, led me again through gloomy corridors to another floor, and deposited me in another ante-room. By now it was noon. I was in an agony of fatigue, and desperate at the thought that I might have to sit there until French officialdom had had its lunch. But this time I was called in promptly.

I faced a younger and apparently higher official, no more than forty, clean-shaven and rather elegant for a Frenchman. More tiresome questioning. Growing impatient at length, I threw my policy of good-humour out the window and said half angrily :

"Please, monsieur, have pity on me and let me go. I can't stand it any longer-I must have a bed, and sleep." And then I took the plunge and told him why I needed sleep. My lady, I said, was waiting anxiously for me to appear for lunch. It was now five minutes to one and I was at the other end of Paris. He was a man of the world, and would understand that I couldn't keep a lady waiting. There was no reason for holding me any longer; where was the famous French politesse? "This has all been very interesting-in a way I've enjoyed it-but now I feel that too much is being made of it. It seems to me now as if I were just being handed round as a curiosity-not as the Flying but as the Crazy Dutchman."

He so far forgot his correctness as to laugh at that. But he was not going to let me go without putting me in my place. His voice had an edge when he said:

"You are right-we mustn't make too much of it. But it seems to me that you are yourself inclined to make too much of some things. Your wide range of acquaintances here in Paris-so contradictory. . . . And then all these women to account for your movements. . . " He looked at his notes. " One at the Meurice-a Russian; one at the Continentale-English; another at the Claridge - 'voyons', it's too much. A little more discretion, monsieur; you might easily get yourself entangled in something and find less humorous listeners than you have to-day-and then all your wit would be in vain."

I rejoined with some heat that the results would probably be shocking if some of the most 'respectable' people in France were to be followed day and night, and he had the grace to agree, with a laugh.

"You may go now, but you'd better pay me another visit before you leave Paris."

'What did that imply for me?'-I wondered numbly as I tumbled down the stairs. My taxi was still waiting, the chauffeur swearing, the meter something fantastic.

Thinking back over the inquisition on which the caustic catalogue of my lady friends had been based, I realized that one of them and her respective hotel had escaped notice. Madame X, the wife of a diplomat, was living at the Carlton and was about to start on a motor-trip to the Balkans, by way of Switzerland, to join her husband. The diplomatic immunity of her car would, in case of need, get me smoothly out of France. I stopped at the Carlton long enough to write a note to her; then I went across the street to the Claridge. Ten minutes later I was asleep on an American shoulder.

A few hours' sleep cleared my head. My observed contacts with French Fascists and White Russians, I decided, had been responsible for my trouble. But I must turn my back on France. German-French relations were sharp, and the police would be certain to keep a short rein on me as a German.

Being a Nazi, I could expect no help at all from my Government if I got into serious difficulty.

Next day I left Paris with Madam X in her limousine, en route to Geneva and Lausanne.

In Switzerland I paused long enough to make a French translation of the official

Nazi programme; I had it copied in quantity and arranged for its distribution wherever it promised to do the most good, especially in France and Italy. Then I bolstered up my bank account by liquidating my very last holdings. The amount which this brought in represented my total resources. Where new money was to come from when this was spent I did not know.

From Lausanne I went straight back to Munich.

Things had happened during the months of my absence. Rosenberg had resigned his office as Hitler's deputy. In early July, Hitler had withdrawn from the leadership of the Party, announcing that he would refrain from all political activity until his release-obviously a gesture toward the authorities in the hope of hastening his parole. Ludendorff, after conferring with Hitler, had made a serious effort to unite all the Nazi, folkic, and Nationalist groups under a three-man leadership, consisting of himself, Graefe, and Gregor Strasser, with Ludendorff the public sponsor of the movement. The attempt failed. Some of the Nazi groups in particular openly refused to take orders from Ludendorff. Strasser, who had taken over Rosenberg's duties, adopted a wait-and-see attitude, counting on Hitler's early return. There can be no doubt that Hitler opposed the unification, and made his influence felt through Esser and Streicher, the leaders of the opposition force.

Rosenberg's resignation was a surprise to me. We had been in constant touch, and one of his most recent letters had been a request that I serve as witness in a libel suit against Hermann Esser, which he was determined to press in court. At the last moment apparently he could not face the prospect of the brawl, and going to the other extreme, retired from his exposed position. Instead of narrowing his Party work, however, he had launched a new bi-monthly, Der Weltkampf, dealing with the Jewish question in all countries.

"By the way," I said, when he showed me a copy of his magazine, "you can count on netting some mighty queer fish in your subscription list. Some little anti-Jewish school-master up in Pomerania has put me on his private blacklist and is out gunning for me. Look at this..."

Rosenberg laughed while he read the long letter I handed him. It had been addressed to friends in London, who had given it to me to use as I pleased. The author, a German and a member of the Pan-German Association, a man unknown to me, had seen a letter of mine in the British Guardian and had taken it upon himself to denounce me in the quaintest English-not for my anti-Judaism, with which he was super-abundantly in sympathy, but for my work as an international spy! My old shadow again!

...Ludecke in the last time was chief press man to Hitler. In South Brazil this man is well known. Still better he is known in Buenos Aires. Best known he is in Danzig. He is the same Ludecke who handed over the German secret code to Washington. Ludecke after the war banished from the Argentine because of heavy immoral crimes returned to Germany and wrote for Nationalist papers. This double traitor is now in the intimate circle round Hitler, whose press office he was the chief of. Now he sojourns generally abroad, since he is an old fox. That also Hitler was deluded by this swindler, explains very much. Certainly Ludecke has crept into many guileless national circles, in order to spy upon them. The working of his present Munich actions will only become known, when it is too late. I enclose a clipping from the Deutsche Post of Sao Paulo, Brazil, which says all I am writing here.

The Ludecke of the British Guardian signs himself as Kurt L., the man from South America is known as ... L., but I am perfectly convinced it is the same man. The Milan Panjewish Moscovite-socialistic Avanti shortly reported Ludecke was in Rome, frequents the Mussolini surroundings and stirs up there 'religional and racial unrest.' I send you this warning, beseeching you to be careful. This man is one of the most dangerous existing in this country and the world at large. . .

Rosenberg grew suddenly serious.

"Ludecke, there's one lunacy in this letter which is worth considering. That spy story crops up more and more frequently; why not scotch it now? See how it travels-from here to Brazil, from there back to Germany, only to be sent along to London and God knows where else."

Facetiously I quoted Hitler's maxim: "Any morning when I don't see myself vilified in the Jewish Press I blame myself for not being sufficiently active as a Nazi." Had we thought it worth while, we could have spent all our time bringing suits for libel against the Press. From Hitler down, the Nazis were stripped naked, painted black, crowned with thorns, and dished up to the public as horrible examples of rowdyism and graft, lechery and treason. No restraint of decency or truth held our enemies back in their efforts to besmirch our private characters. After such a lesson, with ourselves as Exhibit A, it is no wonder the Nazis learned to reply in kind later on.

As it happened, the time was exactly ripe to reply to the calumny which linked me with my unfortunate double. According to the papers, the latter had recently been arrested and sentenced to six years at hard labour. Patiently I composed a long resume of the case, pointing out the reasons why I was not, could not be, and refused to be, the same person as the man then in custody. On 30 November the Voelkischer Kurier of Munich, a substitute for the still forbidden Voelkischer Beobachter, gave its front page to my article, under the main headline, 'The Ludecke Case.' Though the libel against me was really damaging (foreign newspapers, for instance, circulated the despatch that I had been shot as a spy!) I could do nothing more to set matters straight. I did not have the money to start a series of libel suits, and as far as the rest of the Party was concerned, such libels were regarded almost as honourable endorsements, coming as they did from our enemies. Whether it was ever possible to correct a misapprehension by publishing anything so unsensational as the bald facts of the case, I gravely doubted.

To go back to Party affairs of larger importance:

With Rosenberg disaffected, the Party was also in danger of losing the co-operation of Captain Roehm. This was a serious prospect. Roehm had extended his Frontbann all over the Reich, and had already built it up to thirty thousand men. He held himself aloof from the political intrigues inside the Party, but aloofness was difficult, and the politicians, who resented his attitude and feared his strength, intrigued against him. The breach between the two parts of the movement was so visible that the Bavarian Government took advantage of the weakened condition of the Nazis to arrest some of Roehm's chief lieutenants for 'illegal activities'-for example, Wilhelm Brueckner, who to-day is Reichsfuehrer Hitler's chief personal Party adjutant. The arrest was seized on as a pretext for delaying Hitler's parole, which in ordinary course would have been granted him automatically on 1 October of that year.

It was now November, and Hitler was still in Landsberg. Party prestige had dwindled to zero, while the Berlin Government had retrieved and extended its power and was now in a much stronger position. The most disturbing inner problems had been settled, at least temporarily. The long-standing conflict between the Reich and Bavaria had been adjusted, with Kahr, Lossow, and Seisser dropped, and the official anti-Marxist policy of Munich more or less abandoned. The mark had been stabilized. The French had evacuated the Ruhr. The precarious relations with the Entente had been eased, for the time being, by the adoption of the Dawes Plan, a cynical scheme of the international bankers which converted the official political debt, into a private one" with the entire German economy as a commercial guarantee for payment of reparations-indeed, a very profitable business transaction for the international money trust.

Quick to calculate that these new conditions had robbed the radical opposition of its most valuable talking-points, and well aware of the decline of the Nazi movement, the Marxian-Centrist coalition decided that this was the moment to go to the polls again. The new elections of 7 December showed in cold figures the Nazi defeat. Out of a total of two million votes in the May, election, the movement recaptured only nine hundred thousand, and lost eighteen of their former thirty-two deputies.

It seemed clear that Hitler was a dead lion. His movement was finished, and no sensible purpose could be served by continuing his 'martyrdom.'

Accordingly, on 20 December he was released.

Hitler's return lifted our hopes out of the depths, but the traditional Christmas holiday, during which everything stands still throughout Germany, prevented any immediate planning. In the lull, I accepted an invitation to represent Hitler and Ludendorff at the convention of the 'Awakening Hungarians' at Budapest.

The moment I arrived there, the police offered their usual civilities by taking me to headquarters for interrogation. Fortunately, I was accompanied by a Hungarian colonel whom Tibor von Eckhardt had sent to meet me, and he was able to cut the red tape in which I might otherwise have been indefinitely entangled. The acting chief of police, Dr. Emmerich Hetenyi, learning that I was the invited guest of the powerful 'Awakening Hungarians,' joking, waived the recent ban which Hungary had imposed on Nazi emissaries, and improved 'the occasion by satisfying personal rather than official curiosity. I told him what he wanted to know.

"Well," he said, "I'm pleased to meet the German who spent the night in a charming lady's room last time my men were looking for him. I'm really sorry that we've caused you this second inconvenience. But about that other time-tell me-was she blonde or brunette?"

And then the chief, who had picked me up to expel me from Hungary, ended the interview with a brotherly kiss on each cheek, to the astonishment of the correct colonel, and let me hurry off to the first session of the congress.

Over twelve hundred delegates were gathered in the Town Hall, an impressive body of prominent men which constituted a real political force. My speech followed that of Bishop Prohaszka, a man of striking appearance, with beautiful, white hair and a fine voice. The difficulty of succeeding such an accomplished speaker was not lessened by the envy that filled me as I compared the Nazis' pathetic come-down with the growing ascendancy of the Hungarian folkists. But von Eckhardt gave me a glowing introduction, and, encouraged by the obvious sympathy of the audience, I devoted my allotted time entirely to a refutation of the idea that the Nazis were defeated. Hitler and Ludendorff, names to conjure with in Hungary until the putsch, had been caricatured by the enemies of the 'Awakening Hungarians,' until the Nazi connection was more of a liability than an asset. That damage I repaired as far as was possible in a single speech, excusing our failure by magnifying the forces which opposed us, and insisting that Hitler was the heroic victim of treason and duplicity. He was not out of the running, I said; on the contrary, new circumstances were at that moment opening a new road to victory, and in our success we would not forget Hungary, our noble ally in the World War. This speech, delivered with the necessary quota of allusions to brotherhood, destiny, and so on, roused such applause that I knew at once that the delegates had heard what they most wished to hear from me.

More difficult was it to convince cunning, cool-headed Julius von Goemboes,[1] then already a key-man in politics and later Premier, that I had not been talking through my hat. Closeted together for hours at his headquarters in their impressive club, where I felt like a poor relation of the rich Hungarian racialists, we went over the ground in detail. Goemboes was sceptical, with reason.

Three times, he pointed out, I had appeared in Budapest to announce the

1 Died 6 October 1936 at a sanatorium near Munich

imminent triumph of the Nazis. Largely on the basis of my representations, Goemboes and his party had played up Hitler's importance, claiming him as an ally whose success would contribute to their own-and now they found themselves linked with a failure, a strategic handicap which the enemy Press had not neglected to capitalize. In view of the Nazis' past performance, not to mention their present lack of leadership and unity, how could I hope to find further confidence abroad?

It was rough going, Goemboes yielding no more than a point now and then.

"You may say what you like," he said, "but even with Hitler at liberty now, you have to begin all over again. And frankly, Hitler's role in the Beer Hall Putsch was-to put it mildly-so discouraging that I don't want to compromise myself through him again."

At last, after I had used every possible argument to bring him round, he gave a guarded assent to my interpretation of the Nazis' ill-fortune, and agreed that it was not irreparable.

"But," he warned, " I may as well tell you that I have not been alone in my attitude. It would be profitable for you to talk with other political friends here. We are having a dinner tonight at the club, where you will be able to address our inner circle without the restraints which a public meeting imposes. Why not take the opportunity? But remember, many of our men are staunch Catholics. Take the Church question easy, and don't paint the cardinals too red."

I took his advice, spoke before his colleagues for about an hour, and found them very receptive. During the lively discussion that followed, Goemboes kept me on edge by posing the trickiest questions his sceptical mind could conceive; but when the meeting broke up at last, I had the satisfaction of knowing that the rehabilitation of Hitler was well begun in Hungary.

"I made it pretty hard for you, didn't I?" Goemboes twitted me afterwards. "But you came through all right. Now why not come down into the country with me over Christmas, to get your breath back? I'll have a little surprise there for you."

Next day, when we arrived by motor at Goemboes' country home, the surprise turned out to be an introduction to 'Herr Schmid.' The police would have envied me that introduction, for Herr Schmid was in reality a lieutenant of the former Imperial German Army, and one of the two assassins of Mathias Erzberger, the German Minister who as plenipotentiary had been chief signer of the Armistice. Schmid was sought by the police of every country, and the mere rumour that he was hiding in Hungary had raised a new man-hunt for him.

I was drawn to him at once. It was difficult to accept the fact that this slender, handsome man, modest, soft-spoken, and mild, had committed the crime which threw Germany into terrific commotion and led to the Draconian laws 'for the protection of the Republic.' Even now the police were hot on his trail; Goemboes had pointed out two Secret Service men as we entered the grounds.

"They aren't sure he's here. But they dare not enter to find out," he assured me. "My immunity as a Deputy bars them; my guest is safe."

In spite of his half-amused certainty that the police must cool their heels at a distance, it was unsettling to think that only an invisible bar, a mere parliamentary convention, protected the fugitive.

After supper on Christmas Eve we sat together drinking hot punch, and heard as macabre a tale as was ever unfolded by the light of a Christmas tree. The huge room was dim in the flicker of the candles; the fire burned low, throwing wavering shadows over the Lieutenant's face as he told us the story of the killing. We saw the mists of a drizzly afternoon . . . . Erzberger walking in the Black Forest beneath his umbrella . . . thrusting it towards his assassin's revolver in one last tragi-comnic gesture, as a pathetic shield between himself and the bullet. . . .

Whether or not you can bring yourself to regard the political assassin with a special tolerance, I submit for your compassion, as a tragic figure, this man who gave up honours and career to strike a blow which in his mind seemed a duty, necessary for his country's welfare. After the crime, hounded like a wild beast, deserted by the 'German Patriots' for whom he had acted, he finally reached Hungary without money, without hope, to find a dangerous asylum in one hiding-place after another, moving on each time the police crept up with extradition papers. This Christmas interlude, which Goemboes had offered him at great personal risk, would end in a day or so, and back he would have to go into the underground world.

"Remember all this, Ludecke," said Goemboes. "When you get back to Munich, tell them how quickly your revolutionaries forget their own people. Schmid is not the only German refugee we have to look after, though we cannot afford the money or the risk. After all, the moral obligation is yours."

Goemboes, already denounced as a Germanophile, for he was a Lutheran and his wife and mother were German-born, later had a hard time weathering the storm that arose when it was whispered that his house was an asylum for assassins. But by that time his guest had moved on, this time into Turkey, and I did not hear of him again. When Schmid and his accomplice finally returned to Germany in 1933 under Chancellor Hitler's amnesty decree, I myself was in prison by Hitler's order. A year later I thought of this once-hunted man when I, too, was fleeing without money and without papers, starving and homeless.

XV

THE NEW HITLER REBUILDS THE PARTY

With the new year, 1925, Hitler resumed his political activity. The hostile Press called him 'a fool maddened by imprisonment,' and in fact it did seem madness to try to carry on with the means at hand, in the face of the completely new conditions which prevailed in the Reich.

The three principal circumstances which had helped the Nazi Party to gain a strong hold on the masses were no longer effective. First, Mussolini's triumph in Italy, which had made a tremendous impression on the German mind, was no longer news. Second, the Ruhr invasion, now that the French had withdrawn and Hitler had failed as an avenging angel, was no longer a burning issue; it had been half-forgotten, though the wound was still open. Third, and of prime importance, the inflation was over and the re-established mark had brought to the country a general but evanescent relief. The middle class and especially the peasants believed their insecurity ended.

Moreover, the conflicts with the Entente seemed settled, on the basis of the Dawes Plan. Selling the plan abroad by propagandizing the Germans as a thrifty and industrious folk who had regained political sanity and were ready to work for industrial recovery and payment of reparations, the international 'experts' brought a flood of foreign gold into the country, creating a mock prosperity which actually lasted several years and fooled the majority of the plain citizens. Ground down by the insufferable poverty of the inflation, they can be forgiven for not asking too insistently why this wealth of foreign coin came so suddenly-and how they were to repay it in the end.

But the experts who saddled Germany with the Dawes Plan must have had a guilty knowledge of what the ultimate results would be. It was inconceivable that a defeated Germany, stripped and impoverished, could possibly pay a regular annual tribute amounting to £125,000,000 in gold for an indefinite period, as provided by the Dawes Plan. Germany's economic sovereignty went the way of its military sovereignty when the plan forced foreign financial control of the Reich.

The German Reichstag ratified this infamous pact in August 1924, against the violent protest of the Nazi deputies, who warned the world that the pact bore no signatures which really represented the will of the German people, and that when the Nazi day of power arrived, they would repudiate it. They publicly branded as a lie the assurances of the dominant parties that foreign loans under the plan would increase national prosperity, banish unemployment, lift wages, reduce taxes, and save agriculture. In vain they prophesied that reality which time revealed only too well-national bankruptcy under the burden of unpayable interest rates, crippled industry, ruined farms, widespread unemployment, and crushing poverty-a nation headed for the ultimate debacle.

But when Hitler surveyed the scene early in 1925, these disasters, which later were to serve him admirably as campaign material, were still to come. Many years might pass before a general unrest would offer him a new stepping-stone to power. Meanwhile, to entrench himself in preparation for whatever chance might come, he had no choice but to worm his way up through parliamentary channels. He must continue the 'legal' process.

Hitler's obvious strategy of dividing the power of his followers during his imprisonment had succeeded in holding the leadership open for him. The resultant quarrels, however, had so weakened the Party that it was no longer an effective instrument for his use, and it was no secret to Rosenberg and to me that Hitler had resolved to ignore the existing organization headed by Ludendorff and start anew from the very bottom, building a new Nazi Party with himself as the only leader.

The prospect troubled us deeply. After talking it over, we were far from sure that the refounding of the Party was not to be undertaken along most unsound lines. As for Hitler, there was, even in our somewhat disillusioned minds, no change in our belief that he was then the only leader capable of really leading. But he intended to call back as many of his old followers as possible, uniting under his banner the same dissonant elements which had wrecked the Nationalist movement. We had little faith in the efficacy, or even the possibility, of this Pax Hitleriana.

Rosenberg was adamant on the question of resuming collaboration with Esser and Hanfstaengl. When Hitler tendered him the office of editor-in-chief of the Voelkischer Beobachter, which he intended to revive, Rosenberg reserved his decision. But he continued to work along Party lines by publishing the Weltkampf, widely read among the more intellectual adherents of the folkic ideal in Germany. Would I write an article for him which might serve as a timely word of warning about the fundamental problems which would confront the reorganized Nazi Party, and the methods by which they could be met. It would be helpful if, in passing and without mentioning names, I were to hold up a mildly admonitory finger toward Hitler, whose increasing shift from idealistic to material motives worried us.

The article appeared in the Weltkampf on 1 February 1925, and also was reproduced in full in Ludendorff's daily, the Voelkische Kurier. As the first candid critique authored by a Party member, it aroused widespread comment inside and outside the folkic camp. It will suffice to translate here a few passages which show the major premise advanced-in brief, that the Party would be able to do constructive work only when the destructive practices and elements which weakened it had been eliminated, so that the men we needed would enter the work cooperatively instead of standing on the sidelines sniping at us for our sins.

Though the Nazi movement expanded after the Hitler trial, in its present condition it is no longer a factor to be taken seriously.

The experience of the past year has proved that before the inner and outer liberation of Germany can be achieved, a tremendous work has to be done within our movement, partly because of its deficient organization, but equally because of the overweening ambition, lack of character, unscrupulousness, and stupidity of certain so-called leaders and countless sub-leaders--shortcomings which are aggravated by the distressing lack of funds and the absence of the absolute authority of a real leader.

A liberty movement which arrogates the right to represent the real people against a confused, degenerate, besotted, and Judaized majority, must demonstrate spiritual and political values in order to swing the scales for the spiritual and political renascence of the nation. To understand the ruin which threatens and to wish for salvation will not suffice; only when understanding and will are united with practical knowledge and ability can the tremendous difficulties be overcome.

Only the proof that the fighters for liberty are really folkic in their conduct and thinking can give them the right to demand the highest sacrifices from their people, because the fight for German liberty is not only a fierce political fight, but also a mighty spiritual struggle.

We are lost, and deserve no better fate, if we do not unite all the best folkic forces as soon as possible, and create an organization of spiritual and practical value which represents an actual power. Germany has now entered into a decisive period which makes this imperative.

Guarding against that 'German objectivity' which paralyses us, we must cease fighting against all fronts at the same time. For instance, it is impossible to destroy in one blow the ultra-montane power and the clerical reactionary monarchists in Bavaria, and still contend with Capitalism and Marxism in the Reich. Our main enemy, however, is Marxism; a one-sided fight against Marxism in Bavaria would be wasted effort, because there is no longer a serious danger. Hence the field of attack ought to be transferred as early as possible to the Protestant North, where religious questions will not divide our strength, where the Centre Party is almost identical with Marxism, and the concentration against Marxism will become a logical step.

The folkic state's plan in its fundamental principles lies clear before our eyes; it only remains for us Germans to give the leader the necessary weight to seize the political power. The Nazi element has been the only real activist force within the folkic movement. Whatever criticisms may be levelled against us, it cannot be denied that Hitler has the ability to lead the movement to victory. But precious time and strength must not be lost; we must unite; both arrogance and Byzantine servility must be stopped. It is urgent that this man should have the help of every man and every means. One thing is certain: there is visible nobody to replace him. In the end, the strongest personality will win.

Marking a copy of this article, I sent it to Hitler with a memorandum amplifying several points which it would have been impolitic to treat fully in print. I stressed the fact that it stated not simply my personal opinion, but that of a considerable group of his chief followers-by no means the least important group-and asked him to arrange an interview for me, when we could discuss my journeys and Party problems.

Though I had seen Hitler several times since my return to Munich, I had not managed to talk seriously with him; he had been too busy orienting himself, seeking money, and feeling his way toward the tactical course best calculated to get him what he wanted. As always at such times, he was very secretive and, if he chose, beyond the reach especially of those who had opinions of their own and whom he thought it better to leave in the dark until they could be faced with an accomplished fact. I was in an advantageous position in those days because I was practically the only one who could give him first-hand information about other than strictly Party matters-for instance, the attitude toward his release in folkic circles outside Germany, of which he could not read in German papers.

On the afternoon he had appointed, I went to his quarters at Thierschstrasse 41, where he was staying with a married couple, old members of the Party. Here he lived for years, sleeping in a small bedroom in the rear of the flat, and receiving his visitors in a tiny study in the front, where he also worked. Nothing had changed since my last visit before the putsch except that shelves of books now filled the last inch of space. The etching of Frederick the Great-my Christmas present of two years before-still hung over the work-table.

Julius Schaub admitted me to the study. He had replaced Ulrich Graf, Hitler's former bodyguard, too severely wounded at the Feldherrnhalle to resume his duties. Schaub, then about twenty-seven, was, I suppose, as good a choice as any-an average, middle-class Bavarian, who, though slightly lamed in the war, had shown special courage as a Nazi bouncer and had never swerved from his fidelity to Hitler. He had gone from pharmacy into the war, and thence into Hitler's fledgling S A. On the eve of the Beer Hall Putsch, he had carried important orders from Hitler to Gregor Strasser, and next morning was entrusted with the job of arresting the Socialist mayor along with the Socialist and Communist aldermen. For all this, he was sentenced to a year and three months of imprisonment, the last half of which he served at Landsberg with Hitler. On his release, he began that career of handyman-secretary-bodyguard for Hitler which has carried him up to dizzy heights along with his master. The important role he plays today is unique, and a trifle bewildering to those who remember him in his stamp-licking days.

Realizing the value of such a man, however, I cultivated his good-will from the start. Like the original Poo-Bah, he did not disdain a tip now and then.

While I waited for Hitler and talked inattentively to Schaub, my mind was busy with the things I meant to find out. I wanted, for example, to know about Ludendorff, toward whom Hitler now was taking what seemed an ignoble attitude. From his own point of view, Hitler unquestionably was right when he vowed that he must start the Party over again with one member-himself. And yet his summary treatment of Ludendorff was more than questionable. He had begun to go straight over the head of the man who, when all is said, had ruined himself for the 'Bohemian corporal' and had loyally done his best to keep things going while Hitler was in Landsberg.

But the great General had served his purpose. Hitler simply dropped him. For those of his sincere followers who knew the true facts about the putsch and Hitler's responsibility for its failure, this attitude was a distinct shock. Within me, and within Rosenberg as well, a certain inner break with Hitler became a fact then and there. We continued to cling to the Fuehrer for his positive qualities and because there was no one else. But things were never to be quite the same.

Ever since doubt of Hitler's flawless greatness had begun to creep into my mind, I had been wanting to get under his skin and learn more about his real self. This time I meant to satisfy my burning curiosity. Determined not to be dominated, I would shoot direct questions at him if other methods did not work. And I recall distinctly that while I listened to Schaub, I rehearsed in my mind certain tactics I might use.

Then Hitler came in, and Schaub discreetly vanished. The Fuehrer clasped my hand, tapped my shoulder, and asked me to tell him more about Henry Ford, and Budapest. In detail I explained why it was useless to hope for money from that side, or to expect anything from German-Americans. I emphasized the poor prospects from a foreign political viewpoint, the wholly dormant potentialities in England and elsewhere, and in general the foolishness of counting on anybody or anything outside Germany, so long as we were without power, without prestige, and so hopelessly divided as we were at present.

During this glum recital, Hitler had been interrupting me frequently, appearing irritated and nervous. 'The healthy air he had in Landsberg was gone, and with it his poise. He looked almost fat; his cheeks seemed flabby and his chin weak, and as usual plenty of dandruff adorned collar and shoulders of his dark blue suit. For the first time I felt a distinct dislike for him, and proceeded to bear down harder.

"No use," I said, " to cherish any illusions about our foreign prospects. Things couldn't be worse. Our good friends in Budapest are in fact the only ones with any influence who look at us with sympathy. But, believe me, I had a hard time to undo some of the damage done. You've no idea how effectively the entire Press everywhere has ridiculed and pilloried you, taking it for granted that you're dead, stone-dead."

"Ha!" he cried, "I'll show these dogs how dead I am!"

"Yes, that's well enough "-and I continued rubbing it in-" but you must admit that things look rotten now and that much of what is said is true. And I mean especially the way the Ludendorff affair is being handled. Do you really think it's to your credit and to the advantage of the movement?"

The avalanche fell over me.

"Bah! Generals!" stormed Hitler. "I've had enough of generals! Not one of them was a truly great statesman; even Frederick the Great made surprising blunders and did his thinking more with the head of a general than a statesman. So did Napoleon-"

And now he went off at one of his quick tangents. "Beethoven exploded when he heard Napoleon had crowned himself emperor-threw the manuscript he was going to dedicate to him on the floor and trampled it under his feet--" Here Hitler was so overcome with histrionic rage that he became Beethoven and fairly crushed Napoleon into the carpet. Seeing the astonishment on my face, he quickly added: "Thank God he didn't destroy it-he later called it the 'Eroika.'"

With scarcely a second's pause, he was back on the track again. "Look at Bismarck"-here I shouted unheard that Bismarck had never been an active general-"with his 'Politik ist die Kunst des Moeglichen.' That's a cheap subterfuge. If a statesman only attempted what seemed possible he wouldn't get very far."

And so it went on for a long while, with Hitler pacing around as much as the miniature room permitted. I was now on my feet; in fact, through most of the interview we were standing. Wearying of a tirade which criticized everything and everybody except himself, I threw the name of Cromwell in his face.

"There was a man, you must admit," I said. "I don't know of any revolutionary who could touch his greatness as general and statesman. He never compromised-he took the Government by force. Look what he flung at the Rump Parliament when he closed the House of Commons. When the battle-scarred general who was his adjutant went to remove the mace, Cromwell told him to shake the Speaker's gentle hand with his iron fist and tear his baby's rattle off!"

"Cromwell, Oliver Cromwell ..." Hitler mused for a moment. "Yes, he made England-but even he couldn't do without the Jews!"[1]

And I had to listen to another lecture on statesmanship and Jews. Finally I said impatiently that was all beside the point; I had mentioned Ludendorff, who after all had stuck by him to the last and hadn't hidden in an automobile and run away.

"Do you mean me by that?" Hitler shot back furiously.

"Exactly," I said. "Do you think for one moment that I would have staked myself and all I had on you so unreservedly if I had suspected that the March on Berlin could end in such a miserable fiasco? Please don't interrupt me now-don't shout at

---

1 *Cromwell, about 1650, re-admitted the Jews, who had been barred from England since 1291*

me! I'm not Schaub. Let's discuss this quietly-believe me, I am not the only one who wants to know where he stands."

Pointing to my article, I stressed the dishonesty of assailing the corruption and disunity of the parliamentary system while our own ranks showed the same qualities to a lamentable degree. Another stumbling block, I told Hitler, was his alleged secret bargain with Dr. Held.[2] I admitted that he needed him for two reasons: first, to avert expulsion as an 'undesirable alien,' and second, to rebuild his own National Socialist Workers' Party. No easy matter to win his good-will, since Hitler had long been baying at the heels of the 'Pope's frocked politicians,' and it was right enough for him to make his bow and come to an understanding. But the question was: at what price? Without mincing words, I went on point by point with what I had resolved to get off my chest, winding up by saying how unbearable it was that Hitler was going to proclaim the new Party within a few days and nobody knew exactly what he really intended doing.

Hitler was growing visibly calmer, and finally came round.

Taking a more conciliatory attitude, he spoke almost humorously. On the premise that I, having been abroad all that time, could not possibly have authentic information about the putsch itself and the later trial, he began to belittle Ludendorff more subtly, by innuendo. I was made aware of the General's 'stupid performance' during the putsch, of his 'poor show' at the trial when he denied knowledge and responsibility 'to avoid punishment.' It did not matter to Hitler that Ludendorff really did not have 'full knowledge and responsibility,' and that this had been wise strategy for the sake of the movement. He scoffed at Ludendorff's 'face-saving,' apparently unaware that he himself, to save his own face, was now impugning the motives of the once-cherished General whose prestige he had ruined.

"And now Ludendorff's senseless attacks on the Roman Church and on Crown Prince Rupprecht are forcing me to separate myself from him. For the moment they are the stronger-what else can I do if I want to resume my work? I must come to terms with them-otherwise I should be out of the picture. And what then? Ridiculous to expect me to drop Streicher-they must be crazy! Who is going to win Nuremberg for me? Professor Meyer, perhaps, or Herr Geheimer Justizrat Dr. Class? Nein, meine Herren, daraus wird nichts! I'll do as I please-no dictation for me."

By now he was in his old element again, talking himself into a fury. Gone was that awkwardness, that false undertone which occasionally had showed through his ill-temper. He had regained his persuasive, almost compelling countenance, displaying again his usual sureness and that mask of captivating sincerity which has deceived so many.

"And this outcry, this idiotic indignation about Esser gets on my nerves! That

---

2 *Doctor Heinrich Held, Bavarian minister-president after the liquidation of the Kahr-Lossowregime; an old Catholic Party leader, separatist, and monarchist.*

fellow has more political sense in his fingertips than the whole bunch of his accusers in their buttocks. Everywhere and always, politics has been a hard and ruthless game. Even to achieve a worthy end, we must sometimes adopt strange methods and use dubious ways if we want to stay in the race. You are too much of an idealist-you'd better change your temperament a bit. I have to take people as I find them, use them as best I can according to their talents, and forget about their bad points. Otherwise I wouldn't get very far, my friend."

Why not, I pleaded, move the field to Protestant Thuringia? There he would be safe. Dr. Dinter had made a good start and the Nazi units there were getting stronger every day. It was the heart of Germany, a splendid strategic position, and Luther and Weimar gave it a unique, historic, and inspiring background. There he would be more readily accepted by North Germany. If we were to combine all our forces on Thuringia we could get the little state in not too long a time. Once in power in that state, we could launch a concentrated drive on Marxism with much better prospects of success, and could put down roots much faster in other parts of the Reich than if we were to spend our energies on small, impotent, and persecuted units scattered all over the country. Why launch the new Party under a terrible handicap? If we must proceed legally, let us also proceed planfully and systematically. Such a beginning would be harder, I admitted, but promised much quicker results than sitting in 'gemuetlichen Muenchen' and playing ball with Jesuits.

Hitler turned to gaze for a moment out the window, then brusquely back to me.

"There's some sense in what you say. Such a step might facilitate things and avoid unnecessary complications-who knows! But I can't leave Munich. I'm at home here; I mean something here; there are many here who are devoted to me, to me alone and to nobody else. That's important."

"To be sure," I conceded, "proclaim the New Party here, but at the earliest possible moment aim every effort at the conquest of Thuringia."

"No, no ! " he cried impatiently. "I shall not alter my plans; I don't want to."

But, I asked, could he really be sure of his Bavarians? It seemed so clear that he was going to need the North Germans more than any others if he wanted to vote himself into power. And there was another ticklish point about this business. To destroy democracy by democratic means looked very tempting but had dangerous pitfalls. It might well undermine the very fundamentals of the movement, surrendering the aristocratic principle of the Party to the instincts of the masses, or-what might be worse-to the highest bidder. "Let me worry about that," said Hitler. Sarcastically he added: "You'd better see to it that Rosenberg comes to his senses and stops playing the offended innocent."

"That's not so easy," I snapped at him. "That cut went deeper than you think."

"Ja, ja, we'll see." And he laughed. "But what about you? I've talked with Amann about you. He agrees with me that you are the best man to put the Beobachter over in Berlin. The reorganization of that is one of our most important tasks. We must invade Berlin. It's a tough job, but I know that you can do it. Besides, I need an intelligent observer in the capital, whose judgment I can trust. You could act at the same time, discreetly, as my representative. What do you say?"

"Interesting, but sudden," I replied, and asked for a day or two to think it over. "I'll tell you right after the Party meeting. Let's see how that turns out."

That ended the interview, and I left unsatisfied, though with somewhat mixed feelings. February is a gusty month, and toward the end of it, the stormy Beobachter began to blow again. Its appearance on the stands was surprising in view of the ban laid upon it, and those who suspected Hitler of making a deal with the authorities pointed to his renewed Press-freedom as proof of concessions on his part. The Beobachter was indeed less strident than formerly, due to the dearth of burning public issues to editorialize; but it served to prepare the public mind for the first step in Hitler's second campaign for power-the re-founding of the Nazi Party.

On the 27th of the month, he called his mass-meeting, the first since his release. Shrewdness, bravado, and love of drama made him choose the Buergerbraeukeller, the actual scene of his recent failure.

Again the great hall was crowded with Nazi followers and leaders. But there were conspicuous absentees. Rosenberg, who had stood at Hitler's side on the fateful night of the putsch, was not there. "I won't take part in that comedy," he had told me in the afternoon. "I know the sort of brother-kissing Hitler intends to call for" Ludendorff and Strasser, who had resigned their leaderships on 12 February, stayed away, and so did Roehm. But the others gathered in full force, sensing that this would be the night to get in on the ground floor of a rebuilt organization.

Max Amann, Hitler's trusted friend, business-manager, and banker, opened the meeting. Naturally, the most prominent and most ardent Hitlerites crowded the tables nearest the speaker's platform, which, being rather large and very low, was well adapted to the last act Hitler had in mind. But he began his speech by talking to the back of the hall and to the gallery where the anonymous rank and file were packed. As his voice rose, their response became more fervent. No apology or embarrassment marred the practised technique with which he gathered them again into the palm of his hand. Long before the end, I saw that he could count absolutely on their support. .

Next he turned his forensics on the Party officers at the tables directly in front of him. He did not ask for their loyalty or their service; he suggested no compromises. He ordered them to come with him and work for him-or get out.

"This is an absolutely new beginning. You must forget your personal quarrels. If you will not, I shall start the Party alone, without you."

The crowd yelled and cheered in excited approval.

Then Hitler affected to soften somewhat, and his harsh commands gave way to an extraordinary stage-play. Like a revivalist exhorting sinners to hit the sawdust trail, he called on his quarrelsome men to bury the hatchet then and there. Pathos flooded the gathering, women wept, the crowd pressed from the rear, climbing on chairs and tables. Singly and in pairs, men who had been bitter enemies mounted the platform and shook hands, some of them unable to restrain the tears which Hitler's magic voice had worked up. In groups they avowed their forgiveness of each other and swore undying loyalty to the Fuehrer.

The spectacle should have been Comic, but somehow it wasn't. From the inconspicuous corner where I sat, I watched the crowd revelling in this emotional moment, and reflected that Hitler had not staged such a scene without purpose. It was, in effect, a dramatic tableau planned to show the most simple-minded as well as the most cunning Nazis that there was, and could be, only one leader for them all.

The lesson was not lost, even on the absentees. A few days later Rosenberg, who had vowed to stay aloof, accepted the Beobachter editorship. Gregor Strasser also took up Party work again, albeit reluctantly. Loyal to the cause, he joined Hitler with the Bavarian Nazi deputies and his own district of Lower Bavaria, which really was the kernel of the new Hitler Party, the nucleus of the second epoch of the Hitler movement. As trustee, Gregor Strasser had held it together during the crisis; now, at the decisive moment, he gave it back to Hitler. Doubling his efforts, the trustee became the missionary of National Socialism in North Germany. Strasser organized the Party there, but it developed into a movement largely his own, with a Press and propaganda machine independent of Munich.

Captain Roehm, who had progressively withdrawn from Party ties, conferred with the chief men of his Frontbann and, with their acquiescence, offered to unite the organization with the new Party if Ludendorff would be the military chief and would act again as the sponsor of the movement, while Hitler retained political leadership. Ludendorff declined. Then Hitler talked privately with Roehm, asking him to bring his Frontbann into the Party and take charge of it as the new S A, but requiring his unconditional submission to the Fuehrer's authority. Cogent practical reasons made Roehm spurn what seemed a very bad bargain. Fed up with the whole system of partisanship into which the folkic movement had degenerated, he decided to break all connection with it. On 1 May he transferred the command of the Frontbann to Count von Helldorf, and literally cut himself off from every sort of political activity for a period of years. One of his chief men, Oberleutnant Wilhelm Brueckner, loyally resigned with him.

How they eventually re-entered the Nazi Party, and what the consequences were for each, comes later in the story.

Ludendorff retired to his villa again to nurse his disgust. But first he made one more effort in behalf of the folkic movement-a hopeless effort not aided by the tactics the Nazi Party adopted. Some said that he was wilfully betrayed; others that he was undone by circumstance. In any event, he ran for the Reich Presidency, and failed dismally. But his failure is interesting because of the circumstances surrounding the election, and because it introduces again the name of Hindenburg, the old Field-Marshal and legendary figure of Tannenberg fame.

Fate seems always to be weaving a strange net of fortuitous events to catch fish for Hitler. The day after his triumphant reappearance on the platform, the Berlin authorities, alarmed by such visible proof of his latent power, quietly decided to instruct the states to grant him no further permits for public speaking. This would clip his wings for a time; other and more serious steps against him were probably being planned. But on the very day the ban was laid on the Fuehrer, Reichspresident Ebert died in office, and in the scramble to capture the Presidency the Nazis were forgotten.

Grateful to have attention diverted from him, the Hitler who but a few days before had scoffed at Ludendorff now accepted him as his candidate for Reichspresident, and plunged into the electoral contest along with the other party bosses. It was an unequal battle. The Nazis were quite unprepared, and even though they worked with the whole folkic movement to elect the General, that courageous soldier stood no chance. The two million votes of May 1924 dwindled to a paltry 285,793. These were cast for the General on 29 March 1925, in the first but indecisive balloting. Ludendorff's wretched showing decided Hitler to swing his group to Hindenburg, who, in the second election, was nominated by the Right, while the Left and Centre were backing Wilhelm Marx, then chief of the Centrists, and the Communists their party leader, Thaelmann.

Hitler had no further use for Ludendorff. It is inconceivable that so astute a politician expected the General to reap anything but disaster from his candidacy. Whether or not Hitler foresaw and deliberately engineered the War Lord's humiliation the defeat furnished a sufficient excuse for breaking the last thread of common interest which bound them. A venerable general is a good advertisement for an armed political party, but a defeated candidate is only a liability for a regular vote-getting machine. Coldly and cruelly Hitler shut the door in his face.

Since I had done my share in bringing Ludendorff among us at a time when Hitler needed and welcomed his personal prestige, his ouster filled me with anger. The problem of my own relation to the Party occupied my thoughts. It became clear that any decision I might make must be on the basis of several cold facts. To continue Party work, it would be necessary to earn my livelihood within the Party, since my personal funds were almost gone. The raw zeal which originally had inclined me to accept without examination every plan Hitler proposed had evaporated; from now on, while my greatest desire was to speed our programme, I must weigh and judge each new project. The Party could count on me, but I wanted to count on results. My attitude was so cooled toward those Party men with whom I must co-operate as long as I remained in Munich, that it became increasingly difficult to accept them as co-workers. In other words, I wished to continue in the Party, but not in close touch with headquarters-and I had to earn a living.

Consequently I decided to accept Hitler's proposal. On 8, April I signed an agreement with Amann to represent the Nazi publishing house, the Ether Verlag, in north Germany, organizing the distribution, advertising, etc., of the Beobachter and other publications. I was also to act as Hitler's contact man in Berlin.

With relief I turned my back on Munich. I found Berlin in the grip of the second election for the Presidency. The Right had staked all its hopes on Hindenburg, convinced that his defeat would mean the end of Germany, while the Left was equally sure that his election would spell the end of the Republic. The campaign was the most violent that parliamentary Germany had seen. Feeling ran high, and clashes were numerous.

On April 26 1925 a wooden giant, Field-Marshall Paul Ludwig Hans Anton von Beneckendorff und von Hindenburg, in his seventy-eighth year, was elected the second President of the Reich. But it had been a close race, and it was dawn before the final result was known. Marx obtained 13,751,605 votes, Thaelmann 1,931,151, and Hindenburg 14,655,641 - less than his two opponents combined.

In those days I became close to Arno Schickedanz, a Balt and an old and intimate friend of Rosenberg. I had known him in Munich, where he had worked with Scheubner-Richter, the most prominent Nazi victim of the slaughter which marked the end of the putsch. Not yet naturalized, Schickedanz had been expelled from Bavaria before the Hitler-Ludendorff trial, and was now living the hard life of an impoverished political fugitive in Berlin, trying to get German citizenship papers. He was a man of poise and grace, combined with a certain Baltic arrogance. His was a keen mind in a well-formed head, with finely chiselled features. I discovered in him an interesting and valuable companion, for he was familiar with the political undercurrents, the personalities and intrigues of Berlin, not only in our camp but elsewhere. Almost timid, reserved, cool and impassive like Rosenberg, he was nevertheless able in a quiet, inconspicuous way to gather excellent information. Being somewhat vulnerable as "Baltic outsiders," Rosenberg and he stuck together; the former found him highly useful.

I made it a point to renew old acquaintanceships and make new ones. From them I gained a deeper insight into the perplexity of German politics. One of the highlights was a talk with Reventlow-still a lone wolf. Through decades of politics the Count had known everybody and everybody knew him. Without ever achieving real prominence as a leader or as working executive within a party or a government, he was a veritable walking encyclopedia of politics. With his political energies "restricted mainly to writing, which he did unceasingly, sometimes brilliantly but for the most part in heavy style, he had grown embittered and dissatisfied. In the past several years his poker face had turned slightly sour, the furrows had deepened along his witty nose and ended now in the sarcastic corners of a tight mouth which had a sceptical sag. His lips could twist in a peculiarly dry and caustic smile while his cool grey eyes looked as amused and innocent as ever.

We had quite an argument about Hitler, for I opposed his view that Hitler was through.

"All right," said the Count. "Even if he gets on his feet in Munich again, here in the North he's finished for good. The hard-headed North-German Protestants won't stand for South-German Catholic leadership. There are too many shouting Bavarians already. It's a good thing Goering's out of the way. I hope he stays out. Almost the only one of the whole bunch I can digest is Dr. Frick. No, young friend, no use your breaking a lance here for Hitler. I tell you he's through."

"I'd agree with you," I insisted, "if there were anybody better than Hitler in sight to take his place. There's no one, definitely no one. You haven't seen him since before the putsch, but I have. I grant you he's disappointing in some ways, but there's more to him than to any possible rival."

"What about Strasser? He's promising enough," said Reventlow.

Strasser, I agreed, was promising, but would never go the limit. He would go far, but Hitler would go farther. Strasser had missed his great chance to take things in his own hands while Hitler was in prison. He hadn't that driving force, that leader complex to get to the very top no matter what happened. And he lacked Hitler's dynamic impulse.

"What's the good of ignoring Hitler or fighting him, if you haven't a better man to do it with? It will delay but not arrest developments. It's certainly a better policy to support Hitler and push men like Strasser, so that Hitler's trees won't grow into the sky."

I wanted something definite from Reventlow-I wanted him to help me establish for Hitler a working relationship with Doctor Class and other important Nationalists, men whose influence under a Hindenburg regime could do much to smooth the Fuehrer's path. "Class is an honest Nationalist," I said. "He wants what Hitler wants, and has a lot that Hitler hasn't. But he needs Hitler. Neither he nor any other old dignitary of his class can line up youth and the working man. But Hitler can."

"Yes, that's all plausible enough," Reventlow said patiently, "but don't forget that with Hindenburg President, things have changed greatly. I have no special illusions about Hindenburg, yet people in general have, and they don't think that a Hitler is needed any longer. On the contrary, they think that he might spoil things. However, do as you wish. You know I'm sceptical, but I won't stand in your way. Perhaps you can impress the old Herr Justizrat, though I doubt it."

The various tentatives I then made in that direction were not at all discouraging. Dr. Class and Finanzrat Dr. Bang, the financial expert of the Pan-German

Association and an important figure as founder and head of a new folkic association of industrialists, listened to me with understanding and declared that they were ready at any time to discuss with Hitler a basis for co-operation if his men would cease their defamations and malicious attacks.

I trod on thorns in my other work, however. Unfortunately, one representative in Berlin, a man who had been chosen by Hitler, showed himself incompetent and jealous of interference. He resented not only my representing the Beobachter, on which he had counted for revenue, but my very presence; he seemed to think that I was there solely to check up on him. Instead of helping me, he intrigued against me and made trouble wherever he could.

In no time at all we found ourselves in open conflict. With typical inefficiency, the Party had given me responsibilities which duplicated powers already granted to this man. He and his people were unfit for the work in hand; in a city of four millions, he was selling less than fifty copies of the paper; yet his resentment when I tried to organize a creditable distribution had its echoes in Munich. After a controversial exchange of letters, there arrived from the Bavarian capital an 'arbitrator' who simply stirred up affairs even more hopelessly. A former Communist of the usual type, whom Hitler had selected because he could 'talk' in meetings, he was later kicked out of the Party. But when he arrived to represent headquarters in a difficult situation, my respect for the Party sank almost to zero. How on earth could we dream of achieving anything if we put so much as a fraction of our fate in hands like his?

At this juncture, an opportunity came my way to get out of the Berlin mess and completely away, out of Germany and out of the petty back-biting of local Party politics. A German art-publishing house asked me to represent it in Canada and the United States, assuring an immediate income and the promise of rebuilding that financial independence so necessary if I were to continue my political activities in a manner consistent with my code.

The future in Germany was obscure, but there could be no doubt that for the Party and its members all hope of earning a reward must be postponed for several years at least. In the meantime, rather than live precariously by claiming a share of the Party's puny war-chest, I preferred to earn my own way, meanwhile working as best I could for the cause. So I prepared to leave, and returned to Munich to confer with Hitler again.

But first I saw Roehm. A long conversation with him strengthened my belief in the wisdom of my course.

"You have a good grasp of things and men," he said. "No need to tell you what Hitler is like. Believe me, I didn't mince words when I last talked with him. But it's useless; if you try to tell him anything, he knows everything already. Though he often does what we advise, he laughs in our faces at the moment, and later does the very thing as if it were all his own idea and creation. I've never seen a man so magnificently unaware that he's adorning himself with borrowed plumage. Usually he solves suddenly, at the very last minute, a situation that has become intolerable and dangerous only because he vacillates and procrastinates. And that's because he can't act as clearly and logically as he can think and talk-no system in the execution of his thoughts. Hitler wants things his own way, and gets mad when he strikes firm opposition on solid ground. And he doesn't realize how he can wear on one's nerves, doesn't know that he fools only himself and those worms around him with his fits and heroics. But nobody is perfect, and he has his great qualities. Apparently there's nobody else who would do better than he."

Here was a man, probably second only to Hitler in the Party, who had preferred to abandon his career rather than blindly to accept the 'leadership principle' under a leader who appeared not ideally fitted to hold unlimited power in the movement. Roehm's personal doubts had been re-enforced by his awareness of Hitler's low credit throughout the Reich, which he thought could be restored to its former level only by cautious plugging over a period of years.

"And if this is the situation in Germany, how much he must need an advocate abroad! By all means go," said Roehm.

Rosenberg agreed also, though with a touch of bitterness. His decision to abandon Party work had crumbled under pressure of the necessity of earning a living, but his opinions had not changed.

"The men around Hitler are still what they were," he said ruefully. Take Amann. As editor of the Beobachter, I have to deal with him as business manager-yet our personal relationship is such that we communicate only by notes! But what can I do? I have to accept the measly salary. I'm married; it's too late to discover a new career for myself outside the Party. Besides, the work is my life, I cannot give up the cause. I'm stuck here, no matter how badly Hitler lets things slide. Consider yourself lucky to get clear of this mess. Once you're abroad, you'll find plenty to do for us.

Hitler and I lunched together in a braeuhaus, and fortunately I found him in a pleasant mood, despite my very sharp letters to Amann about the Beobachter situation.

"You don't seem to think much of my Berlin district-leader," Hitler said, taking a gulp from his bierseidal. "Don't you see that he puts on a good show in the meetings, with his rolling bass, his duel-scarred face and war-crippled arm, and an Iron Cross, First Class, on his chest?"

I couldn't help laughing. "That's so typical of you. You're a brilliant politician and you have a fine instinct for the mass, but you surprise me sometimes in your individual judgments. The man is the type of the eternal German student. You can't expect an old corps student to be a leader and build up an organization."

Hitler listened to my account of my difficulties in Berlin, and to my reasons for going abroad.

The foreign field suited my temperament better, I said finally. During my long absences I had somewhat grown out of the German rhythm-not enough to feel myself a stranger in Germany, but enough to acquire a slight impatience with some of the 'typical' German habits of thought and action. It made me writhe to have idiots who found nothing else to criticize declare indignantly that I couldn't be a Nazi because I rode in taxis and wore a gold wrist-watch. "But they don't mind riding with me," I told Hitler, "or wouldn't mind wearing the watch themselves if I were to give it to them. I am as I am, and obviously my attitude, which I cannot suppress, will not smooth my path or add to my value at home."

My job lay abroad. America offered a better field for my talents than Germany, now that the prospect of a coup de force had given way to the long, dull grind towards parliamentary power, which would demand of me more petty compromises than I could stand. I was more interested in Germany's role in the van of the folkic world struggle than I was in wages, local scandals, and internal quarrels. And I was more than ever convinced that our main weakness lay in the foreign political situation; that was my field and hereafter I'd stick to it. When, in a more or less distant future, our domestic hopes were beginning to materialize, he would: find that foreign policy would need much more of his attention than he could give it now. There was a lot to do-more than I· could ever dream of doing alone. But he could count on me not to be idle; I would do my share as his missionary abroad.

Hitler did not answer for a brief space. Then he said: "I believe that our world programme, in the far future, needs England more than any other country. Don't you think it might be better for you to begin in England?"

"No-I've thought of that, too, but it's much too early now. The mere fact that I'm a German would nullify, as German propaganda, even good work on my part. The British are slow-Americans live faster and they are far away. My job gives me an opportunity for wide travel, and I can make a first-hand study of America and get acquainted with people. Much better to work the English via the Americans, for the time being at least."

"I suppose you're right," Hitler nodded. "By the way, I read that booklet you gave me, Two Days with Ludendorff-good job, good propaganda. I'm glad that you won't desert me. No matter what happens, we have to go on, haven't we? It's in our blood, we can't get away from it. I wish there were more like you. Keep in touch with me. Good luck to you!"

Gregor Strasser alone advised against my leaving Germany. "I believe that it would be better for you and for the Party if you were to hold on. You're a Berliner and we need men like you in the capital. I myself am thinking of moving up North pretty soon. I wouldn't mind your doing some good pioneer work in the meantime," he said good-naturedly.

I saw an opportunity to tease him a little.

"By the way, if you take your man Himmler with you, tell him that there's quite a job waiting for him-I mean the proscription list for Berlin." And I showed Strasser a letter his henchman Himmler had recently sent me.

MUCH ESTEEMED MR. LUDECKE:

Excuse my bothering you with this letter and taking the liberty of addressing a question to you. Perhaps you know that I am now working in the management of the district of Lower-Bavaria of the Party. I also help with the editing of the local folkic paper, the Kuricr fuer Ndb.

For some time I have entertained the project of publishing the names of all Jews, as well as of all Christian friends of the Jews, residing in Lower-Bavaria. However, before I take such a step I should like to have your opinion, and to know whether you consider such an undertaking rich in prospects and effective. I would be much indebted to you if as soon as possible you would give me your view, which for me is authoritative, thanks to your great experience in the Jewish question and your knowledge of the anti-Semitic fight in the whole world.

I enclose two copies of a speech of Reichstag deputy Strasser. Expressing to you in advance my very best thanks, I am with respectful regards and treudeutschem Heilgruss. Faithfully

(Signed) HEINRICH HIMMLER.

Strasser laughed, then rumbled in his blunt Bavarian dialect: "That's just like him. He sees in every creature who doesn't 'think' Nazi a Jew or a Jew serf, a Jesuit or a Freemason. He's devoted to me and I use him as a secretary. He's very ambitious, but 1 won't take him along-he's no world-beater, you know."

That was 1925. Today this young man who was no world-beater and whose pointed nose and pince-nez gave him more the look of a little country schoolmaster than of a crusader, rules over the formidable 'Gestapo' or secret police, over the entire German police and the SS, and is one of the most powerful figures in the Third Reich. If anyone had told Strasser then that in 1934, nine years later, this modest fledgling would be able to arrest and execute him through his henchmen, he would instead have died of laughter.

"But joking aside," Strasser said, growing earnest again, "you'd better change your mind. We could do things together-I mean it. It's tough now-but who knows? Things may turn out better than we think. Mind, once gone you're soon forgotten, and it won't be so easy to get back in the swing again. Better join me and fight with me instead of getting lost in the Canadian woods or scalped by savage Indians."

His words had impressed me, but my plans were laid. A few weeks later I was in London on my way to Montreal.

XVI

SIMPLE INTERLUDE

April of 1926 found me in California seeking retreat with the Franciscan monks at the Mission of San Luis Rey. If that seems a surprising step in the story of a Nazi, the state of mind which led me there is comprehensible enough.

My new business venture, which had carried me all through Canada after several trips to New York, had taught me another lesson. I had come to America eager to regain my financial independence. But I had not the slightest intention of neglecting my work for the cause, and I learned that it was impossible to do justice to both aims at the same time. When I realized that my business affairs needed all my attention, all my energy, and, if I wanted to succeed, demanded nothing less than my giving up political activity, I did not hesitate a moment in making my choice. The revolutionary in me was on top again.

The mentality of a revolutionary is indeed a curious thing. He moves and acts under one impulse, guided by one maxim: the end justifies the means. Again I was ready to sacrifice my personal interests; I knew now that I preferred an uncertain but adventurous life for a real cause to an uninteresting, hard, and useless struggle for my own security, an aim which seemed to me meaningless and, commonplace at a time when a world was going to pieces.

Looking back now at my former activities, impelled as I then was by two opposing forces-a temperamental inclination to live as I pleased, and an idealist's obsession to save mankind-I am amazed that I had as much singleness of purpose as I did. One idea was uppermost after all: I must do my share to reforge this lying, crazy world; I was ready again to subordinate everything else to it. Having acquired the habit of thinking more and more in terms of centuries and continents, I was inclined to see in men and situations nothing but pawns to serve an end.

It is necessary to keep this in mind if one wants to understand the attitude of thinking Nazis. It explains why I had no scruples against using my business connections to the utmost. Without entirely forgetting, I hasten to add, the interests of my employers. I arranged to extend my travels to San Francisco, because I thought it imperative for my future activity to gain a working knowledge of the land and people of America. The more I saw of the American colossus stretching from the Atlantic to the Pacific, the clearer became my perspective of Germany and Europe. This broader view naturally could only deepen my conviction that the Nazi fight would grow eventually into a world struggle for a new order, which some day might change the face of this earth.

In this mood I would be of no further use to my business friends in Germany, and so I severed the connection, a decision which relieved my conscience and restored independence to my spirit but not my purse. I had only a few shillings, and nothing to draw upon except my faith in the cause. But now that was enough. Rich within, I had a heart for any fate. . I was dissatisfied with myself, however. As a Nazi, I had not been idle; I had lectured to Germans and German-Americans in Montreal, Toronto, New York, and other places, doing what I could to spread our ideas and gain sympathy for our cause. Yet the progress I had made was insignificant. What had been my impression after former visits to the United States was now my conviction: the German and German-American element was not the right vehicle for our propaganda. There was only one way to gain American sympathy and support. We must approach the American-born through native Americans, with an American folkic programme. That would be a hard job for an alien. At that time I was not even an immigrant with his first papers; all I had was a visitor's visa for a six-months' stay, which had been once extended. With such a problem before me, I wanted simply to get away and think. I needed a real rest after all these hectic years without a holiday, but most of all I needed a spiritual retreat in which I might meditate and gain strength to conquer myself before I tried to conquer others. One afternoon while I was walking through a park in San Francisco, I observed a Franciscan Father coming towards me. On impulse I stopped him.

"I knew some Franciscan Fathers in South America who were very kind to me. It is a real surprise to see you here; you are the first monk, the first Franciscan, I have come across in this country. I am a foreigner, please pardon me. If you have time, I should like to talk to you a little."

The good Franciscan looked puzzled for a moment, but answered good-naturedly: "Yes, of course, my friend."

He was a nice old man with the eyes of a child. I told him only that I was on the threshold of a new life and needed advice; I was going to Los Angeles, and hoped to find a quiet place to think in peace. He wrote a note and handed it to me.

"This Father is a German and I am sure he will help you. Perhaps he can find a place for you in one of the missions."

Los Angeles restored my interest in the objective life somewhat. I went about getting acquainted. With my newspaper credentials it was easy to visit the studios. I watched Eric von Stroheim directing the Wedding March, and even displayed my talents as an extra for eight dollars a day; I visited with my old friend the Grand Duchess Polavska, alias Pola Negri, whom I had known in 1919 when she filmed Madame Du Barry in Potsdam, just before my departure for Buenos Aires.

But two weeks of this sort of thing was enough, and I went to find that Franciscan Father, at a monastery or church whose name I have forgotten. The German monk was not there; another came in his stead and read the note. After a short talk he wrote a letter warmly recommending me to the Father Guardian of the Mission of San Luis Rey.

So it happened that late in the afternoon of Holy Thursday in 1926 I rang the bell of the mission. A novice opened the door and took my letter while I waited in the hall.

A few minutes later I was sitting opposite Father Guardian Albert. I liked him immediately. This tall, slender monk, healthy and tanned, with kind grey eyes in a strong face, had a poise and dignity which inspired confidence. Again I was welcomed without one question. He showed me to my room, and said: "You must be hungry. You can have your dinner here. Later in the evening we will continue our talk." Then he left me.

I was alone in a room which was almost bare. There were just a cot, a table, and chair, a Bible on a little shelf, and a crucifix on the whitewashed wall. The window looked over wide fields in bloom.

The last rays of the setting sun were flooding this peaceful cell. Soon the swift California dusk began to come down. It was the hour of contemplation; the stillness was intense with the chirping of a million crickets; the air was warm and fragrant, filled with all the hopes of spring.

At first a sense of unreality pervaded me in this new remoteness from the world. Why had I, Nazi crusader and pagan at heart though Protestant by birth, found refuge in a monastery of the Franciscan monks? Had I a right to be here? I wondered whether they knew that I was not a Catholic. They must, I thought. But then, even a pagan may seek his God with a deeply religious soul.

After a while a novice brought my dinner and withdrew without a word. It was a frugal but tasty meal, and the wine was good.

The ringing of a lonely bell reminded me that I knew nothing of the rules and duties in a monastery. Was this a summons to the evening devotions? What should I do-how ought I to behave? Another novice solved the problem by summoning me to Father Albert.

We sat in a little tower, the cloister court on one side, the garden on the other. There was a feeling only monks can give. Sipping our wine, we talked late into the night.

Father Albert was of German descent, and I happened to be the first German he had seen for many years. We spoke of my country and the war, and I told him of Hitler and the Nazi struggle. Still maintaining his reserve, he put questions and made comments which revealed his interest in a world of which he had never heard before.

"Let us take a walk through the garden before we retire," he said finally. "Morning is not far away and soon you will hear the singing of the birds."

218

The air had the freshness of the hour before the dawn. My soul was quiet and my heart felt warm. Beside me on the garden path, Father Albert looked almost like a ghost in his monkish garb.

"Giving it new thought," he said, "I believe it would be better for you to go With me to Pala day after tomorrow instead of staying here. Pala is the ideal place for you. It lies in the mountains some eighteen miles away, in the beautiful Pala valley, near an Indian reservation. It is a small, abandoned mission; only the chapel is left and part of the main building. A romantic old place, with only two white people. One, a doctor for the Indians, lives two miles away. The other, a very pleasant man and an old friend of mine, runs a general store which occupies the left wing of what remains of the mission. Most of the Indians are very kind. They are like children, and devoted to the Church.

"I am going there on Saturday to celebrate Easter Sunday Mass for the Indians and the farmers in the valley. When I have left you there, you will be alone to collect your thoughts, and you can stay as long as you like. But I warn you, it is very simple, it has no conveniences, and you must sleep on a little iron cot. And," he added, with a twinkle in his eyes, " if you really want to fast and live on oranges, I'm sure it can be arranged."

Of course I accepted gratefully. Indians, adobe walls in ruins, mountains, woods of oak and pepper trees, orange groves-it seemed the promise of a perfect haven.

But before I left for Pala, I received perhaps the most mystical impression of my life. After Father Albert and I parted in the garden, I slept and awoke refreshed, to spend a solitary afternoon. In the evening I went to the Good Friday devotions.

All the Fathers, Brothers, and Novices were assembled, kneeling before the altar with heads bowed low, fervently murmuring their prayers. The chapel was dim in the flicker of the candles burning in the seven-branched candelabra. The praying grew more intense when a monk began putting out the candles, one after another. Presently there was utter darkness.

Suddenly from near the altar a faint light threw on the wall a wavering shadow which steadied into the profile of a humble monk-the spirit of Saint Francis of Assisi.

The monks had ceased praying; there was absolute stillness. I could hear the pounding of my heart. Then shadow and light vanished, and there was darkness again. Now the monks were intoning their prayers in ecstasy, beating their brows against the stone floor. The acolyte slowly relighted the candles.

I had witnessed a ritual observed every Good Friday in memory of Saint Francis, founder of the order. It had almost as much emotional effect on a Nazi pagan as on the praying monks.

On Saturday afternoon Father Albert and I set out through a lovely landscape on our way to Pala. We dined on a ranch with friends of the monk's. Darkness was settling in the folds of the hills when we took the trail again, climbing steadily. A little stream murmured beside us. Soon the night was touching everything with mystery, and boyhood fancies came back to turn the Franciscan into my Indian hero Winnetou, and me into Old Shatterhand, on mustangs sure footedly carrying us uphill.

It was almost midnight when we reached Pala Mission. I was thoroughly weary now, and under no illusions about stepping down from a rattling old Model-T Ford.

Two days later Father Albert had gone. I was alone in my new quarters, within walls over a yard thick. My room had a fireplace, a large, rough table and several rude chairs, a shelf with a few religious books, and, of course, a crucifix. The skins of two rattlesnakes and a coyote adorned the wall. My iron cot stood in a tiny cell, near a small kitchen with an earthen stove. Outside the back door, an old pump furnished water. Huge pepper trees stood in a garden gone wild; a wooden fence separated it from the courtyard of the general store. Beyond lay adobe walls in ruins.

The Indians were kind; I was a friend of their beloved Father Albert, and they were curious to see the German who had come from far away over the great waters. Within a few days I had a horse, a chestnut mare caught from the many running around in the large valley. And I had oranges, more than I could eat. Riding through the grove, I picked them myself from the overloaded boughs.

At once I began my fast, living only on oranges and water. And I stopped smoking, which was far harder, for I had been a 'chain-smoker,' consuming from forty to sixty cigarettes a day. The change was so violent that my whole system revolted. I did not give in. The fifth day was apparently the crisis; I felt ill and almost crazy. But after that I recovered rapidly, feeling better every day, until I gained a vigour of health and a lucidity of mind unknown to me before-or since.

I got up with the sun and pumped cold water over my tanned body. Then I ate at least two oranges, and worked naked in the neglected garden for an hour or two. After a sun-bath I had some more oranges, and then would study Indian life, or rest in the shade near my horse, 'Swallow,' reading or working on a manuscript - a sort of a political manual which I intended to use for my activities and to publish, if possible. From two to six or later I would spend rambling on horseback, or bathing in the Pala stream while Swallow grazed near by. Home again, I would tie Swallow to a pepper tree and give her some fodder. Then I had my own meal of five oranges or more. I consumed between twenty and thirty oranges a day. When it was dark, about nine o'clock, I went to bed.

For once I was leading a healthy life, and I felt strong and happy. But flesh was soon to vanquish spirit.

On the seventeenth day, after a long ride, I was washing myself under the pump when I saw a man coming from behind the barn on the other side of the fence. He had a canteen slung over his shoulder and carried a heavy stick; the oldest of felt hats almost hid a leathery face. I observed his overalls, so stiff with patches that they could have stood alone. He disappeared into a little wooden shack which clung to the adobe wall like a bird's nest.

He had not seen me.

Curious about my new neighbour, I went over, and through the open window watched him smoking his pipe and handling a frying-pan. He looked between fifty and sixty, lean and of medium height, with weather-beaten features, heavy eyebrows, and deeply furrowed brow and neck.

"Good evening, sir," I called at a venture, but he did not even look up. I tried twice again without result. Determined now, I banged at his door and entered, introducing myself as his neighbour and wishing him good appetite for his supper. He growled something unintelligible into his pipe, and I continued to talk casually on. Finally he said that he was a prospector, and had come here to look over the Pala mines, part of which were drowned in water. What was a prospector. Grudgingly he told me-it was evident that he did not think much of the greenhorn in his presence. But I stood my ground and said that I would like to go with him one day. Throwing me a contemptuous look, he barked:

"Well, if you can get up at four o'clock and walk five hours to the place and back, you can come along."

Obviously he didn't expect me, but when I joined him next morning he barely gave me a glance. At quarter to five he started off with long, even strides. Hour after hour he kept on, until we reached a fire-break not cleared for years, grown over with heavy underbrush. Up we went. I was beginning to wonder what this fellow was up to, and I was having the devil of a time. Thorns and brush were clawing my legs and ruining my trousers-and I was afraid of rattlesnakes. And so I trotted behind him under a blazing sun, anxiously looking right and left, ready to jump if I heard a rattle. But my prospector did not bother about such things. It was about ten o'clock when at last he stopped, took a long draught from his canteen, handed it to me without a word, and then went on again. I was fatigued now and trying hard not to show it. When the trail was once more winding round the mountain he spoke.

"There are the Pala mines."

And on he went.

It was almost two o'clock when we got there.' I had only one orange left. While I was tasting the dubious pleasure of watching him eat his sandwiches, Bobby Tritton - I think that was his name-began to open up a bit. He even talked. Finally he said:

"You're a better guy than I thought you were. I didn't believe you'd make it. Now I'll show you the mine and tell you what prospectors do."

When we started home near four in the afternoon, we were friends. But the way back was strangely easy and swift. At a quarter past six we crossed the yard and he asked me into his hut, with a grin on his face.

221

"Now you know," he said, " what it means to go with Bobby Tritton to the Pala mines. But don't mind my having fooled you-you're all right. Don't go picking any oranges. I'm going to make a regular mulligan for both of us."

That ended my fasting. I was too hungry to resist. I don't think I have ever eaten so much of anything, and with such gusto, as I did of his mulligan, the first and best I ever had. Over our coffee, he smoked his short pipe and told me of his prospector days along the coast and in the Rockies, spicing his narrative with incredible jokes. Bobby Tritton would have fitted perfectly into Bret Harte's tales of California.

Father Albert, when he came again, asked me to give a talk at the Mission of San Luis Rey. I spoke twice on Germany and the Jewish question. It was interesting to watch the faces of those monks and of the elder pupils of their school when I told them of Hitler and of our struggle to create a new concept of the world. Here was a curious thing indeed: a Nazi revolutionary and pagan on the platform before Franciscan monks.

The weeks passed quickly. Never had I felt better in body and mind, and I knew it was time to go back to my task. I should like to write more about Pala. But this book is dedicated to more serious business.

Back in Los Angeles, I faced a new problem. How was I to finance a trip to Detroit? It was important that I be present at a Jewish libel suit against Henry Ford. Having already pawned all my valuables, I had just enough cash to pay for one meal.

I took the only thing I could find at the moment. A casual acquaintance introduced me to the maitre d'hotel of one of the big hotels and asked him to give me a job. I thought it not a bad idea, for I hoped in a few days to make enough in tips to carry me to San Francisco. Being inexperienced, I was put on the floor-service.

My new colleague, also a garfon d'etage, lent me a uniform which did not fit me very well. Tanned almost coffee-brown and looking the picture of health, I felt ridiculous. After a nearly nudist existence in the mountains a stiff collar and a starched shirt were torture.

But I was heartened by the memory of an experience I had had as a waiter. Years ago, before the war, a distinguished and beautiful but unapproachable lady had refused to take the slightest notice of me. Her charm was such that I had to meet her, but I had to be quick, as I was leaving for London the very next day. She happened to live on the same floor of the hotel where I was staying, and I decided that my only chance to force the issue was to take her breakfast to her room next morning. Money talked, and I was able to persuade the waiter on my floor to let me play his role. When she rang for her breakfast shortly after nine o'clock, I answered the call. Clad in a khaki suit, the last word from London, I must have looked anything but a waiter. I recall my sinking sensation when, carefully balancing the tray, I knocked at her door and went into the room. To this day I can see the picture that greeted me when, wheeling round, I discovered her still in bed, looking at me with wide, astonished eyes. I almost lost my nerve; it was the crucial moment. But before she could scream or reach for the telephone, I lowered the tray to her bed and said:

"Beautiful lady, don't be afraid. No use complaining to the management-you'd only compromise yourself. Besides I've already checked out and am leaving for London at noon. I had to see you before I go."

The ice was broken, her curiosity was aroused. My boldness, her bizarre situation, and perhaps other favourable factors combined to weaken her natural resistance. I have the pleasantest memories of that encounter.

Perhaps I would have a bit of luck again, despite my grotesque appearance. But the reality proved a grim contrast to the dream. After serving several dignified ladies and gentlemen with more good-will than skill, I answered an order for ice and Canada Dry, and found a strange, resolute lady well along in her fifties, of the aggressive type. Despite her gorgeous pyjamas, she looked anything but desirable, to put it mildly. And evidently she liked to drink. I stood waiting for my check to be signed or paid, but she leisurely mixed her highball, looking me over, and started to talk in what impressed me as a very silly way.

"Madame," I said after a while, handing her the check, "will you please sign? I must go and serve other guests." She handed me two one-dollar bills.

"But the check is only twenty-five cents," I told her.

"Keep the rest for yourself, but be back here as soon as you can," she said, with a speaking look.

I left hurriedly in some consternation, feeling that I had not made good my escape. I was right. In half an hour or so she asked for more ice and another bottle of Canada Dry. It was the same story, except that this time she was more outspoken and insistent. On my third visit I found her decidedly aggressive and in a nicely advanced state-she must have had at least five highballs. "Now sit down here," she said. "Have a drink. I won't let you go this time." "But madame, I cannot," I protested. "I must attend to my duties."

"Rubbish," she said, and pushed me into a seat. "You're on duty now, right here. I pay you."

"But madame," I cried with rising desperation, "you forget--" And then she interrupted me to state matters in words too plain for these pages. And I, feeling myself really at bay, lost my temper and bellowed at her in language even plainer. Whereat she began swearing and throwing things at me, and I ran out of the room.

That finished my career as a garçon d'etage. I quit that very evening. I had made over six dollars, not so bad for one day.

My next job was a loftier one-window-cleaner in an office building. On the fifth or sixth day I almost fell from the ninth floor into the street. I had finished a window, and after getting back into the room decided that the outside of the lower sash was not quite satisfactory. Being a Prussian and accustomed to doing a first-class job once I start, I went back, but this time did not attach the safety-belt. Somehow I slipped, and would have fallen into space if my feet had not caught the lower edge of the window. It took all my strength to pull myself slowly back into the room. That was enough of window-cleaning.

I counted my money. I could just about get to San Francisco by bus, without paying my hotel bill. The manager of my second-rate hotel was a good old soul who liked to talk to me; he had even advanced me ten dollars. I told him that I should like to depart at once without paying my bill. Having far too much luggage, I offered to leave my trunks with him; I would send for them as soon as I was in funds. He obliged me, and I started north without my two trunks, which I never recovered. Among the things I lost was an album of pictures which included a large photograph of Hitler inscribed to me in Landsberg-the first ever circulated.

In San Francisco I conceived the idea of giving lessons in German and French; so when a friend joined me from Los Angeles, a young and personable Englishman, we worked it out that he was to present himself as my secretary and I was to be traveller and writer. An advertisement in the paper brought me three women pupils from whom I asked five dollars a lesson. Eventually I made about seventy dollars a week for two or three weeks.

As a Nazi, I continued trying to make contacts with the Press and with people who might later be useful. For my meetings and speeches I still had to use the German-American element, being without means or plan for reaching the native American.

In most American cities there was no German newspaper, but wherever there was one it provided a point of contact. Or there would be German clubs, and through them I would look for 'good' Germans to interest in our movement. Then I would suggest a lecture, under whatever auspices I could muster.

In general, the German societies were either purely social organizations, such as Gesangvereine, Turnvereine, Kegelvereine, or tribal organizations-Bavarian, Swabian, and so forth, politically more or less uninterested in Germany. They felt themselves to be good Americans and had only a cultural link with Germany, chiefly one of music. But they were a boring and philistine lot. The more intelligent Germans were completely Americanized and cut off from the body German. I soon saw that the capture of these societies was out of the question because the liberal-democratic spirit was overwhelming. Most of them were opposed to the former monarchy and satisfied with the Weimar Republic. In a way, it had been the creation of Wood row Wilson, and it had always had a first-rate Press in America.

Naturally, an intelligent German Government could find in the numerous German societies excellent instruments for certain purposes if it knew how to use them. Actually, however, when the Nazis came to power and Hitler tucked me away behind bars, they had no one who really knew how to enlist help from this source.

My position was always unenviable. Even in Germany the folkic movement was in complete debacle and had lost hundreds of thousands of its followers. I had nothing but my inner faith-not even comradeship, for I was in the most forlorn of all situations: that of a lone prophet in a strange country. I found it advisable to announce myself not as a Nazi but as a, well-known German writer:

In San Francisco three hundred people attended my meeting, which was held without sponsors; I simply put an advertisement in the local newspaper and arranged with three or four people to publicize it in the local societies, which centred about a 'German House' with large and small halls, restaurants, and so forth. Some German communities, such as those of New York, Detroit, Chicago, Cincinnati, Milwaukee, and St. Louis, boasted a real theatre with German players which was the focus for all the various societies. There were also the German: Masonic lodges. Anyone could hire a hall.

My San Francisco audience was enthusiastic, and as usual, I allowed free discussion afterwards; in debate I was always happy and could carry even a hostile crowd. The success was such that the 'Allgemeine Arbeiter Bildungsverein,' a purely Marxian Socialist-education group, called a meeting for 12 August 1926 to answer me.

A typical Marxian functionary from Berlin was the principal speaker. I had been challenged to debate, and accepted with the stipulation that I be allowed at least thirty minutes' speaking time. My opponents had distributed thousands of insulting handbills all over the city; my answer was to begin handing out my own leaflets when I got to the hall, which soon was crowded with more than twelve hundred people. It was an organized opposition such as I had encountered once before, in Montreal.

My Marxian was already on the platform. He read my pamphlet and shook his finger at me. There was hissing and heckling. In the whole audience there were certainly not more than fifty or sixty sympathetic to me.

I sat down next the speaker on a chair provided for me in the centre of the stage-an exposed target for abuse. For almost two hours I listened patiently to ridicule. After several vain attempts to get the chairman to give me the platform, I decided to take matters into my own hands. Jumping to my feet, I interrupted the speaker by shouting into the hall:

"Attention! Attention!"

There was general uproar.

"Silence!" I cried. "Don't you want to hear me? I was promised an opportunity to speak to you for at least thirty minutes. This treatment is cowardly and unfair."

New uproar and shouting. "Throw him out!" But now many other voices were crying: "Let him speak. We want to hear him!"

"Are you afraid to hear me?" I yelled, and that finished the opposition.

I always introduced quite a new tone into such meetings, talking in the hardest and sharpest way, attacking vigorously; at first I invariably had to overcome interruptions, but usually I was successful. And I was this time. To the dismay of the 'leaders' on the stage, I got the platform and spoke to rising applause. After the meeting, I remembered Hitler's veto of my ambition to be a Nazi speaker in Germany, and wished that he could have heard me.

A few days later, I was warned to clear out of the city if I did not want to be 'bumped off or deported.'

From San Francisco I started east, now a real hobo 'thumbing for lifts'; with luck I could still reach Detroit in time for Ford's action. In a lunch-wagon in Sacramento I met two outright hobos, a novice and a veteran. The veteran initiated me into scientific hoboing. From this graduate of Dartmouth, a trained engineer, I learned that the hobo army has its own esprit de corps, ethics, codes, and comradeships, and comprises all degrees of society from regular criminals to the unemployed and those who merely do not like bourgeois life. The fellow was a real philosopher. His greenhorn companion, Otto, was a German sailor who had jumped ship, and had decided to beat his way to Chicago to find his relatives there. He had been in the submarine service of the imperial navy during the war. A Communist idealist, he was, in his own way, a splendid chap.

We three joined forces. I was learning a strange, new aspect of America-its nomad horde that follows the seasons, travelling on foot, by auto, by rail, in freight cars and coal cars. I encountered men who lived entirely by their-wits, some who relied on seasonal labour, others who depended on theft.

In a cave in Nevada I stayed in a hobo camp equipped with blankets and tinned food. If you had money, hobo ethics required you to restock it before moving on. I saw two such camps and believe there are many more. Walking and bumming our way in motor-cars, we three stuck together as far as Denver. The hospitality of the road was to me, a German, fantastic. I had never encountered anything like the kindness and willingness to help.

I still had some money and had recovered some valuables I had pawned. But it was getting towards the end of September and the nights were growing cool. I realized that if I was to make Detroit in time, I would have to travel faster. In Denver the sale of my field-glasses bought me a ticket to Chicago, and I bade my two good hobo friends a sad farewell.

XVII

SELLING HITLER IN AMERICA

By the time I got to Chicago, after stopping over to try for a hearing in the larger cities en route, I was broke again and had to pawn what jewellery I had left. I reached Detroit late in November 1926 with two dollars in my pocket.

I had always wanted to spend at least a week in the Ford works, but the best I could get was the night-shift in the papermill. They set me to splitting and pulverizing with a hammer the blocks of resin used for paper fabrication, or carrying the heavy loads of waste paper collected throughout the plant. Ruining my good suit of clothes, I struggled with work beyond my strength. On the fourth night-Friday-I fainted. By Monday I was a real-estate salesman on a drawing-account of thirty dollars a week.

That was one of the oddest experiences of my life. My first victim was a Frenchman who played a monkey-act in one of the theatres, a skilled acrobat who knew nothing about real estate. He has my sympathy. He paid almost two thousand dollars for those lots and probably is still stuck with them. But I learned much about the advertising racket and the American science of salesmanship, thrusting my nose into many things, discovering more about American mentality than in all my previous visits put together, but keeping away from making Nazi propaganda. Since I was to attend and report the Ford libel suit as a newspaper correspondent, I did not· want to become conspicuous.

Henry Ford was being sued by a Chicago lawyer, Aaron Sapiro; the libel action was based on a series of articles criticizing the 'Sapiro Plan' for the marketing of farm products. I believed that Ford would be obliged to back up his position, and that then I might find him approachable. In the worldwide burst of publicity bound to result, I might be able to be of service to him. My present aim was simply to keep myself afloat until something materialized here.

After the trial had finally opened in March 1927 I had several talks with Ford's editor of the Dearborn Independent W. J. Cameron, who introduced me to Senator James A. Reed of Missouri, one of the counsel for the defendant. Senator Reed was a handsome and distinguished looking man and a remarkable speaker, with a beautiful, deep voice, and perfect gestures. But he had one amazing habit. At regular intervals in the midst of a flowing, polished speech before a packed court-room, his lips would purse into a strange shape. Then, with perfect control, he would shoot a mass of yellow liquid unerringly into a spittoon almost three yards away-so expert a feat that I almost shouted with excitement. But nobody else seemed impressed.

Soon it was evident that Ford was really on the defensive, and didn't want to make anything out of the affair. The papers reported that it had been impossible to subpoena him; then, one fine morning, it was announced that he had had a motor accident and that it would be impossible for him to appear. The trial was adjourned. I was not surprised to be told confidentially that the matter would be settled out of court.

By the middle of May I knew definitely that Ford had made up his mind to discontinue, finally and permanently, the anti-Jewish campaign and all articles that might give offence to Jews. Of course it was a blow to me; Detroit was meaningless now. To cap it all, the news from Germany was most discouraging: the Nazi movement was all but dead. Here was a quandary: should I stay in America or go back to Germany? Deciding at last to stay, I was told I must return to Germany and apply for an immigrant's visa. Fortunately I do not believe everything I am told. When I learned that quotas are also provided for Germans living in Canada, I went across the border and established Canadian residence.

In this time of gloom I did an amazing thing. I married.

Colonel Lindbergh is directly responsible. He had made his transatlantic flight, and my mind saw future political possibilities for this young Norseman. His father, it developed, had been a congressman and a man of exceptional courage; he had even written a book, now out of print, called The International Money Trust-to a Nazi a most interesting and intriguing tide. My search for a copy finally led me to the Detroit News, reputed to possess the finest newspaper library in the world.

When I went there one afternoon shortly before five, I found the book, and I also found in the librarian a quality that interested me more than the elder Lindbergh's international money trust. She was about to close up for the day; so I hung around and walked down the street with her, pleased with her charm and poise and well-modulated voice, noting how definitely her fine hands and delicate feet expressed her personality. She was not beautiful, perhaps not even pretty. But she was aesthetically and gracefully feminine, intelligent and real.

We spent two hours together, to meet again the next day. On the fourth day I cooked for us a Mulligan stew ala Bobby Tritton in my Faustian room. In the twilight I kissed her gently. Later, when I kissed her good night on the porch of her father's house, I said on impulse, only half seriously:

"I don't see any reason why I shouldn't marry you."

"Yes, why not? " she answered, looking straight at me.

I liked that, and the idea began to grow in me. Several days later we discussed it in utmost frankness. Wanting above all to be honest, I told her I was dedicated to a cause which would always come first. After all, I was only an almost penniless revolutionary, who could not give her security and peace. All I had to offer was my faith in the future, and a life full of fight and contrast.

My dear, reasonable, but essentially romantic little Mildred was too involved with her crazy foreigner to weigh all the consequences. Three days later we were married in Bowling Green, Ohio, without her family's knowledge, for I knew we should never have their consent. I had an American wife of good stock, of intelligence, and judgment, who combined an almost lyrical temperament and a generous heart with character and will. Her natural pride and aloofness, her almost touching modesty, were especially endearing. I had a wife who would be helpful to me in my work in America. And she, for her part, had a husband who brought with him the certain prospect of an uncertain future.

Mildred had thought that our marriage would not get into the Detroit papers. A week later she telephoned to say in a trembling voice that her mother had read the news. "Good Lord!" I said. "Now I'll have to face the music. I'll be over after dinner."

My wife was the favourite of her father, a Yankee of English-Scottish stock, six feet tall, a man of few words, honest, and competent; his kind, strong face looked very much like the Mark Twain whose picture hung in his den. He would have resented anyone's taking his daughter away from him. But for a German, a foreigner, a crazy Nazi without a position, to marry his daughter after only nine days...!

I prepared myself for a hurricane, and I got it. Mildred was sitting with her mother in a corner of the living-room; both had been weeping. Her father charged as soon as I had dropped my hat. In his deep, roaring bass he stormed at me for some fifteen minutes, and I took it in silence. When he had finished, I said that from his viewpoint he was right. But Mildred and I were both mature and knew what we were doing; the future would prove to him that I was not such a bad sort. With that I left.

He was a grand old man. Later he gave us his blessing, and died within the year.

I had not forgotten about Lindbergh. He was likely to become a national hero and idol; if he should prove to have qualities of leadership he might have tremendous political possibilities for the furtherance of our folkic ideals in America. But one day I dropped him entirely from my calculations. In the 29 July issue of the American Hebrew, I found a significant photograph of Lindbergh and Harry F. Guggenheim; the young flyer was to tour America by air under the auspices of the Daniel Guggenheim Foundation for the Promotion of Aeronautics in America.

The late T. E. Shaw - 'Lawrence of Arabia' - was another object of speculation. He could have been the unchallenged leader of British youth. For years I tried to get in touch with him. Finally, in 1932, he sent me word through a mutual friend that in England the time was not yet ripe for action. I am convinced, however, of the truth of the rumour that his sudden death interrupted negotiations looking to a meeting with Hitler.

The real shock came early in July, when, along with a surprised world, I read the colossal news of Henry Ford's retraction and apology to the Jews.

Ford's signed statement had been sent to a Detroit attorney with a letter authorizing him to transmit it to Louis J. Marshall, a recognized leader of Jewry in the United States and throughout the world. He confessed himself:

'... deeply mortified that this journal (the Dearborn Independent). . . has been made the medium for resurrecting exploded fictions, for giving currency to the so-called Protocols of the Wise Men of Zion,[1] which have been demonstrated, as I learn, to be gross forgeries, and for contending that the Jews have been engaged in a conspiracy to control the capital and the industries of the world, besides laying at their door many offences against decency, public order, and good morals.

'Had I appreciated even the general nature, to say nothing of the details of these utterances, I would have forbidden their circulation without a moment's hesitation...'

There was much more, but what I have quoted was the core of the statement. Though I had already abandoned every hope of Ford, I had never expected one of the richest men in the world to be willing thus to repudiate his editor and to make such a humiliating kowtow to Jewry. Determined to get to the bottom of this, I rushed to Dearborn to catch Cameron before he could make himself invisible. Successful in dodging the usual routine of writing down name and purpose of visit at the information-desk, I found him alone in his office; even his secretary was so thoughtful as to be absent.

Cameron did not notice my entrance. Seated in his desk chair, turned half away from the door, he was gazing out the large window. Instinctively I stopped to watch him, thinking for the tenth of a second of Schopenhauer's Parerga und Paralipomena, in which he tells somewhere how revealing it is to get the impression of a person when he believes himself alone and unobserved. It was indeed revealing. Cameron was looking worried, his round, sour face resting in his small, soft hand, his short, rather stout body almost crumpled in the chair. He looked forlorn and weak. I felt instantly that Ford's recantation was as much news to him as it had been to me.

Walking in, without preamble I showed him the screaming headlines. "What is this? Did you know about it?"

His face took on an expression of helplessness, almost of guilt. Shaking his head, he said in a feeble voice: "No-no, I did not."

"Well, is there nothing you can do about it? It puts you in a terrible position!"

"Don't I know it?" said Cameron. "But what can I do? I'm still so stunned that I haven't made up my mind yet."

I pressed him hard. He must not, I said, regard this as a purely personal matter between himself and Ford. It was history-history in which he had played a very important role. He owed it to himself and to the world to come out with the present

---

1 The much-disputed Protocols represent a programme, alleged to have been composed at the First Zionist Congress in Basle (1897), for the Jewish domination of the world, and pointed to by anti-Jews as one of the principal evidences of a Jewish world-conspiracy.- K. L.

truth for the sake of the historical truth.

Cameron was avoiding my eyes, showing increased embarrassment, and nodding his head slowly, as if consulting with himself. Softening a little, I told him I knew he was in a bad spot; his bread and butter was at stake. And, of course, Ford was practically at his mercy.

"But you must force his hand," I urged. "You can turn the whole thing to the advantage of the cause for all of us if you have the guts."

But looking at him, I knew that he would not.

"I don't know yet what I am going to do," he said finally. After a moment he added in a firmer voice, with visible emotion: "But it is certain that I for my part will never make any retraction. What I have written will stand. Not one thing will I take back. You can be sure of that."

Cautious Cameron was becoming almost militant. ,

"All right," I said, "that's fine!"- and asked if he remembered our talk about his article, 'What About the Jewish Question?' published a year earlier. He had told me that this article in particular, which he had styled 'a frank exposition of the present status of this situation,' had been inspired by Ford himself and exactly expressed his views. Had Ford, since then, ever indicated to him or to anyone else that he had changed his attitude, or that something had happened to put doubt in his mind?

"No, decidedly not," Cameron said spontaneously. "The whole thing is a mystery to me. I know Ford too well not to be absolutely sure that the views set forth in that article are still his views, and that he thinks today as he always did simply cannot understand his alleged statement."

Producing his own article, I read him long passages from it, excerpts which emphasized the fairness of his view, made careful distinctions among Jews, brought out the fact that America's many socially minded Jews were a definite asset, declared the Dearborn Independent ready to defend all Jews who wanted to be Americans. It was a just article, true to fact and generous in spirit. Cameron, as he heard his own words repeated, had taken a brace; he was now on his feet.

It was Ford, I pointed out, and not Cameron, who had been quoted as saying about the disputed Protocols: 'Forgery or no forgery, they fit in.' If we Gentiles who accused international Jewry as a world-menace had not ourselves the courage of our convictions, we were worse than the Jews we accused. Cameron simply must not maintain silence. If it was true that he had written those articles in good faith, after a careful investigation of the facts, with Ford's explicit consent and on his order, then he must make himself heard; the world would listen. If it was not true, it was imperative that he say so, candidly and publicly. In either case he could not escape his responsibility to stand up and speak the truth.

With that I left him.

The world knows that nothing happened. Cameron is still in the employ of

231

Henry Ford.

Not satisfied with my personal observations, I went further and interviewed several people who had been at the source of the facts. The man from whom I learned most was E. G. Pipp, former editor-in-chief of the Detroit News and Ford's first editor of the Dearborn Independent. Pipp insists that he resigned because he disagreed with Ford when he learned of the contemplated anti-Jewish campaign. He talked to me freely, confirming my own findings. Several weeks later, in the 15 July issue of the American Hebrew, he wrote:

I am not saying that Ford knew as to the truth or falsity of every statement published in his 91 articles against the Jews. I am saying that the campaign was ordered by him and carried on with his knowledge.

So much for a sorry business.

Admitted to the quota at last, I entered the United States from Windsor as a regular immigrant. Though I say 'at last,' I had in fact been lucky to get my papers so quickly, within a few weeks after my application; in Germany I should have had to wait from one to two years at the least. At once I took out my first papers, eager to be off for New York.

In early August I left by the Buffalo boat. Gazing down at Mildred looking up at me from the dock with so much love and light in her eyes, I swore to myself that I would not betray her faith in me.

In New York, however, things were less easy than I expected. Week after week went by, and I could not find a job. And I, in view of all the languages I could speak and write, and my experience, had thought of $150 a week as the very lowest I would accept! I still had good clothes and could talk my way to the top. Presidents of concerns received me, but no one would give me a first-rate job, and I would not ask for humble ones.

After more than three months of job-hunting I decided in disgust to take any job I could get. Analysing my case again carefully, I found that I had something definite to offer in the travel business. But I was still top-lofty. For example, I did not offer my services to Thomas Cook & Son. Oh, no, I was one of those people who have an aversion for Cook's tourists!

Top-lofty or not, I was lucky. One day early in December a good wind blew me into the smart office of a travel service at the Plaza Hotel. Presently I found myself engaged at seventy-five dollars a week to edit their house-organ, which they wanted to develop into a real travel magazine. Though I had never been an editor, I felt that my good Nazi training would help me to bluff it through. Mildred joined me in New York and soon became my assistant. By hard work we built up a regular travel magazine which won recognition from the trade.

One of the boys who went to the ships to look after our clients came into my office one morning and told me that a German had arrived with a beautiful wife.

"Perhaps you know them," he said. "They're at the Plaza - Mr. and Mrs. Quandt."

In the midst of my amusement at the idea that I knew all the Germans travelling the earth, the name began to have a familiar sound. Presently I was wondering whether this Quandt could be an old school-friend of my boyhood. Within a minute I was talking over the phone to Dr. Guenther Quandt, brother of my friend Gerhard.

I lunched with him and his charming young wife. He was now one of the richest men in Germany, with the mentality typical of internationally and economically minded business machines. Of course he had become at once another object for speculation for me-I wanted to get him and his money interested in our cause. But he was sceptical.

Well, I thought, if I can't get you directly, I shall get you indirectly through your wife, who seems to be much more open to suggestion. Her eyes sparkled when I told her about Hitler and the Nazi heroics. By the time I said good-bye to them on the ship which carried them home to Germany, Frau Quandt had become my ally. She promised to read the Nazi books I had given her and to work on her husband, and warmly invited me to visit them in Berlin.

We became close friends during my visit in Germany in the summer of 1930, and I made a fervent Nazi out of her. Together we went to Party rallies, and I took her to the Nazi headquarters in Berlin, where she signed up for regular Party membership. With nothing to do and a good income to do it on, she became an active Nazi supporter. I introduced her to the leader of the Nazi Women's League.

Soon she was at work in the office of the district-leader of Berlin and chief of the propaganda department of the Party. A year later she was the wife of this cynical little Nazi demagogue, today the powerful minister of propaganda and public enlightenment in the Hitler Cabinet. She is now addressed as Frau Minister Doktor Goebbels.

In 1928, while I was engaged in my editorial venture in New York and still maintaining active touch with Nazi activities, three young Germans calmly cabled to Munich that they had founded the New York branch of the Party. After months of writing to Germany and greatly exaggerating the importance of their group, which actually numbered only three members-themselves-they were recognized by Munich, in direct violation of the Party principle prescribing a minimum of fifty members for the formation of a new unit.

The group sought me out and implored me to attend their meetings and make speeches. They had by that time only from ten to fifteen paying members, and the attendance at their meetings was between twenty and forty.

Though I disapproved of Nazi organizations in the United States dependent in any way on Germany, I spoke a few times at their meetings to test the reaction, and the attendance soon grew to three hundred or more. Eventually I severed my connection with them because I was opposed to the form the unit was taking and also to the character of its officers. Munich ignored my advice to dissolve the unit, and used it instead for internal propaganda in Germany. Nazi papers played it up: 'Our Branch in New York'...'Our Idea Also Marching On in America'...and so forth. As a matter of fact, no well-thought-out or consistently planned organization had then been started outside Germany, though the Nazi Press gave an opposite impression.

Another attempt at an American organization on a basis of National Socialism took place in 1929 in Chicago. This was the 'Teutonia.' Three of the leading spirits, later identified with the 'Friends of New Germany,' had left Germany between 1923 and 1925; though they had been Nazi followers, none of them had been an inscribed member of the Party. They were now acting on their own initiative, without direct authority.

But it is absolutely natural for a Nazi or a Nazi-minded German to make propaganda wherever he is. Only his own intelligence can tell him whether it is advisable to do so where he happens to be, and how to go about it. Any Nazi, like any Communist, is driven by his life-philosophy to advance the cause. He does not recognize the idea of 'national sovereignty' or of 'popular sovereignty' in the liberal sense, and he is bound to seek out people of the same viewpoint. And so small cells sprang up in every community where there were Germans, and most of them disappeared again for lack of leadership.

In all this time I alone was definitely commissioned by Hitler-although it would be misleading to give the impression that I was under strict orders and in continual contact. From 1926 to the spring of 1931 the German organization was so concerned with its own affairs that it had neither time nor interest to plan any foreign programme. The undertakings of the Nazi foreign expert, Alfred Rosenberg, remained in the main theory and slumbered in his desk in the form of projects and memoranda. What happened abroad in these years depended exclusively upon the initiative of individuals, recently emigrated Germans, who, for the most part, especially in America, had discovered their Nazi hearts only after bitter disappointments in the country of their adoption.

The picture began to change somewhat after the Party's first great electoral victory in September 1930, which put one hundred and seven Nazis in the Reichstag where before there had been twelve, In the spring of 1931 the Nazi' Foreign Department for Germans Abroad was founded in Hamburg under Dr. Hans Nieland, a fresh-baked Nazi deputy in the Reichstag.

The Teutonia in Chicago then had sixty or seventy members, but still had not been officially recognized by Munich. Operating under the same rules as any local group in Germany, it was making every effort to get Party recognition. In contrast to the New York Nazi group, it was an entirely independent organization with its own leader and council. Dr. Nieland eventually recognized it and appointed Walter

Kappe, the president, as his representative in America. But he did not notify the New York Nazis of the new arrangement, which put the New York unit under the Chicago Teutonia.

And now rivalry sprang up between the Chicago and New York organizations to determine which was the real leader. The chief aim of each group was to be head of a movement amounting to nothing; that was more important than really to do anything. They proselytized from each other, held meetings and Sprechahende, but got nowhere.

Germans in America and Nazis in Germany continued to think that in view of the large number of Germans there it would be easy to build up a powerful Nazi organization. As usual, the bureau wasn't getting a cent from Munich; that was the privilege of a powerful few inside the Party. Any new department had to justify its right to exist by its competence to support itself, and Nieland's first concern was to get funds.

This ambitious little bourgeois, who was only thirty years old, had never been abroad. He spoke not one foreign language and had no training whatsoever for his very important office. Scenting membership fees, he named his price for recognition of the Teutonia: they would have to turn over to his office in Hamburg two-thirds of what they took in from members, and submit completely to his rule. Under such an agreement, the people in Chicago would never be able to build up anything.

The little people in Chicago and New York who attached such importance to getting a letter from the powerful Nazi Party were now spending a small fortune on postage, and rivalry between them was becoming ridiculous and potentially dangerous. In 1931, when it was clear that they were failing to make headway and I had definitely declined to have anything to do with the New York group, I was approached by the president of the Teutonia and asked to aid that organization, which had begun to publish a monthly bulletin. Being unwilling to judge the Teutonia from hearsay, I accepted their urgent invitation to attend a 'German Day' in Chicago sometime in September of that year.

Kappe and Gissibl, the leaders, impressed me as young men who wanted .to do things, but didn't really know how; they needed the prestige of authority from Hamburg-Munich to get ahead. I agreed to interest myself in the Teutonia only if they would break with Nieland, make themselves definitely independent of Germany, and proceed as a truly American organization-one which would not try to keep Germans from becoming Americans, but on the contrary would promote citizenship and try to permeate American life.

It was my viewpoint that it would never be easy to interest Americans in specifically German problems. In my dealings with the Teutonia and other Nazi elements in America, in reports to Munich and communications to Dr. Nieland, in articles in the German-language Press, I elaborated the reasons for my conviction that Nazi organizations founded and led by 'aliens' linked with and dependent on Germany, could not possibly accomplish anything worth while, would create nothing but trouble, and in the end would prove a boomerang to Nazi interests.

While there were clear signs in America pointing to a coming awakening, an awareness of the need of an inner conversion and of a new way of thinking, Germans would have to realize that a 'folkic' movement in this country, strong enough to produce a new state synthesis, must needs be an entirely American affair. ' In judging American conditions, Germans must understand that the structure, development, and mentality of the American people were very different from their own.

The National Socialist movement in Germany had been born under very special conditions; as the natural reaction to the intolerable spiritual and economic burden imposed on the German people by the Versailles Treaty, it had a meta-physical and historical background centuries old. But America· had no Gothic domes, no great painting and music, no Eckehart, Luther, and Kant, no Schiller and Goethe, in short, no traditional but living body of culture to stir souls, arouse longings and show ways to new liberty. America had experienced no anti-Jewish movements such as Europe had known in all ages; on the contrary, the United States, perhaps more than any other land, might be said to be brimming with the Jewish spirit. Werner Sombart had written: 'What we call Americanism is nothing less . . . than the Jewish spirit distilled.'[2] America had not lost a world war, and had not yet felt the horrors of Bolshevism. Nor did it yet know that horrible spiritual and physical distress which was forcing Germans to think, bringing buried riches of spirit to the surface again, and creating an indomitable will to freedom.

Again, if Germans were to understand this great people, they must reckon with the biological background of America. Until the Civil War, the structure of the American nation had been predominantly Nordic, that is to say, Anglo-Saxon-Germanic; but in the last sixty-five years both appearance and potential heredity had undergone an extraordinary change. An ever-increasing influx of Alpine, Latin, and Jewish blood had modified the American make-up and, perhaps even more, the American temperament. The Americans of today were children of the sun as well as of the mist, and it would be a long time before they acquired a surface finish, a patina of age. Their future must wait upon the outcome of an imperfectly visible fight between two Americas.

Though the World War had created in America a deep craving for national unity-not so much for political unity in the formal sense as for that solidarity of ideals and culture which is the necessary foundation of a real and lasting political stability - Germans must realize that a corollary of that craving was the fact that alien influence and alien activity were becoming increasingly taboo. Homogeneity of thought and of daily customs was being built up at amazing speed from coast to coast, by Press,

2 *The Jews and Modern Capital*

motor, film, and radio.

Repeatedly I pointed out that Germans in Germany and Germans in America must never forget that this was a land in which the ruling culture was Anglo-Saxon, a land in which English was spoken. If they must blame anybody for that condition, let them accuse their own forefathers, who had failed to perceive the historic moment to Germanize this country. It might astound them to learn how relatively slight had been the influence of German thinking and of German institutions, a fact only partly due to the over-adaptability of the German, to his readiness to allow himself to be absorbed. The Germany which sent its best wave of immigration over the ocean was a torn and divided country; her sons went forth with no political tradition to guide them in the formation of new states. England and France, for centuries united politically and culturally, could give their departing sons a firmer character in customs and manners, in tradition and political instinct. That would explain why the Anglo-Saxon element in the United States, and to some extent the French element in Canada and even in Louisiana, had potentialities for lasting effect which the German petty states had not been able to impart to their emigrants.

There was in America no effective German-American element which could be won over in a German 'folkic' sense. The German emigrants before 1870, for the most part higher types, were now completely Americanized; it would be wise to forget them. Those coming between 1875 and 1914 had been, biologically, of a relatively inferior quality; their children, moreover, had been Americanized, and most of them could not even speak German. Only after the war had the higher type of German begun to arrive in large numbers again. But these people were still alien from American life; they had all they could do to keep alive.

Among those of German birth in America there was no organization which offered an effective vehicle for Nazi propaganda. The Steuben Society, the only important political organization of German-Americans, was not in good repute. The many hundreds of German clubs and societies, representing mainly the German immigration from 1875 to 1914, were for the most part such a dull and philistine lot that nothing could be accomplished through them. There remained the relatively small number of German-folkic immigrants who had come over after the war, scattered all over the country, and appearing in groups as 'Steel-helmets,' 'Werewolves,' and the like. Only a very small part of them were Nazis. And when these groups existed as disparate cells in the same community, they either quarrelled with each other or wasted their time in petty club affairs.

The German element in America would never furnish a folkic organization able to exert any real influence on American politics. And even if the impossible were achieved, the fact that such a political organization would be subject to Nazi leadership in Germany would only harm the German cause. It could be dissolved on legal grounds, its leaders and members deported as undesirables if they were not citizens; even citizens would be vulnerable for violation of the oath which had given them American status. It would be idle to hope, moreover, that this postulated organization could exercise any influence on American foreign policy in an anti-Jewish cause, since any great political action in this country was possible at present only with the support of Jewry or with that of existing nationalist forces.

It all came down to this: A folkic movement which would work toward the aim of the German world struggle was not yet possible in this country. America was not ready. When such a movement arrived, it must be under American leadership, and compliant with American laws. Americans could not be induced to concern themselves with the German world struggle for German interests; we must be content for the time being to find an American leader who would undertake to show that the American destiny is bound up with the European destiny, that the success of the Nazi movement would be a bulwark against Communism in Germany and Europe, that if Germany went under, all Europe would follow. The failure of Nazism would mean that billions in American capital invested in Europe would be lost, and that sooner or later Communism would grip America as well.

These were the views I tried to pound into German heads. Naturally, Dr. Nieland in Hamburg did not relish them. My attitude was interfering with his plans. Being a comparatively new member of the Party and a very minor one at that, he probably had never heard my name before, and, of course, knew nothing of my direct relations with Hitler and Rosenberg.

But America never became his milch-cow. Except for one detailed report to Munich, I did not bother about him. I knew the structure of the Nazi Party too well, and knew, moreover, that from a distance of four thousand miles it was useless to put proposals on file; to achieve anything you simply had to present an accomplished fact.

Early in 1932 Kappe, discouraged and disgusted, resigned, and in a long letter implored me to take over the leadership of the Teutonia. I accepted merely because I wanted to seize this opportunity to smash Nieland's whole Nazi scheme in America.

Here is an example of how affairs were being conducted:

Nazi cells were being organized on German ships travelling the seven seas. A steward or sailor would act as liaison-officer to carry information to Nieland. Decisions sometimes hung on the fact that one of these liaison-men was supplying a German in some group in America with liquor-it would determine which side his report would support! He would favour his regular clients, and so would his chief, Dr. Nieland, in Hamburg. The whole thing was idiotic, small, and sad.

Declaring the Teutonia dissolved, I founded the Swastika League with the sole purpose of wrecking the Teutonia in Chicago and the Nazi group in New York by recruiting members from them and letting the remnants fight each other. That accomplished, I decided that neither of these groups was worth bothering about.

At no time, before or after this coup, did either of them have more than a hundred regular paying members, except for a spurt by the New York Nazi group in the few weeks after Hitler's appointment as Chancellor. Finally, late in March 1933, after my return to Berlin, I brought about the dissolution of the Nazi organization in the United States by decree of Rudolf Hess, Hitler's deputy.

It goes without saying that my activity in this matter added some enemies to my list.

But I am getting ahead of my personal story.

Some time in 1928 I left the travel service to look for a job which would give me more leisure to continue my Nazi work. I didn't find it as a customers'-man in a well-known house in Wall Street, but I did find an amazing insight into how fortunes were made and lost, and how accounts were juggled by the brokers. It was possible then to see at first-hand the necessity of a law which would truly supervise the dealings and ethics of the Stock Exchange. The theory of demanding a margin of at least 25 per cent was ignored even by the 'good' firms; customers'-men who worked on commissions and had no fixed salaries simply had to trade in order to justify their drawing accounts. Our Jesuitic-looking 'Analyser' made solemn speeches to our Friday conferences scientifically proving by charts that the boom would go on forever.

Symptomatic of the situation at that time was the installation of brokerage offices on the big transatlantic liners, and a project-I don't know whether it was ever carried through-for establishing a regular ticker-tape office in the Vatican! The customers'-men, too, were a story. Assigned to a most luxuriously outfitted branch office in Fifty-seventh Street which had a special ladies' department, I was just a commoner. The customers'-men were almost exclusively dukes, counts, princes, and barons-Russian, Austrian, German, and French. Their lady clients were numerous.

I gave up my researches in Wall Street to become editor of an international travel year-book, a guide to travel by water, land, and air throughout the world-a reference work greatly needed by the travel trade at large. Having conceived the structure of the book, from June of 1929 into 1930 I worked like a dog on it, for my arrangement with the publisher was such that the year-book, if successful, might well bring me in a revenue for life.

Made to sell at a high price, it came out at the worst possible moment-during the second slump in May 1930. My hopes never materialized. Having arranged, however, to go to Europe in July to represent the book, I managed to visit most of the European capitals by air and to live in good style while I attended to my business-never forgetting, of course, that I was a Nazi agent.

I stayed in Germany only a few weeks, from late August into early September. From Berlin, where my old friend, Arno Schickedanz, put me au courant, I went to Munich to meet Hitler and Rosenberg. Unfortunately, Hitler had left unexpectedly on the day of my arrival; so I was able to see only Rosenberg and Strasser. Both were optimistic; it was evident that the movement was at last well under way. But even they, even Hitler himself, did not anticipate the extent of the forward stride the Party was to make three weeks later in the Reichstag election of 30 September. If I could have foreseen it myself, I should certainly have managed to stay over until after the election, in order to obtain from Hitler at least part of what I got out of him during my next visit in 1932.

The foreign political situation, however, remained as loose and as vague as ever. Hitler and Strasser were so absorbed in the election campaign and the ever-growing internal fight that they hadn't time, money, or energy for outside preparations; in vain I urged the organization of a foreign political bureau of the Party.

Observing that Party intrigues were still growing apace, I was glad again to absent myself from strife. This had its disadvantages, of course, for I created no following within the Party, and continued dependent solely on the good graces of Hitler himself. Every district-leader and group-leader now had his own entourage and party-machine, which rendered him secure in his position within the Nazi Party.

By October of 1930 I was back in New York, and severed my connections with the publisher. Having a car, I decided to become a travelling salesman as the best way to get about. Selling building-material, perfumes, and what-not, I sailed through many States, working for the Nazi cause whenever I possibly could.

I would work intensely for three or four days to make my quota of sales, then try to interest people in what I had to say about politics; often I would get small and occasionally larger audiences. In summer I would make my chief headquarters in resorts. Moving from place to place according to plan, I frequently spoke before the guests of my hotel. Soon I had worked out an effective system for getting about, selling my stuff and making propaganda. No university within reach was spared; through the German department or by some other approach I would get to the students and sometimes to the professors as well, in order to leave my eggs with them. I cultivated newspaper men and editors in the smaller cities, some of whom gave me valuable information. Thus I established my contacts, building cells wherever I could, seriously studying American history and Americans from a Nazi standpoint, closely following magazines and newspapers, and collecting clippings and other material which might be helpful in the future. I made card-indexes of writers, journalists, college professors, business men, and men in public life who seemed to be susceptible to our approach or were outspokenly hostile -according to whether they were red, pink, communistic, or fascistic.

Often I had to cover large distances to carry on my political activities. For example, I was selling perfumes north of Boston when I was expected to attend the 'German Day' in Chicago at the beginning of September in 1931, a round-trip which by motor would take from ten to twelve days. On such occasions I would work frantically to get ahead of my quota; then, to spread my sales for the period of my absence, I would arrange with someone to send in my antedated order and reports on prescribed days. Or I would have a sprained ankle or some other disability-and on my return find a touchingly sympathetic letter from my sales-manager wishing me quick recovery.

It was hard work. There was only one amusing intermezzo -a sojourn with Count Luckner, the Sea Devil. I had a gorgeous time going down to the Bahamas on his Mopelia to hunt sharks with him, his Countess, and some friends. Incidentally, I wanted to know Luckner better in order to determine his possible usefulness after the Nazi regime in Germany should have become a fact. I can confirm something the whole world knows: Luckner is one of the most hilarious fellows and best story-tellers walking the globe; there wasn't a day that we didn't roar with laughter. He is a marvellous actor, with the apparent guilelessness of a small boy.

Mildred was experiencing the insecurity I had promised her; she was having a far from settled life with her revolutionary. But she bore it all with kindness, understanding, and patience, helping me whenever she could. When, at the beginning of 1932, I moved our domicile again, this time to Brookline, near Boston, she came with me without demur, and was an invaluable assistant in detail work and in revising my copy for a new magazine which I intended to launch.

The time now seemed ripe for a more concrete and active propaganda programme to utilize the experience and connections I had made. All this time I had looked in vain for a possible American leader. So I prepared to issue a magazine in order to gauge the reaction; moreover, it would be useful to have some sort of organ round which something worthwhile might crystallize. After long consideration I decided that Boston with its Revolutionary background would be the best place to start American propaganda; I was planning later to move to Washington, first launching an active movement in the Middle West.

My magazine was to go to a selected list of about ten thousand names, spreading in the right proportion over every State in the Union, and covering mainly the middle class with an eye to the younger people, representatives of the army and navy, the colleges and schools. With my available funds and the money promised me by friends, I would have enough to finance six or seven issues.

But while the first number was on press, my bank failed, and promises were not kept. I was able to put out only one issue of five thousand copies, and to do it I had to sell my furniture, pawn my car, and borrow. I got nearly two hundred subscribers and more than four hundred letters from all over the country.

The announced purpose of my American Guard was 'to maintain, defend, and advance American ideals, Aryan concepts, and culture; to further the cause of national unity and social justice.' The reaction came from collegians, clergymen, business men, war veterans, army officers, both active and retired, and patriotic organizations. Naturally, there were letters from cranks and from other strange birds also out to save humanity. But I was encouraged in my idea of building up a purely American organization with a magazine to serve as its mouthpiece.

Meanwhile, developments in Germany had become acute. Hitler apparently was at the threshold of power. Now the moment had come to return to him and find out once and for all what he really intended to do in foreign policy.

In June of 1932 I sailed again for Germany.

XVIII
HITLER VERSUS HINDENBURG: I

While I had been out of the jungle of German politics, Germany had been fermenting in a hotbed of emotions. The history of those seven years from 1925 to 1932, from Hindenburg's first election to his second term, has a wealth of dramatic detail, both tragic and comic, that cannot be imprisoned in any brief sketch. It is the story of a continuous and ruthless struggle for freedom waged by conflicting forces amidst a great people-a people confused and torn by unbridled passions, but intent on its right to live despite oppressors within and without.

At first the ferment was slow. The early years of Hindenburg's 'reign'-the Stresemann period, up to October 1929-were comparatively calm. International relations had been greatly bettered by putting the load on the back of the common man, the German 'Michel,' and an increasing but unsound prosperity was instilling specious hope into the nation. The policy of 'fulfilment' and 'reconciliation' was being anxiously pursued; all the obligations resulting from the Versailles Treaty and the Dawes Pact were assiduously carried out, without the slightest regard for the needs of the German people, rapidly being bled white.

Until the Beer Hall Putsch, Hitler had been riding a wave of national despair, with the support of the army. In this new era of false calm, however, he found himself practically deserted by his 'big' friends, who were advising 'loyal co-operation' with the 'consolidated republic.' Now that the drummer was no longer wanted, it is one of his great achievements that he did not go under.

The Party continued to grow steadily but very slowly. Its inscribed membership in December 1925 was 27,000; by the end of 1929 it was only 178,000. From the Nazi viewpoint, the Reichstag elections of May 1928 looked superficially most unimpressive. Consider for a moment the, make-up of that Reichstag as an illustration of what I have termed the jungle of German politics. Out of a total of 491 deputies, there were 153 seats for the Socialists, 78 for the Nationalists, 78 for the Centre Party and their Bavarian friends, 54 for the Communists, 45 for the People's Party, 25 for the Democrats. The remaining 58 seats were divided among the so-called 'splinter' parties, and of these last the Nazis were one. The elections had brought in only 800,000 Nazi votes, and of the former fourteen folkic deputies only twelve remained. But there was one fact of great significance: they were all Nazis, and the Deutsch-Voelkische Freiheitspartei was as good as dead. And there was another fact of even greater significance. Though the great folkic movement had dwindled to an insignificant party, Hitler was now its acknowledged leader, its only chief.

Actually, in those years of surface quiet, Hitler had been concerned not so much with fighting other parties as with the task of subjugating or eliminating possible rivals within or without the Party, so that he might be the recognized head of the entire folkic movement throughout the Reich. He was hedged about by restrictions; he was pledged to 'legality,' and any change of existing conditions by violence was forbidden. There was now only one way to power: to win the people to the Idea by incessant and insistent propaganda. He was heavily handicapped, however, by the order prohibiting him from speaking in public, rescinded in Bavaria only in 1927, and in Prussia not until September of 1928. This forced him willy-nilly into the background.

With Hitler's voice thus muted, a major development occurred which held both promise and threat for his political future. The real founder of the political structure of the Nazi Party, Gregor Strasser, with the help of his brother Qtto and of his young assistant, twenty-eight-year-old Dr. Paul Joseph Goebbels, built up National Socialism on a firm foundation in North Germany, which had been the folkic domain of the once thriving Deutsch-Voelkische Freiheitspartei. Strasser had, in effect, created a party of his own, very few of whose members had ever seen Hitler's face. Moreover, North Germany was Protestant, and Hitler had been branded there as a 'servant of Rome'; stubborn Count Reventlow in particular called him the 'Party Pope.'

Reventlow, who still had great influence and a considerable following among the rebel intellectuals, was opposed to the 'new' Hitler of the dictatorial manner, and utterly disliked the Byzantine servility of his cheap entourage. He joined the Strasser group, which now began to think seriously of depriving Hitler of his sole authority and of forcing him to oust not only Streicher and Esser but Rosenberg as well. Rosenberg's violent anti-Soviet policy clashed with the sympathies of Reventlow, who favoured the Reichswehr's pro-Soviet course; in general, the Strasser group was disposed to stress the socialistic rather than the nationalistic aspect of the Party programme.

This group now laid plans to bring the various nationalist groups of northern Germany into one movement which would have its own party programme and be under the leadership of Strasser and Reventlow. Hitler was then to be confronted with an accomplished fact. In fairness to the Strasser group, it must be pointed out that the contemplated step was not one of duplicity; it was inspired rather by the desire to resolve a confused situation in which their arbitrary 'leader,' dictating the second volume of Mein Kampf in his enforced public silence on his 'Magic Mountain,' his retreat on the Obersalzberg, apparently could not lead. Even in the South, Hitler was losing his grip on the Party; whole sections and even districts, such as Wuerttemberg, were breaking away from him.

But Hitler still could lead. Learning of the threat in the North, he met it in masterly fashion, saving his dictatorship without risking the destruction of the Party by the loss of Strasser and Goebbels, who were just as indispensable to him as were Rosenberg, Streicher, and Esser. At the first opportunity, he struck. In February 1926, on short notice, he summoned a leaders' conference to Bamberg, in Bavaria. It was an adroit move to outmanoeuvre the Party opposition; travel costs were high, and representation from the North German faction would be slight, for in the North, as elsewhere, Nazi purses were slim. Hitler would be on firm ground among his stalwart Bavarians.

At the meeting, Goebbels, seeing the revolt nipped in the bud, and with it his own chances, deserted Strasser and went over to Hitler's side, offering himself to 'our Leader, the instrument of a divine will.' The Party platform of twenty-five points was declared unalterable, thus ending all agitation for more or less of Socialism in the Nazi programme.[1] In the autumn he shrewdly separated Goebbels from Strasser entirely by making the ambitious little Doctor district leader of Berlin, responsible to Hitler alone. Strasser, until then the Party's chief of propaganda, was appointed to the post of chief of the Party organization. Eventually even Reventlow did penance and sought admission as an inscribed Nazi. Though the danger of revolt had been averted at least temporarily, Hitler evidently perceived that he must break the chain that bound him. The prohibition against his speaking was a matter for enforcement by the various states, and in Thuringia he could expect a friendly interpretation of the ban. On 4 July 1926, in response to his call, the first congress of the Party since the unsuccessful Beer Hall Putsch assembled at Weimar in the very hall which had seen the constitution of the republic adopted. Despite sharp protests from the Government in Berlin, Hitler was heard by the congress, and Nazis again recognized their master's voice.

Hitler had learned his lesson; he was building securely now.

All through that year he strengthened his hold on the Party organization. As early as January he had begun to organize the SS, or Schutz-Staffel, throughout the entire Nazi Party.

The SS was designed to take over the duties of the S A, now almost defunct. At first the main function of the SS was to constitute, in every district of the Reich, a block that would be unswervingly loyal to Hitler, upholding his rule as against any other Nazi who might become too popular or dare to jeopardize the leadership principle embodied in him alone. The 'Hitler Youth,' the 'Order of German Women,' and the 'League of German Girls,' all founded in this period, did much to attach the movement more and more to the person of the Fuehrer. Already a somewhat legendary figure, Hitler was beginning now to reveal a singularly romantic appeal to

---

1 *Reprinted in the Appendix.*

the imaginations of youth and of women.

Rosenberg organized the 'Fighting League for German Culture' to win over the intellectuals. There came into being unions of Nazi lawyers, of Nazi physicians, of Nazi teachers, and finally the Nazi German Students' League, under Baldur von Schirach, with the aim of conquering the universities.

All these organizations played important roles in crystallizing the movement for the long struggle for power over the Reich.

The Press of the Party was' developed; Hitler's Voelkischer Beobachter was built up, and the semi-monthly Illustrierter Beobachter became a weekly. The S A was reorganized, the SS formations strengthened. Propaganda was intensified. Even in red Berlin, the stronghold of Marxism, the Nazis visibly gained ground.

The German ferment was growing now. Developments on every side were proving with increasing force that Hitler had been right. The fiasco of the policy of rapprochement, pursued by Stresemann for Germany and by Briand for France, began to be apparent. The illusionist Briand gave way to an extreme germanophobe and nationalist: Poincare once more gathered the reins of French politics into his hands. That gave Hitler a tremendous opportunity which he exploited to the utmost, denouncing Stresemann as a dupe.

The burden of the Dawes Plan grew; unemployment leaped from month to month, and with it a new wave of political discontent. The reparations calamity began to proclaim itself. Hitler hammered into the heads of his followers the conviction that the Dawes Plan was the cause of the national misery and disgrace. In his assault on the existing system he directed especially violent attacks at the senseless ruining of the farmers and of the middle class.

While a bewildered Germany saw the monarchist Hindenburg, elected by the Right, become separated from his supporters and march away with the Centre Party and the Sozis, Hitler carried on the struggle, prophesying the catastrophe that was to fall on the home markets, reiterating at hundreds of meetings that the policy of 'fulfilment' was sheer lunacy and would make an utter wreck of German industry.

The fourth Party congress, held at Nuremberg in early August of 1929 on a tremendous scale, ended in a parade of 60,000 Brown Shirts, a striking demonstration of the grandiose development of the Party. It gave great impetus to the movement. The multiple Nazi organizations were making converts, and this growing following was soon apparent in the numerous state, county, and municipal elections. Nazi doctrines were penetrating deeply into the national consciousness. Despite continuous internal difficulties the Party was progressing.

Now deeply alarmed, the 'Reichsbanner' of the Sozis and the 'Red Front' of the Communists, both semi-military organizations, well equipped and well armed, were clashing with the Nazis in an increasing tempo of violence. The Nazis answered terror with terror.

And now we come to the Young Plan. Probably no other blunder on the part of Entente statesmen after Hindenburg's election had such far-reaching consequences. This new scheme for forcing payment of reparations had been conceived in Paris at another conference of 'experts' in the spring of 1929. By that time, even experts could no longer overlook the fact that with· two million unemployed roaming the streets of Germany, the 'Michel' had lost faith in the panacea of the Dawes Plan. The German situation had become impossible. The budget problem was insuperable. The inflow of foreign credits ceased entirely. The financial difficulties of the Reich, of states, of communities, were aggravated. Factories shut down, money exchanges slowed up, bankruptcies multiplied.

The Dawes Plan simply was not working; it had to be replaced by something else. But instead of giving Germany a square deal at last by redressing her grievances and assenting to her legitimate aspirations, the substitute merely perpetuated the stupid policy of suspicion, vindictiveness, and greed. The world can no longer blink at the fact that the Versailles Treaty, with all its studied outrages and humiliations, and the subsequent 'agreements,' all signed by German governments under duress, were dictated with the definite purpose of crushing Germany beyond hope of recovery, of holding her down forever in bondage. This blind policy did more than bring Europe to the brink of ruin for the sake of ruining Germany: it was in no small degree responsible for a world depression of colossal proportions. And it gave Hitler his chance, kept him on the march, until masterly propaganda and a ruthless policy assured his final victory.

Let the observer of today's world face the fact that an international policy which aims to hold any proud and potentially powerful nation in subjection must always prove a boomerang. As someone else has said, if another treaty had been framed at Versailles, the world would not now be alarmed by the roll of Nazi drums, and Adolf Hitler would still be an obscure artisan.

The Young Plan, though it purported to settle the reparations problem once and for all, was so impossible, the general attitude of the Allied powers so discouragingly hostile, that the political front which had supported the policy of 'fulfilment' began to break up. Now many of the powerful Haves again reoriented themselves and joined forces with the Have-nots to defeat the adoption of the Young Plan. Junkers and barons of industry opened their eyes and stopped snubbing 'that plebeian, Hitler.' It was time to use that forceful parvenu!

And so it came about that Alfred Hugenberg, the Nationalist leader, approached Hitler. The overtures were made by one of Hugenberg's confidants, Finanzrat Dr. Bang, well known to the Nazi leader.

Hugenberg had everything but the masses; Hitler had everything but the money. Financial difficulties had in fact continually hobbled the Nazi movement. Allocation of Reichswehr funds and large gifts from industrialists had virtually ceased with the failure of the Beer Hall Putsch. From 1925 on the Party had been dependent mainly on membership drives and private contributions. The shortage of funds had at times been so acute that collapse seemed certain. It was of the utmost importance to open up new resources.

Yes, Hugenberg the monarchist and Hitler the Nazi dictator needed each other, and each was perfectly willing to use the other in the final onslaught on the despised Republic. They had, up to a certain point, a common aim: both wanted to annihilate Marxism and destroy the Versailles Treaty. They had, for the present, a common method: each appealed to the unanimous rebellion of German opinion against the treaty, to the deep resentment provoked by the Ruhr invasion, the growing aversion to the policy of 'fulfilment.' And they had a common ambition: each wanted the power in the Reich for himself. Which would outwit the other in the end?

But Hitler had learned a lot since prison days in Landsberg ; he was determined not to be fooled again by anybody. He still thundered against 'contemptible opportunists' and 'dirty politicians,' but he himself was becoming an opportunist par excellence. He was practising more and more skilfully the strategy of the admired model of his youth, the remarkable burgomaster of Vienna, Dr. Karl Lueger: 'Make use of the means of influence' already existing to bring powerful institutions over to your side, so that you may derive from such long-established sources of strength the greatest possible advantage for your own movement.'

Thus Hitler was quick to see the opportunity offered by an alliance with that tragi-comic figure, that bristly-haired, moustachioed, sealion-faced little Geheimrat. Hugenberg, nicknamed the 'Silver Fox,' was a powerful factor behind the scenes. A former managing-director of the mighty Krupp's, he had been since 1928 the official leader of the Nationalist Party, which in that year had carried seventy-nine seats in the Reichstag. Lord of Film and Press, he had immense influence in every phase of the nation's economic and political life. He had long worked in secret understanding with his friend, Justizrat Heinrich Class, the quiet schemer and influential leader of the Pan-German Association, who kept a finger in every pie and, like Hugenberg, preferred to work behind the scenes. Both Hugenberg and Class had powerful friends in industry and commerce and among landholding Junkers and generals-friends who had direct access to Hindenburg or, better still, to the Hindenburg camarilla. Moreover, they practically controlled the Conservative Stahlhelm, of which the old Field-Marshal was honorary president.

To be sure, Hitler must think of the radical left wing of his Party-the Strassers, Feders, and Reventlows, still rather independent fellows who would not approve of an alliance with Nationalist reactionaries which might jeopardize the Party's integrity. But they must be made to understand the expediency of his policy, knowing only too well that propaganda costs money, and that somebody has to pay for it. Hitler was sure of himself and of his subordinates. He would explain. And he did. So Hitler, playing his game carefully, made truce with the bourgeois Nationalists, named his price, and in the autumn of 1929 joined Hugenberg's Committee of Action. He had stipulated that his Party should be free to wage the fight of the 'people's petition' against the Young Plan in its own way.

The Young Plan was stubbornly defended by Hindenburg, who proclaimed that by it Germany would be saved. Hitler prophesied ruin. Exploiting Hugenberg's mammoth political organization to the utmost, he conducted the campaign throughout the Reich with a more powerful propaganda machine than he had hitherto possessed. In this struggle which naturally was completely dominated by the Nazis at the expense of Hugenberg and the Nationalists, he really mastered and developed organized propaganda, or, if you like, organized demagoguery for the mass-production of what we call public opinion.

The referendum was a failure, registering only six million votes against the Young Plan. But that did not matter; Hugenberg's defeat was Hitler's victory. At last political funds, dependable and abundant money sources, were open to him. Moreover, the incredible had become a fact: Hitler found himself firmly established in North Germany, in Prussia. He could be sure that at least half of those six millions who had voted for the Nationalists would go Nazi at the next election. Hugenberg had given Hitler his chance to make the Nazi movement a really popular Party.

The Reichstag accepted the Young Plan in April 1930, against the violent protests of Gregor Strasser, now speaker for the Nazi deputies. When Hindenburg, in opposition to the nationalist element which had elected him, set his signature to the Young Plan, it finished him in the eyes of the Nazis and of all national activists. The Hindenburg cult dwindled, the idol grew blurred in the hearts of millions of Germans; his picture disappeared from its place of honour in their homes. The old Field-Marshal, who as the elected President of the Reich had once been Germany's national symbol and the great hope of the Nationalists, became more and more a bulwark of the Left against the Right, a dike against the menace of the growing Nazi power.

The Diet elections in Thuringia in December 1929 had revealed the rising Nazi tide to all who had eyes to see. The same Hitler who once had violently denounced the whole parliamentary system, now, as the cool and calculating realist, designated Dr. Wilhelm Frick, the leader of the Nazi faction in the Reichstag, for the proffered post of Thuringian Minister of the Interior. The firm and energetic rule of this first Nazi minister, tireless in his efforts to eradicate Marxism in all its ramifications, brought many new converts to the cause. The Party's base was broadened by a proclamation to the farmers in March 1930, and by the appointment of R. Walter Darre, now Minister of Agriculture in the Hitler Cabinet, to organize the peasantry.

The growing economic crisis speeded the Party's progress. There were now three million unemployed, and those who had cherished illusions about the Young

Plan were fast losing them. It had become impossible to continue the financing of reparations by long-term credits and short-term loans. Without American and British capital, Germany could pay only in blood and sweat, and that involved an ever-decreasing standard of living for the working people. The masses became increasingly suspicious and radical and flocked either to the Nazis or the Communists. The youth of the land, despairing of the future and embittered by Germany's helplessness, rebelled at the thought that their country must forever be the football of international interests and foreign powers. Out of their revolt, Hitler emerged as youth's champion. They saw in him the expression of their will to live, and they gave him their hearts.

The SS and the S A, growing from month to month, were now an important political instrument in Hitler's hands. But they suffered heavily under the Marxian terrorism, and were always at a disadvantage. Though they answered violence with violence, courts and police, everywhere except in Thuringia, were dominated by hostile parties, and sided with the anti-Nazis.

In this turmoil, the Party acquired a major saint. On 23 February 1930 the Berlin 'Storm-leader' Horst Wessel died of wounds inflicted by Communists. A young student and the author of many S A battle-songs, he had been outstanding in the struggle for the conquest of red Berlin. In time, clever propaganda made of him a greater Nazi martyr than the national hero Albert Leo Schlageter, and when the 'Horst Wessel Song' was adopted as the Nazi anthem, he became a permanent symbol.

The lines tightened between the Nazis on one side and the Bourgeois and Marxists on the other; often the bourgeoisie and the 'class-conscious' proletariat would form a united front against their common enemy. The wearing of Nazi uniforms was prohibited by the various states, flags and materiel were seized, Party offices and meeting-places closed, chicaneries of every sort practised to put obstacles in the Nazi path. But the spirit of sacrifice and the energy of the rank and file grew with persecution.

On 5 July 1930, in Munich, the swastika flag fluttered for the first time over Nazi headquarters on Nazi property. An old palace was remodelled into the now famous 'Braunes Haus' at 45 Brienner Strasse, one of the most beautiful streets in Germany.

The growing opposition to the Government's fatal course and the announcement of the new and heavier taxes necessary to carry out the Young Plan had put the Sozis in a tight spot. Caught in their own net, they had no choice but to quit. On 27 March 1930 the last Socialist Chancellor of the Republic, Harmann Mueller, had resigned, after presiding over a coalition cabinet made up of Social Democrats, Centrists, Democrats, and the People's Party.

Three days later, Hindenburg, who in nine years of office ran through seven chancellors, made a new appointment. Under the influence of two generals,

Reichswehr Minister Wilhelm Groener and his chief aide, the 'Swivel-Chair General' Kurt von Schleicher, he designated another Roman Catholic chancellor. This was the leader of the Centre Party, Dr. Heinrich Bruening, ascetic bachelor-a sensitive, intellectual type, thin-lipped, with cold eyes behind heavy glasses. A lieutenant in the war, he had fought at the front and preferred the exercise of authority to parliamentary debate, but looked more like a professor of theology than a fighter. The old Field-Marshal could be sure that Bruening would look up to him with civilian reverence.

So Hindenburg set up his first 'presidial cabinet,' entrusted Bruening, his man of special confidence, with special powers, and with his typical countryman's cunning set about using him as an instrument for freeing himself from the evil shackles of the Left and winning back his friends of the Right, who had elected him and then abandoned him.

Invoking the famous 'Paragraph 48' of the Weimar constitution, the new 'bourgeois dictator' vainly sought by emergency decrees to master the crisis and put the State on a solid foundation. But Bruening's semi-dictatorship, based on the authority of an almost senile President, became so unpopular with the people that the Reichstag demanded cancellation of the decrees; even the Sozis joined in the vote. Whereupon Hindenburg, counting on the elections now in the offing, dissolved the Reichstag.

But the elections, held on 14 September 1930 were a cruel disappointment to suave, civilized, correct little Bruening. The Nazis polled six and a half million votes, leaping with one enormous stride from twelve apostles to 107 deputies-alarming news for an astounded world. "What had happened?

	1930	1928
Total Deputies elected	577	491
Social Democrats (Sozis)	143	153
National Democrats (Nazis)	107	12
Centrist, and Bavarian People's Party	87	78
Communist	77	54
Nationalist	41	78
People's Party	26	45
Democrats	20	25
'Splinter' parties	76	46

Here follow the figures for the 1930 election as compared with those of 1928: Europe woke up to the existence of the Nazi Party. After a long interview with

armed and spiritually immunized its people against Bolshevism: namely, Italy. All other European states possess neither political means of attack nor political gas-masks against Soviet propaganda. The question of overcoming Bolshevism is one of Fascistization of all European states: the European states of today, infected with Marxism, cannot resist for long the decomposing influence of this world plague.

For a fight against Bolshevism particularly, a German-French military convention, in my opinion, should be the last consideration. The most important is to remove from among European countries the curse of the Versailles Treaty, which splits civilized nations and divides them into masters and slaves-and not to create new divisions inside Europe by such limited and one-sided military alliances.

A military convention for the maintenance of a new European status would have..meaning only if all great European nations were united in the alliance with equal rights-including, however, the United States as well as Japan, at least as far as concerns the proposition of human culture against Bolshevist barbarism. A league eliminating those countries must, I fear lead to the opposite of the desired end.[3]

Though Hitler here showed himself a man of vision, though all signs pointed to the rising Nazi tide, his enemies within and without Germany continued to under-rate and ridicule him. A few days after the elections, he was a witness during a trial before the Supreme Court in Leipzig and gave sensational testimony whose real significance was understood by only a few. The defendants were three young Reichswehr officers charged with making Nazi propaganda in the army. The opposition saw a welcome opportunity to expose and compromise the Fuehrer, but Hitler brilliantly turned the precarious situation to his own advantage. Testifying on a platform from which he could be heard by the world, with newspaper men present from every corner of the earth, he weighed every word, emphasizing again the legality of the Party, his intention of crushing the opposition and achieving power legally, of fighting the treaties by any and every means.

"Another two or three elections," he declared defiantly, "and we shall have the majority in the Reichstag. . . . Then the power will be ours, and a people's tribunal will judge the November criminals.[4] And I frankly predict," he added almost casually, "that you will see heads rolling in the sand."

And yet the' November' Republic took no action to arrest this man. Was it weakness or stupidity? It was both. Depending entirely on the co-operation in the Reichstag between the Sozis and the Centre Party-the latter being now more or less delivered into the hands of the former-Bishops and priests belonging to the Centre Party launched a fanatical attack against the Nazi movement, excommunicating its followers and even refusing them Christian burial.

---

3 *The italics are Hitler's*

4 *The socialist instigators of the revolution in November 1918 which sealed the German defeat.*

Indeed, much of the present hostility of the Nazi regime to the established churches of Germany can be traced to the memory of much un-Christian treatment at their hands in the years of struggle. But such obstacles could not halt the Nazi avalanche. Whenever they were called upon to decide between Church and Party, Catholic Nazis almost invariably chose the Party. They even made an issue of the identity of the Church with the Centre Party, denouncing the political activities of the clerics as ruinous to Germany.

XIX

HITLER VERSUS HINDENBURG: II

When the year 1930 closed, the Nazis had 389,000 members, with the structure of the Party unshaken by two serious attempts at revolt. The first of these revolts had come in May. Hitler's growing comradeship with Big Business, his new tactics of compromise and 'legality,' his increasingly opportunistic policy involving participation in coalition governments, were stirring up much disapproval within the Party. Eventually there was open conflict.

The Strasser brothers, who had been active in the incipient revolt of 1926, were still left-wing, still in dead earnest about the Party's socialist programme. Their string of official Nazi papers had a large following, particularly in northern Germany. Dr. Otto Strasser, a brilliant and erudite journalist and a more original and independent thinker than his brother Gregor, had continued openly to proclaim the social revolution and to champion confiscation of war profits, appropriation of land for public use, municipalization of department stores, nationalization of trusts, and abolition of the thraldom of interest-all proposed in the original Nazi programme. Pushing into the foreground the question of the economic structure of the future Nazi State and emphasizing the predominantly socialistic character of the Party, he tried ably and forcefully to impose his views, denouncing Hitler and Goebbels as 'Fascist' and 'capitalistic.' Otto Strasser's attacks on Hitler's policies eventually became so alarming that the latter sought to settle their differences at a long conference with him on 21 May in Berlin. Strasser stuck to his guns, refusing Hitler's repeated offer to make him Reich Press-chief of the Party.

The result was a showdown. Strasser was expelled from the Party and founded his own organization of 'revolutionary Nazis,' known as the 'Black Front,' which he still actively conducts from exile' in Prague. Gregor broke with his brother and remained loyal to Hitler. But now there was mortal enmity between him and Goebbels. Goebbels had his triumph. The liquidation of the Strasser Front, with its string of news papers, including a daily paper in Berlin, left him a clear field for his own Angriff. His struggling weekly soon was a prosperous daily.

The full consequences of the Strasser revolt possibly lie in the future. The Stennes revolt, in part an outgrowth of the other, entailed more serious immediate embarrassments. It came just a few days before the September elections. Captain Walter Stennes, supreme leader of the SA for East Germany, was a capable army officer and former police-captain. He had married well and was independent, but was an inept politician. His men were overburdened with work, exhausted by the strenuous campaign, and generally dissatisfied and distrustful of the Nazi leadership; most of them were exceedingly poor and had not even enough to eat. Stennes demanded of Munich more pay for his troops. When his just request was ignored, the Berlin S A refused to carry out their Party duties, stormed Goebbel's new headquarters and completely wrecked them, to the hilarity of all Berlin. Leaflets proclaiming such headlines as 'Down with the Bonzes!' and 'Goebbels' Betrayal of Awakening Germany,' accusing Goebbels of unwarranted luxury and dishonesty, passed from hand to hand.

This was an awkward scandal for Hitler to face just before the elections. He flew to Berlin and settled things personally driving from one SA post to another, promising, beseeching, upbraiding-and the revolt was halted. Stennes, still a power in Berlin, resumed his duties, but his superior, Captain Franz Pfeffer von Salomon, chief of the entire SA, was made the scapegoat and lost his job. From then on, Hitler kept this key position himself, to the dismay of Goering, who, with the help of Goebbels, had worked for the office. Goering had been back in Germany ever since the political amnesty of 1926 had terminated his exile. Until he gained one of the twelve Nazi seats in the Reichstag in the 1928 elections, he had made his living in the aircraft industry.

But Hitler had other plans. Before Roehm had left Germany in 1928 to become military adviser to the Bolivian general staff, Hitler had become reconciled with him. He now recalled Roehm, to become chief of staff to the SA on 1 January 1931.

Before Roehm's organizing genius had time to take hold of the situation, new trouble broke out. Goebbels and Goering, whose plans had been frustrated for the moment by Roehm's appointment, had not given up their ambitions. Goebbels needed control of Berlin as the first step to higher powers, and swagger Captain Goering, not satisfied with the insignificant Reichstag deputy's job worth only six hundred marks a month and a first-class railway pass good for the Reich, still aimed at the leadership of the SA. Playing each other's game, they used for their opening pawn the unsuspecting Stennes. He and his subordinate SA leaders were still sick and tired of Hitler's 'legality complex' and craved action-with machine-guns. Counting on the support of the S A for all of eastern Germany and on the backing of Goebbels and Goering, Stennes again defied Munich by refusing to be dismissed by the 'homosexual' Roehm.

Stennes, however, was no match for Hitler, who stood staunchly behind Roehm. Carte blanche to crush the mutiny and restore discipline was given to a lieutenant, an able man of action and an expert in secret organization, who had been condemned to death as a 'Feme murderer'[1] and after five years of agony in prison had been

_____
1 *The 'Black' Reichswehr, as a secret military organization created in violation of the Versailles treaty, though with the knowledge of the government and the support of the authorized Reichswehr, could judge individual*

released. Now he cleansed the Party and the SA of undesirable elements. When the job had been thoroughly done, Edmund Heines, an old friend of Roehm's and a veteran SA leader from the days before the putsch - incidentally, also a 'Feme murderer'- replaced Stennes. The latter denounced Hitler and allied himself with Dr. Otto Strasser's 'Black Front.'

But Goering's hunger for power had still to be appeased. Hitler dulled its edge not by the gift of a Party office but by commissioning him to act as his 'ambassador' in Berlin. Though the job meant little at first, it was a sop to Goering's vanity, and he soon made it a very important one, despite his bull-in-a-china-shop propensities. (Eventually he and Goebbels proved to be the ideally suitable fellows to serve Hitler in certain obscure dealings which the Fuehrer could not afford to have known.) Goebbels now ran true to form, lined up with the stronger side at the right moment, hailed the Fuehrer, and made himself agreeable to Roehm, who as chief of staff of the SA and one of the two men privileged to address Hitler as 'du,' was a great power.

And so Goebbels and Goering welcomed Roehm with both hands. They were, however, the first and secret instigators of the campaign against the homosexual. They arranged to have some very compromising material regarding the SA chief's private life fall into the hands of the opposition. Much was made of Roehm's letters from Bolivia. In them he frankly admitted his 'peculiarities,' which he had ' discovered' only in 1924 at the age of thirty-seven, and bemoaned his loneliness in La Paz, 'where they know nothing of this sort of love.' The letters were published in every paper in the Reich hostile to the Nazis, and reprinted on thousands of handbills. Though doubtless shocking to many unsophisticated souls, their naivety and lack of the obscene must have disappointed sensation-seekers.

Hitler again stood by Roehm with amazing loyalty, publishing a personal declaration promising 'legal expiation' for a, disgusting and dirty slander . . . Roehm is and will remain my chief of staff, now and after the elections.'

As a matter of fact, Hitler greatly needed Roehm to organize a strong and well trained S A ready for any emergency, which the Fuehrer could make a factor in his political game with both Government and Reichswehr. If he should be unable to come to power legally, if the masses should grow steadily more radical, flocking either to Nazis or Communists, making a showdown by force with the latter or with a united Marxist front inevitable, then the Reichswehr would have no choice but to join the Nazis. In view of his excellent connections with the army, Roehm was the ideal man to patch things up with the Reichswehr. He could bring them to the realization that a well disciplined S A would be most useful as an auxiliary

infractions only in secret courts. The Marxist opposition, harking back to the 'Feme' or secret tribunal of medieval Germany, called the executions ordered by these secret courts 'Feme murders,' and Nazis who had carried them out were in later years victims of persecution at the hands of hostile courts.

army, and that only a Nazi Government could and would take the necessary steps for rearmament on a grand scale. Aside from his military qualities, intelligence, and political experience, Roehm was well acquainted with General Kurt von Schleicher of the Reichswehr ministry, and Schleicher in turn was a regiment comrade and intimate friend of Colonel Oskar von Hindenburg, the old Field-Marshal's son and adjutant. Schleicher was also a friend of Dr. Otto Meissner, the President's Secretary of State.

Moreover - and this was decisive - Roehm was a genuine Nazi and absolutely loyal to Hitler.

Whether he was to achieve power legally or by force, Hitler needed three things- money, the masses, and the support or at least the benevolent neutrality of the army. He had gained access to the money resources of big business, and he had torn away large blocks from the other parties; success along these two lines lay in the continuation of his well-tested policy of incessant, bold attack. To make friends with the Reichswehr, however, a more subtle policy was needed. And so Roehm stayed.

Hitler had gained a powerful recruit in Dr. Hjalmar Schacht, one of the shrewdest business politicians of all time. After the acceptance of the Young Plan, Schacht resigned his office as president of the Reichsbank and brought his international reputation and world-wide connections to the side of the Nazis.

The Fuehrer's influence grew steadily, and the Party's inner development proceeded 'organically' - to use a pet word in the Nazi vocabulary. New organizations in labour and industry were created to counterbalance the highly developed trades unions of the Sozis; an economic-political department came into being, in fact, everything which would serve to make of the Nazi Party a veritable state within a state. With consummate skill, Nazi cells were being formed on the Communist model to serve as a leaven throughout Germany. Propaganda which valued the spoken over the written word swept the land from the Rhine to the Vistula, from the North Sea to the Alps.

The close of 1931 saw eight hundred thousand inscribed members and more than ten thousand local units in the Party.

That year had shown the decline of the regime more and more clearly. Chancellor Bruening ignored the Party's demand for power, and attempted, always with the support of Sozis and Centrists, to starve the movement out. Finding themselves systematically barred from recognition, the Nazi deputies ostentatiously walked out of the Reichstag in February 1931, and the Nationalist opposition followed. Thus was Hindenburg finally and openly abandoned by that part of the nation which had elected him and which was dearest to his heart.

Willing to violate the fundamental rights of the constitution in order to eliminate the opposition, Bruening issued an emergency decree 'to suppress political excesses.' It prohibited meetings and wearing of uniforms, and put posters and newspapers under censorship. Hitler ordered strictest compliance. The Party discipline held like iron.

In July, the collapse of large banks froze credits throughout Europe and contributed to the economic crisis, making changes in Bruening's cabinet advisable. He himself took over the Ministry of Foreign Affairs, while General Wilhelm Groener, the Reichswehr Minister, assumed also the Ministry of the Interior. This was clearly a consolidation of the executive powers for the final fight with the Nazis.

The opposition struck back with the famous 'Harzburg Front.' On 11 October, in the charming little town of that name in the Harz mountains in Brunswick, Hitler, Schacht, Hugenberg, and Franz Seldte - the leader of the Stahlhelm who now is Minister of Labour in Hitler's cabinet-met and formed a 'united' national opposition, demanding Bruening's immediate resignation, cancellation of the emergency decrees, and new elections.

This somewhat compromising alliance with such reactionary forces as the Nationalists, the agrarian Landbund, and the Stahlhelm, was explained to Nazi followers openly and without constraint as a policy of expediency. The Nazis would seize political power with their help, but would throw them overboard at the first opportunity, just as Mussolini had done. This should have been warning enough to Hugenberg and his confreres, but eventually they were to be the victims of their own over-cunning and self-confidence.

The significant Harzburg meeting was immediately followed by a huge Party rally in Brunswick, possible there despite the emergency decree because a Nazi was Minister of the Interior.

With Nazi planes circling overhead, Hitler and Roehm reviewed a six-hour parade of one hundred thousand Brown-shirts, while Germany and the world took note.

Roehm's diplomatic skill and valuable connections now began to bear fruit. He arranged to have Hitler meet Hindenburg and General Schleicher. Though without immediate results, these meetings were preparatory to wider moves on the political chessboard-it was fitting that the leader of the second party in the Reich should know the President and the man whose hand really moved the pieces.

The latent civil war continued. On Christmas Eve the Sozis founded their 'Iron Front' for a fight to the finish with the Nazis. The Marxist Karl Severing, Prussian Minister of the Interior, made his famous threat that he would drive Hitler out of Prussia with a dog-whip, an ill-considered remark which eventually cost him dearly.

Thus ended 1931 - with a snarl.

A new and useful acquisition was Hitler's press-chief, Dr. Otto Dietrich, whose excellent family connections opened many doors. As son-in-law of the influential owner of the Rheinisch-Wesifaelische Zeitung, the organ of heavy industry, he was linked with powerful economic organizations. Dietrich became the Fuehrer's constant companion on his endless criss-crossing of Germany by motor and plane, and was at his side through all the election campaigns, of which there were twelve in 1932. Eventually he wrote a book, With Hitler into Power, a vivid personal narrative of those days. Especially interesting is his description of Hitler's ' invasion of economics':

From the lofty pedestal of their Realpolitik the captains of industry looked down pityingly upon him as an impractical idealist and dreamer. Having grown up to their position at the helm of industry under the protection of a powerful empire and being unused to responsible political thinking, they had forgotten that German industry had not conquered the world unaided, and that the power of the State had first created the requisite conditions for the prosperity of the national economy. Living now in the republic, they had accepted a paradox, that of ' building life, economically speaking, upon the idea of achievement, upon the value of the personality and therefore practically upon the authority of the personality-but politically denying this authority of the personality and replacing it by democracy, the law of the majority.'[2] Now, while the nation was struggling for existence with its life's blood, they were still thinking in terms of figures.

Adolf Hitler, who more than anyone else has from the beginning kept the value of the personality in the foreground of his thinking and doing, soon perceived that he had to conquer not only the masses but also the personalities of economic life, as the strongest pillars of the system. Some progress had been made in the last several years, but in the summer of 1931 the Fuehrer resolved to work systematically on the leading figures in industry and on the bourgeois middle-ground parties supported by them, who formed the centre of the opposition; he meant to demolish the Government building brick by brick.

In the months following this decision, Dietrich tells us, Hitler toured all Germany in his Mercedes, bobbing up everywhere for confidential talks with outstanding figures, meeting them wherever he could be sure of absolute privacy from the Press, sometimes even deep in the woods. His efforts were not without effect. 'The beams of the Government structure began to creak-uncannily, invisibly, almost impalpably.'

On the evening of the 27 January 1932 Hitler had a memorable success. At a meeting in the Industry Club at Duesseldorf, he managed to break through to the West German captains of industry.

Hitler and Dietrich drove into the court of the Park Hotel in Duesseldorf amid booing from the Marxists, and entered a hall overflowing with the elite of the West German industrialists. On a few of the faces, which they recognized as those of men whom they had already won, there was friendly expectancy, but for the most part they looked out upon a sea of cool reserve. These men had come for the pleasure of being confirmed in their own opinion of the Nazi leader.

Hitler was given a perfunctory greeting. He spoke from a projecting balustrade,

---

2 *Quoted by Dietrich from Hitler.*

resting his hands lightly on the railing, and Dietrich sat behind him, taking notes on the reaction. The Nazi began to develop with forceful logic the relationship between economics and politics, their effects upon each other and upon Germany. He told them why things had come to their present pass, and the only way they could be changed.

Within an hour, the cool reserve had vanished, and Hitler's audience was listening with intense interest. He went on to tell them of the heroic fight of his political soldiers-poor, persecuted in hatred, but ready to sacrifice everything, even their lives. He set the selfless idealism of German youth as embodied in National Socialism and in the new nobility of its workmen, against the lack of comprehension, the materialism, of the merely economically minded bourgeoisie.

He was seeking to sharpen the social consciences of his hearers without wounding them.

From his post, Dietrich could see faces begin to turn red; he saw that eyes were intent on the Fuehrer's lips, he could feel hearts growing warmer…'Now they are following inwardly. Now they are touched to the depths. At first hands move timidly, then beat out salvos of applause. When Hitler finished he had won a battle.'

Hitler had definitely won Fritz Thyssen. The powerful industrialist rose and made to this audience his confession of faith in National Socialism and in the spirit of its leader; in them lay Germany's salvation. It was a body-blow for Bruening.

Next day the Jewish and Marxist papers published brazen accounts of Hitler's champagne-and-lobster revels with the great industrialists, despite the fact that a few minutes after the meeting the two men had been back on the road, driving through the night toward a new task.

At Godesberg he won the silk industry. A triumph before the National Club in Hamburg followed. The plan was working, he was breaking through. Waverers suffered a relapse after Bruening's next broadcast, but Hitler had succeeded in planting the seed of the Nazi idea in the rich soil of Germany's economic life.

It is incredible that those in power could have continued to misjudge and underrate Hitler after his widely publicized Duesseldorf speech, which in clarity and logic, in interpretation and sheer appeal, was really a masterpiece. Most of them, of course, had never even bothered to read his Mein Kampf, let alone study it. The opposition now belittled the speech, representing it either as a fiasco or a sell-out to capitalism. In the ensuing months, much was made-as it still is to-day-of the Nazi leader's alleged dependence on the moneyed interests.

Fairness to him impels one to say that such slurs are rank injustice. In its inception, and as it developed under Hitler's guidance, the National Socialist Party was never one of class interests; its aim from the beginning was to serve as a reservoir for the national and social energies of all real Germans, out of which there might be moulded a political will toward the liberation of Germany. Hitler saw clearly that this liberation was possible only through a resurrection of the German spirit; a people in a state of spiritual collapse-confused, disunited, bewildered by false ideas-could be saved only by the triumph of a new ideal, a new concept of government based on the principles of performance and of authority, and on the value of the personality. This new concept could be made effective only by the eradication of the opposing Marxist concept. To win this fight, to forge a unified will for the reanimation of a prostrate Germany, Hitler needed the help of all classes. The poor man's gift was welcome, the rich man's doubly welcome, for it made possible a longer forward stride. What mattered was: Were there strings attached?

In most of the criticism levelled at Hitler during the years of struggle, there is abysmal ignorance of the facts. Hitler was making his fight as best he could, enlisting help where he could find it, and, at least up to this time, keeping his skirts surprisingly clean. Even his enemies, if they are honest and well informed, must admit that on his road to power, at least until the summer of 1932, the Fuehrer acted in the main with great intelligence, with dynamic energy combined with foresight, with a high sense of the realities-as an idealist-realist. But what he did when the power was within his grasp-that is another question.

One more word in extenuation:

Adolf Hitler had asked the fine gentlemen at Duesseldorf to think of his hundreds of thousands of men climbing on their trucks at dusk and setting out to protect meetings, sacrificing themselves night after night, returning at dawn to their work in shop or factory or to receive their stipend as unemployed, and out of their pitiful means buying uniforms and insignia, even paying their own fares to do the Party's business…, Believe me, in this lies the force of a great ideal!'

His picture of sacrifice was all too lightly brushed in. To be a Nazi in those years meant poverty and persecution, endless indignities. He who confessed himself a National Socialist was ostracized from the community of the State, from the decaying bourgeois society, from the life of the 'class-conscious' proletariat. It took courage to wear a Nazi badge in towns where Reds patrolled the streets. Mere suspicion of being a Nazi was enough to cost a man his job, to bring boycott and business ruin down upon his head. Hundreds and thousands were thrown into the prisons of the republic. Many died for the cause. The churches were mobilized against the Party; devout Nazis went to their graves without the assurance of peace for their souls.

True, as the Party grew, the inevitable bureaucracy developed, and with it the average integrity of Nazi officialdom probably suffered the equally inevitable decline. The movement gathered in many hooligans, camp-followers, and cheap opportunists. But through the years of struggle, the vast majority were splendidly loyal, ardent, disciplined, and brave. Each man, from Hitler down to the humblest SA trooper, might well have chosen for himself an easier life than that of being hunted down throughout Germany, always with one foot in prison, hounded by numberless decrees, unable to appeal to the state for protection, Sure of hostility in the courts.

The world has been asked to regard with compassion the lifelong self-immolation of the handful of 'Old Bolsheviks' in preparation for their death-grapple with Czarism. The years of the National Socialist struggle were briefer, but let me say that the sum-total of the Nazi sacrifice was great.

In the embittering hell of those years, Nazis learned to return blow for blow. The Nationalsozialistische Deutsche Arbeiterpartei was forged to steel. Nazis withstood the test of fire, but they grew hard. They remember, and the world forgets, what made them· so.

Facing a world of enemies, the Fuehrer had hammered the movement into a mighty instrument. The year 1932 would be decisive. In his New Year's proclamation to the Party, he made this prophecy:

'Germany is about to become National Socialist, and the world is facing a decision which may confront it only once in a thousand years.'

The coming presidential election dominated the political scene. On 6 January, Hitler was called to Berlin for a conference with Bruening and Groener. They asked him to lend his party to make up the two-thirds majority in the Reichstag necessary to proclaim a prolongation of the term of the Reichspresident. He refused, on the ground that such procedure would be a violation of the spirit of the constitution and would compromise Hindenburg.

The Fuehrer openly attacked Bruening's efforts by sending the Field-Marshal a memorandum which was a masterly expose of the Constitutional weaknesses of the chancellor's proposal; in two open letters to Bruening he put the matter in the right light before the German people. The President's reply was noncommittal, and Bruening remained his Chancellor, but Hitler had won his first diplomatic victory. Hindenburg had been forced into a distasteful open fight against the parties of the Right.

It meant that Bruening, willy-nilly, had now to bite into the sour apple, face an election, and offer the Field-Marshal the support of the Sozis to bring about his victory. Hindenburg was now the candidate of the Left, and it was necessary that he be opposed by the strongest man of the national opposition. Hitler's great opportunity to gain the power legally had come. If he could win the Presidency he would be master over army, Reichstag, and Government.

On 22 February, Hitler came out for the Presidency. He was now no longer a 'foreigner'-his appointment as a Brunswick official had automatically made him a German citizen. By a stroke of the pen, a Nazi minister in a small state had been able to legalize Hitler's candidacy-a useful survival from the days of German separatism.

The campaign proceeded violently. At its centre was the fantastic spectacle of Hindenburg, the God-fearing Protestant, the national hero, presenting himself for re-election in his eighty-fifth year as the candidate of the Catholic Centre Party and of the godless Social-Democracy.

The old man had gone pitifully astray in the German political jungle. In 1925, when he had been the candidate of the Nationalist element, the influential Deutsche Zeitung, mouth¬piece of the Pan-German Association, had said: 'Hindenburg will restore to the German people a form' of State which will inspire respect in the foreign world.' In 1932 the same journal could say: 'The question at issue is whether internationalist traitors and pacifist swine, with Hindenburg's express approval, shall bring about Germany's final ruin.' And Nazi papers called the one-time idol of the German people 'the candidate of the mutineers and deserters.'

The first balloting on 13 March was inconclusive. With 18,651,497 votes, Hindenburg had not reached a majority. ' The candidate of the Stahlhelm and of the Nationalist Party polled 2,557,729 votes, the Communist candidate 4,983,341. Though the 11,339,446 votes for Hitler represented a tremendous increase for the Nazi Party, the 'legal' march on Berlin had failed, and discouragement took hold of the Party.

A crisis in the movement was at hand, and a decline seemed inevitable.

But the Fuehrer did not lose his head. The constitution required another election. With his habitual fortitude he called his followers to the second assault; the attack must be resumed at once with utmost vigour. He himself took the lead, carrying the main burden on his shoulders. Dietrich tells us that the propaganda methods employed in this second campaign were more spectacular than anything heretofore known in political life. Using the fastest of modern planes, Hitler took to the air. In the last week before the run-off election, he addressed giant mass-meetings in twenty-one cities.

The balloting on 10 April brought him two million more votes. His figure was 13,418,547 out of a total of 36,771,787 votes. But Hindenburg was re-elected.

After his zealous campaign on behalf of the old gentleman, who had refused to leave his throne either to travel or make speeches, Bruening now thought himself firm in the saddle.

When the Government of Prussia declared that police raids at the homes of various Nazi chiefs had furnished evidence that the Party was preparing for civil war, and demanded prosecutions for high treason, the Chancellor thought that the moment for his decisive coup against Hitler had come. Three days after the second election, under pressure from the Left and from the Centre Party, General Groener, as Minister of the Interior, declared the Hitler Youth, the SS, and the S A abolished throughout the entire Reich, as a 'private army.' General Schleicher withheld his approval of the decree, but Hindenburg ill-advisedly signed it.

This was a cruel blow, the worst the Party had sustained at the hands of the Republic since 1923. But only weak organizations are destroyed by attempted suppression. Bruening had his answer ten days later in the Diet elections-a Nazi landslide. National Socialism was now by far the strongest single party in Prussia, where the Nazi leaped from 6 to 162 deputies in the Diet. It was also the strongest party in Wuerttemberg, Hamburg, and Anhalt. Even in 'Black Bavaria,' the Nazi strength equalled that of the Bavarian People's Party.

Even now Bruening sinned against right and reason in his 'Democratic-Parliamentarian' Germany. He allowed the Prussian cabinet of the Marxian ministers Braun and Severing to remain in office against an opposing majority. Bruening's Centre Party thus cheated the Nazis of their legal reward for a legal fight. The bill was presented to them later.

One of Hindenburg's old war comrades was now to make his exit from the political scene with a touch of comedy. General Groener refused to ban the Reichsbanner of the Sozis as he had the Nazi organizations, and made a fiasco of his defence of this discrimination before the Reichstag. Schleicher, now the leading spirit of the Hindenburg camarilla, decided that Groener must go, and was doubtless aided with Hindenburg by a circumstance which the Field-Marshal must have found very disturbing.

Deserted by Schleicher, his beloved protégé, who all this time had cannily kept up personal contact with Hitler and who now coolly declared that the Reichswehr Minister's action against the Nazis had cost him the confidence of the army, Groener threw up the sponge and resigned. His fall sealed Bruening's fate as well. The Chancellor was isolated now, and the camarilla, jealous of his influence over Hindenburg, could encompass his downfall.

In the final overthrow of Bruening, Captain Roehm played a skilful hand. In those days of plotting and intrigue, he was Hitler's chief negotiator with Schleicher, whose name very aptly means 'creeper' or 'crawler.' Before Groener's resignation, Roehm had already reached an understanding with Schleicher and his proposed new chancellor, Franz von Papen. On 8 May Hitler confirmed the agreement in a secret but decisive conference with Schleicher, in the presence of Doctor Meissner, the President's Secretary of State, and of Hindenburg's son.

These were his terms: He would tolerate a Papen cabinet if the Reichstag were dissolved, if the decrees against the Nazi organizations were lifted, and if complete freedom were allowed for agitation. Needless to say, both sides in this truce meant to double-cross each other when the time came.

Hitler won another election in Oldenburg with an absolute Nazi majority, visited the navy in Wilhelmshafen to find officers and men all Nazi-minded, and then went into hiding away from Berlin; he did not want his continued presence there to rouse the Chancellor's suspicions.

Schleicher laid his plot against Bruening. The centre of the drama now shifted to Hindenburg's favourite home, Neudeck in East Prussia. Here the old President had gone, as was his wont, to spend his holiday and meet his friends. It had not been in vain that Baron Elard von Oldenburg-Januschau, almost as old as Hindenburg and owner of the adjoining estate, had collected funds for a national gift to the popular hero. On the Field-Marshal's eightieth birthday, this East Prussian gentleman and speaker for the Junkers had presented him with the old Hindenburg family place, freed now of debt.

With Hindenburg now at Neudeck, it was easy for members of his own order to remind him of his loyalty to his class. Of course he must drop Bruening, that Catholic who was daring to plan the break-up of large estates and turn them into peasant settlements! And here, pat to the moment, the Supreme Court in Leipzig had cleared the Nazi Party of the charge of treason which Bruening had presented to Hindenburg as the legal basis for the banning of the SA and SS. Why hadn't Bruening asked for the dissolution of the Reichs-banner of the Sozis as well, which was just as much a private army?

It worked. When Hindenburg, back in Berlin, received his Chancellor on 29 May, Bruening did not know that his master had already accepted the complete list of Papen's cabinet. He got a cool reception, and bystanders witnessed an embarrassing situation. The oaky old giant, eyes on the paper in his hand, bellowed out in his deep bass a chiding lecture to his little Chancellor with the Jesuitical face-the man who had helped him to a new lease of power by securing for him the aid of the despised Left. Now he was accused of 'agrarian Bolshevism…unpopular government.' In growing bewilderment behind his glasses, Bruening at length lost patience and tried to explain, but did not get the expression of confidence he sought, or support for his programme.

On the following day, at a second conference which lasted only fifteen minutes, the Chancellor announced the formal resignation of the entire cabinet. Hindenburg accepted at once. And on 1 June 1932, exactly seven weeks after his re-election by the Left, the Reichspresident appointed a be-monocled Junker cabinet of the Right, with Franz von Papen as Chancellor and Kurt von Schleicher as Reichswehr Minister. It was called the 'Cabinet of National Concentration.'

XX

FATAL BLUNDERING

Overnight the Conservative 'Herren' element, the gentlemen's clique, moved into the cabinet offices. The power of this new cabinet rested only on the favour of the President, the force of the army, and the support of the 'Herrenklub,' an ultra-fashionable social-political club of the landed and moneyed elite-Junkers, generals, and magnates of heavy industry. From the outset, this 'Barons' Cabinet' had no hold on parliament and no support from the people. They could, however, count on the backing of the industrialists and of the great landowners-two mighty groups who had worked hand in hand for fifty years, ever since the beginning of Germany's protective-tariff policy.

Schleicher, master of intrigue and Reichswehr Minister in the new cabinet, was now the real power in the State. Papen was virtually unknown to the masses. He had achieved a name of a sort, for as military attaché in the German Embassy in Washington he had been the enlightened diplomat whom the United States Government had expelled as persona non grata. He was rich by marriage, popular with the ladies, and endowed with the suppleness and charm of the elegant and independent man of the world. There is a description of him in Captain von Rintelen's absorbing book, The Dark Invader -the war-time reminiscences of a German naval intelligence officer with an admirable record, who played a lone hand and lodged eventually in the Federal 'Grand Hotel' in Atlanta for six years of suffering after a brilliant career.

But Papen became chancellor, and now, for the first time, Hider was not in outspoken opposition to the Government. By his temporary alliance with the State authorities, he was hoping to get at least one foot of his Trojan Horse inside the wall. And yet, in this present manifestation of Hitler's newer opportunism, one sees a certain shadowing, a quality that does not comport with one's earlier concept of Hitler the uncompromising fighter.

To understand that statement one must look again at the parliamentary situation under the Republic, that absurd mass of complexities which the commentator on the German; political scene must needs explain repeatedly in English-speaking countries.

The Bruening Government had been the last coalition cabinet under the Republic, the last to have a majority, however slim, in the Reichstag. The maze of parties had then been reduced to twelve, grouped roughly in three broad divisions-Right, Centre, and Left, the Nazis forming the radical wing of the Right, the Communists the radical wing of the Left. Party blocks would shift back and forth from group to group until the whole game became as intricate as chess. For example, in the make-up of the Reichstag at this time, the Right had some 227 seats, the Left about 220, and the Centre 107 - which explains the unique strategical advantage of the Centre Party in German parliamentary history, enabling it to maintain, ever since Imperial days, a political strength far exceeding its numerical strength.

From 1919 on, until the rising Nazi tide forced a regrouping, a coalition of Left and Centre had ruled against the Right -the Catholic Centre Party, with its monopoly on God, in alliance with the Marxists who know neither God nor country.

The new Papen cabinet, however, had only 227 seats, including the Nazis, against the 327 of the combined Left and Centre.

Papen hoped that the coming elections would bring in a sufficient increase of seats for the Right to give him a majority in the Reichstag, and accordingly asked Hitler to sign a written pledge to tolerate his cabinet after the elections. It was a naive request, and the Fuehrer refused it on the ground that the elections might create a completely new situation for which he would need a free hand. But his refusal meant that he had exacted concessions for a valueless concession on his own part. Hitler had stipulated the dissolution of the present Reichstag; that body would not function again until the elections had brought in another Reichstag, and for that new parliament Hitler declined to bind himself.

From the beginning, the entire bargain had been bound to set the parties of the Right at odds and to work for the benefit of the Centre and Left. Schleicher and Papen hoped, of course, that during the truce they would be able to steal Hitler's thunder and with it much of the Nazi following, while the Fuehrer on his part was sure that his Party, freed from the shackling decrees, would emerge from the elections the strongest in the Reich and that the Chancellorship would be his.

They all were mistaken.

As was to be expected, Papen made no haste to keep his own promises. Although he dissolved the Reichstag on 4 June, he set the election date for as late as 31 July, and failed to lift the ban on the SA and SS until 15 June. Even then the Governments of Prussia, Bavaria, and Baden continued for a while to ignore the revocation. Papen's tactics of delay, his continued reliance on emergency decrees, the increasing Red terrorism encouraged by the unconstitutional Marxian Government in Prussia, were seized on by Hitler as pretext for rescinding his original pledge to tolerate the Papen cabinet until the elections. By the beginning of July the Party was again in violent opposition to the State, and everything was tainted with an odour of bad faith. Hitler had undoubtedly lost face through his abortive bargain. Even among Nazis it was predicted that it would cost him two million votes. It is easy to pass judgment after the event. Hitler of course needed the elimination of Bruening, new elections, and a free hand in them. These things he gained. The things he lost are among the imponderables. The election campaign got under way in a sea of bitterness. A state of virtual anarchy prevailed in the streets of Germany. With the ban lifted, Brownshirts were everywhere in evidence again, and now four private armies, equipped at the very least with jack-knives and revolvers, daggers and knuckle-dusters, were shouting in the squares and rampaging through the towns. Processions and meetings, demonstrations and protests, festivals and funerals, all wore the same face but a different uniform-except that the SS and SA of the Nazis and the Red Front of the Communists marched more obstreperously, the Sozi Reichsbanner more fatly, the Stahlhelmer more sedately. The Reichswehr, the one legal force, was least in evidence, even though it was, in a sense, the private political tool of Hindenourg. Everywhere the swing was towards the radical wings. Thousands of Sozis flocked to the Communists, thousands of Nationalists joined the Nazis. Among the private armies, the enmity between those Marxian brothers, the Sozis and the Communists, grew more deadly; the hypocritical truce between those hostile brethren, the Nazis and the Nationalists, was about to end. The parties were all at each other's throats.

And what of Germany? Swarming with unemployed, now nearly six millions of them, preyed on by adventurers, desperadoes, and gangsters, but alive with the resolution of an idealist youth. All over the land, young spirits were rearing up in defiant protest against the wretchedness of a life that their fathers seemed to have spoiled for them. This was the generation grown up under the sign of war; these were mystic, ardent souls. Whether they marched with the Nazis, as they did in increasing numbers, or shouted the battle-cry of the Communists, they were resolved on change, on a new order. In Germany, as elsewhere, the mass is soft and inert; in all countries it is always the youthful activists, forming not an elite of the intelligence, but an elite of the will, which determine the movements of the mass, bring on rebellions, and carry revolutions.

From Right and from Left came the cry: 'Things must be different!' The spirit animating the Nazis was strongly anti-capitalistic. In a great speech for the Nazis before the Reichstag in May, Gregor Strasser became in a sense the voice of rebellious Germany:

The anti-capitalist yearnings which animate our people do not signify a repudiation of property acquired by personal labour and thrift. They have nothing in common with the senseless and destructive tendencies of the Internationale. But they are a protest against a degenerate economic system, and they demand from the State that it shall break with the demon GOLD, with the habit of thinking in export statistics and in bank discounts, and shall, instead, restore a system that gives an honest reward for honest work . . .. If today the economic system of the world is no longer capable of properly distributing the wealth of nature, then the system is false and must be changed. These anti-capitalist yearnings indicate the dawn of a new age: the conquering of Liberalism, the rise of new thoughts for economic life, and a new concept of the State.

The Marxian epoch was fading in retreat, revealing neither courage nor imagination. The Communists in particular were making a bad fight, showing lack of leadership and ideas, and wasting their energies in strife with the Social-Democrats. The fact that they were taking orders from Moscow kept many potential recruits out of their ranks. On 20 July Marxism sustained a body-blow, for on that day the remains of the unconstitutional Red power in Prussia were wiped out. Reichswehr moved into the capital with armoured cars and Maxim guns; a state of emergency was declared, and the Braun-Severing Government dismissed. Papen, appointing himself State Commissioner, took over the duties of Prussian Prime Minister and made Dr. Franz Bracht, Mayor of Essen, Minister of the Interior. The Jewish chiefs of the Berlin police were ousted, certain provincial police-heads and governors were deposed, and executive powers transferred to the army. The coup d'etat met with no resistance, no general strike-nothing but protest. The Marxian giants made a cowardly retreat; it was a miserable exit of a miserable regime. Its haggling parliamentarianism had installed favouritism and corruption everywhere, had demoralized German officials, disorganized finances, ruined State enterprises, blinked at scandals in the municipal administration in Berlin-all, by the way, Jews out of the East. Marxism had been routed from its stronghold. It held fast to one hope: a decisive defeat for Hitler in his fight with the Nationalists, now in power, which would throw his battalions, deserting a lost cause, into the camp of Bolshevism for a joint onslaught against a capitalist Fascism.

This struggle between the Nazis and the Nationalists for the ultimate ascendancy in the Right was in fact the supreme feature of the campaign, for its outcome was to determine Germany's future. Before we proceed to the final act of that drama, let us understand clearly the nature of the opposing forces. The men who formed the general staff of the Nationalists were drawn from the privileged or formerly privileged groups. They were the heirs of the leading elite of the old regime; they comprised the landed or military aristocracy, high functionaries, university professors, representatives of heavy industry and high finance-men of conservative or reactionary tendencies, essentially monarchists aiming to re-establish the old order by an authoritarian regime which would restore to the traditional cadres their one-time influence and power.

Hitler, on the other hand, was the tribune of the people; he had behind him the great crowd of 'little men' who had been the real victims of the revolution of 1918 - the discontented, the disinherited, the declasses, revolutionaries of every kind. He had concentrated his propaganda machine on the mass of bourgeois suffering from the economic crisis, on working-men stricken by unemployment, farmers more or less ruined by debt and unfavourable markets, the numberless intellectuals who could see no way out of their distress, the unfortunates and adventurers whom the dissolution of the army had thrown into the streets. His followers had every¬thing to gain, nothing to lose. They wanted only to push a dying, crumbling epoch into the abyss; they did not think of restoring the past. No more did Hitler. His ambition was to create a Third Reich resembling in no way the old imperial Germany. He himself must be the new chief-not one designated by birth or elected by a majority, but created by his own will and confirmed by the free choice of the people in recognition of his superiority.

"Hello!" I said as I entered the Berlin office of the Voelkiseher Beobachter. Arno Schickedanz, still Rosenberg's close-mouthed scout, and Hans Hinkel were sitting there, discussing the election to be held on the coming Sunday.

"Heil Hitler!" they returned, which sounded somehow amusing from old comrades like Schickedanz, the Berlin representative of the Beobaclzter, and Hinkel, a deputy, and correspondent for the Nazi Reichstag faction.

"Well, you've spread out since I was here last. All the way down from Bremen I saw swastikas flying. The country seems to be going Nazi. Coming from abroad, I can feel a change in the air."

"Yes, things have moved along. You arrive at a good moment," said Hinkel. "There's no doubt we'll get the election next Sunday. Hitler has the whole country in ferment. If he isn't Chancellor within a fortnight, it will be an unholy miracle. You should see the campaign shows we put on nowadays! He's speaking tomorrow at three, beginning in Brandenburg, where I am to be the first speaker. Drive down with me and see for yourself. Good opportunity, too, to shake hands with Hitler-he's scarce nowadays, you know!"

Indeed, the methods by which the Nazis were wooing the German voter were impressive enough, even without counting the spectacular mass-meetings. As I walked through the Berlin streets, the Party flag was everywhere in evidence. Huge posters, pictorial homilies, and Nazi slogans screamed from windows and kiosks, blazoning forth messages about honour and duty, national solidarity and social justice, bread, liberty, and the beauty of sacrifice-all proclaiming the consummate skill with which Hitler had been leavening the masses. Passers-by wore tiny lapel emblems; uniformed men elbowed their way through the crowds, the swastika circling their brawny arms. On every news-stand the Beobachter and Angriff were piled high.

In the years since Hitler's release from prison, Berlin had become the hub of the Party machine, the centre of the parliamentary thrust as well as its goal. Munich remained the business and spiritual stronghold, as it had been from the beginning; but the heavy political barrage was now being directed from under the shadow of the Reichstag itself; Hitler was waging a hand-to-hand battle with the elected leaders of the Republic. Everything was keyed to the highest pitch. The whole city bore evidence of the intensity of the battle, and showed how close the Fuehrer was to victory.

If I thought that the campaign was going strongly in the capital, the next day's experience taught me how expertly the Nazis had extended their lines throughout Germany. Hinkel drove me up to Brandenburg, through villages where the bright summer air seemed to bubble with expectation-not the usual pre-election excitement, but more intense, more concentrated, and concentrated notably on the emblem of Nazi promises. As we approached Brandenburg, the roads became crowded with cars and wagons headed in our direction and hemmed in by people on foot.

A broad meadow had been marked off with banners, and a high platform at one end was draped with flaming swastikas. Below the platform, in the centre of the huge circle, spruce Storm Troopers were ranked in solid squares. Bands played while the audience pressed into the rough wooden benches ; and those who could not find seats stood up, row behind row, around the field; among them were thousands of peasants, and many women and children with shining eyes.

Hinkel addressed the crowds. While he was speaking, an aeroplane zoomed over the field; every head turned to follow its descent. And when Hitler hurried to the platform, he was greeted by the loudest cheer I had ever heard in my life. Sixty thousand arms were lifted in the Roman salute which the Nazis had adopted. Sixty thousand faces of country folk made a bright blur as they looked towards him-the composite face of Germany, bending its composite ear to catch the words of one man.

Hitler spoke with such furious power that I wondered if he would not lose his voice, hoarse enough already. The crowd roared approval whenever he paused, and at last, at the psychological moment, he stepped down, leaving the whole audience suspended on the oratorical heights to which he had lifted them. He had no time to wait for the applause, for that same afternoon he was scheduled to speak in Potsdam, and that night in Berlin. As he left, he stopped only long enough to pat a child tendering him flowers and to clasp my hand.

"Ludecke, how are you? I'm glad you are back in time to be with us. But now I'm rushed. Look me up, first thing after the elections."

Hinkel and I drove back to Berlin to witness the great Grunewald Stadium rally which was to wind up the entire campaign. Enormous preparations had been made by Goebbels, the Nazi director of propaganda. This was to be no medicine-show for peasants and farmers, but an event which must make sophisticated Berlin open its eyes in amazement.

Only Hinkel's official position got us through the throng which jammed the approach to the stadium, though we arrived well in advance of the meeting. When we took our seats near the platform the long July day still lingered over the open amphitheatre in its beautiful setting of trees. By the time night began to steal over the field, more than a hundred thousand people had paid to squeeze inside, while another hundred thousand packed a nearby race-track where loud-speakers had been set up to carry Hitler's words. And at home millions were waiting at the radio, open to the Nazis for the first time in this campaign.

Inside the stadium, the stage-setting was flawless. Around the entire perimeter of the vast stone arena, banners were silhouetted against the darkening sky. Row under row, the seats stepped down to the centre field, a murmurous, vast acreage of Germans, merged by the dimming light into one solid dun-coloured cliff of humanity. The long oval was broken on one side by an opening which framed high poplar trees, through whose branches shone the level rays of the setting sun. Directly opposite reared a dramatic speaking-stand, its bold, cubical masses hung with giant swastikas which gained significance through sheer magnification. Draperies likewise flaunting swastikas made a simple and thrilling background. Picked men from the Schutzstaffel were drawn up in close ranks below the stand. Twelve huge SA bands played military marches with beautiful precision and terrifying power. Behind the bands, on the field itself, solid squares of uniformed men from the Nazi labour unions were ranged in strict military order, thousands strong.

Here in this vast bowl, so carefully and with such theatrical genius arranged for the occasion, the intensity of the long election campaign was compacted and brought to a focus. The hundred thousand citizens had but one mind. Their thought was as directly apprehensible as though a finger were writing it upon the sky in letters of fire. And yet not every one in the throng was friendly to the Nazis. In the boxes especially I could see tight little groups of men, obviously political observers, or industrialists and business leaders who had come here only to watch and corroborate the deep mistrust, the fear, which Hitler still inspired in many men of their class. And it was interesting to observe, as the play went on, how the mien of these hard-boiled fellows took on softer tones; some even showed undisguised emotion. One and all, however, were fascinated by the final preparation for the climax of a struggle far more profound and far-reaching than a mere state election. One simply knew that this was a decisive moment in history.

Scarcely daring to lift my voice or remove my eyes from the platform, I waited for Hitler to appear. Presently Goebbels, a fanatic-looking, emaciated dwarf, and yet, in such a set-up, a fantastic figure in spite of his grotesqueness, began to pinch-hit for tile star in his penetrating, clarion voice, comparing Hitler to Cromwell.

Suddenly a wave surged over the crowd, it leaned forward, a word was tossed from man to man: Hitler is coming! Hitler is here! A blare of trumpets rent the air, and a hundred thousand people leaped to their feet in tense expectancy. All eyes were turned towards the stand, awaiting the approach of the Fuehrer. There was a low rumble of excitement and then, releasing its pent-up emotion, the crowd burst into a tremendous ovation, the 'Heils' swelling until they were like the roar of a mighty cataract.

Hitler had stepped through a passage-way on to the tribune, bathed in light, hatless, brown-shirted, briskly saluting. When the tumult subsided at length, like a thunderstorm receding, he threw defiance and appeal, with his whipping, cracking speech, over loudspeakers and microphones into the falling darkness of the night.

Within five minutes the destiny of Germany was sealed.

When Hitler had first swept me off my feet, I had been ten years younger. Now I was astonished how cool I remained in this vibrant atmosphere, looking at him as though he were contesting a race, weighing him for the last time, but jubilant that after all and in spite of everything he was to be the winner. And yet I felt again, but in a different way-more abstractly and impersonally than in former years-the invisible lines of force which radiated from Hitler. To be within sound of his voice, as I was clearly aware this time, watching the response from the masses, was like being within the field of a powerful magnet. Whether one was repelled or attracted, one was electrified.

I listened closely, checking an impression which the Brandenburg meeting had given me. I watched intently. This was the same Hitler speaking-a little heavier, his hair thinner, his voice hoarser. But not the same speech. Gone was the invective of his earlier rabble-rousing orations. He never spoke the word Jew, nor did he pause to attack individuals. With hard, almost disdainful self-assurance, he launched out on a high philosophical plane, rising into ever more rarefied regions of almost abstract theory as he spoke. No need now to stoop to the level of the dullest clod among the crowd, as before he had done with deliberate purpose. Even if his passionate periods about a dying epoch, State concepts; world outlooks, and the imminent Nazi millennium went over their heads, they were clearly moved and would take the trouble to untangle their bewilderment next day by reading his speech in the Nazi Press. He spoke with the freedom, the fire, the certainty of a victorious leader who knows that he is followed by millions to whom his most obscure parable will seem like an inspired prophecy. The work of electioneering was finished; this demonstration was just a superlative finishing touch, a seal set on the thousands of rallies which had been held in every corner of the Reich in the last week. And so, with millions straining to catch his words, Hitler dared to soar.

The change in his speaking routine amazed me. His pantomime had not changed-clenched fists before his expressive, working face, heaven-pointed or threatening forefinger, pleading hands. But his speech was a new one to me. No one had grasped better the fundamental principles of propaganda, which-in his own words-depends for its success on its intelligibility to the dullest, least-educated listener. Now he spoke like an inspired statesman and a professor of ethics, yet still he held the crowd. If I had wanted proof of his inner conviction that power was almost within his grasp, I had it now. For only a man confident of his own destined success would have presumed to speak in so bewildering a fashion to a mixed congregation of average voters.

Hitler had finished. The dozen massed bands struck up his favourite march, the 'Badenweiler,' and the ceremonious last act of the meeting began. Two sleek, huge Mercedes thrust their long black noses from the tunnel through the break in the tiers under the platform. Hitler stepped down into the first car, with his adjutants. Beside the chauffeur, he stood upright in the moving car, smiling yet serious, simple and sure of himself, his arm at salute to the madly cheering audience. The second Mercedes followed, crowded with eight giants - Hitler's personal body-guard. Slowly the little cavalcade made a circuit of the field. The roar of cheers did not diminish during the whole time.

As the cars finally disappeared through the breach under the stand, a broad stream of flame emerged from the passageway beneath the poplar trees. A column of fifteen thousand black-uniformed SS troopers carrying torches, it divided into two streams of light flowing slowly along two sides of the arena. At last, after forming a fiery pattern, it dissolved into a single border around the whole stadium. Bugles sounded in the darkness far and near, and suddenly the bands broke as one into the 'Grosse Zapfenstreich,'-the Great Tattoo. Then a burst of fireworks shattered the zenith, the torches flared, the bands blared again, and the crowd rose to its feet to join in the most tremendous rendition on record of 'Deutschland Ueber Alles' and the Nazi 'Horst Wessel' song.

The election campaign was at an end. There remained only the formality of casting and counting the votes; that Hitler would win was a foregone conclusion.

I was thoughtful on my way back to my hotel, and staggered in retrospect by the display which my old party, once so pinched for placard paste, was now able to afford. No doubt this great circus would have drawn many into the movement if they had not been Nazis already. Fifteen thousand torches are no mean beacon to follow...

The election proved more of a landslide than even the most optimistic of Hitler's followers had ventured to expect. The Nazi Party polled 13,748,781 votes out of 36,882,354, capturing two hundred and thirty seats-ninety-seven ahead of its nearest rival, the Social Democrats. It was now by far the largest party in the Reich, with a comfortable block of almost two-fifths of the entire parliament. The Communists had gained twelve and the combined Catholic parties ten seats, but the Social Democrats had lost ten seats, the Nationalists four, and the splinter parties had almost disappeared.

By tradition if not by law in Republican Germany, the cabinet resigned after an election if it had not attained a majority, and the President asked 'the leader of the strongest party in the new Reichstag to form a cabinet. The people's mandate had

REICHSTAG ELECTION, 31 JULY 1932	
Total of Deputies elected	608
Nazis	230
Sozis	133
Communists	89
Centre	76
Bavarian People's Party	21
Nationalists	37
Splinter parties	22

been given to Hitler's Party decisively. At last he could feel that he had succeeded, after seven years of parliamentary strife, in winning by legal means the power he had failed to seize by force of arms in the Beer Hall Putsch.

He had justified his methods to himself, and had justified himself before the people. The high office should follow. The world knows that it did not follow.

With not even ten per cent of the new Reichstag in support of the Government, Papen should immediately have presented the resignation of his cabinet. The Hindenburg camarilla, however, saw with dismay that by observing this democratic custom they would be forced to work with Hitler, whom they still held in suspicion and contempt. Moreover, another coalition cabinet was apparently impossible, since no party had a clear majority in the Reichstag, and a parliamentary alliance between the Nazis and the Centre Party seemed most improbable. This unpromising situation provided the camarilla with a nominal excuse for falling back on the old trick and continuing to govern by emergency decrees under the same Paragraph 48 of the constitution, now so threadbare in Hindenburg's hands. The fact that such measures required a two-thirds majority of the Reichstag and that no such majority existed, did not trouble the gentlemen of the 'Presidial Cabinet,' though they must have realized that they could not long hold to a course against the constitution, against parliament, against the overwhelming majority of the people.

Hitler waited. He knew, of course, as the camarilla knew, that he could not think of a coalition with the Centre Party, which then would again be the balance of the scale-an intolerable dependence in view of the revolutionary nature of the Nazi programme. With Nazis holding practically two-fifths of the Reichstag, however, there was precedent for his being designated the head of another 'Presidial Cabinet.'

Nothing happened. The Fuehrer went to see Schleicher and stated his demands: the Chancellorship for himself; the Ministries of the Interior, of Agriculture, Air, Justice, and Propaganda to be filled with Nazis, as well as the offices of Prussian Prime Minister and Prussian Minister of the Interior. The response was evidently more positive than negative, and Hitler returned to his 'Magic Mountain' to confer with his Party chieftains,'

Behind the scenes at the Wilhelmstrasse, the bickering, bartering, and plotting went on. The wires were busy. Schleicher and Papen shifted and shuffled. One flimsy excuse after another was given for their dilatory conduct: Hitler had promised that he would tolerate the Papen cabinet; Hitler could scarcely head a 'Presidial Cabinet' in view of his one-sided dependence on his Party-and so forth.

The whole nation was feeling the suspense. Though the people might continue to hope despite the delay, the Nazi leaders should have known better. It was becoming increasingly apparent that the camarilla did not want Hitler as chancellor under any conditions, and meant to cheat him out of it. He himself could scarcely cherish illusions about his standing with Hindenburg. 'This Austrian-this Bohemian corporal' the President had called him only a few months before. 'Post¬master-general if the worst comes to the worst' was the sour political plum the old man would hand him if he needed to quiet the aggressive upstart.

While Hitler waited for the customary summons to the President's palace, the Nazis grew restive. Their Fuehrer was being ignored-the rank and file saw it more clearly than the leaders. The SA pressed for action, and the whole Party held itself on the alert to seize the power if necessary. Thousands of men left their work to get ready, and their political officers were equally prepared for the great moment. Daily workouts in the form of pitched battles with Sozis and Communists kept the men of the SA at the top of their form.

As the temper of the relations between Munich, the Nazi capital, and Moscow, the Communist capital, grew hourly more violent, a condition of latent warfare developed. Bombings, shootings, knifings, raids, and murders increased. Finally there was issued from Berlin a new emergency decree proclaiming martial law, forbidding all political demonstrations, making political murder and arson punishable by death, and providing heavy penalties for other disturbances. As the courts were chiefly anti-Nazi, this measure would fall heaviest on Hitler's men.

Sixty thousand Brownshirts were concentrated in a ring round Berlin, their arms and trucks in readiness for instant action. Keeping them in leash became a delicate task. Mixing strategy with truth, the Fuehrer let it be known that his troops might get out of hand if the due rewards of the election were much longer withheld. The prospect may have hastened his opponents' final move, but it is probable that their plans were already laid, and that before burning their bridges behind them they had been trying to decide whether Hitler would act or only threaten. Now they evidently made up their minds that this was, after all, mere bluff, and took heart. They intended to treat Hitler to a cold shower of contempt, with enough publicity to let the public in on his humiliation. They were going to sneer him into the discard.

Eleven days after the elections, the Fuehrer apparently was still hoping that the

Chancellorship would be his. The crisis was now at hand. It took a form least anticipated by him.

Contradictory reports abound as to the details of the famous Hindenburg-Hitler interview of 13 August 1932. The existing accounts of it are more or less clever reconstructions. On Hitler's movements in the two days preceding it, the best-informed Nazi sources are at variance. These are Goebbels, who as propaganda chief was in continual contact with the Fuehrer, and Dietrich, who as Press-chief accompanied Hitler on all his travels and was always in the latter's immediate entourage.

Goebbels' diary[1] represents Hitler as resolving on 11 August to leave his 'Magic Mountain' for Berlin, there to wait in seclusion. They rested briefly in the Fuehrer's flat in Munich; then Goebbels departed for the capital by the night train; Hitler was to follow by car. Towards evening on the twelfth, Goebbels drove out from Berlin to Caputh, a small suburb near Potsdam where he had a cottage, and waited for Hitler to join him. The Fuehrer arrived at ten o'clock, in darkness, and listened to Goebbels' detailed report.

All evening long he paced with huge strides up and down the room, up and down the terrace. The importance of the decision he must face on the morrow was visibly working on him. Would the reward of ten years' labour be his at last? Nobody dared to believe that it would, says Goebbels.

Trying their best to wait calmly, they had some music and talked over old times. It was late when they separated. Hitler was to stay there overnight; he would drive into Berlin early next morning with Roehm, his chief of staff.

Dietrich reports[2] that on 11 August a telephone call from Berlin reached Hitler at his retreat on the 'Magic Mountain' telling him to be in the capital on 12 August, for discussions and decisions regarding a new government. "Not yet able to penetrate the situation, we could only believe that Adolf Hitler's hour had come," he says. He further relates that Hitler, coming by motor from Munich, arrived at Caputh at eight o'clock on the morning of the thirteenth, there to meet Roehm.

Of these varying accounts, it is pleasanter to choose Goebbels'; one is reluctant to sacrifice the picture of Hitler pacing up and down for hours on the fateful eve, and finally resorting to music to quiet his nerves. We must leave undetermined the question whether Hitler was summoned from Munich or left for Berlin of his own accord, since Goebbels and Dietrich do not agree.

Concerning Hitler's movements in Berlin on the thirteenth, however, we have facts. By noon he had completed an interview with Schleicher and one with Papen, had been offered the Vice-chancellorship, and had refused. Then, with Roehm and Frick, he had driven to Goebbels' city flat to await developments.

---

1 *Vom Kaiserhof zur Reichskanzlei.*
2 *Mit Hitler in die Macht.*

At three o'clock that afternoon, Goebbels' records, Secretary of State Planck telephoned to summon the Fuehrer to the President. He was told that if the decision stood as announced, it was useless for Hitler to come. "The Herr Reichspresident will talk to him first," was the reply. That revived a vague hope. Perhaps after all the "Old Bull" would bow to the voters' mandate and entrust Hitler with the Chancellorship! He set off, again with Roehm and Frick, for the President's palace.

Hindenburg waived all formalities, as well as all courtesies. He did not ask Hitler to sit down. Standing with the support of his cane, flanked by his son and Meissner, his secretary, he asked the Nazi leader point-blank whether he could accept the Vice-chancellorship and support the national government in accordance with his promise. Thus was the fiction of the "promise" maintained. Hitler again refused; co-operation in a position subordinate to Papen was out of the question-it must be chancellor or nothing. Few words were wasted. Speaking sternly, Hindenburg replied that he could not square it with his conscience and with his duty to the Fatherland to appoint a party leader head of a "National" government. Hitler was admonished to conduct the opposition in a chivalrous manner. Then he was dismissed.

The interview had lasted less than ten minutes.

Hitler had barely reached Goebbels' flat again when the newsboys in the streets began screaming headlines: "Hitler Demands the entire Power"–"Shocking Pretension"-"Hitler's Breach of Faith"-"Hitler Reprimanded by the Reichspresident." The accounts were based on an official bulletin, issued at such bewildering speed that it had evidently been in readiness in the government Press office when Hitler left the palace. The whole thing had been a plotted manoeuvre. But it worked, and within an hour the Press of the world resounded with Hitler's disgrace. 'And the world believed it,' wrote Dietrich.[3] In vain we tried to set things straight. We could not penetrate with our Press-it was shouted down,'

The peerless Nazi propaganda machine had been caught off guard, unprepared to counter an exasperating humiliation. The whole Party tingled with it, and waited feverishly for a signal from the Fuehrer. Now at last the S A would have a chance for direct action.

But Hitler thought otherwise. Late that afternoon the SA leaders assembled in a rear room of Goebbels' fiat to receive his decision. He told them what had happened, and also that the situation was not ripe for direct action. They must obey orders. The S A must go home.

There was at first blind rage at Hindenburg, then growing dismay among the S A leaders when they remembered their Brown shirts just outside Berlin, held in check for so long by the promise of a triumphal entry into the city under their Fuehrer's chancellorship. How would they take this disappointment? The climax had been

3 *Mit Hitler in die Macht.*

reached and they knew it. More than one captain declared emphatically that he would no longer be able to maintain discipline. But Dietrich who was present, relates that the Fuehrer was ready with striking arguments to convince men sick and tired of the eternal electioneering, men who wanted to be on the march, that they must go on with the fight legally. And it was Roehm, says Goebbels, who as chief of staff of the SA now had the hardest task ahead of him.

Then, taking up the public aspect of the afternoon's humiliation, Hitler and Goebbels swung into a programme for explaining away the rebuff. Speeches were drafted, procotols drawn up, articles written, proclamations dictated, and soon the whole formidable Nazi propaganda machine was whirling at top speed to correct the prevalent impression that Hitler had been worsted. With the colossal effrontery which was rapidly becoming more and more characteristic of Nazi officialdom, Hitler was portrayed as the saviour of the Party and of Germany by his astuteness in avoiding the trap of the offer of the vice-chancellorship.

By midnight the Fuehrer had left for his little chalet on the, 'Magic Mountain,' and soon Goebbels' apartment, which that day had been the scene of so much storm and stress, was dark. If Goebbels himself was able to sleep in the face of the terrific job of rehabilitation which had to be done, it was only because the Nazis were used to crises by now. For the stark fact was that everyone feared that the Fuehrer had come as close to power as he ever would in his parliamentary orbit. Nothing could wipe away the impression that Hitler had suffered defeat, and it was a heavy problem to know how to proceed.

August 13th had been a black day not only for the Nazi Party but for the entire German nation. Again Hindenburg had played a poor role. For two years he had been exceeding his powers; his autocratic regime, completely eliminating the Reichstag as a legal authority, had been a flagrant violation of the constitution and of his oath. One is tempted to point out the ironical fact that while Hitler, in a sense, had been playing the game legally, Hindenburg had been playing it illegally. His statement that his sense of duty and his conscience forbade his entrusting a party leader such as Hitler with the executive power of the Reich was dishonest-but of course one must remember that the old man was merely the figure-head of the camarilla.

The blindness of some of these gentlemen would pass comprehension if their selfish motives were not so apparent. The Papen cabinet was in an untenable position, opposed as it was by the parties of the Left and of the Right, and supported only by the small group of Nationalists led by Hugenberg. Their parliamentary situation was hopeless', for, under the existing constitution, at any given moment a hostile Reichstag could compel them to quit. Modification of the constitution would require a two-thirds majority, impossible without the Nazis. And if by repeatedly dissolving the Reichstag they thought to prolong their stay in office and start a decline of the Nazi Party, the Communists would be the gainers; it should have been clear to them that a complete disintegration of the National Socialist Party would only throw the nation into the clutches of Bolshevism. If they were planning recourse to a military dictatorship, where had they a man strong enough for that role? They had no Cromwell, no Napoleon. Moreover they would have found the army already too 'Nazified' from the bottom up to serve them as a sure instrument against the Nazis.

Events were to prove that eventually they would have to compromise with Hitler anyway. If they had chosen the historical moment, they would have been in a far stronger position. As it was, they elected to capitulate when a malign constellation stood over each side. Had Hitler been made Chancellor after the July elections, German history and even world history might have taken a far better course.

But the reactionary clique preferred to resort to trickery. Even Rudolf Olden, one-time editor of the formerly Jewish Berliner Tageblatt, a man outspokenly hostile to Hitler and to everything Nazi, admits the injustice of it. In his biography[4] of the Fuehrer, he writes:

Now that the National Socialists had reached the ante-chamber of power, and were taking part in political parleys, they encountered a measure of haughtiness, contempt and trickery which, if they had not come out victorious, would have earned their just indignation. For all the doors that were thrown open to them, for all the hands that shook theirs, there was not one of the 'respectable people' who received them who did not want to exploit them, and usually to trick them. It was exactly as it had been ten years before in Munich: the others wanted to rule, and Hitler was to take over the propaganda department. But it was far from certain that he was to keep even so modest a province for long.

On 13 August Adolf Hitler made his own cardinal mistake, a blunder whose historical consequences may perhaps become more fully apparent in the future.

It was not the refusal of the Vice-chancellorship; from the first it was obvious that he could not and would not rise to that bait. Even Goebbels admits in his diary[5] on 13 August:

'The suggestion that Hitler could be Vice-Chancellor in a bourgeois cabinet is too grotesque to have been made in earnest. Rather fight another ten years than accept this offer.' Dietrich, however, proceeds to romanticize about the Great Refusal:

On this day the Fuehrer saved the movement by his firmness of character … August 13… not only turned out to be a triumphant victory for the character and personality of Adolf Hitler, but was felt by himself instinctively and immediately as one of the happiest days for the movement … while the sceptics were believing everything lost … He did not then, as the whole world thought, feel like a loser,

---

4 *Hitler, by Rudolf Olden, p. 247; Covici-Friede, New York.*
5 *Vom Kaiserhof zur Reichskanzlei, pp.145-6.*

but glad and free, like a man who has fortunately escaped a great danger ... The movement had become great through fight, and only through fight by complete attrition of its opponents, could it conquer. That had been, and continued to be, the battle-cry of the Fuehrer....[6]

These are fine words, but precious nonsense, an absurd inflation of a decision that was a foregone conclusion. More-over, Dietrich's book was published in 1934, over a year after Hitler's rise to power, when it was a matter of history that the Fuehrer's fight after 13 August was anything but heroic, and that his final 'triumph' was bought by a questionable bargain unworthy of a Nazi, a disgrace to that Nazi concept of 'Blood and Honour' which had been proclaimed ad nauseam.

To take Hitler's measure in this crisis, let us examine two questions: Was he duped by Schleicher and Papen? Did he miss his unique opportunity to seize the power in a bold and honest way worthy of a Nazi revolutionary? To the first query, the answer is a qualified 'yes,' to the second an absolute 'yes.'

In view of Hitler's keen sense of the realities, it is difficult to believe that he seriously expected his appointment as Chancellor. He has, however, as Lenin had, a fine instinct for mass psychology, but, also like Lenin, often a poor judgment for individuals. He had stated his demands and entrusted his negotiations to Schleicher. It is reported that in their conversations before 13 August, the two seriously debated forcing Hindenburg's resignation and making Hitler President of the Reich, with Schleicher as Chancellor and three Nazis in his cabinet. Whether or not Schleicher lured him into a fool's paradise with this rosy dream, Hitler should have known that he was dealing with an intrigant, and should have been prepared to be the victim.

When the Reichstag was dissolved on 3 June, Hitler could reasonably expect an astute and vigorous campaign to yield at least two hundred and twenty seats in the coming election. That is plain arithmetic. He had polled 13,418,547 votes in the second presidential election on 10 April, and sixty thousand votes were needed for the election of one deputy.

Demanding of Hitler only that he show himself as much the realist as he had in the past, it would seem that he should have envisioned three certainties. First, a vote that would not yield him a majority but still would make the Party the strongest in the Reich. Second, the camarilla's refusal to entrust him with the Chancellorship, despite all parliamentary precedent. Third, the fact that the July elections would bring his legal campaign to its climax, and that further elections would only jeopardize his chances. Actually, in the ensuing November elections, the Nazis lost two million votes, and in later by-elections proportionally more. His instinct for mass psychology should have told him when his parliamentary star would reach its zenith.

Ergo, it was both logical and imperative that Hitler be prepared in early August

---

6 *Mit Hitler in die Macht.*

to abandon the 'course of legality' for a final showdown. If, immediately after the election, he had convinced Schleicher and Papen that he meant to force the issue, they would almost certainly have yielded. They dared not precipitate a civil war which they were bound to lose either to the Nazis or the Communists. Hindenburg was moved to make Hitler Chancellor on 30 January 1933 at a time when the Nazi movement was on the decline and with it Hitler's star. There can be no doubt that he would have made the appointment in August if the camarilla had told him he must bow to necessity.

What would Hitler's chances have been if Schleicher and Papen had accepted his hypothetical challenge and had preferred bullets to ballots?

By 1 July the Fuehrer had an efficient force of more than 500,000 men in the SA and about 75,000 in the SS; he could easily have had a total of 600,000 troops in a short time. The Nazi automobile corps was excellent. The spirit of the entire Party was ripe for a coup de force; indeed, everybody was waiting for it. Nazi Governments, with control over the police, were established in the States of Anhalt, Brunswick, Hessen, Thuringia, Mecklenburg, and Oldenburg; the Party, including the SA and SS, was very strong in Berlin, as well as in the Prussian provinces of Silesia, Saxony, Brandenburg, Pomerania, and East and West Prussia, where the farmers and peasants were overwhelmingly on the Nazi side. Local authorities in towns where the Party was not in actual control could have readily been expelled and replaced by Nazis. Thus Berlin could have been completely cut off and starved into capitulation, while Nazi forces were seizing strategic points, if not the actual power, in Bavaria and other States. This was, in fact, a plan which had been under serious consideration.

Most important of all, the Marxian Government in Prussia (remember that Prussia comprises two-thirds of the German nation) with its powerful Prussian police, always one of the strongest factors behind ·the Weimar Republic, had already been eliminated at the time of the election. The cowardly exit of the Marxian might had disillusioned millions of its followers and had almost paralysed its fighting force.

What forces could the Hindenburg-Papen-Schleicher regime have relied on?

It could not expect the unqualified loyalty of the army, in which Hindenburg's prestige had rapidly been sinking and sympathy for the Nazi cause rising; here disaffection would have been certain. The Centre Party had already expelled the Catholic Papen in fury at Hindenburg's disdainful discharge of their leader, Bruening. The Social-Democracy was in fiercest opposition. The camarilla could count as assets only the doubtful support of the army, the Nationalists under Hugenberg, the Steelhelmets under Seldte, the Junkers, heavy industry, and high finance-except where Hitler had made inroads on these last. Stalwart action on Hitler's part would assuredly have won large blocks of the Nationalists and Steelhelmets. In the face of a bloody civil war, with Bolshevism waiting round the corner, thousands of them would have joined the Nazis, and thousands of others would have adopted a wait-and-see attitude.

All this is conjecture. Unmindful of the German nation, the camarilla ran their selfish bluff, and Hitler backed down. The Fuehrer missed his historical moment, and the consequences are apparent in Germany today.

XXI

'HEIL HITLER? QUATSCH!'

In that tense period between the elections And Hitler's rejection by Hindenburg, I went down from Berlin to Munich; I wanted to talk with Rosenberg and others whose insight into Party affairs might help me to chart my future course. Before leaving the capital, however, I spent a full week surveying Nazi affairs from underneath, so to speak -from the viewpoint of the man in the street and the man in the ranks. On what sort of foundation did the towering Party structure really rest?

Everyone was taut those days, and politics was the only subject of discussion. Total strangers would accost each other in cafes to exchange opinions, and private arguments on street-corners would grow into mass debates and sometimes into brawls. In Communist circles and meetings, where curiosity led me, I heard Sozis attacked as violently as Nazis, and the existing Government mentioned with contempt rather than fear. It was strange to find that certain responsible Communist leaders really seemed to desire a temporary Nazi regime as the 'last stand of Capitalism,' which they believed a necessary evil before Communism could seize the reins of power. Instead of forming at the twelfth hour a common front-'The Popular Front'-as they later did in France and Spain, the Marxists in Germany then were fighting each other with such hatred that they were easily beaten in the Nazi's final onslaught.

Next I visited the Leaders' School of the 'Horst Wessel' Standard ('standard' corresponds to a regiment in the army) which had its quarters in a country inn near Berlin, belonging to an old Party member. Here, as in many other similar schools, SA men were put through a rigorous training, with enough of the Nazi Weltanschauung drilled into them to make them political soldiers and unquestioning servants of the Party. In such camps, for a period of fifteen to thirty days, many thousands of Brownshirts lived, ate, slept, and laboured, under strict discipline along military lines. True, they handled no weapons, since their arsenals were secret; but they learned how to use bayonets and hand grenades by means of painted wood imitations. The authorities pretended to believe it was all in sport. For the most part, people of the neighbourhood, hoping that Hitler would some day roll his growing brown juggernaut over the Government which they abhorred, kept the camp commissaries supplied with gifts of food.

I spent the whole afternoon witnessing their remarkable performance during a final inspection of that particular group, which was under the command of Karl Ernst, who then was still a minor officer, but later became the well known SA leader of Berlin-to be murdered in the Blood Purge of go June 1934. The adjutant of the standard had been showing me around. When the inspection was over, I sat with him in the side-car of a motor cycle riding slowly ahead of the men who were returning singing to quarters after their hard day. I asked the adjutant about the financing of the SA, and the really astonishing discipline for a voluntary troop.

"You see," he began, "the driver of this motor cycle owns it. He is a former policeman who was dismissed because he was seen reading the Nazi Angriff. This man doesn't get a penny for his vehicle or for the time he gives us. He even buys the petrol whenever he uses it for us. There are thousands like him. This spirit of devotion and sacrifice has made us great. And the discipline is not based on punishment but on an appeal to their honour. The first reproof is made quite privately; if another is needed, it takes place in front of the assembled troop; if that doesn't help, wearing of the uniform is forbidden for a fortnight, and only then, if this also fails, does degradation and expulsion from the ranks follow. But that is very seldom necessary."

But what about the SA pay? The American Press had reported that every SA man received an average daily pay of four marks.

The astounded face of this sunburned old soldier who wore the Iron Cross, First Class, was something to see. "What! We-? Pay? That is fabulous!" He stopped the car and jumped out. "Boys!" he cried. "How much daily pay do you get?"

For a moment they didn't grasp the question, it was such a novel idea. He had to shout it a second time.

"What! We-?" they echoed. "But we don't get any pay!" They bawled it at me, turning out their empty pockets.

I saw many examples of the admirable sense of duty which at that time seemed a matter of course among the soldiers of the Nazi movement, at least among the rank and file of the SA and the SS. Nobody paid them wages; no military oath bound them legally to their service, like the regular army soldier; no military law hung over their heads, no superior officers had disciplinary power over them. Yet they were the most disciplined, zealous, loyal, and courageous soldiers an army ever possessed. Now they all seemed to take it for granted that this time Hitler would 'make it.' And whenever I asked, and I asked many of them, "But what if he doesn't?" there was only one answer: "Then we'll smash the gates in for him!" Remembering all too well my anxiety in Rome in November of 1923, when I feared that history was being made without me, I now made arrangements to be with them in the hour of action.

Wherever I went in and around Berlin, one impression was re-enforced: there were only two contestants for power in the Reich. Except for its nominal hold on the army, the constitutional structure upholding Hindenburg and von Papen was as hollow as a papier mache throne. It would crash any day without being dignified by direct attack, but almost incidentally, as it were-if the two real forces of German activism should rush into open warfare around it. Namely, the radical Right, the Nazis, despite cunning, reactionary Nationalists, and the radical Left, the Communists, despite vacillating Sozis. German politics were like a dumb-bell; only the extremes had weight. The masses were weary of mere words and were choosing sides. If the showdown came, it seemed clear to me that the Nazis must triumph, because they were supported by a greater section of the people and were far better organized. The SA knew this, and were living for the day when they could prove their strength. Hitler had created a potent revolutionary force, but he had not swerved from his parallel effort to create a public sentiment which might make the use of force unnecessary. Here too, every straw in the wind indicated that he was on the verge of success. Not every one liked him; but fewer still liked the Communists. It seemed not impossible that the Hindenburg camarilla would show some common sense.

Thoroughly heartened by the results of my survey, I went on to Munich in a fine glow. I wanted to get, before talking with Hitler, moral and material support for my plans in America from the organization chiefs whose common effort to realize our ideals had made possible such splendid progress. What I found, however, was a common effort to cut each other's throats-each one professing the most altruistic motives as he sharpened his verbal knife.

An able American journalist went with me, expecting to get some useful interviews in Munich with my help. It was time to provide Americans, through an American writer, with intelligent and honest first-hand information about the Nazi movement, its structure, its aims and philosophy, its domestic and foreign policy, and its leaders.

We planned to present the whole matter in the form of concise questions, especially those which would be the most interesting from an American viewpoint, and concrete answers from the heads of the various Nazi departments. These last two questions Hitler himself was to answer: What would you like to say to twenty-five of America's leading citizens? What would be your message to all the 120,000,000 Americans, if you had the opportunity to address them? The scheme would provide an excellent framework for vivid sketches of Hitler and his chiefs. We were going to syndicate the material in newspaper and magazine articles, and perhaps use it as the foundation for a more comprehensive but equally readable work on Hitler and National Socialism.

I thought the idea would prove effective, and was moreover well aware that it would serve as a handy re-introduction of myself to the inner Nazi circle, and would put me in a favourable light before my old Nazi friends and the new leaders as a practical and useful man. I was sure that everyone of them would welcome the opportunity to be publicized in America.

First we called on Rosenberg, whom we found willing to give the matter his immediate attention and to answer all questions coming within his province. Armed with his signed recommendation that we be granted all possible assistance, my American friend and I proceeded to the former Hotel Reichsadler. This huge building, now rented by the Party, housed the political organization headed by Gregor Strasser, the propaganda department under Dr. Goebbels, the agricultural department under Walther Darre, the labour service under Colonel Hierl, the Hitler Youth under Baldur von Schirach, and many other departments. The Nazi organization had grown to bewildering dimensions and complexity. The apparatus was now a state within a state. Not counting the SA and SS, it was puffed up with a staff of functionaries and Party officials numbering well over a hundred thousand throughout the Reich.

The instant we stepped into the building I had the sensation of finding myself in a beehive. There was a constant coming and going of orderlies and visitors, civilians and uniformed Nazis, each apparently bursting with importance. There were guards outside the entrance and inside the hall, and two fierce-looking fellows at the information desk. Standing there taking it all in, we must have looked slightly amused at the incessant clicking of heels and booming of 'Heil Hitler,' and we were sternly asked what we wanted. Fortunately, at this moment an old Nazi came along who had known me well in bygone days and had now advanced to the position of housekeeper of this new Nazi palace. He took us under his wing and showed us around, up and down corridors where at every corner new guards clicked heels and shouted 'Heil Hitler' until it got on my nerves to have to shout back 'Heil Hitler' to all and sundry. From now on we progressed smoothly, simply going wherever we pleased, unmolested and received with utmost respect as the 'two Americans.'

But it was another story with our little besogne. The first day we were shunted from pillar to post because it happened that none of the 'big shots' was in town. Strasser had left for Berlin, Goebbels was on his way to Hitler, and Roehm was already with him on his 'Magic Mountain.' I had to talk to assistants and underlings, gaining thereby a good look into the inner workings of the Party machine, but no very favourable impression. On the second day I managed to get through to Gregor Strasser's staff manager, Dr. Alexander Glaser, likewise destined for murder in 1934, and I saw Dr. Robert Ley, who today is Strasser's successor and one of the chief potentates of Nazidom as leader of the powerful Nazi Labour Front and holder of many other offices.

From the first moment I got on famously with Dr. Ley; it was evident that he liked the 'Amerikaner' who declined to wait in antechambers, knocked at the door, walked right in, sat down, and stated his business. When even he did not dare give me what I asked, I realized how far red-tape and evasion of responsibility had gone.

"We are not allowed to give out any more interviews for information for foreign publication without permission of the Fuehrer," he said. "The best you can do for the moment is to leave the questionnaire with the various departments for reply in writing as soon as you have obtained authority for it from Hitler."

My good American grew impatient and on the third day returned disappointed to Berlin, with my promise to get the material together as soon as I could. Though my personal business was faring better, and I had made the contacts and obtained the information I required, I could accomplish nothing final for the present. I needed Hitler himself, and it was out of the question to approach him before the political situation cleared. But I wanted to see Strasser and Roehm before talking to Hitler. In the meantime I would try to get closer to Rosenberg and to get Amann on my side.

Munich, the Nazi capital offered a sad contrast to the splendid spirit I had observed everywhere else among the rank and file of Party members and in the SA and SS. While countless deeds of devotion, sacrifice, and courage on the part of Nazi men and women were echoing through the Reich, here I smelled the foul breath of politicians. Everywhere I encountered little political machines, with their own jealousies and intrigues. Glimpses of nepotism, back-scratching and even venality appalled me, as did the overdone military aspects of the SA and SS. The one oasis of welcome relief was, surprisingly enough, the headquarters of the SA, a large building next to the Brown House. Here, due no doubt to Roehm's personal influence, a more business-like atmosphere prevailed.

But in all this obsequiousness, this incessant heel-clicking and Heil-Hitlering, I saw that spirit which had been utterly distasteful in pre-war Germany coming back in a most virulent form. Something false and specious had crept into the upper

(Left) A SINISTER HITLER With his 'Grobian' whom he could never dominate - Gregor Strasser, killed in the Blood-Purge.
(Right) A SMILING HITLER Whose hand holds both flowers and a dog-whip, walking to his plane with his faithful henchmen, Wilhelm Brueckner (centre) and Julius Schaub.

stratum of the movement. For years the Party had advanced on nerve and bluff, using them as definite political weapons.

Now I found myself unable to distinguish between truth and bluff. And the terrific over-organization! For years we had fought against 'Bonzen'-and here was the Party, so 'over-bonzed' that an old member like myself couldn't get through all the offices.

I discussed all this at length with Rosenberg, who put the situation in a nutshell.

"Hitler has sown the dragon's teeth," he said.

Rosenberg was himself the object of continual attack.

"I think that half the time Hitler doesn't know what a circus he's running. Neither do you-so far. It's a three-ring affair with more clowns than lions. When you understand this, you'll know better why I'm not breaking my heart to get a ringmaster's job. On the contrary, the Party has become such a sad spectacle in some ways that I'd prefer to be out of it altogether. But when I sent in my resignation, stating my reasons in plain words, Hitler refused to let me go. As you see, I'm keeping on with my work-but only reluctantly."

"That's bad news," I said. "I'd supposed that you at least were sitting firmly in the saddle. Don't think for one moment that Hitler will forget your thrust. His dropping you from the Reichsleitung[1] is serious."

Rosenberg shrugged. "We'll see. Anyway, we're near the goal at last. Once we've the power, we can look further. And confidentially-don't worry about me. Only the other day Hitler told me something very reassuring-but I'd better tell you about that another time."

Coming from outside, from another world and with a cooler perspective, I could not share the general optimism, and said so. "You all seem to be so hot on one thing, on one idea, that you take too much for granted. It's almost a fortnight since the elections, and still no summons for Hitler. That looks fishy to me. What if he isn't called to the Chancellorship? Will he force the issue?"

"I really don't know myself," said Rosenberg, drawing endless diagrams on a pad, as he does when he is warming up to a subject. "But it's high time now that we stepped into power. If we don't, God alone knows what will happen. Opposition has lasted long enough-too long, in fact, to be good for the organization. Longer waiting will make things much worse. We can't feed the people ad infinitum on beautiful phrases and heroic election battles. The last one was our apogee. Another election will lead us downward, and that would be the beginning of the end."

"But why sit here and wait-why not get together and do things!" I said impatiently.

"There's nothing I can do," Rosenberg replied in his cool, impassive way, head bent over his diagrams. "You know how Hitler is. If he prefers to have Goebbels and

---

1 The Reichsleitung is the highest council of the Party; its members are called Reichsleiter. Rosenberg was not reinstated until April 1933.

Goering around him, all right. I won't run after him."

"Don't pretend such indifference," I said, beginning to get angry now. "I know your ambitions. But you won't get what you want by sulking in a corner. I know what I want, and I'm going to get it. I've already told you about my plans in America. We need Amann and Schwarz[2] to pay the bill. What about Amann? You know we didn't part friends in 1925."

"I can fix you with Amann," he said, almost smiling. "Our relations are excellent now; we buried the hatchet long ago. I grew to know him better-a rough diamond. In fact, he likes your spunk. I talked with him this morning. He thinks you are a real Nazi, and said so to Hitler. Don't worry about him, he's curious to see you."

This was all so reassuring that I should have known that I was going to step right into the shadow of my Nemesis. I was turning to leave when Rosenberg said:

"By the way, did you get my last letter, mailed to you some two or three weeks ago?" His tone was so carefully casual that I sensed something unpleasant ahead.

"No, I was on the water then. What was it about?"

"I apologized for letting a most unfortunate reference to your name slip into the Beobachter two months ago," he said.

"With the whole Party at sixes and sevens, fantastic mistakes occur, and sometimes show up in the routine news columns. This particular item was a report of the perjury trial of Abel.

A very delicate affair. You know, of course,"-this in a voice of veiled irony, accompanied by a suggestive smile-"that Hitler has declared in court that he never received foreign pay from any source and never even asked for it.

"Christian Weber was called as a witness against Abel and the rough fellow lost his temper and balked at cross-examination by a Jewish lawyer. When asked what he knew about Kurt Ludecke, he shouted: 'Ludecke? Why, he's just another swindler!' He didn't realize his mistake until later, when the defence for Abel called as witness Kurt Ludecke. You can imagine the tension in court. But the man who appeared next day was a dark little fellow with a moustache, a jailbird in prison garments, handcuffed and under guard. He had never even been a member of the Party, and his name was not Kurt, but an altogether different Ludecke, and he was serving a prison sentence in Luckau.

"I personally added to the record of this session a specific statement that all suspicion concerning Kurt Ludecke had been without any foundation whatsoever. But I'm sorry to say that no one thought to correct the record of the previous day in connection with you, which was the damaging thing, and it was printed in the Beobachter. I'll call for a copy if you want to see it."

"But," I said tensely, "when you became aware of the error, you published a correction in the paper?" Rosenberg now looked really embarrassed. "Well, I must .

2 Franz Xaver Schwarz, Reichs-treasurer of the Party.

confess, what with the many things on my desk, I've forgotten about it."

After my days of misgivings in Munich, this was all I needed to boil over. The general run of readers would be entirely justified in taking such an error at face value, since it was the sworn statement of a well-known Party member, printed in a Party paper about a brother Nazi. All my pent-up irritation came pouring out.

"I've had ten years of trouble with this damnable and confusing slander on my name. I insist that you bring out at least a full statement and apology from Weber, which I'll produce as soon as I get hold of him. This is going too far. I wouldn't be so furious if it weren't so significant for all of you. Yes, sir, you included. Believe me or not, I've never seen such brutal selfishness, such boorish manners as among the Nazi bosses. I noticed it as early as 1923. For example, I would never have been arrested, that whole mess for me and all the foreign pay rumpus for Hitler would never have happened, if Hitler weren't such a stupid egotist. It makes me laugh to see you Nazi knights crusading for truth, honour, integrity, urging and expecting sacrifice and self-denial from everybody but yourselves, shouting that you alone can reform, re-forge, re-make our Germany, when you can't even be honest among yourselves, and waste your time in petty jealousies and intrigues at a critical moment which more than ever demands united action! If a Goebbels and others can push themselves between you and Hitler, it's partly your own fault. I admire your brain and your knowledge, but if you want to stay in the game you've got to snap out of your aloofness. Sorry, if I've said more than I should, but I like a clean situation between friends."

Rosenberg seemed honestly contrite, and Weber gladly wrote a clear statement of apology saying that the careless confusion of names was doubly regrettable since 'the probity and good motives of Kurt Ludecke, the writer who is active in Party work, have long since been established.' It was published a few days later in the Beobachter. But there is no way to side-step the working of human perversity. A year later, when Weber's correct version had long been forgotten, the little one-line libel was to come out of limbo to damage my reputation again-this time four thousand miles away.

But I had no time to brood over my wrongs. Max Amann, the Hercules of the Nazi publishing business, and one of the foundation stones of the Party, was next on my list. He was Hitler's banker and close friend; to my knowledge, he and Roehm were the only Nazis to whom the Fuehrer ever said 'du'. Aman was in on Hitler's personal financial affairs as well as his secrets. A top sergeant in the army, he had carried the manner into his business life. People dreaded an encounter with a man whose voice could be heard out in the street in front of his offices.

During my absence from Germany, the Eher Verlag had mushroomed out to a huge concern, and was now one of the largest publishing houses in the Reich. Amann was its manager, Hitler the principal owner. It was the conspicuous success among Nazi publishing enterprises, which in the main were then still the weakest aspect of the organization. Out of some five thousand German newspapers; there were only sixty Nazi dailies and sixty Nazi weeklies, whereas there should have been six hundred. Except for a few brilliant writers, the journalistic staffs were mediocre, and the various editorial policies were confused and contradictory because of the lack of a uniform political alignment. The various publishing firms were privately owned, even though they might function for Nazi districts. Very few of them had prospered.

The Eher Verlag, the central publishing house of the Party and the business centre of its huge propaganda machine, was the shining exception. Most of the effective placards, hand-bills, and pamphlets which were poured over Germany in gigantic quantities came from the Eher Verlag, as did most of the Nazi literature. This was already impressive in bulk, and consisted chiefly of Hitler's Mein Kampf Feder's dogmatic economical essays, Goebbels' clever and scurrilous lampoons, Strasser's political-economical studies, and Rosenberg's political-philosophical treatises and polemical pamphlets. Of the various newspapers, trade journals, etc., published by the Eher Verlag, the Voelkischer Beobachter was by far the chief publication, and still Hitler's mouthpiece.

The whole secret of the Eher Verlag probably never will be known. Certain it is that Hitler's extraordinary rise from an obscure nobody to a national leader and Mikado over sixty million Germans could never have taken place without Amann's aid.

Another man must also be given his due of credit - Adolf Mueller, Adolf Hitler's printer. Though Mueller was a member of the Bavarian People's Party, he was first of all a business man, and he had done the printing for the Party since the acquisition of the Beobachter. Until the putsch in 1923, business had been good and the two Adolfs had become friends. This friendship was to prove valuable. In the critical time after Hitler's release from Landsberg, it was Adolf Mueller who advanced cash and printed the paper on credit until it was afloat again. Herr Mueller, who is stout and almost deaf, must have an excellent nose, for he became a millionaire.

When I entered the ante-room of Amann's private suite, who should greet me but Ludwig Schmied, my old factotum of years ago, now private Cerberus to the big boss. All dressed up in a well-fitting sport-jacket and knickerbockers, he was clean shaven and neatly combed, beaming from ear to ear. There was a big sandwich in his hand, but no cigarette-stump hanging from his mouth.

The good old soul! I embraced him cordially, really happy to see him.

"I knew you were coming-Herr Amann told me," he said in slight confusion, "and-and-yes, I've prepared this for you"-showing me a table piled with papers, magazines, and pamphlets. "I thought you'd like to see all our latest publications. And I always saw to it that you got your papers regularly." He concluded his

SOME PROMINENT NAZIS

(Clockwise from top left) Frau Magda Goebbels; Dr. Paul Joseph Goebbels; Dr. Ernst F. S. Hanfstaengl ('Putzi'); Alfred Rosenberg.

unusually long speech with a broad, proud grin.

I barely had time to invite him to bring the assembled publications to my hotel at seven that night, for a meal and a long talk, when a nice-looking girl came in to say: "Herr Direktor Amann laesst bitten." I followed her into a large and beautiful corner room, with four or five big windows.

Behind a heavy desk stood Amann, all smiles. I hadn't seen him for seven years. He was the same little man, strong and active looking, with a heavy head on a short neck almost lost between his shoulders. I was aware again of his prominent nose and small, peculiarly brilliant blue eyes, which constantly wandered about as if roving for game. I knew that he was an enthusiastic hunter, and that his hobby had cost him an arm. Climbing up a hunting-stand in the forest to shoot a roebuck he had slipped, his rifle had been discharged, and he had almost bled to death before he was found.

His welcome was hearty. "That was a nice letter you wrote me when I had this accident. I still have it-I appreciate it. And you were dead right about that fellow I sent years ago to Berlin. He was no good, and I kicked him out. He was a Communist spy and later died of syphilis. And that 'mistvieh' who warned Hitler against you is a swine, a mean hound, a blackguard-I'll throw him out if he ever dares to set foot in here again, that scoundrel."

Thus did we bury the hatchet-in the bodies of two wretches we disliked in common.

"But there are others-it's time for a good house-cleaning."

All the while, the spitting of his extraordinary vocabulary went on at terrific speed, in a voice which seemed to rebound from frightened walls.

Then came an interruption. The telephone rang, and from what I heard I gathered that Amann was being informed that a certain person, who also carried on a thriving business with Hitler's enemies, had printed for Ludendorff a pamphlet insulting to Hitler and the Party. Amann fumed and almost broke the instrument in his haste to get this man on the wire. But he-wisely-was not in. What followed is indescribable. Amann in a rage is a spectacle one never forgets. I cannot translate the load of invective he heaped on the poor chap.

"What can I do?" Amann finally said, calming down a little. "Hitler likes him, they drink tea together, they eat cakes together, and this man tells him all the dirt. But I won't pay him this time-no, I won't-I'll take the business away from him, I'll ruin him. I'll let the fish flounder until he goes down on his knees." And suddenly, perhaps at his own crazy metaphor, he grinned so madly that his nose fairly jumped and his eyes almost disappeared in his crinkling face. "You should see him when he begs for his money, when he adjures me by the love of heaven and moans that I am bringing him to an early grave-it's a sight."

For a moment there flashed into my mind the memory of that day ten years earlier when I had given Amann the last of my precious French francs to appease his printer.

"Yes, you have missed a lot," said Amann. "Things are happening here and we're having fun."

Our interview seldom rose above the level of personalities. But we discovered ourselves in agreement on many questions, political as well as personal, and to my satisfaction Amann heartily endorsed my plan for America.

"I'll use any influence I have to put your idea over "with Hitler," he promised. "As for money, you can draw two thousand marks [then nearly one hundred pounds] a month from the Verlag treasury. But I'm afraid you'll have trouble getting the rest from Schwarz, even if Hitler asks for it. The Party is very low in funds right now, and even in the best of times, it's a work of days just to get a cheque signed. Well

-I'll see what I can do with him."

Half the necessary sum gained in one interview! Things were coming my way, and thanking him, I moved on to drum up further support for myself. I understood by this time that having the right friends in the Party was far more important than having merely the right idea.

Back at my hotel, I found a note saying that Hitler had left for Berlin. At last it had come, an end to the unbearable suspense! In a day or two Hitler would be Chancellor-or rifles would speak. I booked a place in a sleeper at once, to be there in time for the historical moment.

When I arrived in Berlin on the morning of 14 August, however, it was all over, and Hitler's humiliating rebuff was a historical fact. And Hitler's only answer had been paper protests. A challenge in print-but the SA had been sent home! I was stunned.

Now I knew that I had lost my faith. Wherever I went, I found disappointed, discouraged, or disgusted Nazis. What had they been mobilized for? Surely to get into action if those swine in the Wilhelmstrasse were to dare to cheat Hitler; surely not just to quell disturbances in case of his appointment! Oh, no-for then the SA would have had their three-day carnival, their chance to wet their long knives in the blood of the Kommune! Now Hitler's captains made no secret of the fact that this had been their promise to their Brownshirts.

The SA and SS leaders of all degrees and the great brute force of the ranks had been ready for a coup de force; they lacked the subtlety to understand or honour a leader who would allow himself to be cheated. Only a very few were able to console themselves with the thought that Hitler's mind was not an open book, and that his decision against an armed move perhaps might, after all, be wisdom.

Wondering what Strasser would have to say about it, I went to my appointment with him at the Hotel Excelsior, the rendezvous of many leading Nazis. When I was admitted to the salon of his suite, I found him still busy with a late breakfast and a hearty appetite. Here was a new Strasser. He looked prosperous in his almost elegant suit.

"Hallo, Ludecke, Gruess Gott!" was his welcome in true Bavarian fashion. "You blow out on us every time the Party is between the devil and the deep sea … Anyway, it's good to see you-old rascal!"

"By Joe," I said, reverting in my relief to Count Luckner's favourite English expletive, "it's good to hear you say 'Gruess Gott!' That's real music to my ears. I was getting so tired of 'Heil Hitler'-"

His booming laugh interrupted me. "Incredible, what? I'm getting used to it now, though it makes me very mad every time I think of it. 'Heil Hitler'? Quatsch! If it were 'Heil Deutschland,' all right-that would please me. But 'Heil Hitler'-no-no-no!" Shaking his head vigorously he took another mouthful, inviting me with a friendly gesture to join him.

"How on earth could it become so popular?" I asked. " Who invented the stunt?"

"Popular!" He blinked at me. "Well, that's very simple. Don't you know, the crowd shouts 'Heil' to anyone of us when we appear in the area-' Heil Strasser' or whoever it happens to be. So our little Mephisto, our little Goebbels, made it a permanent thing and earned a new feather for his hat. That's the story of the 'Hitler Gruss,' mein Lieber, and a true story at that."

"But it's too absurd. How can Hitler…?"

"Ja, how can Hitler…?" He laughed again. "See for yourself, and you'll find yourself asking that question many times. But please let's forget politics for a while, I'm sick and tired of it. Ley has talked about you quite a lot, and how you joked together. He likes your ties and shirts, and thinks you're a very smart fellow. 'Der Amerikaner,' he said, spitting with laughter, as he usually does-I advise you to keep an umbrella with you when you go out with him- 'knocks at the door and just walks in on you.' Mein Gott, you didn't even knock at my door! Let's see, yes-you did. Now, tell me about America. I want to hear about your ranches and how you are getting along with the Indians …"

And so he went on in his rolling bass and his peculiar sense of humour-one of the few Germans I ever encountered with a taste for 'kidding' in the American style.

We had a long and friendly talk. When we finally reached politics, I noticed that even he maintained a certain reserve. But he did not mince words when I touched on Hitler's predicament.

"A serious impasse," I said, feeling my ground. "It doesn't look so good for Hitler."

"Yes," he growled, "now we're in a mess. First the big show of teeth, then back into the mountains with your tail between your legs. Downright monkey-business! And we're left here to shovel out the dung. 'Eine dolle Schweinerei!'"

Carefully sounding him out, I knew before long that he was Goebbels' mortal enemy and in earnest inner opposition to Hitler. At that time, of course, Hitler's cardinal mistake in not having reckoned in advance on a possible rebuff by Hindenburg was not so clear in my mind as I have expressed it in the preceding chapter, but when I voiced my concern for the future, Strasser remarked almost disdainfully: "Hitler's game is sheer bluff-call the bluff, and he'll crawl. Yes, he'll shout, but he'll climb down. I always was opposed to really believing it. Now I'm certain of it. But it's not too late to revise my course."

And with that rather mysterious hint he shifted to something else. We talked about Rosenberg, and he confirmed my impression that Rosenberg had lost ground with Hitler.

"But Rosenberg is no journalist," Strasser said. "The Beobachter is far from what it should be. And yet, Hitler still thinks the world of him. Not long ago he told me that only once in centuries is a man born with brains like Rosenberg's. I think you're right-the Party needs a foreign office. Hitler can't abide Reventlow, and maybe Rosenberg is the right man for it."

As head of the Party organization, Strasser was second in importance only to Hitler, and I needed his co-operation in several aims. One particularly troublesome matter came under his jurisdiction-the abortive little Nazi cells headed by obnoxious 'leaders' in certain American cities.

"Oh, Nieland's international," he laughed, when I mentioned them. "I don't think we need worry about him.

I only gave him the job because I needed someone to answer the letters from abroad, which were threatening to swamp my own desk. He was young and willing-and besides, you know, he comes from Hamburg."

"But he's never been out of the country," I objected. "And surely you don't mean that he qualifies for foreign work simply because he had seen foreign ships sail into the Elbe!"

As a matter of fact, that was exactly what Strasser had thought.

"I was pleased with the way Nieland took hold of the work," he continued. "Right away he hit on the idea of organizing Nazi cells in America. He hoped that out of the millions of German-Americans there, thousands would join and pay dues, which would carry the expense of his office and add handsomely to the Party treasury."

Having already seen Amann, I knew the answer to this.

"Amann told me in Munich the other day that Nieland has asked for a new fund to meet his expenses for a new publication, Der Auslanddeutscke Beobackter - but didn't get it. What he brings in wouldn't pay for one cablegram. Their combined labour has netted less than one hundred paying proselytes in all America. But I'm not complaining because the list 'is skimpy. I'm worried that it exists at all."

Strasser, so clear-sighted on internal questions, demanded that I explain my meaning. To ask for the dismissal of a hundred Nazi foreign missionaries seemed like sabotage to him.

"They're no credit to the Party," I told him. "They strut through the streets of German neighbourhoods puffed up and loud-mouthed, parading their Storm Troop uniforms. As propaganda, they're pretty bad. America doesn't like strong-arm agitators, especially aliens. And most German-Americans are proud of being peaceful citizens; they get on well with the Jews, ignore the Communists, and resent being identified with the rowdy Nazi-Americans."

More serious still, I pointed out, was the fact that these foreign cells, puny though they were, would inevitably drag the home office into conflict with foreign governments. In America they were making so much noise that sooner or later there would be an investigation. If Hitler were Chancellor then, Strasser must realize how compromising it would be for the Fuehrer to have to admit that he was supporting subversive groups abroad. And yet Nieland was sending them charters and membership-blanks and enough letters to prove the connection absolutely.

"Cut them loose now," I begged. "They're utterly irresponsible, and before they goad the American-Jews into retaliating by raising a hue and cry against them, the connection must be dissolved. Let them talk their way into jail if they want to, but take steps to prevent the Nazi Party from sharing the scandal-or more likely, the ridicule."

My own work in America would be wasted so long as every unemployed butcher and grocer's boy who took the fancy could occupy his idle hours by posing as Hitler's spokesman before amused or indignant Americans. If my plans were successful, and if Hitler sent me back to Washington as the official agent of the Party, I insisted on having a clear field, without being hampered by a lot of misplaced and stupid Brownshirts. But in any event, they ought to be dismissed for the good of the movement, and the sooner the better.

Strasser agreed to order their dissolution.

"We'll have to follow the routine, though. I'll ask Dr. Ley to do what's necessary; it won't take long. Nieland will be mad-but you're absolutely right, they must be dropped. I'm glad you hit it off with Ley. Hitler already knows that you're here. He likes you and thinks you are very capable; you'll find it easy to get him on your side. The money of course is another question. But we've time to see to that, if you get stuck. A miracle that Amann is willing to untie the purse-strings for you-that's something. We'll get together again after you've seen Hitler."

He looked thoughtful for a moment.

"Just think-if you had only stayed here instead of leaving us after Hitler came back from Landsberg .... You remember that I told you to stick it out with me. See where we are today. You, too, would have gone far. I even thought of calling you back, years ago. But you know how it is, and then we've been living at such a tempo that I can't even sh-in leisure. You'd have your foreign bureau by this time, and wouldn't have to worry. Well, no use-water under the bridge. It's too late."

He made several scathing remarks about Goebbels, ridiculed Goering, expressed his displeasure over Roehm's increasing notoriety, and even ventured a few keen criticisms of Hitler for surrounding himself with such aides. Painful evidence again that the Party was riddled with dissension. Scarcely any six of Hitler's followers could gather in friendship and confidence.

"And your brother Otto ... ?" I ventured to ask Gregor, as I was leaving him.

"I don't like to discuss that business. But you may as well know that we have broken completely, I'm sticking with Hitler."

XXII

A MEETING WITH GOEBBELS

Strolling through the streets to sniff the wind of Berlin, I found the picture changed overnight. There was the usual hustle and bustle; but gone were the bold faces of yesterday. Today Jews were again walking with their chins high, looking down with triumphant disdain on us poor Nazis. The city was apparently returning to its normal state of indifference, to its absorption in the trivialities of everyday life.

Only the news-stands told me that the country was still on the verge of insanity. Here were racks stuffed with a weird, mushroom growth of publications. The superstitious Germany of the great crisis was opening its arms to every art of sensation-monger and charlatan, to fortune-tellers, astrologers, graphologists, chirologists, numerologists, phrenologists, clairvoyants, spiritualists-all that occult lunatic-fringe who can hear the growing of the grass.

Suddenly my eye fell on Gregor Strasser's picture, and his name in huge, front-page headlines. I grabbed the paper, half suspecting that I, too, had been infected by some sort of psychosis. Here was a long article about Strasser as the man of the hour; he, and not Adolf Hitler, was the coming leader of Germany. And then my startled attention relaxed into amusement, for what I held in my hand was an astrologer's publication, and this was a reading of Gregor Strasser's 'stars'.

At my hotel, I found a message from Frau Goebbels, a postcard view of Hitler's retreat on the 'Magic Mountain' She had written:

MY DEAR LUDECKE,

I'm sorry that your kind letter reached me only yesterday, as I've been motoring for two weeks with my husband. For the last five days we have been up here with Hitler, and are returning to Berlin on Saturday. I hope you will still be there. I shall be very glad to see you. We have spoken of you often here. As soon as I reach home I shall try to get you by telephone.

Cordially, with Hitler Heil, your

MAGDA GOEBBELS.

And so, a warm afternoon in August saw me turning into the Reichstagplatz, here the Goebbels now lived in the same apartment which Magda had once presided over as Frau Quandt.

In spite of the Fuehrer's outspokenly Nietzschean opinion on the proper place and function of women, the men of the Party were cultivating the ancient and universal custom of spending considerable time with the ladies. A delightful coterie of gentle

Nazis was already much in evidence during the hours when Hitler's captains relaxed at public restaurants and theatres. In private, I had heard, these same ladies wielded an influence which was not the less potent for being invisible. When power fell into our hands, they would automatically become the First Ladies of the Land, since Hitler himself was unlikely to bestow that pre-eminence on anyone woman. It was inevitable that political intrigues would then be launched by the flutter of an eyelash, and carried to successful conclusion by a ripple of feminine laughter or a sigh. The German has no substitute phrase for the Frenchman's 'Cherchez la femme,' though he has fully as much occasion to use it. Even now, I was told, the National Socialist hierarchy had its priestesses as well as its priests.

My first inclination after my arrival in Berlin had been to avoid a meeting with Magda Goebbels, but this thought had been dispelled by Arno Schickedanz, who had met her with me in 1930, and by Rosenberg. "But you must!" they insisted, and argued that it would be interesting and useful to renew acquaintance with a woman now so near the source of things.

Her cordial reply to my letter made me wonder at my own diffidence. Marriage scarcely could have diminished the warmth and charm with which nature had endowed her. After all, she had been married when we first met-and to a man much older than Goebbels. Yet she had been a gay and understanding friend in those days, and no doubt I should find her so again.

Goebbels I had never met, and I was already definitely prejudiced against him, partly because I heard him condemned from many sides, but chiefly because I knew him to be an enemy of Rosenberg and Strasser. For the time being, however, his unparalleled talent for communicating his own fever to the public made him useful, despite his frequently grotesque exaggerations. He could safely be permitted to help us to victory, but he must not be allowed to be too prominent after our final triumph.

A renewal of my friendship with Magda Goebbels would precipitate a personal meeting with her husband. It would do no harm to be on good terms with him and have a better knowledge of his character and methods. He was a bad influence within the Party-but still an influence. He was district leader of Berlin, publisher of the Angriff, next to the Beobachter the most important Nazi daily, and as chief of the Party propaganda machine a good word from him could only help my plans.

It might even be possible, by means of an amicable relationship with him or by enlisting the interest of his wife, to bring about a truce in the Goebbels-Rosenberg feud. Not for their sakes-I knew that each loathed the other beyond hope of change-but for the sake of the Party. Now that we were on the verge of success, Party feuds were a dangerous business. Personal scores could be settled after a united effort had put the movement over.

I was quite shameless in my hope that Frau Goebbels, unfamiliar with my alignment in the Party, would enlighten me concerning her husband's private attitude toward Rosenberg, Strasser-and Hitler.

I arrived at the Reichstagplatz apartment certain that Frau Goebbels' husband would not be present at my first meeting with Magda in two years. She received me alone. My last trace of uneasiness vanished when she greeted me graciously, calling me Kurt and using the familiar 'duo' At first we spoke of trivial memories. Then the talk veered to the burning question of current politics, and her husband's name came up naturally.

"So you're on your way to a great position in Germany," I chaffed her. "Surely you'll be 'Frau Minister'-with myself and the others courting your favour! But tell me, Magda, how did it come about?"

Lightly and amusingly she told me that her interest in Party work, for which I had been responsible, had continued until at last she began to work in the Berlin office. There she caught the eye of the leader-Joseph Goebbels. She became his personal secretary, he her ardent suitor. (And why shouldn't he, I thought, as her story unfolded. She was beautiful, cultured, intelligent.)

"My congratulations come late," I said, "but please accept them now. At the time I didn't feel like cabling compliments. You can imagine my astonishment when I picked up the Illustrierter Beobachter in New York and saw your picture on the front page between Hitler and Goebbels, and the story of your wedding. And now I find you already a great lady in the Party, with greater things to come. So I fly here to sue for your blessing. One word from you will soon be enough to make me an ambassador!"

"Hitler spends so much time here; frequently he and the Doctor discuss their work together for hours, while I sit and listen. Or Hanfstaengl plays the piano, if he isn't rolling on the carpet or amusing us with some other buffoonery. We like to have Hitler think of this apartment as his second home."

I had been told that one of the most appreciated services Frau Goebbels rendered Hitler was the preparation of special meals, difficult to get elsewhere. Hitler was by now a confirmed vegetarian, finicky to exasperation over carrots and spinach, and Goebbels, by baiting his hospitality with a tasty vegetable-plate, so to speak, had managed to get and hold the Fuehrer's ear as no one else had before. I chanced to ask why Magda didn't find a pretty friend for the lonely Adolf.

"My husband asked exactly the same question some time ago," she replied. "He was most anxious to get Hitler interested in some nice girl-it would have done him good to be able to relax and pour out his troubles to a sympathetic woman. Alas, I was no good as a match-maker. I'd leave him alone with my most charming friends, but he wouldn't respond. Putzi tried too, but didn't do any better than I. In some ways Hitler simply isn't human-he can't be reached or touched. My husband was terribly disappointed when we couldn't get him to choose a confidante."

I agreed that as far as I knew Hitler was a born solitary. "It's discouraging for the ladies, though," I added. "With Hitler out of reach, there are scarcely any high Party men left unmarried, are there?"

She laughed.

"There's always Captain Roehm."

It was no longer a secret from anyone that the captain's apple-cheeked recruits interested him inordinately. When he brought suit for libel against the slanderers who had invaded his private correspondence, Roehm increased rather than dispelled his notoriety by abandoning the case at the last moment, evidently not daring to let the courts pass upon his homosexuality. In private he was always frank enough about the subject. Nor were his friends likely to be too shocked, since a notable growth in homosexuality was one manifestation of the appalling licentiousness which gripped Germany under the Republic. In Berlin, the centre of every sort of social disintegration, male prostitutes could apply for police health-cards along with the female street-walkers, and the breakdown of public standards which this cynical system summarized existed unconcealed in every stratum of society.

But however tolerant the general public might be toward ordinary citizens of doubtful sexual inclinations, Roehm was an exception. His success as head of the much-hated SA made him the target of a savage attack through the loophole of his personal habits. His notoriety was pitilessly exploited by the enemy. The better he did his work for Hitler, the more he suffered from sneers, ridicule, and condemnation which he was powerless to answer because they were at least based on fact. Hitler had always defended him vigorously. But there was no ending the stories or evading the truth that Roehm's vulnerability was bad advertising for the Party.

"We've given up hope of finding a wife for Hitler. Maybe it's true that he can't get over Geli's death.[1] It's too bad, because he needs an intimate woman friend, if only to tell him the things that no one else can mention. His clothes, his manners-and for that matter, his associates. You know Heinrich Hoffmann, his staff photographer, who can be so funny with his jokes in his spicy Bavarian dialect that Hitler shakes with laughter? Well, Hoffmann is always with him nowadays, wherever he goes."

Magda Goebbels was now well launched on the stream of Party gossip, and I was not unwilling to let the current take her. It was increasingly evident to me that her husband's inventive mind, rather than her own, was the source of what she said; so deliberately I dropped names into the conversation, to see what ripples they raised. Rosenberg and Strasser drew not ripples but a flood-tide of sarcasm and contempt. As I had expected, she was unaware of my close association with them, and spoke unreservedly. These were of course Goebbels' opinions, and by the time she had completed her inventory of Rosenberg and Strasser-their ideals, motives, activities,

---

1 'Geli' was Hitler's pet name for his niece, Greta Raubal, daughter of his half-sister Angela Raubal, who kept house for him. Greta lived with them. Her attractive cheerful nature had won her uncle's affection to the point of devotion. She was ambitious for a stage career as a singer, and this one wish he sternly opposed. Late in 1930 se shot herself in her bedroom in Hitler's home in Munich.

persons, families, and prospects-I was in dismay. So these were the ideas with which the crafty little witch-Doctor was priming Hitler!

Worst of all, I was convinced by Frau Goebbels' self-assured attitude that her husband, more than anyone else in the Party, really had the ear of Hitler. Those pleasant evenings over the vegetable-plates in the Reichstagplatz apartment promised no good for Goebbels' enemies-or for the Party. By now I realized all too well that from Goebbels' point of view I had placed myself on the wrong side of the fence, simply by allying myself with his opponents, and I knew that his opposition could be a serious obstacle to any plans of my own. Thus far, I was exempt from the poison which he was dripping into Hitler's mind, and if possible I wanted to maintain this fortunate status. Whether Goebbels was to be a mortal enemy or an aid depended on me. Therefore I accepted at once when Frau Goebbels suggested a meeting with her husband.

"With your talents, your zeal, you ought to be at the top," she urged. "But you must be more of a diplomat on your own behalf. You must look out for yourself. Everybody does it, I see it every day-why not you? Hitler has spoken of you so often, with such friendship and appreciation, that I'm sure you have every chance in the world. And the Doctor is eager to know you-he likes your work abroad. Right now he is down at Heiligendamm, resting from the campaign, but he telephones every day. It's a good place to have a real talk with him. I'll arrange a time for you, if you like."

And so it was arranged. I left her with compliments-genuine in view of her enduring charm-that made her eyes shine with pleasure, and I carried away with me her kindest assurances of friendship. It had been, in a way, a successful afternoon. But I was aware of a subtle malaise within me. It was the realization that I, too, was now a politician. One's sense of the realities rejects certain compromises, demands others; in twelve years of active political work, I had evidently learned to square the minor demands with my conscience. Magda Goebbels, my good friend, had proved useful.

Arno Schickedanz was much pleased at the news that I was to meet Goebbels. Being now one of the Nazis privileged to have a car of his own, he suggested driving me down to Heiligendamm, which is on the Baltic, and waiting for me at Arendsee, a nearby beach.

A few days later I presented myself at Goebbels' hotel in Heiligendamm, having reserved a room there for an overnight visit. But before I describe our meeting, let me tell what I had been able to learn about the man who clumped across the terrace of the 'Kurhotel ' to greet me.

Paul Joseph Goebbels was then nearing thirty-five, and was the youngest of the Nazi overlords. He had been born in the Rhineland in 1897, son of a factory-superintendent and grandson of a blacksmith.

His dwarfish stature and clubfoot early barred him from physical pursuits. It is easy to fall into the error of ascribing the entire development of his personality to revolt against this handicap, and yet certain of his traits are obviously conditioned by his misfortune. Probably the cynical quality of his intelligence and the bitterness of his disposition are largely the product of sensitiveness about his bodily affliction, which his enemies, myself included, never forbore to mention with an almost malicious satisfaction. Mental agility became his substitute for physical power. The cult of the heroic became an obsession with him: he worshipped the idea of large men performing bold deeds, and in fact his chief value to the Nazis lay in the amazing success with which he managed to present them in this light to the public. A helpless minuscule himself, he was so carried away by the beauty of brutality that his ecstasy overflowed in speech and print, turning the most ordinary Brownshirt street brawl into an epic of heroism.

A Catholic by birth but furiously anti-clerical by inclination, Goebbels had been able to enter his first university on a scholarship awarded by a Catholic society. Courses in six other universities followed, usually on German literature and allied subjects. At Heidelberg he had taken a degree of Doctor of Philology, and was commonly referred to by his Berlin crowd as 'Der Doktor.' He had become master of a peculiar style of high-flown, flowery prose, as allusive and figurative as a revivalist's exhortations. If Hitler's speeches in their content can be described-and Goebbels would so describe them-as bread for the masses, then Goebbels' own are cake, but cake that is all icing. Apparently very little of his schooling really entrenched itself in his mind. His serious literary efforts are unimpressive. He has a bright veneer of superficial information on almost any subject, a peculiar gift of brilliant presentation, but real knowledge of nothing-unless it be of the cynical principles of ballyhoo and spellbinding, at which he is a veritable genius.

Goebbels is an unanchored personality, impulsive and unstable in his loyalties, gullible in his beliefs, but quick to respond to a new enthusiasm and well fitted to be the glib interpreter of ideals which he himself cannot share. His mind is keen, and a certain dynamic quality about the man would make of him a most useful instrument if his scope could be severely limited. No resource of irony, satire, invective, casuistry, and clarity of exposition is beyond him; it is the content and not the form of what he says that betrays his weakness.

As a formal speaker he is subtler and better than Hitler, but this is chiefly because he is so adept at polishing second-hand thoughts. Hitler is often carried away by sheer force of temperament, whereas Goebbels' every effect, however excessive, has been carefully thought out beforehand. Hitler seems real, Goebbels artificial. The critical and detached auditor can always detect the undertone.

It is difficult to point to a true parallel to Goebbels in the American scene. One American reporter called him 'just another Jimmy Walker with a German dialect

'-doubtless thinking of their use of wisecracks, gibes, and platitudes, of their sometimes subtle, often rough-and-tumble agility. But in other respects the analogy falters, for the one-time mayor of New York is far more sympathique than the major showman of the Nazi circus. It is only when I survey the field of journalistic writing-and in that sphere Goebbels' efforts outrank those of any other political journalist of Nazidom-that I am able to fasten on my own candidate.

Gentlemen, I give you Westbrook Pegler.

That inimitable battler for 'liberty, freedom, and justice' will reject with disgust my comparison of him to a man he abhors. He far surpasses the Doctor in style, in humour, and in the bite of his sarcasm. Yet both have certain peculiar talents in common, and both are irritable to the extreme; both criticize everything, hitting hard at what they dislike-and that can be almost anything. Each dips his pen in vitriol, to spread it with gusto and cynical satisfaction, and each, probably against his better judgment, is often flippant and superficial for the sake of getting in a passing dig. And each takes a devilish delight in indicting a whole people when it suits his prejudices. To Goebbels every Jew is a Bolshevik and an object of physical loathing, while Pegler is so kind as to brand every German a coward and cringer, or a hypocrite and liar.

My own direct impressions of Goebbels had been gained from hearing him speak. On the platform he is pure wizard. There the only ample thing about him comes into play-his penetrating voice, a great, sometimes sonorous, sometimes clarion tone that emphasizes his physical meagreness by contrast. When he opens his lips to orate, it is as if Niagara came pouring from an eye-dropper. His most characteristic gesture, no doubt carefully studied, is to lift his right arm rigidly erect with forefinger and middle finger straining heavenward-a fatiguing pose, but one which serves to add to his height.

With eyebrows lifted in heroic wrath, he would stir the masses to a frenzy, assailing the rottenness of the regime with hard-hitting phrases. Or with eyeballs rolled to the skies, in a strain of utterly reckless demagogy he would promise a rapt crowd heaven and earth through Nazi 'socialism.' He could tear his opponents to bits with biting parody and satire, hurling abuse and extravagant taunts at parties and men while his audiences seemed crazed with excitement and laughter. When he chose to insult, he was without restraint. The reader of these pages bows me for no admirer of Hindenburg, but I fully shared the widespread resentment of the brazen public indignities which Goebbels heaped on the old Field-Marshal.

Sometimes he would take a humble pose, exalting the Fuehrer or the men of the SA with praise which would have been disgustingly fulsome in print, but which, from his lips, charged the air with awe and emotion.

All these effects were sure-if you were not one who could detect the undertones. I had been at pains to inquire into Goebbels' Party background.

Actually, Goebbels seems to have first heard of the Party in 1922. He did not join the folkic movement until 1924, and then he became a Ludendorff adherent. Later he switched to the Hitler Party. Gregor Strasser discovered his talents. Together they published Nazi literature, playing up especially the socialistic aspect of the Party programme. The Strasser-Goebbels combination formed a strong unit of opposition to many of Hitler's policies. In 1926, as has been related in an earlier chapter, Hitler decided-not without justification-that they were potential if not actual rebels. Thereupon he broke the combination by winning over Goebbels with the district leadership of Berlin. Later Goebbels, sensing which way the wind blew, publicly repudiated and condemned Strasser and his friends.

His brilliant work as propagandist unquestionably merited recognition and advancement. And yet there was for me something almost of black magic in his success in twining himself upon Hitler. Probably Hitler has no idea even now of the degree to which Goebbels has gained influence over him.

The man who came limping across the terrace in Heiligendamm shook my hand affably and welcomed me with gracious phrases. There was in the first moment an impression of a bird of prey-an angular, cadaverous face which seemed to slope from all sides toward the tip of his fleshy nose; large, feverish, dark eyes, curiously lidded; a loose mouth heavily creased at the corners; ears like wings, projecting at an angle; a putty-coloured skin, and hair of a dingy black, brushed back. His continual half-smile revealed his proudest feature-good teeth. His voice was pleasant, and consciously modulated to give an effect of quiet self-assurance. And suddenly I saw in him one of Sem's famous caricatures of a well-known 'Maquereau du Monde'-a herring-bone dangling down from a huge head with Jewish features. It was a discomfiting flash. For a moment I felt awkward, and was glad of the diversion when Harald, Magda's beautiful boy, with hair like ripe corn, came running and threw his arms round me.

Goebbels was in civilian clothes, but nearby several black-uniformed SS men were loafing. They were his bodyguard. The 'Kurhotel' is an exclusive hostelry, a favourite resort of high-born and wealthy Germans. While the three of us were having dinner in the pleasantest corner of the terrace but in full view of the other guests, I caught more than one baron and countess discreetly craning their necks for a glimpse of the Doctor-they wanted to see the Nazi who brought along a sample of a private army when he came there for a rest.

Apparently neither Goebbels nor the particular Black Guards whom he had chosen were making a good impression. He would seem ill at ease, and again he would not-or was it that I was not at ease because I saw that he was pretending to be at ease? At any rate, by an occasional brusque gesture or by the way he admonished Harald for his table manners, he would betray himself as a parvenu. His beefy bodyguard, who at least had no social pretensions, seemed by their mere presence to annoy the usual patrons. And indeed it would have been difficult to assemble a more unattractive squad.

That evening and the next morning, when we loafed about in bathing-suits--all except the Doctor, of course-he was the centre of curiosity. We chatted with Prince Otto von Bismarck, counsellor at the German Embassy in London, and with his beautiful Swedish wife. Prince Louis Ferdinand, son of the Crown Prince, approached Goebbels with courteous deference.

It was easy to see that he loved his role. I knew him now for a snob who liked great names and was ready to kowtow to them in salons, but equally ready to thunder in public against the stupid arrogance of the monocled nobility, or to ridicule the fat bellies of the moneyed elite. This was the man I had heard call the labourer his comrade, the man who had bellowed from the platform: "Arise, young aristocrats of a new working class! Clench your fists! Square your jaws! You are the aristocracy of the Third Reich and the seed you have sown with your blood will bring a glorious harvest!" And I was secretly amused at the tasteless spectacle of this loudspeaker for the poor working man parading himself before the high-born and the rich.

I had my talk with Goebbels. Through him I hoped to discover Hitler's inner conviction concerning the consequences of Hindenburg's rebuke, and whether constructive steps had been planned to prevent the situation from crippling the Party. I knew that he was privy to Hitler's attitude, and indeed had probably helped to mould it. His own opinions, if he could be made to reveal them, would answer me.

I was reserved, but flatteringly polite when I spoke of the efficiency of his work and the punch of his style. My negative reply to one of his first questions-Had I already talked with Hitler? - visibly determined his attitude. Not knowing exactly my potential value nor how important a rating to give me, he was non-committal and evasive, and took on the patronizing air of a routine statesman.

My mention of Hindenburg drew sarcasm, and he affected to dismiss the old man's resistance as senile obstinacy, annoying but harmless. Propaganda had become second nature with him, even in confidential talks with a Party member like myself Soon, however, a few concrete question about the disaffection of the SA and the voters showed him that I was not ignorant of the facts, and he consented to discuss realities with more frankness. I decided that we could now get down to brass tacks.

"In Munich," I said, "the Nazis have built up a tremendous complex machine for political action, and have geared it with auxiliary machines throughout the Reich. Our Party is virtually a state within the State. On a moment's notice we are prepared to switch the machine into legal motion. It looks to me as if, simply by changing our letterheads, we could operate as the actual Government of Germany. You know how narrowly we failed a week ago. Yet suppose we had not failed. In that event, the Party would already have been in power for seven crucial days-and not one agency exists which would have been able to explain this power in foreign countries!"

I pressed on. "But do the Nazis think: that Germany exists in a vacuum? Or do they hope to be represented sympathetically and intelligently by the present ambassadors of the Government we expect to oust?"

"Alfred Rosenberg is the Party's Minister for Foreign Affairs, not I," Goebbels replied. "At least he thinks he is. He should be familiar with these problems."

" Of course, he should," I said, "but the man seems over-burdened with work and has a thousand other things on hand. Besides he has as yet no apparatus to operate with, as far as I can see."

"Have you been in touch with Dr. Nieland?" Goebbels asked. "I mean the director of the Auslandsabteilung in Hamburg. His office and his organization could be used, no doubt."

"Nieland! Why, he's nothing but a motherly hen whose entire duty is to cluck after Nazi chicks who've strayed into foreign parts! He has never been abroad; and in any event, as you must know, he has not been empowered to formulate or exercise anything approaching a foreign policy. Yet such a policy, with an effective organization for carrying it out, is the most pressing problem before us, and will become of critical importance the moment Hitler attains power."

Specifically I pointed out that the Nazi programme called for social and military changes sure to arouse formidable opposition outside the Reich, even in countries usually indifferent to our internal politics. Powerful forces would be aligned against us. Jews in America and England would not look calmly on the suppression of the co-religionists in Germany. France would react ominously to the first sign that we intended to carry out the complete rearmament to which we were pledged. Financial interests in the United States would temper their friendship or enmity largely according to the prevailing public opinion. For a hundred reasons just as cogent, the foreign aspect of our problem could not be ignored or postponed any longer without unfortunate results. And with a courteous gesture towards Goebbels, I added that I had hoped to find in him-the expert and authority on propaganda-special interest and support for what I proposed to do.

I asked what steps he might have considered taking along these lines. "Rosenberg has ideas-" I began, wishing to sound him out, but he, interrupted me.

"I believe you'll find Rosenberg to be purely a theoretician, not a practical man. He has a good mind, but he fails to understand the true nature of politics. As for handling propaganda work abroad-why, he's not even a journalist! I direct the domestic propaganda, the foreign not as yet. You see, things have changed a little since you were home here; for instance, Rosenberg hasn't quite the influence he used to have."

Goebbels has a way of packing his words with greater venom than they reveal in print. His voice conveyed the contempt he felt.

"You'd better talk this over with Hitler. His quick grasp of things will see the advantage of your proposition. Tell him that you have discussed this matter with me and that I share your view of the foreign problem. Something must be done. But Hitler is the only one to decide the what, the when, and the who.

"Besides," he went on, "Gregor Strasser is really the man who should settle the Nieland affair and pave the way for you in that direction. As Reichsorganisationsleiter he has charge of that department. No doubt we could work together with good results-but my hands are tied when it comes to the foreign affairs of the Party, for the time being at least. The best we can hope for the moment is that Strasser will understand enough of what you say to give you his support. From his past performance I should not rate your chances too highly."

Money also complicated the problem, according to Goebbels. The election campaigns had seriously depleted the treasury, and no one dared calculate what effect the Hindenburg incident would have on future contributions.

As he talked, my quandary grew. The most exasperating thing of all was the obvious fact that really no one, not even the highest members of the inner council, had power to act independently on any large problem, especially when money was involved. They never had enough for their own wants. All authority came from him and returned to him. On paper the organization looked as logical as an algebraic formula, but in practice the leadership principle paralysed constructive work no less than it did destructive plots. The Reichsleitung, or upper circle, which derived its authority directly from Hitler, was outwardly a sort of smooth-running secret cabinet, united in vision and loyalty. Jealously it guarded this reputation.

But inwardly it was reft by every possible division. Hitler was a genius at keeping his right hand from knowing what his left was doing. Antagonisms, suspicion, jealousies, and their emulation of Hitler's policy of secretiveness, held his Reichsleiters at loggerheads. In the confusion, not one of them was quite sure where his duties began or ended.

Either Goebbels or Rosenberg or Strasser might be the proper man to approach with my plans for a foreign bureau. Since I must make my choice, wisdom told me to expect more practical help from the Doctor-but not even from him unless Hitler could be lined up for the idea.

Another circumstance also had a vital bearing on the plans I was trying to make. How soon could the Party recover from its recent setback? Nothing could hold Hitler down, I knew; as long as he lived, he would renew his battle, along one line or another. And if he should die, somebody else would take his place. We were bound to win in the end, for the cycle was with us and ours the move.

But how long would the rebound take? I asked Goebbels outright, and his reply compacted all the cynicism of the man.

"If Hitler insists on following the parliamentary path instead of compromise or using guns to blow down the Reichstag walls, it will take months, many months perhaps. No one can say when there will be a new election, for one thing. But this is certain: if it proves necessary to wait so long, we will have our voters at the polls when the day comes. In a week I shall have made them forget that Hider allowed himself to be snubbed; in a month, they will be crying louder than ever for him to save them from the Jews, the Communists, the Capitalists, the French, and the dandruff. Bugle-calls, battle-cries, and catchy shibboleths! Nothing is easier than to lead the people on a leash. I just hold up a dazzling campaign poster and they jump through it like a trained dog through a hoop. As the Fuehrer says: 'It is impossible to underestimate the intellectual capacity of he masses. Tune your propaganda to the level of the average voter, and you will succeed.' That is a truth our opponents either don't understand or disdain to follow. And that is why we shall win in the end."

XXIII

A TANGLE OF ANIMOSITIES

There is a world of difference between the give and take of living talk and the stale, dead ashes of conversations raked over and subjected to a frigid post-mortem after many months. The whole atmosphere and emphasis are changed. Transitions from one subject to another are blurred. Critics may reasonably object that to resuscitate in cold print parts only of conversations, as I admittedly am doing, inevitably will distort the whole focus.

My answer is that these were, for me, no mere casual conversations. I had returned to Germany after a long absence to find myself afloat in a sea of change. Each talk was like a voyage of discovery. I was steering my way cautiously, gauging the wind and trying to chart the new currents running beneath the surface. I was constantly trying to digest and assemble everything I heard.

The reader may be willing to concede my claim to a memory of those days derived from sensitized perception, but he will have to take my word for it that I am trying to draw on it as truthfully as I can.

Sometimes, in the course of my explorations, I arrived at destinations mildly astonishing.

Take the famous Braunes Haus in Munich, the Party's official headquarters. When I first joined the Nazis, they enjoyed literally none of the world's luxuries, and consequently made much of the Spartan ideals of simplicity and frugality. Discomfort was more bearable if it could be called a virtue. Nazis' ethics demanded that the lowest follower and the highest leader alike be willing to go hungry, shed their blood, or give up sofa-cushions with equal readiness. Many of US thought that hardness was a fundamental tenet of Hitler's Weltanschauung.

But when an errand carried me to the Braune Haus for the first time, only the Swastika flag floating over the roof convinced me that this was not a cardinal's palace or a Jewish banker's luxurious residence. It faces the residence of the Papal Nuncio on Brienner Strasse, the most aristocratic avenue in Munich. Three stories high, set back from the street between narrow, fenced gardens, and elegantly reconstructed according to Hitler's own plans, it offers tardy proof that the Fuehrer might have been a good architect if he had not become what he is.

Through a haughty doorway, where two Brownshirts eternally stand guard, I passed into a large foyer where swastikas were scattered like confetti on the ceiling, on the windows, the hardware. A grand staircase led me to the second floor, on which are the offices for Hitler and his staff, and the Senatorensaal, or senate

313

chamber. At the door of the latter are two memorial tablets for the fallen heroes of the movement. The chamber itself is all in red with rich red leather arm-chairs at the front for the leaders, flanked on both sides by rows of similar chairs for the senators. A modern Dogensaal - very beautiful indeed, but practically useless. Why trouble to go through the form of convening a legislative body when Hitler, in his study next door, considered himself equal to every decision?

Everything had that air of richness which comes only from expensive materials simply used. Hitler's remodelling job had cost forty thousand pounds, not counting the interior decoration, also designed by him.

There were more offices on other floors, and long one-storied buildings under construction in the garden at the rear, for the Brown House, was already inadequate for the needs of a rapidly growing organization. One of the distinctive features, however, is the casino, a cosy, wood-panelled, typically German beer-cellar restaurant, below stairs at the front. It is for visiting Nazis, with one smaller room reserved for officials. Here Arthur Kannenberg and his pleasant wife were then preparing meals to suit every taste, from Hitler's meagre herbs to Goering's gargantuan feasts.

There was always an atmosphere of jollity in the Brown mess-room, with witty Kannenberg circling from table to table, making you laugh merely by a look from his eyes ill a pumpkin-like face.

Like Caeser, Hitler likes fat men around him, and Kannenberg is one of his special protégés. His is one of the many priceless Nazi stories. Son of the proprietor of a one-time famous wine restaurant in Berlin closed up by the inflation, he started a little 'Lokal' in Berlin West, where Dietrich Eckart used to take Hitler in bygone days. The mere fact that Hitler eventually chose so comic a character to run the Brown mess shows that he has a sense of humour. In fact, Kannenberg's typical Berlin mother wit made him indispensable to the Fuehrer. He spent week-ends on the 'Magic Mountain' to entertain the Mogul and cook for his guests; when Hitler moved into the Wilhehnstrasse as Chancellor, he imported Kannenberg into his palace. In 1933 the jester was running the menage, and he and his wife were living across the hall from Hitler's bedroom.

The whole air of the Brown House proclaimed the fact that Nazis were now living the larger life. I became even more aware of expanding Nazi tastes on the various occasions when I dined with Dr. Ley. In the old days I had been conspicuous among my National Socialist comrades because I dressed well and dined well. "You're too much of a swell-you wouldn't go over with the masses," Hitler had once told me bluntly. Now, by an ironic reversal, I felt some alarm at having to hold up my end among the Party spendthrifts when Ley took his lavish meals. High-powered official cars would whisk us to the finest restaurants, and champagne now moistened conversations that once would have been floated on beer. Obviously, the

Nazi Weltanschauung was paying dividends at last--cash dividends, welcome to a man of Ley's stamp.

Dr. Ley had rented a very attractive villa in exclusive Ludwigshoehe, near Munich. Ley is short, paunchy, and roundheaded, with a somewhat Jewish cast of features.

He was then Strasser's man. Today, so far as the functioning of the Party is concerned, he is Strasser's successor-and therein lies an example of the strategy by which the Fuehrer keeps supreme control of the Nazi organization. The contrasting characters of the two men are significant of the trend of Hitler's Germany. Within Nazidom, Gregor Strasser was, next to Hitler, the most powerful man and the most effective speaker. He was the undisputed leader of the Nazi deputies, and his speeches and writings rank among the best intellectual achievements of National Socialism. But he was also the political force of highest potentiality in all Germany, the dynamic spokesman of the socialist wing of the Party, strong-willed, independent, creative, with a mind of his own-ambitious, but unwilling to sell his soul for the sake of advancement.

Ley, to be sure, was capable, inventive, agile. But his was a subaltern nature; he preferred to act on orders rather than on his own initiative.

In early September I saw Hitler for the second time, again only briefly. This time it was by appointment in his carpeted study at the Braune Haus, a magnificent corner-room, in which a fine portrait of Frederick the Great hung over a massive desk and a painting of a battle in Flanders adorned the opposite wall. I went in with some apprehension, wondering how I would find him at close range, this leader of the Nazi Party who so many people assured me had forfeited his chance of ever becoming Chancellor of the German Reich. But as he stood there, smiling with outstretched hands in front of a bronze head of Benito Mussolini, he did not look as though he felt himself a beaten man.

"You see, I haven't forgotten you," he said. And for a few minutes we talked about casual things.

"I must run now. I know about what you want - Amaan has told me. And Strasser and Rosenberg have endorsed your proposition. You haven't wasted your time, have you! I like that. We must have a long talk, but not today. I couldn't make a decision anyway, right now-there are still too many things in suspension. I'll know more in a week or so. It can be done, I think-well, we'll see.... You'd better get hold of me in Berlin next week-we'll get together then."

"Can I count on that?" I asked.

"Positively."

My praise of the Braune Haus brought shine to his eyes. "Yes, Ludecke, we have gone a long way since you were here last." And with a sweeping gesture: "This is only the beginning-I plan buildings which will last a thousand years."

As he showed me to his private lift, the dramatic expression of his face changed to one of his boyish looks that can be so winning. "Don't miss the casino downstairs. Kannenberg has 'Weisswuerste' today-you still like them, I imagine!"

Or was it 'Leberknoedel'? No matter-I am fond of both.

Whatever it was, as I was eating it Christian Weber barged in, grown now into a veritable mountain of flesh, but always ready for more food and drink. We sat behind steins of beer 'kidding' each other-Christian is another of the few Germans who could match any American at the art-the while Brother Kannenberg went on making faces at us like the man in the moon.

I felt that I was beginning to get a fairly accurate picture of the lay of the land, and to envisage the plan by which I might build a foundation for the bold project for Nazi world propaganda that was taking shape in my mind.

Strasser, Rosenberg, Goering, and Goebbels would all play important roles in coming events, and I would have to cross the path of each of them. They presented a complex problem.

Both Strasser and Rosenberg were implacable enemies of Goebbels and were in opposition to Goering-bonds which still held them together despite their natural drift apart since 1925. Strasser's curve of power was rising, Rosenberg's declining. The Balt now had almost no direct influence on the domestic policy of the Party, which was decided among Hitler, Goebbels, Strasser, Frick, Darre, Goering, and of course Roehm and the district-leaders. A practical working foreign policy did not exist, and Rosenberg's importance now rested mainly on his editorship of the Beobachter and on his prestige as writer and the outstanding thinker of the Party.

To aggravate the confusion, Strasser and Goering were strongly opposed to Roehm, who in turn was not on the best of terms with Rosenberg, disdainfully calling him a 'noisy moral hero.' Goering and Goebbels co-operated with or intrigued against each other according to their personal interests of the moment.

It was clear that I was going to have to pick my way carefully through this tangle of animosities.

And yet it seemed equally clear to me that in most of these Nazi chieftains the revolutionary spirit still lived, despite a perceptible sag under the weight of years. No man with forty-five years on his back has the spirit of sacrifice he had at twenty-five-and he who claims to have it lies. But that peculiarly German, idealistic impulsion to save the world, expressed in 'Am Deutschen Wesen soli die Welt genesen' - so severely commented on by non-Germans-was still alive in these Nazis. Goebbels and Goering, incapable of the true crusader spirit, were the exceptions; before they could possibly think of creating a new world they would have to make something entirely new out of themselves.

More serious was the divergency of the personal ideals of these men. Here was Rosenberg, by far the deepest thinker of the Party, interested in the spiritual aspect of the German struggle as part of a coming world struggle; Strasser, fervently intent

Hitler as Parsifal. In another image which is often misunderstood Hitler is depicted as a banner carrying Parsifal with the dove of peace descending from the heavens.

on social justice, was an uncompromising socialist - Roehm, the soldier, a socialist and a man of remarkable general intelligence, was centring his heart and soul on the problem of Germany's military rehabilitation. And so on down the line, to Dr. Wilhelm Frick, the professional bureaucrat, patiently biding his time until he could give wider scope to his liking for administrative activity.

They were a secretive lot, each of them jealously guarding his standing with the Fuehrer. And Hitler, more secretive than any of them, never definitely took sides with one or another of his quarrelling groups.

What was the mainspring of Hitler's revolutionary nature-now? I knew that he was spurred on by an almost fanatical love of politics and by a dynamic "Drang" toward personal fame. He was a man in step with the march of time-but was his vision beginning to be blurred by success, by the secure conviction that he was riding an irresistible wave of human emotion? I meant to find out-from himself.

Meanwhile, I had no choice but to throw in my lot with Strasser and Rosenberg, try to keep clear of the Party snarl of intrigues and conflicting ambitions, and get along as amicably as possible with the other Nazi leaders. I wanted particularly to keep on friendly terms with Roehm, whom. I still believed to be the most intelligent, energetic, perhaps even the most honest and independent, of the figures then close to the Fuehrer. Back in 1925 he had seemed to me to have a clearer, more practical grasp of things than Hitler himself. It would be wise to try again to patch things up with Hanfstaengl; I needed at least the benevolent neutrality of the man who was foreign Press-chief and Hitler's court jester. We met in his office in the Brown House. Rudolf Hess, whom I encountered now for the first time, was present during parts of our conversation but did not share in it. I gave up all hope of ever establishing a basis of co-operation between us.

Heart-to-heart talks with Rosenberg raised my already high opinion of his mentality and his integrity of principle. Oddly enough, because of this integrity and because of his quiet bearing in contrast to the shouting Nazi leaders, he commanded more respect from some of our best political opponents than from many of his own Party colleagues. Striving always to keep in the foreground those ideals and convictions which had originally been ours, he was, in effect, a Nazi fundamentalist. So was I. We both knew that this was not the most profitable stand to take in a party whose dogma was becoming an accordion in Hitler's hands. The glib conformists who could change their principles with their neckties would get ahead much faster, and more safely.

On the other hand, I could see why Hitler simply could not depend on men like Rosenberg for his front-line fighters. The detached thinker lacks the springs of action. That was plain to me when I asked Rosenberg how he had developed the Nazi foreign bureau, which Hitler had agreed to on principle.

He had done nothing but establish archives, with a zealous young man, Thilo von Trotha, in charge. He hadn't even office space-probably only the three of us remembered that the foreign bureau existed-on paper.

"I simply haven't the money to get things going," said Rosenberg.

"That's scandalous. If Hitler can find the money for a senate chamber nobody uses, he ought to be able to scratch money together for a foreign bureau."

"Well, I've talked to him about it and I've sent him a memorandum."

That made me laugh. "You ought to know by now that writing letters won't get you anywhere in this party," I said. Here he was, author of pamphlets and books read by hundreds of thousands; his Mythus[1] had sold over sixty thousand copies, phenomenal for a book of that kind. He was the editor of Hitler's mouthpiece, the Voelkischer Beobackter. For twelve years he had been moulding Hitler's mind-and yet he would lose out for a lack of a personal following in the Party to push him forward, as if on the point of a wedge.

Rosenberg clearly wasn't relishing my analysis of his practical weaknesses, but I continued to press him.

"Intellectual prestige and moral strength would suffice if this were a sensible,

_____

1 Der Mythus des 20. Jarhhunderts by 1337 had sold well over half a million copies.

moral world. But it isn't. Every day you can see how much tangible strength counts. What will you do when Goebbels gets you into a really tight place? Your newsboys won't be any use against his henchmen. In two days I'm going to see Hitler. I hope for a showdown on certain questions, if I can manage it, and I'd appreciate it if you'd tell me honestly where you stand and what you expect from him."

"I'm no pusher," he said, " and I don't expect any serious clash with the ones who are. My work is to exercise the souls of our followers, not their muscles. And I don't itch with ambition. I think I can count on Strasser. Hitler told me that Goebbels might get the ministry of education, which would eliminate him as my immediate rival. As for personal advancement, I know definitely what to expect. Hitler has promised to make me his Foreign Minister when he is Chancellor."

"Hitler has definitely promised you the Ministry of Foreign Affairs?" I asked in some amazement.

"He has - and I'm already working on a visit to London."

Not sure whether this was good news or bad, I tried all the more earnestly to impress on him the importance of being prepared. And then I put the direct question. "Then you really believe that Hitler is going to make it? I want an honest answer."

Rosenberg hesitated. Finally he said: "Yes, I do. Hitler is a very lucky man. Time and again I've seen him in a terrible mess, but he always gets out of it, and at the last minute does the right thing."

"I know that Hitler's views on foreign policy were largely based on your concepts. But does he still subscribe to those concepts, which you have continued to set forth so precisely in your writings?"

"Evidently he does," replied Rosenberg, pallid satisfaction on his face, "if I am to be his Foreign Minister."

"All the more reason then for having a foreign bureau of the Party-a practical, functioning organization that you can draw on the moment you step into a Hitler government. Any time now you may be called upon to act as a buffer between a Nazi Germany and the world, and yet you're totally unready."

Again and again in our talks I returned to the subject, always to go away unsatisfied. One of the prize packages of Nazi power lay in the palm of Rosenberg's hand; yet he would not close his fingers on it. My own success might depend on his success, and his fatal detachment baffled and irritated me.

Rosenberg told me one day that he had heard from Hess that my talk with Hanfstaengl had been a failure. "It's unfortunate," he added, "for Hess is constantly around Hitler, and his influence with him is growing."

This was the first intimation to reach me that Hess was a coming power-I had in fact been so busy with Putzi that I had scarcely noticed the other man.

My talks with the men around Hitler in my attempt to understand the significance of the changes coming over the Party were bringing me to one definite conclusion. There could be no doubt that Hitler was on the threshold of success. No mere snub by Hindenburg could block his rise for long. Either by force of arms or by compromise-perhaps by the exercise of some pressure which only his secretive genius now foresaw-he would step upward to the supreme control of the government of the German Reich.

This conviction was growing in the face of discouraging developments. The futile bargaining and bickering were continuing. A conference between Hitler and Bruening, looking toward a Nazi-Centrist coalition, led to nothing. Repeated interviews between Papen-Schleicher and Hitler showed plainly that these gentlemen hadn't the slightest intention of giving him a chance at the helm. Their game was to wear Hitler down, to force him to abandon his claim to the Chancellorship because of the fear that new elections would give him a setback and start the disintegration of the Nazi Party. But Hitler stood firm-Chancellor or nothing. The result was an impasse. Hitler was not allowed to govern, and Papen, with Nazis, Sozis, Centrists, and Communists against him, could not govern.

On August 22 a new tempest had arisen. Under Hindenburg's emergency decree against terrorism, a special tribunal tried five Storm Troopers charged with killing an innocent working man in a small hamlet of Upper Silesia, under bestially brutal circumstances. The Nazi Press claimed that they had executed a Polish insurgent, a Communist.

The men were sentenced to death, and the fury of the SA was so intense that Hitler was forced to act. He telegraphed to the condemned men as 'comrades,' solemnly promising that their freedom would be made a point of National Socialist honour. Even friends of the Nazis criticized him for thus identifying himself with 'murderers.' In a violent manifesto to the Party, he denounced the 'bloody objectivity' of van Papen, and threatened a national uprising to deal with this system. The SA took heart; the revolutionary activists in the Party hoped that their great moment was at hand.

But an alarmed government commuted the death-sentence to life-imprisonment, and the crisis passed.

Three days earlier, the new Reichstag had convened under grotesque circumstances. It was customary for the oldest member to act as provisional president until the permanent president was elected. The honour devolved on seventy-five year-old Clara Zetkin, a Communist deputy, who left her sickbed in Moscow for the occasion. She was carried into the Reichstag on a stretcher and propped up in the president's chair.

What followed was heroic from one viewpoint, but a ghastly tragi-comedy in the eyes of the majority. For a never-ending half-hour an uneasy house listened in silence to a haggard old woman stammering out a shaky appeal for world revolution and the dictatorship of the proletariat. The moment she was carried out, commotion broke loose in hall and galleries.

Balloting for the permanent president ensued. Paul Loebe, the bespectacled, sly little Sozi who had clung to the Reichstag presidency for twelve years, had to make way for a brown-shirted, blurting Nazi colossus-Captain Hermann Wilhelm Goering.

The Reichstag was adjourned; its dissolution was a forgone conclusion. In vain Goering tried to thwart it; the old man at Neudeck would not even receive him. Papen probably already had the signed order for it, for he was now boldly threatening new elections unless the Reichstag gave him a free hand for at least six months. The Government had succeeded in strengthening its position somewhat. Relying on the authority of the Field-Marshal and on his Chancellorship and Premiership of Prussia, and supported by the Nationalists and the Steel Helmets, Papen continued his wearing-down tactics and his political 'Erbschleicherei,' adopting Nazi slogans, doing everything possible to steal the Nazi thunder, and claiming to have saved the Reich from ruin.

Deep depression again settled over the Party, a state of nerves that would yield to crazy elation at the wildest rumour. For the first time in two months, Hitler addressed the public, in the Sportspalast, the Madison Square Garden of Berlin. He was in great form that night. For two hours he tore the monocled cabinet, the barons, and the reaction to pieces, and for two hours a storming crowd interrupted him with indescribable outbursts of applause.

A few days later I was present at another Nazi rally in the old Zirkus Krone in Munich, when Hitler went further still and inveighed against Hindenburg with scorn and hatred.

"I can wait," he shouted. "I'm only forty-three, not eighty-five, like this venerable Field-Marshal, his Excellency Herr Reichs President Paul von Beneckendorff and von Hindenburg. Yes, I can wait. These old Excellencies can't frighten us. Let them dissolve the Reichstag ten times, a hundred times! We will not give in; we will fight. We must win. I believe in my destiny…"

Words … words ! When was he going to follow them with action?

I made up my mind that I was going to ask him.

Before I saw Hitler, Count Reventlow, to whom I confided some of my doubts and apprehensions, opened my eyes to the importance of the 'Kampfgemeinschaft Revolutionaerer Nationalsozialisten,' in other words, the so-called 'Black Front'- the seceding organization formed under the leadership of Dr. Otto Strasser, Major Buchrucker, and Herbert Blank, in combination with Captain Stennes and his insurgent SA men active in the 'Stennes Putsch.' I had known of this movement, but had not realized its full significance.

Otto Strasser had published a report[2] of his debate with Hitler which had led to his break with the Fuehrer and to his manifesto, TM Socialists Leave the NSDAP.[3] I found it startling reading now, for here were all my own misgivings. Two other dissenting pamphlets also impressed me - Ernst Nickisch's Hitler: A German Destiny, written by a patriot of knowledge and responsibility, and Adolf Hitler, Wilhelm III, by Weigand von Miltenberg, pseudonym for Herbert Blank-brilliant, exaggerated, distorted, but full of meat.

All this served to make me the more wary. I wasn't ready to agree with Otto Strasser on many points, and I hoped to convince myself that he was wrong. I must get inside Hitler and make him talk. I would have to keep my wits about me, stand my ground, and fight things out with him if necessary. I would have to keep my head and heart cool-most of all, be on my guard against my old attachment, that dimming glow which he could sometimes so easily restore to incandescence by a mere inflection or a moment of simple friendliness.

Only perfect naturalness and spontaneity would bring the response I wanted. I had the advantage of being involved in no Party intrigue; though a member of long standing, I stood for no particular group. In past years I had enjoyed a very personal relationship with him, and I knew there was a certain congeniality in our temperaments. In a sense, my position was unique.

But I must be ready to meet this man's almost feminine intuition, his fine sensitivity, his acute shrewdness. His alert and speculative mind, which could work with almost lightning swiftness on any subject, had grown so suspicious that he would avoid discussing issues methodically unless he saw selfish advantage in doing so. He would shy away into aloofness if one touched on the personal or knocked on the hidden chamber of his secret thoughts. His naturally impulsive and generous nature was now controlled by automatic locks.

This man's indomitable spirit would never acknowledge defeat. His ego was inflated by an incredible success. But he never got drunk, never indulged in familiarities in moments of weakness; he could get intoxicated only with himself when his imagination was afire. His conviction that his triumph would be the triumph of Germany made all things right.

While I was thus analysing Hitler, I took a good look at myself. I had always thought of myself as a genuine revolutionary, intent on the folkic aims of Nazi philosophy. But so far, compared to the miseries and sacrifices of many others, I had got off easily. I had known anxieties, difficulties, despair - but I had never suffered deeply for very long. I had been in tight places, but they had been largely of my own making. I had always managed to find enough to eat, even in hard times, and usually to sleep in a good bed. I had always liked having money to spend, and had

---

2 *Ministersessel oder Revolution, July 1930, Kampf-Verlag, Berlin.*
3 *Published in the Nationale Sozialist, Nr. 110, 4 July 1930.*

spent enough of it, but I had never been a snob. I had often been frivolous, but there had been nothing to cause me shame for all my life. I had done plenty of vacillating between the material and the spiritual; I certainly was no selfless idealist-and yet there was something in me that was forever trueing me up again, bringing me back to a cause that I believed would lift this machine-driven, money-ridden age to a higher level of social justice.

Yes, I decided, I was still enough of a revolutionary to pass judgment on Hitler. And I went over the problems of my talk with him again and again, setting the important points down on paper to make them come clear in my mind. Hitler liked, silently even admired, thoroughness-in others.

XXIV

ALONE WITH HITLER

"See me in Berlin," Hitler had said. The time eventually appointed was half-past ten on the morning of 12 September 1932, and the place was the famous Kaiserhof Hotel, near the chancellery, and only a few steps from the 'Palais' of the President of the Reich. Here, for decades past, ambassadors, foreign ministers and kings had stayed; here Bismarck made friends with Disraeli. And here Hitler had established his headquarters in Berlin. For that reason, I had found it convenient to take a room in the hotel.

To sample the atmosphere surrounding Hitler on a busy morning in Berlin, I arrived almost half an hour early. Outside the suite, two of the Fuehrer's bodyguard stationed in the corridor grinned recognition at me. In the anteroom I was received by Schaub and Brueckner, who were acting as secretaries. Hitler's days were so crowded with callers that his time had to be strictly budgeted.

There was much coming and going. Brueckner cursed into an insistent telephone. I was chatting with Schaub and Heinrich Hoffmann, Hitler's photographer, when Gregor Strasser and Dr. Frick came in for a final word with Hitler before going on to the Reichstag.

"Hello, Ludecke!" Strasser boomed, on his way into Hitler's private rooms. "Put your project across-good luck! I haven't a minute now-this is going to be a great day. Call me tomorrow at the Excelsior."

Talking over his shoulder as he went in, Strasser almost collided with someone coming out. The man was tall, slender, and well-dressed, and I recognized him with amazement. This was the Count von Alvensleben, and he seemed equally astonished at sight of me.

"What a coincidence to find you here!" he said. "Indeed?" I said with a laugh. "But how on earth did you get here?" "Well, you know-things happen," he drawled, adjusting his monocle. "How have you been?" "Oh, excellent. You look splendid. ... And how is Canada?" I couldn't help adding, maliciously.

He looked slightly embarrassed. "Why can't I ever get rid of that silly story? I know you people here don't trust me; Strasser certainly doesn't. I'm a friend of you Nazis-I'm doing things for you. Time will tell. You're a man of the world-you understand, don't you?"

"To be sure," I said reassuringly, almost absently ... I was musing on the strange turns our lives take, when Strasser came out and told me Hitler was ready to see me.

"Wasn't that Alvensleben who left you a minute ago?" I asked Hitler when our greetings were over.

"What! Do you know that fellow too?"

"Slightly. But for the most part I know about him-as who doesn't, on both sides of the Atlantic! He used to be one of the best-known promoters in Canada. You still find old-timers standing at bars and bragging of the lavish parties he used to give in his marble palace at Vancouver. His brother, by the way, is president of the Herrenklub."

"Yes, I've noticed how we're branching out lately." And then I sailed boldly in. "The Party appears to have overlooked nothing-except one vastly important matter. And that's what I want to discuss with you to-day."

I began to talk steadily and carefully. There was much I must say to establish the ground-work for our talk. I must say everything I wanted to say without irritating or antagonizing him. Above all, I must keep myself perfectly in hand, somehow contriving to control the discussion. I knew from experience how unmanageable a conversation with Hitler could be when he was afire-it would move and jump too rapidly. His mind works very fast, reacts immediately, and in general is extraordinarily responsive. His imagination is keen, and he anticipates so quickly that he will snatch at your meaning before you have been able to get out more than a word or two. This I must avoid, if possible, for things needed to be talked through between us.

First of all, Hitler must be made to understand that I was thoroughly informed on the Nazi situation in all its aspects. I succeeded in talking uninterruptedly for a while. What I said I mean to set down here in substance. It was in effect a prospectus of Nazi possibilities, a guide-post for a Party at the crossroads. My interpretation of the signs drew from the Fuehrer an unequivocal declaration of the direction he meant to take. Today, five years later, the informed reader will be able to note where his footprints have left the trail.

"Of course you know," I said, as we settled into chairs at a table, "that my immediate and personal concern is foreign policy, once you're Chancellor-the foreign policy that will best help us to our ultimate goal of a powerful German Reich on a national and social foundation, as we Nazis conceive it. But foreign and domestic policy are so inter-related, so interdependent, so tied up with the complex situation facing an eventual Nazi regime, that we can't discuss one without the other. And so I'm going to go into the entire problem confronting you. And I'm going to talk frankly, if you don't mind."

Hitler nodded approval. "Go ahead, by all means," he said. He was looking rested that day, and in excellent humour. "The things that make the problem so complex for you are four-the shackles of the Versailles treaty; Germany's military impotence coupled with her geographically vulnerable position; Germany's extreme poverty; and the challenge inherent in the Nazi philosophy, in reality a challenge

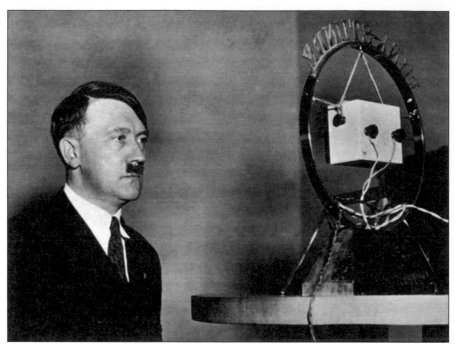

Hitler speaking on the election trail in 1932. This picture was taken at the time when Nazi electoral fortunes were approaching their highest ebb. At this point the infighting with the SA and the events of the blood purge still lay in the future.

to the political, economic, social, cultural, and spiritual systems of the white World-in fact, to its whole structure. For your new German State, you "will have to establish the Nazi regime firmly within the Reich, and give it absolute internal and external sovereignty. You will have to get rid of the Versailles treaty, rearm Germany completely, end poverty by solving the problem of expansion, and at the same time carry out the Nazi programme, step by step. And you can do these things only if you are not stopped by a preventive war."

Here Hitler gave me a keen look, and I realized that he had seen the shadow of this 'preventive war.'

The 'eastward drive,' I said, was a definite necessity for Germany. We could solve the problem of expansion only if our domestic policy permitted our foreign policy to bring about a constellation of world powers that would allow us to achieve this old German 'Drang nach Osten.' If we were to do that, internal and external policy must be basically right, founded on realities, both at home and abroad, and not on hopes. Otherwise, our whole struggle and all our sacrifices would have been in vain.

So far so good. The Fuehrer was listening intently, with no sign of wandering attention, and I went on.

"There are only three possibilities worth considering. You have a choice of three combinations. You can ally yourself with England against Soviet Russia. Or with

Japan, and eventually Italy, against Soviet Russia and her probable allies. Or you can come to an agreement, and ultimately a close alliance, with Soviet Russia."

This last brought me an enigmatic look, and I pounced quickly on Possibility Number One, which could easily be dispatched. Would it be possible, even probable, that England could be induced to join a Nazi dictatorship in a crusade against Soviet Russia? Why should England help to Germanize eastern Europe as far as the Urals? For biological-racial reasons, perhaps? To re-establish the lost Nordic supremacy against an advancing Asiatic-Bolshevistic peril? To save India and the British Empire by helping to crush Russia?

No, all that was sheer romancing. In the first place, the Englishman didn't trust his poor German cousin. Why should he ally himself with an anti-Jewish, anti-Christian juggernaut to bring all of Central Europe and parts of Soviet Russia under Nazi control, make Germany the most formidable power in Europe, and build up thereby a threat to himself? Absurd to expect such a step from democratic England, from jealous, perfidious Albion. So long as Italy, France, Germany, and Russia continued to hold each other at bay in one world sphere, and Russia, Japan, China and America did the same in another, England had a better course to follow-sit tight and hang on to her Empire. Why forsake that policy to lend a hand in bringing about a terrific upheaval with unforeseeable consequences?

No use to cherish the hope that England would voluntarily surrender any part of her colonies to meet the legitimate German need for expansion. Herr Hitler well knew that in economic life, the Haves' never yielded any of their privileges to the Have-nots except under compulsion. No more would nations. And in dealing with England, the Nazi philosophy would offer a special obstacle.

"We must remember that Englishmen and, for that matter, Americans as well, are reared in the tradition of liberalism and of personal ethics; they will not yield to Fascism, let alone Nazism, to regimentation, to social morality, until forced to do so by inner and outer pressure. And that time is still a long way off."

As I said that, I realized more clearly than ever this man's tremendous handicap in his complete ignorance of the English language; all ideas from the vast English-speaking world could reach him only at second-hand.

Hitler was pacing the room by now, still listening without once interrupting me. I was encouraged by that, and even more when he responded to a telephone call with instructions not to disturb him except for something of special importance.

Thus heartened, I set out to demolish Possibility Number Two, fully expecting here to draw his fire. An alliance with Japan, I said, would undoubtedly put the Bolsheviks in a pincers, and the combination might be extended to include Finland, Italy, Austria, Hungary, and Bulgaria. It might possibly take in even Yugoslavia and Roumania, but never Czechoslovakia and Poland, for Rosenberg had publicly condemned those two states to liquidation. The alignment would, however, eventually menace vital British interests in the Far East and in Europe, and sooner or later would force England and France to side with Russia. China certainly would not relish a German-Japanese alliance, and, encouraged by England and probably America, might definitely throw in her lot with the Soviets, thus diverting a large part of Japan's military strength from an offensive against Russia.

But such a policy held a more subtle danger, already foreshadowed in Russia's visible trend under Stalin's dictatorship toward nationalism, at the expense of Communism and the Comintern.[1] The German-Japanese threat would accelerate this tendency, for Russia would need to make herself acceptable for an alliance with democratic Western powers.

"What if Stalin should openly abandon the theory of world revolution, and dissolve the Comintern? Wouldn't that cut the ground from under your feet? In any case, a Nazi crusade with the help of certain European powers against a ' Godless and Communist' Soviet Russia will obviously be impossible if your regime undertakes to pursue an anti-Jewish, anti-Christian, anti-capitalist policy-the philosophy expressed by you and by Rosenberg. The Catholic, Protestant, Jewish, and capitalist forces of the world will then raise the cry against you rather than against Stalin, and Nazism will supplant Communism as the world-bogey. Even if things never quite reach that pass, there will be a line-up of Nazism and Fascism against a line-up of Democracy and a modified Communism, and the United States will be sure to swing definitely away from Germany, for obvious reasons."

But could Herr Hitler pursue the plan of a German-Japanese-Italian alliance, the purpose of which would be obvious from the outset, and re-arm Germany before he was stopped by a preventive war? Expert opinion said that it would take years-at least four and probably six-to build up a German military establishment capable of defeating Russia and holding France at bay. It was true that for the time being England, France, and the United States were not ready for hostilities, and public opinion in those countries was definitely against war. Within several years, however, that condition might change completely.

Even if no preventive war halted him in his tracks, even if the German-Italian-Japanese combination were allowed ample time to get ready, the outcome would be most doubtful, the slaughter terrific, the price of victory too high. And I personally did not believe that victory was likely. So much for Possibility Number Two. Hitler, still pacing the room, had heard me through, to my surprise. Now I must venture out on thinner ice.

"Before I come to the third possibility - an understanding and eventual alliance with Soviet Russia - I want to touch briefly on another most important matter. Everything I have said assumes that once you are Chancellor, you will be at liberty to choose what you want to do. That depends largely on how you become Chancellor.

---

1 *Communist Internationale, aiming at Red world revolution.*

If it is on the basis of a compromise with the Papen-Schleicher-Herrenklub clique, you will be restricted in questions of domestic and foreign policy.

You'll be bound by some sort of agreement-however temporary on your part-that will be interpreted as a coming to terms not only with reaction at home but with capitalism abroad.

Obviously these gentlemen won't hand over the Chancellorship to you without conditions-if you fail to take it yourself by that revolutionary act which alone will give you freedom of choice. The very future of National Socialism may depend on how you come to power."

There was by now more than a suggestion of irritability on his face, and I said quickly: "I'm analysing only because I'm pointing toward an inevitable conclusion."

Hitler sat down abruptly, still looking nettled. I must not let him crash through me yet, and I decided it was high time to feed his ego a little. To create a diversion, I got up in my turn and paced as I talked.

"You, of course, hold all the strings in your hands, and you alone will know what is best to be done. But remember that I come from outside, and in a way I know both sides of the fence. My findings can't fail to strengthen a few points in your calculations."

He let me sketch briefly my analysis of his situation. Papen and Schleicher were certainly not enjoying the existing deadlock, but apparently thought Hitler in a worse plight. They were doubtless hoping to wear him down with another election which would cost him millions of votes and bring him to terms. He would have no further chance to vote himself into power, and he had no time to lose. Continuance of the policy of negative opposition would lead eventually to a complete debacle for the Party.

But the deadlock could be ended in one of two ways. Since a 'Presidial' cabinet with himself as Chancellor was out of the question-a coalition with the Centrists being not even conceivable-he must choose between the alternatives of compromise and force. Compromise with the Reaktion would mean either permanent or temporary renunciation of the socialist part of the Nazi programme. Complete abandonment of the social revolution would lead to an explosion and certainly to the end of Hitler. Even postponement until the reactionaries could be outmanoeuvred and thrown out of office would create, no matter how expertly handled, a complex situation full of hidden dangers. Hitler himself might survive it, but the men around him, the Party itself, would crack under the strain after so many years of fighting. The masses, even his truest followers among them, would not understand a compromise at this stage; they would take it for surrender, for betrayal, and most of the Nazi leaders and sub-leaders would take Hitler's own compromise as an excuse for compromising with themselves and taking it easy. That would be the end of the Nazi Party.

"I don't need to tell you that the Party is weighed down by the deepest depression.

Adolf Hitler as Lohengrin in Der Bannertrager (The Standard-Bearer), by Austrian artist Hubert Lanzinger. This famous painting is another heavily stylised hagiography of Hitler from 1935. This image is usually described as Hitler as a generic knight. In reality the Fürher is rendered as Lohengrin the Wagnerian hero. This painting with it's pure white background clearly identifies Hitler with Lohengrin "the Knight of the Swan", the eponymous hero of the Wagner music drama "Lohengrin".

Incidentally Lohengrin was the first Wagner piece which Hitler heard performed. He attended a performance in Linz at the age of 12. In the pages of Mein Kampf he describes the experience at Chapter 1, "I was captivated at once. My youthful enthusiasm for the master of Bayreuth knew no bounds. Again and again I was drawn to his works, and it seems to me especially fortunate that a modest provincial performance left me open to an intensified experience later on." The Fürher liked the painting a great deal; it was first exhibited at the Great German Art Exhibition at Munich in 1937, and afterwards was sanctioned for official reproduction and distribution as a postcard image photographed by Heinrich Hoffmann known to posterity as Hitler's "court photographer". After the war, the painting was captured by the US Army, and is now preserved in the US Army Art Collection, German War Art Collection.

There are crucial days ahead of us. I'm your pupil, I've learned a lot from you. I'm recalling now what you told me, years ago, about the danger of compromise on fundamental issues however temporary. 'The National Socialist Programme is unalterable. Tactics and methods may and will vary, but never the goal!' Those were your words, Herr Hitler. What choice do they leave you but to use force?"

At this point Hitler, who had been listening with eyes fixed on me, scratching his knees or rubbing his hands as he does when excited, got up and began to pace again. I stopped talking, stood stock-still, and waited. Presently he came to a stand in front of me.

"Don't worry," he said, with an expression of malicious satisfaction. "Today, this very afternoon, Herr von Papen will be the one in disgrace. He won't dare remain in office, even if a hundred senile Field-Marshals back him up. He must resign after the crushing vote of non-confidence he's going to get today. And then what can they do-I ask you? They'll have to come to me; there's nothing else left them. Perhaps there will be some compromise-why not? What of it? Mussolini started with a compromise, but not for long. I can do the same thing; perhaps I'll go him one better. I've fooled these gentlemen so far, I'll show them that I can fool them further."

With that he took his seat again across the table.

"I refuse to see black," he went on. "Of course, there are things that trouble me. Possible foreign complications give me headaches. Can I also fool these gentlemen abroad for any length of time? That's the question. What will England say, France, the United States, once I'm Chancellor with Hugenberg in my cabinet? Oh, I'll set that worthy's chair outside the door fast enough-but will I be able to rearm Germany before they get on to me and strike at me with a preventive war? That depends largely, I suppose, on whether they have the leadership and guts to strike-if they can get the people to go to war again, and that I doubt."

I heard him with dismay. Obviously, his mind was set on compromise; he was taking it for granted that the deal was within his reach. I realized I must make another effort to shake his optimism and unsettle his assurance. It was time to sting the Fuehrer in a vulnerable spot.

"I always looked to you to do greater things than Mussolini," I said, speaking slowly. "But there are plenty of fools who say that you're just aping him. However, you're not quite true to fact when you say that Mussolini began his rule with a compromise. In the first place, the Duce forced the issue by a definite revolutionary act." And I reminded Hitler that Mussolini's ultimatum to Minister-President de Facta, demanding resignation of the whole cabinet, had been sent after the Blackshirts had taken possession of strategic points and provincial capitals 'throughout the kingdom. Twenty-four hours after the ultimatum, de Facta and his ministers had resigned, on 26 October 1922. On the same day Mussolini had publicly ordered a general mobilization and had declared the martial law of Fascism. Public buildings were occupied in all important cities and an army of one hundred thousand Blackshirts began the march on Rome. Mussolini had then been invited to enter a 'cabinet of concentration.' His reply had been: "In a few hours Rome will be in the hands of a hundred thousand Blackshirts." He had rejected a second offer in the night of the twenty-ninth. And that had been the end of the liberal regime in Italy.

"Now listen to this." I took a magazine from my brief-case lying before me on the table, and read:

Shortly before noon of the thirtieth there came an urgent telephone call from Rome: Mussolini was invited by the King to accept the commission to form a new cabinet. And Mussolini answered: I am very grateful for this invitation, but I want it confirmed by telegram. The telephone often does not transmit exactly.' Then, at 2 p.m., came a personal, urgent telegram: 'On. Mussolini, Milan. His Majesty the King requests you to come to Rome immediately, as he wishes to entrust you with the composition of the new cabinet. Faithfully Gen. Cittadini.'

"An article in one of your own publications, Herr Hitler 'What We Ought to Know About Fascism.'[2] Here it is -" and I handed it to him.

I remember that as he perused the two pages I had marked, he wore the vacant expression often typical of him when he is intently reading or listening-mouth open and underlip drawn in. When he had finished them and began to leaf further, I fairly snatched the magazine from him; I did not want his attention wandering to extraneous things. He submitted without a word, and looked up at me with an expression almost of docility. Something told me I had won this preliminary round, and in my excitement I came near losing the thread of my argument.

"No, Mussolini's triumph was won by a definite revolutionary act, not by bargaining with an irresponsible camarilla. He compromised after he had forced his appointment. He included some nationalist monarchists in his cabinet-moderation at that moment was wise. You must admit that you are much stronger now, on a broader foundation within the nation, than Mussolini when he marched on Rome. That's natural enough-you've been preparing for over twelve years, whereas the Duce had only three.

"Now you must crown your struggle for power with a revolutionary act! It's the only possible solution, the only one worthy of you, the only one worthy of the Nazis!"

And I let the excitement of the idea carry me away on a flood of words. What a bombshell! Instead of going to the polls, order the March on Berlin, with a ringing manifesto to the nation, to all nations! An end to the ridicule and contempt in which the world now held him, a purging of the humiliation the old Field-Marshal had

---

2 'Was Wir vom Faschismus wissen muessen,' National sozialistische Monatshefte, Herausgeber Adolf Hitler, Heft 26, Mai 1932, pp. 223-7.

heaped on him! It would throw all responsibility on Hindenburg and the camarilla, would proclaim their right to govern forfeited by their blindness and stupidity, by their unpatriotic willingness to throw Germany into the horrors of anarchy rather than yield to a leadership established by the franchise. Hitler's appeal to reason had been thwarted. Now guns must speak! "No possible doubt of their capitulating," I almost shouted at him. "Papen and Schleicher will resign, Hindenburg will invite you to form your cabinet and-"

And here, for the first time, Hitler brought me down in mid-flight. "That's all very well and good, mein Lieber, but you're forgetting one thing, and that's very important. I need Hindenburg - I need that feeble-minded old bull, that senile dodo, that -"

I got back my wind in time to interrupt in turn. " But what if you had won the election against Hindenburg? He might be smoking his pipe in Neudeck by now, almost a forgotten man."

I thought I had him there, but he flashed back at me without a moment's hesitation.

"Oh, if I had become President, Hindenburg's prestige would, of course, be in the basket. Besides, I knew I couldn't make it-but it was priceless propaganda, a splendid springboard for the sweeping elections in July. (But they didn't sweep you into power, I thought.) Aber dieser sture Bulle -"

And he began to imitate the old man's rumbling bass, bellowing wordless syllables-a sort of 'hou-uh-hou-hou, in his deepest voice, while he stalked slowly and stiffly round the room, left arm folded behind his back and right hand resting on the head of an imaginary stick. Finally he looked up at me and said:

"Don't you see? Don't you see that I need the old cab-horse? Say what you will, his prestige is still priceless-a fabulous reputation that must be exploited. Here's a symbolic picture I don't intend to miss: Hindenburg representing the Old Germany and I the New, the Old Germany reaching out its hand to the New-the old Field-Marshal of the World War and the young Corporal from the trenches pledging themselves to the swastika at the tomb of Frederick the Great! A marvellous tableau, with tremendous potentialities! I'll stage such an act in Potsdam as the world has never seen! If I force a showdown, the old idiot might resign, and I can't afford it. Don't you see?"

I was dumbfounded. He had it all figured out. "Certainly a beautiful spectacle," I said feebly, "but really-I can't see that you need it… What if he does resign? All the better for you, for then-"

"Ach!" Hitler broke in, impatiently now. "Why can't you see it? I need his prestige for the transition period, until I've solidified my power. With his prestige behind me I can proceed step by step-I can get rid of Versailles, I can re-arm, I can get allies. I don't care what they think and write about me abroad-better for them to keep on underrating me until I get strong-I'll be ready to strike before they know it, the fools! Austria will be the first fruit to drop into my lap; I'll settle things with Mussolini myself. You wouldn't mind going to Rome with me, would you? Who knows!"

And he laughed heartily, all good humour again. I was still floundering, and could get out only a few ineffectual words.

"There can be no doubt of Mussolini's siding with me," Hitler went on. "He must, and that checks France. As for England-why worry about her? If she doesn't want to join with us, she'd better keep quiet and stay neutral - Mussolini could raise hell in the Mediterranean!"

Here I found my legs again. "I can't quite share your optimism," I said. "A lot of water will flow down the Spree before you can strike. They're Latin sisters, France and Italy-don't forget that. Don't count too much on Mussolini; he'd be less interested in helping you to build a Nordic colossus than in using you for pressure on England to further his Mediterranean plans. Besides, there's the Vatican. I've seen and learned a lot since I last saw the dome of Saint Peter's."

"What do you mean by that? " Hitler said sharply.

"The Vatican, religious capital of the world's most powerful Church, happens to lie within the walls of Rome, the political capital of Italy," I reminded him. There was no Protestant-Catholic conflict in Italy, because there were only a few Protestants. Mussolini's struggle with the Pope had been only to set up Fascist ascendancy in Italy as against that of the Vatican. Once sovereignty was achieved, he had stopped fighting the Pope, whose political world importance he was fully aware of: Fascist Italy could certainly profit by the Pope's prestige and power in the world at large. That had a bearing on Austria. 'Anschluss' with a democratic Germany had already been thwarted, for political reasons. A Nazi anti-Christian Germany would be in itself a menace which the Church would fight tooth-and-nail, even though it was Germany's internal affair. A union of Austria with a Nazi Germany would be opposed by Mussolini not only for political reasons - the Brenner and Trieste - but to safeguard the interests of the Pope. The break-up of the old, almost entirely Catholic Austro-Hungarian empire had been a cruel blow to the Vatican; it had been followed by reverses in Mexico and Spain. The relic that was Austria, the Church would be resolved to keep. "By the way," I said, "what will you do 'with Vienna if Austria should become German?"

"Austria will be like Bavaria or any other state in the Reich, and Vienna a Free City like Hamburg' he replied, a bit snappishly.

I dropped it there, and went back to the fetters he would forge for himself if he were to come to the Chancellorship through compromise. His objectives could not all be achieved at once; some of them would have to be deferred, and he must be free to choose among them. That he could never do if he came to terms with the Reaktion, for these gentlemen would demand their price. "There are so many pitfalls, so many tangles ahead," I said. "In any case, you'll be slapping half the world in the face-Moscow, Warsaw, Prague, Rome, Paris, London, Washington-when you make Rosenberg your foreign minister."

"Who told you that? " he shot at me, frowning. "Rosenberg himself, only a few days ago," I said. "Why shouldn't he, if it's true? "Visibly unsettled, Hitler began pacing again without replying.

"Don't misunderstand me," I went on, watching him intently for storm signals. "I admire Rosenberg-his Mythus is a really epochal work. But he's the avowed arch-enemy of Moscow, of Rome, of Jewry. It will be like a declaration of war. Marshal Pilsudski and Comrade Stalin will jump into action. Jews and Jesuits will move heaven and hell against you. All right, if that's what you want-but do you think for a minute that you'll be at liberty to do that if you compromise now?"

Hitler did not reply. He was looking far from pleased, but not yet antagonistic.

"I'm grateful to you, Herr Hitler," I said, "for allowing me to talk to you so frankly, and honestly relieved to find you so open-minded as to listen to me; in fact, 1--"

"But of course I'm listening," he broke in. "Your approach interests me-I've always liked to talk with you." And we both smiled. He sat down. The atmosphere was easy again, and I ventured on.

"A compromise, even temporary, will oblige you to muffle, if not to drop, one or more of your most publicized issues-German socialism or the Jewish question-and to adopt a more conciliatory attitude toward the Pope. I doubt if the Party, keyed up as it is, would stand for it-I foresee a state of confusion, to say the least. By the way, I heard about the Schwarze Front the other day. Is Otto Strasser-"

I was cut short. "Oh, he is as good as finished!" he snarled. But I thought the opening might yield some inkling of his attitude toward Gregor Strasser.

"Gregor Strasser is a big man today, but he's devoted to you. I should say he's all right …"

"Mm - there's a 'Grobian'[3] - I'm not so sure…" and he drew a long breath. His expression didn't encourage further exploration. I left it at that; after all, I had to stick to my muttons. I began to stress again the necessity of his being at liberty to decide what part of the Nazi programme he would tackle first. He must be free to lead off with Socialism, instead of with Jew-baiting and racialism, which would antagonize the whole world. With Socialism he would be on solid ground. The Church could not quarrel with him. The few thousand German capitalists, of course, would crawl into their holes, but the support of millions of Communists and Sozis would go to him. As for the Jews, let him break their power, but do it without fireworks. Jews everywhere were afraid of him now, and expecting persecution; if he did not start right in wringing their necks, he would avoid immediate reprisals in Paris,

---

3 There is no exact English equivalent for Hitler's epithet. 'A rough, bearish fellow', conveys the sense.

London, and New York. He would gain time; it would mean credit, raw materials, smoking chimneys-employment, bread, and self-respect for the masses, who cared more about these things than about Jews and race. Hitler would have an easier time persuading the relatively small number of really earnest racialists in the Party that we would have to go slow on their pet issue than he would convincing the millions that they must tighten their belts, perhaps for years, to the glory of Nordic blood and honour.

"Don't tie your own hands," I pleaded. "I don't believe in Machiavellian methods at this point, considering the power you have behind you. Make yourself chancellor, and preserve the integrity of Nazism-it's the only consistent and honest course! A heroic movement with a historic task must choose the heroic way."

But Hitler was sitting impassively in his chair, looking at me with hard eyes. I was getting nowhere. And I must go on now to very thin ice indeed: the question of future relations with Soviet Russia, my original Possibility Number Three. I recalled to mind something that might help me: Hitler's talk with Otto Strasser in which he had affirmed the right of the Nordic race to govern the world, a right which must be the guiding star of our foreign policy; it made an understanding with Soviet Russia impossible while a Jewish head surmounted a Slav-Tartar body; one could go along with Russia, as Bismarck had done, only if a Germanic head sat upon this Asiatic trunk. Today, the Fuehrer had said, such a policy would be criminal. Perhaps I would be able to make Hitler see that this condition was undergoing a change.

I began again, in as detached and impersonal a manner as I could summon.

"I believe, as you do and as Rosenberg does, in racial values. But we're still so vulnerable that while we must be very bold, we must also be very wise. Rosenberg said to me the other day that we Nazis were fifty years ahead of other nations. If that's true, we must not rush things, we must plan carefully, and above all we must make 'Realpolitik.'

"I'm coming now to what, a while ago, I called an inevitable conclusion. I'm convinced that Bismarck's policy still holds good, even though Russia now has a Stalin instead of a Czar-from Russia's point of view perhaps even more than ever. The isolated Communist regime, bereft of its old intelligentsia, going through a period of fundamental change and struggling hard to get on its feet, needs us as friends more than the Czar ever did. Two other countries headed by dictators have been shrewd enough to take advantage of Russia's need. Mussolini recognized Soviet Russia because he needed oil and other things. And Kemal Pasha, another dictator and certainly not a Bolshevik, maintains definitely amicable relations, if not a secret alliance, with Moscow. After all, they are neighbours, and there's always the Russian threat to the Bosporus. That's 'Realpolitik.' You've got the Rapallo Treaty[4], which

---

4 The Treaty of Rapallo in its modified form of 1926 and the secret military protocol were still in force at that date.

336

wasn't so stupid. Rathenau may have been a Jew and may have had his own idea about what he was going to do with it, but it exists, an instrument ready for your use, to exploit and expand as you see fit."

Hitler was listening intently, evidently meaning to let me have my say on this subject too, and I began to warm up to it. I told him that I thought it would be easier to convert a Bolshevik revolutionary activist to National Socialism in a Russian sense, than it would be to win a British capitalist to our faith in a British sense. It would be a mistake to run after the English-Rosenberg didn't understand English mentality. If you wanted to impress an Englishman to the extent of getting anything out of him, you had to show him a good fist and the prospect of a kick in the groin. If you weren't able to do that, keep hands off'. Avoid antagonizing him, avoid cultivating him-simply be cool and courteous and bide your time.

Neither Britain nor Italy had any need of a Nordic giant. Russia had. Faced with the alternatives of a brute assault by Germany, Japan, and perhaps other powers-a war to the death-or an understanding with a Nazi Germany, perhaps even a close military alliance at the cost of certain concessions and modifications, Stalin, I believed, would choose Germany, provided the approach were made earnestly and intelligently. Hitler would have a foundation to build upon in the existing collaboration between the German and the Soviet general staffs. Such an alliance would be truly invincible-a system extending from the North Sea and the Baltic Sea down the Danube to the Bosporus, and east as far as Vladivostok. It would mean a perfect counterpoise to the British Empire, and would establish at last that non-existent political and economic world equilibrium, unattainable so long as England's predominance should be able to prevent it. It would mean peace for Russia in the West, a final check to Japan in the East, recapture of the Baltic countries-excepting Finland, of course at relatively little cost. It would give the Soviets security to work out their tremendous inner problems.

For Germany, the advantages would be almost incalculable. Politically, economically, perhaps even biologically, Hitler would be able to solve his own problems more easily with Stalin than against him. Russia would offer a tremendous hinterland for our industry and Wirtschaft. Czechoslovakia would be liquidated, perhaps Roumania as well, and that would be certain to appeal to Hungary and Bulgaria. Poland, under pressure from both sides, would have to return to us every inch of ground, including Danzig - to be compensated perhaps by Memel or Riga and parts of Czechoslovakia. A definite and binding agreement regarding the Ukraine would be an essential. Germany would then have the sphere of influence she long had sought, from the North Sea to the Black Sea, and a real voice in the world. And she would avoid the necessity of an alliance with Japan, really contrary to Nazi philosophy. Vulnerable and impotent as we were, we must at all costs avoid antagonizing England and America, and, at least at the start, we must make the

National Socialist thesis as palatable and digestible as possible, for it was all that a Nazi regime, beginning with a prostrate Germany, had to offer to the world.

The combination would put an end to the absurdity of England's holding the balance of power in practically any and every situation. And yet England and the other Powers would see that it offered a solution obtainable without war-that new world-war which might mean the end of all of us. The few minor States liquidated, Czechoslovakia, for example, had no real political right to existence-although perhaps one must except the buffoon kingdom of Roumania. And it would jeopardize no existing combination, political system, or sphere of influence without offering an effective substitute. England would keep her empire. To safeguard her Gibraltar-Suez-India life-line she would have to maintain amity with us against an eventual Latin combination of France, Italy, and Spain, which would control western and southern Europe, the Mediterranean, and North Africa. The Japanese could extend their sphere of influence in China, even though Siberia would be secure from them and the 'Yellow Peril' checked. The common interests of the two Americas, a world in themselves, would not be endangered. Five spheres of influence, five organic and independent units.

Moreover, in view of America's prime importance in the Nazi struggle, such a solution of the European problem would be more palatable in the United States than any other. Not only would it save American investments by rendering Europe solvent; it would open new and profitable markets, protect American interests in the Far East, and help in the solution of Far Eastern problems.

Finally it would bring to this fear-ridden world a feeling of security-a psychological factor of incalculable value.

All this I said, and more, while Hitler listened closely, interrupting me now and then with a pertinent question or brief comment. It was time to wind it up. I said:

"The most serious question of all is whether Bolshevism could be developed and modified sufficiently to make it compatible with National Socialism. I believe it could: the gap can be bridged. After all, both philosophies aim at a total revaluation; both are revolutionary and seek to create a socialist state, a new structure from the bottom up. It depends on whether our nationalism will truly be socialistic and whether Russian socialism will become sufficiently nationalistic-and it is tending that way now.

"Another thing: you once spoke of the impossibility of going along with a Russia in which a Jewish head animated a Slav-Tartar body. I think that state of affairs is changing. Trotsky is in exile, and on the whole the Jewish influence in Moscow seems to be on the wane. Possibly you'd find that Stalin might be disposed to accelerate the process, and likewise to taper off the Comintern, which is an increasing liability to him in his new policy of Russian nationalism.

"Russia offers you two alternatives: a war which may be the end of Germany,

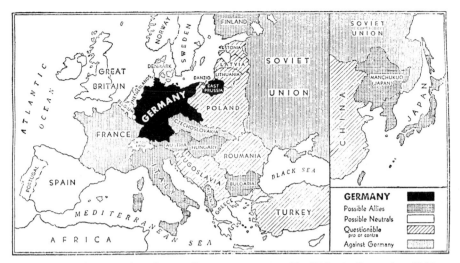

Germany's foreign political constellation as envisioned by Hitler in September 1932.

or an alliance which may open up a road of peace for the triumph of a greater Germany. But if you come to power by a compromise with capitalism, Herr Hitler, you close the door on the second."

There it was. I had had my say, and I stopped talking. I knew there were gaps in my reasoning, and I had made debatable statements for the sake of carrying my points, but in its main outlines I believed that my idea was practicable.

I waited. Presently Hitler spoke.

"I've encountered similar lines of thought," he began slowly, in an emotionless voice. "But your presentation is interesting and original. There may be a fallacy in your synthesis, or there may be in mine-who can tell? But I like mine better. Suppose I came to an agreement with Stalin and proceeded accordingly. What if I were to be attacked by Italy, France, and England, and Stalin should betray me -instead of helping us, should line up with our enemies? What then? You're right-a Nazi regime will be most vulnerable in the beginning. For that very reason it would be better to ally myself with Italy and Japan, and play along with England, even if I can't get her friendship-a course which you yourself, by the way, advised years ago.

"The economic power of the Versailles· States is so enormous that I can't risk antagonizing them at the very outset. If I begin my regime with socialism, Paris, London, and New York will be alarmed, the capitalists will take fright and combine, and I'll be whipped before I know it. A preventive war would ruin everything. No, I've got to play ball with capitalism and keep the Versailles Powers in line by holding aloft the bogey of Bolshevism-make them believe that a Nazi Germany is the last bulwark against the Red flood. That's the only way to come through the danger period, to get rid of Versailles and re-arm. I can talk peace, but mean war."

He was on his feet by now, back at his nervous pacing.

"If England opposes a greater Germany at all costs, all right. I still think that Mussolini might be interested in making Germany so strong that together we could force John Bull to his knees. And it will be easier to overthrow Moscow and take the Ukraine if the capitalists are on my side. If the capitalists are forced to choose, believe me, they will prefer a greater Germany, even if it means the end of Moscow, to an alliance of the two against themselves-for that would spell the finish of capitalism the world over. Never fear-faced by such an alternative, capitalism would rather have me than Stalin, and will accept my terms."

He paused, and seemed to reflect. Then: "It would be a strange thing to go pro-Bolshevik now after our furious propaganda against them ... But I can frighten those gentlemen in Paris and London and New York if they won't leave me alone..." After a moment he went on more vigorously, leaping from idea to idea.

"The primary thing is to get rid of Versailles and re-arm socialism must come in the second line. Re-arming costs money, and so would what you call a revolutionary act. [As if elections didn't cost money too, I thought.] And I've very little now, I tell you ... No, it can't be done ... Besides, I need Hindenburg, as I've told you, at least until the worst is over ... And furthermore, I don't trust the Russians, just as Stalin probably doesn't trust us. The Machiavellian method is the only one possible, the only one by which I can accomplish anything in our plight ... What if the Reichswehr should shoot again? (But it wasn't the Reichswehr; it was the Landespolizei, something quite different, I corrected him in my mind.) No, mein Lieber, the Feldherrnhalle was enough-I've learned since then. No use being heroic in this world; if you want to get something done and get anywhere yourself, it's better to talk about it and let others do the work. If you can achieve something by cunning, don't try noble deeds-they might knock your teeth out."

Now he was in full spate, speaking in a harsh voice and throwing his thoughts into the room with more of contempt than passion.

"I'm a 'Politiker' and not a reformer or religious fanatic. I know what I want, and I think sometimes I know what's possible. Why should I bind myself to Stalin so long as there's the slightest chance of winning for Germany the room she deserves? I won't forfeit that chance."

Then, in a sudden, fierce outburst of the passionate energy of his nature:

"And if it's going to take bombs to show these gentlemen in London, Paris, and New York that I mean business, well, they can have them. Don't be afraid-I'll go the limit when the time comes, but not before.... Oh no, not this time-I've learned to wait ... If they don't understand any other language, they'll learn something if a dozen of these gold-hyenas swim in their own blood in every capital of Europe and America. I have only one thought, one will that animates me day and night-to make Germany great, the greatest power on earth. And if you visualize a greater Germany side by side with Russia, I tell you that I can see a German Reich stretching from the

North Sea to the Urals, but without a Stalin!

"I was aghast. I felt the chill in my veins that I had felt in Linz, nine years before, when Hitler had been carried away by the idea of bombs. He stopped talking, but continued his nervous pacing. I kept still; I only wanted this fit of fury to subside. Presently he sat down again, and after a moment began to question me calmly enough about America.

The Presidential campaign of 1932 was then gathering momentum. I said that Roosevelt's election seemed certain. The situation in the United States was serious, and if the promised New Deal did not meet the crisis, a revolution was not unthinkable. In any case, Washington could not and would not interfere in a possible European imbroglio.

Amann had asked me if I could sell the rights of Mein Kampf in the United States for $50,000; the Hearst syndicate had already offered $25,000, I think he said. I spoke of this to Hitler. There was, so far as I knew, no foreign edition; an American edition would be excellent propaganda, but shouldn't it be considerably revised? A full translation of the German text would be embarrassing-so frank an exposition of so sweeping a political programme might be prejudicial, and it might even be advisable to modify in future German editions some of the passages most offensive to foreign ears.

"As a matter of fact," I said, "I've never come across a foreigner of consequence who has troubled to read your book, and only one or two foreign correspondents who have. Once you're Chancellor, however, they'll begin-it might even occur to diplomats to stick a nose into it."

"I don't see any particular danger in the book as it stands," said Hitler. "If you can get fifty thousand for it, go ahead-the money would be most welcome right now. Of course it would be up to the American publisher to condense and abridge, provided that doesn't falsify or distort the original meaning. I don't need to retract what I wrote years ago, like a professional writer-I make politics, not books. And like any other Politiker, I've a right to modify or correct my domestic or foreign policy any way I choose."

He got up and went to the bell. "And now," he said, " I think it's time we ordered some lunch brought in."

XXV

TIME OUT FOR LUNCH

I remember little about my lunch that day except a cup of not very good Mocha. Still too tense to do more than touch the food, I watched Hitler eat a vegetable omelette, with a cup of Hag.

There was bottled water on the table. "I've been doing without alcohol for a long while," he said. "It can't be good to take alcohol with meals; it ferments in your stomach, and that doesn't help your digestion. That doesn't mean that you shouldn't have some wine if you want it." But I declined. "I'm glad you've stopped smoking," he went on. "You used to smoke like a chimney, and I can't abide the smell of cigarettes." I asked about his vegetarianism. He said that he had tried it during the first presidential campaign that spring, and it had so increased his efficiency and endurance that he had decided to go on with it.

From where I sat I could see the old chancellery on the other side of the Wilhelmplatz. I began to wonder if Hitler had had the power of suggestion in mind when he established his head-quarters within sight of his goal. Was he a Hannibal before the gates, as his opponents hoped and some of his followers feared? Or was he just a demagogue, flouted now by his enemies as 'The Labour Leader in the Hotel de Luxe' disposed more to talk than to hammer at the door of that building from which Bismarck had once ruled the German Reich?

"You have an exciting view from here," I said casually. "A good pair of field-glasses might show you Papen squirming, and wiping the cold sweat from his brow. He must have nightmares about your Brown-shirts storming the gates. Or does he keep his shutters closed?"

Hitler laughed. "I don't know whether I give him bad dreams. But I'm staying here less to frighten him than to be comfortable. Here I'm relatively safe, for the Kaiserhof lies within the Bannmeile, and no demonstrations of any kind are allowed. That's an important consideration, in view of the wretched Berlin police and the mock-authority of the State."

We fell to talking easily about old times, and Hitler told me again of his pride in the miraculous growth of the Party. Suddenly he said:

"It's a great pity that you can't stay over until the tenth of October. I'd like you to be with me at the tenth anniversary of Coburg - that will be a great day. I've designed a beautiful badge. Every one of the old guard who was there will get it, and surely you deserve one.... Can't you possibly make it?... Well, I'll see that one is sent to you, photographs and everything."

I said I hoped he wouldn't forget it, never dreaming what an ironical twist Fate had in store for me in connection with that Coburg decoration.

"Oh, don't worry, I'll see to it - I'll tell Hoffmann today to remind me of it. You saw him today? He's a remarkable fellow, always ready for a joke, and I like him.... Coburg is one of my dearest memories, and I'll never forget it. I can still see everyone of us-you in your long coat, and Ludwig trudging at your side.... Yes, for a while you were right beside me, with Dietrich Eckart and Rosenberg, until the fighting started and you jumped at somebody... Dietrich Eckart shouting furiously... My good friend Dietrich Eckart-what would he say if he could see us now, and all we've achieved! I'd give a great deal if he could be here. We often talk about the old times - Hoffmann, Weber, and good old Graf - he never forgets! And your beautiful new boots, that hurt you so when you were with us in Landshut - do you remember?"

I remembered those boots very well, but in this affable moment I was looking for a way to bring the talk round to other personalities in the movement, to Rosenberg, Strasser, Roehm, Goebbels, and Goering-the men who seemed destined for the most important posts in the coming Nazi Government. I wanted especially to know how he felt toward Strasser and Goebbels as individuals. I knew that Strasser's growing popularity and influence didn't please Hitler. It was hard for me to imagine the two of them in his future cabinet, with Strasser Minister of the Interior and Minister-President of Prussia-the posts he was expecting. Only the other day Strasser had said to me: "Ludecke, get this straight-the gap between Goebbels and me can't be bridged."

Presently Hitler himself switched the talk back to his present situation.

"It's a good thing that Papen has already carried out parts of my task for me, by means of the very steps he took to defeat me," he said with satisfaction. "Hindenburg and Papen have set up a half-way dictatorship-an impractical one, but it gets the people used to the idea. Take Prussia, for example. Papen is literally a dictator there, and Prussia will fall to me in turn as chancellor. The Prussian police are a powerful tool to possess. And only last month, at Lausanne, the Government wangled a moratorium on reparations payments - virtually a cancellation. That's another problem I won't have to tackle."

Now I mentioned Strasser. "Strasser will make a fine minister in your cabinet," I said. He's been giving a brilliant presentation of the socialist aims of the Party, and of course the masses will expect sweeping changes in the ownership system, once you come to power."

Hitler frowned. "Strasser would do better to attend to the smooth functioning of the political organization, and stop trying to formulate Nazi policy. He's extended himself too far, and I'll have to dock his tail pretty soon. If the masses want socialism, let them expect it-and vote for it. Strasser is committing the Party to more than we shall be able to give. That Grobian simply won't understand that the masses are only a means to an end. Having not even a gleam of aristocratic consciousness, he doesn't share our contempt for the street and for democracy ... No, I don't like his rawness, and our contacts are now limited to official business.

But we were now on the subject of wives, and I spoke of having known Frau Goebbels for years, and of my visit to Goebbels at Heiegendamm. Hitler's face grew tense with curiosity. Seeing that I was disposed to be reticent, he said: "You can talk to me freely-I know you're no gossip, and I respect you for it. But I'm very much interested in what you may have to say. Goebbels is one of my most important men, and I like to know about things touching him."

I told him about my former friendship with Magda Goebbels and mentioned the animosity against both Goebbelses I had encountered in the Party.

Hitler gave me a shrewd look. "Ludecke, I understand you very well. But you needn't worry. Schauen Sie: Goebbels ist ein vom Schicksal geschlagener Mann."

I spoke of his friendship with Magda. He met that with a simplicity which disarmed me completely. "No," he said. And after a moment: "In those days I was the happiest man in the world,"-and it was plain that Magda Goebbels had nothing to do with that happiness. When he spoke again there were tears in his eyes, and he was clearly unashamed to have me see them. "You remember what Schiller says about the envious gods: 'Life's undiluted joy is not granted to a mortal'... Geli - you never knew her. She was very dear to me."

In this moment I was facing a transparent man. 'Geli' was the adored niece whose unhappy death he can never forget.

We came somehow to the vexatiousness of petty critics.

"I'm utterly sick of these gossip-mongers and moralists," Hitler told me. "Women and clergymen complaining about all the women-chasers among the men of the SA! Good Lord -if they'd only stop bothering me about such things! I'd a lot rather my good SA men took the pretty women than that some fat-bellied moneybag should have them. And by the way, there's no lack of talk about your triflings with women -someone was even so kind as to advise against you-'Ihre Weibergeschichten waeren skandaloes!' Do you want to know what I replied? I said that it was better for you to have women than men!"

Here was a neat entrance to a subject which I had not known how to broach for myself. I said that I had heard from many sources that homosexuality in the SA had assumed really serious dimensions, likely to prove embarrassing even abroad. Two prominent Berlin physicians holding rank as doctors in the SA had told me in confidence that they had ostentatiously resigned from the organization as a protest against Roehm's conduct. Their protests to the Fuehrer had not been answered, and they had given me a memorandum on the matter and had begged me to present it to Hitler privately. The situation was especially distressing to me, I said, because I had a high opinion of Roehm's capabilities.

Obviously not pleased at my following up the opening he had given me, Hitler dismissed the subject with a wave of his hand.

"Ach, why should I concern myself with the private lives of my followers! My concern is their service to the cause.

In times of crisis one can't make changes in important posts for such reasons. Ridiculous! I love Richard Wagner's music-must I close my ears to it because he was a pederast? The whole thing's absurd .... And quite apart from Roehm's great achievements, I know I can absolutely depend on him."

In other words, said my mind, Roehm is vulnerable-his perversion has delivered him into your hands; when his usefulness is over and the Reichswehr is yours, you can finish him off at will. If I had not realized it before, I would have known in that moment that Adolf Hitler, who people still said would some day be destroyed by his loyalty to his friends, was no longer the star-storming idealist but an ice-cold opportunist prepared to use situations and men without scruple. Strasser, the unassailable, had been thus far the only one of his lieutenants who apparently was not persona grata to the Fuehrer.

Next I tried Goering. A few days before, I told Hitler, after I had put some one on the train in Munich, I had been hurrying down the corridor to get off, with only a second to spare, when I found my way blocked by a mountain of flesh. It was Goering. "Oh, Ludecke-" he had said, "now that's handy! Please attend to this telegram-I won't have time for it.... Thanks, that's nice of you. See you in Berlin some day. Good-bye."

"And of course," I said to Hitler, " he forgot to give me the money for it. Lucky for me it wasn't a radiogram to Tokio."

Hitler laughed. "That's Goering, all right," he said with relish. "An extraordinary fellow-there you have another case. Why must he live so high! But he has his points and he's very useful at times, even if he is guilty of awful asininities now and then. I'm glad he's now well taken care of-the Reichstag-presidency should fill the bill. I hope he makes good today!"

"Do you think he'll be satisfied with the presidency of the Reichstag?"

"He can be glad he's got that," Hitler replied. "I've been ready more than once to give him the air-and perhaps he would make an excellent Air Minister!"

Then we began to discuss in earnest my project for establishing a Nazi press bureau in Washington. I said that we could no longer neglect our problems abroad; the goodwill of England and America would be an essential counterweight to French enmity. Our programme was loaded with international dynamite, and by its very nature would arouse deep antagonism everywhere unless we were prepared-to meet that condition with judicious propaganda. With his authorization, I could proceed at once with concrete plans for setting up an agency for gathering American news for the Party press and, what was much more important, disseminating Nazi news in the United States.

"Amann tells me that he's ready to contribute five hundred dollars a month for your office in Washington," Hitler said. "I'll see if I can get an equal amount for you from Schwarz. I doubt very much if I can squeeze it out of him for the present-good old Schwarz sits on his treasure like a hen on her chicks. Well, he's obliged to, for the elections have swallowed everything, and we have debts."

I thanked him, and said that he of course realized why I had thought it vital to ascertain his views on foreign questions, particularly on long-range developments, for I would constantly have to be building foundations for such developments. I could do intelligent and effective work only if I understood Hitler's objectives, and one or two things still needed to be cleared up for me. I now produced again the May issue of the National-Socialist Monthly, which contained several interesting papers on the general subject: 'The Struggle for the East.' In the introduction to his article, Rosenberg had said: 'It gives us National Socialists great satisfaction to be able to affirm that we have been right in the question of foreign policy. I have absolutely nothing to retract from my book.'[1] These words I pointed out to Hitler, and another sentence, which would be meaningless if quoted here without its full context, but which implied that Rosenberg, for considerations of caution, had indeed always understated his views.

"Did you see that? " I asked Hitler.

"No," he said, looking rather distrait. "I didn't."

This I thought strange, for Rosenberg was generally acknowledged to be Hitler's spokesman in matters of foreign policy. But I didn't say so. I merely reminded the Fuehrer that the book which Rosenberg was now so stoutly reaffirming contained these extreme statements:[2] 'The liquidation of the Polish State is the most urgent necessity of Germany,' An alliance between Kief and Berlin and the creation of a common border is a national and political necessity for a future German policy.' ... 'After a severance of the South (and of course of the Caucasus) the Russian State can still be a colossus...' Then I added :

"If you come to power committed to the policy of your future foreign minister, the preventive war that you dread may be on you sooner than you expect; neither Paris nor Warsaw nor Moscow will permit realization of such a plan if they can help it. That's why I've been stressing the possibility that you might find it easier to attain the solution of our room-problem with Stalin and Pilsudski than against them."

It was all I could do to keep from bluntly putting the fundamental question: To what extend did the Fuehrer really stand behind the man from whom I was apparently to receive my instructions for foreign propaganda?

But Hitler sat with impassive face and said nothing.

---

1 *Der Zukunftsweg einer deutschen Aussenpolitik, Verlag Frz. Eber Nachf., Muenchen, 1927.*
2 *Ibid., p. 97.*

"It's a pity you've made up your mind about Russia. I saw myself going from Washington to Tokio and on to Moscow on a mission to sound out Stalin. Newspapers are full of contradictory reports about Russia. We don't really know what Russia is like today. We condemn everything because it fits in with our present policy, but there may be possibilities. At least you'd be sure of getting honest first-hand information."

Hitler looked as though he were undecided whether to give me a good dressing-down or to take my insistence in good part. Finally he said sarcastically that he couldn't very well change his plans just to gratify my travel whims, adding in a more friendly tone: "I see what you mean. It's not a bad idea. You'd made a good ambassador - you have the equipment for it, and you know how to treat the women. Do you know Russia too?"

I confessed that I didn't, and admitted that an ambassador should know the language and the country. "But I've no ambition to become an accredited official ambassador-in his capacity, such a man couldn't very well do what needs to be done. Anyway the haute volee bores me to tears, and besides I prefer women of my own choice. It's more the job of a handsome young attaché to satisfy amorous matrons."

We talked easily for a while about Nazi prospects, but whenever I pressed for precise instructions or for information which might guide me, Hitler at once became reserved or evasive. I had the impression that this was due less to his secretive nature than to the fact that virtually nothing had been planned, either in practical foreign policy or in diplomatic personnel. He did concede that something should be done about building up a foreign office for the Party. He would discuss the matter with Rosenberg. For the rest, I was able to elicit only general suggestions that the Bolshevik menace be emphasized in America, with the bulwark of a Nazi Germany as a safeguard for American investments, and that the idea be disseminated that capitalism and Jewry need not look too fearfully toward a National Socialist regime. But what was Hitler's real intention regarding the problem of Jewry? I had learned with the years to take a calmer view of the Jewish question in practical politics, and I wondered if Hitler still accepted the idea of a Jewish world conspiracy as unquestioningly as he once had. I told him about publishing the American Guard in Brookline, and what it had taught me. When I pointed to Arno Schickedanz's attempt to solve the Jewish riddle in his study (Sozialparasitismus im Voelkerleben) of the biological laws determining the Jewish character-an exposition of the actual origin of the Jew as a human parasite, similar to the scientifically accepted theory of the existence of parasites in animal and plant life - Hitler interrupted me before I could finish my thought about an error in Schickedanz's analysis. " Ach, der Schickedanz!" he said, and made a depreciating gesture. He added, with a mysterious air: "I am working on a book, a work-well, you'll see when it's finished!" And he looked at

347

me as though to say that the world was soon to be presented with the last word of wisdom about everything. Later I was reminded of this potential brain-child when Amann mentioned it to me in awe. "As I see things now," I resumed, "after years of practical experience and observations in Europe and America, I wonder if it is intelligent to attack the Jewish people as a whole. I know for a fact that the Jews do not present a united front against the Gentiles, and the belief that there is a universal policy for destroying the Gentile world, thought out and enunciated in detail by a super-council, is a delusion. I talked with Rosenberg about it the other day, and even he admits now that the authenticity of the 'Protocols of Zion' is doubtful. "The Jews are, in a sense, as divided and differentiated as we Gentiles are. In the main, it's their extraordinary status, their vulnerability combined with their peculiar Jewish intellectuality and persecution complex, that drives them together instinctively in times of crisis. I believe we can achieve quicker results, with less risk to us, by trying to divide them further and by helping those Jews who want to escape Jewry-there are many of them-if given a chance. That can be done without jeopardizing our plan for breaking the established Jewish power in Germany." Hitler was again giving me his closest attention, and I began to feel that perhaps there was a chance of persuading him to adopt a more cautious policy toward the Jews. I told him I had interviewed prominent Jews in various countries, with the intention of finding out what was in the back of their minds, and I had failed to find conformity of opinion as to either their own status or their attitude towards the Gentile world. I mentioned specifically my talk, early in 1930, with Louis Marshall, the head of the Jewish Committee to whom Henry Ford had directed his apology. Hitler sat bolt upright in his chair. "But that would interest me very much," he said. "Tell me about it." But before I could begin, there was a knock at the door-it was just a few minutes past three o'clock-and in came Heinrich Himmler, Strasser's one-time secretary, now head of the SS, in his gorgeous black uniform with a prosaic pince-nez riding his face, which beamed now with importance; he clicked his heels, heil-hitlered, and announced that the Reichstag had recessed for half an hour and that the Fuehrer was needed at once for an important decision. Goering, Strasser, and Frick were waiting for him in the palais of the Reichstag-President. Hitler jumped to his feet, my presence forgotten. "We'll get that fellow now," he said excitedly, and stormed out. I found myself alone. In some bewilderment, I slowly gathered my papers into my brief-case and went to my room. Several hours later, I heard newsboys screaming extras: "Reichstag Dissolved!"

XXVI

I BECOME A DANGEROUS FELLOW

Everybody was asking questions. Had the Reichstag actually been dissolved? Had lack of confidence been voted? Would Papen be forced to resign? What had really happened?

Acting under instructions received from Hitler during the recess, Goering had staged what he regarded as a single-handed coup d'etat.

As soon as the session was reopened, he electrified the house by proceeding at once with the vote on the Communist motion of lack of confidence in the Government, which, to the surprise of everyone, had met no opposition in the chamber. Papen, with Hindenburg's signed decree of dissolution ready in the famous red portfolio, realized that he was in a serious position. He asked for the floor. Goering ignored the request, though it came from the chancellor of the Reich. In a fury, Papen took the document out of the portfolio and put it on the desk in front of Goering, who did not deign even to look at it, thus brushing aside Hindenburg's decree. Papen and his colleagues left the chamber in outraged protest.

The voting was completed: 513 against Papen and only 32 for him. It was the worst parliamentary defeat in the history of republican Germany-a crushing rebuke for the cabinet's emergency ordinances.

Goering's arrogant gesture had an aftermath of confusion. The Nazis demanded that Papen resign, insisting that the decree of dissolution was invalid because the cabinet had already been voted out of office. Papen maintained that the vote was meaningless and Goering's coup unconstitutional, since the Reichstag had already been dissolved. It was a ridiculous impasse, with each side accusing the other of violating the constitution. Goering threatened to reconvene the Reichstag, Papen to use force if Goering dared try. But Goering did not dare. It was finally settled that dissolution of the Reichstag had technically been decreed before the vote, that therefore the vote of lack of confidence did not exist, and that the Government was still legally in power. A niggling and hair-splitting business.

Thus was the Reichstag dissolved once more. New elections were ordered for November 6.

I learned about all this in some wryness of spirit. From my impassioned plea for a 'revolutionary' and 'heroic' solution of his difficulties, Hitler had rushed straight into another bout of parliamentary trickery whose net result for him was a further loss of prestige in activist circles, even though it obliged Papen to face the elections with an illegal but fat vote of lack of confidence on his back.

On the thirteenth, Nazi headquarters at the Kaiserhof resembled a beehive. The whole Nazi council discussed the situation late into the night, debating tactics and preparations for the coming campaign. The situation was clear now; Hitler had made his final choice. It was to be the 'legal' course.

The Press was mirroring the reigning confusion throughout the Reich. Every newspaper accused somebody. It was evident by now that the entire bourgeois Press had joined the Reaktion and was swelling the anti-Nazi chorus. Hitler had opened the battle in true Homeric fashion that day with a flaming speech before the Nazi deputies on the slogan: 'Gegen die Reaktion!' And the Nazi Press, following its well-worn practice, was already glorifying the Fuehrer and the cause in the dramatic language of German war-bulletins.

As I sat in my room early in the afternoon of the fourteenth of September perusing newspapers of all shades of opinion, one thing seemed plain: the last chance for a real Nazi revolution had been forfeited. The whole spectacle so disgusted me that I was almost physically ill. I was in a quandary what to do. Too late to quit the whole business-I was too deeply involved. Besides, despite my disillusionment, I had to admit to myself that it was fascinating to watch history in the making from the inside. I must go through with it, and play my own game as best I could.

Reflection showed me one last possibility of changing Hitler's course. Speed could be necessary. I remembered 1924, when I had tried to move Rosenberg, Strasser, and Roehm to join in action of their own without Hitler, when the Fuehrer in his Landsberg prison was frustrating every attempt at a clear-cut policy. Now the only combination that, could force Hitler's hand would be one of Gregor Strasser, chief of the political organizations, and Ernst Roehm, chief of the SA and SS. Their organizations would practically control the coming election campaign; if the two presented a united front to Hitler he would have to yield.

Could I put it over? Things had changed since 1924; these two men had gone ahead, each in his own way, and I was now a midget compared to them. Strasser was no longer on friendly terms with Roehm-was, in fact, in definite opposition to him. But I felt that I must try. Before I talked to Strasser I must see Roehm and find out where he stood.

Hitler had asked me to leave with him that night for Munich. I wrote a note to Strasser to say that I had big news for him, but that I could not see him until after my return.

Dismally I surveyed my immediate problem. I had only a few marks in my pocket. What about my hotel bill and railway fare? I had been reluctant to ask Hitler for money, intending instead to ask Amann for an advance. But now I needed cash right away.

As if in answer, the telephone rang, announcing Ellery Walter, a young American writer who, by means of my letter of introduction, had met Hanfstaengl and had obtained an interview with Hitler. Now he wanted information for some articles he was preparing, and asked me to join a party that evening. Learning that I had to leave for Munich and needed money at once, he graciously offered to help me. We went downstairs and cashed a traveller's cheque for fifty or sixty dollars.

Walter was a charming and handsome young man, the perfect image of a Nordic knight, whom I had met in Nassau at a party on Count Luckner's boat. One leg had been amputated, the result of blood-poisoning contracted while he was with the rowing crew at the University of Washington. Though in practically constant pain after more than twenty operations, he was always ready to joke about the jungle of German politics whenever I tried to explain it to him. He finally died in Florida several years ago, after much suffering.

Next I ran into a young acquaintance who insisted that I help her to get a glimpse of Hitler. She was in luck, for Hitler had come down a few minutes before and was now in the 'winter garden,' sitting with his staff at the round table in the rear right corner, always reserved for him when he was in Berlin.

We sat down at a table near the entrance from which my companion could watch the Fuehrer. He saw us at once, and returned my salute with a friendly smile and a wave of his hand. Presently I was aware that the Nazi dictator was displaying considerable interest, showing us his best face and looking keenly at my companion. I could only come to the conclusion that the Fuehrer was trying to fathom the personality of my guest. Actually the whole table was looking at her. She was so excited that she squirmed in her chair.

"Hitler is very disappointing," she said. "He has such a funny face, and his mouth is ugly. I like Brueckner much better."

I put her in her car, promising to arrange a dinner with Brueckner, whose six-foot stature and broad smile had interested her more than the eyes of the Fuehrer. When I returned to my table to pay the bill, Hitler beckoned me over.

"Why didn't you join my table? Was that your wife?" he asked, all naive curiosity. "A striking woman-beautifully dressed."

So that was why he had shown such interest! Apparently he assumed I had married a rich American. I explained that she was no wife, only one of a million German females who were yearning to look into the eyes of the Fuehrer. He was visibly flattered.

"But who is she? " he insisted. "She's very good looking."

I let him have the truth with some relish. "She's good looking indeed, her legs most of all. She's a dancer. She wasn't so ambitious as to look higher than Brueckner, but of course, I said jokingly, if I had known…" And I looked meaningfully at Hitler.

"Enough, enough!" he said, laughing. "Ludecke, you're incorrigible."

"Judging from Schaub's eyes and Brueckner's anticipatory sigh, they understand me well enough," I returned. "But she said that Brueckner would have to lose some

351

weight."

Brueckner blushed slightly, looking down at his huge frame.

"I can see it's a blessing we're leaving tonight," Hitler grumbled. And to Brueckner: "Have you the sleeper for Ludecke? " And to my pleased surprise, Brueckner handed me the tickets.

When we met again on the train, I found that my compartment was next to Hitler's. He was sharing his with Schaub, and they had the door open into the adjoining compartment, which was occupied by Brueckner and Dr. Otto Dietrich, the Party's Press-chief Dietrich I now met for the first time-a rather frail-looking, well-groomed young man with brownish eyes. He had a suave manner but was somehow nondescript.

The five of us talked long past midnight in Hitler's compartment, helping ourselves from a large basket of apples, oranges, and bananas. There were also sandwiches and bottled water. It was plain that the Fuehrer and his entourage were used to travelling in comfort.

Hitler was in an optimistic and expansive mood, based apparently on a positive conviction that he was to be chancellor of the Reich, and some day President.

"Oh, no," he said, "chancellor or President, I don't intend to be treated like a glass doll packed in cotton-wool, riding only in special trains at fixed times -" And here he got up, again the perfect mime, and advanced on Schaub in a take-off of the typical German station-master, red-capped and moustachioed, coming to pay his respects to a Travelling Personage. "Watched and guarded all the time-mustn't do this, mustn't do that-oh, no, not for me. I'll keep on doing as I please." His pleasures, he said, were too precious to him-motoring, flying, going places and seeing people, and always returning to his retreat in the mountains, his little chalet on the Obersalzberg between Berchtesgaden and Salzburg, the only place where he felt really at home.

I said that I had never seen it. When, with Dietrich Eckart, I had visited the Platterhof, which lies a little higher on the Obersalzberg, Hitler had not owned Haus Wachenfeld,[1] then almost hidden in mountain woods.

"But you must come and see Haus Wachenfeld," said Hitler. "The autumn landscape is incomparably beautiful up there-a panorama that fairly carries you away."

As usual, the mention of Dietrich Eckart, who had first discovered the Platterhof, the old farmstead which became a refuge for many Nazis in times of persecution, filled the Fuehrer with sentiment. "I'll set up a beautiful monument to him between the Platterhof and Haus Wachenfeld, on the hill he loved so dearly and where he finally died, broken-hearted and alone … His Lorenzaccio is a glorious poem … Some day I'll build a theatre to carry his name- 'Die Dietrich Eckart Buehne.'"

---

1 *Now completely rebuilt and called 'Der Berghof.'*

Then he told me about his police-dogs at Haus Wachenfeld-Blonda, Muck, and Wolf. Blonda was his special pet, and like a boy he imitated her wiles for wheedling favours from him.

During an evening in which he talked almost continuously without giving me even a moment of boredom, I kept sufficient detachment to observe the expertness with which Hitler created his effects-drawing forth details from a mind which had them ready in nice order, modulating his voice, using his body, his head, his hands, his mobile face. It was not so much conscious acting as the perfect co-ordination of impulse and expression, something that had become second nature with him as a result of his many years before the public. Even in this intimate and cozy moment, I sensed no attitude of familiarity towards him on the part of his staff; there was always a certain distance about him, that subtle quality of aloofness which unquestionably contributes to his unusual ability to deal with individuals. It is one of the gifts of a statesman.

That gift was neatly in evidence towards me on the way from Berlin to Munich. While he seemed entirely unconstrained, and I had the reassuring feeling that nothing I had said in Berlin had seriously annoyed him, he made not the slightest allusion that would have encouraged me to touch again on political matters. Wondering how much in earnest Hitler was about me, I found occasion to ask him whether I should take out my second papers in America, explaining that though I was still a German citizen, I had my first papers in the United States and was now eligible for full citizenship-in some ways a very desirable status.

"Better for you to remain German," he said. "Yes, I'm sure it's better, but I'll think it over."

When I left for my own compartment, a man followed me into the corridor to ask me to arrange a meeting for him with the pretty dancer of the afternoon. "But not a word to--" and he pointed over his shoulder at the door behind which the Fuehrer might already be standing in his unmentionables.

While I was silently preparing for bed, careful not to disturb my fellow passenger-a Jew, and a very fat one-I was amused to observe that he was wide awake and covertly watching me in the mirror. What a story he would have to tell about his night ride from Berlin to Munich-a Nazi under him, doubtless a brutal bodyguard, and Hitler almost within reach of his hand, only a thin panel between him and the Haman of the German people!

I had already subsided into my lower berth when there came a gentle knock at the door. I reached out and opened it to find Schaub's grinning face.

"Sie haben eine gute Nummer bei Hitler -"

"Sssh!" I motioned toward the berth above me, and with my forefinger described a reversed six over my nose. Schaub began to flounder in an embarrassed undertone. "You didn't come in here to flatter me," I whispered.

"What did you really want to say? Out with it!"

"She had her eye more on me than on -. I'm certain of it-he can't fool me. I must meet her, even if it costs me two bottles of champagne."

I promised to help him, privately resolving to do them both the same good turn. Hitler, once Chancellor, would not be easy to reach. These two men would be able to take things to him directly, without red-tape, and from them I might be able to hear things I could not learn otherwise.

When we parted in the morning at the Munich station, Hitler told me to meet him at Amann's office. "And about your American citizenship-I've thought it over. You'd better remain German."

Two hours later, when I reached Amann's office, my good Ludwig told me that Hitler was already inside with the boss. He emerged pushing a bundle of miscellaneous papers into the inside pocket of his suit. Seeing me in the ante-room, he came up, beating the inevitable dog-whip against the equally inevitable raincoat.

"It's all settled. Arrange the details with Amann. I'll talk to Schwarz today or tomorrow, but I doubt if we can get money from him now-we'll need every penny for the campaign. However, I'll try, and let you know. You're at the Continental, I suppose? We'll get together soon and continue our talk of the Kaiserhof. Gruess Gott!"

I called after him: "Herr Hitler, what about the credentials? Are you going to sign them?"

"Oh, no, not I." He shook his head vigorously. "No signatures from me for anybody any more. Amann and Rosenberg will tend to that. I must run now. Auf Wiedersehen."

Amann was again affability itself, and amazed me by agreeing at once to pay me three months in advance. He would draw up a regular contract, and arrange for a permit to take money out of Germany; Rosenberg would sign the necessary credentials. But he did not offer me immediate cash, and so I was obliged to turn to Rosenberg, for whom I had often done as much in the old days.

I had luck getting Roehm. He arranged for us to meet quietly in his flat, and we had two long talks. Not having met for seven years, we had much to tell each other, and we quickly hit the old tone. Besides our old acquaintanceship and the fact that we were about of an age, we had a new common ground of sympathy: each of us had been abroad, and coming home had found things different.

Roehm was a little stouter, the lines in his battered face a little deeper. Outwardly he had changed but slightly, yet his demeanour was not quite the same. He was a little less definite, less positive, less sure of himself than I remembered him. His judgment was still sound, his mind still showed the realist, with a wide grasp of things; in certain aspects, he had grown. He still had his poise and his winning personality. But there was something vaguely disturbing. Perhaps the vicious attacks on him had sickened his healthy ego, perhaps the tarnish on his reputation had eaten too deeply. It was as if a sense of guilt hovered over his countenance, which now and then looked forced. I had the feeling too that something of the politician had crept over him.

"Yes, in a way I loved being in La Paz. It was most interesting, but terribly lonesome. I was unbelievably bored at times-you know those parts of the world. Naturally, I was only too glad to accept Hitler's proposition, though it meant I was to be only second-fiddle."

When we touched on recent developments and the current crisis, we found ourselves speaking the same language, and I no longer hesitated to lay my cards on the table. I told him in detail of my conference with Hitler. Even though I could see that I was touching a raw surface, I didn't mince words when I voiced my impression.

Roehm, because of his absence in Bolivia, was not familiar with the pamphlet and manifesto issued by Otto Strasser for the Schwarze Front after the latter's break with Hitler.

"Read it now," I said. "I don't subscribe to everything in it, by any means. But I want your reaction."

He read it, shaking his head now and then, and I asked him point-blank if he too accepted the principle that the Idea must always stand higher than the Leader, who personifies that idea only so long as he is the servant of it.

" If we put the leader above the idea," I said, " we declare his infallibility-and I for my part must decline to do that just as I reject, in accordance with the Nazi concept, the infallibility of the Pope."

"Of course I agree with you," said Roehm, without hesitation. "That's common sense, and certainly true Teutonic-Rosenberg would say Nordic-thinking. I don't see how Hitler can seriously object to it. Yet he does-and Otto Strasser's report looks genuine to me because Hitler's answers are so characteristic of him. Note where Hitler says, for example: You wish to give every Party member the right to judge the idea, the right even to judge whether or not the leader is faithful to this so-called idea. That is the worst sort of democracy, for which with us there is no place. With us Leader and Idea are one, and every Party member must obey the command of the leader, who incorporates the idea and alone knows the goal.'

"Now that's a very clever but superficial and false interpretation of Strasser's very clear statement. Of course Hitler wants to see it that way. You're absolutely right-by no deed or accomplishment has Hitler proved that he's worthy of the unlimited confidence we give him so blindly."

He paused, and when he went on his voice was shaking: "It's also true, and I admit it to my shame, that the vulnerability you mentioned has delivered me into his hands.

It's a terrible thing ... I've lost my independence for always ... You know as well as I do how Hitler can wear you down-he's incomparable in the art of making people believe in him. Now the situation is such that there's none among us who would dare throw the truth in his face, defy him openly, and fight it out. . . . And we, we ourselves, have made him what he is.... my position is so precarious I can't be too exigent; I'm becoming more and more an ostrich with my head in the sand. I stick to my job, following him blindly, loyal to the utmost-there's nothing else left me. It's wrong, I know, and believe me, I suffer under it. We do strange things sometimes to escape from ourselves."

I was by now almost as moved as Roehm was, but dared not let him survey his own wreckage too long. I said firmly that there was a way out if he would only use his power for the good of the cause. Briefly I outlined my now familiar basic course for our domestic and foreign policy. Roehm steadied and became alert, arguing a point here and there, but in the main agreeing.

"Of course I expected a showdown after the thirteenth of August," he said, in answer to my question. "But my hands are tied-now I'm only a soldier who obeys. I must confess that Hitler didn't find it hard to persuade me to his course, though I had a tough time keeping my men in check.

"What worries me as much as anything," he continued, "is that Hitler really is no executive. He hates details now as much as he always did, but they're damnably

Hitler on the speaker's platform at Nuremberg. He is accompanied by Ernst Roehm, who was destined to fall victim during the Night Of The Long Knives. Ludecke dedicated this book to the memory of Roehm.

important. The truth is that he's incapable of them; only when it's a question of outright propaganda or when his immediate interests are involved does he look after details himself. In everything else it's still the same 'Oesterreichische Scblamperei'! I wonder how that same Austrian sloppiness is going to show up when he's Chancellor."

Roehm's old spirit seemed to be coming alive as he talked.

"For ten years Hitler's been striving to build up political credit. He knows only too well that the more effective the propaganda and the more sensational the publicity, the better the credit. But when he should have proved what he could do with it, he failed-in November 1923, as well as August 1932. Nothing but words, and yet millions of hearts beat for him-fantastically enough, he's still my only hope.

"Never did a man have better material to work with!" Roehm's eyes were burning with pride now. "Look at the Nazi Youth, the SA, the SS-splendid stuff, ready to fight, to die, to conquer! And now he asks them to fight with the ballot again! Instead of giving us the order to march, Hitler makes us wade into the morass of parliamentarianism. He's taken so much out of Mussolini's book-why can't he imitate his March on Rome? And they praise his 'legality' as a ruse, as clever strategy! He tells you he needs Hindenburg's prestige. What a farce! As if foreign correspondents and diplomats didn't know what a putrid role Hindenburg's playing!...

"Oh, but what's the use of talking! There's nobody to replace Hitler, even less now than in 1924. We can't do without him, but something ought to be done. If I could see a way out, I wouldn't hesitate. What have you to propose?"

There must be no question of deposing Hitler, I said, even if we had power to do so; it would be a stupid and difficult thing to tear him down after doing so much to build him up. But if Hitler made mistakes, there must be some way to stop him should he refuse to listen to reason. Admitted that we couldn't do without him-he also couldn't do without us, and must be as loyal to us as we were to him. Two things needed to be determined: what course Hitler should adopt if his present one was wrong, and what to do to make him change. Then, satisfied that Roehm had accepted the logic of facts, I let him have it.

"I see only one combination that can force the issue-you and Strasser."

"But, mein Lieber," said Roehm, "that won't work. Don't you know that Strasser is now very much opposed to me? Even if I were willing to ally myself with him, he wouldn't be, I'm sure."

"But it's worth trying," I pleaded. "You're chief of staff of the SA and SS, Gregor Strasser heads the political organization for the whole Reich. You must get together. By God, if you're willing, I'll take care of Strasser-I'll bring you together. Will you give it a try?"

"You're asking a great deal of me." Roehm spoke slowly. "But you're right: Strasser is the only one with real power, the only one who doesn't depend on Hitler's favour.

Moreover, he's got no weak spot - Hitler can't pick a hole in him and drop him like an old shoe. Yes, we two together could swing it."

He said no more for a moment, and I knew that he had silently weighed and accepted the risk to himself when he added quietly: "I'm ready to go ahead with it, but I'm afraid Strasser won't be."

Our time was up, and we agreed to go into practical details at our next meeting. When I turned to go, Roehm showed himself in a characteristic moment. "But what about yourself, in the meantime?" he said. "You're probably travelling on your own purse, as usual, and more than likely a little short. I'd be only too glad to help you out."

That touched me. I told him I had all I needed until Amann should come through. But Roehm was the only Nazi leader who had been considerate enough to think of that. "You'd think that Hitler or Rosenberg might. But no-I had to ask Rosenberg for some."

He laughed. "Well, don't hesitate to call on me. And don't forget that Amann's also given to sudden lapses of memory. Amnesia is a well-developed art with us, ready for use at a moment's notice. Get what's coming to you and get it quickly-that's my advice."

Between my two talks with Roehm I did not see Hitler. On the nineteenth, as I later learned, he had made a mad dash to Vienna on a sudden impulse to visit Geli's grave. I met Roehm for the second time some afternoon before the twenty-fifth, and we worked out a definite plan. I was to approach Strasser at once. If I succeeded, we three were to get together and put a binding agreement on paper. On the strength of that, we were to plead our cause before Hitler. Should he, against our expectation and against all reason, meet our frank approach with a flat refusal to explain his intentions, or reject our programme in toto and fail to convince us that his course was better, we would break with him at once and put the whole question before the Party and the German people.

These were to be the basic points of our programme:

1. Immediate mobilization of every force and potentiality for revolutionary action before the election on November 6. (Roehm was convinced that a revolution was feasible, and that the Reichswehr, having everything to gain from a Hitler regime, would declare fur us rather than against us.)

2. Possible deposition of Hindenburg in favour of Hitler.

3. A balanced policy of social revolution, liquidation of Versailles, rapid rearming.

4. Immediate organization of a foreign office of the Party, and an attempt at rapprochement with Soviet Russia.

If I had been undecided before, I would have felt myself compelled to try to bring matters to a head, whatever the cost, when Roehm said soberly:

"Practically and technically, for military, political, and economic reasons, it will take at least three and probably four years for Germany to regain full sovereignty and an adequate condition for defence. And it will take five and more likely six years to prepare Germany for an offensive campaign against Russia. And even so, we would have not a ghost of a chance with a hostile France at our back and England cutting us off from war materials. It's doubtful if even an alliance with Japan and Italy would give us victory. Of course, there's the hoped-for possibility that Russia, attacked on two fronts, would collapse. But who can tell about Russia? How many times a Bolshevik collapse has been predicted within the last fifteen years-and today the Soviets are stronger than ever!

"There may be many details I don't know, but believe me, while we're working feverishly the general staffs in Paris, London, and Moscow aren't asleep. If you'd care to, you might have a talk with X,[2] who keeps me au courant. He'd be interested. In his opinion, an alliance with Russia is a life-or-death matter-he's certainly no friend of Rosenberg's.

"Even with new inventions and the improvement in transportation facilities, Russia would always have the advantage of the inner line, whereas we'd constantly be moving away from our bases, and Japan would even have to cross a sea-let alone the fact that we'd first have to beat Poland or Czechoslovakia to get at Russia. No, it would be sheer insanity, so long as there's the slightest chance of coming to an understanding with ' Russia."

When all the important points were settled, we pledged absolute secrecy. I was to talk with Gregor Strasser as if I had not approached Roehm-a necessary precaution in case Strasser should prove unwilling. If Strasser acceded, Roehm strongly advised that I become Strasser's chief of staff, replacing Dr. Glaser. That would bring Dr. Ley and Schulz under control and guarantee effective collaboration between Strasser and himself.

These two meetings with Roehm will always live in my memory. I honour the man-he was a soldier and a man of his word.

It was the day after my second conference with Roehm that I sat down with Strasser in Berlin.

What I was trying to do, if successful, might have reversed developments entirely and brought about a political world constellation vastly different from the one we see today. And yet, looking back now on those burning hours, it is hard to know what really prompted me to it. Certainly I wasn't taking the risk to fatten my ego. Was it out of genuine conviction that Hitler was wrong, resentment at his spoiling my cherished picture of a German revolution, hidden ambition to elevate myself in the belief that I might not do worse than others? Probably it was, more than anything else, the Nazi complex for saving the world.

_____

2 A higher officer in the general staff, whom I cannot name, for obvious reasons.

Strasser and I clearly were not cut from the same wood, and an observer-if there had been one-would probably have found the two of us amusing. I simply can't eat when I am excited. But Strasser, whenever we got together, would settle down in his jovial way and have something to eat and drink, a habit that was beginning to tell on the circumference of his limbs. On this occasion, while I was playing all the tunes in my register, assaulting him with cold reason or trying to topple him over with impassioned pleading, the gemuetliche Bavarian calmly went on swallowing Schnapps. The man simply was not to be jolted out of his composure. .

We argued it hither and yon, uselessly. Strasser turned me down flat.

"You're right on many points-on most points, if you like. But I cannot do what you ask. Even if I were able to bring myself to join forces with Roehm, I couldn't do it now. It's too late; two weeks earlier I might have considered it. Of course we can't do without Hitler-that goes without saying. Certain things need to be changed: he must be made to listen to us when he's wrong. But I doubt very much if the way you propose would solve the problem for good. Roehm is too much involved with Hitler. What if he had to choose between Hitler and me? I'd be left in the lurch. I cannot take that chance so long as there's another possibility which I'm sure will work better than your plan, without the same risk."

He took a good swig and went on.

"Don't fancy for one second that Hitler would ever forgive us this. He simply can't be wrong-he's crazy on that subject. He'd never willingly submit himself to permanent control at the first opportunity he'd heave Roehm or me overboard. Or Roehm might become too powerful, which would be equally bad. Besides, Hitler still can have fits, you know. What if he should tear the Party to pieces? Or what if he really did commit suicide? Probably it's only theatricals-yet he's incalculable as far as his own person is concerned."

"Are you telling me that Hitler has actually been threatening suicide?"

"Yes, just the other day.[3] We can't afford that," said Strasser. "At least not now," he added ironically.

These hints of things hidden maddened me. "For heaven's sake, can't you tell me what you're up to? I've looked at this question from every possible angle, but I can't read riddles. Won't you give me at least an inkling?"

Strasser had a last pull at his glass. "Rather not talk about it," he finally said, and leaned back in his chair, stretching his legs, folding his arms over his rounded belly, and belching out of sheer well-being. "But don't worry, you'll know in due time. It's as good as certain that Schleicher is going to drop Papen and make Hitler chancellor. You can see that Roehm doesn't fit into that picture. And that's all I can

---

3 There are other testimonials to occasional threats of suicide on Hitler's part, threats perhaps genuine, perhaps calculated. Goebbels' published diary reports another one on December 8th, 1932, after Strasser's resignation.

tell you for the moment."

"Do you mean to say that you are trusting Schleicher?" "Keine Sorge, mein Lieber," said Strasser, with all the assurance in the world. "I'll see to that. And believe me, there'll be no Goebbels in that cabinet. Goering might get the Air Ministry, as Hitler said, but that's about all."

It was plain that I might as well give it up, and I said so. "Frankly, I'm not at all thrilled, and you'll forgive me if I'm still sceptical. You won't even talk to Roehm before it's too late?"

"Nothing doing, and don't insist-I know what I'm up to. I'm not so crazy as to compromise myself with Roehm at this stage. What if he should talk? Anyway, why should I confer with him when I don't need him? He'd only be in the way. No, mein Lieber, knock that idea out of your head for good and all."

He'd done a very thorough job of knocking it out himself, I said. "But it would be a good thing if you'd stay here," Strasser said amiably. "Things will come to a head soon after the elections-only a few weeks longer. Then you can have everything you want. I think you'd do very well at the head of a foreign office. Rosenberg has no push, he's not a practical man and we all know it. He'd make a better Kultur-Minister and director of spiritual education in the Party-if he'll only learn to face facts."

There was no need of my hurrying off to Washington, I admitted, but at least it was something definite. Who would pay my bills if I stayed?

"Why not take the money from Amann and stay? It would be perfectly all right with me. By God, the Party owes you enough; you've gone it entirely on your own up to now," he rumbled stoutly.

Well and good, I agreed, if everything turned out as he expected; but if it didn't, I'd be the culprit. In any event, it would be taking money under false pretences. "No, I've a better suggestion. I'll stay if you install me in your organization."

"As what?"

"Don't you think I'd do as well as Dr. Glaser? In fact, I think I'd make a better chief of staff."

Strasser was staring at me in amazement. I had finally jarred him.

"Chief of Staff? You're crazy! Hitler wouldn't understand-he'd see through everything. That would be a dangerous step. That would be the wrong way to show Hitler who his true friends are."

"A matter of opinion," I said. "You appoint me, I'll do the rest. I swear to you we'll see the thing through then."

"Impossible," he growled. "There's Ley and Schulz to be considered, and you're practically unknown in the Party."

I argued that I didn't want to be put in the limelight. My appointment could be made quietly, as an inner Party matter. It would be enough if I became known to every one of his men by being with him during the campaign. There were stormy times and plenty of trouble ahead of us, and Strasser would need a man who wasn't afraid to go the limit.

"How many deputies, how many district-leaders can you count on?" I insisted.

"Well over a hundred deputies, and some of the best district-leaders," Strasser said, beguiled in spite of himself. "I'm also on good terms with the SA, and Himmler of the SS is my friend, as you know-it's I who made him." Then he stiffened.

"But what are you driving at? Useless to talk about it-I'll never lend my hand to break up the Party-I'll never betray Hitler and-"

"That's just it-and Hitler knows it!" I shouted in exasperation. "Who's asking you to break up the Party? Who's asking you to betray Hitler? It's only a question of making him do the right thing. You can be sure he'll yield if we go about it the right way. And if he doesn't, it's better to break up the Party than have him betray the cause and all of us!"

Strasser was up on his feet now, speechless, dislodged from his Ruhe at last.

"You're a dangerous fellow!" he finally bellowed. "Here I'm calmly awaiting developments, and you have to blow in to disturb my peace! It sounds good, but it can't be done. Maybe you can do these bold things in America, but not here-and that's final!"

Then, never ungemuetlich for long, he relented.

"I'll tell you what I'll do, if you can't stay in Germany. I'll keep in touch with you and the moment things are ripe here I'll cable you. I'll need you then-my position towards Hitler will then be a stronger one."

Cryptic still. But that about ended this conference. We discussed a few matters, and then pledged each other to absolute secrecy regarding our talk. I, of course, had to give my promise with a secret mental reservation: I would have to make my doleful report to Roehm.

XXVII

FAREWELL DEFERRED

The Reichstag restaurant at lunch-time next day was a busy place. Things were fairly buzzing everywhere, except at the table where Count Reventlow, Alfred Rosenberg, Arno Schickedanz, and I were sitting.

I had been too sure of Strasser-so sure, that I had arranged this lunch to bring Reventlow and Rosenberg together, in the hope that they would make a start toward reconciling their widely divergent views on our future Eastern policy. It had seemed to me intolerably stupid for these two potential moulders of Nazi foreign relations to go on stubbornly avoiding each other instead of trying to find a basis for co-operation. I had thought, moreover, that this lunch might get us somewhere in the organizing of a real Nazi foreign office.

But having failed so dismally as a marriage-broker for Strasser and Roehm, I could no longer see any point in trying to heat up a Rosenberg-Reventlow courtship. No sense in burning my fingers at this stage. Now that I was to leave Germany, it seemed wiser to let things ride and wait until Strasser was ready.

Thus our lunch was inconsequential, and uninteresting save for the amusement of watching the two Nazi diplomats. They knew perfectly well why I had brought them together. The reserved Count and the Balt showed each other the utmost consideration. But I had resolved to make no effort to steer the conversation, and so these two latent rivals sat stiffly and made dull talk about insignificant things. I could only think of two cats circling warily about a too-hot dish of pap, each with a watchful eye on the other.

Later, when I was alone with Reventlow, who looked almost pathetically ludicrous in brown shirt and black civilian trousers, without a jacket, I remarked on the meagre outcome of the Party.

"After all, you can't expect me to begin it," said the Count in his demurely acid way. "When Rosenberg was penning his first articles in awkward German, I already had grey hair."

I admitted sourly that while I had perhaps hoped for it, I hadn't expected it. "But if you won't take the initiative, I don't see how you can do the things you want to do and which your experience entitles you to. That lunch was typical for me of how little common sense even the highest figures in the Party can show."

"Well, it's no wonder," said Reventlow, unruffled. "You can't blame the novices when the High Priest sets the example. Some time ago I wrote to Hitler about an important matter and didn't get so much as an acknowledgment. He knows my address, he can find me if he wants to-but he prefers subaltern creatures around him. If he's so sure of becoming Chancellor, I'm not so sure that he'll fill the bill. My God, Hitler can't govern - he can't sit still behind a desk and work steadily for two hours!"

Once more I was on the night express to Munich, feeling thoroughly deflated now, but never dreaming that this might be my last trip to the gay city on the Isar. Oberleutnant Paul Schulz, Strasser's intimus, was on the train, and we talked until after midnight. I studied this stocky man, so quiet and self-controlled, with low forehead and sharply jutting nose. Here were character and determination, something strong and something secretive, and that indescribable look that lives in the eyes of men who have suffered for years in prison.

During the war Schulz had been one of the very few German privates to become an officer for extraordinary bravery in the face of the enemy. He had been one of the principal organizers of the Black Reichswehr. He had spent five long years in a lonely cell under sentence of death, until the untiring protests of the Nationalists had at last extracted his release from Hindenburg. He had immediately joined the Nazis. Death relaxed its vigilance for a while, to make another snatch at him in the massacre of the Blood-Purge.

Through all our casual talk I could see the man behind bars; five years under the constant threat of death would either drive a man crazy or harden him for anything. And this one was impenetrable, though I tried to get some idea of the extent to which Strasser might be under his influence! Without stinting criticism of conditions in the Party and around the Fuehrer, he really committed himself in no way, except to show outspoken opposition to Roehm, for personal and practical reasons.

No word or gesture betrayed knowledge of my last interview with Gregor Strasser, and I was glad that Strasser's mouth was tight.

Roehm was deeply disappointed by my news. Of necessity, I had to give him half-truths, for the whole story of my interview with Strasser would have made the mess complete. I merely said that Strasser, though at first receptive, had told me that he would never lend his hand to a coup which might disrupt the Party. When I had insisted on discussing it, he had blown up and as much as advised me to mind my own business, then had relented and told me that he had his own plan, which he could not reveal - something that would assure the Chancellorship for Hitler much sooner and without risk to Party morale. And, of course, I had been careful not to reveal to Strasser the fact that Roehm had already been approached.

"I wonder what he's up to," Roehm mused. "I'll bet the fool is staking everything on Schleicher-the good Strasser is overrating himself. It's the old story of shifting the responsibility, just as Hitler does. These men don't know what they hold in their hands! Now I suppose all we can do is sit on our hams and wait. You had me so convinced that I'd already put down on paper, to the very last detail, a plan for the mobilization of six hundred thousand men at a moment's notice. Damn the politicians!"

We should have to wait, I agreed. But we must hold ourselves alert, and Roehm's hands were by no means tied; even alone he was a power. With a press bureau and a newspaper, he had the facilities for launching, somewhere outside Germany, an article pointing out signs of a reorientation in Nazi foreign policy and of rapprochement with Soviet Russia. If it were to emanate ostensibly from 'Warsaw, for example, it would make news throughout the world and perhaps lure Hitler into thinking things over.

Roehm liked the idea, and suggested that I stay and do the trick. "Why not head my press bureau? Dr. Scholz, who has it now, was one of your men back in 1923 - Reiner[1] told me so just the other day. It's not an important job, but you could make it one, and you'd be at hand when we're ready for other things."

It was too late, I said. I had got my money for Washington from Amann just that morning, and my credentials from Rosenberg.

"But you ought to stay," Roehm insisted. "Something could be arranged. Of course there's always Hitler to reckon with. He might smell the roast-he's uncanny sometimes. But that would be my worry. What if Strasser comes a cropper and makes a mess of things? Hitler will jump at the chance to get rid of him - I know he's afraid of him. With Strasser out of the way, Hitler can do what he likes with the Party, and then we will be in the soup. Hang on at least until after the election - on any pretext ! "

With Strasser and Roehm both urging me, I should have contrived somehow to remain in Germany; I am convinced now that I committed one of the great stupidities of my life. I do not delude myself into thinking that I could have altered the course of events - and who can say what the effect on my personal fortunes would have been? Yet I should have held on. Instinct told me to stay, reason to go - and it is probably instinct that keeps a man from missing his life's historical moment.

Next morning I visited Hitler in his luxurious, modern flat of eight or nine beautiful, large rooms covering the entire second floor of 16 Prinzregentenplatz, in one of the better sections of the outer city. His body-guard was quartered somewhere on the ground floor. The same Frau Winter who had looked after him in the Thierschstrasse was now keeping house for him; his sister was spending most of her time at Haus Wachenfeld.

While Hitler was showing me round, I thought, and perhaps he did, of his admiring envy back in 1922 when he had come from his hall-bedroom to visit me in my modest studio apartment. This flat showed for pure legend the idea that

---

1 Rudolf Reiner, Roehm's adjutant, also murdered in the Blood-Purge.

Hitler was still living simply. The furniture had been designed by Ludwig Troost, the architect of the Braunes Haus, and Hitler would not have accepted such a service for nothing, since he always made a point of refusing important gifts. It was legend likewise that he still lived exclusively on his earnings as a writer. He had a fleet of private cars at his disposal; his petrol and travel bills were always paid by his adjutant, Brueckner, out of an expense account provided by Party funds. Though occasionally he kept to second or third-rate hostelries, endeared to him from the old days, for the most part he stayed at first-class hotels.

In 1932, this was also the scale of living of all the important Nazi leaders-a striking contrast to what I had seen in 1925 and even in 1930. Now they all had chauffeurs, orderlies, body-guards, and huge cars, representing the most powerful party in Germany in truly grand style. Schwarz evidently kept a tight grip on the purse-strings except for the expense accounts of the higher-ups.

Nazi Germany, like Soviet Russia, points pridefully to the frugality of its officials, to their low salaries, to the fact that a Secretary of State gets only a hundred a month. But flats, dinners, automobiles, travel, sanitariums, all go on the accommodating expense account. 'That irritated me then was not this system-for indeed most of these men worked like slaves, and amply earned their keep - but the hypocrisy of all the talk about Spartanism, folkic simplicity, and self-discipline. Hitler doesn't eat meat, drink, or smoke, but his vegetables are the very choicest and are fastidiously prepared, and in his rooms there are always dishes of the choicest fruit, of the varieties that are far more expensive in Germany than meat.

With visible pride, Hitler conducted me to his library, an attractive, cosy room, lined With several thousand books, many of them gifts, ranged in built-in bookshelves. I was delighted when, leading me straight to a section filled with atlases, geographies, and travel books, he pointed out the inscribed copy of Ashwell's World Routes that I had sent him from New York. "I'm told this is a very fine job of editing. However did you do it? I wouldn't have credited you with the patience to deal with so much detail." He waved me on into his study, a room which, despite its simple and practical furnishings, somehow reminded me of a college-bay's study fitted out by rich parents.

" Perhaps playing chess and those months in jail taught me to be patient when I must," I replied. "I wish you were able to read English. I hear that Mussolini has improved his German considerably, and even has a working knowledge of English now. It would be a great advantage to you if-"

"No use," Hitler interrupted me, cutting the air with his hand. "I've tried, but I can't do it-I've no language sense."

We sat down near the window. "I'm glad everything's settled for you," he said. "I suppose you're ready, to leave for Washington. Sorry I couldn't do more for you" - and he rubbed his thumb briskly against his first two fingers, in international sign-language - "but Schwarz said it was impossible. After the election I'll see to it that you get what you need."

When I touched again on the scope of my work in Washington and again tried to pin him to something specific, he waved his hand and made a characteristic remark. "Ludecke, bear in mind that I have an old principle: only to say what must be said to him who must know it, and only when he must know it." And he gazed at me with that odd look of remoteness which baffles many people who talk with him.

"After all, you know what it's all about," he added. "We must gain time but not lose a minute. You've good judgment - stick to what I said the other day; it's the best line to take. We want peace, but Versailles must be wiped out. We're the last stand against Bolshevism, and that practically covers everything - other matters will come of themselves. As for the rest, be a conciliating influence, when you must, without committing yourself. Of course, things will change when I'm in command - I'll let off a propaganda campaign such as the world has never seen - and then you can come to me with proposals. To talk about it now is just a waste of time."

"I understand perfectly. The moment you're Chancellor we'll have a completely new situation, and I'll catch the first boat to remind you of what you're saying now. At least, I hope you'll give me the opportunity to do that."

Hitler laughed. "You never miss a trick, do you? But - I'll see you - never fear."

I produced a memorandum on Poland, 'The Danger in the East,' which Rosenberg had given me for guidance. I had read it only the evening before. It affirmed the necessity of doing away with the eastern boundary limit set up for Germany by the Treaty of Versailles, and declared that the age-old German room-problem would have to be solved in that direction.

"Would you like to look it over?" I asked Hitler. He took it and began to scan it rapidly Of course I was trying once more to get clear in my mind the puzzle of his attitude toward Rosenberg. A certain coolness had arisen between them, I knew- but was it fundamental or superficial,or perhaps purely personal? By this time, my observation had led me to believe that it was personal, in this sense:

National Socialism, as a movement of protest, had become a clearing-house for various widely divergent philosophies of discontent, and among them, Rosenberg's ideology represented the aristocratic principle in National Socialism. In reality he was seeking a Nazi ethic. Hitler's temperament, his contempt for the mass, naturally brought him closer to Rosenberg and his conception of government by elite than to Feder, the other outstanding Nazi philosopher, and his socialistic interpretation of National Socialism. In 1923, Hitler had often said in private talks: 'I shall never give in to the street.' But even while he was in prison in Landsberg, he had begun to give in. Willing by now to employ any and every weapon in his fight for power, he presumably was finding less discomfort in the company of men like Goering and Goebbels, who had no scruples, than in that of Rosenberg, the unyielding fundamentalist. And the Balt, who saw everything, doubtless realized that he was now giving Hitler a sort of spiritual nervous indigestion. For Rosenberg was an uncompromising critic; he took Feder with a grain of salt, and was no great admirer of the Hitler intellect. I recalled his condescending appraisal of Hitler's Mein Kampf: 'A freshly written book.'

Hitler handed the memorandum back to me. 'All in order. Everybody knows that we can never renounce our claims in the East. Poland has just as little right to existence as Czechoslovakia."

"Well and good-but Poland is the ally of France. Perhaps we're disposed to be a little less noisy about Poland?"

"Aeh, diese dreckigen Polacken - mit denen werden wir schon Schlitten fahren!

"So Hitler was planning to take the 'dirty Polacks' for a sleigh-ride. That didn't sound as if he and Rosenberg were far apart in questions of foreign policy, and I decided to explore ·no further in that direction. (And yet, when the Fuehrer was Chancellor, under pressure from Pilsudski he made a pact with Poland renouncing vital German territory in the East and recognizing the Polish Corridor - a humiliating blow to German pride, and a renunciation which would have thrown Hitler himself into fits of the most violent and hysterical flagellation if it had been authored by anybody else.)

Once established in Washington, it would be necessary, I said, for me to make a special effort to keep in touch with developments; there was no Party bureau adequately equipped to look out for me, Rosenberg being so overburdened with work.

"It's too bad," said Hitler, "that you're also in wrong with Hanfstaengl." He laughed. "You know Hanfstaengl has always considered himself the expert on America, and when he heard that you were going to Washington, he threw his arms in the air and said: 'What! That Hochstapler ?'. . .

Since 'Hochstapler' can be translated with fair accuracy as 'four-flusher,' I was nettled. "I know Hanfstaengl's supposed to be very amusing," I said, "and I can well imagine him waving his arms like semaphores-but the fellow's beginning to get on my nerves.

"Well, you should know him by this time," I said. "I'd be perfectly willing to co-operate with him, but I don't see any possibility of it so long as Rosenberg-"

"Ach, Rosenberg!" Hitler interrupted. He must have seen my own eyes widen at this revelation of feeling, for he exclaimed, half-annoyed, half-amused: "What's the matter with you? Has Amann infected you, perhaps? You know, he once couldn't bear the sight of Rosenberg, but now he flies into the air red as a turkey if I say one tiny word against him. Of course," he hastened to add, " I appreciate Rosenberg very much."

But I had seen the flash of resentment. At that moment Schaub came in to remind Hitler that it was after one o'clock, and others were waiting for him. He excused himself, asking me to come to see him in the afternoon at the Braunes Haus.

Wanting to get some books for Hitler that would relax his mind, I taxied to the Odeonsplatz. I liked my final choice: German translations of Sterne's incomparable Tristram Shandy and Sentimental Journey, and of the hilarious Mon Oncle Benjamin, by Claude Tillier. Then I strolled leisurely to the casino of the Braunes Haus to join Brueckner and a few others for lunch. Among the guests was Schwede, the giant, blond Burgermeister of Coburg, the first Nazi mayor in Germany and a master-machinist by profession. He told us with the greatest enthusiasm of his colossal preparations for the coming Coburg celebration, and I was more than ever sorry that I had booked my passage and would have to miss it all.

The Fuehrer came in late, looking very preoccupied, and restraint fell over the table. He ate hurriedly and said little. The moment he left, reminding me to come upstairs to his study later, the jollity welled up again. Few people ever seem really at ease in Hitler's presence.

When I was again sitting opposite him in his study, I took the plunge, fortified by the thought that he could not have forgotten the financial sacrifices I had made for the Party or the donations I had given him personally in the lean years. I told Hitler I was in a dilemma: I had been forced to borrow money to make this trip; the advance received from Amann was my allowance for October, November, and December, and did not cover my travelling expenses or my expenses in Germany. Hitler's friendly mien cooled visibly. He deplored again - this time in formal phrases - the scarcity of funds, and promised once more to see to it that I got more after the election. Then he took a thousand-mark note from his pocket and handed it to me with a significant look. Mon Dieu, I thought ruefully, scarcely boat-fare-what magnificence! But he autographed a copy of Mein Kampf for me, and gave me some photographs of himself.

The time for farewells seemed to have arrived, and I felt a strange jumble of emotions come over me, partly a sad, deep disillusionment, partly a resurgence of the old affection. Hitler too seemed genuinely moved, and his eyes were moist. With as much spontaneity as I had ever seen in him, he clasped my hand and asked if I were free to take a cup of tea with him. I was, of course, and as we walked downstairs and out of the Braunes Haus, I was acutely aware, in my emotionally sensitized state, of the extent to which all of his personnel idolized him. It was in the eyes of everyone we passed-a sense that this man was always superior to any situation, an embodiment of courage, of something indomitable, that inspired them all to zealous devotion despite his occasional terrific outbursts of temper. It was in the shining eyes of the office-girl who dashed up to the car after the driver had started the motor, laid a bundle at Hitler's feet, and said: "Herr Hitler, here's the rug you wanted - it came just a moment ago," and then scurried shyly away.

As usual, Hitler sat in the front seat beside the driver. He adores automobiles and knows everything about them, but told me regretfully that he dared not drive, for in case of accident he would be personally responsible. Systematically he was subduing everything to his plan, and I realized again how amazingly he had learned to discipline himself.

First we drove to the Mercedes branch works in the outskirts of Munich to inspect a 'special bargain' - a huge touring-car. Hitler's coming electrified the whole plant. Executives, clerks, mechanics, all eyed him with excitement and curiosity or with undisguised devotion, and he chatted good-naturedly with them, shaking hands here and there, intensely interested in everything.

Then we went on to the Carlton tea-room, the best place in town, patronized chiefly by English and American residents and travelling foreigners. Soon we were joined by Heinrich Hoffmann, the official Nazi photographer and Hitler's constant companion.

These two had met as early as 1920, when Hitler was still refusing to be photographed. Hoffmann had finally convinced him of the propaganda value of the camera. Since 1923, when he made the first official portrait of Hitler, he has taken literally thousands of pictures showing the Fuehrer in every sort of mood and situation when I had visited Hoffmann's office to choose from his files a collection of subjects for use in America, I had been amazed at the richness of his material; it was the unique story of the Nazi movement in photographs, from the very beginning. Hoffmann later made use of them in an excellent book of propaganda, The Triumph of the Will, with text by Baldur von Schirach, Hitler's protégé and the leader of the Hitler Youth.

Schirach, who is married to Hoffmann's only daughter, presently came into the tea-room with his wife, and they sat down at our table. Frau Schirach is a pretty, blue-eyed blonde with finely chiselled features in a serious face.

This seemed to me that day an oddly assorted little group - Hoffmann, a small, very agile man with piercing blue eyes and a sharp nose in a lean, intent visage; Schirach, tall and young, his aristocratic good looks somewhat marred by a low forehead; and Hitler, completely at ease and saying little plundering the pastry with great gusto, content to indulge his sweet tooth and his fondness for cakes and 'Mehlspeisen.' Relaxed as he was, he gave me the best opportunity to study the physical man since my return. He wore no jewellery, as always, and looked very neat and clean in his dark blue suit, which fitted him none too well. His once lean and serious face with its individual mouth was beginning to be caricatured by furrows along his nose and cheeks and by the start of pouches underneath eyes and chin. For the first time, I observed that he seldom shows his teeth, probably because they are bad; there are several prominent gold teeth that one never sees in photographs. And I noted especially that, contrary to the prevalent impression, he is not 'alpine' either in stature or head. He is narrow-faced, and dolichocephalic rather than brachicephalic.

The conversation was trivial until Schirach asked: "Herr Hitler, you're going to be in Potsdam Saturday evening, aren't you?" He was referring to the first great Hitler Youth Day, to be held in Potsdam on the first and second of October, with a parade and a review.

"No, that's out of the question," said Hitler. "I'm engaged -it can't be done."

Young Schirach's fresh, eager face sagged. Looking terribly upset, he began to plead. "But Herr Hitler, the whole programme is arranged, and you are expected- boys and girls from all over Germany, even Austria - I assure you you're scheduled to speak at eight in the evening in the Stadium ! "

"Very sorry, I can't, I tell you. And you must accustom yourself to putting on such things without me. I can't be everywhere." And Hitler shrugged his shoulders.

Poor Schirach made another try. "But please understand! There'll be forty-five thousand there-yes, that's the last report, forty-five thousand-but I expect far more than fifty thousand!"

"You and your fifty thousand !" Hitler, laughing now, was beginning to tease him. "You'll be lucky if fifteen thousand come."

"No, I swear it-we're sure of more than forty-five thousand, and thousands of' them are already on the road. They're coming from everywhere-by foot and by truck. Please think of the propaganda, the colossal propaganda-the opportunity for Hoffmann, the pictures he can take, showing the discipline, the enthusiasm, the racial quality of our youth! Marvellous propaganda, right at the doors of Berlin - 'fabelhaft'! You must come-it's so terribly important just before the election!"

That went home. Hitler's negative attitude changed to keen interest. "Na - when must I go, you-you tormentor?

"Schirach's troubled face brightened as if touched by the sun. "It's all set," he said eagerly. "If you leave tomorrow by motor you can make it easily. Those boys and girls are coming to see you-it will be the great day of their lives-boys and girls from every state, from every district, from every-"

"Yes, yes, from every town, every hamlet, every family," Hitler broke in amusedly, but obviously impressed by Schirach's enthusiasm and persistence. "Well, I'll go. I'll take the plane Saturday - that will give me one more day here."

We all protested. He must go by train or motor; flying was too dangerous now, in the autumn fogs and storms.

"All right, all right," Hitler gave in. "I'll go by motor, tomorrow. How about it, Ludecke - you ought to see that, too. It will be a sight worth seeing - give you something to write about in Washington. Come along!"

Of course I wanted to go. I accepted eagerly, our farewells again postponed. And everybody was happy except Frau Schirach, who still sat there listlessly playing with her handkerchief.

371

XXVIII

THE TEMPO TAKES ITS TOLL

S o I stayed over, and Spent a pleasant evening with Hoffmann. We had dinner and lots of fun at the Oktober-Wiese, the immense, two-week fair held every fall outside Munich. The October Fair is the greatest folk-festival in Germany, and probably the greatest in Europe. There is a colossal slaughtering of meat in preparation for it, a tremendous brewing of an especially potent beer. Mountains of food are consumed, dozens of kinds of sausages, thousands of chickens roasted in the open. There are carousals, fortune-tellers, shooting-games, side-shows, and circuses. Then is when the carefree Muenchner pawns his valuables, his bed if need be, and doesn't mind if his wife fails to sleep at home.

For this robust occasion Hoffmann was an ideal companion, humorous and amusing, a good story-teller, with plenty of what the Germans call 'mother-wit.' At Haus Wachenfeld, Kannenberg with his accordion and Hoffmann are said to be a team that can make Hitler laugh himself sick. I found plenty of horse-sense behind his jester's mask, however, and we had a rollicking time. I was sorry Hitler wasn't with us, for he adores this sort of thing.

Of course we talked of the Fuehrer, for Hoffmann probably sees more of him than anyone does. "Yes," he said, in answer to my question, "it looks as if Hitler were very kind, and in a way he is. But it's terribly difficult to work with him. He's constantly keyed up, constantly in tempo. You never know when he's going to dash off-and you with him, of course. Yes, he's kind to his people, but, in a way, utterly inconsiderate. None of us can have any other life-we must be forever at his disposal. Well, you'll have a taste of it tomorrow."

It was almost midnight when we returned to the city. We went to the Cafe Heck, in the Ludwigstrasse, where Hitler was spending the evening with his party. They were just leaving as we came in, but Hitler did not feel like ending the evening, and invited us all to his flat. "It's too early for bed," he said.

Captain Roehm was one of the few who begged to be excused. When we shook hands in a last good-bye on our way out to the street, we looked at each other soberly, and I felt that he was thinking with me of the water that would go over the dam before we should meet again.

"I'm sorry I can't stay," Roehm said, "but I've a lot to do-I'm leaving for Vienna early tomorrow. He's in form tonight, and it will be a long session."

Among the six or seven guests at Hitler's flat, I recall only Hoffmann, Adolf Wagner, now Bavarian Minister of the Interior, and Hitler's architect, Professor

Troost, now dead. I had a little tête-à-tête with the Professor in a corner of the library; I was interested to know what this academic, cultured man of late middle age, aside from his personal and professional sympathy for Hitlerism, thought of Hitler as a man. I told him that I had been surprised to discover that Hitler, who had never seen it, knew more about the lay-out and structure of the Pads Opera than I did myself, who had been inside it many times, and that he even had an architectural idea of Quebec and the Chateau-Frontenac.

"Yes, it's extraordinary," said Troost, "the scope of what he knows. I've found, for example, that his theoretical knowledge of architecture exceeds mine. He has a remarkable sense for effects, and his building plans are really gigantic. Let's hope that he'll soon be able to realize his great ambitions in this field as well."

We were cut short by the arrival of wine, coffee, sandwiches, 'and cakes, and we all settled down round Hitler, who had 'stretched himself in a chair near the window, obviously enjoying 'his role of host and master, with disciples at his feet.

Our talk ran on at random for a while, until I was able to tug it round to a subject I was much interested in. Something gave me occasion to remark that it was fortunate for the Nazi movement that it had been born in Catholic Bavaria, which was more Church-ridden than Protestant Prussia; it would have been harder to bring Bavaria into a racial movement which hadn't originated there. I was thinking of an article in which I had said that religious and social energy must be developed in equal strength in the German liberator, and I wanted to see how clearly Hitler was foreseeing the religious controversy that must inevitably come, and also to know what role he was going to play in it.

The Fuehrer took my bait and began to lecture rather professorially.

"Yes, it was indeed good fortune that National Socialism started in Black Bavaria, and that's why Munich will always remain the capital of the movement. Naturally, practical politics demands that, for the time being at least, we must avoid any appearance of a campaign against the Church." He was careful to emphasize again that he was a Politiker, with no ambition to become a prophet. But National Socialism, he said, was a weltanschauung and in fact a religion which was now building itself up and disseminating itself, except that its forms of activity and of propaganda were different. In ancient Rome, for example, Christianity had been able to mobilize masses in a way that the old polytheistic religions never could. "And now in turn," he added, "National Socialism is able to influence greater masses at once than the Church possibly can." By this time he was talking entirely to me; it is his habit to centre himself on one person when he gets warmed up. The others were listening intently enough except the good Hoffmann, who seemed slightly bored and had concentrated on the wine with such good effect that just about here he dumped the bottle over, and the precious liquid spilled over the priceless little table at his side and on to the priceless rug. Hitler stopped. He looked up frowning, lifting his shoulders in annoyance, but said nothing. There was an awkward silence, in which Hoffmann blushed like a child, mumbled something, and disappeared.

Hitler spoke at last. "Na-ach-where was I?" he said, snapping his fingers. "Oh, yes, Ludecke, if you want to see my meaning illustrated, you need only go to the funeral of a fallen Nazi and watch the Storm Troopers ranked about the grave. Watch their faces, blank while the priest is reading the service"-and here he stopped long enough to imitate a priest mumbling the litany, fingering an imaginary rosary, and spreading hands in blessing (an excellent performance, as always)-"and then see them light up when the Nazi leader lifts the flag and begins to speak words of flame over the dead.

"Yes, National Socialism is a form of conversion, a new faith, but we don't need to raise that issue-it will come of itself. Just as I insist on the mathematical certainty of our coming to power, because might always attracts might, and the traditional wings, whether they be Right or Left, constructive or destructive, will always attract all the activist elements, leaving only a juiceless pulp in the middle-just so do I insist on the certainty that sooner or later, once we hold the power, Christianity will be overcome and the 'Deutsche Kirehe' established. Yes, the German Church, without a Pope and without the Bible-and Luther, if he could be with us, would give us his blessing."

Hitler was ablaze now, and I could see the ideas of Rosenberg's Mythus working in him. When he shouted with passionate energy: "Of course, I myself am a heathen to the core!" it seemed to me that the form this church might take was implicit in the words.

"No, Ludecke, we don't need to declare this fight openly. It would be political stupidity to show the masses too many enemies at once. The political victory can only follow if the fight is concentrated against the fewest possible number of enemies-for the time being, the Marxists and the Jews. Then will come the turn of the Reaktion, and the end of that will mean the end of the Christian church-and the opening of our own temples, our own shrines. The French Revolution, Bolshevism, all of Marxism, in fact, our whole deformity and atrophy of spirit and soul would never have come into being except for this oriental mummery, this abominable levelling mania, this cursed universalism of Christianity, which denies racialism and preaches suicidal tolerance."

Someone remarked here that the Jews were pointing to Christ as the first Communist.

"Quite so," Hitler nodded. "Jesus Christus," he said thoughtfully, in a quieter, almost solemn voice. "It is the tragedy of the Germanic world that no German 'Heiland' was born among us; that our organic, spiritual evolution was suddenly violently interrupted; that Jesus was judaized, distorted, falsified, and an alien Asiatic spirit was forced upon us. That is a crime we must repair."

The Brown Mess in The Brown House.

There was much more talk that night, but none so portentous as that I have reported here. I thought of Hitler's words months later when, as Chancellor, he put on the great show in Potsdam that he had foretold in our talk at the Kaiserhof-a tremendous, solemn celebration to proclaim the epochal nature of the great change in Germany. It was done in full harmony with tradition; the ceremonies were opened with both Lutheran and Catholic services, attended as a matter of course by all the potentates - Hindenburg and all the dignitaries of Church and State. But while these preliminaries were in progress, Hitler went with Goebbels to lay a wreath on the grave of Horst Wessel in a Berlin cemetery. As the act not only of a party leader but of the Chancellor of a Christian country, it was an intended affront to the Christian nature of that country and a challenge to the Catholic Church, of which the Fuehrer was nominally a member. The story went about that Hitler did it because he had been refused communion by the Church -sheer nonsense in view of the fact that for years he had not set foot in a church to confess and pray, probably never since the war. He was plainly throwing down his glove to the Church that had refused church funerals to dead SA heroes and had threatened Catholic Nazis with excommunication. And the Catholic Church evidently weighed the gesture and realized its own situation, for it adopted a more conciliatory attitude.

But I am anticipating events. It was after four in the morning when our party in Hitler's flat broke up. The Fuehrer escorted us to the foyer. When he shook hands with me he said: "Meet me at Hoffmann's office at five tomorrow afternoon-no, what am I saying? Today at five. And don't be late. We'll be off at five sharp."

I wasn't there by five sharp, however. I had only a few hours of sleep, and a busy day. There was some delay about that pesky money-permit, and I battled my way from one financial fortress to another, only to have to give it up at last and hope for better luck in Berlin.

It was five o'clock when I reached my hotel, to find there a message from Hoffmann saying that Hitler refused to wait any longer-I must show up at once. Hitler had gone when I reached Hoffmann's office, but the photographer was still waiting for me in the darkening street. My things were quickly transferred from the taxi to his brown Mercedes, and we tore off, with Hoffmann at the wheel.

After a mad drive of nearly two hours, we slowed down at sight of a man standing in the glare of our headlights, one arm akimbo, the other waving a dog-whip. It was Hitler, with his caravan alongside.

We drew up, our lights picking out a fantastic-looking group. Hitler was in a long leather coat, with a leather cap over his ears and motoring glasses pushed up on his forehead. Beside him, feet planted firmly on the ground, stood the Fuehrer's ever ready, ever faithful dummy, his sturdy, strong-faced driver, Julius Schreck.[1] This blunt Bavarian was to me the most sympathique and sincere person on Hitler's staff. Brueckner was there, arguing with Schaub, while mild little Dr. Dietrich was beating his sides to keep warm. There was also a Sepp Dietrich in the party, the short, and burly commander of the bodyguard. He was giving orders to his eight giants, fine, athletic German types. They had zipped motor-car overalls over their black-coated uniforms and wore close-fitting aviators' helmets. Armed with revolvers and sjamboks-hippopotamus whips, terrible weapons capable of knocking a man out with one blow-they looked like men from Mars.

Hitler growled at me a little, but shook hands good-naturedly enough. I told him of my troubles, which had almost brought me to fisticuffs with an official of the Deutsche Bank.

"I can imagine how you bawled him out, the poor fellow. People are slower here than in America, you know. Now let's eat - Brueckner's as hungry as a bear."

We trooped into a typical German wayside inn, a place where Hitler often stopped for a brief meal. We seemed to be the only guests, and soon all of us were sitting like one big family round a long table, with a guard left outside to watch the cars. The innkeeper and his wife served us. Hitler ate some scrambled eggs and a sandwich of black peasant bread, with excellent appetite. Brueckner, who was the travelling marshal with all arrangements in his care, rushed through his meal and then fought with the oldest telephone in the world, trying to get Nuremberg in order to tell Streicher when to expect us, trying to reserve our rooms at Berneck, our overnight

---

1 *Julius Schreck died in 1936 after an operation necessitated by an inflammation of the brain, according to an official bulletin, and was buried with highest Party and military honours. It was rumoured that he had been the victim of a murderous attack intended for Hitler, whom he resembled at a distance, except that his hair was black and his eyes dark.*

(Left) The former chef of the Brown Mess: Arthur Kannenberg, Hitler's man in the moon.
(Right) The Brown House in Munich.

stop, trying to find out from Berlin if Goering, who was to meet Hitler in Berneck, had left on his way to Vienna.

"Ha, Goering ! " said Hitler. "I can hear him cursing at having to spend the night on the road." Then to me: "Pity we can't stop to say hello to Frau Wagner....

In no time at all we were off again. I sat in Hitler's car right behind the Fuehrer, who was in his accustomed front seat. Beside me was Schaub, and behind us were Brueckner and Dr. Dietrich. We were followed by the car carrying the bodyguard. Sepp Dietrich had taken my place in Hoffmann's car, which was third in our caravan.

Hitler, turned half towards me with his arm over the back of the seat, asked me to talk about America. He was delighted to hear that as a boy I had devoured Karl May's stories about the Indians, Old Shatterhand and Winnetou, and said that he could still read them and get a thrill out of them. He was all ears for my experiences with the Franciscan Fathers and the prospector with the seven-league boots. Whenever I mentioned books, such as Prescott's Conquest of Mexico and Conquest of Peru, Denny's America Conquers Britain and Tile Fight for Oil, or Frank H. Simonds' Can Europe Keep the Peace? he would ask Schaub to write down the titles. He questioned me about the Roosevelt campaign, the American crisis, the probability of a great change in the United States. He was much interested in Prohibition. Though a teetotaller, he was no bigot on the question, and accepted my arguments against it. I tried to organize my talk somewhat to show Hitler the United States from a Nazi view-point, in order to give him a background for calculations of international policy. And so I told him of America's utterly different structure and tremendous resources, and suggested that even if Germany were to become a desert,

America could get on without us despite the conviction of many worthy Germans that it couldn't, and that furthermore God wouldn't permit its destruction.

Delivering a lecture in an open car rushing through the night at top speed is a fatiguing business. But it pleased me to see how well Hitler had learned to listen. He was at once alert to what I was saying and intent on the road. Between Munich and Berlin he seemed to know every curve, every roadside tree and shrub, and would point out bits of special beauty as we approached them.

It was past eleven when we stopped at the Deutscher Hofin Nuremberg, where Streicher and two of his lieutenants were waiting for us. Hitler and Streicher seated themselves at a separate table, and I was surprised to note how chummy they seemed.

From my own table, I studied Julius Streicher closely. When I had first known him, he had been, apart from his fanatical anti-Jew complex, a harmless and good-natured fellow. I recalled the time when he had been glad to drink a glass of wine with me, and when in our crazy enthusiasm we had fasted on cherries. Back in 1922 he couldn't praise me enough for bringing him back to Hitler, nor be grateful enough for my gifts of money to the cause. I remembered that he had endured persecution in the years of the Nazi struggle, had spent much time in prison, and still carried the marks of the abuse he had suffered.

For Streicher, the Jewish question is the Alpha and the Omega, the key to the whole history of the world; it is practically the only aspect of Nazism to which he brings both passion and any considerable knowledge-in this case, a vast amount, well mixed with misinformation. He has become a terrifically demagogic speaker, and no one in the movement can stir the masses against the Jews so effectively. He is still the publisher of the notorious Der Stuermer, a frighteningly sensational anti-Jewish weekly which does not hesitate to assure its readers that Jews are stealing their children and murdering them for ritualistic purposes, or that they are raping and perverting blonde Gentile women in orgies of lust. Like Hitler, he carries a heavy dog-whip, and in his leather jacket and badly cut breeches and puttees he always appears, whether in parliament or in society, a terrifying figure.

Hitler owed much to Streicher. In the dark years he had been instrumental in holding for the Fuehrer the Nazi element in northern Bavaria; in conquering Nuremberg, next to Munich the largest Bavarian city; and finally in winning over all of important Protestant Franconia. Hitler himself had to admit that Streicher wasn't fitted for an important administrative post as a minister or a state secretary. But the district-leader was compensated. He had remained the uncrowned king of Franconia and the chief scourge of the Jews.

Hitler and Streicher were discussing some matter in subdued voices. Presently one of Streicher's men put before them on the table come small object of art, apparently a figure of Nazi symbolism and probably the work of some Nazi.

We sped on through the moonless, crisply beautiful autumn night. Schreck asked me to tell them some more about America, and so I talked about the extraordinary contrasts to be found in this amazing country. It kept me awake to watch their faces, as much as I could see of them. Shreck, with eyes intent on the road, had his ears pricked up so as not to miss a word; the Fuehrer, visibly fatigued, was trying to follow but would doze off repeatedly, rousing himself each time with a grimace. Whenever he nodded I would stop gladly enough, but Hitler would say: "Go on, go on-I mustn't fall asleep. I'm listening," and I would prod myself to speech again. After a long time, they let me fall silent.

It must have been well past one when, after travelling through open country, we plunged into inky darkness. In the glare of our headlights, the road seemed to cut through the dense forest like a blade of white-hot steel. Leaning back to look up into the alley of stars overhead, I dozed off into the infinite. But my dream of the eternal was short. Hitler's very earthly voice was jarring on my ears, and I roused enough to realize that we were slowing down. We stopped. The Mars men and Hoffmann were right behind us.

Trees reached ghostlike high into the sky. I was aware of the moist breath of mother earth, pungent with autumn scents, of the voice of the night wind in the forest - and then of the embarrassed giggle of someone sneaking away into the bushes, and of other sounds. Then men were all out of the cars. Wide awake suddenly, I realized that I was missing what was, in its way, a moment of quasi-historical interest. I stepped out and advanced a little. Yes... Hitler too, like any ordinary mortal . . . head bent. Over his shoulder he said to me: "We're lucky, Ludecke-not one drop of rain." I had always been delighted by the transparency of the association of simple ideas. And then, taking a deep breath, he added: "A beautiful night, sparkling with stars." Was this, I asked, also one of the favourite stops he had told me about? "Yes, very likely," he said cheerfully. "Of course I've passed here at all times of the day." And laughing we climbed back into the car.

At last our way opened out into a starlit valley. I could hear a little stream, and in my sensitized state was ready to imagine elves dancing in the night-haze hanging over the meadow. But we tore through this peaceful mountain idyll and thundered over a frightened old bridge into the 'Luftkurort und Kneippbad Bemeck im Fichtelgebirge.'

The Hotel Bube was expecting us, and our luggage was quickly carried to the rooms. Hitler disappeared. A few minutes after a handful of us had settled into the agreeable bierstube for a little supper, commotion again invaded this tranquil place, and in stomped Hermann Goering with his retinue. He went directly up to Hitler's room.

Among Goering's entourage I remember only its outstanding figure, his gentleman-in-waiting Paul Koemer, who joined our table. Today he is staatssekretaer

379

THE CANDID CAMERA SNAPS A DICTATOR UNAWARE

(Photographed with the author)

(Top) He saw his name in fat letters;
(Centre) 'This sort of thing can't go on!';
(Bottom) His tight-faced look.

(Top) A mouthful.;
(Centre) 'Who is this Mrs. Lewis, anyway?';
(Bottom) 'I don't care what they call me as long as I get what I want.'

381

and Goering's confidant.

Bed at last. There was still a light in Hitler's room at four in the morning. Finally I fell asleep, but it seemed as if I had been lost in dreams for only a few minutes when Schaub was pounding at my door.

"Raus der Amerikaner! Out of the feathers! The Indians are coming-we're off at nine I Himmelherrgottsacrament!"

It was such a resounding oath that I had none ready of my own when I discovered that it was already a quarter to nine. A quick shave, a short breakfast, and off we went at half-past. Now, however, I was riding in Hoffmann's car. I had been glad to accept Sepp Dietrich's suggestion that I let him take his seat in Hitler's car again. I was too tired to talk.

"We're coming into Saxony, red country," he explained apologetically. "Now I must be on the job. I'm responsible, you know." But in his eyes and manner I seemed to read the suggestion that if I made myself pleasant enough I could stay on in Hitler's car.

Our car managed to follow closely most of the way, but Hoffmann had to step on it. About noon we saw their cars stopped by the wayside, and Hitler, swinging his whip, again standing in the middle of the road, feet planted wide apart.

Hoffmann is a fairly good but decidedly abrupt driver, and he missed running Hitler down by only an inch. The car stopped at the precise spot where the Fuehrer had been standing before he made his frantic leap away. And what a jump-terror, amazement, outraged fury on his face all at once! Hoffmann, ruffling the sharp-pointed nose that always seems to me to express consummate impudence, made the funniest face in the world. Hitler was gasping for breath.

"Hoffmann!" he bawled. "You are crazy-positively, you are crazy!" That was all he said. And a minute later he was obligingly consenting to pose for a picture when some fat ladies and gentlemen, descending heavily from their car, approached him humbly, their eyes filled with curiosity and excitement at being so near the German miracle.

An hour later we turned aside into a lonely track cut through a forest, and stopped in a clearing screened from the road, a spot where Hitler often halted for a picnic. Blankets were spread, and we settled at ease in the grass under the trees for a rest and a lunch of sandwiches, eggs, and fruit.

Hitler and I sat together, a little apart. Between bites we talked, both unaware that Hoffmann was surreptitiously snapping pictures of us. He sent them to me in Washington weeks later as a complete surprise.

Knowing the Fuehrer's passion for newspapers, I took from my coat a well-known Norwegian daily containing an article about him. As soon as Hitler saw his name in fat letters on the front page he asked me about it. And here I put the finger on Hanfstaengl.

"Oh, yes," I said casually. "It's by the Scandinavian journalist whom Hanfstaengl introduced to you in the Munich Opera House. But it's rather annoying. Rosenberg gave it to me-he thought it might interest you."

"But what does it say? "

"Perhaps I still have the German translation . . ." and after a moment of pretended searching I pulled out the typed pages that Thilo von Trotha, Rosenberg's archivist, had given me at the last minute with his malicious best wishes. Hitler read it in growing fury. It was Hanfstaengl's responsibility to bring only trustworthy people to him, and this article ridiculed him mercilessly.

"This is impossible! This sort of thing can't go on," he growled. Then I mentioned an incident as a matter of common gossip among those in the know - Flick-Steger's shove that had sent Putzi sprawling into a tub of shrubbery at the Kaiserhof.

"Ach, ja," Hitler grumbled. "That was an awkward moment. But I couldn't do anything-the man's two heads taller than Flick-Steger. So I just walked out."

He was looking gloomy. "Here's something interesting," I said. I pulled out a copy of my paper, The American Guard, and turned to an article headed 'Hitler's "Pet Names" in the American Press.'[2] These were the quoted epithets I read off to him, translating into German as I went :

"Little man - world menace - messiah of absurdity - reactionary-demagogue - adventurer – desperado - would be dictator - drummer of a jazz orchestra - fanatic product of the jazz age - mystical nonsense monger - drummer-boy - mischief-maker - dapper quack doctor - German Rasputin - clown-terrorist of the streets - brazen charlatan - mad apostle - Bolshevik-Monarchist. "

Hitler's tight-faced look had given way to one of amusement. He took such things more lightly then.

"… a little selection"- I read on, touching only the high spots - "culled at random from newspapers and magazines… These pleasant epithets… all highly contradictory… remind us of the Press reports when Mussolini made his bid for power. Those who told the truth about the genius of the Duce ten years ago and predicted his fame and lasting influence on world affairs were laughed off as morons and lunatics… Hitler's pet names indicate the amazing ignorance in which the public is kept… For instance, The Boston Transcript… editorially branded Hitler as an 'adventurer' who 'fought in Cuba against the Spaniards, and in Africa, with the Boers, against the British.' Considering that Hitler is today only forty-three years old, he must have been a remarkable child!"

And here Hitler laughed out loud. Then I read him this quotation which I ascribed simply to 'Mrs. Lewis, the wife of one of America's best known novelists':

"When I walked into Adolf Hitler's salon, I was convinced that I was meeting the future dictator of Germany. In less than fifty seconds I was sure I was not."

---

2 Published in May 1932.

Hitler looked puzzled. "Who is this Mrs. Lewis, anyway?" he asked. I reminded him of his meeting Dorothy Thompson in Berlin when she was correspondent of the, New York Evening Post.

"Ja, ja, now I remember. Hanfstaengl again! He brought this woman to me. Den Burschen werde ich mir kaufen!"[3]

There was much more. Eventually I came to this of my own:

"Hitler is ... essentially a man of peace. His vast programme for the reconstruction of his country economically, politically, socially, and culturally, leaves no time for war. He is the German Man, who is neither a Reactionary nor a pseudo-Fascist, but the leader and prophet of Young Germany."

I added, with a slight emphasis: "This was written five months ago."

But that was lost on Hitler. "Excellent!" he exclaimed spontaneously. "I don't care what they call me so long as I get what I want." Then, more thoughtfully: "Fools believe that politics operate by the laws of reason. No, they're predominantly a matter of passions and emotion. Who could understand us without being one of us? Today and tomorrow you'll see our youth-my boys. We'll take the children away from the old fogies-we must control the youth. A great statesman must be an artist to be able to mould the mind of the people as clay takes form in the sculptor's hand."

He started up suddenly. "Let's go-it's time. Before I forget it, Ludecke, thank you for the books. I've already glanced at them-very interesting."

We broke up and went back to the cars. Hoffmann and Schreck came up to me with congratulations.

Now we were flying through Saxony, the reddest section of Germany. Nearing Zwickau, we found the road broken up for repairs, and ahead of us was a column of more than twenty trucks waiting to proceed. They were filled with Communists waving red flags.

We slowed down. It was apparent that because of the state of the road we were going to have to pass this long line at low speed. I could see Sepp Dietrich whistling through his teeth. Everybody stopped talking, and I noticed that the right hand of each of the Mars men in the car in front of us disappeared at his side. We crept by. Every one, the Fuehrer included, looked straight into the faces of the Communists. Recognizing Hitler, they raised a great howl against him but never a hand. It was obvious that they were unwilling to take chances with his body-guard.

Late in the afternoon we began passing trucks full of Hitler Youth, who went wild with joy when they saw the Fuehrer. The last miles were a triumphal procession. A few kilometres from Potsdam we were hailed by men waiting in two big cars; it was Baldur von Schirach and his entourage, anxiously watching for Hitler. In their wake we drove into Potsdam at a few minutes past eight. The place looked as though an army had occupied it-tents and trucks everywhere, children on all sides, each of

3 In the sense of 'I'll let the fellow have it!'

them in uniform. For the most part they were from fourteen to eighteen years old, but many were even younger.

When we drew near the stadium the human mass was so dense that the regular police and the SS could scarcely keep our way open. The moment Hitler stepped out, the human wave closed in behind him. I jumped from our still moving car, but it was too late-I was cut off. I had a terrific time fighting my way through to a gate which I found already closed, but the Ehrenkarte signed by Schirach got me in, just in time to see Schirach saluting and making his official report to the Fuehrer-some sixty-four thousand boys and fifteen thousand girls. Hitler was still wiping the road-dust from his eyes.

The stadium was a blaze of torches. Tens of thousands of boys and girls stood in formation on the field, surrounded by a vast ring of humanity. When Hitler stood alone at the front of the platform, a fantastic cry went up into the night, a sound of matchless jubilation. Then he raised his arms, and dead silence fell. He burst into a flaming address which lasted scarcely fifteen minutes. Again he was the old Hitler, spontaneous, fiery, fully of appeal.

Immediately after the exercises we started for Berlin. We had been joined by Prince Auwi (August Wilhelm), the Kaiser's fourth son.

It was interesting to observe Hitler's manner with the Prince, who had joined the Nazis several years before, was now a Reichstag deputy, and held the rank of brigade-leader in the SA. He was in uniform; the Fuehrer was not. Hitler was courteous, addressed him as 'Royal Highness' but was absolutely poised. The Prince was exceptionally respectful but equally at ease, even when his elbow sent a wine-glass to the floor.

Hitler was distressed when the Prince, who lives in his villa in Potsdam, told him of the difficulties the meeting had created. The town was prepared to take care of forty thousand children at most. Twice that number had arrived, and thousands of them had been on the road for days. The affair had been badly organized.

"I was afraid of this," said Hitler in a troubled voice. "Schirach is too young for this job. After all, he's only twenty-five-he hasn't the experience. What are we going to do? Those thousands of children mustn't sleep under the open sky."

"I've taken fifty-five into my house-impossible to take more," said the Prince, looking equally worried. "Perhaps we could make a house-to-house canvass."

The Fuehrer was so concerned that after he had eaten something he drove out to Potsdam again at midnight, and did not return until he had made sure that everything possible was being done for the comfort of the children. Thousands of them, however, had to sleep in the open, in the squares or under trees in the fields-no joke on 1 October.

Hitler wasn't in bed until well after four, but at seven he was again in Potsdam, walking about to animate the weary children.

At eleven o'clock the great review began. I had never seen anything like it, and know I never shall again. It was a gloriously sunny October day. From out the forest behind the stadium there began flowing across the golden meadow a steady column of brown-shirted Hitler Youth. For seven hours they came on, boys from every part of the Reich, even from Austria and Bohemia, from Memel and Danzig, their thousands of banners fluttering in a light breeze. Their young voices were raised in marching songs until they neared the Fuehrer; then they would march by in earnest silence.

When one sturdy lad came on leading his section and bearing on his shoulders his five-year-old brother, who clutched a flower in his tiny fist, a storm of applause tore the air, and Hitler beckoned to the two brothers to approach and shake hands with him.

With unflagging joy I watched each section of the endless column. Here was the warmest breath of our youth, here was our pride. 'He who has the youth has the future.' Here were the sons of workmen, of artisans, of officers, of peasants. I saw whole groups of blond, blue-eyed, long-headed boys, strong and lithe as osier switches-a homogeneous type, the same boys, the same faces, the same stride. Oh, I thought, if only they in America could see this! How clearly it would show them what we hope to achieve by our racial ideal! And how feeble my words will seem to me after this!

It was a spectacle so thrilling that only now and then did one remember the physical ordeal involved. The Fuehrer, for example, stood reviewing the parade with his arm constantly lifted in the Nazi salute from eleven in the morning till six in the evening, letting it fall at rest only in the gaps between sections. Through all this time, five bands-more than six hundred men-stood deployed on the field, playing old martial airs and Nazi songs. Behind them were fifteen thousand Hitler girls, from fourteen to eighteen years old, massed in squares, and uniformed in brown blouses. Now and again a girl would faint and have to be carried out. During a brief pause, Hitler walked out among the formations, talking to girls here and there, bringing life back into tired eyes. He himself was smiling continuously, obviously tremendously uplifted. Once, after a section had passed, he came over to where I was standing with Count von Helldorf, SA group-leader of Berlin, and Count von Wedell, group-leader of Brandenburg. Touching my arm, he said :

"You see, Ludecke … No fear-the German race is marching."

Yes, the race was marching! It was at moments poignantly moving to see some of the smaller fellows, so beautiful racially, many of them probably supperless, sleepless, and breakfastless, draw themselves erect under their rucksacks as they neared the Fuehrer, and then march proudly by, all traces of weariness gone from their bearing.

In the fading light, six thousand SS giants drilled past in a parade-march that the

THE AUTHOR'S CREDENTIALS FOR WASHINGTON

Signed by Alfred Rosenberg, authorizing the author to represent the foreign political interests of the Party in the United States, Canada, and Mexico.

old Imperial Guard could not have bettered, and the show was over. Its propaganda value, after Hitler's reverses, would be incalculable. No spectator could escape its pull. There was no longer the slightest doubt in my mind that, whatever the political setbacks ahead, the Fuehrer would triumph.

Hitler, I believe, had dinner with Prince Auwi in Potsdam and later spent a while at the Goebbels' before going to his train. In the evening I drove back with Hoffmann to the Kaiserhof. The good Heinrich had put in a desperately active day, jumping around like a cricket to snap every aspect of the marching youth.

With a jerk we were off. In a few minutes we were at the Potsdam station, and I rushed with Hoffmann to the waiting train. He wanted to give Hitler the films, to be developed in Munich, as he himself was staying over in Berlin for a day or two.

As we stepped into the railway-carriage, Brueckner blocked the aisle. "Leave him alone," he said. "The man's played out." But the Fuehrer had seen us through the window. He was sitting in a corner of the compartment, utterly spent. The tempo had finally taken its toll.

Hitler motioned weakly to us to come in. He put the films in his pocket, nodded to me, but said nothing. Seeing how exhausted he was, I sat down for the barest moment only. He looked for a second into my eyes, clasped my hand feebly, and I left.

When next I saw him he was Chancellor.

XXIX

DISTANT THUNDER

Two days later, in the early afternoon, my train moved smoothly out of the Zoologischer Garten station in the west end of Berlin. Still gasping for breath, for I had barely made it, I counted my bags and then sank into a corner by the window, thankful to find myself alone in the compartment.

As my pulse slowed down, things left undone began to leer at me. Yesterday had been one long and frantic rush; this morning had been just as bad. I had finally got the money-permit, the certified check and the cash for the journey at the very last moment. Then straight from the bank to the station to catch my train, missing the lunch engagement with Magda Goebbels that we had arranged at the Potsdam stadium on Sunday afternoon. No time even to stop in the appointed restaurant near the Zoo and make my excuses. For all I knew, she might be waiting there still, and I writhed at the thought; I'd send her a wire from the boat. Then I realized that I'd forgotten to return his money to Ellery Walter, and resolved to mail it as soon as I touched London.

In the course of those crowded hours I had visited Flick-Steger's office and there had talked with crusty old Karl von Wiegand, Hearst's chief foreign correspondent-a man who 'knows everything,' and who really does know quite a lot. He had just come from the United States after a tour through the Far East, and had seen and heard many things. The veteran globe-trotter was pessimistic about our chances, as positive that Hitler would never make it as I was certain that he would.

"Hitler had better listen to people," he said. "He has many things yet to learn. I have interesting news he ought to know, but I won't beg for an interview. There's been too much red tape here lately. I have no trouble seeing a Mussolini, a Stalin, or a Prime Minister in London."

So I had talked by telephone to Schaub in Munich, and had arranged for von Wiegand's interview with Hitler-reflecting that once you're a man of importance, once you're at the centre of things, you have it easy in many ways. Everybody comes to inform you, to warn, to advise; it needs only instinct, psychology, and experience to sift out the stuff left at your door.

For almost forty hours there had been literally no chance for me to think. Now I had time to examine the emotional impression left on me by Hitler, sitting so fagged out in the corner of his compartment. Had his performance really been so incredible, so superhuman? Couldn't almost any man have done as much if his ego were being so magnificently fed? This was strong meat, this sense of being the glorifying presence, the heroic centre of devotion, of hope, and sacrifice, the focus of thousands of shining eyes, thousands of stirring voices. The fortitude, will, and discipline of this host of youth, undergoing an even harder ordeal than the Fuehrer's, were sustaining him as well. Impossible to collapse so long as their strength was his.

All over this country that was slipping past my window, were millions of eyes, ears, and tongues, millions of hands and feet, minds and hearts working for the Fuehrer, fashioning him into the leader who would lift a people out of its misery, make Germany free and great again. Blunder as he might, it was too late for him to fail. He was now being upborne by the resistless force of a people intent on creating a hero.

But there was another and more cynical reason why Hitler would not lose: he had so many Germans fettered now in the bonds of interest. They might not see it yet, but they would. I thought of that play of Jacinto Benavente's in which Leander, handsome young ne'er-do-well, arrives in a gay and rich city, penniless but with fine clothes on his back. The guile of his servant Crispin promptly spreads the illusion of Leander's fame and wealth through the town; unlimited credit is his, and the love and the promise in marriage of Sylvia, the richest man's daughter. Then comes suspicion; soon certainty spreads among those most concerned. An impostor! Father and tradesmen storm Leander's house, where Sylvia at that moment is secretly visiting her betrothed. They are all for throwing the fraud into prison, but Crispin's ingenuity saves him. Repudiate my master and you debase your daughter! Send him to the galleys as a debtor and you lose your money! Why are you all so determined to bring about your own ruin? The happiness of each of you depends on this illusion. Save yourselves by keeping it up. Let them marry!

Capitalists, accept this Hitler, this concept so elaborately built up. Take him, use him, make sure of your money. About face, Churchmen; stop fighting him. Ruin him and your Church is lost in the general chaos. Nazis, this may not be quite the man you thought him. But you have put your whole stake on him; now you must go through with it. The Bonds of Interest!

It would be something like that. No use pressing the analogy too far. But everything would be tainted with cynical compromise, and what was really fine in Nazi idealism would fly out the window. And yet the certainty of it seemed to be biting less deep now than the fear of it a few weeks ago. Was I accepting my own bonds?

Or was the magic of travel already at work, the softening illusion that comes of distance? Hills were swelling and then sinking away. Soon grey evening was bowing over the fields, blurring the German land and with it the contours of my own inner world.

Mildred was waiting for me on the dock at Quebec. She had spent the summer with friends in Maine, and had driven up in our little Ford to meet me. It was a happy reunion. Dawn found us still awake in our room at the Chateau Frontenac. I had so much to tell her, and at last I could be the bearer of good news. Her crazy, stubborn, impetuous German husband had been right for once, and I think a feeling almost of security came over her. I was careful to give Mildred only my good impressions. We built our own castle in Spain, and I was willing enough for the moment to crowd my misgivings about Hitler down its oubliette. Hitler would get to the top, the Nazis would win out … We are both optimists by nature, anyway.

We were in a happy mood when we drove to Montreal to keep an appointment with Adrien Arcand, the fiery leader of the 'Ordre Patriotique des Goglus' This was a violently anti-Jewish, in the main Catholic folkic movement which at that time was growing rapidly in French Canada, with three publications, all very demagogic and clever.

I liked young Arcand at once-his vibrant, intelligent fine-featured face, his genuine fighting spirit. He was greatly pleased when I gave him an autographed photograph of Hitler. We understood each other perfectly, and agreed to co-operate in every way.

When I had appointed several representatives to serve as contacts and to supply me with material, Mildred and I continued our journey down along Lake Champlain, and then on through the final splendour of the gloriously dying woods of Vermont and New Hampshire. These were the last of our halcyon days, for after we had wound up our affairs in Boston, we went on to New York, and there a jolt awaited us.

I had left Germany with explicit assurance from Strasser that the order dissolving all Nazi units in the United States would precede my arrival in Washington. Now I was surprised to learn that nobody had heard about dissolving anything, and on that question the rival New York, Detroit, and Chicago Nazi cliques were now banded together in a common front.

Urging the New York district leader, who was janitor of an apartment house in Elmhurst, Long Island, to stop all public activities, I continued to Washington. There I found a friendly letter from Oberleutnant Schulz containing the information, along with cordial greetings from Strasser and Ley, that 'Ausland' affairs and 'Seefahrt' affairs (these represented the Nazi organization respectively outside Germany and on the high seas, and had formerly been comprised in one department) had now been revamped as separate districts under his direction. He would appreciate any proposals I cared to make about further organization in the United States, Canada, and Mexico.

This development did not increase my respect for the Party organization, in view of the carefully prepared memorandum I had given Dr. Ley, which undertook to show that Nazi organization in the United States had got off on the wrong foot and that it was best to make an entirely fresh start. I decided now to waste no further time on it, and to let things ride.

In Washington, where I set up housekeeping and office simultaneously, my status was officially that of the accredited representative or the Nazi Press; I was admitted to the Capitol Press galleries, and received the usual passes, including a White House card. I released a statement through the news-channels oft he country announcing that the National Socialist Press Service in Washington would function as a news agency for the Nazi Press in Germany and would supply the American Press and public with authentic information about the character and aims of the National Socialist movement and its relation to the Germany of today. For the rest, I did everything possible to establish a working agency for making the United States conscious of our movement, its power and importance. There were talks in clubs and before students, interviews and articles in papers, wide correspondence and personal contacts with senators, representatives and key newspapermen.

It was amazing to find that Hitler was still not being taken seriously; he was practically unknown, even in comparatively well-informed circles. The ignorance and indifference were at times so overwhelming that I had often to fight the feeling that I was working at a quixotic, impossible task. Slowly but surely I established my position and gained ground, for now I had tremendous accomplishments to point to. Yet my situation was always difficult, for the German embassy was definitely against me, and others were at best only polite, with sceptical reservations.

There were, however, a few exceptions. Dr. Kurt Sell, of Wolff's Telegraph Bureau-the former semi-official German news agency-was always courteous and helpful. A journalist of experience, of attainment, and ability, the only German Press man of importance in Washington, he had been in the diplomatic service before he joined the WTB. He was important to me because he was generally popular and was persona grata in the German embassy and in the consulate-general in New York. As he had been absent from Germany for several years, his own picture of the situation was strongly influenced by the WTB and the liberal Berliner Tageblatt. Eventually I succeeded in convincing him that National Socialism was a factor for friend and foe to reckon with, and that a Nazi Government was certainly in sight.

Two other men were useful: an Austrian, Dr. Carl Smetana, a collateral descendant of the composer and a student at Brookings Institute, and Dr. Georg Leibbrandt, a Volga German, who was working for Carnegie Institution on a stipend. They both came to see me and put themselves at my service. Intelligent and sincere men, they were definitely helpful, and I had plans for both of them when the great day should arrive.

Among all the people who sought information from me about Nazi affairs and personalities, I remember with especial pleasure a very resolute little lady of advanced years who offered a significant and sympathetic example of the influence of American women on American life. This was Miss Janet Richards, the popular lecturer on current affairs, who seems to have interviewed every worthwhile European in the last fifty years. I recall her astounding collection of signed photographs of every sort of celebrity, statesman, and royalty, and her pride in them, lightened by touches of caustic wit. Hers is an original mind, mellowed by experience and travel, and it probes deeply and thoroughly. I painted for her, as always, a most sympathetic picture of Nazism and its leader, and had rather a time convincing her that neither the Kaiser nor Hugenberg would play a role in the 'Nazi Revolution.'

Then there was my encounter with Heinz Spanknoebel, who later stepped into the limelight as official spokesman for Minister Dr. Joseph Goebbels, after Hitler had assumed the Chancellorship. He was now leader of the Detroit Nazi unit and 'the representative of Dr. Nieland in Hamburg.' He wrote me an arrogant letter from Detroit. But the little man was tame enough when he visited me in Washington on his way to New York to 'out-dictate' the other Nazi dictator of America, the Elmhurst janitor, who also claimed to be Dr. Nieland's representative. Spanknoebel graciously accepted my indifference to his struggle for supremacy, and promised not to start the publication he had in mind.

The news from Germany did not make my task any easier. As we had expected, Hitler had passed his peak at the polls in July. The Nazis lost heavily in the November elections, declining from 234 to 196 seats, whereas the Nationalists added fifteen and the Communists eleven, giving the latter a total of 100 seats in the new Reichstag. But the Social Democrats and the Centre Party sustained losses, and the Nazi Party remained by far the largest in the Reich. Nevertheless it was a set-back, and Hitler's prestige declined. The spell was broken; the Tribune of the People no longer looked invulnerable. Astonishment rocked the country. The Herrenklub drew a breath of relief. In the new Reichstag, however, the 'Cabinet of National Concentration' again failed to win support. On 16 November Papen finally presented his resignation. Schleicher was ready to drop him like an old glove, but Hindenburg was intent on carrying his favourite Chancellor over into a new Government. For the next two weeks, the Wilhelmstrasse was deep in the fog of parliamentary deadlock. The old President summoned Hitler, receiving him on 19 November with no one else present -'under four eyes,' as the Germans say. Goebbels' diary calls this 'a great advance.' This is modesty indeed. Possibly this time they even sat down!

The interview led to further negotiations with Hindenburg or rather with the Hindenburg camarilla, which Hitler conducted by letter lest he again emerge the victim of another August 13. He was staying off thin ice, conducting himself with real skill in a delicate and precarious situation.

On 21 November there was another conference with Hindenburg. Goebbels records that the crowd massed outside the Kaiserhof believed that Hitler had already been appointed Chancellor. 'What a terrible illusion!' he laments.

The upshot was a letter from Hitler refusing to accept anything but the

Chancellorship in any cabinet, declining also to attempt the forming of a Parliamentary Government, and demanding a Presidial cabinet headed by himself and invested with the powers Papen had enjoyed. Hindenburg refused in turn, likewise by letter, insisting that a Presidial cabinet must be headed by a man above party and one in whom he could repose special confidence; under a party leader it would perforce develop into a party dictatorship with consequences that he could not square with his oath and conscience.

Both sides immediately made statements to the Press containing the exchange of notes. This time Hitler, mindful of his August fiasco, reached the public first.

That ended the parleys and what had really been a cautious duel between Papen and Hitler. But the deadlock continued.

Now the Fuehrer was for the time being out of the running, and the race was between Papen and Schleicher. The murk of intrigue again enveloped the Presidential palace. The old man was obviously weary of the impasse; there were rumours that he was threatening to resign, that a regency was being planned, that the Hohenzollerns were to be restored. The country grew restive.

But where, during this muddled interval, were Gregor Strasser and the mysterious plan about which he had been so complacently reticent?

In complete accord with Hitler (Strasser later assured me of that with his own lips), he was maintaining contact with Schleicher, the man who, of the whole camarilla, was considered least antagonistic to the Nazis. He also conferred twice with Hindenburg, in the presence of Schleicher and Staatssekretaer Meissner. At the second of these two interviews, when Strasser asked Hindenburg point-black to state his attitude towards Hitler, the old man is alleged to have said:

"I give you my word of honour as a Prussian general that I will never make this Bohemian corporal Chancellor of Germany."

Blunt words, obscurely charged with ruin and death for the two men who said they had heard them uttered. Schleicher, much too loose-tongued for his role of intriguer, cynically whispered them about. Strasser of course repeated them to Hitler. Months later, when they had done their work of ruin, he affirmed them again to Otto Strasser.

The brothers Strasser had not seen each other since July 1930, when Otto had separated himself from Hitler. They met again, for the last time, in May 1933, shortly before Otto fled from Germany. In 1935, declaring that he had added nothing and changed nothing, Otto Strasser published an account[1] of what his brother had told him in this last talk. That account is an important source. What immediately follows here is derived from it.

According to Otto Strasser, his brother was carrying on these private negotiations with Schleicher by the Fuehrer's order. In November, the General suggested to him a

1 *Die Deutsche Bartholomaeusnacht*, 1935, pp. 39-44.

Schleicher-Strasser-Leipart[2] government, with Papen or Bruening as foreign minister. Strasser took the view that he could discuss participation only if Hindenburg could not be brought to change his negative attitude towards Hitler. At the second conference with the President, in response to Strasser's direct question, those words were spoken which seemed to shut the door on the Fuehrer so long as Hindenburg should hold office. Strasser at once reported them to Hitler.

The Fuehrer had let it be known that he could neither tolerate any other Chancellor nor assign members of his Party to a cabinet not headed by himself. Hindenburg's adamant position altered the situation; however. Strasser and Hitler weighed the advantages and disadvantages of Nazi participation in the prospective government. The result was a tentative agreement that Gregor Strasser was to enter a Schleicher government either as Chancellor or Vice-chancellor. But Hitler reserved final decision on the question until he himself should have conferred with Schleicher in Berlin. The latter was expecting him there on I December.

As a result of rumours which had reached him, Hitler confronted his chief aide in Berlin. The man accused was so utterly dumbfounded that all he could do was to ask quietly:

"Herr Hitler, do you really believe me capable of such a dirty trick?"

"Yes", said Hitler.

Strasser walked out of the room. He sent the Fuehrer a letter saying that he resigned all his offices, but would remain in the Party as a simple soldier of National Socialism.

So much for Otto Strasser's report of his brother Gregor's version. The truth of this extraordinary affair can never be known. Otto Strasser I regard as a man of honour. It must, however, be admitted, for the sake of historical truth, that a man so passionately active in politics as the surviving Strasser is to this day, and so beset by the innumerable difficulties encompassing an exile, can hardly remain independent, however high his personal integrity.

Hindenburg, Schleicher, and Strasser are dead. The old President, though a rock of stubbornness, was being overtaken by senility and may well have been inconsistent. Schleicher was capable of any duplicity. Gregor Strasser I knew for a man of probity. He told it, however, when he was completely out of the picture; it would have been only human to depart from fact sufficiently to put himself and his fiasco in the best possible light.

But what had Schleicher and Strasser really been up to? And what had been the motives of each? One can only conjecture. Perhaps they were sincerely acting together to resolve a hopeless situation; even so devious a politician as Schleicher can sometimes be genuine. Possibly Schleicher was using Strasser as a dupe, to bring about the complete break-up of the Nazi Party-an improbable aim, since at

2 Theodor Leipart, leader of the Socialist Trades Union.

this juncture the Communists would chiefly have benefited. Possibly the 'Social General,' as Schleicher liked to call himself, was aiming at a socialist-military dictatorship, based on the military power he commanded, and on the Catholic and Social-Democratic trade unions, which were receptive and already were considerably under the influence of Gregor Strasser. The latter, as Vice-Chancellor and Prime Minister of Prussia, would be expected to bring the Left wing of the Nazi Party fairly intact into the combination.

Strasser, whose disapproval of Hitler's 'rule-or-ruin' attitude and distrust of his entourage were no secret, may honestly have believed that his alliance with Schleicher was the only means of forcing Hitler into line and saving the Party from collapse. His resignation of all his offices seems the quixotic act of an outraged man whose motives had been misinterpreted. Such an ebullition of feeling would have been natural to the Gregor Strasser I knew. And yet his withdrawal may have been due to over-confidence; too sure of the outcome, he may have decided that for events to come he preferred to be clear of the charge of abuse of his position as Hitler's chief executive. Whatever his motives, his resignation and subsequent inertia in the most critical phase of his career, in a time when he needed every ounce of his energy and every advantage of his position as second in command in the Nazi Party, shows bad judgment and an absurd naivety. It was a mistake which eventually cost him his life.

In all this imbroglio, one sees Hitler's incredible luck at work. First in the paralysing of the Reaktion that resulted when Schleicher and Papen parted company and embarked on conflicting intrigues. Then in the fact that Strasser and Schleicher, despite a political constellation most favourable to themselves, simply did not know how to play their game. They could not measure up to a situation which demanded men of passion, with a sense of the imponderables and a dramatic impulse for action. Goering and Goebbels, whatever their faults, were guilty of no such blundering. They struck while the iron was hot.

There is significance in the steady rise, from then on, of Goering's and Goebbels' stars in the Nazi firmament. To this day Hitler either believes or-what is more likely-keeps up a pretence of believing that these two saved him from a trap. History does not yet tell us that they did not. But historical intuition does tell us that Hitler must have found it gratifying to see Strasser go forth into outer darkness wearing the convenient brand of' traitor.'

The crisis could not last for ever. Reluctantly Hindenburg let his favourite Chancellor go. Papen carried away with him a photograph of the President on which the old man had written in a trembling hand: 'Ich hatt' einen Kameraden!'

On 2 December Schleicher was named Chancellor, at the head of another Presidial cabinet. This second soldier-chancellor since General Caprivi in 1890 had more power given into his hands than any previous Chancellor. He was not only the Federal head of the Reich, but Minister of National Defence and Federal Commissioner for the State of Prussia, with control over the Prussian police. Now the master-intriguer and minister-maker, the wire-puller behind the scenes, had at last stepped into the open. Now the' man without nerves' would show what he could do.

What followed is the most farcical interlude in German history, a comic curtain-raiser to the drama of Nazi dictatorship. Instead of leaping into action at once, making himself independent of Hindenburg, arresting Papen, Goebbels, Goering, certain gentlemen of the Herrenklub, certain 'key' Communists-instead of doing these things, the 'man without nerves' made a poor, thin speech over the radio to the nation.

Strasser, his resignation in, went into hiding. Hitler, with his own chances diving towards zero, was rushing feverishly with his aides from place to place, fighting desperately to fend off a complete Nazi collapse. One calamity followed another.

The Thuringian elections of 4 December showed an ominous loss of 40 per cent from the figure of 31 July. Goebbels' diary from the beginning of December to Christmas shows the despair that gripped the Party and its leaders during those days. These are excerpts:

December 6: 'The (Nazi) situation in the Reich is catastrophic.'

December 8: 'Severe depression prevails ... Financial worries render all systematic work impossible. . . . The danger now exists of the whole Party's going to pieces ... Dr. Ley telephones that the situation in the Party is becoming more critical from hour to hour ... [Strasser's] letter to the Fuehrer [resigning his offices] is dialectic pettifoggery ... Treason! Treason! Treason! ... For hours on end the Fuehrer walks anxiously up and down the hotel room ... Once he stops and merely says: "If the Party should ever break up, I'll make an end of things in three minutes with a revolver."'

December 9: 'On all sides the Fuehrer and the Party are given up as lost ... One is almost ashamed to meet an acquaintance ... Everywhere the rats emerge, ready to leave the sinking ship.'

December 10: 'The financial condition of the Berlin district is hopeless ... Strasser's demarche has created great alarm in the public.'

December 15: 'It is hard to hold the SA and the Party officials to a clear course ... If we succeed in holding the movement together we shall also succeed in saving the situation.'

December 17: 'We decide to work with all our means on the Party organization ... and see if we cannot lift the organization up again, in spite of all.'

December 20: 'We must summon all our strength to rally the Party once more.'

December 21: 'Altercation and discord ... The financial crisis continues.'

December 29: 'It is possible that in a few days the Fuehrer will have a conference with Papen. There a new chance opens.'

There, indeed, a new chance opened. A heroic movement, animated by a heroic ideal, a movement with a decade of heroic struggle behind it, a movement whose leader had failed to seize in heroic fashion his historical moment-now had its chance to win back some of the ground it had lost.

I was in a tight spot in Washington in that month of December. When I read a despatch from Berlin to the New York Times saying that Strasser had resigned and that Hitler had taken over the Party organization, appointed Dr. Ley his chief of staff of the PO, I was simply flabbergasted.

Though I had managed fairly well to keep au courant and had been aware of an aggravated situation, I naturally did not know the circumstances surrounding Strasser's step. But I sensed an irremediable blunder. Now only a miracle could save the Great Cause.

An agony of uncertainty ensued. The Berlin correspondents understood little of what had happened and were cabling the wildest and most contradictory rumours, enough to fray, anybody's nerves. For weeks I was in the dark as to whether Strasser's elimination was an accomplished fact or whether he was planning to spring a surprise. The Fuehrer's enemies inside Germany and out were making the most of the Party crisis and were predicting Hitler's finish. I cabled Hitler personally for enlightenment. Significantly, no answer came.

No word came from Strasser. Weeks later there arrived a letter from Roehm wishing me a happy New Year and mentioning, only in passing, Strasser's 'incomprehensible blunder' and the fact that he had left Berlin for (horrible phrase in politics!), a long vacation.'

That had the ring of finality. All I could do was wait, and eventually revise my whole personal policy. It looked now as if Strasser was really down and out. His withdrawal involved the retirement of his intimates, notably Oberleutnant Schulz, his right-hand man; I could expect a lapse in active interest in the United States. Hitler created a new office, the Political Central Commission, under Rudolf Hess, his closest private secretary, who thus stepped with one stride from comparative obscurity into prominence and power. The repercussions of the Nazi crisis greatly increased my difficulties in combating unfavourable news in the Press. And to make matters worse, I was left more or less in the lurch. Fighting against collapse, the Nazis had scant thought to spare for their foreign agent. The home office slipped up on my remittance for January and again for February. My plight would have been desperate if Dr. Sell had not come to my rescue. In view of the strong interests working against me, notably the German Embassy, it was humiliating to have to borrow money.

After repeated cables and letters to Rosenberg and even appeals to Hitler, the money would arrive, weeks late. Financial uncertainty capped the sheaf of worry.

My brave wife, who at first had seemed so happy, began to show the strain.

Towards the middle of January details had begun to leak out about Hitler's solemn reconciliation with his erstwhile opponent, Franz von Papen. The international clubman was now seeking his revenge on Schleicher; the unseated Gentleman Jockey was now out to tumble the General.

Hitler and Papen had conferred in Cologne on 4 January 1933 at the house of Baron von Schroeder, the international banker. They met in the greatest secrecy, but not secretly enough to hide the fact from Schleicher. But the General was doomed; the spider was caught in the web of his own weaving.

Hitler's declining star was rising again; so much was clear to me even in distant Washington. But another thing was clearer. Hitler now ruled the Party as unchallenged Dictator. Whatever Strasser had planned, whatever I had hoped might develop, had evaporated into thin air.

XXX

THE FIELD-MARSHAL AND THE BOHEMIAN CORPORAL

"I've big news for you!"

My good friend Kenworthy of the United Press on the phone, sounded a trifle more excited than is usual for a newspaper man.

"What news?"

"You're the first I'm telling it to."

"All right-but tell me!"

"HITLER IS CHANCELLOR!"

I dropped the receiver. It was ten o'clock in the morning of 13 January 1933.

No use now to try to describe my emotions-they were too jumbled. For eleven years I had lived in the faith, fairly constant despite ups and downs, that some day Germany's destiny would rest in our hands, but now, when at last the great dream had become a reality, anxiety began almost at once to cast a shadow over my first joy.

Soon screaming headlines confirmed both the news and what I had feared. One glance at the names in the new Government told me the story. Three Nazis - Hitler, Frick, and Goering - against nine non-Nazis. Dr. Wilhelm Frick became Reichminister of the Interior, then still an office with little power, since in the Weimar Republic executive administration lay in the hands of the various states. Hermann Goering was named minister without portfolio, Federal Commissioner for Air Transport, and Prussian :Minister of the Interior. Thus he was subordinate to Papen, who being still the Federal Commissioner for the whole Prussian Cabinet, now became Prime Minister of Prussia and Vice-Chancellor of the Reich. So far, Goering's position was of dubious value, except that he had direct access to the Prussian police, the one instrument of power in Nazi hands. The Reichswehr had been entrusted to a general, the divisional commander of East Prussia, Werner von Blomberg. He was the new War Minister. The leader of the Stahlhelm, Franz Seldte, became Minister of Labour. Alfred Hugenberg, the chief of the Nationalists, received the two Reich Ministries of Economics and Food, as well as the corresponding portfolios in Prussia, which made him practical dictator of commerce and industry, in fact of the whole economic policy of the Reich. All the other ministries - foreign affairs, finance, justice, etc., remained in the hands of Ministers of the Papen-Schleicher Governments - Nationalists and representatives of the feudal gentry.

What a compromise! I was eager to know the inside story of the interesting deal arranged at that Cologne banker's home, the deal which Goebbels rightly calls a coup. Papen and his friends must have felt themselves perfectly secure, with Hitler so nicely encircled that he could not move.

Not until months later, when I was back in Germany, was I able to ferret out the story of that deal. The Reich had been surrendered to Hitler on certain 'conditions,' and it will be long before the actual history of that surrender is written. Perhaps the diaries, letters, and notes that would shed full light on the transaction will always be obscured. They are now protected by a conspiracy of silence in which there are three classes of partners: men who prefer not to speak because they are the beneficiaries of present conditions, men who dare not speak because they still have something to lose, and men who cannot speak because sudden death has sealed their lips. Papen knows, of course, and his knowledge is a Damocles' sword over his head, and-so long as Papen lives-over Hitler's as well.

At the beginning of his brief Chancellorship, Schleicher, though lacking parliamentary strength, had certain powerful forces behind him. He had the army; he had Hugenberg's Nationalists, heavy industry, and Junkerdom. Sadly over-estimating the potentialities of his role as 'social general,' he promptly began to alienate this support. Industry took fright over his threat that the Reichswehr was 'not chained to the capitalistic system,' and over his known dealings with Gregor Strasser, 'that national Bolshevist.' The landed aristocracy was infuriated by his colonization plan, a menace to their large estates. And when, to whip them into line, he opened a Pandora's box - the 'Osthilfe' scandal - Junkerdom and Hindenburg's entourage were thrown into sheer panic.

The 'Osthilfe' was a fund originally created to succour the poor peasants and impoverished landowners in East Prussia. Most of the millions that the Government fed into it, however, found their way into the pockets of the Junkers as sheer loot. Partial details of the scandal were made public, and a Reichstag committee began to investigate. Schleicher's refusal to muzzle this committee cost him the friendship of important people.

When I pored over the news in distant Washington, I did not know these things. As I studied the situation, however, it began to look more hopeful. Perhaps these fools would soon wake up in wonder. For there were to be new elections. That had been Chancellor Hitler's first demand, and it had gone through after a stormy debate, against Hugenberg's stubborn opposition.

Under the circumstances, skilful hands could use the new Reichstag as a lever to real power. With Goering head of the Prussian police, the key position to power, a striking Nazi victory at the polls was almost a foregone conclusion. Goering wouldn't hesitate to act. Who would stop him? Not Papen! 'Fraenzchen' certainly would be no match for our heavy-handed Hermann.

So Papen's intervention might develop into something really interesting after all. Hitler's bombastic proclamation sounded confident enough:

... The National Socialist Party knows that the new Government is no National Socialist Government, but it is conscious that it bears the name of its leader, Adolf Hitler. He has advanced with his shock troops and has placed himself at the head of the Government to lead the German people to liberty. Not only is the entire authority of the State to be wielded, but in the background, prepared for action, is the National Socialist movement of millions of followers united unto death with its leader....

Yes, the set-up showed distinct promise. It looked as if the Fuehrer had at last got his Trojan Horse inside the walls. Five and a half months ago he could have marched in with banners flying-but I resolved to think no more about that. It was clear that Hitler's final test had begun. Now he was in the vortex of his most crucial struggle.

At my desk in Washington, I devoured every paper I could find, trying to share in the wave of joy that was sweeping the German people. I read that on the evening of that historic Monday, the SA and the SS had staged, instead of the dreamed-of heroic 'March on Berlin,' a gigantic torchlight parade. Through the Brandenburger Tor, down Unter den Linden, and through the Wilhelmstrasse flowed the endless columns, like a river of fire hedged in by masses of humanity -men, women, girls, and boys, fathers with little children on their backs. Hour after hour they surged along, past the Chancellery, where at one of the windows stood the old Field-Marshal, nodding his head in salute and now and again tapping with his cane to the rhythm of the blaring military marches. Suddenly, grave of mien, he turned to Meissner and said: "I didn't know that they were so many-you should have told me . • . !" From another window only a few yards away the 'Bohemian Corporal,' Adolf Hitler, beaming with happiness, greeted with, outstretched arm the jubilant crowds streaming by to pack the Wilhelmplatz.

After all, I was only reading at a desk, four thousand miles from the storm-centre in Berlin. Now the time was ended for speculating, for brooding over lost chances or planning things that never could be. History had spoken. I was only a cog in the wheel, and mine was the duty to get into gear.

Under the circumstances, I had done about all I could to prepare for such an occasion. Though I had been warned against Dr. Sell, I had followed my instinct. Shortly before Hitler's appointment, I decided the time had come to suggest to him that from now on he should definitely work with me-secretly, of course. As I was convinced that the foreign office at home and its representatives abroad, partly through ignorance, partly through ill-will, would sabotage the Hitler regime, I appealed to Sell's common sense. I told him that Hitler's assumption of power would be only a question of weeks and that therefore he would do well to ally himself with us rather than with the ambassador.

Dr. Sell responded satisfactorily; he himself didn't think much of Dr. von Prittwitz und Gaffron, an outspoken anti-Nazi with no interest in any activist German programme, who preferred to spend his time on the golf-course. Of course we agreed that Sell should not allow it to appear that an understanding existed between us. On the contrary, he was to speak only sarcastically of me, the better to learn what people really thought of us. He did this very neatly. On 2 February, however, after Hitler's rise to power, he turned over to me five minutes of his monthly broadcasting programme to Germany, allowing me to tell Germany the reaction in America to Hitler's success.

With great excitement, I took the air for the first time in my life, a day or two after Chancellor Hitler's broadcast in Germany, relayed to this country by short wave. I told my countrymen :

'America, too, needs a Hitler or a Mussolini! Yes, if I were a German, I, too, would be a Hitlerite!' So say many Americans today. The sudden coming into power of the Hitler Government has had the effect of a bomb in America, has aroused tremendous interest everywhere and undoubtedly has evoked sympathy, surprise, and admiration. Confused for years by false Press reports about Germany, and misinformed by articles and interviews of so-called Germans who have travelled through this country posing as experts on German affairs, the American public could not help but have a false conception, or no knowledge, of the new, young Germany, of its leader, our Reich Chancellor, Adolf Hitler ... and of the powerful National Socialist movement ... What an experience for me to hear over the wide ocean the voice of my leader, the only man who can save Germany! ... The American Press has taken the news much more calmly and moderately than might have been expected after its rather hostile attitude of the last two years.

Naturally, my talk over an American network was criticized as 'the radio exuberances of the Nazi ambassador.' But I was thinking of the millions of Germans listening in, and of the potential influence on the coming elections in March. That my broadcast had some effect was proved by many letters from home, still being forwarded to me weeks later.

In Germany and Italy, the offensive power of the Fascist groups had originally come almost entirely from the veterans' organizations, the old front-line fighters. Very early I had come to the conclusion that the corresponding organizations were the most likely nucleus of an American movement, particularly since they were held together by a common grievance-the bonus that had not yet been granted. At any rate it was important that the activist organizations should not fall into the hands of the Communists, who were trying, though with scant success, to capture them. It is an historical lie to brand the veterans' march on Washington as a Communist undertaking. That march had accumulated an immense and changing crowd in the capital. I had looked it over in 1932, and talks with several leaders had convinced me that it held tremendous possibilities in an America seething with revolutionary currents.

Now I got in touch with some of the 'bonusers' who still were maintaining loose contact with most of the groups of dispersed veterans. We arranged a meeting for February, and

W. W. Waters, the former chief of the 'Bonus Army,' came all the way across the continent to attend it. In the many hours we spent together, I explained National Socialism in relation to the world situation, pointing out especially the racial implications. Germany was the torch-bearer in a world programme; if it was to be pushed through, America must wake up. In short, I initiated them as best I could and felt that I had won them over completely. Seeming to perceive the value to them of my practical experience abroad with problems more or less similar, they were ready to undertake preparations for an organization in America, and agreed with me that veterans who had been bombed with tear-gas and treated like Communists were now good soil for a movement as Americans rather than as veterans.

Now that Hitler was Chancellor of the Reich, my position had become much more interesting and important overnight. I found myself being sought out from all sides by literally hundreds of Americans of every rank and station, from senators to bootblacks. In talking with them I tried always to put aside my own prejudices and passions; I too had learned to listen.

Americans are badly informed about Europe, just as Europeans are about America. In time I developed a regular method for furthering sympathy with Germany. Most effective was the argument that historical forces and geographic conditions largely determine a nation's ideology and its concept of state; therefore the so-called German militarism was not the excrescence of an innate ferocity but was the result of Germany's geographic realities. My country was the heart of Europe, limited in room and hemmed in by hostile neighbours richer than she. Capitalistic individualism was a luxury for rich and strategically invulnerable countries like the U.S.A.; but even in America, despite her seemingly boundless territory, the question of form of government would become a paramount issue as soon as the land should become filled and the social problem should become acute with the emergence of the room-problem.

My relations with the German embassy, however, grew more strained, and the New York consul, Paul Schwarz, a Jew, was appearing on all occasions as the official representative of the Hitler Government. I did not object to that, for I was not blind to the potential value of a Jewish consul in Jewish New York, provided he showed himself a diplomat. But I did object to the tone of affairs. The German consulate-general gave an official dinner in honour of Lion Feuchtwanger, the novelist, who was a violent anti-Nazi. The German guests were all Jews, and the conversation produced such a vehement cursing of everything Nazi that native-born American guests had to come to our defence. And Feuchtwanger - so read the report I received- boasted of having been offered ten thousand dollars by Jews for four broadcasts on 'The Menace of Hitler.'

When I learned that Feuchtwanger had been invited, with Albert Einstein, to be a luncheon guest at the embassy in Washington, I decided that the German diplomatic representatives were carrying things too far; they seemed to be brazenly ignoring the new Government and conducting themselves exactly as if Hitler were not its Chancellor. So I took the initiative, and did what I could to emphasize the fact that the wind was now blowing from another direction. I made this clear at a 'Bierabend' which Dr. Sell gave at my instigation for a number of important Washington correspondents, and at an equally lively evening in my own house, attended by a different group of interesting people.

The anti-Nazi propaganda was gaining momentum, however, though I was doing all I could to anticipate and forestall it. Men in several embassies were sympathetic to us, and from them I gained ideas for the conduct of our propaganda campaign, and also, on occasion, guarded co-operation.

Towards the end of February I decided that Party reasons and my own interests required my going to Berlin. I appointed Dr. Leibbrandt as my confidential man in Washington; Sell and Smetana were to maintain touch with him. They were to keep me informed and act discreetly for me when necessary.

It seemed cruel that our shortness of funds again made it impossible for Mildred to accompany me. She was to keep an eye on things in Washington for a while and then go to Detroit to spend the few remaining weeks of my stay abroad with her family.

I left Washington by motor immediately after a hurried dinner. Mildred came down to the car with me for a last good-bye. There were no tears, for I was not to be gone for long and would surely come back with everything in secure order. How little each of us knows what lies ahead of him! Through a misted glass I had a final glimpse of my wife waving to me with her tender, child-like hand, the first soft flakes of a gentle snowstorm powdering her hair.

W. W. Waters and one of his friends went to New York with me on business of their own; Waters was to drive my car back to Washington. The trip brought us closer together. Waters had made up his mind to go ahead with new organization plans, and was eager for me to get back. He inscribed for me his first copy of his book, B. E. F. : The Whole Story of the Bonus Army.[1]

In New York I was the guest of a vice-consul at the German consulate-general whom I had known for some time as an able man and a secret member of the Nazi Party. On my way through New York the preceding October I had made an

1 As told to William C. White, The John Day Company, New York, 1933.

arrangement with him and had found him very useful. From his home, I now gave last instructions to the men I had organized in many places over a long period of time, for example, employees of the various steamship lines.

From one of these representatives I learned that Lion Feuchtwanger had been planning to leave on the Europa but had changed at the last minute to the Alhert Ballin, on which I was also sailing. We promised to make interesting shipmates. Roosevelt's inauguration was to take place within a few days, and I made a point of getting in touch with persons who, directly or indirectly, had access to him. That done, I sought out other people of interest and influence. At his New York home I saw Colonel Edward M. House, whose fame in Europe had reached almost legendary proportions, especially in Germany, which he had visited as Wilson's emissary during the World War. I had a long and stimulating conversation with him. The little old man, with his gentle manner and the intently watching look of a mouse, listened to me with the greatest interest, and, though he did not commit himself, expressed sympathy with Hitler; he definitely saw that there was a great force behind our movement. He invited me warmly to see him again after my return, and to greet his old friends in Germany. "Only," he added, "they will not be exactly in Nazi ranks."

A splendid lady was the late Mrs. Henry Loomis, an aunt of former Secretary of State Stimson, and grand patroness in the United States of the White Russians; I had, in fact, met her through a White Russian of rather dubious authenticity. The Grand Duchess Victoria, wife of the Grand Duke Cyril, had been her guest in the United States, and had made a propaganda trip throughout the country under her auspices. In a letter to me, Mrs. Loomis expressed her interest in all that was being accomplished in Germany, and invited me out to her home at Tuxedo Park. I spent an afternoon there and stayed to dinner. She was active and intelligent, a tall impressive woman, with the head of a lion. Her position was strong in the old wealth of the East and among important and influential Americans all over the country. It was planned that after my return from Germany I was to meet many of these people through her, and talk before groups of those who were definitely anti-Communistic and conservative, and before other groups who could be won over.

Definitely nationalistic and folkic in her sympathies, Mrs. Loomis promised to be a most valuable contact. She offered me whole-hearted co-operation, and we discussed a programme of talks before women's organizations. I was to open my campaign with a talk on Hitler and the Nazi movement before a picked audience which she would invite to her house; I expected to be ready for her party by the end of April at the very latest. She was planning to go to Europe in the summer, and I was to arrange for her to see things in Germany at first-hand.

On 1 March, the date of my sailing, I had an appointment with Victor F. Ridder of the New Yorker Staats-Zeitung, the largest German language daily in America.

I courteously pointed out to Mr. Ridder that it had been the policy of the Staats-Zeitung to support whatever government was in office in Germany at the time, but that he had broken this custom when Hitler came in, and had continued his violent anti-Hitler campaign. I suggested that in the interest of German-Americans, it might be wise to moderate his tone until he knew the results of the 5 March election, but I permitted myself to inform him, majority or no majority, Hitler would stay in power. Mr. Ridder was irritated and freely expressed his condemnation of the Nazi policy as ridiculously anti-Jewish and anti-Catholic. Our interview developed into a heated argument, and in the midst of one of his tirades I got up and walked out.

On my way out of his office I was accosted by his secretary, who certainly had overheard the conversation, but who now expressed enthusiasm over the way things were going ill Germany. Having apparently discovered sudden but deep sympathy with Hitler, he offered me his services. Then, in the waiting room, a Colonel Emerson introduced himself as one eager to aid. He was an American-born citizen and former war correspondent, a Germanophile in the employ of the Staats-Zeitung.

At the consulate in the Battery I sent in my card bearing the swastika insignia of the Nazi Party to Consul Schwarz.

The presence of "Hitler's representative" had thrown the outer offices into quiet consternation. I went from room to room speaking separately to each subordinate official, most of whom I knew to be anti-Nazi-simply saying that no one would insist that they become Nazis, but that they must remember they were Germans, and act accordingly. If Hitler should fall, chaos would envelope Germany, and as Germans we must all pull together and forget old disagreements. It was embarrassing to see each one shrink into himself, thinking of his future, preparing to change his opinions in order to hold his job. After all, I held no office. But they listened.

Two hours later I had a laugh. I learned then that the door had hardly closed behind me when Schwarz called the whole personnel together, made a written record of every word I had said to everybody present, and telephoned the incredible affront to Washington. His Excellency the Ambassador was furious, and poured his rage into his end of the wire. "The impudence! You should have thrown the fellow out!"

I arrived at the dock late. The gong was already calling visitors ashore, but I found my cabin filled with people. The moment they left, there suddenly appeared in the door a huge fellow who looked like a gangster; he was accompanied by a more civil-looking man. They asked me to come out of my cabin to hear something in confidence, insisting that it was important. Unsuspecting, I went out with them. The corridor was empty. They took me under the arms and began marching me along. I shook myself free, but they grabbed me again and said brusquely, "We want an interview. We must know what it's all about. Come along."

I did not move. "Who are you, anyway?" I shouted. The gorilla took a badge out of his pocket, while I did some quick thinking. "You know what that is," he snarled. "Any one can have that," I shot back at him. "I'm a diplomat-you had better be careful!" And I stuck my White House Press card under his nose. They looked at each other and disappeared; the bluff had worked.

With so much on my mind, for the moment I attached no particular importance to the incident, and went about seeing to my luggage, telegrams, and letters. The ship had been moving for some time when I recalled that Feuchtwanger had booked on the same boat-the Albert Ballin. I sent for the chief of the Nazi cell, which on this vessel was securely established amongst officers and crew. He told me that Feuchtwanger had arrived with all his luggage, but that a messenger had come with a letter for him which was delivered to his cabin. Thereupon Feuchtwanger had collected his bags and had cancelled his passage.

At any rate, it was a relief to me not to have Feuchtwanger on the same ship. But not to the Nazi sailors. They were disappointed that he had slipped through their fingers-fingers that looked rough and hard enough to me.

"That Judenschwein would never have reached Cherbourg - he would have fallen overboard," one said grimly, with a telling gesture. "Ha, even sharks couldn't digest that corpse!" said another, with a grin.

That startled and disturbed me. Nazis had much to learn. They were surprised when I told them how foolish that would have been - it would have caused an international outcry.

"Why?" they said. "Who cares? Nobody would have known how, when, and where he had disappeared." But Schwarz had been astute, for a German boat is German territory, and Feuchtwanger could have been arrested.

It was a rush to catch up with the newspapers I had neglected in New York, and all I could manage was the headlines. But there was news. The Reichstag had burned! Immediately there flashed through my mind: Clever! Well done! I took for granted, of course, that the Nazis had done it. But I couldn't guess how badly they were going to muff it, when the clumsy trial of Van der Lubbe was to stir the world.

Reading between the lines of Berlin despatches, I could see that developments in Germany were running according to plan. Preceding the Reichstag fire, Nazi Storm Troopers had been armed as 'auxiliary police'; even stronger curbs had been placed on Nazi foes, and only the Government and its spokesmen were allowed to be heard on the radio. Right after the fire, Communist deputies were arrested all over the land, Red leaders were jailed, the entire Leftist Press was banned, and four or five thousand Communists were thrown behind bars. It looked like the end of the Communist Party, and, more than that, the destruction of Marxism in Germany. Yes, the Reichstag fire had meaning; ethics aside, it all looked like good politics to me. Good politics, too, had been Hitler's final campaign speech at Koenigsberg, in East Prussia. With a great show of emotion he had recounted how he, the simple grenadier who had done his duty on the Western Front, and the venerable Reichspresident, who had freed East Prussia from the enemy, had clasped hands and had pledged themselves to work together for the salvation of Germany.

But the foreign aspect looked less promising. There had been a silly outburst from Goering in answer to a Swedish paper's attack on him, and Hitler had given an incautious Press interview. He had also made an infelicitous statement on our Italian policy which had raised almost no echo in Italy. It seemed to me as though forces were at work encouraging Hitler and his men to expose themselves to ridicule. And I remembered the remark of a friend in the foreign office. For years, he told me, this had been a common saying among the higher officials: 'Let Hitler come into the Government; we'll see to it that he makes a fool of himself.'

But I made up my mind not to worry, and to enjoy a new experience-that of casting my vote. I had been abroad at every election except the July 1932 poll, and then I had arrived in Germany too late to register my name. Now, for the first time, I voted on board ship-far from thinking that within the year I would have to vote for Hitler in a concentration camp.

The ship's radio was in constant touch with Germany, and we on board probably knew the results as soon as the people at home.

Of the 647 deputies elected, the smaller parties won 13 seats, the Communist Party 81, the Social Democrats 120, the Centre and Bavarian People's Parties 92, the Nationalists and Stahlhelm 53, and the Nazis 288 seats. This was not quite enough to secure for Hitler a clear majority in the new Reichstag; we still needed the Nationalists' votes. But the elimination of the Communist Party would serve. Now I understood better why all the Communist deputies had been arrested!

But I had expected an even greater Nazi victory. Hermann's little fire, Joseph's great tattoos, Adolf's heart-rending final appeal from old Koenigsberg, where German kings had been crowned, the bogey of Bolshevik revolution-all these had yielded much, but they should have yielded more. Swift action followed, however. State after state surrendered to 'Nazi Commissioners' appointed by Hitler, and by the time my ship docked at Hamburg, stubborn Bavaria, the last to oppose the assault, had fallen under Nazi control.

My country was 'conquered' before I put foot on its soil. It was mid-afternoon when I arrived at the office in Hamburg for Nazis in foreign lands, curious to meet Dr. Nieland at last. But instead I met Ernst Wilhelm Bohle, a handsome young man in his early twenties.

"Nein, Herr Polizeipraesident Doktor Nieland ist nicht hier. I have taken his place in this office," he informed me with an important air.

I was floored. "What-what did you say?"

"Don't you know that we are having a revolution here? Herr Dr. Nieland is now the new President of Police."

Astounding-that fellow President of Police in the second largest German city! Was this Nazi nepotism, or, more probably, just one of those absurd toss-ups that will happen in revolutions?

It was easy to make the young man talk about himself.

"Oh, I," he said with some pride, " I was born in Australia. My father was a German, I just happened to be born there. I came to Germany before the war, when I was still a small child. I had a British passport once … Oh, no, I haven't been back since."

Apparently, for an engaging youth, to have been born among kangaroos and to have travelled on a British passport was qualification enough to place him at the head of the Nazi Auslands Organization. I didn't know then that he was a special protégé of 'Fraeulein' Hess, as certain disrespectful Nazis sometimes called Hitler's deputy, Rudolf Hess, who likewise was an Auslandsdeutscher, born in Egypt.

When I told Herr Bohle who I was, and advised doing something quickly to stop the silly but nevertheless dangerous doings of American Nazis, especially in New York, who now were responsible to him, he said that my name was very familiar in that connection. He had heard a lot of me, and that Herr Polizeipraesident Dr. Nieland certainly would want to see me.

"Please wait a minute," he said eagerly. "I'll telephone him that you're here."

He left the room, and when he returned said in a tense manner: "Herr Polizeipraesident would like very much indeed to see you. He can come here, or, if you prefer, you might see him at police headquarters."

Just then the telephone rang in the room where I was sitting. The thought flashed through my mind: "Why hadn't he used this telephone?"

"That's fine, thank you. I've a taxi waiting outside - tell him I'll be there shortly."

With that I left. Putting two and two together, it occurred to me that the chap might take the fancy to arrest me. Crazier things than that have happened in revolutions, and for all I knew there might now be dozens of Nielands and Bohles ruling in Germany. So I decided to drive to the station and entrain for Berlin.

Long after midnight I 'was still reading German newspapers in bed at the Kaiserhof, the same bed in the same room that I had occupied during my last visit, when Hitler had also been staying there.

XXXI

HINDENBURG'S TROJAN HORSE

Would I find Hitler changed? Would he even see me? I had a feeling that he would, and while I shaved next morning I ran over in my mind what I must say to him, even talking aloud to him as if he were there.

Entering the chancellery, I perceived that the Fuehrer's bodyguard, somewhat augmented, had already moved in. Sentries who recognized me greeted me and passed me on. At the wide staircase inside stood liveried lackeys. Everywhere in the corridors were men of the secret service of the SS, everywhere an impression of power and wealth. The whole tempo and atmosphere smelled of change.

On the first floor, adjoining the Chancellor's rooms, I walked into the office of Brueckner and Schaub, who greeted me with loud hellos. They were not great personalities; triumph beamed on their brows. And there in the corner was brave Colonel Hierl, later Unter-Staatssekretaer as chief of the labour service and labour camps organizations, but then visibly a little down in the mould because nothing had come to him yet. I was to meet more of these figures, slinking around with depressed mien but with hope not yet relinquished.

Looking at this scene-telephone ringing without stop, people coming and going - I knew right off the bat that nothing had changed with the Nazis. Every individual would have to fight for his own position in the general grab, and if he had a mission, he would have to fight for the chance to fulfil it.

"Not today, old man; there isn't a chance," Brueckner told me. "But I'll put you down for an appointment… Yes, I'll tell him you are here."

"Fine," I said, "I'll wait outside." I still felt that Hitler would see me, and I wanted to collect myself in case he did. So I sat down in the hall on a bench placed in the semi-darkness of a niche.

I was just laying my overcoat and hat beside me when a door opened and Hitler came out. I got up. Recognizing me, he came up and exclaimed: "Oh, Ludecke, Sie sind's - wie geht's?" And putting his hands on my shoulders, he said, looking straight into my eyes: "Are you satisfied now? "

"Gewiss," I replied warmly, and such is the magnetism of the man that at the moment I meant it wholeheartedly. "My very best and sincerest congratulations -"

" Excuse me," he interrupted, smiling. "Wait right here - I'll be back in a moment. 'Ich muss mal…'" and he pointed to a door behind me, through which he disappeared.

I called that luck! If it hadn't been for necessity's little prompting just at the right time, I might have had to wait God knows how long to see him. I looked at my watch; it was a little after ten o'clock. In less than a minute he was back and took me into his working-room.

This room was large with several windows, furnished in elegant but rather modernistic style, not too much to my taste. I sat in a comfortable arm-chair near the window, while Hitler perched easily on the arm of his chair, a low round table between us, and we chatted as if this were a most ordinary event. He looked well; a quiet energy lent strength to his appearance.

I told him I had just arrived and that he was the first person I had wanted to see. "I feel very grateful for your giving me the chance, and I'd better use every minute. I'll plunge right into telling you what I want you to know, if you don't mind."

"Yes, go right ahead," he said.

I reported concisely on America, its grave national crisis, the likelihood that in the United States as well the Roosevelt administration marked the end of an epoch and the beginning of a new one; emphasized again the enormous importance of winning the sympathy and good-will of America, which now offered more parallels with Germany than ever. For many reasons the potentialities were great; if we acted intelligently much could be achieved, not only in the United States but also in England. That country would be increasingly obliged to shape British policy to conform with American policy, for Canada's sake, if for no other reason. Canada was the link connecting the British Empire with America, just as England was the link with Europe, and Canada was showing a growing tendency to identify herself with the American system rather than the European. I touched lightly on having been left in the lurch about money, whereupon he patted my shoulder, saying: "We've had our own difficulties, believe me. From now on things will be different."

"Of course," I said. "And then that Strasser affair."

At Strasser's name that foxy expression flashed over Hitler's face. Although he has learned to exercise marvellous self-control, he is by nature too impulsive entirely to control his eyes and mouth. Whenever something really touches him and he passes over it without a word, one who has known him from the early days can read a lot in the expression of his mobile face.

"Yes - that Strasser affair," he said, suppressed anger and contempt in his voice. He added, as if to himself: "What luck that it happened then - what if it had happened now!"

That was enough: I knew that only a most unusual situation could bring Strasser back to the scene. This was plainly a ticklish theme; so I switched to the anti-Nazi propaganda in America, and its rapidly growing momentum. "And the whispering campaign branding you as a megalomaniac is common talk now. It -"

"Tstse... Tstse..." Hitler interrupted me, looking annoyed. "Incredible!" He clearly wanted to hear no more of that.

I accused a certain person of incompetence. "He really is a 'Scheisskerl'" - I blurted out, but when my own ears heard it - for 'Scheisskerl' is a bad word - I was shocked at myself and stopped. Hitler raised his eyebrows a little.

"I apologize - it slipped out - I'm sorry, Herr-Herr" - "Never mind," he said, smiling. "And just call me Herr Hitler, plain Herr Hitler, always, for my old friends."

Reassured, I said: "I realize that we cannot change ambassadors and consuls overnight, but a change in Washington is imperative…"

"Very good. How would Luther do? I must get rid of him; I want Schacht in his place. Washington takes care of Luther - I must give him something if I show him the door!"

I did some rapid thinking. Luther's removal would be a delicate matter, since the position of the President of the Reichsbank was somewhat subject to international considerations, the Bank of International Settlements, in Basle. I happened to know that Luther, once a burgomaster who had been lucky enough to play the role of Chancellor for a while, had never been in America and did not know English, and I figured quickly that he would have to depend on me somewhat.

So I said that if Luther had to be compensated with an ambassadorship he would perhaps do best in Washington, where a man with known liberal and democratic tendencies would be well received. But he must be under the eyes of a trusted Nazi. And if Hitler considered it favourably, I should like to return as Press attaché of the Embassy, a position which would afford me diplomatic immunity and at the same time permit me to be ' the eye of the movement.'

"Excellent," Hitler said. "A good solution. Prittwitz must go; you'll have things much easier with Luther. Of course, I haven't control over the Foreign Office as yet, you understand."

"I understand perfectly. I can make it so hot for Prittwitz that the Foreign Office will advise him to resign before it's too late."

"Yes, that may be," Hitler returned, "but the 'Gleichschaltung' of the Foreign Office will be along and tedious business."

That was the first time that I had heard the word ' Gleichschaltung,' which meant co-ordination in the Nazi sense the Nazification of the administration, of public offices and the national organizations; in short, the preparatory step to the Totalitarian State. The idea gave me a welcome opportunity to broach the subject which was most important to me.

"It will," I said, "because there's no Party agency which could do the work for you without your compromising yourself in the least. A foreign bureau of the Party would come in handy now. I could act as the Party's ram against the Foreign Office if we had a Party foreign bureau. We must proceed very carefully in that direction, but there are some things which simply have to be done. Don't you think it's high time now to organize such a bureau?"

"I don't know," Hitler replied thoughtfully. "It's a delicate matter at this stage."

I argued that there were things to be done which must not be connected with Hitler or with any government office. There was one trick we could learn from the Bolsheviks their Comintern Office. Out of the side of their mouths they were denying any connection with foreign propaganda, but out of the other they were preaching world revolution. Whenever anything happened abroad that seemed to prove the duplicity of Moscow, the Government would say that it had no connection with the Comintern and was therefore not responsible. It seemed to be one of the Bolshevik tactics we should adopt; we'd be accused anyway. Why not organize a foreign bureau now? Many things could not go through the regular channels of the Foreign Office for the simple reason that many officials here and abroad were our declared enemies, and would sabotage Nazi policy and discredit Hitler wherever they could-at least for some time to come. "I really think this is a very important matter which should be attended to at once," I insisted.

"Oh, I hear that from morning to night," Hitler cut in a little impatiently. "This must be done, that is essential. After all I can't do the impossible. A little patience, please - for the present I can't do more than pick from among 'the most important' those that I think really are the most urgent."

"Don't I know it," I said appeasingly. "I don't envy you. But if I am to act as a ram against the F. O. I must have some authority, and there are a few things that cannot wait. If I could act for Rosenberg as the chief of the new bureau -"

"There's no need for an office now. You can go ahead; I know about it, that's enough. But this, mark well, is my silent consent."

Now I had him where I wanted him: it was obvious that he wanted to avoid committing himself about Rosenberg. "That's very well," I said, "but if I cannot use your name, I'll have to act for somebody; I myself am still unknown. Who besides you and Rosenberg knows what I am doing? I must represent something, somebody, and that can only be Rosenberg."

" Good - I'll think it over," he conceded finally. "You go ahead and talk with Rosenberg, but be careful."

I thanked him, and said I would also have some definite suggestions to make about foreign ·propaganda, the Foreign Office, and so forth; if he preferred I'd give him a memorandum. "And then, of course," I added, "there's the money question - I would need quite a lot."

"Fine - do that. Yes, make your headquarters with Rosenberg. Those suggestions about your needs, you understand, will have to go through other channels. I'll put you in touch immediately with Funk; he is the connecting link with the F. O. He'll see to it that your appointment as Press attaché goes through promptly - he'll take good care of you."

Hitler walked over to his desk and instructed Funk by telephone that I was in Berlin and would return to Washington as Press attaché; that he was to do everything necessary, and that I would tell him the rest myself.

He had hardly put the receiver down when the telephone rang. "I'm having callers," he said. "That's all for the moment - I'll see you soon." He shook my hand in dismissal.

As I closed the door behind me, two tall figures were approaching it: the smiling, blond civilian with the lined countenance was Vice-Chancellor von Papen, and the taller, darker officer, cool and erect as a rifle-barrel, was the War Minister, General Wemer von Blomberg. They were talking intently, voices lowered, arrogant assurance in their faces.

I was disappearing round the corner, feeling myself an important personage to have snatched forty-five minutes from the chief, when I heard a hail. Brueckner came running after me.

"Do you know a Dr. Somebody from California?" he asked. "He left just a minute ago. Hanfstaengl urged me to see him. I sent him flying back and told him not to pester me with gossip. The man had a letter from Dr. Nieland and said he was the representative of a certain person."

"Yes", I said, "I expect you mean 'G'."

The fervour which surrounded the appearance of Adolf Hitler at a major appearance can be sensed from this powerful image captured as Hitler attempted to leave the venue swamped by adoring sympathisers. The parallels with modern rock stadium concerts are obvious. Ludecke first heard Hitler speak at a huge outdoor event like this and was mesmerised by the combination of the spectacle and the power of Hitler's oratory. On the day following the event he sought an audience with Hitler which led directly to the events described in these pages.

"That was it - 'G'. He drivelled about your having been in prison in America; he must warn me against you, and similar rubbish. But you ought to know about it. Chummy with Hess, and now has his office with Goering in his Palais. So watch your step!"

Thanking him, I went straight to the Kaiserhof, for I had an idea that my detractor from America would be staying there. He was. I left a polite note asking him to see me. The usually dignified and conventional Kaiserhof was a beehive, chockfull of Nazis from all over Germany, each with the Nazi eagle in his buttonhole, each coming to make his connections and his fortune. I took a good sniff of the atmosphere and then hurried over to see Rosenberg, now permanently located in Berlin in the branch-office of the Voelkischer Beohachter, though the South German edition of the V. B. was still being published in Munich.

Rosenberg was clearly surprised to see me. "I'm glad you're here," he said. When I told him in detail of my interview with Hitler, he did not conceal his satisfaction, and I think I jumped degrees in his esteem. I knew that, for personal motives, I was welcome as an ally in a pivotal position respecting Nazi foreign policy. For Rosenberg had no 'elbows' and knew me for an activist. Now definitely outstripped by Goebbels, he was in the distasteful position of one of the oldest Party members who has been pushed aside. My elbows would be useful.

He emphatically confirmed and extended my impression that Hitler was still far from being a dictator. "The situation is extremely delicate, and we must be very cautious. The composition of the cabinet includes relatively few Nazis and therefore, from a revolutionary viewpoint, is a compromise. Hitler has made important concessions. The Foreign Office is one of them, and under the circumstances it was quite impossible to appoint me Foreign Minister."

He agreed that we were in a bad way without a definite foreign bureau of the Party to exercise pressure on the Foreign Office, which was in itself a power in Germany. Carried over more or less intact from the old monarchy, surviving the revolution of 1918, it was the traditional stronghold of Capitalism, of the Centrists, of Junkerdom, and, to some extent, of the Jewish influence. The few Socialists whom the German Republic had established there had been moulded to form. Jealous of its privileges, it might sabotage our foreign policy, and its co-ordination in a Nazi sense would be impossible for some time. We concluded that we must try to squeeze concessions from the Foreign Office by systematic bullying and bluffing. I was to act as Rosenberg's spearhead; he himself would undertake to wrest from Hitler prompt authorization to organize a Party foreign bureau.

Then Rosenberg told me with sarcasm and unconcealed ill humour that Goebbels' official appointment as Propaganda Minister in the cabinet was only a question of days; that was probably why Hitler had been so reluctant to empower Rosenberg himself with the Party's foreign bureau.

"Of course." I said. "I see it clearly now. There is the question of foreign propaganda, and the secret fund which the Foreign Office controls. And the Ministry of Finance is in the hands of the Nationalists. I had been wondering how Hitler could solve the problem of the huge amount of money needed. A foreign bureau of the Party makes sense only if we handle the foreign propaganda. I don't know Funk, though I think I saw him once with Strasser. Who is he? What do you think of him?"

"Funk is a spent man, but his position is important; he's Press chef of the Reichsregierung and as such reports daily to Hitler."

"Apparently he was not a Strasser man?"

"Mein Lieber - that is a delicate point I'd rather not discuss."

I exploded. "This damned mysteriousness! How can I proceed intelligently if I don't know who's who or what's what? I'm going directly from here to see him. Is he a Goebbels man, or what?"

"I really don't know myself. For a time he was Hitler's economic adviser and served as connecting link with industry. Very useful in fishing for money. He joined the Party only two years ago, leaving the Berliner Boersenzeitung where he was editor of the economic section. No, he's certainly not a radical; on the contrary, his appointment was a sedative for timid souls."

"This is very important news, you know," I said. "If he falls into Goebbels' claws, it's good night!" I told Rosenberg of my broad propaganda programme for America. A national paper, the Washington Post, was for sale, and there was a chance of getting control of it with certain Americans. I spoke of the possibilities with W. W. Waters, and so on, and added that when I had hinted to Hitler that larger funds were needed he had cut me short by saying that I had better talk that over with Funk. Though I felt that Rosenberg's position was not what it should be, I said that I would throw my lot in with his.

"With good teamwork we can get somewhere, but you must get going. We must play party politics now, otherwise we're whipped. I like it as little as you do, but we must do it. Hitler is in a favourable mood. Strike while the iron is hot; you should have his O. K. for the foreign bureau next week; without it we can do nothing. You know how he likes to juggle with two rival groups, and your best argument is that the foreign bureau would be the only weapon with which he could keep the Foreign Office on the defensive; besides, it will take care of things which cannot be done through official channels."

So we planned our campaign together and came to a definite understanding. It was now so late that I postponed my visit to Walther Funk to the following Monday.

Rosenberg had put a stenographer at my disposal. The next afternoon, a Saturday, I was dictating the first memorandum for Hitler in my room at the Kaiserhof when the doctor from California announced himself, and very politely I asked him to come up.

When I walked into Funk's private office on Monday, in the beautiful old Schinkel-Palais, now being reconditioned to house Goebbels' new Propaganda Ministry, I recognized the bald-headed man with the drooping shoulders as the one I had seen for a fleeting moment in Strasser's apartment at the 'Excelsior' the year before Funk received me as kindly as his careless and indifferent manner allowed. He looked indeed 'spent,' with flabby cheeks and sagging mouth, but behind his tired eyes worked a shrewd and practical mind, and except for a tendency to quibble I found him rather likeable and matter-of-fact. He informed me that he had arranged for my appointment as Press attaché, which now would run through the ordinary routine. "It will take only a few weeks," he said. "In the meantime, we can discuss those other things you need."

Then he introduced me to Geheimrat Aschmann, next to himself the most important man in the Reichs Press-bureau; he would take care of me. Aschmann was a gentleman and impressed me as a pleasant personality, well-groomed and good looking, with the polished manner of the professional diplomat of the old school. Our first meeting was more of a feeler on both sides, but I had several more business-like interviews with him in the ensuing weeks. That first talk, however, held an incident which showed me the touchiness of these non-Nazi officials and their sense of personal, insecurity. We went into Aschmann's office, and there I told him that unfortunately I hadn't understood his name. When, in repeating it, I innocently drawled the word a little, he drew himself up and said:

"Herr Ludecke, you do not mean to insinuate that perhaps my name has Jewish connotations?" Such an idea had never crossed my mind.

During the next few days I finished the memoranda for Hitler and to avoid red-tape sent them to him personally through Julius Schreck, his chauffeur, who was also a guest at the 'Kaiserhof.' Rosenberg and I carefully planned our offensive against the Foreign Office. As an opening gun, I prepared several articles for the Voelkischer Beobachter, and they were set up ready to print; they would be sure to give the Foreign Office and some of its representatives in the United States a headache.

Aschmann arranged for me the appointments I wanted at the Foreign Office, and I went there repeatedly. I wasn't particularly welcome, for I was using my elbows, by giving them to understand that National Socialism was now governing.

You must see the Foreign Office. There is tradition. There and among the great international industrialists and financiers you see the relatively few people of Germany who know how to dress and have a certain form, a certain style. From their one-sided and superior viewpoint, they regarded National Socialism as something they would soon finish off. Nazis had learned their tactics in fights with Communists and Sozis, where they were splendid. But they didn't feel very comfortable in a salon. It was relatively easy for these gentlemen of the F. O. to deal with a typical Nazi dare-devil by politely complimenting him out the door with profuse promises, never kept. "Really, they are very polite, very nice," he would say, wonderingly.

But I was immune to compliments and good suits. Herr Geheimrat So-and-So and His Excellency This-and-That almost lost their tempers at my persistence. After a promise had been made, I followed the practice of calling up twice a day if necessary to ask if it had been carried out. Naturally, they disliked the proofs of my articles.

Whenever they yielded a point, they would sabotage their own decisions. Thus one diplomat, for example, was not recalled to Germany, as I had requested, but was relieved of his office, permitting him to play the role of martyr rather than subjecting him to the .odium of declining to obey orders in case he refused to return. At any rate, Prittwitz resigned, Luther resigned from the Reichsbank, and Schacht once more became its head. The astute Schacht always knows what he is doing. He knew when he said in an interview, in November 1932: "If Hitler does not become Chancellor now, he will four months hence; he can wait."

Still resolved to bring about the dissolution of the Nazi units in the United States, I went to see Dr. Ley in his suite at the Hotel Excelsior, and found him talking over the long-distance telephone with a subordinate on each side. He looked up to say, "Hello, Ludecke! Fabulous! I'm governing," and then, as always, shook and sputtered with laughter.

Six months earlier, this mighty man had agreed to the disavowal of the Nazi units in America. But when I asked him now what had become of the dissolution order, he tried to shunt me off to Goebbels, on the ground that Goebbels, as Propaganda Minister, would probably take over foreign propaganda as well. I pressed him to telephone the little Doctor for an immediate appointment for the two of us.

Ley tried, but couldn't reach him. "Why not try Hess?" he said then. "He's now at the head of all the affairs of the Party, and takes great interest in the welfare of Germans abroad." So I arranged an appointment with Hess for the next morning.

"But if I don't get immediate action from him, we'll both go to see Goebbels. Is it a promise?" "Okay, Mister Americano," Ley said in English, and I left him howling with laughter. My meeting with Rudolf Hess in his new office of the Verbindungstab at the Wilhelmstrasse was less amusing.

Hess was then barely thirty-seven years of age. He had been brought up in Alexandria, Egypt, until he was fourteen, and had continued school in Germany in preparation some day to take over his father's business. In the midst of his apprenticeship the war broke out, and he volunteered with a Bavarian regiment in Munich. He was shot through the lungs, promoted to officer rank, and was admitted to the Imperial Flying Corps towards the end of hostilities. Back in· Munich after the revolution, he entered the commercial fields studying on the side at the university.

419

In May 1921 he joined the Nazi Party as an SA man. In the Beer Hall Putsch of 1923, he was the leader of the student group within the SA regiment 'Munich.' He was close to Hitler during the imprisonment in Landsberg and became the Fuehrer's private secretary soon after his release in 1925.. Later he was elevated to the post of Hitler's first adjutant, and after Strasser's resignation rapidly rose to the most powerful position within the Party, next to the Fuehrer himself. On 27 April 1933 Hitler made him his general representative, with full powers in Party matters.

I knew Hess but slightly; in 1932, at the Brown House, he had sat in for a while at one of my talks with Hanfstaengl when I was trying to smooth things out with Putzi. And he hadn't particularly liked me. "Ludecke was perfumed - I don't like perfumed men," he said to Rosenberg afterwards. When I heard about it I recalled vaguely that I had gone to that meeting straight from a hair-cut and shampoo, and I was amused.

Anyway, when I called on Hess that unfriendly March morning in 1933, I tried to smell and behave as Nazi-ish as possible. But I had a hard nut to crack. There sat a man not easy to read. I couldn't quite see the epithet of 'Fraeulein,' for he was virility itself Luxurious, dark hair crowned a strong angular face; he had grey-green eyes under heavy, bushy brows; a fleshy nose, a firm mouth, and a square determined jaw. Slender and lean-limbed, he was good-looking and rather Irish in appearance. There was a restrained fanaticism in his eyes, but his manner was collected and quiet. I recall him as a commanding presence, a compliment one can pay to only a few of the higher Nazi chiefs.

Hess did not put me at my ease. I couldn't make him out, and he didn't help me a bit. He was polite, too polite, very cool, and I couldn't get at him, couldn't draw anything out of him. When I told him that it was imperative to dissolve the American organization, at least the Nazi units depending on Munich, he was evasive. "I'll think it over," he said. "It seldom pays to destroy something if there's nothing to put in its place." It was almost to the word what Hitler had said.

"But I have something to put in its place. Much better, much more effective, to have influence in a rising native American organization than to try to impose any Nazi organization on Americans. It won't work!"

But it was useless. I was unable to kindle his humour. He remained non-committal, elusive, not once looking straight into my eyes, which I held fixed on him. After a shifting, manoeuvring talk of fifteen or twenty minutes I left him dissatisfied. I now knew for certain that he was not my friend.

So I held Ley to his promise, and we went to the chancellery to try Goebbels. When a guard told me that Goebbels had just left Hitler's private quarters upstairs to go to a ministers' council on a lower floor, I ran after him, though I didn't succeed in dragging Ley with me. I stopped the little Doctor as he was reaching for the door-latch of the council-room. He returned my greetings with friendly courtesy. When I rapidly explained the purpose of our visit and the necessity for prompt action, he agreed at once.

Going back, I found Dr. Ley chatting with Max Schmeling, who had just had an audience with Hitler and Goebbels before sailing for New York. It was a pleasant surprise to find the German boxer a likeable, soft-spoken gorilla.

And then someone else appeared on the scene-my good friend Dr. Hanfstaengl. Seeing me, he quickly turned his back and made off. I shouted after him, half in earnest, half in jest, but he hunched his shoulders and sailed down the stairs, long arms and legs swaying, and we roared with laughter.

But even when I told Ley that I had Dr. Goebbels' consent, I couldn't move him to act. Eventually, after receiving alarming warnings from American friends, I went with Rosenberg to Hitler himself and got his O. K. And then at last, in the presence of Rudolf Hess, I drew up the text for the dissolution order, and Hess signed it. I had finally got through the snarl of red-tape.

Naturally, the official dissolution of the Nazi Party organization in the United States stirred up bad blood against me among the American 'Little Hitlers.' 'G' and a few others took ship and came over to play their own games. But they found no ground under their feet; Nieland had withdrawn into the office of the Hamburg police, and young Bohle was then still hanging in the air.

Every American observer will know that I was right in putting an end to the nonsense in the United States. My difficulties serve to show how, from the beginning of the Hitler regime, Party intrigues, individual rancours, personal sympathies and antipathies, conflicting ambitions, and an ever-growing Party bureaucracy hampered a sound development in the quickening tempo of events.

"I'll stage such an act in Potsdam as the world has never seen," Hitler had told me the summer before.

His great 'Potsdam Day' was held on 21 March. The sober, quiet city, symbol of Prussian greatness, discipline, and order, seemed submerged in a veritable sea of flags. Joyous crowds surged through the streets. The little baroque Garrison Church was the scene of the solemn celebration of the national resurrection. Here took place the symbolic inauguration of the Third Reich, the union of the symbols of ancient glory and of young strength - of tradition, personified in the venerable Field-Marshal von Hindenburg, and the movement, personified in its youthful leader Adolf Hitler.

After the religious ceremonies, from which Hitler absented himself to make his gesture of laying a wreath on Horst Wessel's grave, there assembled in the church diplomats and officers in resplendent uniforms, scores of high government officials, high dignitaries of the old regime, the deputies of the new Reichstag, most of them Nazis in brown shirts - Sozis and Communists being excluded. The Crown Prince, conspicuous in his Death's-head Hussar uniform with its tall fur cap, occupied the old Imperial box. Inside the chancel, facing the marble altar and surrounded by his cabinet, sat Hindenburg in a uniform covered with decorations, holding his field-marshal's baton in his right hand. His last Chancellor, the Bohemian Corporal, dressed now ill a cut-away, stood facing him behind a little pulpit.

When Hindenburg had read his message to the deputies and to the German people, Hitler read a moving address which brought tears into the half-closed, deep-set eyes of the old knight. Dead silence ensued, to be broken by a jubilant ovation when the Marshal extended his hand to the man he had rebuked six months before. The solemn climax came when the oaken old giant, with the organ playing softly, descended alone to the tombs of the Prussian sovereigns and prayed at the cold sarcophagus of that cynic soldier-king, Frederick the Great. Outside, over the heads of endless crowds, guns fired salutes. Then came the finale by the hob-nailed boots of Reichswehr, Stahlhelm, SA, and SS, goose-stepping past the Imperial Field-Marshal and the Bohemian Corporal, to the flourish of trumpets and the roll of drums.

It was impressive enough. But the real political business was transacted two days later, on 23 March, when the Reichstag convened to consider the Enabling Act, the so-called 'Ermaechtigungsgesetz,' which would invest Hitler with dictatorial powers to put his 'Four-Year Plan' into effect.

The Kroll Opera House, the temporary Reichstag building, was decorated with evergreens, flowers, and Party emblems. A huge swastika banner formed a background for the speaker's tribune. Outside, a solid rank of black-uniformed SS troopers encircled the building; inside, brown-shirted men of the SA enclosed the entire assembly. The rows were filled with members of the Reichstag; only the Communists were absent. The brown-shirted Nazi deputies were at the left, holding half of the stalls. The whole Cabinet was present in the first two rows of seats on the tribune, where Goering, bulging under his brown blouse, had enthroned his fleshy frame in the towering chair of the Reichstag-President. Honorary guests admitted only by special card packed the balconies. I had a splendid view from my seat near the Diplomatenloge. In a box nearby was Magda Goebbels; I bowed to her and she smilingly signalled me to ring her up.

At last Hitler came in, this time in the simple brown shirt of the S A man, and sat down next to Vice-Chancellor von Papen. Goering opened the session and after a short speech gave Hitler the floor.

As he had in Potsdam, the Nazi Chancellor read from a prepared manuscript. His carefully worded address, though moderate in tone, was forceful and much to the point. It was the first and last time that Hitler ever crossed swords in public with his enemies. He closed his demand for dictatorial power for the four-year-plan with a challenge: "Now, meine Herren, it lies with you to decide for peace or for war!"

He returned to his seat. We were witnessing a dramatic occasion, the best-staged parliamentary play I have ever seen. Yet the outcome was still in doubt. What would the Centrists do? What about the Sozis?

After a long recess for deliberation, Otto Wels, former paper-hanger and the last chairman of the Social Democratic Party, took the platform. He was in an unenviable position, facing a hostile house and surrounded by strong-armed Nazi troopers. Under the circumstances his vote for his party against the bill showed courage.

But this moment of terrific tension offered him his last opportunity for a blast that would be heard by the world; it was a moment demanding supreme leadership and aggressive boldness. The leader of the Sozis failed wretchedly as the bugler of his party. Speaking monotonously, he protested that his party had never lacked patriotism nor feeling for national honour. He cut a poor figure; his voice seemed the last squeak of a beaten and miserable group. As critic spectator at a marvellous play, I was disappointed, and recalled how superbly Hitler had risen to the occasion when, in 1924, he had faced the court a beaten man.

Hitler had followed Wels's every word with mobile face, jotting down a few notes. Now he rose briskly for an improvised reply. Speaking impetuously, bitterly, ironically, he quoted at the outset the famous phrase: "You come late, but yet you come!"

It was a rhetorical masterpiece. As he talked, I watched the people in the house, the foreign diplomats in the centre loge, and most of all the men on the tribune. How they stared! I saw Papen's curious, lean face, Neurath's intelligent, jovial mien, now so intent. I saw Blomberg's eyes, keen and cool, and the feverish eyes of the dwarfish Nazi Mephisto, his chin cupped in a nervous hand. There in the second row was Hugenberg, the grizzly little silver fox, twiddling his moustache.... In that duel, Hitler simply overwhelmed his enemies, lashed them to shreds, and threw the tatters in the air. If ever a party was annihilated by a speech, it happened then. The house swelled with cheers, with roars of laughter, with enthusiasm and derision. And when he ended: "I do not want your votes! Germany will be free, but not through you!" the storm of applause was a cyclone. One had heard that sort of thing in great mass meetings, but this was a German elite.

Whoever did not yet realize that the hour had struck was either blind or deaf. The Trojan Horse that Hindenburg had received into his citadel had come to life and was thundering over Germany. The old Field-Marshal, like his imperial master before him, had signed his own defeat.

The show was over when an embarrassed Dr. Ludwig Kaas - bespectacled professor, papal house prelate, apostolic prothonotary - rose and capitulated, meekly though with evident reluctance, for the mighty Centre Party.

The vote was 94 against and 441 for the Enabling Act. Hitler had his dictatorial powers. The Nazis leaped to their feet, and the whole house, trembling with emotion, arms outstretched, sang with them the Horst Wessel song:

"Raise high the flags! Stand rank on rank together,
Storm troopers march with steady quiet tread...."

XXXII

DISILLUSIONMENTS OF A REVOLUTIONARY

S o far, so good. Striking scenes - oh, yes! Marvellous tableaux, sweeping strokes, bold contours, strong colours. But these were all on the surface. The carefully designing hand of the great master, the discerning and combining mind of the superior executive, were missing. The detail work was sloppy. 'Gleichschaltung'- co-ordination - was indeed the thing needed. But the co-ordinating genius was not there.

Hitler had been ruthless and shrewd, clear-headed, and consistent in his struggle for personal power first as Party chief and then as Chancellor. From the beginning of his regime, however, his indecisive, contradictory, and inconsistent leadership in statecraft reflected other facets of his character. It was the baleful fruit of compromise. There were conflicting tendencies within the cabinet, conflicting aims and interests within the Party, and they were bound to create general confusion under a Fuehrer who was failing to develop the compelling qualities necessary in one who sets himself up as sole leader. Soon Germany was revolving around a struggle of rival groups all trying to govern through Hitler.

Hitler was dictator in his Party. And yet, paradoxically, too many horses were pulling the Nazi team. The foreign field showed it all too clearly. The Foreign Office, as was soon apparent, could not cope with an increasingly difficult and complex situation. It was failing partly because of ignorance resulting from the existing confusion - and this through no fault of its own; partly because of its own incompetence and ill-will; partly because Goebbels was sticking his beak into everything and Goering insisted on splashing in alien waters. And Rosenberg and I, who realized what needed to be done, were trying to sail without sails.

I did not fool myself for a moment. Our foreign bureau was still in the clouds. Rosenberg had not seen the Fuehrer since my return. "I cannot reach him," he said, in his quizzical and peevish way. "He's rushed from morning to night. And week-ends he must fly to Munich!"

Meanwhile the atrocity propaganda was assuming dangerous proportions throughout the world, and Germany was threatened with complete isolation. On one of my jaunts to the chancellery toward the end of March, I talked briefly with Goebbels about the seriousness of the situation. Cocksure as ever, he announced that something gigantic was about to be decided on, something which would surprise the world and throw Jewry into a panic. "I plan a tremendous blow," he boasted, "that will end the crisis!"

He was referring to the Jewish boycott, that puerile venture for which he later patted himself on the back in his diary, calling it a 'great moral victory for Germany.' Only one who has seen the little Doctor at work can have an idea of the early days of his ministry. To see him performing before the film world at the Kaiserhof, for instance, holding court after a speech. He was even planning to visit the Chicago Exposition and take advantage of the occasion to tell Americans a few things. But we succeeded in restraining his Wanderlust, and two minor officials in the propaganda ministry were sent in his stead. I thought it fortunate then, but today I am not so sure; in Chicago the little Doctor might have met an early Waterloo. He really ought to be grateful to me.

The boycott, scheduled for 1 April, was absolute news to Rosenberg. He was the Party's recognized authority on the Jewish question; yet he had not even been consulted. Apparently it was one of those decisions concocted by the Fuehrer in the seclusion of the 'Magic Mountain', with the puny Goebbels whispering in his ear. I saw in it a glaring example of how little real co-operation existed.

The kudos of directing the Jewish boycott was bestowed on Julius Streicher - the most impossible or, from another viewpoint, perhaps the best person Hitler could have thought of for the job. Hitler had decided that he must give old Streicher something to do. Actually it was better for Streicher, who had no prestige to lose, to be exposed to the odium and ridicule the task entailed than Rosenberg - even if he would have accepted the task, which is doubtful.

Thus were matters of the utmost consequence in world politics decided. The whole idea of the boycott was childish and stupid. It was chiefly responsible for giving the world the idea of using the boycott against Germany. It was ill-timed in that it disturbed Mussolini's negotiations for the Four Power Pact which he had proposed to London on 20 March.

Furthermore, it was mere bluff, an impossible thing to carry through. What was the sense of boycotting a little Jewish shop when the great Jewish department stores and banks couldn't and wouldn't be boycotted? Goebbels' 'tremendous blow' blew itself out in one day, never to be repeated, at least not in the same silly and noisy form.

April Fool's Day brought another surprise which temporarily threw certain people into a panic, while the nation's attention was centred on the boycott. Rosenberg had at last talked with Hitler the night before. The cool, impassive Balt was really excited, and actually smiled when he showed me a little piece of paper bearing one line of writing under which Hitler had scribbled his name. It was an historic document: it created the 'Aussenpolitische Amt,' the Foreign Bureau of the Nazi Party, with Rosenberg as chief.

But the step was made at an unhappy moment. Coinciding as it did with the proclamation of the boycott, in a way it linked Streicher to Rosenberg, whose uncompromising opposition to Jewry and to the Christian Church, especially that of Rome, was well known. And, of course, Rosenberg's appointment, as the adverse effect of the anti-Jewish boycott became apparent, was feared to be the beginning of a radical Nazi foreign policy. Although I did not say so to Rosenberg, I believed that Hitler had yielded partly to give him a sop and partly to use him as the wolf at the door of the Foreign Office, but with no intention of giving him concrete authority. I still hoped, however, that with perseverance and skill I should be able to manoeuvre Rosenberg and, of course, myself with him into real power.

The great event was proudly announced on the first page of the Voelkischer Beohachter of 1 April. Naturally, von Neurath saw in Rosenberg's appointment the first drastic step toward seizure of the Foreign Office. He offered his resignation as foreign minister, and was with difficulty persuaded to remain. Of course the Foreign Office didn't know how much power or how little - Rosenberg really had.

Now an under-cover fight began. The Reichs Press-bureau had been torn away from the Foreign Office and attached to Goebbels' ministry, which now included radio, Press, film, theatre, and general propaganda: five large departments, practically the whole field of mind-forming agencies of the nation. Though Hitler was showing Goebbels preference, the question of which office was to handle the foreign propaganda, and with it the secret funds which at that time were still at the disposal of the Foreign Office, had not yet definitely been settled.

In the fight for this function, Goebbels, who had executive power as a Government minister, was in a much stronger position than Rosenberg, whose reserve and passivity were no match for the little Doctor's methods. But we had certain points in our favour. Goebbels knew neither foreign countries nor foreign languages. Moreover, if he, a cabinet minister, were given the foreign propaganda, making Rosenberg's office superfluous, the Government would be held responsible for all foreign activities. The shrewder plan would be to imitate the Bolsheviks and create an office of which the Government could wash its hands. And although Rosenberg had travelled but little, he at least had been out of Germany, knew Russia and the Russian language, had a working knowledge of French, and had a far deeper knowledge of foreign affairs than Goebbels. Furthermore, Goebbels had no men to draw upon for such a task, whereas Rosenberg had a few he could put to work at a moment's notice. And he had the prospect of considerable help in my own person, since for years I had specialized in this particular field.

It all seemed so obvious that I wondered how there could be any argument about so simple a matter. Why waste ourselves fighting each other when we should be using all our wits and every ounce of our strength on the gigantic task before us? But the explanation lies in the peculiarly distorted character of the National Socialist movement at the beginning of Hitler's regime. In order to understand that movement and its leader in the spring of 1933, one must understand the successive phases of the development which Nazis had undergone.

First phase: The movement had been called into being to liquidate the Treaty of Versailles and to win for Germany her inward and outward liberation. Hitler knew that outward liberation would not be possible until the German nation had been reforged. For that task, new men with new ideas would be necessary, men embodying the best virtues of strength, endurance, loyalty, and courage. Thus the first conception was the building of a resolute minority, for obviously only a minority possesses these qualities.

The masses were despised. The appeal was less to social justice than to morality. When Nazi revolutionaries spoke, for example, of the confiscation of war profits, they were less concerned with social justice than with the punishment of corruption and of the war profiteers who flourished during and after the war. They aspired to introduce a new moral tone into the nation.

An ideal of this kind can be made to appeal to only a limited number and for only a limited time. Until the putsch of 1923, National Socialism was not a party but a heroic movement, instinctive and passionate. But this spirit subsided to a large extent when the glorious 'March on Berlin' dwindled to a demonstration march and ended ingloriously under police bullets in Munich. Although this decline was not clear then or later to the Nazi activist, he often felt it instinctively, even though he was ready again to break a lance for Hitler - all unaware that his Fuehrer had changed in prison.

Second phase: During the hard years after the putsch the so-called 'normal' person would have been incapable, in so desperate a situation, of carrying on the struggle. Without its adventurous characters, the Nazi movement would then have died. Many other Nazis, some of them from time to time in exile, were living by their wits, borrowing money here and there, or collaborating with other kindred revolutionary movements.

As it became clear that the fight might last for years, even the truest revolutionary had to adapt himself and make compromises and concessions if he wanted to stay in the race. And these very compromises, accompanied as they were by a sense of self-degradation, made his hatred of the enemy greater victory seemed for years to retreat rather than to advance, a fanatic attitude developed. Loss of all feeling for legality, contempt for the existing system, which in turn became contempt for all law connected with the system-these were but natural results. The psychology of the Nazi who felt himself unjustly persecuted became the psychology of the outcast. Only those who were convinced that they were right-so right and so oppressed that the end justified any means only they could stand the gaff, could go on with the fight.

And it would be hard for such a Nazi to lead a normal life again.

The system did not liquidate the movement by arresting Hitler and again charging him with treason. Instead, it let the Nazis live, and fought their movement with chicanery, with prohibitions of newspapers and meetings, with individual and wholesale arrests. In a sense, the fight ceased to be political and became intensely personal. It was a crusade that divided families. And the longer the fight lasted without a showdown, the farther one seemed from the goal, the more fanatic, disingenuous, and tricky did the movement become, and the more it retreated from its original heroic attitude to adopt instead the forms and technique of the enemy. The activists of the Party, who really drove it forward, were decent fellows to begin with; eventually they were men with no moral inhibitions. To break a political word of honour was nothing; for them, only the Nazi comrade was a human being. We considered ourselves in those days almost above morals, ready for any measure which would serve the cause. The saying 'I'd steal horses for it' well described our attitude.

This is a wonderful spirit with which to make a revolution. But what does one do with these people when power has been achieved by compromise and not by revolution? Some outlet must be found for this accumulation of passion.

The Fuehrer had been going through his own metamorphosis. In prison, a courageous man like Hitler accumulates spiritual power from his experience but at the same time becomes shrewder, more calculating, less inclined ever again to trust his whole fate to the play of one card. The heroic passion grows cooler and cooler.

Hitler entered prison a crusader; he came out a politician with the cloak of a hero on his shoulders. He could not, however, permit his followers to be politicians; he must keep the revolutionary spirit alive among them. With his help, Nazis went on deceiving themselves into believing that they were making the 'German Revolution'. The reality was to be very different from the dream.

In a sense, Hitler lost control. The bigger any movement becomes and the longer it fights, the more difficult is it for any one man to supervise it and keep it on the track of a clear idea. As the Nazi movement degraded into a demagogic mass movement, it eventually became a reservoir for all the malcontents. Shrewd opportunists who wanted to make use of the movement became its sub-leaders. And National Socialism, which was a feeling, a yearning, quite as much as it was a programme, was increasingly subject to conflicting interpretations. As the aims of the movement grew more confused, Hitler himself grew less concrete, appealing more and more to generalities heroism, blood, honour, soil. Flying from east to west, from north to south, he became in the end an abstraction, a legend. Men, women, and children flocked to him. Mass feeling had been worked up to a point where Hitler could have said anything to deafening applause.

Meanwhile, his movement had grown into a huge party machine, expensive, overstaffed, disunited, with hundreds of lesser speakers, trained as carefully as book salesmen to sell heroism to the masses. It was inevitable that the effect should become calculated, theatre reduced to mathematics, and that the original Nazi veracity and fortitude should be distorted by heroics, mendacity, and bluff. Popular agitators who were by no means the finest moral natures in the movement became its district-leaders, not because they were the best men, but because they could move the largest number of people.

But it would be wrong to give the impression that in 1933 there were no fine men in high positions in the Nazi Government and in the Party. There were many of great competence and idealism, comprising much of the best blood and virtue in Germany. They were not dominant, however. Tragically, Hitler had been caught in his own machine: at the climax of its development it had as leaders its most articulate but by no means its noblest personalities, and he was obliged to fill important posts with mediocre and even contemptible figures who were not representative of the best type of German. Goebbels, for instance, had played a useful role in the movement as a brilliant speaker and a superb demagogue.

Invariably, men who can move the masses are mass types. Only rarely does there appear in history a man like Lincoln, of the people and speaking with its voice, but nevertheless not of the mass. Germany almost produced one in Hitler, but in the end the mass go him.

Finely conceived truths from the brain of a really great mind like that of Rosenberg had become, in the mouths of those who parroted them, mere superficial platitudes. In the early days of National Socialism, men had sat together and discussed the philosophy of the movement, striving to clarify and develop it. Now, in 1933, the gift of gab reigned supreme.

These observations had begun to be clear to me in 1932. Now, with the Third Reich a reality, they became startlingly apparent. I saw them plainly at the first reception given by the neugebackene Excellency Dr. Goebbels in his propaganda ministry. Everyone of importance was invited - the Cabinet, the diplomatic corps, the army and navy, big business, the foreign and German Press, and, of course, the Party.

Here was the elite of Nazidom. Though there were certain pleasant exceptions, I was dismayed to see what sort of characters had pushed their way through to bask in the limelight. I saw 'proud revolutionaries' bowing with smug satisfaction to uniforms and titles, insinuating themselves with sugary smiles into a once despised society. Walking through the wide rooms, I observed little groups getting together, compromise obvious in every gesture, as they chatted and served themselves from the lavish cold buffets. It was more than a mere effort at sociability; it was compromise. But was it merely a phase, a breathing-spell together strength for a new forward stride? Or was it the outcome?

The first part of the evening I spent with Geheimrat Aschmann. He asked casually after Rosenberg, one of the few Nazi Noble Lords who weren't there, "Apparently he isn't coming," I said. "He's conspicuous by his absence." Aschmann gave me a knowing glance and remarked in his cautious way that Rosenberg unfortunately had no practical diplomatic experience. "Perhaps he might be interested in an ambassadorship as a preliminary" - he said, as if sounding me out. "London might do, perhaps -"

Wondering if he knew of Rosenberg's ambition to pay a visit to the British Foreign Office as Hitler's special envoy, I decided this was a good opportunity to intimate something I knew he would pass on; it would further my own plans.

"I see Rosenberg almost daily. I'm quite sure he isn't interested in an ambassadorship," I said - emphatically. "We need him right here. He ought not to be away when things are in the making - at least I shall advise strongly against it." That was clear enough.

Aschmann introduced me to some interesting people, among them the late State Secretary Bernhard W. von Buelow, next to von Neurath, the most important man in the Foreign Office. I avoided, however, an introduction to the Foreign Minister himself. I wanted first to study him in an inconspicuous way.

My opportunity soon came. The guests had moved into the main reception-room, where Hitler and Goebbels were speaking about the so-called freedom of the Press. As all the chairs were occupied, I posted myself near the entrance to study the heterogeneous crowd. Presently I felt myself being observed. A casual side-glance showed me a tall, well-padded man standing a little behind me. It was Baron von Neurath. He was sizing me up, I realized, and so I moved, as though unaware, to a position which allowed me to watch him without his seeing me.

I liked him. He had the bearing of a gentleman, a true aristocrat, with a large, full face and regular features. His expression was frank, his eyes intelligent and sympathetic. There was an air of joviality and kindness about him; he looked the bon vivant with a fine touch of reserve, the widely travelled, open-minded man of the world. Encouraged, I resolved to talk to this man openly as soon as I was ready.

After the speeches, Dr. Ley and I strolled out to help ourselves to drinks. Goering, as we passed him, beckoned to Ley as one would signal a waiter. And Ley, subaltern that he was, trotted meekly over and listened as though Goering were the Almighty himself. As they stood there, Goering talking softly but with commanding gestures instinct with self-importance, Ley listening with head devoutly bent, the tableau revealed to perfection the character of the Nazi bureaucracy.

Hitler went from room to room to shake hands with old comrades, and then left. Ley and I joined Amann to go to a private salon upstairs, where the reception ended in a drinking party with Funk as host. The drooping Funk was in high spirits and engaged in animated conversation with some other Nazi Go-Tos, of whom I remember only the Minister President of Brunswick. The drink was strong and the jokes stronger. Amann gave his account of the Nazi revolt.

"Ludecke, you should have seen Christian and Maurice when we dragged Stuetzel and Schaeffer[1] out of their beds! That was a sight…" and he went into a laughing fit, ably seconded by the unrivalled Dr. Ley.

When Funk withdrew for the evening, the party continued in the 'Excelsior' bar with girls and champagne until early morning. But it was worth it. Amann and Ley were priceless, and I heard much interesting gossip that set a number of things straight in my mind.

But the evening had been symbolic. I had found in it nothing but moral discouragement, and my revolutionary instincts laughed at me.

Next day I told Rosenberg that Aschmann had suggested an ambassadorship.

"How convenient that would be," he said acidly. "In London I'd be well out of the way! Sorry I can't please these gentlemen. I've every intention of staying right here in Berlin."

"Well and good," I agreed. "But I don't see that you're making any headway. You've had Hitler's O. K. for a week and practically nothing's been done."

" I've talked with Schwarz about funds. I can't do anything without money."

"It's money you need, all right, but you won't get it from Schwarz, unless you want to wait weeks and months-and then it won't be enough. Every day counts. No use to fool ourselves. It's almost certain that Goebbels will get the secret fund and with it the foreign propaganda."

Rosenberg admitted the weakness of his position. He could not afford to have two cabinet ministers - Goering and Goebbels - and the Foreign Office as well, against him. Goering was now demanding the Prussian premiership of Hitler, and that meant the ousting of Papen. If necessary, Goering would want to compensate Papen with the office of foreign affairs, which Hitler had promised to Rosenberg.

And there were other reasons why Rosenberg was in way. The mighty Hermann had his own diplomatic ambitions, touching eastern and central Europe and Italy.

"Here's a proposal," I said. "If you'll give me full power to proceed, I promise you two things: first, you'll have a million marks at the least within three weeks, and second, your position will be strong enough to talk business with Goebbels and von Neurath. You might even come to some understanding with Goebbels, divide the sphere of interest, and get part of the secret fund for our purpose."

I explained. Rosenberg was to call on Baron von Neurath in a conciliatory and co-operative spirit, implying that von Neurath had nothing to fear from his side. He must also come to an understanding with Goering. We were going to harness the entire national economy in all its international ramifications to carry our propaganda

---

1 These were, respectively: Christian Weber; Emil Maurice, who, a clock-maker, was Hitler's oldest SA commander and his first chauffeur; the Bavarian Minister of the Interior, who for years had persecuted the Nazis; and the Bavarian state councillor, a monarchist and a violent anti-Nazi who only a few days before had boasted that an Reich commisar sent to Bavaria would be arrested at the frontier.

to every country. Shipping, commerce, banking, insurance, and so forth, all had their own branches and agents in foreign lands with many thousands of employees who could be used, directly or indirectly. The whole framework was there.

My proposal was that Rosenberg invite all the important economic leaders of the nation to a luncheon at the 'Kaiserhof' to hear his report on the foreign political situation. I would then draw the practical conclusion: get their money by pointing out their own need of an effective foreign bureau able to function at once and to cope with existing difficulties. The luncheon would take place in the last week of the month.

"You're an unknown quantity to our big men," I said. "But I know your prestige is good, and they'll be curious to hear you. So far they have seen only the incredible nerve of the Nazis, their political cunning, their ruthless brutality. They're nonplussed. Let's show them that we also possess some brains, and are capable of systematic thinking and foresight. They want facts, figures, common sense, a practical plan. If we show them that, we'll win."

Rosenberg's face lit up. Money is a magic word in all parts of the world, and even a philosopher understands its value.

"But mind You," I continued, " you must see Neurath before that luncheon, and you must talk sense with Goering. He can be just as clever and practical as he is sometimes clumsy. And he has one good point: he does things and he isn't afraid. But we can use him. Play up to him!"

If we made a success of our luncheon, we would go to Hitler with a detailed, practical plan. Rosenberg would express his readiness to co-operate with Goebbels provided a clearly defined field, upon which we would have to agree, were assigned to him. Faced with something tangible and concrete, Hitler would consent.

Rosenberg agreed in full. When we had planned our procedure, I mentioned having seen Dr. Luther twice before he left for Washington. The first time was at his villa in Dahlem. A round little fellow, nearly bald, he rolled toward you like a barrel, speaking in a ridiculously squeaky voice. The next time had been in a magnificent room in the Foreign Office, where he had been entrenched behind a huge desk, with his legs dangling in the air. He had asked many questions about America, but I had been reserved.

"It's hard to realize that he has been Chancellor, President of the Reichsbank, and now is sailing as ambassador to America," I said. "Symbolic of the mediocrity of our time," observed Rosenberg dryly. "I hope he won't make things worse over there."

In Rosenberg's name I immediately got in touch with the secretary of the Federation of German Industries, and with his help made up a list of the most influential economic leaders of the nation. Within a day or two the invitations, signed by Rosenberg, were in the mail. Between the lines in invisible ink, there was printed on them my personal doom.

The conflict between Goebbels and Rosenberg had reached the stage of sabotage. In their frantic search for good people for their new bureaus, they were trying to take away each other's men.

For politics' sake, therefore, I thought it expedient to get in touch with Magda Goebbels and, through her, prepare the ground for a better relationship between Rosenberg and Goebbels. A friendly tête-à-tête between the Doctor and myself, arranged by Frau Goebbels at her home, would be a good preliminary step.

I drove out to pay my respects to Magda Goebbels. I was expected for tea. She received me graciously, accepting my excuse of over-work after scolding me a little for not having got in touch with her earlier. The conversation moved smoothly. Goebbels' sister, a swarthy but not unpleasant little person, was there, and later tactfully withdrew.

Presently I told Frau Goebbels of my disillusionment over the unworthy rivalries within the Party at this critical time. We were seated on a large, comfortable sofa, with a low tea-table before us. I had spoken with feeling, and sympathetically, in a friendly way, Magda put her hand on my arm. I was just about to speak of my wish to bring Rosenberg and Goebbels together, when suddenly the door opened, and there stood the little Doctor.

He paused for a moment, his hand still on the door-latch, looking at us with wide, staring eyes in a pallid, tired face. There was a moment of awkward silence. Slowly I rose, withdrawing my arm from under Magda's hand. Goebbels advanced, ill-humour written plain on his face. He accepted sourly my rather stiffly spoken congratulations on his successful reception, and declined the cup of tea his wife offered him.

" No, thanks, it's almost dinner time," he said curtly, sitting down. "I am very tired."

He was obviously not pleased to find me there. His wife suggested that I stay for dinner, but I excused myself, and presently rose to go.

"I should like to have a talk with you some time when you've a few minutes to spare," I said to Goebbels.

"Any time you like, next week," he said, as though taken slightly by surprise. After a moment's pause, he added pointedly: "In my office. I'll tell my secretary to put you down for an appointment."

Frau Goebbels went with me to the foyer, obviously annoyed with her husband. "I'll call you tomorrow morning," she said. "I want to talk to you. Let's lunch together somewhere else."

"Yes, call me - I want to talk to you too. I'm sorry - I'm afraid you'll have a little family scene presently."

"Nonsense," she said, with a twinkle in her eyes.

That was the last I saw of her. Next morning she telephoned to say that there had been an argument after all. Impossible to see me that day; she would positively arrange a meeting for tomorrow-we might drive out into the country. She would let me know. But the following' morning she telephoned again to break the engagement, asking me with some embarrassment to call her in a few days. When I tried, I found that her private telephone number had been changed, and the new one was of course unknown to me. That told me enough. I did not try to communicate with her again.

The Goebbels opening in my little game had not developed as I had hoped. Probably it would be better now to postpone my talk with the little Doctor until after the Kaiserhof gathering. But I thought it time to bring myself again to Hitler's attention and to make another move.

A day or so before he left for Obersalzberg to spend Easter on his 'Magic Mountain,' I had a cup of coffee with the Fuehrer on the terrace of his apartment above the chancellery. We talked of the huge propaganda project I had in mind in connection with the coming Kaiserhof meeting. He was pleased with the memoranda I had prepared for him, copies of which had also gone to Rosenberg as my chief.

"Good work," said Hitler. "Some of your suggestions are excellent and feasible, others are not. It's too late now to change our course, but, as you say, the possibility of a rapprochement with Moscow can be held under John Bull's nose whenever necessary."

When Hitler agreed with me that for the time being our only active asset was the National Socialist ideology and the successful application of the Nazi state concept at home, I stressed the necessity of helping the Americans to achieve a movement with a purely American facade, personnel, and programme. The National Socialist propaganda must not concentrate merely on awakening sympathy for Germany. We must also create a world movement around National Socialist ideas, adapted in every country to the peculiar history, mentality, needs, and problems of that country - a White International to set against the Red International, each movement to be absolutely sovereign in its own country. There were writers, ideologists, and even incipient movements in America and elsewhere 'Which gave promise of such collaboration and development if intelligently approached.

By now we were walking up and down the terrace, which had a good view of the chancellery garden and the larger park of the adjacent Presidential palace. Suddenly Hitler gripped my arm.

"There! You see? There he is-the old one..." he said, half aloud, leaning forward with pointing finger. Yes, there was old Hindenburg stumping along the path, leaning on his cane. We watched him silently until his tall frame disappeared round a curve, behind trees. And Hitler stretched himself and turned to me with a strangely hypnotized look in his remarkable eyes. Slowly he said again, as if half to himself: "Ja-Ja, da geht der Alte!"

I felt history running down my spine.

We resumed our promenade. I spoke of the letters that were pouring into the foreign bureau from all over the world denouncing resident Germans and officials abroad. It was evident that among many honest and justified complaints, there were also a great number incited by personal malice, gossip, and stupidity.

"We must know whom we can rely on abroad," I said. "When things get more settled here, I believe that a trip round the world to look over the ground will be absolutely necessary if we want to do properly what has to be done on the spot. Within a month or so I'll be ready to leave here for America. I don't need more than six or eight weeks at the most to get things going there, for the ground-work is done. I propose then to return to Berlin. Developments here meanwhile will have reached a stage to allow you to see clearer in certain things. Then I could discuss in detail with you or with Rosenberg a world trip of the sort."

Hitler was silent for a while. "The idea is good," he said at last. "Has your appointment come through from the Foreign Office?"

"No, not yet. Under the circumstances I'm in no great hurry about it; nevertheless, I'd like to have it soon for several reasons. It would raise my prestige with the Foreign Office, which apparently doesn't like me very much-you know I've been rather aggressive. It would be helpful if you would mention it to Neurath in passing."

" Yes, yes," he said. "I'll talk to him, tell him that it is my personal wish. I'll see to that after Easter. And about that world trip-I consent in principle; I'll see you about it before you leave for Washington. But mind you, officially I know nothing about it." Then Hess approached Hitler, reminding him of urgent matters awaiting him, and I was cordially dismissed.

I went away with the complete conviction that Hitler stood behind me; in all respects I had his agreement in principle. What was to be done must of course be left to my own initiative.

As I left the building, an acquaintance from the SS Flying Corps rushed by me.

"What's the hurry?" I asked.

"Flying to Koenigsberg - important orders - thick weather over there." And off he went in a waiting car.

I had forgotten that there was real fear that a preventive war might start on the Polish border, and that feverish preparations were going on, the details of which I didn't know, nor was it my business to know them.

Somehow I didn't believe in a war-yet. Our enemies were too blind. But I could see that the Nazi Chancellor had quite a lot to think about.

435

XXXIII

NAZI ATROCITIES

Hitler's forty-fourth birthday, the twentieth of April, was declared a public holiday, and with unerring instinct the Tribune of the People manifested his wish that nobody go hungry on his anniversary. There were free meals in restaurants in every town and city; kitchens of private homes were opened to the needy, and Nazi organizations everywhere distributed food among the poor. The nation decked itself with flags, and turned out to show the Fuehrer's extraordinary hold on the German people. Eulogies flooded the Press to the point of mawkishness, Hitler's picture was everywhere, bands played; at least every other person wore an edelweiss - the Fuehrer's favourite flower.

The object of all this adulation passed the day far from noise and intrusion in his beloved mountain retreat.

A more cynical observer might have found plenty of disturbing contrasts on that day, but I, still unaware of Nazi terrorism, saw only comic ones. On the Friedrichstrasse, I was accosted with a boisterous "Heil Hitler!" by a prostitute. "Na, Kleiner," she shrilled, "how about it? Only five marks tonight. We, too, can make sacrifices on the birthday of our Fuehrer!"

In those days, people were arriving from outside Germany on some 'mission' or other to 'study conditions within the Reich.' Among them were my good friend Victor Ridder of the New Yorker Staatszeitung and Herman A. Metz, coming as an investigating committee from the German-American Chamber of Commerce. Mr. Ridder's face showed a suggestion of surprise when he walked into Rosenberg's private office and found me there, cordially inviting him to have a seat. He did not stay long. But before he left Berlin he replaced his Jewish woman correspondent, at Hanfstaengl's suggestion, with one Margreve, a Harvard colleague of Putzi's, a German-American journalist out of a job.

Margreve was one of many who called on me to beg for fair weather; I was organizing the North American and. South American division of the foreign bureau- though at that time we hadn't even office space. Of Margreve more anon.

Another visitor was Ernst Wilhelm Bohle, Dr. Nieland's successor in Hamburg, anxious to justify his existence by pointing out the invaluable work done by his organization. He didn't like the idea of being incorporated in the foreign bureau, however, preferring to rule by himself.

Bohle has certainly been more successful than I have. Today he is the chief of the Party's foreign organization and the first Nazi official to enter the Foreign Office. As director of a new Foreign Office sub-division, he now sits with the Cabinet when questions affecting Germans abroad come up for consideration. The youngster whom I judged so lightly has made a career for himself.

The increasing activity forced on me by Rosenberg's passive attitude did not add to my popularity. I knew I was in an exposed position, and I made two more calls at the musty, forbidding quarters of the Foreign Office to try to smooth things out a bit. Dr. Hans H. Dieckhoff, who now has replaced Dr. Luther in Washington, was then head of the Anglo-American division. As brother-in-law of Joachim von Ribbentrop, later Hitler's special envoy and ambassador in London, perhaps he had some knowledge of Nazi ways. At any rate, he received me kindly and seemed not at all antagonistic.

State Secretary von Buelow was another story, however. Tall, stiff as his white hair, a correct, hard, unbending Prussian nobleman of the old school, he gave me a polite hour of his time, but his every tone and gesture betrayed hostility to what he knew of Nazidom. He would not ease my path; to him I was an intruder.

Buelow's attitude more or less determined my course. I could only hope that the Kaiserhof gathering, now a few days off, would bring home to the Foreign Office that I was someone to be reckoned with. Then I would have a frank and open talk with von Neurath. Meanwhile Rosenberg's reserve brought to nothing a lunch that I arranged for him with State Secretary Funk, Aschmann, and another man In his department -a lunch that had been planned to keep things moving.

The anti-Nazi atrocity stories in foreign countries were increasingly distressing. Especially damaging to Nazi prestige were the syndicated articles of H. R. Knickerbocker,[1] then correspondent of the New York Evening Post. I knew that Putzi called Knickerbocker his friend, and that Knickerbocker's relations with Goebbels were also of the best; the little Doctor had a nicely inscribed copy of his book, The German Crisis. But Knickerbocker was suspected of pro-Soviet leanings; someone in the general staff had warned me that he was believed to be working for the American intelligence service. Since he was the one man on whom my American correspondents were concentrating their reports, I thought something had to be done.

I talked the matter over with Rosenberg, who asked me to take care of it. Now it must be stressed that, strange as it may seem, both Rosenberg and I were then convinced that the atrocity stories were perfidious lies; we didn't even think it necessary to investigate. I went to Funk, who, as the Government's official Press-chief, should have been the deciding authority. But he didn't wish to decide anything. He sent me to Goering's pack-mule, Koerner, Prussian State Secretary of the Interior, who sent me to 'Herrn Regierungsrat' Sommerfeld, Goering's Press-chief, who sent me to the Presschief of the Reichs ministry of the interior, Dr. Frick, who sent me to'

---

1 Now of the Hearst publications.

Herrn Staatssekretaer Reichspressechef' Walther Funk as the only competent official in this grave affair. But nobody sent me to Hanfstaengl.

If Socrates was right when he reasoned that Aspasia's little boy-who governed his mother, who governed Pericles, who governed Athens, who governed Greece, who governed the world-really governed the world, it should follow that I in similar fashion had reached the centre of things. But I was still hanging in air. My journey from the beginning back to the beginning had brought me nothing but a headache.

It was the old story: there was no real policy for the treatment of foreign correspondents, no real authority, no real competence, no real organization of censorship. Rosenberg and I decided we must attempt to make a test case of Knickerbocker. Either there must be a consistent policy of trying to win the foreign correspondents individually or we must make an example of correspondents who, though they knew better (so we thought then), wilfully distorted truth in their reports, or allowed their reports to be distorted or garbled by editors at home. Knickerbocker's atrocity stories-had gone through the Government censorship approved, and continued to do so. We wanted not only to create a precedent for foreign correspondents, but also to force the hand of the proper authorities.

Let me emphasize that if I had known then what I know today of Nazi persecutions, I probably would never have picked out Knickerbocker, and after re-reading his articles, I herewith apologize.

Now my point is not who was right or who was wrong, but that lack of esprit de corps which was so largely responsible for getting Hitler's regime off on the wrong foot in foreign countries. The foreign bureau sent a cable in English, written by me and signed by Rosenberg, to the editor of the New York Evening Post protesting against the distortions which were seriously jeopardizing relations between the United States and Germany. We appealed to journalistic ethics, and begged the editor to instruct his correspondent to adhere to the truth, lest we ourselves feel obliged to take other steps. We were at pains to tell the propaganda ministry what we had done. Dr. Hanfstaengl, who as the Party's Press-chief was, or should have been, in daily contact with the propaganda ministry, thereupon ostentatiously invited Knickerbocker to lunch, and also included him in a semi-official dinner at which Rudolf Hess, Hitler's deputy, was present. The illustrated papers did not fail to show pictures of this dinner, which Hanfstaengl boasted was his victory over Rosenberg, 'the alien Balt.'

Busybodies in the Foreign Office began whispering criticism of our 'threatening' Knickerbocker, and spared the much more damaging activities of the Reichs Press-chief Walther Funk. That worthy was actually threatening the president of the Foreign Press Association in Berlin, Edgar Ansel Mowrer of The Chicago Daily News, because of his book, Germany Puts the Clock Back, even though it had been published before Hitler was named Chancellor. Funk asked Mowrer to resign, but the Foreign Press Association unanimously rejected his resignation. Funk-then threatened to force his resignation by boycott, with the result that instead of one, he found a hundred and thirty-five foreign correspondents arrayed against him.

Obviously 'Knick' was sacrosanct and Mowrer was not. And ironically enough, though Knickerbocker's damaging atrocity stories were passing approved through the censorship, nobody realized the value, on the positive side, of his book The German Crisis, an analysis of the German situation as seen at the end of 1931. Having been absent from New York while the articles of which it was composed were running in the New York Evening Post, I was not familiar with its content. When later I came upon the book, I found it an extremely able presentation of the German problem, one which could have been used, in a sense, as an argument for the Nazi cause. It is food for thought even today. But it had never been published in Germany. Nazidom was apparently unaware of it - Goebbels, who had an inscribed copy, Rosenberg, who reads innumerable books, Hitler, who had given Knickerbocker an interview which comprises an entire chapter and had never even mentioned it to me.

We found ourselves frustrated in our attempt to induce the various Press bureaus, whose multiplicity must be bewildering to the reader, to adopt a common line of co-operation. We wanted to curtail and co-ordinate the Press conferences which everyone was giving-ministers, state secretaries, governors, Party and SA leaders, now overly polite, now bullying. Foreign correspondents, largely liberal in sympathy and by tendency anti-Nazi, continued to go to their accustomed liberal or Jewish sources for final information. Planlessness and muddle persisted in Government and Party, with irreparable damage to the Nazi cause abroad.

Take the case of S. Miles Bouton, former Berlin correspondent for several American papers. In 1932 I had read an article by him in the American Mercury which was excellent, and fair to National Socialism. I thought it so important that I translated it in full with comments, and the Voelkiscker Beobachter published it in a series some weeks before Hitler became Chancellor. Now, months later, when I saw Bouton, I told him how much I appreciated his attitude, and mentioned my translation.

"Oh, yes," he said, "I saw it all right, but I never saw a cheque for it."

Articles are the journalist's bread and butter, and I asked Rosenberg to see that a handsome cheque was sent to him. Weeks after that, I found that it still hadn't been done. Schlamperei! Negligence on the part of the official Party organ and the stupid handling of certain political issues eventually turned Bouton against National Socialism, and in 1934, by order of the Hitler Government, he left Germany, a sworn enemy of everything Nazi.

More devastating was the stupidity with which the Dorothy Thompson affair was handled. Sinclair Lewis's wife was expelled from Germany in a polite but unmistakable manner. Her bantering booklet I Saw Hitler, published as early as 1932, had aroused the ire of the Fuehrer and Putzi, who was responsible for introducing her to his master. I have heard Dorothy Thompson's own account of the matter. She, as publicist, and her husband, as one of the foremost American novelists, exercise considerable influence on American public opinion, as I've had the honour of pointing out to Hitler himself Both had substantial interests in Germany which would have made them think twice before cutting the tablecloth between themselves and the German Government. Unquestionably the affair could have been smoothed over, with diplomacy. Hitler, who takes the time to see so many people, could have granted her another interview and gallantly ignored her earlier faux pas. Eventually the bill was presented. Irrespective of its merits as a novel, Sinclair Lewis's It Can't Happen Here has not made Nazis more popular in this western hemisphere. And Dorothy Thompson has continued to be the most telling critic of Nazi Germany among American journalists.

The German newspapers, which have always functioned as party organs rather than as news sheets, had been co-ordinated overnight, to be gradually moulded into a one-voiced instrument of the Totalitarian State. There was utter incomprehension of one essential difference between the German and the Anglo-American Press: the latter's relative freedom, if not complete independence, from Government interference, especially in the United States. It was a mistake to suppose that Anglo-American correspondents would go along as a matter of course with whatever Government came to power, or could be bullied into it. If the foreign correspondents underestimated the Nazis, Nazis also underestimated the foreign correspondents. Soon the whole situation had broken over the Nazis' heads. They were unable to cope with it; so they lied, and one lie gave birth to another, until the whole structure was riddled with mendacity. Some of the leaders were either utterly unconscious of the outside world or didn't care a fig' about it.

By now it may even have dawned on the Minister of Propaganda and Public Enlightenment that he is still very far from the goal he set when he wrote in his diary on 2 April 1933:

"There lies before us a spiritual war of conquest which must be carried through in the world in exactly the same manner (I hope not!) as we have carried it through in Germany itself. In the end the world will learn to understand us."

In the midst of busy preparations for the Kaiserhof gathering, my eyes were opened to .

I was working at 'key' men, not only to win their sympathy and support, but also to make sure of their willingness to come openly to our support at a critical moment.

One day one of the big men introduced me to an influential foreigner, who asked me, with casual caution, whether I knew of terrible things going on at the Colombia

Hitler captured in front of the adoring crowds in the Hauptplatz at Nuremburg.

Haus,[2] in the General Papen Strasse, in the cellars of Nazi headquarters at the Hedemannstrasse, and elsewhere - beatings with steel rods and rubber truncheons, torturings, altogether horrid illegalities. I answered honestly that I had read about them in foreign papers, but that they had not come to my own ears, and I didn't believe them. He insisted that he knew them for truth; it was amazing that people like Rosenberg and myself should be unaware: perhaps Hitler himself was unaware. There should be an investigation. Didn't I realize that there had been official protests to the Government?

Still incredulous, though somewhat shaken in my faith, next day I ran into an

2 *A former military prison.*

old acquaintance, Dr. von Langenhan from Vienna, still a nationalist with great sympathy for awakening Germany. Naturally we celebrated the wiedersehen. The charming causeur and gourmet, whom I had last seen when we Nazis had gone into a confused little huddle in Vienna after the failure of the Beer Hall Putsch, was still excellent company. Good food, good wine, and good music loosened our tongues and we talked freely. I told him what I had heard the day before. These things were true, he said, and profoundly disturbing. Finally he informed me confidentially that a great industrialist,[3] principal owner of Silesian mines and smelting-works, had been arrested and was being kept incommunicado in Breslau, accused of fraud and other offences. Langenhan swore he would put his hand in fire to affirm the man's innocence.

Next day I lunched again with Langenhan and one Herr von Bismarck, whose Christian name I have forgotten, but who was, I believe, related by marriage to the arrested industrialist. They produced evidence that the man had been arrested without indictment and was being tortured into handing over his fortune. It was sheer criminal coercion - I could not escape the truth.

I telephoned to Edmund Heines, whom I had known for over ten years. As one of Captain Roehm's oldest and most trusted friends, a high officer in the SA and president of police for Breslau, he was a man with great power. Heines promised an immediate investigation and fair treatment meanwhile for the man in prison. A few days later he reported that Brueckner claimed he had a real case against the industrialist, but admitted that the charge might have been a frame-up.

"Ludecke," said Heines, "all I can do is see to it that he is well treated. Or, if you like, let him escape." But I argued that this wasn't the proper solution if the man was innocent. So I introduced Langenhan to Dr. Luetgebrune, who was Heines's and Roehm's personal lawyer, official attorney for the entire SA, and commissioner of justice for Prussia. Luetgebrune accepted the case. To my amazement, after several days he confessed in complete bewilderment that he could do absolutely nothing.

Heines kept his promise and let the prisoner escape. Later I learned that the Silesian concern had dismissed a minor employee, a Nazi, who had recourse to his Party and through them was applying pressure in the hope of instating himself as director and turning the foundries over to the Party.

On the day of the Kaiserhof gathering I was enjoying a leisurely breakfast, convinced that I had done everything possible to insure success, when the telephone rang. It was Dr. Fritz Mertens, whom I had known for many years, now pleading so earnestly for help that I hurried down to his office in the Getreide Industrie & Commissions AG., probably the largest banking concern for the grain industry in all Central Europe.

The concern was managed by four directors, two Jews and two Gentiles, Dr.

3 *I do not recall his name.*

Mertens being one of the latter. The status of this grain-handling corporation was somewhat complicated, for it was controlled by two large banks representing two different groups. One of them was connected with Jewish interests politically powerful during the socialist regime in Prussia; embezzlement on the part of one of its directors, a former Prussian finance minister, had involved it in a great scandal. The other bank was conservative-nationalist and was linked to the Hugenberg interests. The Jewish orientation predominated, however, and since 1931 the bank had been the target of concentrated Nazi attacks, let by the weekly Landspost; the mouthpiece of the present Reichsminister Dam!, who at that time was chief of the agricultural division of the P. O.

After the 'revolution,' the leader of the Nazi cell in this organization emerged into the limelight. A small clerk who saw his chance to make himself one of the directors, he declared himself Nazi commissar and brought pressure to bear on the two Gentile directors. Hugenberg, however, was still Reichsminister of economics, and the Nationalists, displaying remarkable boldness, installed a commissar of their own. The organization was thus saddled with two commissars, one an upstart Nazi, the other a Hugenberg man. They were at each other's throats.

I was solemnly assured that grain-jobbing in the international markets was almost a monopoly of the 'sacred seed,' a particular art developed through age-long experience, and seldom mastered by 'goys.' Therefore, I was further informed, the services of experts were indispensable-otherwise an adequate grain supply for sixty-seven million Germans would be jeopardized!

My panic-stricken, perspiring companion of former days insisted that he had received an anonymous warning that the Nazi commissar was planning a coup de banque that very day; if I would prevent the Nazi berserk from taking full possession of the institution and throwing both 'goys' and Jews into the street, I should have his undying gratitude.

"But," I said, "you don't need me! If this fellow is crazy enough to attempt such a thing, why don't you throw him out? You have people enough in your organization to do that. What's the matter with you - have you lost all your spirit?" And I rose to go.

"Please - lieber Kurt !" Mertens insisted, holding on to me. "Don't you understand? He's coming with SA men-nobody will dare touch them! Can't you see that this is serious, with the constitution practically suspended?"

So I sat down again, and was told in detail how Nazi commissars were invading commercial and industrial establishments all over the country and preparing to rule business.

"Their tactics are very simple," said Mertens. "The Nazi who has the nerve and sufficient backing will march into a directors' meeting followed by a half-dozen Storm Troopers, declare himself 'Commissar,' and appoint a new board of directors with himself at the head. I assure you, Kurt, this is happening now in hundreds and thousands of cases, and if it isn't stopped soon the entire business structure will fall to pieces!"

I decided to stay for the showdown. But the tension with which the atmosphere was loaded burst like a paper-bag; the performance of the little Hitler was a flop. When he finally appeared, he was alone. Probably none too sure of the impression they would make, he had left his martial Storm Troopers below in the vestibule.

When the 'Nazi Commissar' stormed in, he found the proposed directors' meeting adjourned, and me seated in a big leather chair alongside Dr. Mertens. He let loose a barrage of words at his apparently none-too-popular boss.

"Stop that yelling, young man!" I said.

"Who is this man?" he shouted at Mertens who had regained his composure. Adjusting his monocle, Mertens told him in an icy voice. The little man was losing countenance visibly. One more Donnerwetter and the lion would be tamed.

"If you don't behave," I warned him, "I'll report your conduct as unworthy of a Nazi to Darre himself-You know what that means." With that we dismissed him, and he retreated in confusion.

But I stepped out of the building into the Herr Direktor's waiting limousine with a bad taste in my mouth. Before I left, I had exacted from Mertens the promise that there would be no reprisal against the little Nazi commissar who had overplayed his hand. What cowards they were, these smug, bourgeois Haves! After all, the fury of the 'little man' seemed not entirely unjustified. And yet, if he had changed seats with the Herr Direktor he surely would have been worse than my distinguished friend.

Though I had been heart and soul for the socialistic aims of the Nazi programme, I was now facing the riddle of the reality. How could it be solved? Only if the governing concept of 'private property' were modified and readjusted in accordance with common sense and social justice, and the present leaders of business were allowed to remain at their posts only so long as they fulfilled their duties towards the commonwealth - duties and responsibilities definitely fixed by Federal law.

At the Kaiserhof I crawled out of the car wondering how the leaders of Big Business were going to receive us - for we were going to present ourselves, in a sense, as their eventual 'Foreign Commissars.'

The suave manager of the Kaiserhof took me into a well-arranged salon with an ample ante-chamber. About fifty couverts had been laid. Everything looked perfect; the show could begin.

Gradually the rooms filled. There they were-the elite of leading Gentiles in industry, commerce, finance, agriculture, shipping, and banking; among them were some of the newly appointed Nazi Reichs-governors from Hamburg, Lubeck, and so forth. It was a remarkable assembly, and I saw some fine, proud figures among these gold-blooded aristocrats. But for the most part I saw fat-bellied, money-making fatheads, and I saw too the irony of our readiness to mobilize the very forces against which the socialist aims of the Nazi revolution were to have been directed. Here were we, true to this era of Nazi compromise, trying to make a revolution with the help of our enemies!

More guests arrived, and couverts had to be added. Rosenberg sat at the head of the table, flanked on one side by Germany's famous industrialists, the 'cannon king' Dr. Krupp von Bohlen und Halbach,[4] white-haired, spare, and earnest. On his other side was the new Reichsbank president, high-collared, witty Dr. Schacht, who, only a few years before, had been branded by Rosenberg, his present host, as an 'exponent of international finance' and as a 'criminal against the German people.'[5] I was seated somewhere in the centre, where I had a commanding view. An excellent lunch with few courses was quickly served, and wine-glasses were not refilled too often; I did not want the older men dozing off during Rosenberg's speech.

My concern was groundless. Rosenberg delivered an interesting, well-conceived and finely rounded discourse; everyone listened with close attention, and there was genuine applause. Speaking freely and simply as usual, without tricks or showmanship, he gave a matter-of-fact, general picture of the foreign political situation, dealt with the atrocity propaganda and the dangerous potentialities of Jewish world politics, frankly discussed Germany's political and possible economic isolation, emphasized the necessity of intelligent and immediate world propaganda, and built his climax on the danger of a 'preventive war,' something at least theoretically to be reckoned with.

Closely watching the faces intent on the speaker, I saw that all looked seriously impressed and some definitely alarmed. That was good; that was what we wanted.

Then I rose to draw the practical conclusion - in other words, to get the money - and to emphasize a few delicate points which I wanted my hearers to pass on to the Foreign Office immediately after the meeting.

Very briefly I said that I had just returned from America and could assure them that experience and observation bore out every word of Rosenberg's argument; I had proof, however, that in our country's difficult and precarious situation, certain officials and representatives of the Foreign Office were treating these facts with an amazing indifference and lack of comprehension. I hinted at conscious or unconscious sabotage, and observed that these same gentlemen were committing a grave error if they believed that they could survive 1933, as they had 1918, without soon falling in line. I argued that the proposed world-wide counter-propaganda should not, for obvious reasons, be directed through the official channels of the foreign office or of any other governmental department, but should be handled by

---

4 *On May 1923 arrested without causes by troops of La Grande Nation, during the French Ruhr invasion; spent six months in the Essen jail, treated as an ordinary convict.*

5 *30 November Koepfe, von Alfred Rosenberg Kampf-Verlag, 1927.*

the unofficial foreign bureau of the Party, since many activities must be carried on in a manner not traceable to the acting government. Our whole national economic system, with all its international ramifications, should be utilized for this gigantic work. In my appeal for funds, I stressed the point that their own material and personal interests demanded prompt, intelligent and far reaching action, and that without it they might lose everything in a preventive war. Free and generous contributions now would do great service not only to our beloved country but also to themselves.

To most of these men I was unknown, and as I spoke I observed surprise in many faces, approval in some, disapproval in others, and business-like and appraising eyes everywhere. Evidently they were not used to bold, frank words, and what I was saying was definitely a challenge. I believed that I could count on Hitler even if the consequences should spell trouble for me.

Immediately after my address I nodded to Lieutenant-Colonel W. Sichting, one of the Party's military experts. He rose to expound the seriousness of the situation from a military angle, with force and persuasive effect. Any German audience, high or low, will applaud an officer who presents his case cleverly and knows how to prod German emotion in its most vulnerable spot-its military consciousness. These men were scared and impressed.

Coffee, liqueurs, and cigars had made their rounds and the temper of the audience now seemed exactly right. Schacht of the Reichsbank, Diehm of the potash trust, and others made neat supporting remarks. I went over to Schacht with the list. It began to circulate and I with it, so that there could be no escape.

Right there over a million marks were underwritten. Some of the congratulations warmed me through and through. One sturdy old gentleman with a strong face, who had spent many years in foreign lands and part of the war in British concentration camps, said to me: "That was bully! It's time to take those monocled AA's[6] by the ears. These walls have ears - be sure of that! They'll take notice!"

Another man who had changed seats to become my neighbour at table took me aside. "I am Kiep, of the Hamburg-American line, brother of Consul-General Kiep in New York. I've heard you're not pleased with him. Good man, though. My company of course will do its best to be of service. My brother -"

"I've nothing against your brother," I reassured him. "He has charming manners, and he may be a good diplomat, but I'm afraid New York is a little tough for him."

I noted especially that Rosenberg was talking earnestly with Geheimrat Schmitz, then the head of the I. G., the German dye trust, largest chemical trust in the world and long a potent influence in the Foreign Office.

When our guests dispersed, Rosenberg, Schickedanz, and I withdrew with some of the most important men into private conference to lay down in broad outlines

6 AA – abbreviation for Auswaertiges Amt, or Foreign Office.

the plan for the organization of a world-wide campaign. I proposed that the Nazi foreign bureau should work out the details, and it was agreed.

Rosenberg was all smiles now; it was the first and only time he ever thanked me for anything. "By the way," he said, "Hitler asked me to tell you that he has spoken to Neurath, who will rush your appointment through." And Schickedanz, grinning from ear to ear, said: "Ludecke, you carried that off most adroitly!"

But had I? Unquestionably this Kaiserhof gathering put the Nazi foreign bureau on its feet. But it also was my undoing.

XXXIV

DER MAI IST GEKOMMEN

A few days later, at the end of April, we were Hitler's luncheon guests. Rosenberg and I, the first to appear, arrived together punctually at two o'clock, Hitler's usual luncheon hour, but he was still downstairs in his office. Not knowing who else had been invited, we were looking at a picture in one of the salons of Hitler's flat, which covered the entire top floor above the chancellery, when Dr. Goebbels clumped out of another room.

Rosenberg's back was turned, and I tapped him on the shoulder. 'There's Goebbels.' And it flashed through my mind that his being there was no mere chance-perhaps Hitler had arranged an opportunity for our getting together. Goebbels walked up to us smiling, but Rosenberg greeted him icily and turned back to the picture. I was so dumbfounded that instead of trying to save the situation, I only bowed. There was nothing left for Goebbels but to pass on.

Then, angry with myself for not having shown more presence of mind, I went after the Doctor to see if I could repair this asininity. But by now he was engaged in conversation with Hess and someone else. I lingered beside them for a while, but the opportunity had gone by.

So I went back to Rosenberg and spoke my mind.

"Here I'm struggling with all my wits to get us somewhere, but your damned stubbornness spoils everything. I'm losing patience with that passive, philosophic attitude of yours. Perhaps people are right in saying I ought to change colours - Goebbels is at least a practical man..."

"You wouldn't do that!" the imperturbable Bait cut in, looking a little alarmed at last.

"I should, and still I can't. But you must change your attitude, otherwise we'll be whipped yet."

"You're right, but what can I do? I am as I am - I can't get out of my skin-"

"You can carry your skin to Goering and set things straight at least with him. You promised me weeks ago you'd talk to him. Don't tell me you've had no opportunity - it's more important to do that now than to fuss with things you haven't the power to carry out anyway."

Of course Hitler was more to blame than we. I still believe it was his intention to bring the two men together, but the way he did it was typical of him, illustrating his lack of candour, his habit of dodging responsibility, of avoiding being pinned to anything. He did not go up to the two men and say openly: Look here, I've asked you here in order that you may iron out the differences I know exist between you.' Instead he let things drift, and the luncheon merely made things worse.

We were still arguing when Hitler's voice sounded outside. Going out in the hall, we found him with his printer, Adolf Mueller, and Goebbels. In a manner almost affected he was praising a new police-dog which had been brought in by two of Goebbels' body-guards. Then we all went in to lunch.

Hitler sat at the head of the table, putting the half-deaf Mueller - one of his special pets - on his right and Rosenberg on his left. I was next to Rosenberg and facing Goebbels. Schaub, Hess, and Brueckner - all members of Hitler's household - made up the rest of the table. Rosenberg, Goebbels, and I were, except for Mueller, the only guests, and I was convinced that the Fuehrer must have brought us together of intention. Yet he made no effort to draw Rosenberg and Goebbels into conversation with each other.

The shoulders of Hitler's dark suit showed that the Chancellorship had not cured him of dandruff. While he ate his special food - a kind of vegetable stew, with eggs and mushrooms - the rest of us attacked one of Kannenberg's incomparable meals, with desultory talk, chiefly between the Fuehrer and Mueller, a pursy, cheerful man and a good story-teller. Politics were barred at Hitler's table during meals.

Kannenberg, a born comic, was serving us, and slyly clowning it for my benefit, making faces or waggling his behind with indescribable effect. Presently I caught him in one of his little tricks near the kitchen door, and at the same moment heard Hitler teasing Mueller: Could he really see what he had on his plate over the arch of his paunch? Suddenly the pretensions of this little group struck me as utterly ridiculous. Was I really to believe that the man jesting with the fat printer was the Nazi dictator and self-proclaimed saviour of the German people? That the immovable statue next to me was the Nazi evangelist predestined to down Christian universalism with the Nordic Myth? That the caricature opposite me was the Nazi trumpeter chosen to proclaim the new faith to the four corners of the earth? It all seemed too preposterous, and when Kannenberg grimaced at me again, rolling his bulbous eyes and knitting his brows, my laughter broke through.

"Nanu, Ludecke," Hitler said. "What's the matter?"

Feeling foolish, I hesitated in embarrassment, casting about for some plausible explanation.

"Come on, let's have it," he insisted.

So, under the spur of necessity, I began to invent aloud a train of thought ostensibly suggested by Hitler's gibe at Mueller's girth, which had led me to someone whom discreetly indiscreet English writers call 'A Very High Personage,' a man who likewise could see his feet only in a mirror. The story was building to its scandalous conclusion, having to do with a specially designed chair installed for his convenience at the famous Maison Chabanais in Paris, which would permit him -

"Stop, Ludecke - stop!" Hitler cried. "Leave the rest to our imaginations. That reminds me of a present I have in store for you - I'll wager you can't guess what it is!"

" I don't dare try," I said, "because I'd suggest something I'd like to have -"

"You'd better not, then," Hitler laughed, "because what I mean is a muzzle!"

Spoken in jest - but was there a deeper significance to it, I wondered? I only said that if the muzzle was intended to prevent me from tasting more of Kannenberg's culinary art, I humbly protested, but if it was meant to shut my mouth, I accepted it with apologies - quod licet Jovi non licet bovi!

"You see, you see!" Hitler said. "He must have the last word." He rose. "Let's have coffee on the terrace. It's warm today the sun is out." Still laughing, we followed him out.

We had barely finished pouring ourselves coffee when Roehm and Frick arrived. Hitler at once withdrew with Roehm into his study, and Frick sat down with us. Goebbels was speaking of the huge May Day preparations which were to convert the traditional holiday of Europe's revolutionary proletariat into a legal holiday, the 'German Day of National Labour.' As he talked, he began to develop the idea of a national donation of one or two marks to each of the unemployed on 1 May - to be paid by industry, of course. He speculated on how much it would amount to. Frick looked at Rosenberg and Rosenberg looked at me; it was obvious that Goebbels was not interested in the social value of the idea but was thinking in propaganda values only - headlines in the Nazi Press. Rosenberg said dryly: "What would one or two marks actually mean to one of the unemployed?" It would be alms, he added, more likely to create scorn than gratitude among the receivers and needless anger among the donors, who would pay wages for 1 May as it was, and were being fleeced incessantly for one thing or another.

So the idea of a national May Day donation for the unemployed fell under the table, and the rift widened.

But I was more interested in an excited debate going on behind the closed window at my side. Hitler always shrieks when excited, and Roehm was shouting back at him. Gradually I made some sense of the words I could pick up now and then. There was disagreement over measures taken by Roehm concerning the SA; apparently the SA chief was resolutely opposing the projected seizure of the Labour Unions, to be carried out immediately after May Day throughout the Reich, in accordance with Hitler's plan. Roehm's disapproving voice was music to my ears, and I resolved to have a good talk with him soon.

When Roehm left, Hitler reappeared for a moment just as an SS guard was bringing in a new issue of the Angriff. He grabbed it at once. I have said before that you can't have a conversation with Hitler if there is a fresh newspaper in the room; if it catches his eye he will stop in the middle of a sentence. Now he literally devoured the head-lines, skimmed the inner pages, and then, taking Frick and Goebbels with him, went back into his study without once looking at us.

Gloom came over Rosenberg's earnest face. I felt sorry for him, for his judgment in many respects was superior to that of either of the other two. Once he had been Hitler's closest adviser; now he was obliged to witness the Fuehrer consulting with others and disposing of far-reaching issues and important affairs of State without even noticing his presence.

The others were gradually drifting away. Rosenberg was called to the telephone, and I was left alone with Hess. Leaving, he said casually, with no perceptible overtone, that he would have come to the Kaiserhof gathering if he had known more about it. I replied that he had been invited.

When Rosenberg returned I was alone. He was in bad humour. "Now I've wasted two whole hours here. I came to have a talk with Hitler, but all I get is a vis-à-vis with that creature."

"Rubbish," I said. "If you've wasted your time it's your own fault. By the way, what about those admission-cards for the Hitler Tribune on May Day? We must have at least ten. You know I've invited some of those smoke-stack barons to go with us."

"Ach Gott! I've totally forgotten it." Provoked, I rushed to telephone to Dr. Ley, but found he had none left. When I came back, Hitler was still closeted behind his study door, casual toward his guests, as always. We were tired of waiting, and left without saying good-bye.

Downstairs, I asked Schaub for admission-cards, but he also had none. "But wait," he said finally, "perhaps Sepp Dietrich can help you out. Be nice to him; you know, he's a smart fellow." And as we talked I was forced to accept, as a reality beyond changing, something I had begun to observe with dismay the year before: even in this exalted new State, a subaltern like Schaub possessed extraordinary power through the mere fact that he stood next to Hitler and could, to a considerable extent, determine who was to get the Fuehrer's ear. In a sense, he could shape world policy. It looked to me as though a palace camarilla was in the making.

When Sepp Dietrich arrived, I had evidence of what it meant to stand in well with these gentry.

Sepp Dietrich today is commander of the Hitler Leibstandarte, Hitler's former body-guard, which has been increased to the size of a regular regiment. He has been raised to a very high post in the SS, with tens of thousands of men under him, and is moving in the highest society.

'Der Mai ist Gekomen' - It is the opening of a century-old poem, set to a century-old folk-tune. Wherever there are German schools, boys and girls sing it to usher in the month of May, the lovely 'Wonnemond'. For a German there is magic in the words.

Church bells rang far and wide to wake the German land on that May Day, truly one of the loveliest days of the spring of 1933. Long before noon the Lustgarten, the impressive old square at one end of Unter den Linden, was filled with more than a hundred thousand boys and girls, warmed by a glorious sun. It was a moving and beautiful sight, instinct with a feeling of rejuvenation, a sense of the rebirth of a nation.

But presently the hypocritical note of showmanship appeared: the reanimation of body and spirit was extended to an image which had become blurred in the hearts of German youth. The fading fame of the old Field-Marshal was being retouched. Motoring through cheering crowds came President and Fuehrer, seated for the first time side by side, once more a reincarnation of age and youth as a joint symbol of the Third Reich. The exercises began. The 'Dotard,' the 'Old Bull' whose senility had so recently been the public butt of Nazi scorn, was dragged forth as the biggest attraction of the Nazi circus. Now his phenomenal freshness and mental agility were extolled. Hitler's worn-out adversary was again the venerable 'Teuton Nestor,' the great soldier of three wars, the faithful 'Ekkehard' of the German nation.

The children dispersed, marching, cheering, and singing as they had come, and with the same enthusiasm multitudes of workers and burghers, employers and employees, began to stream to the Tempelhof field outside Berlin, where the evening's show was to take place. Countless processions marched through the Berlin streets, which were flag-hung and decorated as never before. There were contingents of men, women, and girl workers from every factory and every workshop, from every trade and craft; groups of frontier Germans and peasants in their colourful local costumes; Nazi cells from industrial and commercial establishments. Each section was headed by its own band, and shepherded by brown-shirted Storm Troopers, who, as they passed, would shout 'aloud the slogans which spanned the streets on huge banners, one to almost every block:

'Honour Work and Respect the Workers'... 'Chains Must Be Broken'... 'Command Us, Leader, We Will Follow! And this bit of irony: 'For German Socialism: Against Class Warfare and Class Prejudice.'

Oh, hopeless German idealists!

After a very late lunch, Rosenberg and I met our smoke· stack barons in the lobby of the Kaiserhof. Among them were Dr. Carl Friedrich von Siemens, head of the Siemens concern, Diehm of the potash trust, and Dr. Ilgner of the German dye trust. Two limousines carried us to the Tempelhof, into ever-denser crowds singing to the rhythm of marching feet. When we finally arrived it was almost dusk, but airplanes still soared in the skies. The huge Graf Zeppelin, after one more majestic circle over the field, headed for home. The enormous grandstands, hung, with gigantic swastika banners, were already packed; only the Hitler tribune in the centre had a few vacant places.

We took our seats next to the diplomatic corps, almost within reach of the microphone into which Hitler was scheduled to speak at eight o'clock. When the Italian ambassador arrived he sat down between Rosenberg and myself; he was visibly impressed. Below us on the brightly lighted field stirred a vast sea of human faces. The martial music of massed bands mingled with patriotic songs swelling from one and a half millions of throats throughout the wide arena. In the distance, Reichswehr, police, Stahlhelm, SA, and SS were manoeuvring to entertain the patiently waiting crowd, which had been moving in since early morning. Overhead the famous flyer Udet was tirelessly performing his breath-taking tricks.

But May Day had lost its magic. The weather had changed, and chilly gusts were carrying sprinklings of rain down on the delicate gowns, glittering uniforms, and top-hats of Hitler's many guests. I thought of the poor devils below, most of them coatless, who had been standing for five or ten hours after miles of marching to get there.

Dr. Ley, wearing a self-conscious air in happy anticipation of the morrow's coup which would make him king of the , German Labour Front,' spent a few minutes with us. Our top-hats treated him with amusing deference and respect: after all, these Nazis were incalculable people, and nobody knew what they might do. In keeping with the German custom of always carrying an etui filled with cigars, one of our big-shots offered his jovially to Ley, just as you might to your postman or your policeman. And Ley, after ogling it a moment, took out three or four and passed them over his shoulder to his lieutenant, who accepted them with gusto!

At last the waiting ended. A distant murmur swelled quickly to tumultuous applause, as Hitler, standing erect in his car with arm uplifted in salute, moved slowly up through a narrow lane. He descended and walked toward us along a line of more than a hundred labour representatives brought here by plane from all parts of the Reich. He passed the honour company of the Reichswehr, standing like statues with arms presented. I saw his face, the brown shirt, the iron cross dangling from the left side of his coat as he walked up the wooden steps and, looking a little embarrassed, slouched awkwardly to his place, bending his right arm in a loose gesture in response to the wildly cheering throngs in the stands and on the field. 'Heils' rose up to us with the thunderous monotony of the surf.

Goebbels opened the meeting and then ordered one minute of silence in honour of some miners who had perished that very day in Essen.

Suddenly a ring of searchlights reached high into the gloomy sky to meet overhead in a giant cone, a magic tower. Hitler stepped forward, a spotlight resting on him.

"Der Mai ist gekommen…" he began. But what followed was neither towering nor magic. Reading from a manuscript in a declaiming fashion, his metallic voice increased a thousand fold by loudspeakers posted all over the field, he introduced May Day as a symbol of rebirth, of constructive work and national unity instead of division, hatred, and strife, and declared it a national holiday to mark the end of internal class warfare. Then came ideological abstractions. A slogan: 'Honour the work and respect the workers.' Then, vaguely outlined, the cardinal points of his economic programme and disillusionment.

453

Here was no concrete, solid fundament on which the worker of the fist could meet and accept the worker of the brow in a final settlement between Capital and Labour. Every honest, thinking Nazi had expected something more. Hitler offered shop-worn generalities: compulsory manual labour for young male citizens; security for agriculture as the foundation of the nation's economic existence; abolition of unemployment by means of private and public enterprises, chiefly a gigantic scheme of road-building and waterway construction; a commercial policy that would secure the stability of industrial production; reduction of existing interest levels.

My first reaction was a feeling of shame and indignation. Though I had not expected much, I was not prepared for such a brazen insult to intelligence. The gap between what the Fuehrer actually offered and what the Party had promised to the worker was too great, the paltry content of his speech as the colossal climax of the day's programme too pitifully inadequate.

Now the whole spectacle appeared to me as clever camouflage, an evasion of the problem. The masses arrayed before Hitler needed more than food for their emotions; they wanted butter, more meat for their pots, shorter working hours, social security with a better-than-living wage.

A thousand times during the years of Nazi opposition, they had heard Nazis reply, when asked what a Hitler government would do to solve the economic crisis: "Don't expect us to give away our recipe for the solution; our enemies would steal it and take credit for it!" And when sceptical souls would retort: "That means you have no solution," Nazis would laugh. "Of course we have. You wait and see. Remember the element of unexpectedness. Hitler knows… When he springs his surprise, it will be effective."

Hitler had sprung his surprise - but the magic formula remained unspoken.

'Lord, bless Thou our fight for liberty and therefore for our people and Fatherland!" ended the Fuehrer, with arms upraised. The bands struck up, and 'Deutschland, Deutschland Ueber Alles, Ueber Alles in der Welt' roared over the field, followed of course by the Horst Wessel song.

New waves of popular enthusiasm surged about Hitler as he slowly drove away. Then, without a moment's lapse, as if the masses were not to be allowed to realize that they had been duped, stupendous fireworks went off in the distance, ending in an imitation of a hellish drum-fire in the Great War and capping Hitler's solemn May Day with fire and smoke. This time Dr. Goebbels' genius had carried him too far-into irony!

Only three or four of our guests had held out with us to the very end; the others had discreetly vanished. The ranks marched off, the multitudes streamed for home. Our returning limousine barely crawled along; often hemmed in by marching crowds for blocks at a stretch. Our top-hatted guests might easily have been the target of jeering jibes or worse, and in the half-dark of the car I saw concern on their faces. But we heard not one vulgar remark - only a few jokes and some good-natured shouts. This too is part of the extraordinary German nature, I thought, when at last we reached the Kaiserhof without insult.

Rosenberg and I had a late supper alone. There had been little talk in the car; now we talked less. Life looked to me like the circus we had just witnessed. How different May Day could have been if Hitler, instead of cheating himself to the top, had seized power by force!

Showmanship, following its inevitable and cynical curve of decline!

The evening in the Grunewald stadium in July of last year, the unforgettable Youth Day in Potsdam - days of incomparable élan - had led to the symbolic travesty of the Hindenburg - Hitler cavalcade to the tomb of Frederick the Great, to be followed by Hitler's gala performance at the Kroll Opera House, and topped off by the fireworks of May Day, the German Day of National Labour! Was this the prize? Were all our efforts to end in fraud? All this was not German! It was dishonest and false. Now I understood why Goebbels was called the curse of the Party.

In the morning Labour had its grim surprise. Squads of Dr. Ley's NSBO swooped down on the German Trade Unions, took possession of all their offices throughout the Reich without the slightest resistance, arrested their leaders, impounded their funds, and announced their dissolution. The raid, secretly prepared, was carried out with precision and speed. Labour banks were occupied, consumers' co-operatives, with their vast network of stores and factories, were seized; in brief, the chief bulwark of Marxism was wrested away and transformed into another stronghold of Nazism with the militant name, 'The German Labour Front.'

Other developments followed quickly. In a few weeks the solidification of Nazi power within the Reich became an accomplished fact. The liquidation of Marxism and the ensuing liquidation of the party system made the Nazi Party the only political party in Germany. Nazi Reichs-governors were appointed in every state. Hugenberg was ousted. The Stahlhelm capitulated. The German Federation of Industry kowtowed to Nazi control. It was the dissolution of the entire Weimar regime, the completion of the political co-ordination within the Reich, the end of external conquest for the Party.

The way was open for the spiritual conquest of the nation and for the economic and social liberation of the people. Yet the capture of power and of complete public control - press, radio, stage, school, university, art, literature, science, and pulpit - was destined to be used not to imbue the German people with the real substance of the Nazi Weltanschauung of truly German thought and spirit, but to 'co-ordinate' everything into the furtherance of one cause, one idea, one party the Hitler party and the Hitler cult.

The first phase of the Nazi revolution was ended; the second phase, Party dictatorship within the Totalitarian State, had begun - and with it the error and the fraud of identifying Germany with Hitler.

XXXV

I GET INTO TROUBLE

Meanwhile I had not been idle. The day after the Kaiserhof gathering, I was busy arranging for the transfer of the money which had been subscribed. To get a subscription is one thing; to get the money another - an unpleasant but important detail. Speed was necessary, for our enemies had not liked our success. And nobody knew what the next day might bring.

Before the first week of May was over, we had more than half a million marks in a special account at the Deutsche Bank. Rosenberg urged me to act as co-signer, but I refused in order to forestall possible misinterpretations. The amount was, of course, only a fraction of what we needed, but it was enough to start with. We took offices at Wilhelmstrasse 70a, next to the British embassy, in the old wing of the Adlon Hotel. The upper two floors served as the first address of the Aussenpolitische Amt or Foreign Bureau of the Party. The question of personnel was a difficult one, and for the time being we had to be satisfied with the bare minimum. The most important thing was to secure the authority and the means for action.

But I have lost out in my personal fight to make the Party's foreign bureau a weapon in the Nazi world-struggle; so it is futile today to go into detail, except for one rather interesting complication in which my efforts to get the money soon involved me.

One, a director of the I. G., suddenly developed a keen interest in our proposition and offered his active co-operation. He was a busy little fellow, a fledgeling putting on the airs of the old bird. But he was clever enough to see that he would have - to get around me if he was to have clear sailing with Rosenberg.

It was evident that he was acting for the German dye trust, which had great influence with the Foreign Office, as I have said before. I had to know what his scheme was before I could lay plans to thwart it. So I played the role of good-fellow, until he was convinced that I would be easy going.

Assuring me that the promised cheque for a hundred thousand marks had been sent, he hinted that possibly he could arrange for another hundred thousand, since we seemed to share the same views about foreign policy and the best line to follow. Of course I indicated my pleasure and our readiness to consider suggestions. Apparently I played my part well enough, for next he clumsily hinted at a reward for me - perhaps he was simply employing tactics that had proved effective with other Nazi chieftains. Touching on the great work I had before me in Washington and the large funds needed, he gave me to understand that there might be a substantial sum available for my office there if I could personally help to carry out this 'colossal task in a reasonable and practical way.' Again I expressed my pleasure.

"Splendid!" he said. "You're the right man; we understand each other!" And then he let his cat out of the bag. Casually it was disclosed that a very important American of enormous influence had arrived incognito in Berlin. He could not reveal his name, but Hitler ought to see him. Could I perhaps arrange an interview?

I thought: 'Certainly not!' - but said that I would do my best. When I told him the next day that I had been unable to arrange it, he showed irritation, but finally said that he would like to have Rosenberg and me meet the American.

When we met for lunch in a private salon of the Kaiserhof, I was not a little surprised to have the director introduce Ivy Lee,[1] of New York. The late Ivy Lee had been the well-known and successful public relations counsel for the Rockefellers and for many large corporations. In America I had heard it alleged that he had also issued publicity for the Soviet Government, and was active there on behalf of the German dye trust. Now I understood why the director and the interests he represented wanted Hitler to meet this mysterious gentleman.

Having never seen Ivy Lee before, I looked him over with special interest. He was a quiet, elderly man with tired eyes, but apparently very shrewd, an interesting type of anything but a Nazi - obviously a coldly calculating man whose first line of interest was business.

But I was still somewhat puzzled as we sat down to a dull and uneventful lunch. There was a fifth roan present, whose identity I do not recall. Rosenberg, warned by me not to commit himself, was even more reticent than usual. As he spoke no English and Lee no German, the conversation was mostly in English, to the visible delight of the director, who proudly showed off his imperfect command of the language. Lee followed the rule that silence is golden, and I, for once in my life, kept quiet; so the director's eloquence knew no check. Apparently he took it for granted that we were convinced with him that Ivy Lee was the only living person who could turn the tide in America in favour of the Nazis.

When Dr. Kiep, the German Consul-General in New York, was mentioned in connection with George Sylvester Viereck, the well-known German-American writer, I pricked up my ears.

After lunch the director and I had a little talk alone. The dye-diplomat benignly expressed his satisfaction at our finding Ivy Lee so agreeable.

"A fabulous man, but very, very expensive," he informed me in brotherly fashion - and I didn't doubt it for a minute. "But, of course, we're going to take care of that. By the way, the additional money for Rosenberg can be arranged. And we can talk next time about that extra cheque for your office in Washington, when we discuss our plan. I've outlined in detail how we're going to proceed."

---

1 Died in 1934.

That was enough for me. "Marvellous!" I said. "But I'm afraid the I. G. policy isn't quite the Nazi policy. And Ivy Lee may be a fabulous man, but in this case we'd do better without a commercial agency. We welcome suggestions, of course, but we shall accept or reject them as we see fit. Make no mistake of this: the final word about tactics and policy lies solely with the foreign bureau of the Party. Rosenberg is responsible only to Hitler himself."

The director's cocksureness was gone. His round face expressed ill-temper, but he controlled himself and left with a sweet-sour smile.

Ivy Lee's advent in Berlin disturbed me. He must be kept out, come what may; he could ruin the whole game. We did not want a spokesman who would bend his ear in turn to Moscow, Wall Street, and the City of London. And the director's mention of George Sylvester Viereck was equally disquieting. I recalled that Dr. Kiep, a year earlier, had urged Viereck on me as the best man to promote the Nazi cause in America. Knowing Viereck by reputation, I thought the idea bad, and after several very polite interviews with him, arranged by Dr. Kiep, I thought it worse. And instead of recommending his services to Munich, I had done the contrary.

But it alarmed me to see our financial sponsors already beginning to spin their webs about us, with only half their subscriptions in our hands.

To cap it all, I found Rosenberg calmly planning his visit to London.

"I don't like this," I said. "It's beyond me, your willingness to risk a trip to London, when you ought to be here on the spot every minute. You're not sitting in the saddle yet. Please stay at least until this affair is settled. Anyway, you must see Goering before you go - you promised me that a month ago."

"I can't wait," Rosenberg replied stubbornly. "You're getting too pessimistic. Now that Hitler has consented, I must go. I feel confident of good results in London. That will make my position stronger here. My talk with Goering will have more effect after my return; I'll see him first thing then."

I used up most of my ammunition on him. He didn't know the British; the international situation was against him; he couldn't possibly bring back a conspicuous success, and his enemies would do their best to make it appear a fiasco. Hitler might find it a welcome excuse for dropping him. And he was leaving Goering behind his back - Goering, who didn't like him, who was hand-in-glove with the money magnates so long as he needed them. Rosenberg himself had just said that Goering might not be deaf to the suggestions of the I. G. if their price were high enough. And we had already offended them by turning a deaf ear to their suggestions.

But Rosenberg sat there smiling imperturbably and drawing figures on his desk-pad.

"You can't speak even a word of English! You haven't got one decently fitting suit to wear. Your evening clothes are impossible. You can't go to London like that-go to a good tailor first!"

That budged him. Looking up, he said dryly, half angry, half joking: "Hitler was right - it's a muzzle you need. But you talk well. You'd better go to London with me."

But I said hotly that it was more important to collect the rest of the million for our office before we found ourselves all hedged about. And we argued no more.

Rosenberg left for London on 5 or 6 May, boarding the same train that Dr. Schacht had taken some days before. I had wished Schacht bon voyage at the Zoologischer Garten station on his way to New York. Crowded as he was, these were the only minutes the busy financier could spare me. But they were long enough for him to tell me that Hitler, whom he had consulted, was in full agreement with our idea. Turning to the Vice-President of the Reichsbank at his side, he asked him to pay the money.

After Rosenberg's departure, some of the men of the foreign bureau who sensed that there was a quiet, under-cover struggle going on between us, the propaganda ministry, and the foreign office, showed their apprehension about Rosenberg's trip and asked me why I had not prevented it.

"I'm getting sick of the whole business," I said. "I'd better wash my hands of this silly fight and hurry to Washington."

But they would not hear of it. "You're needed here more than in America - without you the foreign bureau is a sinking ship. We can't carry on without you."

That heartened me; everyone's ego yearns at times for appreciation, and I decided to stick it out with them until our ship was well out in the wind.

My great resolution didn't amount to much because of something unexpected.

On Tuesday, 9 May, Schickedanz and I had a dinner engagement with Skoropadski,[2] the former Hetman of the Ukraine. It was about eight o'clock on a rainy evening when I dropped Schickedanz at the restaurant where Skoropadski was awaiting us, and went on to the Kaiserhof to get my mail, saying that I would join them presently.

At the desk I was told that two gentlemen had inquired for me several times, and were still waiting somewhere in the lobby, crowded that evening because Goebbels was scheduled to speak to the Stage and Film Society. Before I could look for them I was called to the telephone. As I emerged from the booth, two men approached politely and asked for a moment of my time.

My eyes took them in with approbation: two tall, lean men, somewhat stiff of manner but at ease in clean, worn suits. "All right," I said. "But I'm in an awful hurry. What can I do for you?"

The one with the grave, grey face motioned at the noisy crowd round us and suggested that we step aside, as he had a very important message for me. I wanted

---

2 Hetman Skoropadski had been rewarded by the German general staff, which had made him governor of the Ukraine in 1918. Goering favoured him and Rosenberg opposed him.

to run up to my room, anyway, and invited them to come with me. When we had stepped from the elevator and were walking down the quiet, soft-carpeted corridor, I said: "Sorry to have to rush you after keeping you waiting so long, but really, I've only a minute-you'd better say quickly what you have to say."

And with that I opened my room. Bidding them sit down, I walked straight to the bathroom. Through the open door I asked: "Who are, you, anyway?" When I reappeared, drying my hands on a towel, they got up and slowly introduced themselves as Kommissar Dr. Braschwitz of the Gestapo,[3] and one Lebrun of the Geheime Nachrichtendienst, the secret service of the SS. There was a hesitant pause. Still unsuspecting, I said, a shade impatiently: "Go ahead, I'm expected - I'm late -"

"We have an extremely awkward mission to fulfil, Herr Ludecke. We must ask you to come to the Polizeipraesidium. My chief, Dr. Diels, would like to see you," said Dr. Braschwitz in the same even voice.

"Impossible now. Perhaps later in the evening, if it's that urgent, or early tomorrow morning."

Very gently, Lebrun addressed me. "Herr Ludecke, I know very well who you are, I've often seen you in the chancellery when I was on duty there. But we have orders to bring you to the police."

Suddenly I realized that I was arrested. It was like the stab of a knife. I sat down to think. Braschwitz, confirming their definite orders to take me to headquarters, said he didn't know whether I was to be arrested or only to be questioned, and that he had to report immediately to Diels as soon as they found me. Now he called police head-quarters to be told that Diels had just left and that he could be reached at his home. But he couldn't reach him there either.

Lebrun was very brotherly. "Don't be upset," he said. "We're soldiers obeying orders. Sorry that we have to take you with us. We'll try again to get Diels from the station."

Cool now in the face of facts, I ordered some sandwiches and drinks, packed a bag with necessary toilet articles, and added some books and a bundle of the New York Times I hadn't had opportunity to read. Perhaps my detention would be merely a matter of hours, but it might be much longer. I thought of my former arrests, and was entirely composed this time. Amazing what practice can do! I thought. But these two were really kind to me. I hope if ever I should be arrested again it will be done with the same consideration - it makes things so much easier.

They talked little while I was getting ready. "I'm afraid this spoils your whole

---

3 Gestapo or Geheime Staatspolizei, the State secret police, created by Goering on 27 April, and headed by Dr. Rudolf Diels, a versatile but able professional official and vice-president of the Berlin police during the Marxian regime. Though not a Nazi, he worked directly under Goering's control. The Gestapo became one of the pillars of Goering's tremendous personal power until, in April 1934 Diels was replaced by Heinrich Himmler, who co-ordinated the Gestapo with the SS and finally was appointed chief of the Gestapo throughout the Reich, under the jurisdiction of Dr. Frick, Reichsminister of the Interior, but de facto responsible to Hitler alone.

evening," I said. "Is that really all you know?"

Diels himself was puzzled, they told me, and hadn't the slightest idea what it was all about. "But if it means anything to you," said Lebrun, "it was Goering himself, about 5 p.m., who ordered Diels by telephone to get you to headquarters and await further orders. He gave no reason."

Goering! That looked serious. I picked up the telephone, and learned that Hitler was not at home. Then we went down to their car and drove to the Alexanderplatz, on the edge of one of the worst districts of Berlin. I felt a chill within me when we entered the forbidding, red-brick bulk of the Polizeipraesidium.

It was past ten before Braschwitz finally got Diels on the telephone. But there were no further instructions, except that I would have to remain overnight; they would try to settle things tomorrow.

I was turned over to the Schupo.'[4] Hell, I thought, here's another calaboose for you. And the same routine began, the same experience of dealing with petty authorities, who are everywhere the same. I had to part with all my valuables, but was allowed to keep my books, newspapers, pencil and wrist-watch, thanks to a good word from the genial Lebrun, who promised to see me before noon if I wasn't free by then.

Then a yawning Schupo took me through a gloomy corridor, dismal with dirty, naked stones, and left me at the cell-block. Now I was just the simple prisoner, a late guest disturbing the good night-warder, who had been smoking his pipe, drinking his chicory-coffee, and reading his penny thriller.

"Get in there," he barked. "Undress!" And I found myself in a dimly lit room, bare except for a little table and a chair.

"Herrgott!" I expostulated mildly. "Don't insist on my getting stark-naked - I've nothing unlawfully hidden in my cavities! And don't throw those books and papers on the floor, good man!"

"Shut up - and take your clothes off, every stitch - I stick to my rules!" he shouted at me. Too late I realized that he had not been informed of the mitigations promised me. One is never through learning. Obviously there was nothing to do but obey quietly and keep my dignity even in Adam's costume.

"A nice watch," he said curiously, taking it from me. "These are not Berlin papers- aren't you a German? What are you in for?"

"How do I know? " I replied, as I put on my clothes, and seeing a chance, I added: "I'm from America."

"Why didn't you say so before?" he grumbled, quiet friendly now. "I've a brother there. I wonder what he's doing... All the cells are full, and the larger ones are filled with bums, but there's one left. You'll be by yourself. Take all the stuff with you... I shouldn't let you... Perhaps you can tell me how I can get in touch with my

4 The Schutz-Polizei, or protective police.

brother… No, the razor and the watch I keep - no gold may be left with a prisoner."

We climbed up a little iron wentletrap three flights and went down a narrow, glass-floored corridor to cell sixty-nine.

The keys rattled. I was inside.

"And if you want that watch, and your own meals from the canteen, report in the day-warder early, at the first round."

"Thank you. Good night!"

With a frightening noise the heavy door fell into its iron lock. I was alone in a tiny cell, shut off from the world. A little glow fell from a lighted court, through a small window so high that my outstretched fingers could not reach the bars. There was a wooden bunk with a straw sack and a blanket, a rickety stool, a tin cup, a water-jug, but no wash-basin. In the corner, at the foot of the bed, a smelly privy.

Radio singing sounded in the distance. Before I could settle down to puzzle over my predicament, a woman began to scream, apparently in the women-prisoners' wing. 'Then she moaned and groaned, and ended in a pitiable whining. Stillness. Suddenly she began again, screeching like mad for a long while. The hysterical performance went on for hours. The prison stirred, doors banged, keys clanked, men shouted, prisoners pounded on walls.

There was no end. It was frightful. At last morning dawned and I fell fast asleep.

XXXVI

I AM GOERING'S PRISONER

A bell was ringing. A voice was bellowing "Aufstehen!" I rubbed my eyes and sat up, my bones cracking. Leaning on my elbow, I looked about me in bewilderment.

Slowly I realized I was in jail. Ruefully I looked at my suit, badly rumpled, for I hadn't been willing to undress in this lousy box. I plumped my feet to the floor. No water-nothing… And I had forgotten my shaving-mirror-couldn't even see my crumpled face. By now I was thoroughly mad.

There was the creak and the rasp of my door being unlocked and unbolted. I looked out, and seeing that my neighbours were putting out their water-jugs, I put mine out too and stared about me. "Inside with you!" yelled the jailer, coming back on his tour of bolting the cells. "But I want to -" Bang! There I was, alone in my cage with my wisdom. Patience, Kurtchen, patience!

After fifteen minutes there was the noise of unlocking again. The jailer stood by watching the trusties serving 'breakfast'; one of them poured a muddy liquid called coffee from a large kettle and the other handed out dry bread from a hamper, two pieces for each prisoner. I thanked them, asked the jailer to put me down for the morning report, and, taking my jug, now filled with water, was locked in again.

It was about seven in the morning. I made a scanty toilet, and lay down to wait. Exhausted, I dozed.

Suddenly the door clanged. Here were welcome guests - Dr. Braschwitz and Lebrun. They brought me some eggs and sandwiches but no news. Then they took me with them to Gestapo headquarters in the Horst Wessel House, the former Karl Liebknecht House, erstwhile headquarters of the Communist Party. A terrible building, especially inside. I had to wait, but I didn't mind-glad of anything that prolonged my respite from that stinking cell. I sat in a small room with three routine officers of the former police force, who took no notice of me. For a while I watched them opening intercepted letters by rolling a pencil under the flap of the envelope, and carelessly closing them again with common glue. Then I read the morning papers Lebrun had given me. But soon I was aware of moans and screams. They sounded far away. I thought of the torturings my Austrian friend had described, and I was glad when Lebrun took me to wait in another room where Braschwitz was interrogating prisoners.

At one o'clock lunch was brought in from outside. There was still no news for me, but I got some significant bits of information. It was clear that Rosenberg was being struck at through me.

"It's really Rosenberg they're after. To down a powerful man you first have to isolate him," they said. "Really, he should have been more circumspect in some things… Rosenberg had better look out. He has been watched for some time."

I listened, goading them on. Crazy rumours - but from the mouths of by no means minor officials. No doubt certain persons were trying to make the Balt unacceptable by working up an ugly scandal.

On the way back to the Alexanderplatz Lebrun told me that the foreign bureau had been busy on my behalf, but that nothing could be done - Goering refused to budge. Hitler was the only one who could give orders to Goering. I realized that I must find some way of getting word to him, for I believed that he knew nothing of my plight.

Lebrun promised to leave word that I was to be allowed to buy my own food and newspapers, and said he would come back next day. So I gave my share of the uninviting prison food to any of my fellow prisoners who wanted it, and then waited in vain for my dinner. Eventually I called a friendly warder by pushing out the signal, a metal disc which drops outside the door, and was told that my name was not on the list for private meals from the canteen. That was a privilege requiring the signature of the prison inspector, which might take a day or more. So I went hungry.

Soon it was too dim to read. I dreaded seeing the light die on the grey walls, for with the dark would come fear and loneliness.

Daylight was welcome, and so was Lebrun, even though he still had no news. But he brought some appetizing food. What he could tell me about Rosenberg's reception in London, of which I had found next to nothing in the few papers I had, was most discouraging. And his report that Hitler was flying to Munich that afternoon deferred my hope of getting in touch With him until after his return on Monday. I had to resign myself to at least four or five days more in my dreary cell.

The plot was too transparent. Probably counting on Hitler's anger over Rosenberg's failure, it was hoped to finish off both of us. It looked rather serious. Yet I was not greatly worried about my personal safety, for I knew by intuition that my detention could be only a question of days. What distressed me was the now almost hopeless outlook for the realization of my plan. Much can happen while you brood in a cell, helpless and shut off from the world.

I spent the next few days reading, thinking, and sleeping. Neither Braschwitz nor Lebrun showed up again. And I had another involuntary experience in fasting. When, on Friday morning, I asked the prison inspector why I was not getting my private meals, I was told that I had the permission all right, but not enough cash. Fifty marks were the minimum for the enjoyment of such a privilege, and I had deposited only forty-nine marks and eighty-eight pfennige. The fact that I was only twelve pfennige short did not influence this brave official - rules were rules. He suggested that I leave a note ordering my bank to forward more money. As the Gestapo censored all the mail of its prisoners, it was unlikely that the money could arrive before Tuesday morning, four days hence.

A charming outlook!

With rumbling stomach I returned to my Cell 69 and had recourse to reading to make me a full man. I had twelve or fifteen issues of the New York Times. Here were alarming and amusing headlines: "Iron Ring Forming Around Germany... Poland, Driven by Fear of Nazidom, Likely to Join Little Entente... Baltic States Ready to Form Block... Hitler Now Seeks Soviet Friendship..."

And this, for my savoury :

"Victor Ridder and Metz End Reich Mission... Leave Berlin Well Satisfied after Seeing All Leaders They Wanted to Meet... Agitation Abroad Decried... The Less There Is ant the Better It Will Be for Victims of Persecution... Hitler's Sincerity Praised by Ridder... 'Hitler One of the Most Sincere, Honest and Open Men I Have Ever Spoken To'" - (this is reference to a twenty-five minute interview with Hitler in Munich).

Victor Ridder!

By Sunday my emptiness was so acute that I appealed to my human-looking and friendly warder. He was all concern.

"For heaven's sake! Why didn't you tell me the last time I was on duty? I knew you had some pull when those Gestapo chiefs spent so much time in your cell... Yes, I'll get something... You'd better go out now with the others and get some air. No sense in refusing the only promenade that will take you out of this pigsty."

I took his advice, and for the first time I had a full view of the small, dismal stone court, part of which I had been able to see from my 'window' by standing on my toes on the rickety stool and pulling myself up with my hands gripping the bars - a verboten practice.

The calaboose was full. These were the prisoners I had heard through the walls, cursing, laughing, crying, snoring. We walked silently in a densely packed circle. Speaking or looking behind you was forbidden. But the two guards could not see everything, and I managed to have a look at all my fellow prisoners, most of them poor, ragged creatures with confusion or fear, stupor or spite plainly written on their worn, unshaven faces. Some had swollen heads and black eyes. I observed only two or three neat and intelligent-looking men. One distinguished and handsome man, obviously a foreigner, looked at me with wide, inquiring eyes and bowed his well-formed head slightly in greeting every time we passed each other. I bowed also, returning his gaze. Later I learned that he was a former staff officer of the murdered Czar, arrested on suspicion of espionage.

The friendly warder had not forgotten. He brought to my cell a frugal meal which tasted good, and when he returned to take the dish away, we talked for a while. He was the best type of the German small official; he belonged to no party and tried to fulfil his duties carefully but with humanity and common sense. I spoke of the bruised and beaten prisoners I had just seen.

"I've seen worse than that," he said. "They arrive like that - we here can't help it. But the very worst, those who can no longer walk, stand, or talk, are kept in other quarters.

Thank your God on your knees that you didn't fall into the hands of the Feldpolizei[1] - real devils in human skins! Here we hold prisoners two days or perhaps five; more than ten is exceptional. Many of them really don't seem to know why they're here. They don't look like criminals to me, and all the jails are overflowing, two and more in tiny cells. I don't know what Germany is heading for."

Alarm was beginning to grow in me. Sure that on the morrow something would happen, I was up before the Monday reveille. The hours crept slowly by. Around one o'clock my lock rattled, and an officer, polite for once, asked me to follow him. He landed me in the ante-room of Dr. Diels's office, where I sat down to wait on a real chair.

People came and went. Count Helldorf came in, in uniform, and strode straight through to Diels's office. Relieved that Helldorf hadn't seen me - if only because it had been three days since I had been under the trusty's scratchy razor - I turned my chair away from the door from which he would emerge. Then in came Aumueller from the foreign bureau, who was also working for the secret service of the SA and co-operating with the Gestapo. He had done all he could for me. "A disgrace!" he said. "Courage! you'll get out of this today or tomorrow. Hitler is expected back this afternoon, and so is Rosenberg. He must speak to the Fuehrer about you this evening. Of course, his London journey, you know…" and his face and the shrug of his shoulders said the rest.

"Chin up!" Said another acquaintance in passing. "There's a dirty intrigue against you. This can't go on…"

I was called in. Diels greeted me courteously, took me in at a glance, and with an apologetic expression invited me to sit down. I felt at ease with this tall, slender, and polished young man, and found his consideration instantly comforting. It was an occasion when good manners were doubly welcome.

"I'm glad to see you - I wanted to meet you," he said in a pleasant voice. "Unfortunately I must tell you that I still don't know why I had to arrest you. Nobody knows, and Goering won't tell me… Yes, it was by his personal order… Your friends from the foreign bureau keep after me, and I'm annoyed to be able to tell them nothing; I'm at a loss to understand it myself," and he shook his head… "Ah; you already know of Rosenberg's coming? I'll try once more."

---

1 Goering's auxiliary, picked from the SA, the later Feld Jäger.

Then and there he did his best to get Goering on the telephone, and when that failed, tried Goering's lightning-rod, Staatsse-kretaer Koerner. Finally he gave it up.

"Since you know Goering personally, why not write him a letter? I'll see to it that he gets it tonight or tomorrow morning." When I asked if I might also write a note to my wife, he said: "Of course, do it right here," and handed me pen, paper and envelope. Without looking at my note he ordered it mailed at once.

Amazing how little things like that help your morale when you are in prison! I went back to my cell feeling I'd rather be shot by a gentleman than drubbed by a churl. A little table was brought to my cell, and in a diplomatic letter I wrote a protest to Goering. It was past six when I turned it over to the warder. Thoroughly convinced now that I would soon be out, and too tense to feel the need of food, I lay awake on my cot for a long while, and finally went to sleep.

Though I have had moments of uncanny intuition and searing sensitiveness, I am in no way 'psychic'. Yet I am sure that that night, to quote Kipling, I 'passed beyond the bounds of ordinance'.

I dreamed that I was lying in my cell asleep, and that I was awakened by a bang at the door and brought before Goering. I had a dream impression of a dramatic scene with the gargantuan Nazi freak in his Palais. He had his hands on my shoulders and was telling me with bleary eyes that I was free - when there came an actual hammering at my actual cell door, the heavy key turned noisily in the lock, and the door banged open. Two officers shouted at me: "Get up at once!"

Gradually coming to, I bellowed back at them: "How dare you yell at me like that? I hate the very sight of you - get out! "

This took them aback, and rather tamely they said they had orders to take me immediately to Goering. I shook with nervous laughter. "Oh, that's good news, I've been expecting it - I just talked with him; he said I was free!" They looked at each other as though they thought I was crazy.

As we stood outside an exit I could hear them whispering together, debating whether to risk a taxi - the Herr Reichsminister was waiting.

"Of course we'll take one," I said, hailing an approaching taxi, "and I'll pay for it!" The one we jumped into was the oldest in Berlin, but it had a light, which my two officers turned on for fear I might escape. We gaggled through the old town, down Unter den Linden, past the Brandenburger Tor to the 'Residenz des Herrn Reichstagpraesidenten und Reichsminister, Seine Exzellenz Hochwohlgeborenen Preussischen Ministerpraesidenten und General in spe,' etc., etc. - Hermann Goering.

A liveried servant opened the door, and other flunkeys ushered us up the handsome staircase to the next floor. There an officer of Goering's staff said that the Herr Minister President requested me to wait a moment. I sank into an arm-chair of softest leather - marvellous luxury after my prison coop. It was now nearly eleven o'clock.

Already I felt like a free man. But considering that Rosenberg's failure in London, of which I knew no details, might have affected my own standing, I was in a quandary what attitude to adopt with Goering. I had seen him several times since my return from Washington, but had never once sought to speak with him. In fact, the last time I had talked with him at any length was during my short stay in the summer of 1930, when, after his lunch, he had sat down at my table in the lobby of the Hotel Bristol. But I had been rather abrupt with him and had ignored his invitation to visit him at the Reichstag for a longer talk - I couldn't abide the fellow. I hadn't thought of this little incident for years. Had my disregard of his weighty aplomb pricked his conceit?

Major Jakobi, Goering's nimble adjutant, ushered me into a large room where the great man awaited me. I have said before that pictures greatly flatter the Nazi Lohengrin. An unretouched close-up of him that night would have shown him in a truer light.

He was without his habitual gaudiness of apparel, being dressed in an ordinary brown suit - an immense, fat creature who hoisted himself to his feet and stumped towards me on elephantine legs, with outstretched hands, an artificial smile around an ugly mouth with inward turning lips.

"Mein tuber Ludecke! I'm so glad you're here. Of course you're free!" Waving me to a seat, he sat down. Striking his hands together in a gesture of regret, he added: "I had no idea that you had been arrested. I am very sorry that this occurred. I only heard about it this very evening and ordered you brought here immediately. Yes, yes, you are free, of course - certainly."

But now I had to say something. I apologized for my unshaven appearance, made a few ironic remarks about the sudden surprises of life, especially in revolutions, and thanked him for intervening in my behalf, with no hint that I believed him the cause of my trouble. He could imagine my bewilderment, I said, at finding myself arrested in the midst of my work, though I enjoyed Hitler's confidence and had been recommended by him personally for the Washington post. Then to be left in the dark for days, and to learn that even Dr. Diels knew of no reason... As I spoke, I looked straight at him.

"Fortunately," I went on (thinking 'unfortunately' to myself) "you have never known what it is to be in jail. Yes, it feels fine to be free again. But it's a most annoying affair, and I'm afraid my arrest will hurt my prestige and make things rather difficult."

He interrupted me. "Oh, Ludecke, take it humorously, not so tragically. You know we're in a revolution, and strange things happen. You were treated well, I suppose? At least I - I" and he stopped in confusion.

I rescued him. "Yes, to be sure. I didn't mind the discomfort and the anxiety - I was certain Hitler knew nothing of this imbecility, and that I would be free as soon as he did. I was worrying about other things. This is an awful disgrace - it's bad to be compromised like this - something I simply cannot afford."

"Nobody knows of your arrest - you're taking the whole thing too tragically, I tell you," Goering said.

"I can't help feeling alarmed," I insisted. "My arrest can't remain a secret; too many people know about it. Odd that it happened during Rosenberg's absence - there must be persons interested in knifing us both, and they've undoubtedly spread the news. I must find out."

"I told you no one knows about your arrest," he interrupted me again, raising his voice in irritation. "Impossible. Nothing has leaked out."

"After all, I'm not a fool, Parteigenoss[2] Goering," I said with emphasis.

His red face went redder. "I explicitly gave the strict order that your arrest be kept absolutely secret," he burst out, and then, visibly furious at his own blunder, entangled himself further. "I didn't know that you stood so well with Hitler - you can count yourself lucky to have got off so easily," he added with an ugly laugh.

"What do you mean by that?" He shrugged his shoulders and walked to a window, turning his back to me. I waited, wondering how I could make him talk without making things too hot for myself, for I was still in his power. I couldn't be sure that Hitler had ordered him to set me free.

Then suddenly he turned, pushed a chair to the table near which I was sitting, sat down, and said in a quieter voice:

"Look here, Ludecke. The thing is like this. There are two groups in the Party, two opinions about you," and picking up a pencil, he indicated the division. "You see, Ludecke, you're a rather unusual type in Nazi ranks, a 'Weltbummler.'

Some think you're an adventurer, a fantastic sort of person, a gambler" and noticing my wide-eyed surprise, he added, not without a touch of humour, "It's said that you gambled at Monte Carlo. I don't mind, I like to gamble myself - all life is a gamble anyway. But even our Party has its old fogies. And they say that you like women too well"- he gave me an unpleasant smile. "And the others think you an exceptionally intelligent, energetic, and useful man. You see, you're a disputed personality."

"Very interesting, but I fail to see why that should land me in jail," I retorted. "Even the most superficial examination of my status would have shown the stupidity of detaining me without cause, without even the pretext of a cause. Such arbitrary insolence would be a flagrant insult to anyone; with me, an old Party member, it's an inexcusable outrage. After all, it's no lark to spend a week in that filthy hole…"

I was talking myself into a passion, but stopped when I perceived that he was now returning my gaze with undisguised amusement, his face showing intent

2 Party comrade.

curiosity and a more natural friendliness than before.

The strain was beginning to show on his nerves; fatigue and impatience reappeared on his worn face. Reaching for my overcoat to show that I was going, I said I hoped to be spared similar experiences in the future, and to see the administration of the law tempered if possible by the saving grace of common sense.

But he did not try to put me in my place. He actually gave me his word in an apologetic manner that I need fear no further trouble from his side.

Then I mentioned having heard that Rosenberg himself was to be arrested.

"Oh, nonsense," he said, unable again to conceal his embarrassment, and looking down at his uneasy feet. He was silent for a moment, biting and compressing his lips, which made his bull's face appear mouthless.

"Rosenberg-tsche-" he finally said sneeringly, with a contemptuous gesture. "He'd better climb down from his high-horse. Hitler certainly did not relish his London performance, nor the echo in the Press.[3] But he seems to like you - I had no idea... Drop in and see me before you go to Washington!"

I indicated my extreme pleasure in the prospect. "The world seems to become more hostile to us every day," I remarked, at a venture. "Things begin to look rather serious, don't they?"

"Couldn't be worse," he growled. "Hitler will talk to the Reichstag Wednesday. His speech should clear the atmosphere somewhat. We need a breathing-spell." Rising, he repeated that he would like to see me before I left for Washington. "And forget what happened - you'd better!" he added jokingly, but with a cynical undertone, and patted my shoulder.

But I needed one thing that would not be easy to get.

"Perhaps you can advise me. My disappearance and my arrest are known, of course - we can't help that. I must be able to give some sensible explanation. My position is of no great importance, nevertheless I've some standing - I'm not quite unknown. You understand that I can't very well tell about our little rendezvous tonight..."

"Hm, hmm," he said, stroking his face with stubby fingers, a crafty expression creeping into his tired, sunken little eyes. Then, with infinite assurance, he unleashed his brilliant idea:

"If the question should come up, simply say that you personally had asked to be taken into protective custody, and that I granted your request, arresting you with your consent while a matter concerning you was being cleared up. Finding it unnecessary to make the investigation you had demanded against yourself, I had released you. That will settle the matter - that ought to satisfy you."

---

3 It served Goering as a good argument with Hitler against Rosenberg, for it complicated his work with Mussolini in fostering his Four-Power Pact in London. Goering, as Hitler's emissary, had visited Rome on 10 April and went again on 20 May after Hitler's speech of 17 May.

"Splendid," I replied. "Suppose you give me that in writing." Now he was all theatricality. "Don't you trust the word of the Minister President of Prussia?"

"Of course," I hastened to say, "but it will be more convincing to others to have it in writing. There's no reason why not - don't you in turn trust me?"

He gave me a sidewise grin. "You sly-boots! You're quite a schemer. No, my good friend, nothing in writing - I gave that up long ago."

The best I could do, as he was escorting me out, was to remind him of prison routine, and suggest that he write a word for the police, so that I might be spared another night at the Alexanderplatz and could get my valuables.

"Don't worry," he laughed, taking me under his arm, "I'll take care of that." He couldn't be induced to part with anything bearing his signature.

In the staircase hall, my two officers were standing in devout posture. Goering, beaming a Lohengrin welcome, greeted them with handshakes like long-lost friends. As I looked at him standing there in pompous joviality, I wondered whether a sausage might not burst if stuffed too hard.

"Herr Ludecke is free!" he boomed in a stentorian voice.

"The arrest was a mistake! Herr Ludecke must be released at once!"

"And you"- turning to the now sweetly smiling Major Jakobi, who had rejoined us - "see to it that there's no delay!"

Some more joviality with the people, a last handshake with me, and the mighty man plumped away.

XXXVII

I FIGHT

My awakening next morning in my old room at the Kaiserhof was pleasanter. The refusal to put my release in writing had almost cost me another night in jail, for the night-warder had insisted on a 'written order.' When at last I had found myself out on the street, a free man, I had taxied to the Friedrichstrasse Station for a bath and a shave, and after that had spent an hour gathering in all the German and foreign newspapers I needed, the English papers especially. Finally, long after midnight I had found time to get something to eat.

Now, in the morning sunlight, I turned to the newspapers.

Everything had contributed to Rosenberg's bad luck. While he was trying to create a better understanding between Hitler's Germany and Great Britain, another Nazi bomb had caused a stir throughout the world. On the evening of 10 May, thousands of 'un-German' books had fed huge bonfires in Germany's thirty universities - the culmination of the Nazi student campaign against the 'un-German' spirit. And Goebbels of course had made it an occasion for delivering an address full of heroics.

No doubt of it: Rosenberg's Press was terrible. English Press and Parliament, from extreme Right to extreme Left, had unanimously turned thumbs down on Hitler's special envoy and had shown themselves openly and aggressively antagonistic to Nazi policy. An 'angry session' between the Foreign Secretary and Rosenberg had been followed by a statement of the British Secretary of State for War which had the tone of an ultimatum to Germany; there had been a demand in Parliament for Rosenberg's deportation as a propagandist; Lady Asquith had given out a sensational story of her personal interview with Rosenberg; a wreath which Rosenberg, in behalf of Chancellor Hitler, had placed at the foot of the Cenotaph War Memorial had been slashed by a British captain.

Instead of appeasing English sentiment, Hitler's envoy had inflamed it. The German non-Nazi Press was cleverly telling the Germans about Rosenberg's rebuff in London by denouncing, with a great show of indignation, a treacherous trap into which it was alleged poor Rosenberg had been led.

But the issue was rather Rosenberg's stupidity in undertaking a mission foreordained to fail. In politics more than anywhere else, nothing succeeds like success. Editorial indictments, such as one stating that Rosenberg had exasperated the British by his mere presence and acclaiming the general relief at his departure, were the final blow.

The news showed that Rosenberg's escapade was tinder for new fires flaring up against Germany. I noticed for the first time that a 'preventive war' was openly being suggested in many quarters, both in London and Paris. No wonder the Fuehrer was disturbed at our complete isolation in a hostile world.

But the papers of that very day were to show that the Fuehrer's fabulous luck had not deserted him. Just at Hitler's psychological moment, the enthusiastic new President of the

United States made a moving appeal to the world. In a message on disarmament and economic peace, cabled to the heads of fifty-four nations participating in the General Disarmament Conference at Geneva and the World Monetary and Economic Conference, to be held in London in June 1933, Roosevelt made high-minded proposals for ending the armament crisis. Now the whole world looked to Berlin. And Hitler, with his singular aptitude for tactical situations, seized the opportunity .

Next day he delivered his Reichstag speech-a diplomatic achievement. Presenting Germany's case against the world, he stressed her will to peace on the basis of equality, security, and dignity as a sovereign nation, and warmly endorsed Roosevelt's proposals. His unexpected spirit of moderation impressed the world and helped to lessen the political tension in Europe. For the first time, editorials in the hostile foreign Press spoke of 'A Different Hitler' and 'Hitler the Statesman.' The Fuehrer appeared stronger than ever, and I was inclined to feel more confident about him and the German future.

It looked now as if the dreaded' preventive war' would not materialize, and Nazi Germany, with no foreign complications to fear for a long time, could safely concentrate on itself, push the 'German Revolution,' and, above all, begin the necessary house-cleaning within the Party. It seemed to me that my case offered an ideal opportunity to set the ball rolling, and I looked forward to a great fight, if I could bring Rosenberg to see eye-to-eye with me.

I did not see Rosenberg until late in the evening of the day after Hitler's speech. Night was always the best time to get the Balt to yourself. He would be shut up alone then in his editorial sanctum, seeing the morning edition of the Voelkischer Beobachter to press, or shaking a last-minute editorial out of his sleeve.

He had little to say about his London visit and about Hitler's reception of him when he had reported to the Fuehrer on Monday evening. When I handed him my translations of some English Press reports, he admitted quietly that he had made a mistake.

Rosenberg had spoken to Hitler about my imprisonment, and the Fuehrer had replied that he had already ordered my immediate release. Another report that came to me from some one close to Hitler corroborated this. Hitler had interrupted his dinner when he learned of my arrest, promptly bawled Goering out by telephone, told him that he approved of my activities, and instructed him to apologize to me.

We discussed our situation frankly. It was plain that there was a tremendous fight on against Rosenberg from many sides - from the Foreign Office, from Goebbels, from Goering, from the clergy, both Protestant and Catholic. Though we could not put finger on a single concrete case of combined planning on the part of these diverse factions, there clearly was method in their drive against 'Rosenberg the God-be-Damned.' Now it began to emerge, the chain of events that linked Rosenberg's journey, that this mission had been sabotaged.

Then, for the first time, the Balt confessed to me that nowadays Hitler never candidly explained his attitude to him, or the necessities behind his moves, and that his own work was suffering under the strain of the uncertainty of their relationship. We discussed the strange conflicts in the Fuehrer's character, his violent urge to be accepted by history as both a giant among intellectuals and a giant among activists. And Rosenberg would quote Goethe's deep words:

"Es sind wenige, die den Sinn haben und zugleich zur Tat faehig sind. Der Sinn erweitert, aber laehmt; die Tat belebt, aber beschraenkt."[1]

Perhaps Rosenberg was perceiving something that then seemed clear to me: he was destined to be one of the tragic victims of Hitler's jerky genius. Perhaps the Fuehrer's intuition told him that Rosenberg was now opposing him objectively as a critic and hating him subjectively as an individual to the degree that he had once admired him. At any rate, that spiritual discomfort which Hitler was now feeling in the presence of the disinterested idealist, who until recently had so influenced him ideologically, was leading the Fuehrer to alienate and torment the man. Instead of using and developing his unique but difficult personality and keeping him morally intact for the inevitable struggle with the Church, Hitler was dragging Rosenberg into the dirty arena of party politics and exposing him to ridicule by allowing him to meddle in foreign politics unaided, and with insufficient means. Once Chancellor, Hitler should have appointed Rosenberg minister of spiritual and ideological education, with the prestige of executive power. Characteristically, he waited until it was too late; then, on 30 January 1934, in a hopelessly muddled situation, he appointed a degraded Rosenberg his 'spiritual' deputy, giving him a new Party office with a high-sounding title but no executive power.

I was able to report to Rosenberg one concrete evidence of the plot to frustrate our plans and cripple our new initiative. Dr. Kurt Schmitt (destined on June 29 to succeed Hugenberg as Reichsminister of Economics)[2] by oversight had not been invited to the Kaiserhof luncheon. He was general director of the 'Allianz,' Germany's largest insurance company. Before my arrest I had sought him out, had been received courteously, and had been promised a hundred thousand marks and

---

1 *There are few who have intellect and are also capable of action. Intellect amplifies but paralyses; action animates but restricts.*

2 *A non-Nazi - but mostly Nordic-looking Minister in Hitler's cabinet.*

full co-operation. Taking me into another room, he had demonstrated, on a huge map of the world covering an entire wall, the physical potentialities of his world-wide organization.

After my release, I had telephoned him. Polite still but a little embarrassed, he told me that he had heard that the situation was now somewhat changed; the propaganda ministry was to take care of 'all this,' - and accordingly he had not transferred the hundred thousand marks.

Rosenberg agreed that my case was now his case, and that we must plan defensive measures together. I had no intention of going to Washington until the cloud of my false arrest had been lifted, and I still clung doggedly to my original purpose of making the Nazi foreign bureau an effective world instrument. Before I could accomplish anything, my prestige must be re-established by at least a moral victory over the instigators of the coup against me. Moreover, mine was not just 'The Case Ludecke,' but concrete evidence of something cancerous within the Party, something that had to be cut out. My case, involving as it did a fundamental principle, would necessitate an operation.

There was only one way to force a showdown. I must bring the whole matter before the Ruschla,[3] the supreme court of the Party, by demanding an inquiry against myself It could not be denied me, and, if properly conducted, could not fail to bring the truth to light. I had done nothing to be ashamed of, but the truth would put our enemies to shame.

I was not so naive as not to realize that I would risk a good deal, possibly my head. But proper clarification of my case seemed worth the hazard, for it meant not only official recognition of my rehabilitation but also our triumph and a definite defeat for our enemies. My case would come before the Party Court and before the highest judge, the Fuehrer himself.

It took a few days to bring Rosenberg round to full support of my intended action. I knew that as soon as our enemies became aware of what my case implied, they would strike at me quick and hard, and that therefore I must have him behind me.

"I can win the battle for us only with you," I told him. "If you let me down, I'm lost. Even if Hitler, hard-pressed, should prefer to desert me - which is unlikely - he can't do it if you identify yourself with me. Hitler may neglect you, but he can't drop you; he knows he needs you in the final struggle. He could do without Goebbels, or Goering, or even Roehm - they're only physical instruments he could replace. But not you. It's you and not he who is the prophet and spiritual leader of our movement, and he knows it. You're the world's most prominent non-Communist,

3 *'Reichs-Untersuchungs-und-Schlichtungausschuss,' or investigation and arbitration committee. Besides functioning as the supreme court of the Party, it swerved also as the disciplinary agency, with local courts and representatives in every district. Its president was Reichsleiter Major Walter Buch, but in reality the supreme judge was Hitler himself.*

anti-Christian leader. Hitler would never publicly abandon you, much less arrest you, for that would mean a tremendous victory for the entire Christian Church in Germany and an open abandonment of the National Socialist Weltanschauung. Even Hitler can't afford that."

He had a unique opportunity, I insisted, to exercise his moral authority and make himself stronger than ever. In the end, even Hitler would thank him if he helped to put them where they belonged. And surely he must see that he had no alternative now but to fight.

Finally Rosenberg came round completely, and we made a solemn pact to see it through together. We would force Hitler to decide whether the Party was to become an Eldorado for racketeers or a clean instrument for a truly greater Germany; whether he himself was to be a fraud or the honest trustee for the German people. The stoic Balt saw his own honour at stake; he seemed aroused at last, and in a real fighting mood.

"A nice occupation, snooping for dirt on each other," he said with contempt, pacing up and down and working his hands behind him, the only sign of emotion he ever showed. "And easy to find if you poke your nose into your friends' bed-pots. Who among us leads a completely blameless life?"

It was agreed that I was to stay in Berlin until the whole matter was settled. If Amann should make any difficulty, my finances were to be taken care of by the Nazi foreign bureau.

The die was cast. In full accord with Rosenberg, I wrote two letters to Major Buch, one demanding an investigation of myself and the other an investigation of the 'Case Ludecke' in connection with my arrest. Then I wrote to Rudolf Hess, chief of the political central commission, informing him of my action.

Now I could only sit and wait.... No, on second thought there was one thing I could do: I could see Hitler and give him my own version of the situation before it could be mis-interpreted by others.

As I turned into the corridor of the chancellery to be booked for an interview, I almost bumped into the Fuehrer, who seemed to be in a hurry. We stopped. I thanked him for his intervention on my behalf. He looked pre-occupied, and stared at me with blank eyes for a moment without saying anything. This was one of those unexpected incidents which always make one reproach one's self for not having done this, or said that.

Suddenly Hitler asked me when I was going to Washington.

"I don't know. I have to see - that depends on - "

"On what?" he snapped. "You'd better get ready instead of losing time here!"

"I don't think I'm losing time," I said coldly, a little vexed by his curt manner. "Besides, the Foreign Office seems to have false information about my case. I've just come from Geheimrat Aschmann - I wanted to find out if my arrest had affected these gentlemen in any way, and might perhaps be used as a pretext."

"Nonsense! " Hitler interrupted me. "Didn't Rosenberg tell you that I personally told Neurath I wanted your appointment rushed through?"

"Nevertheless," I insisted, "there's some delay, and the Foreign Office still has, or perhaps again has, a false impression. Geheimrat Aschmann was significantly reserved at my direct question, and muttered something about a new situation. That was all I wanted to know. Under the circumstances, I don't want to go to Washington - I've something much more urgent to settle right here."

"What do you mean by that?" he asked brusquely.

"Just that," I said, looking straight at him. "I've written to Major Buch, and was just on my way."

"I know, Hess told me," he said, not letting me finish.

"Don't waste your time, I tell you. I'll speak to Neurath. See me before you leave - I must run now."

"Please excuse me," I said, so dead in earnest that my voice was almost choking me. "I cannot go to Washington now. Some ugly rumours are circulating about me - things are going too far."

"Ach, Gott! Why bother about that now?" he broke in, with an impatient gesture. "Don't worry about that!"

"I thank you for the confidence with which you honour me, but I must stand my ground and see this thing through. It is a matter of principle. I owe it to you and to the cause I serve to stay until I've the assurance that there will be no more misunderstandings." He looked at me with an expression of surprise, anger, and impatience. Did his almost feminine intuition sense that contempt which I did not like to admit even to myself? With an abrupt: "As you wish - I'll see," he hurried away.

It was the last I ever saw of him.

Thoughtfully I returned to my hotel, scolding myself for not having been more diplomatic. Today I think that anything I might have said would have made no difference.

A day or so later I learned that a New York paper of 12 May had carried on its front page a libellous article about me, announcing in bold head-lines: LUDECKE ARRESTED FOR SWINDLE AND EXTORTION. It was a cable despatch from the recently appointed Berlin correspondent Margreve, saying that a house-cleaning of the Party was under way, and that it was not sparing persons in the immediate entourage of Hitler.

Again in complete agreement with Rosenberg, I took Aumueller of our intelligence department with me to Margreve's office.

At my request, the surprised correspondent gave me a bundle of still unopened newspapers. When I took out the issue of 12 May and pointed to his cable, he went pale, and without ado surrendered the original of his despatch, which I found conformed in essential facts with the article, though it had been editorialized in New York. I asked Margreve how, as a responsible journalist, he could cable such criminal libel, and demanded his source of misinformation. Was it the police, the propaganda ministry, or any official agency? Cornered, sweating with embarrassment, he admitted stammeringly where he had heard it.

I drove at once to the office of Dr. Alfons Sack, a prominent Berlin attorney, member of the Party and an SS man, whom I knew through mutual friends. He later acted as defence lawyer for the Communist deputy Ernst Torgler in the Reichstag-fire trial, and was among those arrested on 30 June 1934, but apparently escaped the Blood-Purge. Sack was a tall and obviously fearless man who seemed to enjoy giving you the impression of a guzzling Bierstudent and then suddenly to astonish you with the alertness and shrewdness of his mind. I told him that my case would involve important persons, and stressed the fact that it would touch a hot zone of Nazidom. But he accepted with alacrity after assuring himself that the case was clear. For my action in New York against the New Yorker Staats-Zeitung, he advised consulting Dr. Karl van Lewinski, former German consul-general. Dr. Lewinski in turn recommended a well-known New York attorney, to whom I entrusted the case.

In a way, the blunder was a welcome new weapon for us, and Rosenberg and I resolved to exploit it to the utmost. It was evident that the plotters had believed me helpless in my prison cell, and had thought they could safely make me unacceptable in America; then they would be free to pursue the selfish and stupid policy I had opposed.

Dr. Sack had assured me that he could push my libel suit against Margreve to come up in civil court early in July. The article had stressed the fact that I was Rosenberg's collaborator.

Such a revelation in court of criminal intrigue instigated by leaders in the Party would have been a world scandal which Hitler could never allow. We knew that. But we believed that my legitimate use of the right to defend my honour would logically force Hitler to step in at last with the full weight of his authority. At the very least he would have to call these gentlemen and us before him and settle the matter then and there.

Convinced of my moral duty to press the issue, I wrote another letter to Major Buch, pointing to the constitution of the Party and to my rights as a member, and demanding immediate proceedings.

But what if Hitler should see, in this conflict now approaching its climax, a potential danger to his interpretation of leadership? How much had he actually known of this conflict when he ordered Goering to set me free? Had he ever had wind of the 'palace plot' I had planned against him in 1924?

Might he not remember the heated talks we had in 1925 after his release from

Landsberg, and again in 1932 at the Kaiserhof when I had tried to push him into a revolution? Could an inkling have reached him of the attempt I had made to bring Strasser and Roehm together in 1932?

These were disquieting possibilities. To have right and reason on my side now seemed scarcely enough. It was too late to turn back now; I must look for a stronger ally than Rosenberg.

At last, some time in June, I had an interview with Roehm, and found him stouter but in a better frame of mind than in 1932 - more the carefree soldier Roehm I used to know, but grown now a wiser man. On his face were the lines of hard work and also of those occasional, violent outlets which his driving energy seemed to require.

Much depended on Roehm if things should turn out badly - if Rosenberg should fail me, if Hitler should desert me and give Goering a free hand. But would I not meet with another complication if I gave Roehm a frank account of all that had happened and what I was aiming at? A house-cleaning of the Party might not be at all to his liking, since his powerful enemies could then strike at him though his homosexuality. Everything seemed so hopelessly entangled and confusing that it is difficult for me to understand today how I could have been so strangely confident that the truth must win.

Yet I was so convinced that nothing could have stopped me, and said as much to Roehm, making no bones of the predicament in which his homosexuality had placed us.

"You know how I feel about that," I said. "Will you have the moral courage to act if Hitler does not?"

He met me with his habitual sincerity.

"Those hypocrites! I've suffered enough from that. I'll be free of it - that Damocles sword isn't going to hang over me any longer. Homosexuality isn't a sufficient reason for removing an able and honest leader from any position, so long as he is discreet. Such a more or less 'natural' abnormality is nobody's business - I do as I please within my own four walls, like anyone else... But to hell with pederasty. I can and will restrain myself if that's the stumbling-block. Haven't I worked all my life for this land and given Hitler all I had? Where would he be without me? Hitler had better look out -the German Revolution is only beginning!"

And he tossed a yellow pamphlet on the table.

"I suppose you've read this. You know I don't particularly like Rosenberg, but I recognize his value and respect his integrity. He sticks to his ideas and remains the cold idealist he always was. But his optimism is beyond me. Look at this! Compare it with my challenge! His is mere wishful thinking - his clear view of the abstract seems to obscure his view of the realities."

The yellow pamphlet was the 'Deutsche Revolution' number[4] of the National

---

4 N.S. Monatshefte, Heft 39; June 1933.

Socialist monthly - a revealing mélange of Nazi illusions and delusions, with much sheer palaver and some true revolutionary spirit. One could tell a great deal about the various Nazi chiefs by the way they expressed themselves here. I got a sudden headache about Major Buch's qualifications to view my case when I read his mawkish idolatry of the Nazi High-Priest, his praise of Hitler as the 'Miracle Man.' After his sycophantic gush it was a relief to turn to Roehm's message - a warning and a threat, cool and to the point, a blow at 'reactionary opposition, unfitness, and indolence.' Terming the Reichswehr the protector of the Reich, the police the protector of justice, he pointed to the SA and the SS as the third factor of power in the new State.

'The SA and SS, who bear the great responsibility of having set the German Revolution rolling, will not allow it to fall asleep or to be betrayed at the half-way mark... If the Philistines believe that the "national revolution" has lasted too long... it is indeed high time that the "national revolution" should end and become a national-socialist one... We shall continue our fight-with them or without them. And, if necessary, against them! We shall watch relentlessly to keep the "Haves" and the " Co-ordinated" from hanging themselves like so much lead on Hitler's socialistic will... We are the incorruptible guarantors of the fulfilment of the German Revolution....'

The sheer courage of it was tonic. I asked Roehm if Hitler had seen his article. He had seen it, and he knew how to read between the lines. For that matter, Roehm had said more to Hitler than he could put in print.

"The cowardly surrender of the opposition surprised Hitler more than it did me," he went on. "He can't get over it. Why doesn't he put the money-bags where they belong! If he didn't know it before, he knows now that I'll never allow our revolution to fizzle out. Of course he's in a quandary, and, as usual, shuns a clear-cut decision...."

Roehm gave me frank answers to my questions.

"A conflict between me and the Reiehswehr? Not a word of it true, though they're trying to concoct one. I don't need the Ministry of Defence - I've enough to tackle. But I want Hitler to keep his word and appoint me a Reichsminister with executive power - I don't want to be at the mercy of Goering and Blomberg. My SA is growing daily; soon I'll have two million.... No, I've no mass-complex. It's easier to control Communist elements inside the SA than by closing the ranks against them. They can't undermine the SA-some of my best men are former Communists. Let them call them 'beef-steaks'[5] - I like them radical. No fear of that; most of the ones who join us become Nazi revolutionaries, and that's what we want. No better reservoir from which to select our shock-troops....

"No, Hitler doesn't mind the swelling of the SA. On the contrary. He wants to use

---

5 A Berlin witticism: brown outside and red inside

us at will, as pressure on the Reichswehr and on big business here and abroad. But if he thinks he can squeeze me for his own ends for ever, and some fine day throw me on the ash-heap, he's wrong. The SA call also be an instrument for checking Hitler himself.

"But we must be patient. The situation hasn't matured yet to a point where anything can be done. Go ahead with your fight. If Rosenberg stands by you, Hitler will have to yield. That will be the opening battle, and it will lead to bigger ones. I'll be ready - I'll be Reichsminister by that time, and you can count on me."

I asked about Reventlow.

"I haven't talked with him for ages," said Roehm. "I like him; he's no fool. A headstrong and honest man, still the lone wolf. But he's left out in the cold, and has little influence. You'd better see him later...

"Strasser? Judge for yourself. He was an awful fool, but he may be useful yet. Though inactive for the moment, he's still somebody to reckon with."

I saw Gregor Strasser - and judged for myself. It had to be managed carefully, for both our sakes. I had one arrest on my back, and Strasser was now a compromising figure in Nazi politics. He had perhaps as much to lose in being seen with me.

One evening we motored separately to a rendezvous on a secluded road outside Berlin, each of us first making sure that he had not been followed. We sat in my car and talked for nearly an hour, to no great purpose. Tact kept me from touching on his personal debacle, for the subject was clearly painful to him. If I could have known what the future held for each of us, if I had dreamed that his lips were soon to be closed forever, perhaps I would have tried to probe something that now will always be a mystery.

It was a shadowy and unsatisfactory meeting. Each of us was guarded with the other, and I drove back to Berlin uncertain whether Gregor Strasser was still a potential in the future of Germany.

But Major Buch, despite our insistent inquiries, did not move. Finally, after weeks of procrastination, he suggested dismissing the case. When I insisted on regular proceedings, he side-tracked the whole question by turning my case over to Brama, the chairman of the Party's district court in Berlin. Brama was an elderly man who meant well but had neither power nor initiative. He took some evidence in the case - from me, Rosenberg, Hanfstaengl, perhaps from others. I saw him three times, I think. First he adopted an air of secretive importance, which soon changed to friendliness.

"All I'm supposed to do," he disclosed, "is to submit some questions to you and a few others and report my findings to Major Buch. I can't make head or tail of this. There's no case against you. All I have is some ridiculous gossip without basis of fact. Rosenberg spoke very highly of you, and from what I learned from him and hear from you and others, I am disturbed to see what can happen in the highest

481

circles of the Party.... Yes, many cases go through my hands. Some are settled, some are not. The practical functioning of the court is a sad chapter indeed. In certain delicate matters, there are cases that have dragged on for years and have never been settled. Of course there should be regular procedure by the court, as every Party member theoretically has a right to a hearing. But you see, I can't do anything about it. I won't burn my fingers."

"... There's only one thing Buch can do: clear you entirely. You'll hear from him within a few days."

Meanwhile, the Berlin correspondent Margreve asked me to drop the libel suit, and said that Hansfstaengl was also anxious to have the matter settled out of court. I refused on the ground that something more was needed than his and Hanfstaengl's apologies. I received a request from the Berlin court, Amtsgericht Charlottenburg 5, dated 22 June 1933, to pay the necessary deposit for legal expenses, and was advised by Dr. Sack that the case would come up before 15 July.

Before I paid the fees on 30 June,[6] I again made several fruitless attempts to arrange a personal interview with Major Buch. Finally, one day at the end of June, when Brama's report had brought no action, I learned that Buch was lunching at the Hotel Excelsior in Berlin. Employing a ruse, I encountered him in the hotel lobby.

Buch looked like a Jesuit and behaved like one. He was evasive and vague; it was evident that he was not acting on his own, and he stalled for time.

"I can't understand why you and Rosenberg are so insistent. This thing can't go to court. Why not dismiss the whole matter? I must hurry to a meeting. I assure you I'll settle the matter within the next few days - satisfactorily. I see your viewpoint - just a little patience, please."

"Sorry to detain you," I said, just as cool as he, "but I must say one thing. If this matter cannot be aired in Party court behind four walls, I cannot and will not withdraw my libel suit against Margreve in the courts of the Reich unless Hitler takes a stand to keep it out of court. I cannot do otherwise if you, the president of the Party court, declare your incompetence in this matter."

Avoiding my eyes, he asked me to telephone him at seven o'clock to arrange an appointment for the evening. But he dodged me again, and next day he was gone, leaving no message for me. Finally, on Tuesday 4 July, Rosenberg got him on the long-distance 'wire, and Buch said he was dictating two letters, one for Rosenberg and one for me, informing us that he had dismissed the case in a way which would put my full vindication on record. He would send the letters registered "by night mail.

I suspected further temporizing. But now Rosenberg, showing signs of weariness, was so impressed by Major Buch's 'positiveness' that he seemed inclined to give in.

"Of course it's for you to decide," he said, "whether Buch's statement is satisfactory

---

6 *I have the paper and receipt.*

and is to be accepted as the final word. But this affair can take an ugly turn if we are too exigent. I can't help thinking of those aides of Wagner's in the concentration camp,[7] and of Hider's speech on Sunday.[8] That might have been a warning for us too - who knows? This thing is getting tougher than I expected. Perhaps Amann is right. He asked me to tell you to keep away from politics and stay with him; he has an interesting proposition with a great future ahead for you."

I laughed. "Well, Amann at least knows a good man when he sees one. Oddly enough, he said much the same thing to me about you, only a bit more drastically: you were crazy to soil your fingers with politics instead of keeping to your desk. No, I've no interest in helping Amann to make his Eher Verlag the biggest publishing business in the world,[9] his greatest ambition. But don't get cold feet now. Hitler can't treat us like the Wagner men. Ours is a different matter; we want him to protect the honour of the Party and we aren't asking him for a second revolution. Hitler can't arrest you, I tell you - and he won't touch me if you've the guts to stand up for me. By all means, let's first see what's in Buch's letters. But we must see Hitler as soon as he gets back from Munich and I boldly tell him the consequences if he doesn't step in on our side." But I was soon to discover that Hitler had already stepped in - in his own peculiar way.

I celebrated the evening of American Independence Day at a restaurant outside Berlin, with an American and an Englishman - little thinking that this would be my last dinner as an independent man in Germany. It was a glorious night of tender stars, with the scent of summer in the evening dew, and veils of mist floating up from the lake below. The terraces were lively with people dining in the discreet light of little lamps. I saw some foreigners, some Nazis, some real officers in uniform, some of the social set, some pretty women, some plain ones, and some Jews from nearby villas. And I observed especially the smiling, bowing Oriental who owned this beautiful estate and had turned it into the smartest rendezvous around Berlin - in partnership, with, and under the protection of, certain Nazi chiefs.

My indiscreet eyes had already discovered that Harry Bender, owner of the famous bar and restaurant bearing his name and frequented mostly by artists, had, behind a cloakroom, the black guards posted and fed.

That same evening I saw another prospering gentleman - and I say it without

---

7 Four former army captains, aides of Otto Wagner, chief of the economic division of the Party, had directly and indirectly pressed Hitler to appoint Wagner successor of Hugenburg as Reichsminister of Economics, and had been sent by Hitler to the Oranienburg concentration camp. Wagner was dismissed. The 'warning' was displayed in fat letters on the front page of the V. B.

8 Addressing SA and SS leaders in Bad Reichenhall on Sunday 2 July, Hitler declared: "I will crush, brutally and ruthlessly, every attempt... to over-throw the present order. I will turn equally ruthlessly against the so-called Second Revolution... whoever rises in opposition to the National-Socialist State will be hit hard, wherever he is." - As reported in the New York Times, 3 July 1933.

9 Amann's concern has become a veritable octopus. Without my help, he has really made his Verlag the biggest in the world; it now also controls the entire film industry of Germany. It is to be recalled that Hitler was the principal partner in his firm.

malice, for I always liked the man. It was Heinrich Hoffmann and a friend. Hoffmann had opened shops in Berlin and other cities, and as Hitler's friend and the official photographic reporter of the Party, was doing famously. I hadn't seen him since my arrest, and we had a long talk, to which the lady added her word of counsel.

"Beware of Hess," she said. "I'm a woman - I understand men's eyes."

"Yes, she's right," said Hoffmann… Of the men around Hitler, Shreck is the only one I trust… Your arrest was a disgusting affair."

I drew from Hoffmann the information that Hitler had said he hadn't known I was so thick with Rosenberg. As we parted, he added: "Watch your step! You know, if Goebbels has a hand in this... Well, good luck!"

Gloomily I wandered home to the apartment I had moved into three days earlier. Hoffmann's own difficulties in the halls of justice had depressed me. Perhaps I should have accepted the gracious invitation of Madame Charles Cahier, American opera-singer, once so famous in Europe to spend several weeks with her and her daughter in their Swedish country home by the sea - instead of renting an apartment and brooding here in the bed on the futility of life.

XXXVIII

I AM HITLER'S PRISONER

Early next morning they came again. A ring at the door aroused me. Half-asleep, speculating drowsily, I looked at my watch. Only six-thirty. Then the ringing was resumed more insistently, and suddenly I was wide awake in the grip of fear. At this hour it must be they! And then a heavy fist began pounding on the door.

Only they would dare that! Sheer panic now... no escape possible... there was no other door... three flights up, and stones below!

The stoic half of my ego evidently sleeps more soundly, but it waked at last, and in a moment I was able to walk composedly to the door.

"Stop that noise! What do you want?"

"Secret police. Open that door! We have to ask you some questions." "A little early - I'm still in bed. I'll be ready in an hour." "Open that door! We can't wait!" said another and firmer voice.

"You'll have to, until I put on some clothes. You can try battering down the door. It's a solid one, and the chain is on."

I went to the telephone beside my bed.

Rosenberg was not home. Strange, at this hour! But I got Schickedanz. "Wake up!" I said. "I'm in trouble. Listen… Hear that bell ringing? That's the secret police! Try to locate Rosenberg while I get another number. If I don't call back within fifteen minutes, call me here. If I don't answer you, I'm in serious trouble. Help me! Do something hurry!"

Then I got Thilo von Trotha, Rosenberg's secretary. "Herr-gott! Yes, I hear it. What's going on?" he asked bewildered.

"They're trying to break down the door! Wait!" I ran to the door shouting: "I'm telephoning Alfred Rosenberg, who will report your outrageous conduct to the Fuehrer if you are not quiet. I'll let you in as soon as I finish talking."

That worked. I told Trotha what to do and to call me back. Then I rushed through a hasty toilet, though the bell began ringing again.

In full control of myself now, I opened the door to find two men - a short, civilized-looking officer, and a blond young SS giant. Once inside they were relatively polite. After they had identified themselves, the short one placed me under arrest.

"You have no warrant? You don't know why? I refuse to go." "Don't be foolish - you'll only make it worse. Dress and come with us quietly," he said.

"Not before you tell me where you're taking me."

"To the Polizeipraesidium… Yes, the Alexanderplatz… Yes, it's true."

That was a relief - I had dreaded being taken to the Colombia Haus to suffer horrible indignities, or worse. When Schickedanz and Trotha called, I told them where I was going; they must reach. Rosenberg and he or they must inform Hitler immediately.

Though I was sure that this time I was Hitler's prisoner, I hadn't given up hope. Thinking far ahead, I carefully selected and packed my things in case of indefinite detention. The two men were getting impatient, and I rashly displayed to the SS man my new credentials from the foreign bureau and my Party-book showing my Brown House membership. They seemed impressed, but the officer kept these documents along with my passport, which had been in my hand and which I later needed badly. I cursed myself for my stupidity. My other papers I managed to save through all my coming tribulations.

The fact that they did not even pretend to search my room and that nothing else was taken from me, convinced me that my arrest was Hitler's way of disposing of 'The Case Ludecke.'

To gain time, I presented them with some of my books, and told the young SS man that he would do well to learn early of the mutability of all things. Somewhat intrigued, he said: "I don't understand all this, but I envy your living so near the great happenings…"

'What irony'! I thought - and went to take a bath and secretly write some letters to slip into the hand of an understanding janitor when I gave him the apartment keys.

At the Alexanderplatz I was careful to deposit some two hundred marks this time, instead of only forty-nine, and eighty-eight pfennigs. Cool coincidence willed that I be locked up again in Cell 69.

During the three hours behind me, my mind had been so busy with immediate, practical concerns that there had been room only for occasional stabs of despair. But now, in the greyness of my cell, every nerve of my body felt the gravity of my position. Fantastic, this life! Suddenly it grabs you by the scruff of the neck, and you vanish, nobody knows where.

I thought of my young friend from Lahr, the 'Baby' volunteer who had lost an arm in the war. Every three or four years I bumped into him, just as I had the other day. He had married into an Italian family and was now an engineer with a Milanese factory which specialized in telephones. They held the patent for an ingenious and secret telephone-tapping apparatus, something entirely new, and had marvellous contracts with the Mussolini government.

"A fabulous device," he had explained. "It reports automatically both in-coming and out-going calls without possibility of detection. Secret stations which can be connected with any number of private wires are already installed in many cities in

Italy. It's the most extraordinary telephone-spy system in the world. I thought that now in Germany..."

Having just arrived, he had at once thought of my connections (!). And as he talked, I wondered how this charming, warm-hearted young man could praise a heinous gadget which, though it provided him with a good living, would bring misery to thousands of people, both innocent and guilty. And almost in the same moment - for such is the human animal - I began to speculate how I could profit politically by this contraption. It had been arranged that he was to call at ten this morning to bring data and details.... Probably my poor tired bell was ringing this very minute, and he was concluding that I was a most unreliable man.

Days went by - no news, no answer to my letters, no word from Rosenberg. But I learned from the warder who had been friendly to me during my first arrest that I was listed as a prisoner in 'protective custody.' He told me that Captain Stennes had just spent some days in a cell opposite mine after suffering terrible brutalities in one of the Nazi terror stations, and then had suddenly been taken away. (I learned later on good authority that he had been taken out to be killed 'accidentally' but had adroitly thwarted the attempt. Finally released through pressure from the Reichswehr and the intervention of Vice-Chancellor von Papen, Stennes was allowed to accept a commission to reorganize the Chinese police, and left with his rich wife for Shanghai.)

After a week or so, I was brought to the new, palatial headquarters of the Gestapo in Prinz Albrecht Strasse. But they asked me only a few irrelevant questions about a Ukrainian journalist whom I knew slightly through Dr. Leibbrandt; this man and other Russians, mostly Rosenberg men, were also being detained at the 'Alex.' Apparently it had been only a pretext for getting me to the Gestapo, for when I was left alone for a while a stranger came in and said rapidly in a muffled voice:

"Be careful! You're Hitler's personal prisoner-nobody knows why. It's a mystery to us. Buch's letters to you were stopped at the last moment on orders straight from Hitler. You have some friends working for you, but you're up against it, and it looks serious. The swine are tampering with your Munich police dossier. So watch your step, and get that American wife of yours into action. We're trying to get you to Oranienburg, where you'll be safer. Keep your ears stiff!"

So that was why the officer arresting me had looked from me to my picture on that Mexican passport he had taken from his pocket - the one which had been seized at my arrest in Munich in 1923! I was furious at the thought that they were trying to frame me. My despair changed to a fighting mood, and I wrote vigorous protests to Hitler, Goering, and Himmler, which I knew would reach somebody's desk. Trying to forestall dirty work, I hinted that I was not so helpless as one might think.

It was good at lease to know definitely that I was Hitler's prisoner, and almost a

PRISONERS IN 'PROTECTIVE CUSTODY'

Who preceded the author in the Oranienburg Camp, lined up for roll-call. The second man from the left is Fritz Ebert, son of the first President of the Reich. At his right is another former Socialist deputy. The four others are leading officials of the Reich Broadcasting Company, accused of having 'enriched themselves'. All six were forced to exchange their clothes for the rags of the poorest Communists, and their heads were shaved. A tuft of hair was left on Ebert's head to make him look like a Tartar.

relief to realize that I had to battle for my life.

On the twelfth day in the morning there was a great commotion, and my name was called to get ready. At noon I found myself jammed with my belongings "into a room with some seventy prisoners, ranging from dignified priests to lowest tramps. We were being divided up for various transports when I heard my name called again, and in the corridor found a young associate of Dr. Sack's. He told me in haste that it had taken Sack nine days to get permission to see me after he had spoken with Rosenberg, who was worried but totally uninformed.

"Nobody can tell anything about your case. You know the times we live in," he said with a shrug.

And off I went, crammed with others into the semi-darkness of the 'Gruene Minna', the German equivalent of the 'Black Maria'. We had to bow our heads, for the lady was lowbusted. I had interesting companions. The swarthy, broad-faced little man full of witty remarks was 'Fritze' Ebert, Socialist Reichstag deputy and son of the first President of the Reich. And next me was a tall, gentle man visibly fighting against tears. It was Schueler, of the 'Black Front'. We must have bounced through all Berlin before our Green Minnie at last swung through the prison gates of the Ploetzensee jail.

This was a regular prison, a complex of many buildings. Almost an entire structure built in the form of a cross had been emptied of convicts for the reception of us 'Schutzhaeftlinge'.[1] After the usual routine, plus a primitive but welcome showerbath, I was locked up alone in a cell somewhat larger than the, Alex' cell. Altogether my new home was friendlier. The window, though barred, was wider; there was a real little table and a cupboard, a wash-basin and a shoe-brush, and a bunk which folded against the wall. There was a single mattress-luxury! The walls mercifully were white with only a lower dado of grey.

For a few hours I was almost happy. And there hung the prison rules of the old regime, still in force. Yes, here was Prussian order: bed-clothing changed twice a month, a fresh towel every week, and rules for everything - church services, prison library, writing, visitors, cell-cleaning, and so forth. Here the prisoner had a few privileges, however modest.

Ploetzensee was only a prison for lesser convicts, not the dreaded Zuchthaus for the Schwerverbrecher, who live under severer rules and in smaller cells. We were treated like the prison convicts, however, except that we were not required to work and had the privilege of buying tobacco, food, and little extras through the commissary. I read as many newspapers as I wanted. The food was meagre and simple, but eatable, and I sustained myself pretty well with the extras I bought. Meals were brought by trusties who walked from cell to cell with a warder. These were convicts who had been elevated for good behaviour or because they were lick-spittles, and it was important to be on good terms with them. They could sour your life by doling out to you the worst and smallest portions from the pail, or by scooping out your soup without the cubes of bacon swimming on the top - almost the only meat you got.

Though I loathed his visage and manners, I soon capitulated to the chief trusty of my station and paid him 'dues' to get my papers and books and run my errands. There are politics in all walks of life.

Except for the Freigang - half an hour in morning and afternoon in the recreation yard, a large compound with some elms and apple trees - we were left completely to ourselves. By day I would read or lie brooding on my cot, which should then have been folded against the wall, but which I managed to leave open without trouble. At night I would put the stool on the table, which I had moved to the window, and stand on it, holding to the bars and gazing at the sky, feeling the breeze in my face. Looking out was of course verboten, but everybody did it, dodging back when the sentry passed with his police-dog, both clearly visible against the wide, white band of the high brick wall.

_____

1 Prisoners in 'protective custody.'

489

As new recruits arrived daily, the recreation periods had to be taken in sections. Guards enforced the rule of silence and watched for other attempts at communication. Nevertheless, it was one of our diversions to peek out at the silent line wandering around the circle below, or to blink up from below to a hand or pair of eyes making signals, or occasionally even to catch a few words as one passed the array of cells on the lower floor. I did not come across any familiar faces except the Russians I had seen at the 'Alex.' But I made some interesting new contacts with some of the men. One of them, was a Balt and corps brother of Rosenberg who had worked in the intelligence department of the Verbindungstab under Hess. He too had been arrested without cause weeks ago, and had been shamefully treated.

One acquaintance I made at a most impossible moment. I was sitting on a certain seat which I always prepared most carefully-after all, I wasn't living at the Ritz - when suddenly the door opened and in flew a man with a seven-day's beard.

I was furious, but the fellow began to weep so heart-brokenly that I found myself patting his shoulder and holding up my trousers with my other hand. He was a harmless little man, an unimportant municipal official in a Berlin welfare bureau, who had held a job in a socialist youth-group and had possessed Marxian literature which it had taken him years to assemble. They had searched his home, carried him off to the 'Alex,' and confiscated his books. I hate to share a room with anybody, but the little man was so broken up, and begged me so piteously to let him stay with me, that I yielded. He hadn't even a toothbrush, having been dragged from his bed at six in the morning, leaving his wife and two small children behind him. A few days later he was released.

But another cell-mate blew in. This one was an impossible brute, and gave me my sought-for opportunity to make myself known to the Herr Inspektor, who had the Nazi eagle in his buttonhole. I made such a fuss that I was brought before the mighty one. He yielded to my arguments and again I found myself alone, though by now most cells were quartering two or three men.

This may sound selfish. But from the beginning of my imprisonment I fought frantically against indignities of any sort. Since I was not a convict and not accused of anything, I refused, for instance, to scrub my cell. I carried my point, and these chores were done by a trusty. Having done nothing to warrant my arrest, I protested on every occasion against the outrageous and unjustified violation of my liberty. Besides, I knew that I was doomed if I didn't beat my enemies to it. For the struggle ahead of me I needed all my strength, and must protect my sensibilities against avoidable tortures.

After a few days, the Inspektor told me that he expected a new batch of guests. Needing every available bit of space, he offered me for cell-mate one of Hitler's early rivals who had turned 'democratic.' This was Captain Arthur Mahraun, the founder and leader of the once-powerful 'Jung Deutsche Orden.' I spent six: days with him.

And yet he is one who should have been treated generously instead of being driven to life-long bitterness.

Obviously I cannot relate all Mahraun told me, for he is still alive in Germany. But out of my own observation I can affirm that he had been terribly and inhumanly treated. Morose and wrathful, he would brood for hours, his bruised head cupped in his hands, and then write frantically in his notebook. He had gone through the hands of the Feldpolizei, the most dreaded group of all, at the General Papen Strasse. The men had jumped on him with their boots, grinding their heels into his kidneys, so that he continually passed blood in his urine.

There was no case against Mahraun. They wanted him to transfer ownership of his publishing company, and he had refused. During my stay with him he was called out several times to confer with Nazi emissaries. Finally, in September, he gave up, signed away his property, and was set at liberty.

Sheer blackmail, in gangster fashion! This man was merely a political opponent, once an active officer of the army, a wounded veteran, and a knight of the Hohenzollern order for distinguished bravery under fire - the highest order the Emperor could bestow except the Pour Le Merite. This in the face of the new Government's loud proclamations of how it would treat war veterans. To be sure, veterans got free second-class passage on trains - but they also were beaten to a bloody pulp if they failed to fall in line.

From warders who could not grasp this new spirit of justice and were willing to talk a little, and later from prisoners in concentration camps arrested in all parts of the Reich, I learned that the same conditions obtained everywhere. These arbitrary arrests through the Feldpolizei and organs of the Gestapo, and the horrible treatment that accompanied them, were universal and systematic.

Even more disquieting were the sinister tales about men who, like Captain Stennes, were taken from their cells in the dark of night to be 'transferred,' in reality to be shot 'while trying to escape,' or simply to disappear without trace. Soon I began to feel that I too was on the proscription list. I suffered moments of great fear. Night after night I would walk up and down, sit on my bed or lie awake - waiting and listening, steadying myself to meet the inevitable at any unusual noise. I was not so much afraid of being shot as of being beaten. I had always liked the study of history, and now I began to fish grisly bits out of my memory - those strange things that happen in revolutions and make such exciting reading by the fireside.

As the weeks went by, the strain began to tell. Petty persecutions infuriated or depressed me. One day I was called to the visitor's room to be questioned by a Gestapo official about some money I owed Ellery Walter. It will be recalled that I forgot to repay the American a loan of fifty or sixty dollars in Berlin in 1932. From London I sent him all I could spare en route, about seven pounds, in a registered letter which promised to forward the rest from Washington. But in Washington, thanks to Amann's peculiar business methods, I had to borrow money to maintain my office. On my way back to Berlin in 1933 I tried to get in touch with Walter in New York, but he was not in town. From Berlin, I think, I wrote him to inquire exactly how much I owed him and to ask if he would mind waiting until my return; I explained that I was permitted to send only two hundred marks a month out of Germany and those had to go to my wife. As there had been no reply, the thought now occurred to me that Walter's delayed answer had been intercepted and was being used against me.

Having done all I could to deal honourably with Walter, my vexation was beyond endurance. I told the Gestapo man to go to hell if that was all he came for, and to give Hitler and his gang the famous salute of Goetz von Berlichingen.[2]

Even more exasperating events followed. The telegraph office began to hound me with a bill for 198 marks for cables which Dr. Sell in Washington had sent to me collect. I forwarded it to Rosenberg; his Nazi foreign bureau owed me 135 gold marks for the Knickerbocker cables, and I told him that he could collect the balance from Dr. Funk, who had promised to refund my outlays for cables sent in the interest of the Party. Now I was informed that Rosenberg had settled the debt except for 39 marks, 93 pfennigs; if they were not paid within fourteen days my property would be seized. Again I wrote to Rosenberg, telling him what I thought of such niggling treatment of a man, now helpless in prison, who had set his office going by personally collecting over half a million gold marks. Not until January of 1934 was I informed that Rosenberg had settled the bill in full.

About the middle of August, while this elevating correspondence was going on, I received a visit from Aumueller on behalf of Rosenberg. The Balt sent me greetings; he wanted me to know that he was doing all he could. But with Hitler personally involved, his position had become extremely difficult and I had better stop writing to him.

My reaction was violent.

"Now that I'm in disgrace with Herr Hitler, I've become a troublesome customer who is asked to behave like an isolated leper! Why didn't he come himself to tell what he wants? Cowards, all of you! Don't look so scared, and stop trying to shush me. Tell him that what I've seen and heard cries to heaven - and get it into your heads that what is happening to me today can happen to you tomorrow!"

On the way back to my cell, I saw the arrivals in a new transport being lined up. The men were giving their 'Personalien.'

"Major Buchrucker!"[3] said a tall and cultivated-looking man.

"What did you say?" asked the Inspektor.

---

2 Goethe, Goetz von Berlichingen, Act III, end of the 17th scene.

3 Next to Herbert Blank, now doing ten years at hard labour, he had been Dr. Otto Strasser's most prominent collaborator.

A SIGNIFICANT TRIO OF THE OLD GUARD

Members of the 'Blood Order' in memory of the 'Beer Hall Putsch.'
(Left to right) Christian Weber, Hermann Goering, Heinrich Himmler

"Jawohl, Buchrucker, kaiserlicher and koeniglicher Major a.D. im Grossen Generalstab der alten Armee!" The Inspektor looked his astonishment. "Yes, I was the leader of the Kuestrin Putsch, arrested then by the Republic and now by the Third Reich!" the soldier added with a sardonic laugh. After some weeks he was released; apparently the army still had something to say.

Among the prisoners on my corridor was one Guenther Kuebler, also a leader of the Schwarze Front. When I heard that prison rules allowed for day companions in certain cases, I developed an acute claustrophobia and asked for companionship. For about two weeks, Kuebler spent every day from morning until dinnertime in my cell. He was a tall, lean man, agreeable and quiet. We talked, read, or played chess. From him I learned much about the Schwarze Front and the personality of Dr. Otto Strasser, for whom he had acted as a sort of business-manager.

I felt lonely when Kuebler left early in September with the first transport for a new concentration camp in Brandenburg. The lengthening hours of darkness grew harder than ever to bear.

One morning a warder said in his usual phlegmatic voice: "Over there in that cell" - pointing to the other side of our wing - "is one who is waiting for his execution tomorrow at dawn."

I could not get the condemned man out of my mind. As I lay on my cot that night, I saw him waiting… waiting… and finally walking to the block in the little court behind the prison chapel which formed a right angle to my cell. At last I dozed off into a nightmare.

In my dream I saw a huge scarlet poster with large black letters announcing my execution. A foggy night hung over me like a tunnel. I tried to flee but could not move. I saw myself, saw my head lying on the block, and saw in the lifeless dawn a horrid face above me. It was Hitler, his eyes staring at the nape of my neck, his bloody hands swinging the axe high over his bulging head. God have mercy on my soul! I heard the thud of the axe.

Then the sound of a bell jolted me into consciousness, choked in tears. It had happened. The bell was tolling a man's soul into another world.

Soon a real claustrophobia was driving me almost insane, and I was glad to find my name on the list of the second transport for Brandenburg. On the morning of 8 September, we were pressed like the proverbial sardines into several closed Gruene Minnas and rumbled off. The warders who accompanied us told us enough to dampen our hopes for a better life in our new home. It was the abandoned old Zuchthaus in Brandenburg, condemned years before as unfit for ordinary Schwerverbrecher. The convicts had been installed in a new home, the last word in prison architecture, with running water and, for all I know, a radio outlet in every cell.

At noon we halted at the prison gates. I was in the last load. There was commotion and shouting outside. Through a small, barred window behind the driver's seat I watched our new jailers, black-coated SS men, pushing back hundreds of civilians curious to get a glimpse of these sinister enemies of Hitler. Slowly he drove through a narrow alley into a wide courtyard.

One by one, like condemned cattle, we jumped out, most of us carrying our belongings in cardboard boxes. I had barely set foot on the ground when the storm broke. A top-sergeant's bullying reception of raw recruits would be child's play in comparison. A score of SS men rushed at us, screaming and cursing, while others aimed their rifles at the windows of the grim building enclosing us: inmates were forbidden to watch incoming transports.

The Herr Kommandant, a short, husky man with the shoulders of a bull, watched the performance with bloodshot eyes. Suddenly he assailed us, bellowing like an enraged beast and hounding us around like bewildered chickens. Then we were lined up and our names read. Next we were divided into stations, and again driven about until our tongues hung out. Finally we were chased into the building and hurried up the stone stairway with kicks and blows.

My station was prodded to the top of the prison and herded into the attic of the left wing. Dirty and exhausted after the endless 'Hinlegen! Auf! Marsch, marsch!' we were gasping for breath. But this was a dismal place to rest - bare of everything except filth on the rotting floor and cobwebs on the flaking walls. A little light came in through six small openings.

But there was no time to meditate on details. Standing rigidly at attention, we had to surrender everything that had been returned to us on leaving Ploetzensee. One by one we stepped forward and threw into a box whatever we had, including cigarettes and matches. That was sensible enough, for in case of fire we would be trapped like rats. Luckily the SS guard standing by the box was a decent Nazi, and when my turn came I insisted on sealing the envelopes into which I put my valuables and enclosing an itemized list. He barked at me, but I had my way; I had heard too many tales about the disappearance of things deposited with SA or SS men from money to suitcases filled with clothes and shoes.

Then we were examined by a terrible ruffian, a blustering fellow who had charge of the entire dormitory building.

"You have to look after yourselves," he shouted. "The senior is responsible for the order and discipline of the station." His glance rested on me, and he appointed me senior. But managing to find a well-turned phrase, I politely begged to be excused, and stepped back into line - an intellectual in disgrace. A Communist was appointed instead. That was better. I had no desire for the thankless job of playing senior to some fifty 'room-mates,' among whom were Communists and Socialists and Jews.

Relentlessly, insultingly, we were ordered about. Some of us had to clean up the filth; others had to run elsewhere to get spoons and blankets for each prisoner and one earthenware pot which must serve him for coffee, water, and food. I was rushed with another group to a barn in a smaller courtyard to fill burlap bags with straw. Outside, SS men were shouting and sneering at Jews, who were kneeling in the blazing sun and grubbing out the tufts of grass from between the stones with their teeth, goaded on by occasional kicks.

We dragged the straw-sacks back to our stables, which by now had been scrubbed and mopped. In our attic, as in every station in the building, there was a small iron cage completely netted in, from which a guard could overlook the room in safety from a mass attack. On each side were slits in the wall from which spies could watch the room.

In the semi-darkness near the cage was a water-tap. My lips were parched, my mouth, nose, ears, and eyes filled with dust. Water had never tasted so sweet.

Food, like everything else, was an improvisation. It was late that evening before we got something supposed to be cabbage soup. For several days one old table was all we had, and most of us had to eat standing up or sitting on the straw sacks. Those sacks, three long rows of them, covered almost the entire floor, leaving little space to move about.

I had managed to get my sack under one of the apertures. The first afternoon I sat on it with aching limbs and looked around me, too stupefied even to think. Most of the men were simply staring like me into the darkening room. But not for long. A bullying voice swept us to attention. It was a guard with a stop-watch in his hand.

"Out with you, you swine! I give you three minutes to -, one minute to -!"

In groups of twelve we were rushed to the floor below and into a lavatory where stood a row of twelve toilet cans. From then on we were let out three times a day to care for our needs. It had always to be accomplished at terrific speed. If you didn't hurry, you risked being assigned to dirty work, or being chased up and down until your tongue hung out of your mouth. Each of us had to dump his pot, flush the huge sink, and put fresh water in the pot. Just before nine o'clock, which was bedtime, a toilet can was placed at each end of the room. One of them was always in use in the course of the night.

The whole thing was so incredible that I did not come to myself for days. Body and mind moved mechanically. Night after night I could not sleep; every stroke of the old clock in the little tower of the prison chapel found me awake.

For no reason whatever, since there was nothing to do, we were routed out at 4.15 in the morning, and it went hard with the man who did not instantly leap to his feet. Twelve or fifteen had to use one wash-basin; it was weeks before there was a half-way adequate supply. In time we each received a sheet, a pillow-case for the straw-pallet, and a cover to put our worn blankets in.

The day's ordeal began with bed-making. Our tormentors seemed to love playing soldier. As if we were in barracks, our beds had to be 'built' in such a way that cover, head-pallet, and sack were a single unit, absolutely level and smooth, the rows perfectly in line. It was an impossible task. The straw sacks of uneven size lay side by side so closely that you had to crawl on your hands and knees over your neighbour's pallet and then start 'building' from the head, working downward inch by inch with infinite patience, knowing that a cursing SS lout would ruin your painstaking toil with one kick of his boot. Time and again unfortunates had to build and rebuild until their eyes were glazed with despair.

After bed-making, we all stood aimlessly about until roll-call at seven in the courtyard, followed by morning drill to put us in shape - as though we were raw recruits in a barracks. But we were no youngsters. Among us were men old and ill, men who had never practised 'knee-bending with backside on heels and arms stretched out,' or trotting in formation. In between our lusty marchings we had to sing 'merry wanderer' or martial songs. And woe betide you if you didn't sing out in a loud, ringing voice! The guards would bark you out of the ranks and teach you to sing on the run, with SS berserks at your heels. Every day men collapsed, and soon the ranks were combed of those incapable of taking exercise.

A man was forced to roll in the dirt knowing that he had no other shirt, and no soap for washing. That which in the army is hard but bearable because it has a purpose was here utterly senseless, and the smouldering anger grew. Exercise was sensible, but what we got would have been arduous for a corporal. After eight or ten weeks, when the kinder and more reasonable element among the SS guards had gained the upper hand, and when it was known even to the dumbest guard that the majority of the prisoners were not criminals, our general treatment became more human, and only occasionally did the camp become a madhouse.

The daily ration of sour, indigestible bread was a chunk about seven inches thick, which we ate dry. 'Coffee,' a muddy brew of undefinable taste, came after morning drill, when we had been up for more than three hours. Lunch was at twelve, and dinner at six.

All meals had a horrid taste of sal-soda, supposed to decrease sexuality. The spiritual sal-soda of anguish and worry is much more effective, Herr Hitler; you could have saved yourself that expense!

The noon meals always included potatoes, and every evening there was the same coffee-mud, except for tea on Sundays. The man who received no parcels from home and many did not-or who had no money to buy extra food through the SS commissary, was constantly and acutely hungry. Diabetics were not even provided with white bread, as they had been in Ploetzensee or would be in any regular prison. The SS guards, on the other hand, were fed from the police-school in town - frugal but adequate meals of good quality, with sustaining army bread.

Once or twice a week I managed to buy food from outside - cold-cuts, wurst, cheese of better quality and white bread. And yet indigestion and heartburn began to

	Morning	Noon	Night
Monday	Coffee with dry bread	Rice soup.	Oatmeal gruel.
Tuesday	Coffee with dry bread	Cabbage soup with a few shreds of fat.	A piece of cheap cheese 1 ¹/₄ inches thick.
Wednesday	Coffee with dry bread	Noodle soup.	Two inches of the worst wurst in town.
Thursday	Coffee with dry bread	Pea soup.	A small tasteless salt herring; potatoes in jackets.
Friday	Coffee with dry bread	Lentil or bean soup with a few cubes of bacon – if you got them. Best thing of the week	A small smoked herring or bloater. Not bad.
Saturday	Coffee with dry bread	Cabbage or turnip soup.	Two inches of wurst.
Sunday	Coffee with dry bread	A goulash consisting of a big spoonful of potatoes, gravy, and once in a while a square inch of leathery meat. Whether you got meat depended on the good-will of the disher-out. The meat was on the bottom and the grease on the top. If he liked you, he dipped deep.	A soup of grits.

During my entire five months in Brandenburg, this was our weekly menu:

undermine my system. One could only pray not to fall seriously ill in Brandenburg, for not until towards the end of my stay was there a regularly functioning prison hospital. Only when a man was in desperate condition would he be sent to the State prison-hospital in Berlin.

Bit by bit, system and routine were established. Gradually men were assigned to different squads - the kitchen, the washhouse, the hospital, court and indoor duty. Tailors were selected; shoemakers, carpenters, barbers, mechanics, orderlies for the Kommandant and his men, and so forth. Jews were formed into a special 'Juden company' assigned to dirty chores, such as the cleaning of latrines. There were no outdoor squads for road-work.

The artisans, whose workshops were in a separate building, were envied by the other prisoners, for they were free of all dirty work and of morning and evening drill, with opportunities to smoke and to earn a little something - cigarettes or even a few pfennige - by doing things for the guards. The man who could build a uniform or a pair of high boots for a starred, braided, and buckled SS man had a better life all round.

Journalists, bank-clerks, and teachers discovered hidden talents for cobbling or stitching. In the soapy steam of the laundry I discovered a musician who was a good chess-player, and from then on my shirts got special attention.

At least 75 per cent of the prisoners, however, had nothing to do. To find the anodyne of work, one of them would chisel little sailing-boats out of wood; another would chew the soft part of bread to an even pulp, tint it as best he could, and model little Dutch shoes, flowerpots, or ash-trays; still another would sketch or paint pictures for the SS men.

Out of our common misery, no common comradeship arose. In time, looking for favours became a part of every prisoner's psychology, and he would sell his own comrades for the stump of a cigarette. Class-warfare was carried into the concentration camp; denunciations were frequent. When the camp was at last organized so that prisoners could get parcels from home or could buy little extras through the SS commissary, those who hadn't relatives, friends, or money, looked on with envy, and then the rawness of human nature came out. Friendships were made and broken at a moment's notice. The nature of the average man, will, under given circumstances, show its best or its worst side, but it will not change - and it did not in this concentration camp.

Here were all sorts and conditions of men: those who still had something, those who never had anything, and those who for years had been out of work, homeless, and in rags; to these last even horse-meat was an unknown luxury, and they welcomed the 'security' of the concentration camp, with a roof overhead and regular meals. There were workers and intellectuals, men of all parties, accidental and real criminals, the mentally abnormal or subnormal - all mixed together, all living the same life. Comparatively few of them maintained their poise and showed themselves men of generous natures and these few were of all political beliefs. At Brandenburg the psychologist could have probed a bottomless pit of human nature.

The prison grapevine, or, as we called it, the 'Latrinen Parolen,' was an interesting symptom of the general prison psychosis. Shave-days bred latrine rumours; the barbers picked up the news in one station and carried it to another. Everyone had a rumour, and it was a study to watch men pass it on. For the prisoner has a language of his own. He dare not speak his thoughts right out; he uses the expressive gesture, with hand, eye, and mouth - the telling grimace.

The first days of camp life had thrown me into a stupor. My finer instincts withdrew behind the animal in me, making it easier for me to adapt myself to an incredible humiliation. For the moment it was' easy to remain as inconspicuous as possible - a good rule I had learned in the army. In Ploetzensee I had taken to wearing crumpled flannel trousers and a worn wind-breaker - an outfit too ordinary to attract undue attention. Here, in Brandenburg, you learned caution, for in the first weeks most of the guards seemed irrational beasts. Some even seemed to be maniacs. Luckily I avoided being picked out by one of these black brutes; I was one of the few who trotted in the herd almost unnoticed.

The nights were most to be dreaded, with the smell of closely herded men hanging dense under the ceiling. Then I would feel that I must get out of this soon or go to pieces. And yet I was fortunate in some things: at least I could wash myself properly, for I had soap and my own wash-basin. But many of the poor devils stationed with me had absolutely nothing, and lived unbathed for weeks - perhaps some harmless little man who had never dreamed he was being arrested and who had been given no chance to take even a change of socks or a toothbrush. In the weeks that passed before he could get in touch with his family, he would go on wearing the same torn, bloody, pus-stained shirt. Only in December, when biting cold set in, were socks and shirts given to those who had none. It was a miracle that no epidemic broke out.

In the general disorder when we moved in, the heating was not functioning and there was no hot water. It was eight or nine weeks before we could get baths. Gradually things began to appear; we would get a stool one day and a table the next. Finally we had cupboards made by the prisoners - one tiny cupboard for four men, with a few hooks to hang things on.

Our dormitory consisted of a central structure and two wings. Each floor in each of the three parts housed a station; the worst were the three under the roof. On my fourth day I was transferred with some others to the centre station on the first floor - a larger room with regular windows and tables. Here I met Dr. Theodor Neubauer, one of the most prominent leaders among former Communist Reichstag deputies. He was a man of my own age, lean, dark, and quiet, with big, brown eyes. With him and other Communists I had interesting arguments. When I pointed out that the Communists, if they had come to power, would have made short work of the Nazis, he said proudly:

"Exactly! We would have shot the Nazis, but we wouldn't have tortured them. We are German Communists, not Russian!"

But we had to be careful, for among us there were stool-pigeons, appointed or self-appointed, and we were under the constant surveillance of guards and spies. Every time a guard approached we had to pull ourselves up and freeze at 'attention.' One day, from four-thirty in the morning to nine at night, we counted nearly two hundred 'attentions.'

So far, I had dodged assignments, kicks, and blows. My aim was to join the prisoners of the Schwarze Front - 'the Blacks', as they were called - who lived apart from us and enjoyed many privileges, including that of living in cells instead of a common room.

Eventually I succeeded in making contact with some of the decent SS men. When on night-guard they would sometimes call me out to the staircase and talk with me; it was a blessed relief to get out of that stinking room packed with nearly a hundred men, snoring, muttering, or crying out in nightmares.

What I needed was an opportunity to talk with the Kommandant. It came unexpectedly one night.

Usually, for reasons of convenience, I was the last man in the last call to the latrine. One of the two guards on duty was a humane fellow, the other a sadistic brute who rushed and cursed me in the most swinish manner. That night, when he tried to kick me from the pot, I was so angry that I grabbed the heavy thing, and shouted that I would fling it in his dirty face if he dared touch me. He was dumfounded for a moment, long enough to enable the friendly SS man who had heard the noise to come running to my rescue. He had sense enough to take me to a high official of the Prison.

I had studied the official when he roared through the camp or played the monarch during roll-calls, and I felt strangely confident that I could manage this chunky man, with his bulbous eyes of a cow. His sallow face occasionally would show a kindly, slightly roguish expression when he was in genial mood. His whole performance was abnormal. He was at times brutal almost to sadism, at others so sentimental that tears stood in his eyes. His was clearly a weak and highly neurotic nature, of such tension that when he felt incompetent to control the situation he got drunk. In those fits the whole camp would go crazy; the guards' nerves would break and they would then take it out on the prisoners.

I found him sprawled in a chair, scowling savagely, his stomach bulging from an unbuttoned uniform, his finished dinner at his elbow. When the door had closed behind me, standing rigidly at attention I said, soldier fashion, in a firm voice:

"At your orders, Schutzhaeftling Kurt Ludecke, old National-Socialist and Party Representative in Washington."

He looked me over, staring at my bewhiskered face. Suddenly he jumped and yelled: "What did you say? You - National Socialist?"

I did not wince. "Yes, since 1922. The Fuehrer personally ordered my appointment to the German Embassy in Washington. But if you knew my story, you would understand!"

He grasped my lapel and looked at the Nazi Eagle in my button-hole; I had put my coat on for this occasion.

"As a Party official I am entitled to wear it. I belong to the section of the Brown House, and my Party book verifying my statement is with the Gestapo. I wouldn't dare say anything which isn't true."

He retreated to his desk. "Ruehren Sie, ruehren Sie-bitte!" he said, for I was still frozen at attention. "You said you were in America for us?"

His curiosity was aroused. Within five minutes I was 'Herr' Ludecke, and instead of 'flying into the Bunker'[4] I was invited to sit down, drink a cup of real coffee, and eat some cake. I told him just enough to impress him. That evening, to the surprise of everybody, I was moved to the station of the Blacks and was received there with a great hello.

Now I had a cell to myself, one which I could open or close at will. And for the first time in many weeks, I fell into a deep sleep.

---

4 The dungeon-tiny, dark cells in the cellar of the block, originally used for obstreperous criminals who got 'tough.' A wooden bench served as bed and one blanket as bedding.

XXXIX

I MAKE MY PLAN

Next day I sat before an old typewriter in the office of the Kommandant, racking my brains in the effort to think with Hitler's mind when he had ordered my arrest. The very fact that I was said to be his prisoner[1] made my position hopeless. Nobody dared interfere. There was nothing I could be accused of, nothing I could be tried for ; evidently they had failed to concoct a case against me. Perhaps my own attempts from prison had prevented, so far, a move against my life, a move which I feared and which apparently existed, if what I have heard since then is true.

At any rate, the longer I was held the more difficult it became for one of Hitler's peculiar nature to say the word that would set me free. Constituted as he is, what could he say, what could he do with me? Instead of calling Rosenberg and me before him and making a decision one way or the other, he had put me away. For Hitler loathes clear decisions. Away from the platform, he jumps into feverish action only under terrific pressure. He lets things drift, and when they can drift no further, some one has to suffer the consequences.

The letter I finally wrote to him was short and to the point, couched in terms which should have made it easy for him to forgive me in case I had 'without intention, acted contrary to the tact and rhythm of the movement.'

My letter to Rosenberg enclosed copies of my letters to Hitler and to Major Buch, and was more suggestive and explicit, pointing to the serious consequences if I were longer exposed to indignities, and insisting on his immediate and energetic intervention with Hitler. I begged him without fail to hand the Fuehrer the enclosed copy of my letter; someone, I said, might intercept the other.

To Buch I presented my case as the result of an unfortunate misunderstanding. I reminded him that I had an intelligent American wife[2] who had been informed of my first arrest and who certainly would not keep quiet if I were detained longer. If my release could not be effected immediately, I must be given a hearing and be spared further humiliations. At the least, my detention must be made more bearable in quiet quarters for study and reading.

---

1 *Circumstantial evidence that I was actually Hitler's personal prisoner is offered by a letter reproduced in the Appendix.*

2 *In point of fact, I had kept my wife in the dark about my political mishap. Trying to uphold the prestige of the Party, I had explained that my first arrest had been an unfortunate mistake; things were now coming my way, and I soon would be with her and everything would be all right. But she had seen the libellous despatch in the New York Staats-Zeitung, and it had been a cruel shock to her.*

When I had finished, I felt that I had done a good job of writing; it looked all so simple and convincing that I really believed for a while that no sensible and decent person could deny my requests. In my presence, the Kommandant ordered the letters posted by registered mail, and there was no doubt in my mind that they would reach their destinations.

In a far happier mood, I had another cup of coffee with the Kommandant, who by now had taken a warm interest in my case. When I told him that the quarters of the Blacks were inadequate and unheated, he took me to the cell-block forming a right angle to the administrative and workshop buildings, empty except for the frequent guests in the bunker in the cellar. People arrested in the district were locked in cells of the first wing, but the outer wing was unused. It looked cold and forbidding but seemed quiet and remote. With real joy I heard the Kommandant order the transfer of our station to the second floor of that wing.

This was early in the last week of September.

Singing and joking, we settled down in our new quarters, busy as bees in our efforts to make the place more livable. There were five cells on each side of a wide stone corridor; one row looked on the street and the other on a court. At one end of the corridor was a barred door, unlocked during the day; at the other, a large barred window through which one could see part of the other courtyard and the dormitory. The corner cell on the court-side became our mess-room. I chose a cell looking to the street. The cells had iron beds attached to the wall; they were a little smaller than those in Ploetzensee, but the barred windows were larger and lower. By standing on my stool I could see a patch of sky over the tree-tops, catch the dying rays of the sinking sun, and even see a bit of the street. I could hear people passing by and see them look up at the gruesome walls.

There were no guards in our station. Smoking and purchases from outside were allowed. During the day we could walk in the yard or play games in the little court behind the hospital.

I bought us a football and a shot-put, and sometimes the friends we had among the SS would join in our games. It was known to them that the eight or nine prisoners from among the Schwarze Front, which had now been dissolved by decree, were being held merely as hostages for their former leader, Otto Strasser, who had fled to Prague in May and from there had begun to propagandize against Hitler. His men had been seized all over the Reich, in the hope that their plight would inflame them against their leader and force him to stop his activities.

The day before I had joined the station of the Blacks, Schueler had been released and sent by the Gestapo to Prague to urge silence on Otto Strasser. The others, including my day companion in Ploetzensee, Kuebler, had a hearing at Gestapo headquarters in Berlin, and returned to camp in high hopes of being soon set free.

We all looked more cheerfully into the future. The Kommandant often visited us

504

in our mess-room. Wachtmeister Schwarz, who was in charge of our station and of the cellblock, would spend whole evenings with us playing cards or swapping jokes. As a former Stennes man, he naturally sympathized with his one-time comrades of the Black Front.

But our peace was only relative. At any hour of the twenty-four, we would hear yellings and stumbling on the stairs, or the fearful cries and gasps of beaten men, until their moans were stifled in the bunker below. I could make the nights bearable only by stuffing cotton in my ears.

One night the screaming and groaning went on till morning. Some thirty men had been arrested as arson suspects in a village near by. I saw some of them being carried away with swollen heads and bruised bodies. After six weeks of hell, all of them were dismissed; they had all been innocent.

Early one morning the Kommandant raged through the block like a madman, hammering at the closed door of the court and screaming for help. It was because a woman arrested the night before had hung herself. Thereafter, outside the cells of potential suicides, I would see suspenders and neckties thrust into dirty shoes. Two more dead men I saw: one was lying in his own blood and one had hanged himself.

As the days went by without further news of our release, our new cheerfulness abated, and gradually 'prison hysteria' again took hold of us.

Not long after I had written my letters, I was eagerly awaiting the visit of my brother one afternoon. I had much to talk over with him; for one thing, I had not heard from my wife in months. When the voice of a guard called my name, I ran forward. "Has my brother arrived?"

"No, the Kommandant wants to see you at once."

'This time the Kommandant did not ask me to sit down for a cup of coffee. Businesslike, but not unfriendly, he told me that he had just received an order from the Gestapo that I was not to be allowed to receive visitors, and that all my mail must go through their hands; he knew no more. Half an hour later, my brother came, talked with the Kommandant, and was allowed to leave my suit-case and portable typewriter.

It was an ominous answer to my pleas. I believed then and believe still that Hitler himself was behind that order. Of course it is possible that my letter did not reach him, and that Hess or Goering may have given the order cutting off my further contacts with the outside world.

Now I felt the seriousness of my position to my fingertips. If I wanted to leave this or any other prison alive, I would have to get busy. From then on, all my being was concentrated on the one thought of escape.

Meanwhile my station comrades had become even more chummy with Wachtmeister Schwarz, who was in charge of distributing food to all the stations in the camp. Some of them became regular trusties, helping Schwarz in his daily work as our cell-block gradually filled with stations, for new transports were arriving weekly. Occasionally I would go along to carry bread, thus becoming familiar with the layout of the prison and with all the life of the camp.

In the bunker, when prisoners were fed after days of starving, I saw horrible sights. I saw the familiar face of Neubauer, the Communist deputy; he had been there since the day I was first ordered before the Kommandant. They had flogged him on the back with cowhides soaked in water, but he had not broken down. He was accused of having tried to form Communist cells in the camp by contacting certain men, but I think he was too intelligent to try to get away with anything like that. Probably he had been denounced by a stool-pigeon, and the Kommandant, in one of his moods, had decided to make an example of him. I liked the man, and his feverish eyes haunted me for a long time. His lungs were failing now, and he knew he had only a few years to live.

Another enemy of the State I saw in the bunker was an internationally known Jew, the late anarchist and writer, Erich Muehsam. This hapless man had acted on the original but imprudent idea of sending his last will to the prison authorities, with the explicit statement that he was forgiving his murderers. Now his battered face looking out at me showed all the colours of the rainbow, a ghastly shadow in the grisly twilight of the dungeon.

Granted that there were cases which called for bodily punishment by flogging, there was still no justification for, torturing a helpless, exhausted, and starved prisoner by kicking his face and vital organs, and beating him with side-arms, brass-ringed shoulder belts, and heavy keys.

Yet the real guilt lay elsewhere. Adolf Hitler had ten long years to prepare himself for his task. He had reckoned on much more opposition than he actually found. The necessity of concentration camps should have been a forgone conclusion, and the importance of the domestic and foreign reaction to such camps equally apparent. Yet nothing had been prepared. Everything had to be improvised.

Oesterreichische Schlamperei!

I speak of things that my own eyes and ears told me.[3] And if I am to be true to my own observations, I must, in justice to the SS guards and their Kommandant, point out other things I learned.

Our keepers had their own peculiar psychology. Their atrocious treatment of their prisoners can be explained and, if you will, partly excused. They really believed that

---

3 It must be admitted that my report on the Brandenburg camp cannot serve as a yard-stick for the institutions still existing in German,. Far better conditions now prevail, with established order and more reasonable methods. But I feel that there is historical value in my brief sketch of what I observed in a camp from which no prisoner has escaped. So far as I know, there is no other existing picture of something not likely to recur under the Nazi regime. By contrast, convicted criminals serving terms in the ultra-modern American prisons, such as the new penitentiary on Riker's Island, in New York's East River, live in a rest-camp, confined in relative peace and cleanliness, usefully occupied and humanely treated.

these political prisoners were guilty of terrible crimes and of evil designs against the Nazi State. They were, for the most part, very young men with no experience or training for their new duties, and unlimited authority threw them off balance. And they entered on their duties without definite instructions and without provisions. They were supplied only with blankets and dishes, and even these were insufficient and in scandalous condition. To get chairs and even gunny-sacks for themselves, they had to 'requisition' them from confiscated trade union buildings or from the seized properties of political parties which had been dissolved. There was at first no budget allowance for their needs, and what was finally granted was totally inadequate.

The SS guards were overworked and underpaid. When they were on actual twenty-four-hour duty, they had four hours' guard and four hours' rest - in some cases, two hours' guard and two hours' rest. For the next twenty-four hours they were on 'alarm', which required their presence in the barracks ready for any job at any time, such as the censoring or prisoners' mail, examining packages, running errands, doing chores, and conducting military drill. The third day was rest-day, but they would usually be so tired that they slept the clock round, with neither time nor money for recreation. In winter they would have to stand guard without warm coats or sentry-boxes, in windy courtyards or draughty stone staircases.

I have seen dozens of strapping, hearty youngsters go to pieces under the strain. Their dream of glory was gone; they had been cheated in their more practical hopes of a snug security; there was no firm hand to guide them. And so they turned to dreadful excesses. Partly to kill time and partly to satisfy instincts which slumber in all men, waiting only to be stirred. The worst of the 'tormentors,' at least in our camp, were the Maerzgefallene,[4] eager to show their Nazi valour by a false zeal.

It is not surprising that Jews especially had to suffer, for Germans had been assured for years that the Jew was the embodiment of Satan himself. But the percentage of Jews in our camp was small. Of a total of about eighteen hundred prisoners who passed through Brandenburg in less than five months, there were only some fifty Jews. They were insignificant people; I saw not one rich Jew of the international financier class against whom we had been fulminating for years.

A special Jewish company was formed and was drilled separately in a little court behind the hospital. Their lot was hard. But in our camp no Jew was killed, and none committed suicide. Because of the reaction abroad, chiefly because of pressure by American and English Jewry, the Gestapo, some time in October, issued strict orders forbidding the maltreatment of Jews. From then on our Jews fared much better. There were occasional outbursts against a certain few. But it became a byword in the camp that we Gentiles were worse off than the Jews, for we were only 'Germans'

---

4 A nickname used by Nazi veterans for proselytes who, having suddenly rushed over to Hitler after the March elections in 1933, were regarded with suspicion.

whom nobody cared about.

The scandalous conditions in the Gestapo and the incompetence of many of its officials added much to the general suffering and confusion. Arrests were so numerous and so arbitrary that for many months complete chaos reigned in every station of the Gestapo and in those departments of the regular police which had to deal with arrests made by the Gestapo, the SA, or the SS. Officials had no time to wade through all the dossiers, accumulated orders, and counter orders. In many cases they had no vouchers at all to go by. Wives and mothers hunting for husbands and sons were often truthfully informed by Gestapo or police officials that they didn't know where their relatives were.

The majority of our prisoners were, in fact, men who could easily become 'lost'. Insignificant members of the working-class or of the petty bourgeoisie, most of them were victims of private grudges, unfair denunciations, or thoughtless criticism. Often the reasons for their arrest, if indeed any were given, were ridiculous. Held at the pleasure of the Gestapo, without warrant from any court and on charges which indicated only indifference to or dissent from Nazi doctrine, theirs was a harder lot than that of regular convicts who had been duly tried for a recognized demeanour or crime. The latter at least knew where and how long they must serve their terms, and were enjoying the positive blessing of an established prison routine.

One day a transport of over a hundred cripples and invalids arrived. They were housed in cells in the cellars of the big dormitory, which, next to the stations under the roof, were the worst and most unsanitary of all. An order had gone out that all vagabonds and beggars should be rounded up throughout the Reich; and these had been caught in the dragnet. Some of them were scum, but some were men who had become beggars because they had been mutilated or blinded in the war. And some of them were neither tramps nor invalids.

There was one unfortunate youth, a degenerate imbecile and a clear asylum case, around whose neck some grim joker had tattooed these words: 'This neck belongs to the hangman.' And next to him lay weeping a little man, sixty-seven years old, broken by life. He was a country doctor, unpolitical and harmless. But he did not like the Nazis, and he had committed the crime of deleting a Nazi election slogan which had been smeared on his own fence. One morning at dawn he had been dragged away from his wife.

Looking at him, I felt ashamed to be a Nazi.

Escape was a problem. Though I was not in an 'escape proof' prison with modern mechanical safeguards, I was a novice and there was no time to lose, for anything might happen any day. I must not only get myself outside, but safely over the border, hundreds of kilometres away, and then to the United States. I had little money and no passport, and my re-entry permit was to expire on 21 February; I had to land in America before then.

Escape would be worth while only if I could start a new life in America. Without that, I would have preferred suicide, for I had no wish to moulder in the horrible life of an unwanted refugee in Prague or Paris.

Help from inside and outside would be necessary. Obviously I cannot be specific about this phase of my tale, for I cannot implicate men now living who were willing to assist me.

It became increasingly clear that I must get out of the station of the Blacks. In this atmosphere of camaraderie there was not the privacy essential to my plan.

Circumstances were to aid me. In the dark mood brought on by the Kommandant's bad news, I had felt less like singing with them, playing skat interminably in the mess-room, and hearing the same jokes over and over again. I had begun to withdraw, and the beginning of a rift was apparent.

Needing all my money now; I had been obliged to stop buying small necessities and luxuries for the Blacks; I could not explain, and the rift widened. A one-time friend helped the process along. When his release had seemed to be only a matter of days, I had given him a letter authorizing him to draw on my bank account to a total of 150 marks, for he was destitute. By now his prospect of release had faded, and so I asked him to give the letter back to me, again without disclosing my secret need of the money. He handed it over resentfully and became my active enemy. Prison life is like that.

Soon there was open hostility to me throughout the station, and I fanned it deliberately. One evening towards the end of October I observed him and two of his comrades conferring with Wachtmeister Schwarz, their firm friend, behind the closed door of a cell, and knew that something was about to happen.

I had hoped to be transferred to the floor above, which was still empty. Instead, at reveille next morning, under the cold eyes of my comrades, I was packed off to the dormitory, back to the station under the roof where I had started.

This was to be, however, only a temporary set-back.

Not one of my old room-mates was still in the station. Among my new comrades were two foreigners. One was a swarthy, wiry little Cossack, Colonel Ivan von Poltavetz-Ostranitza, full of big tales about his exploits in the counter-revolution against the Soviets. For a time he had been Hetman Skoropadski's secretary, and latterly his rival in the race for Nazi favour. Rosenberg had used him as a pawn in his Ukrainian chess-game, and Goering had arrested him.

The other was also a Russian, a blond and willowy young man, snake-like in body and character, who had been active in White Russian circles in Berlin, and whose confused and noisy tongue had got him into trouble. In the Brandenburg camp he was making himself hated by the prisoners but popular among the guards by his 'expert' handling of the Jews with tricks he pretended to have learned while a prisoner of the Tscheka somewhere in Russia. With him as impresario, the hapless

Jewish prisoners were now forced to present themselves in performances of the 'Bear Dance' and the 'Cock Fight,' or to stage 'Gladiatorial Games' until they collapsed or really knocked each other out-no faking permitted.

The Russian's 'surprise teasers' were dreaded by every Jew in camp. With a devilish smile playing about his feminine mouth, he would hiss a greeting and, like the flick of a whip, crack the fingers of his victims. Or, quick as lightning and with amazing adroitness, he would break a Jew's mouth wide open and spit into its depths.

He was the stage-director of the 'Salome Dance,' a swinish exhibition by a Jew whom his own people despised as a miserable example of his race. In hairy nakedness, under the howling laughter of prisoners and guards, he would prostitute himself in song and dance. With the metal cover of a latrine pot fastened on his head, a twig of fir in each hand, he writhed in ever quickening tempo until, in simulated ecstasy, he would put one 'olive branch' in his mouth and the other behind his back, then reverse them again and again at mad speed until he fell exhausted to the floor.

I had to spend only a few days in this revolting atmosphere. Once more I was called before the Kommandant.

"I've enquired about you," he said. "You are listed as Hitler's prisoner until further notice. Nobody seems to have exact information. There's a lot of hearsay and guesses about you at headquarters." And lowering his voice to a whisper and looking at me with horrified eyes: "I even heard you were involved in a plot against the life of the Fuehrer... Just imagine - if he were to be - No, it's too terrible to think of - we'd all be lost!... Some say it serves you right and others would like to help you, but I was warned to keep hands off your case... Now you've had trouble with the Blacks... Right, if it wasn't for you they wouldn't be in that station... But what shall I do with you? You give me a headache... Yes, so long as there are no orders to the contrary I can treat you at my discretion within the camp, but I can't open a station for you alone... No, I don't know of any charges against the Cossack colonel. It's absurd, he should either be heard and deported, or released... Yes I can do that. The two of you move over to the cell block..."

Then he gave me something beautifully ironic - a letter enclosing a questionnaire from the Adolf Hitler Kanzlei in Munich, which had been sent to Washington, back to Rosenberg's foreign bureau, and from there, by special messenger, to the camp. It was the qualification for the 'Coburg Decoration of Honour' which the Fuehrer had promised me at the Kaiserhof in September 1932. Though the decoration had never reached me, it had found its way to the breasts of some Nazis who had no right to it. Now the Fuehrer was checking up on them; a 'Diploma' signed by himself was to go to the righteous. Out of the Schlamperei enveloping Hitler, in October his own Kanzlei had sent this 'honouring' document to the Kurt Ludecke whom the Mogul himself had thrown into a concentration camp in July.

I could not resist sending a formal letter to Rudolf Hess, ending with the customary 'Heil Hitler,' and with the enclosed questionnaire properly filled out. For the required three witnesses of my presence at Coburg on 10 October 1922 I named Adolf Hitler, Alfred Rosenberg, and Max Amann. Of course I received no answer. But the letter, which had eluded the Gestapo, did much to lift my prestige with Kommandant and guards, for the Coburg Decoration was the oldest and, next to the 'Blood Order'[5], the most coveted of all Party emblems.

A few days after Ivan and I moved to the cell block above the station of the Blacks, the Russian dragged his pallet into our station, having clowned this favour from the Kommandant on the ground that being now left alone, his room-mates would beat him up one night. I had to resign myself to his presence. We must have made a curious trio, myself perhaps the queerest of the three.

My portable typewriter was now helping me into the good graces of the guards. I even wrote letters for them to their numerous sweethearts - and how my parched imagination romped in those billets doux! And I typed petitions for poor devils held without sufficient cause. One young farmer had been a prisoner since 1 May for the crime of herding his geese on May Day, which had been declared a national holiday! Probably the local gendarme or SA leader hadn't liked him.

My relatively quiet existence was ended when the Kommandant put me in charge of five Jews who were locked in cells on our station. Except for a young Zionist, all had been brought up from the bunker. Among them were Erich Muehsam, Kurt Hiller, co-editor of the former Jewish Weltbuehne, and Dr. Hans Litten, who once had cross-examined Hitler in one of his trials, and who had acted as counsel for some Communists accused of murdering several Nazis.

I hated the job. There were savages among the SS guards who came frequently to take a look at the 'Judenschweine,' usually at the 'Geiselmoerder'[6] Muehsam. In his short shirt over wasted limbs, he was a pitiful sight when the night guards rushed him staggering to his feet to exhibit his circumcised penis for the hundredth time - and then to receive a blow.

And the Russian was always lurking cat-like about their cells. I had to be constantly on the watch to keep him from experimenting on them with new tricks. Though I was accused of being too gentle with them and had to administer some nominal punishments, I finally stopped the 'surprise' visits of the Russian and his brutal friends among the guards by complaining to the Kommandant.

Hiller and Litten were transferred to the dormitory. Litten disappeared. I know

---

5 A decoration awarded to those who, during the 'Beer Hall Putsch' of 8 and 9 November 1923 were wounded or took part in the march on the Feldbernhalle. The medal bears the inscription: 'und Ihr habt doch gesiegt!'

6 During the Communist terror in Munich under Jewish direction early in 191, twelve hostages, prominent Gentile citizens, were murdered in dastardly fashion. Muehsam insisted that he had nothing to do with this murder, because he had been arrested before it had happened and was being held prisoner in Augsburg. But to the SS guards he remained the 'Hostage-murderer.'

that he was held for weeks in a dark cell in the prison hospital, and then was taken away after the New Year; I don't know what became of him. Muehsam now looked so ghastly that the Kommandant didn't want the prisoners in the dormitory to see him. He was allowed to keep the door of his cell open, take walks in our court, and have his ears treated at the hospital.

Until his transfer to the dormitory, I played chess almost daily with Muehsam. He was very short-sighted; beatings had broken his eyeglasses and had also knocked him half deaf, making conversation difficult. He was resigned to his fate and convinced that he would die in prison. Yet the mind of the afflicted man was still alert. Though dogmatic, he was witty and original, and especially resourceful when I had him cornered in an argument or on the chess-board. Analytical, sensitive, both sceptical and sentimental, he was an interesting example of a sincere Jewish bohemian and coffee-house-revolutionist. I respected his moral courage. Later I was to see it displayed under peculiar circumstances which probably led ultimately to his death.

My rehabilitation with the Kommandant had not pleased the Blacks. But I was making useful friends among the guards; once they actually saved me from the bunker when the Blacks complained about my refusal to do chores.

These friends had not dropped from the sky; they were the fruit of methodical work and careful selection. In one of my earlier talks with the Kommandant, I had suggested that since a concentration camp was not a penitentiary for criminals convicted of statutory crimes, it should be organized as a 'schooling camp'[7] with the aim of educating and converting political offenders; even in this camp there were many splendid types among the prisoners who could be restored to usefulness. At first the Kommandant was enthusiastic about the idea, and I drew up a memorandum proposing myself as lecturer on the Nazi programme and on historical and travel topics, suggesting also that I give a course in English to those interested among the guards. But the project fell under the table, except for English class - which had been my main objective.

On 12 November we voted in the Reichstag elections, and out of about 1100 votes, less than a score were void or against Hitler. But this was really not to be wondered at: everybody knew that hell would break loose if the result were bad. The actual balloting was secret, however, and was conducted without pressure on the individual.

Some time after the elections, news of a general amnesty for Christmas swept like wildfire through the camp. Even the sceptics were convinced when Goering issued his Christmas proclamation. At the specific request of the Gestapo, the Kommandant prepared a list of three hundred prisoners recommended for release. He made a

---

7 *The Brandenburg concentration camp was never inspected by an intelligent higher official with authority. The only official visitors were men from the Gestapo of no importance, or minor civil servants.*

general inspection of the camp and questioned each prisoner. His 'inventory' and selection lasted for days and threw him into fits, but was fairly made.

We were feverish with unrest. At last we learned that the Gestapo had returned the list, and some of the prisoners packed their belongings. But nothing happened. The guards went about tight-lipped. Suddenly the Kommandant dashed off to Berlin in his little roadster. Consternation seized the camp.

At two o'clock that night he returned. The camp was turned into a bedlam. Prisoners were driven from their beds and hounded through buildings and courts like terror-stricken sheep until dawn.

Instead of three hundred, the Gestapo had ordered the release of only 187, including the Blacks. Of these 187, less than forty were names recommended by the Kommandant. The Gestapo's list contained names of men unknown in the camp, of men who had already been dismissed or transferred elsewhere, and of others who were actually guilty of some crime or violation and had never dreamed of getting out so soon. Many really innocent or harmless prisoners were left out in the cold, although the Kommandant managed to secure the release of some more of them on Christmas Eve.

The gangsters among Nazi chiefs first made sure of their 'legal' exemptions. Each man named for release was confronted with a declaration pledging loyalty to the regime, waiving all claims to compensation for any damage or loss suffered during his imprisonment, and stating specifically that no physical harm had been inflicted on him. And of course each one signed.

When the last group marched out into the open, singing and joking with their paltry bundles in their hands, and the great gate finally clanged shut, the pent-up feeling flared high among the rejected prisoners. Soon a change became apparent, however, a change that seemed infinitely pathetic to me. It was the Christmas spirit, pervading even the cold walls of our camp - the holy feast of love so deeply felt by Germans.

The men left behind decorated the camp with evergreen boughs. Every station had its little Christmas tree, ornamented with makeshift baubles, tiny candles, and tinsel - but with no gifts beneath it. Our Christmas dinner was meat-balls with gravy, and each prisoner received two apples, some walnuts and a few biscuits on a coloured paper plate - the gift of the town. The Kommandant unlocked the bunkers and, sentimental now, went from station to station addressing the men with tears streaming down his cheeks. The gates of the stations were opened and the prisoners circulated freely until ten o'clock.

The New Year was the last bright spot before the final break-up. After a dinner of Bockwurst and potato salad, the prisoners turned the camp upside-down. One corridor of the cell-block had been arranged as a cabaret. Before one of the strangest audiences ever assembled, and with an orchestra as good as any in the trenches during the war, an uproarious entertainment was staged, with jibes which spared neither Kommandant nor guards. Shouts of laughter rebounded hollowly from the dank walls. The director was a really clever Jew who had chutsped himself into grace. Even the visiting guards roared with glee when one of his performers, a Communist in a ludicrous SA uniform (designed especially to delight our SS guards, for relations between SA and SS were strained), threw his arm high in the Nazi salute and, instead of the customary 'Heil Hitler,' shouted: "So hoch der Dreck, Herr Kommandant!"

But I was preoccupied through this grim fun, for I was facing a grave decision.

Everything was set for my escape. I had everything I needed to get over the border; my bills were sewed into the lining of my coat. Two guards were by now so much under my influence that they were ready to throw in their lot with mine.

Again circumstances had aided me. Prisoners in 'protective custody' had been ordered evacuated from Brandenburg by 5 January, to be divided among three other camps. The cripples were to go to Lichtenburg, the physically fit to Papenburg on the Dutch border to drain the moorlands by forced labour, the unfit to Oranienburg. As each camp already had its own guard, our SS keepers were to lose their jobs.

Feeling themselves cheated, and furious with the Kommandant, who had decamped right after Christmas for another position in Stettin, they were in a rebellious mood.

One night, in fact, instead of teaching English to my class, I had to talk horse-sense to some twenty-five turbulent SS men who were ready to drive their truck to the chancellery for a demonstration - steel helmets, machine-guns and all.

"We'll tell Hitler what they're doing to us! And if he won't listen, we'll chase the Gestapo into the street and kill the swine!"

A thought had flashed through my mind. I knew the lay-out of the chancellery.... What might they not accomplish before their mad suicide overwhelmed them? But I argued them into rationality, fascinated all the time with the idea of what might have happened if they had had a leader.

My two friends in particular were fed up. 'America' was now a magic word. They thought, of course, that I had more money than I really had, and knew nothing about passports and immigration restrictions. We could reach the Czech border all right. But what would I do with them then?

I was unwilling to victimize them; it must be my last resource. There was still another hope. Some time before, I had established contact with someone on the outside, and was waiting now for a message. The delay might be fatal to me. If they sent me to Papenburg, I was lost.

At last the hoped-for word reached me: I should try to get into the transport for Oranienburg, where the keepers were SA men and things could be made easier for me in every way. I had reason to believe that the advice had really come from

Roehm, who at last had been appointed a Reichsminister though without portfolio - a fact that might prove very helpful to me.

Intuition pointed to Oranienburg, and after much mental anguish I chose to stay - to the bitter disappointment of my two young friends. The decision had been difficult, for my status in camp had again become precarious. The day after Christmas, there had been a wholesale consolidation of prisoners to save light and coal. The station below us had been moved up to join ours, and among them were men who had known the Blacks. One of them, a young police-officer, brought with him the Blacks' hatred of me and proceeded at once to make my life miserable. He was chummy with a rascal if there ever was one, a bow-legged, swarthy SS man with yellow eyes and yellow skin, a perfect mongrel type. When I looked at him, I could think of nothing but a toad.

The Toad soon hated me like poison. He was the nefarious partner of another rascal, the commissary, an SS man. The commissary was fleecing prisoners systematically; men who had been released would find that he had falsified their accounts, so that they hadn't even money enough to pay their fare home. Alarmed about my own account, I demanded an itemized statement and found an embezzlement of some fifty marks. When I protested earnestly, he sent the Toad to my cell.

"Better forget it," he said. "An SS man can't be wrong."

Chinaman or Jew, Nazi or Communist - a rogue is still a rogue. I told him to go to the devil. He returned to my cell with Wachtmeister Schmid, who ominously closed the door behind him. I relinquished my claim rather than receive a beating then and there.

But now the Toad became my Wachtmeister, and persecution began in earnest. One by one the things I had collected with so much care - the electric light bulb, the table, the chair - were taken from me. When the stations were divided into working squads to clean the pigsty of a prison from top to bottom, I refused, as I always had, to perform such labour. There was a terrible scene which would have ended badly for me if my SS friends had not intervened and taken me to the new Kommandant, a quiet, sensible man who gave orders that I was to be exempt from menial duties.

I was going from crisis to crisis. In the prevailing chaos, prison discipline had relaxed, and morning and evening drill had been discontinued. Now they were resumed, and unwisely entrusted to a brute and a braggart but an excellent drillmaster with a hellish voice. Naturally the prisoners hated being sweated by a fellow prisoner, a 'Schupo-Schwein' at that.

One day when the Kommandant was not in camp, the Toad shouted at me after roll-call to fall back into line with the others. I obeyed, but I was ready for a showdown. When we were in the courtyard of the dormitory, out of sight of the SS quarters, the 'braggart' started his grind.

"Marsch, marsch! " he bellowed. 'Hinlegsen!"

But I did not throw myself down in the dirt.

"Ludecke-hinlegen!" he screamed, now blue with rage.

"Never!' I shouted.

The 'braggart' and the Toad ran up to me menacingly, but I was keyed to such a pitch that I all but hurled my insides at them. The prisoners began to hiss and boo them more and more were getting up from the ground and advancing threateningly. The Toad disappeared; the 'braggart' simply stood there in his zippered green overall like a confounded fool. I took over the command of the company, and with a 'right about face' we marched back to the cell-block singing, In die Heimat, in die Heimat geht es wieder...'

Only some dogged, callous part of my brain was keeping me on my feet. I was near collapse, and in my condition it was not difficult to simulate a nervous breakdown. The Komrnandant ordered an examination by the doctor, and I was admitted to the hospital.

Here, alone in a brighter room and in relative quiet, I could pull myself together for the last chapter in Oranienburg. As a hospital patient, my transfer to Oranienburg was assured, unless there were sudden intervention by the Gestapo. Instructions to the Kommandant in Oranienburg about my special status could also ruin my plans. But somehow I felt that the colossal Schlamperei of the last weeks had thrown me into oblivion. Our SS guards, who had become threatening in their demands for jobs, were giving the Gestapo enough to worry about.

The dispute delayed the evacuation of the Brandenburg camp for a month. On 2 February the transport for Papenburg finally moved out, with detachments of guards marching in front and rear. I watched them go by my window. There was the Toad, stumbling along out of step, signs of a hangover on his abject face. Behind him marched the 'Braggart,' bewildered and silent. The others were grimly singing: Wir sind die Moorsoldaten...'

Next afternoon we unfit were herded into old trucks driven and guarded by brown-shirted Storm Troopers. For hours we stood upright as we bounced over the winter roads. At last, utterly exhausted, we rattled through the dark streets of the town of my childhood and into the courtyard of the concentration camp of Oranienburg.

XL

I ESCAPE

Though Remarque's books had been burned and banned in Nazi Germany, All Quiet on the Western Front was noisily represented in Oranienburg. The camp had its 'Himmelstoss.' That nickname had descended on a man who had a passion for the role of tough sergeant-Troop Leader Petzschner. And yet, after Brandenburg, the welcome he trumpeted into our ears was indeed music from Himmel. In no time our transport was assigned to various stations mine was that of the 'Sonderhaeftlinge,' who enjoyed special privileges.

The administration of Camp Oranienburg, a former brewery and the first Nazi concentration camp, was still under the direction of SA Sturmbann Leader Schaefer, founder of the institution. He was a handsome man in his early thirties, tall, blond, with frank blue eyes. During an inspection of the newcomers on Monday morning, 5 February-my birthday he noticed me and took me with him to his office in the administration building.

I was well prepared for him. Impressed by my Rosenberg credentials and a certificate[1] I had received from Kommandant Grutzeck, he asked to hear more of 'the incomprehensible story.' I began to tell him what I wanted him to know. When lunch-time came, he invited me to eat with him. "I can't offer you wine-but what about a good bottle of beer?"

It was a simple but, to me, Lucullian meal. Over a cup of good, hot coffee I finished my recital. He sat silent for a while, puckering his brow in thought and puffing huge rings from his cigar. At last he spoke:

"In comparison to you I'm a nobody in the Party, but even here, in my position, I come across astounding things. As long as I've anything to say here, you are my Party comrade, and I'll do what I can for you. Tomorrow I'll drive to the Gestapo, and if they don't act within a week, I shall find a way to the chancellery."

I had been afraid of that. It was clear that up to now he had received no instructions about me, and everything would be spoiled if he reminded the Gestapo of me and learned of my special status as Hitler's personal prisoner. So I said that the mere mention of my name at the Gestapo might frustrate my hope of release. But I had a favour to ask: Would he let me go to the American consulate in Berlin, since I must apply there in person for the extension of my re-entry permit into America? And I also wanted to talk with Alfred Rosenberg, who on 24 January, by Hitler's order, had become the Fuehrer's deputy for the whole spiritual and weltanschauliche

---

1 *Reproduced in the Appendix, with translation.*

education of the NSDAP and all co-ordinated associations.' "Rosenberg will talk to the Fuehrer," I said. "If you have the slightest doubt …"

The Kommandant hastened to assure me that what I had showed him and told him had been more than enough. "Kommandant Grutzcck would not certify to you if any charges existed against you. I remember your name now. I've heard of you and have read your articles. Infamous to detain an old Nazi like you for seven months, Go to Berlin any day you like."

He immediately transferred me to the First Aid Station in the same building. There were two rooms, the two SA 'Sanitaeter' lived in the larger one; I was put by myself in the smaller room in the rear, from which a door led to the corridor and thence to the court and latrines, enabling me to slip in and out unnoticed, especially at night-a tremendous convenience. This was the room occupied by the four former army captains arrested by Hitler's order.[2] They had been allowed to leave camp any time during the day without guards, and after a generally easy time of it had been released.

Reports I had received in Brandenburg had acquainted me with the conditions of life here and with the layout of Camp Oranienburg; I even knew of the existence of this room. Seldom in my life has a preconceived plan worked out so nearly as I intended. The situation was even better than I had hoped, and I was determined to exploit it to the utmost. A little more luck, a little more patience, and I would win-barring a sudden change of conditions.

Though I could move about the camp as I wished, I kept to my quarters. The less they saw of me the better. Completely separated now from the other prisoners, I came in contact only with Storm Troopers, and was able to pick out several for special services. My meals were taken with the two Sanitaeter, pleasant fellows who alternated on night duty.

Everything developed according to plan. But I had to be careful; when you make friends you also make enemies. I had to work fast, for my 'exclusive' position soon was drawing criticism. The Kommandant's adjutant, Storm Leader Daniels, began to look askance at me, and a certain Storm Leader plainly disliked me. That worried me, for the Storm Leader was the 'inquisitor,' and liaison-man with the Gestapo.

Possibly an incident involving Erich Muehsam had fired their grudge against me. One Saturday afternoon I was called to the Kommandant, who was in a hurry to get away. Excited and angry, he showed me a pamphlet whose cover bore the title Oranienburg[3] in large red letters all too realistically dripping blood.

---

2 See footnote 7 of Chapter 37 'I Fight'.

3 Oronienburg, published in Prague in February 1934 by Gerhart Seger, former socialist member of the German Reichstag, was published in the United States in 1935 by Reilly & Lee Co., with the title, A Nation Terrorised. In the main, Seger's interesting account undoubtedly is true to fact, but I cannot accept all his interpretations. There were many parallels between the two camps, Oranienburg and Brandenburg, but on the whole I believe that life was much harder in Brandenburg, especially in the early stages of camp life. The sleeping

"You see what happens when you're kind to someone. This man Seger had it better here than most, but the Marxist wretch ran away to Prague on 4 December. And now I get this impudent, mendacious rag! I'll have to reply to it, of course.

"But there's something I should like you to do. A British Fascist, well recommended, is here to see the camp and get some material for his paper in London. A very important matter this, you know. He doesn't understand German, and you could act as interpreter and help him interview some prisoners ...Yes, choose anybody you like ... I'm in a hurry, but I'll introduce you to him."

And his adjutant brought in this person, who later wrote down for me his London address, which I still have. It was hard to conceal my amusement at this Britisher, beaming with importance in his black shirt, for I knew that his organization[4] had no political importance and that the circulation of his publication was two thousand at the most.

But I went to the dormitory to select some prisoners. Muehsam declined until I told him it was the Kommandant's wish and that it might hurt him to refuse. "All right," he said. "I'll answer questions in a way that will not embarrass the Kommandant if I can speak to him before you take me to the Englishman."

I brought him before the Konmandant, who was alone. "Na, Meuhsam," he said, "was ist los? Why do you want to see me? You can tell me the truth-I won't hold it against you. I want to know what's going on in this camp."

"Herr Kommandant, they still beat me," said Muehsam, his voice shaking. "I shall not mention it to the English journalist, of course, but I think you should be informed." He looked straight in the Kommandant's face, on which I thought I saw genuine concern.

"I thank you, Muehsam," Schaefer said, "for coming to see me. Have no fear-I shall look into this! I promise you it won't happen again. Go now and join the others. Herr Ludecke will come right away." And when Muehsam had left:

"He has courage, that Jew-I respect him for it. How often I've given strict orders not to beat anybody! I can't keep my eye on everything-but I'll stop that!"

I am sure he tried, with the best of intentions, and I am equally sure that the final result was redoubled brutality for Muehsam. Months later, after my escape had

---

quarters in Oranienburg, however, were dreadful and unsanitary. They were built into the cement cooling-cellars of a former brewery, veritable rabbit-hutches; instead of beds, there were three tiers high of wooden shelves without space between them, a hundred men or more being packed into each catacomb. But from the beginning, prisoners could circulate freely among themselves in stations and courtyards during leisure hours, could get together in a large community hall, and buy eatables in the camp canteen. The food was more plentiful and of higher quality, the latrines individual and sanitary, with running water; the relationship between guards and prisoners was decidedly better, and there were other advantages. In both camps, among SS and SA men, aside from some alert and relatively well-informed individuals, 'the lack of political interests-not. to mention political knowledge-'as Seger puts it, was 'altogether staggering.' I was amazed to find that in both camps most of our Nazi guards did not even bother to read their Fuehrer's Voelkischer Beobachter, and the few who did, borrowed copies from the prisoners.

4 Sir Oswald Mosley's organization was another group.

519

led to the Kommandant's dismissal and a complete reorganization of Oranienburg under a new Kommandant, I read of Muehsam's suicide. Knowing the fibre of the man, I did not believe it. His old tormentors had now been able to wreak their vengeance on him for having appealed to the former Kommandant, and probably his heart had failed under their punishment.[5]

This was no prison. My new environment-white enamelled bed with real mattress and white sheets, windows without bars, clean wooden floors-were working wonders for my body; slowly my physical resilience was coming back.

But my soul was torn. Every sensitive man is likely at times to feel himself the battleground of two warring egos, and now it seemed as if the inner conflict, which the return of my strength seemed to intensify, would drive me insane. I was indeed two men, each trying to annihilate the other. My newer, cautious self, now the stronger of the two, was intent only on escape, on self-preservation. Accept defeat, it counselled; let the past go; the future will take care of itself. And here, too, was my old, wounded ego, still throbbing under wrong, still thirsting for vindication and revenge. It was Ludecke the revolutionary surging back to rebellious life. Hitler must somehow be forced to listen; then everything would come right. And Ludecke the rationalist saw clearly enough that the other fellow could be strangled only by definite, irrefutable facts. Both men wanted these facts; for one they spelled hope, for the other finality. Now and again suspicion would rise to overwhelm both Ludeckes in confusion. Had Rosenberg really deserted me? If he had, in whom could I put my faith? Could I even trust Roehm? There were certain things I must find out.

Meanwhile I had established direct contact with Roehm's agent. Several times I had managed to leave camp secretly by night; the Kommandant and the two Sanitaeter were completely unaware. It is obvious that I cannot go into details, but it had been amazingly easy. My absences were known only to certain troopers. So long as I paid for their drinks, they didn't care a hang what I did for an hour or two. They thought I was out 'having a good time.'

One night a car picked me up somewhere in Oranienburg to take me to Roehm, who was waiting for me in his car.

At once a little misunderstanding developed. Roehm had taken it for granted that then and there I would drive back to Berlin with him. He would get me out to Switzerland. It was to be as simple as that.

The revolutionary Ludecke reared his head. Must I give up before I was really convinced I was whipped? Moreover, there were papers and documents back in camp; without them I could never rehabilitate myself. And what would this commit me to with Roehm?

---

5 See also the account of Muehsam's death given in the Weissbuch, dealing with the executions of 30 June 1934, Editions Du Carrefour, Paris. John Stone, an English Jew, whose report is given on pp.129-30, was known to me from Brandenburg, from where he was transferred to Oranienburg until his release.

"But, mein lieber Roehm," I said, "I'm not quite ready. Let's talk this over." And the car which had gained the open road and was eating up the miles, slued off into a lonely sidetrack and stopped. Roehm's driver got out and went out of earshot.

We started to talk business. The time has not yet come to disclose everything that was said that night, for I have no wish to encourage further blood-letting in Germany. I shall confine myself to what pertains to my own story, and leave history to grope for the 'missing link' in the mystery of the Blood-Purge, so soon to follow.

"Ludecke," said Roehm, "you must realize that I have a cogent reason for exposing myself to risk in snatching you from Hitler's claws. I also have my little plan. You're of no use to me in Oranienburg, but you could be very useful outside Germany. Are you familiar with the latest political developments? "

More or less, I said; I had read the newspapers; politics had been all I had to think about except my own misery.

Roehm patted my shoulder. "That's over now. I know you've had a raw deal … The luck of the man, as he lurches along!" He pointed to the ten-year non-aggression pact with Poland, the Stavisky scandal and the resulting French crisis, which, for the time being at least, had averted the danger of a preventive war. "Yes, the worst is over. For the present I can't see any potential inner or outer combination that could halt our preparations and wreck our plans."

Our plans? I said that there seemed to me to be a conflict of plans.

"Of course there is," said Roehm, and then with his usual penetration, he stated the conflict succinctly. There was the High Command. Still inclined to be monarchist, they were for an alliance with Russia, but with a military dictatorship to be set up there after Stalin had been overthrown with their help. They were hand-in-glove with Big Business because they thought they needed it for military-economic preparations. "God knows," said Roehm soberly, "what will become of Hitler and the Nazi party if they ever put that over."

There was Hitler. He was aiming at the triumph of the Nazi Totalitarian State and also for the overthrow of Stalin and for conquest to the eastward-but only with the army completely under his thumb, for he must be the unchallenged dictator. Meanwhile he deemed it wise to run after Mussolini, kowtow to London, and antagonize every traditional power at home except capitalism. He would go on playing ball with the money bags as long as they let him. "Schacht already is practically economic dictator[6] - which apparently is helping Hitler a lot in London's City and in Wall Street - and you know what that means ! "

Then ourselves. We were fighting for the triumph of the Nazi idea, if possible with Russia, against the money-bags, and in defiance of England. We believed that in a German-Russian combination, an alliance between two peoples, the German influence would be the stronger and in time the German idea would dominate and

6 *Schacht actually became Minister of Economics a few days after Roehm was murdered.*

muzzle the Russian bear. We would get what we needed by a process of peaceful change without the risk of a war that might well ruin us both.

"The next six months will decide which of the three is going to gain the upper hand," said Roehm. "It may be decided earlier, if Hitler should compromise with Blomberg - in case Hindenburg dies. Hitler will grab the Presidency the moment the Old One closes his eyes. Meanwhile, until Austria falls into his lap, he'll hide behind the broad shoulders of the Old Bull - and then he'll waft him into Valhalla."

I asked about Blomberg.

"Yes, certainly, a capable officer, but conceited and ambitious. He's become wax in Adolf's artist's hands, and now he's just being led along. Only recently Hitler told me he would give Blomberg the Field - Marshal's baton, when and if he became President. You see? And I! I am still minister without portfolio. But that's political expediency - I can forgive him that. But did you see the letter to me that was published in the V. B.?[7] He can't fool me ... Yes, we still need him. Unfortunately half the nation already sees a demi-god in him. But we must push him soon, lest the others push him first...

"You see, Ludecke, I've been thinking a lot along the lines of our talks in 1932 ... Exactly, a reorientation in our foreign policy, a German-Russian combination, will upset all present calculations ... Let London go on wheedling him and trying to undermine me. Hitler can't walk over me as he might have done a year ago; I've seen to that. Don't forget that I now have three million men, with every key position in the hands of my own people. Hitler knows that. Oh, no, it's not going to be so simple as that - Blomberg here and Roehm there. I also have friends in the Reichswehr, you know!

Just what did he intend doing? I asked.

"If Hitler is reasonable I shall settle the matter quietly; if he isn't, I must be prepared to use force-not for my sake but for the sake of our revolution. And that's

---

7 *My DEAR CHIEF OF STAFF:*

The struggle of the National Socialist movement and the National Socialist revolution were only made possible by the thorough-going suppression of the Marxist terror by the SA. If the army must guarantee the protection of the nation externally, then it is the task of the SA to guarantee internally the; victory of the National Socialist revolution, the existence of the National Socialist State and the common weal of the people. When I appointed you, my dear Chief of Staff, to your present position, the SA was going through a grave crisis. Above all it is due to you that within a few years this political instrument has been able to develop that force which by conquering the Marxian opposition made it possible for me to win decisively in the struggle for power. . . .

Hence at the completion of the year of the National Socialist revolution, my dear Ernst Roehm, I feel the urge to thank you for the imperishable services you have rendered the National Socialist movement and the German people, and to assure you how grateful I am to destiny for being allowed to number such men as yourself among my friends and comrades-in-arms.

In cordial friendship and grateful appreciation,

Your

ADOLF HITLER.

(Published in the Voelkischer Beobachter of 2 January 1934.)

where you come in. I need a representative abroad I can trust implicitly-someone so familiar with the whole situation that Hitler will know I mean business. You know he thinks you a remarkable but dangerous fellow … Yes, that's what he said.

Eagerly I asked if Roehm could recall Hitler's exact words.

"Before Christmas, soon after I got your first message, I asked Hitler about you in a casual way. He said: 'Eine dumme Geschichte, dies er Ludecke. Ein sonderbarer Kauz, ein guter Kopf, aber ein gefaehrlicher Bruder!'[8] And then he changed the subject … Yes, it's all he said."

Plenty for me to think about there!

"Now, Ludecke, I want you to go to Switzerland. You will have sufficient money. We'll have time to discuss the details later. What do you say?"

"I agree in principle," I said. "But it seems to me that Gregor Strasser ought to go with me. We two together-"

"You and your Strasser!" Roehm interrupted me, a little provoked. "I don't need Strasser. I've got plenty on them-dynamite enough to blow Hitler and his bosom friends to bits. Don't you know that Strasser's 'intimus,' has plotted against my life at least once? Why should I deliver myself into their hands? It would be crazy. There are only a few men left in this world whom I trust. Herr Gregor Strasser has joined the money-bags.[9] Besides, who knows but what he still may be tied up with Schleicher? I'm through with that gentleman!"

I reminded Roehm that he had told me before my second arrest that Strasser was still someone to reckon with. When I had seen him myself, he had impressed me as anxious to get on his feet again, and confident that his day would come; he had seemed to me to be cured of Schleicher. I had been rather in a quandary about him after our talk, but his name still stood for something-I had heard it mentioned even in concentration camps.

We argued on, discussing Goering and Goebbels as well. When I heard that Roehm was thinking of using Goebbels, I did my best to talk him out of it.

Roehm realized why I needed a little more time, and why I wanted to see Rosenberg and get him to make a last attempt with Hitler before I took the final plunge. If my talk with Rosenberg should prove unsatisfactory, I was to leave for Geneva at once.

Smiling, he gave me five hundred marks "in case you need a little extra money." I shall always remember the strange effect, in the semi-darkness of the car, of that last smile from the man who had lost the upper part of his nose in the war.

RoehIJl returned to Berlin and I to camp.

We separated with a cordial' Auf Wiedersehen.' It was never to be. Five months

---

8 *An unpleasant business, this Ludecked affair. A strange bird, a gopod head, but a dangerous brother!*

9 *Gregor Strasser, politically inactive since early 1933, had become a director of the Schering-Kahlbaum chemical works, a subsidiary or the I.G. Farben, the German dye trust.*

later, Ernst Roehm had been sent beyond all 'wiedersehens.'

Early in the morning of Monday 19 February I took a train for Berlin, only nineteen miles away, for my one-day's leave of absence. One of the Troop Leaders of the prison guard accompanied me.

At the American Consulate, my White House correspondent's card gained me immediate admittance to Consul Raymond H. Geist. This kind and understanding gentleman already knew of my difficulties through an inquiry from my wife, and he had sent her the desired information in a letter[10] dated 3 January 1934. My application for a six months' extension of my re-entry permit was accepted and duly forwarded to Washington.

Then I rejoined my Storm Trooper, patiently waiting in the street, and together we drove to Zimmerstrasse 88. I was in luck, for directly across the street from the entrance of the V. B. building was Rosenberg's Mercedes. I instructed my taxi to park right behind it; we stayed inside.

With my eyes glued on the door of the building, I waited. It was now one o'clock. Rosenberg might come out and take a bite next door, or walk across the street to his car and drive away. He had no idea that I was in Berlin. Not knowing his present attitude, I preferred to run no risk. It would be better to take him by surprise. If he saw me suddenly and unexpectedly, the first flash in his eyes would show me his private feelings towards me.

I waited over two hours. At last he came out. I ducked. He crossed the street. When he was unlocking his car, I left my taxi. He was sitting inside, bending forward with his hand on the gear-lever, when I said through the open window :

"Hello, Rosenberg."

He looked up staring, and a warm glow lighted his cold eyes. It was so spontaneous that my heart rose within me.

"You-Ludecke! You are free! I'm so glad! come in-tell me!"

When I told him I was only on leave, his face sagged with disappointment and regret. We drove to the foreign bureau in the Wilhelmstrasse, followed by my Storm Trooper in the taxi. Rosenberg went upstairs; I stayed below in his car.

After a while Schickedanz came down and sat beside me, and I had one of life's little lessons. He was neither warm nor cold, not at all spontaneous, and apparently didn't quite know what to say. His manner showed that he was wondering what new complication the visit of prisoner Ludecke might bring to Rosenberg and to his precious self, and I began to smoulder. Presently he said:

"Is that the Storm Trooper from Oranienburg with you?

He must be cold. Don't you think he should-"

At that my temper burst through.

"What consideration! You didn't show me that much-not even a postcard during

10 *Reproduced in the Appendix.*

all those months I was facing savages! That Eskimo-dog isn't cold. He could sit in the taxi if he wanted to, but he preferred getting out to see what a real diplomat looks like."

Visibly embarrassed now, Schickedanz gave me a copy of a letter[11] my wife had written to Chancellor Adolf Hitler; she had sent copies, with an accompanying note, to all the Nazi chiefs, to the German Embassy in Washington, and to the German Foreign Office in Berlin. I was reading it breathlessly when Schickedanz remarked that it had been in process of translation when Rosenberg had asked for it, saying that I was waiting downstairs. He was rewarded by another outburst.

"What! This letter was just being translated? It's dated 15 January-you must have had it at least three weeks. And you haven't even acknowledged its receipt![12] Probably you handled my letters from prison the same way... Yes, I know I'm overwrought. But if you knew what I've gone through you'd expect me to knock the teeth out of a fellow like you. Get out and tell Rosenberg what a thoughtful chief of staff he has!"

Schickcdanz left me with obvious relief. And just then an old friend went by on the pavement. It was Count Luckner gesticulating wildly, as usual, and talking volubly to his littleCountess. But I wasn't in the mood to speak up just then, for I hated the whole world.

When Rosenberg returned, after five, I had calmed down. I resolved to avoid antagonizing or frightening him, and from then on I kept fairly quiet and cool. He proposed the evening for a long talk undisturbed.

From eighty-thirty until past midnight I sat in Rosenberg's office. We talked about my case at length and about many other things. For reasons of my own, it is advisable to confine myself here to reporting the purely personal.

"In my letter to you in September of last year, I enclosed one for Hitler. Did you give that letter personally to Hitler, as I asked you to?"

"No," said Rosenberg, rather sheepishly. "I tried to get to Hitler myself, but somehow I was put off. So I gave it to Hess, with the request to pass it on to Hitler immediately ... No, I thought it was important not to lose more time, that's why I asked Hess to do it ... Yes, I am sure Hitler read your letter. Why should Hess conceal it from him?"

"Rosenberg," I said, "sometimes your other-worldliness simply floors me. If Hess did give that letter to Hitler, he probably did it with such prejudicial comment that Hitler promptly gave him carte blanche with me. That's why I appealed to you so earnestly to give it to Hitler yourself and not to leave him before he made a definite reply. Do you know the kick-back I got from that?" And I told him how the Gestapo had cut me off from the world.

---

11 Reprinted in the Appendix.
12 Incidentally, not one of the Nazi pashas showed my wife the courtesy of a reply.

Then I put some straight questions to him. Had Hitler been alienated by rumours about me?

"No, I don't think they were responsible. Last Spring we talked about you several times. I didn't even have to suggest to him that we needed a man of your type. He said so emphatically himself. When he asked me to tell you that he had instructed Neurath to hurry your appointment through, he was all praise of you. 'Ludecke knows a few things,' he said. 'He knows more about America than the whole Foreign Office put together.'"

My revolutionary ego sat there savouring this in bitterness. How characteristic of Rosenberg! This had been said ten months before-why hadn't he told me then? But I only asked him if he had done all he could for me in my plight.

" Under the circumstances, I don't think I could have done more. The last time I approached Hitler about you, his reaction was such that it might have been worse for you if I had insisted. And I have a family, you know, a daughter I'm very fond of. ... No, I never could find out why he arrested you. . . . He turned me down flat and warned me to mind my own business. But you have a staunch friend in Amann. He raged around here in my office, and then went to Hitler. But even Amann, who's on Du und Du with Hitler, was told to shut up."

Rosenberg said that he had made his peace with Goering.

"Yes, this frightful struggle has shattered many destinies and will shatter many more. But things are coming to a head now, and this mess can't last much longer. I see trouble coming; I wish I had you with me. You're right-it's to Hitler's interest to have you alive and free. I'll talk to him-I give you my word ... On Thursday evening, after my speech at the Kroll Oper ... Yes, Hitler will be present ... Arrange it now? As you like."

When he got the chancellery on the wire, he asked to be put down for an urgent interview. I could hear Brueckner's voice, his good-natured laughter, when he said it was impossible for the morrow. It would be Wednesday, 21 February without fail, at ten o'clock in the morning.

"On my honour," said Rosenberg earnestly, "I promise you that this time I shall not leave his room until he at least grants you an interview-if he doesn't release you on the spot."

We discussed what Rosenberg should say and what he should avoid; he was confident and encouraging, and hope surged up in me. At my request, he gave me a word in writing to cover the Kommandant. On one of his personal cards he wrote:

'I have talked at length with Pg. Herrn Ludecke, who is here on leave by your permission. I shall do all in my power to clarify his case personally with the Fuehrer at the earliest possible moment. In the meantime, without wishing to interfere with you, I request that you treat Ludecke with all possible consideration.'

He signed his name.

Of course I did not even hint at my dealings with Roehm, but I told Rosenberg of my concern about my wife. For nearly eight months I had received no money, and had been unable to send her anything. From his desk-drawer he took out a hundred-mark note for me and promised to make it a point of honour to send five hundred to her in the morning.

We stood up. "On my word of honour," he said, " as soon as I have seen Hitler, I shall telephone you. On Wednesday. I shall telephone you at once, whatever he says!"

We clasped our right hands, and I think we both knew that we held human lives within them.

Using the forwarding address through which I had at last established contact with my wife, each of us under an assumed name, I wrote her a letter so phrased that even a censor would suspect nothing, but giving her the gist of the situation, with instructions what to do if by 5 March she did not receive a cable saying I was free.

It was now after midnight, but I still had a very special matter to attend to at the Ziegeunerkeller on the Kurfuerstendamm. We went there, my good Eskimo-dog and I. He was almost shy in the presence of a man who had spent nearly four hours with the great Rosenberg, but his awe soon vanished, what with Tokay, Szegedin goulash, and fiery gypsy music.

"Junge, Junge!" he mumbled, smacking and guzzling. "Next time I'll be in mufti. In this 'Kluft,' with Oranienburg on my sleeve, people give me a wide berth ... Det is Knorke hier. Du vaschtehst's, Kurt, nu noch e draljes, duftjes Mechen zum vaarsen, det wer ene kesse, schmissje, zackje, saftje Sache ...! Junge, Junge, Junge!" And he belched into his glass.

He did not know that the three sturdy men sitting a few tables away from us were waiting there to give him an unexpected 'lift.' But in the privacy of the toilet I told Roehm's man that the outlook was more hopeful after my talk with Rosenberg. The emergency had not yet arrived; he was to tell Roehm that I would be ready to jump if I were not free within a week ... Before I returned to my table, he slipped something into my pocket that made me feel better. It was a flat little Browning revolver.

The Troop Leader and I taxied back to camp over a lonely road.

The Kommandant was much pleased with Rosenberg's card.

"In a few days you'll be a free man!" he said. But I said only that I must go to the American consulate again to sign a power-of-attorney for my wife, and that Amann was coming up from Munich at the end of this week or the beginning of the next. If I should not be free by then, could I...?

" Of course. Just let me know. I'll give you two days' leave-will that be enough?"

On Wednesday at ten o'clock, my heart marched with Rosenberg into the chancellery and up the stairs to Hitler's study-or would it be below, in his official room?

The hours crept by. One o'clock-two, three, five, seven o'clock. No news. One word from Hitler would set me free … one word would end it all … The cold, flat little Browning lay warm in my hand.

A ghastly night passed. Thursday went by, Friday, Saturday. Nothing-and no news from Roehm. I read in the Beobachter that Rosenberg had made his speech on Thursday and Hitler had been conspicuous by his absence.

There was something … wrong.

I could not sleep or eat; I was a wreck again. I watched every move around me, every face going in and out of the building. Every time I heard my name or the ring of the telephone I had an electric shock … There … that must be it! But nothing happened.

On Sunday afternoon I had a message from Roehm: things looked bad-I had better hurry, and send him the word.

It was late Monday afternoon before I could get hold of the Kornmandant. He gave me my two days' leave. This time Sanitaeter Witte was to be my guard. That was better. I knew he had a girl in Berlin and wouldn't stick so close as my Eskimo-dog.

Roehm's man was expecting me in Berlin Wednesday morning on the nine o'clock train. He would tell me when and where I was to be picked up later in the day to meet Roehm. But when, with Sanitaeter Witte, who was in mufti, well scrubbed and brushed, I walked out through the small guardhouse at the front entrance of the camp, the Troop Leader on duty there said that Adjutant Daniels had just telephoned an order that we were to return that evening by ten o'clock.

This new development might ruin everything: the hue and cry must not begin so early as tonight. On our way to the station, I tried to figure out what could have happened. Was it just spite on Daniels' part? Or had there been a message from the Gestapo, or perhaps from the chancellery-and the fool hadn't told me? I decided I must find out-it might be something that would affect my whole life. From the station I telephoned to the home or' the Kommandant: his wife said that he had just left.

We walked back to the camp. It was a hard decision to take, for I had not dared call the Berlin number of Roehm's man to say that I would be delayed. If I escaped the number could have been traced. Moreover, he probably had already left home.

The Kommandant was not there. When he finally arrived, saw me in the corridor, and asked why I had not left, I told him through a throat almost closed by nervousness.

"Nonsense! " he said. "You go ahead. Viel Glueck und Auf Wiedersehen," and he turned away. Apparently on afterthought, he called me back. "Wait a minute, I'll talk with Daniels," and he walked into Daniels' room. In a few minutes he came out. His word stood, he said. I would have two days as promised-and we shook hands.

But by now I had missed several trains. Expected in Berlin at nine, I did not get there until eleven-thirty. And Roehm's man was nowhere in sight.

Through all that anxious day I tried to get in touch with him. At last I had him on the telephone: he had left the station after waiting two hours. It was decided that he would pick me up later in the evening and drive me to Roehm, who was out of town. But everything was arranged.

Meanwhile I had got rid of my Sanitacter, off for his date with his girl-friend. But the day had started wrong and continued to go wrong. It was impossible to get Rosenberg; he was somewhere in Bernau, making a speech. His secretary said she expected him any minute. My need to know what had come of interview with Hitler was so imperative that I risked waiting in his office. In growing agony I waited and waited. Finally I left, but when I reached the spot where Roehm's man was supposed to meet me, I was ten minutes late. My breath almost stopped-for there was no car, no sign of him.

Was the man late or had he gone? I had not slept for nights, and in my exhaustion my nerves were so taut that confusion overwhelmed me.

Holding my wrist-watch in my hand, I paced up and down the dimly-lit street. It was drizzling, and the pavement was wet. Fear and suspicion began to choke me. Every man who approached might be the Gestapo! Those two there, standing at the corner in front of the cigar-store-did they have their eyes on me? I must know; I had resolved to kill myself rather than be rearrested. My hand gripping the little Browning in the pocket of my coat, I walked toward them but they didn't even look at me.

I tried the telephone again but Roehm's man didn't answer. Now he was almost an hour late, and I was desperate indeed.

Suddenly I realized that I must go it alone after all. I remembered my old Brandenburg plan for escaping through Czechoslovakia. Perhaps I could still make the last train to the Czech border. Should I risk it? I tossed a coin. 'Go!' it said. Still I lingered. I heard voices approaching from behind a door, and again I hung my fate on crazy chance. If they walk towards the Zoo, I'll go-if they turn the other way, I'll wait.

The man who came out walked towards the Zoo. I ran, and jumped into a taxi round the corner.

"To the Zoo station-hurry! "

As we neared the station, the large clock under the bridge showed that I could just make it.

I walked briskly to the counter, and as casually as I could I bought a second-class ticket for Goerlitz in Silesia, only thirteen miles from the Czech border.

When I bounded up the stairs, my train was just thundering in. I slowed down, and as I passed a news-stand Rosenberg's Blut und Ehre glared at me. I bought it and climbed into a carriage.

At last the train started to move. I had settled behind a newspaper in a corner of my compartment. Those two young men at the window in the corridor, that round-faced, genial looking pastor over there, that tight-lipped old woman across from me-they were no agents of the Gestapo. But the terrible feeling that someone was watching me persisted.

After changing trains, I reached Goerlitz at four in the morning. I watched too long to see if I was followed, and the town's two taxis left with customers quicker than I. But a porter told me the taxis would return; he would let me mow. So I went into the railway restaurant which was jammed with noisy people. I drank a cup of coffee and wrote a note to Roehm's man, giving a forwarding address in Geneva and saying that I would write from there. The porter approached. I paid my check, and followed him outside, furtively slipping my letter into a mail-box on the way.

It was a battered vehicle, but the young chauffeur beside it looked all right. He had a frank face and an infectious smile, and he would be pleased to drive me. My role now was that of the jovial travelling American, and apparently I was carrying it off. I got in.

"Schloss Schmiedeberg?" he said. "Sure, I know it. It's right near the border. Hindenburg had his headquarters there during manoeuvres. Many tourists go there."

I turned to look back; there was no car following me. I kept him talking; he was selling me Hitler's Germany.

"Yes, Germany is a fine country," I said. "So beautiful, so clean.... Yes, you're right, if it wasn't for Hitler... Yes, he's a wonderful man-I wish there was someone like him in America... Ah, you are a Storm Trooper? Splendid!"

It was from Schloss Schmiedeberg that I had intended to cross the border when I planned my escape from Brandenburg. But when we got there it looked wrong. There was the castle moat, the little bridge, the high wall. But the gate was closed. And where was the path across the park leading to the border?

"Oh, no, mein Herr, there are marshes all round. The border is several kilometres from here."

There stood the Worldly Wise Man and didn't know what to do. It was misting, wet and chilly. In my hopelessness, I was half inclined to drive back to the city and take the first train to Berlin.

But I pulled myself together. The feeling that I was alone against the world suddenly gave me new strength.

"Let's go somewhere else. I want to write a line about this place for my American paper, but I suppose we'll have to return later. Let's get something to eat. Do you know this neighbourhood here?"

"Of course I do. I know every stone around here. I was born and raised in Seidenberg, a little town nearby, right on the border. You'll get a good breakfast at the hotel there-it's only ten kilometres from here."

Right on the border! Could I trust him, I wondered, or did he suspect me? Had I better let my little Browning persuade him to lead me across?

"Okay-drive to the Seidenberg Hotel." We clattered past bleak, wintry fields, bounced across the market-place of Seidenberg, and stopped at the little hotel on the corner. We got out, and my driver pounded at the door. To my relief there was no answer.

"Where does this street go?"- pointing after a bicyclist disappearing in the foggy darkness.

"To the bridge, me in Herr. See where it turns? Then comes the bridge ... Yes, the border line is right in the middle of the bridge. Maybe the Hotel Rose on the other side is already open."

" Let's walk over and see. If it isn't, we can come back and then perhaps somebody here will be up." We walked down the street. The misty contours of the bridge began to emerge. "That house there all lighted up? That's the German gendarmerie and custom house…

I walked faster, 'With each step finding it harder not to run. Now I was on the bridge, with not a soul in sight. The toll-bar was down. I pushed through the turnstile for pedestrians. One more step ... It was done.

So easy! And I had thought that I should have to sneak across the border like an Indian and tramp for miles and miles through snow and woods!

"Yes, Hotel Rose is on the Czech side. It's there to your right, along the stream ... Sure, I will bring your things."

For a fleeting moment I saw my Germany in his honest face.

"I trust you-" But my voice broke, and I gave the astonished youth a bill, and another, and another. He turned back, almost too dazed for thanks. "

It was exactly six o'clock. I had got over none too soon, for just then a big light went on over the bridge. I ducked and darted away. Two shadows emerged from the fog, and I hid behind a fence until two Czech gendarmes had passed.

I wiped the tears from my eyes and walked straight ahead.

XLI

IN A MENTAL STRAIGHT-JACKET

There was a light across the fields, and I tramped towards it. Presently a neat little farmhouse stood out in the misty greyness of the dawn. I knocked and went in.

I found myself in a dim corridor. On one side were the living rooms, on the other the stable. There was a light in it, and a woman, scantily clad, was sitting on a stool, milking a cow. Her blouse was wide open, and the shaking of her firm, white breasts sent a stir through my veins that told me I was still a man. Sensing my presence, she looked up and blushed, and I stepped back into the dark. A man appeared in the corridor and I said good morning to him.

Ascertaining that he was a Sudeten-Deutscher, I took out a hundred-mark note. He was easily persuaded to set out for the Hotel Rose and find a young German who I hoped was waiting there with my things. Meanwhile his wife asked me into the kitchen for some breakfast; hot coffee revived me somewhat.

The farmer returned with the chauffeur, but without my luggage. Genuinely troubled, my Storm Trooper assured me that he hadn't dared bring my things across by daylight. He had left them with the baker's wife on the German side of the line, and of course I could call for them there any time. A glint of understanding crept into the farmer's eyes as he seconded the chauffeur's suggestion. When the youth had gone, he volunteered to go for them himself under cover of darkness that night; since I was obviously exhausted, I could go to bed and sleep in peace until then.

Mind and body were aching for rest, and I turned in. But sleep would not come, for fear was crowding it out. I had been lucky so far-but now I had to be careful. As an alien entering without a passport, I might run into trouble and be held for "months. It was necessary to get quickly to Prague. The next railway station was Reichenberg, cradle of Pan-Germanism, which boasts of being the birthplace of the first National-Socialist movement many years before Adolf Hitler. Now it was the heart of the Nazi Party among those Sudeten-Deutsche who form a thin fringe along the nine hundred-mile frontier that juts into the Reich. I was unsafe among them. This house was too near the border; I wouldn't have been the first or the last to be kidnapped back across the line.

So I got up again, and arranged with the farmer to send my luggage on as soon as he received my forwarding address from Prague. By ten o'clock I was riding on the pillion of his motor-cycle on my way to board the noon train. I had one bad moment, however. The farmer had said that the road almost touched the border at one point, and there we might encounter a patrol. We did. But I was well prepared with a pocketful of cigars. I passed them out, and produced my White House correspondent's card. "Oh, an American," they said, and waved me on. That hurdle had been taken.

By five I was in Prague. At the station I posted two letters I had written back in Oranienburg: one to the Kommandant asking his forgiveness, the other to the Gestapo asking them not to blame the Kommandant for my escape. Then I drove to an attorney to be informed about the police regulations for political fugitives in Prague. After that I cabled my wife, had some dinner, took a bath, posted my address to the farmer at the border, and went to bed-in a room in the apartment of my lawyer's secretary. He had advised against a hotel.

Austria's brutal little Chancellor Dollfuss, later murdered by the Nazis, had drowned the February uprising of the Socialists in blood. Thousands of Austrian refugees were now pouring in, and there were nightly police raids.

In a few days my luggage arrived intact, including my portable typewriter and, best of all, my scrapbook. Though I had my most important papers on my person, that scrapbook contained much that would have been irretrievably lost. One pull of the zipper would have opened the bag: I might have had a million marks in there. Now I knew that the world held at least three honest people: my Storm Trooper, a baker's wife, and the farmer.

On my second day in Prague, I tackled the new struggle with red tape. I needed a passport in order to get to Geneva, and from there eventually, via Paris, to America. But first I had to have a police-permit for my stay in Prague, and that required a certificate issued only on the basis of a properly documented application to an officially recognized fugitive-aid bureau. For fugitives from Nazi Germany there were three such bureaus: Democratic, Socialist, and Communist. But I had been a Nazi, and not an unknown one; there might be a flood of questions; they might suspect me as a super-spy; or the Gestapo, getting wind of my presence in Prague, might set rumours afoot that would get me arrested by the Czech authorities. I decided to be a political nondescript, a German-American who had been sojourning in his home town and who... well, I would know what to say.

The head of the Democratic fugitive-aid bureau, a Jew and a fugitive himself, grew inquisitive when he heard my name, and did not seem entirely satisfied with my explanations.

"Well," I said, "I'm not the only Ludecke in this world. I don't know what my namesakes are doing... You'd be surprised how little can land you in a concentration camp. They accused me of having said that Hitler was an ass. I denied having said it, but agreed that he was one if they said so - and they locked me up. After vainly waiting eight months in jail for Hitler to apologize for causing me such trouble, I thought it was time to run away-and here I am! You see, that's the American spirit."

But his sense of humour - if he had one-wasn't touched, and he dismissed me with a pompous gesture to the ante-room. After a while they handed me my application sealed in an envelope. When I got back to my room I steamed it open. There was a letter enclosed. Perhaps his guardedly phrased 'recommendation, 'with the clause' if you have no doubts,' was only routine caution. At any rate, I presented my application without that letter, and a few day; later I had my police permit. Then came a shock: I was told I might get a passport within four or six months - if indeed I could get one at all.

In despondent mood I started to prowl through the quaint parts of beautiful old Prague. People were looking at me. There must be something in the face and walk of an escaped prisoner that draws attention; there certainly was in mine. With my police-permit in my pocket, I was a free man, and making the most of it. How often in prison had I imagined myself doing just this, wandering at will up and down a street, deviating to right and left as I pleased, peeping into this door or that-and nobody to stop me! There was freedom in the dazzling air of that early spring day, freedom in the flight of the gulls which I watched from the quay on the broad river between the old stone bridges, dipping and swooping across the water, chasing each other for the titbits people threw to them, or snatching them in mid-air with greedy grace.

When the setting sun was burnishing the slow flow of the Moldau, I walked up to the glass-walled coffee-house at the corner to see the ball of fire sink beyond Prague's great hill, crowned by Europe's most royal residence.

All the window seats were occupied. My eyes rested on the profile of a lovely girl sitting alone at a little table. Perhaps she would not mind? When she nodded consent I sat down with my back to the room. She was fresh and cool and clean, so close that I could inhale the fragrance of her youth. There were poise and restraint in her face, but behind the dark-fringed lids of her expressive eyes, smoke-blue and set wide apart under full brows, there was something that promised warmth and sympathy.

The sun was down now; the splendour of colour was fading. I looked full at her, and she at me. I spoke to her; she answered. I learned that she was a medical student. And as we talked, deep comfort came into me, for I knew that here was some one I could trust. At last I could open my soul. She would help an emotionally starved and prison-bound man to become whole again.

The gnome-like, grumpy official I had seen in the foreign division of police headquarters surely could speed me toward a passport if he would only tip me off to the right person to approach. After all, I knew nobody in the city and couldn't speak Czech; I was a fugitive, and a German at that. But when I went back hoping to detect his vulnerable spot, I decided the old buzzard must have got up on the right side of the bed that morning, for he actually smiled, and spoke English and

French to show me how versatile a Czech official could be. His glance rested on a letter from my wife lying in front of me on the rail. "

"Are you collecting stamps, by any chance?" I asked.

"Yes," he said, almost coyly. "Is that a new five-cent stamp?"

He grinned when I tore it off for him, beamed when I returned next day with some rarer ones, and gave me the hint I wanted. Thanks to that, my lawyer's ingenuity, my own persistent energy, and the real kindliness of the Czech Foreign Office, I had a Czech passavant at the end of the month, and with it the needed Austrian and Swiss transit-visas.

In the interim I had vainly tried several times to get in touch with Dr. Otto Strasser, and then had decided that it might be wiser not to persevere. The interlude in Prague had ended. From the window of my compartment in the train for Zurich, I looked into the moist eyes of the girl who had helped my sick spirit to find the way back to life.

'Partir est toujours mourir un peu.'

On Saturday, 31 March, I arrived in Geneva with less than a franc in my pocket. There were no letters. But it was Easter, with the promise of a new world for me. I took a modest but pleasant little room in a pension up in the hills. Here, on Swiss soil, I was safe, and my most fantastic illusion in the dream-world of my cell - the swish of the grass against my feet, the buzzing of a bee, the song of a bird in a rustling nee above my head - had come true. This was no dream! Though everything else might be illusion, this was real daffodils in bloom, hawthorn coming into bud, soft lawns sloping down under trees tender in the sunshine, and a gentle breeze rippling the surface of the happy lake.

Slowly my subtler sensibilities, woven anew with a finer yarn, were returning to my body. But my old ego was still alive. My new spirit had not yet strangled the old one; I still had hope. But I had to move on. The extension of my re-entry permit had been forwarded to me from Berlin in care of the American Consulate in Geneva. Mildred, who had sent me the last dollar she could spare, wrote that nothing had come to her from Rosenberg.

Before I could feel morally free for a new life, however, I had to give Hitler a chance to declare himself. And so I wrote to him from Geneva.

Addressing myself to Adolf Hitler as to one who had explicitly reserved for himself the disposal of my case, I declared my wish to speak openly to him now, as man to man; he had known me well for more than twelve years, and we had often talked in intimate confidence. Regrettably I could no longer call him my 'Fuehrer,' for I could no longer profess adherence to a party which was willing to treat an innocent and faithful member so shamefully, depriving him of his liberty for eight months without legal procedure and without a hearing, brutally and ruthlessly abandoning him to spiritual and physical destruction. .

When my urgent pleas for a hearing had gone unanswered, when even my wife's earnest remonstrances from America had been ignored, I had been forced to act for myself. If this new Germany that was fighting for 'Liberty and Justice, Blood and Honour' was willing thus to victimize a man for his good faith, that man must needs fall back on his instinct for self-preservation.

Giving Hitler a brief account of the history of my case, I said that I was still trying to hold to my objectivity; he had done so much for Germany that I was ready to accept the personal injustice for the good of my soul, and to let it go at that. But there was a principle at stake whose importance transcended my unimportant self. That principle was the honour of the individual, proclaimed by Nazi Germany on one hand, flaunted on the other. Though I might be willing to liquidate the 'Case Ludecke,' to uphold that principle I must insist on these points:

1. Official annulment of my 'protective custody.'

2. Return of my passport and property.

3. Complete rehabilitation and satisfaction, along lines which I specified exactly.

My enemies had engineered my disgrace. But Hitler himself, I reminded him, had told a leaders' conference in October 1933: 'He who courageously demands his right, in the end will get his right.' And in another speech he had said that he would retreat 'only before reason.' In this case reason was on my side. He knew well that the calm admission of error was not a sign of weakness but of strength-a proof of human greatness. And if this last attempt to obtain my rights should also be ignored, I would have to act at my discretion, with only my conscience as my guide.'

To make sure that this letter would reach him, I said, I was sending the original to Rosenberg by registered mail, for personal delivery to him; copies were also going to the chancellery in care of his adjutant Brueckner to Goering, Goebbels, Frick, Hess, and Amann.

The letter had been written with one eye on the future for I did not believe that Hitler or any of the other recipients would reply. I also sent a copy to Roehm's man with a note for Roehm asking him to get in touch with me immediately; I was preparing to return to America if I should not have definite news from him by May.

Finally I raised a little money, just about enough to get me to Paris, and obtained a French transit-visa, an English visa had been rudely refused on the grounds that I had no steamship ticket for America. The Gestapo had ignored my request for the release of my suit-case and other belongings left behind in Oranienburg, but friends in Berlin were forwarding the luggage which had been in my apartment at the time of my arrest.

One day I went again to the railway station to inquire about this luggage, long overdue. As I was turning away disappointed, a man approached me, saying that he come from Berlin and would like to speak to me.

Naturally I connected him at once with my case, He was about my own age, correctly dressed and of the poker-faced official type. His unexpected appearance, after I had ruefully resigned myself to being forgotten, befuddled me for a moment. Wavering between hope and suspicion, I suggested that we sit down in a quiet corner of the station restaurant.

The man moved much too slowly to suit me; it took him a full minute to say ten words. He spoke of a letter I should have received, but did not disclose from whom it came and what its purport was. My insistence that I hadn't received it seemed to disconcert him, but finally he explained that he had been commissioned to bring me to Basle; there I would be given further information.

Beginning to lose patience with this mysterious stranger, I told him I thought it time he identified himself. At that he stolidly produced what looked like 'an ordinary German passport, but gave me no chance to examine it.

When I pressed him to reveal who had sent him-was it Hitler, Goering, or the Gestapo? - he shut up like a clam: he was not permitted to tell me that; my suspicions, he insisted, were unfounded, and I would be satisfied with the information awaiting me in Basle.

But suspicion was now strong; I thought the letter-story only a trick to get me to Basle which lies on the German-Swiss border; there I could easily be abducted into Germany. News of the distressing aftermath of my escape had already reached me: Hitler had raged in fury; Kommandant Schaefer had been dismissed; Sanitaeter Witte had committed suicide. This emissary, I believed, was an agent of the Gestapo, which now, probably as usual without specific orders from Hitler, was trying to repair its blunder and get me back.

How had he known who I was?-I asked. He replied dryly that it was easy enough to recognize me. Impatient now, I told him not to take me for a fool. I was registered with the Chef de la Surete in Geneva, and he would be in trouble before he knew it.

The words were scarcely out when my slow one became quick. He jumped to his feet and hurried away; before I could get out from behind the table, he had reached the door and disappeared in the crowd.

I had let him slip through my fingers-but what could I have done? Could I, after all, be certain? The only certainty was that now I had to pay for the drinks he had ordered. A few days later my baggage arrived, and I set out for Paris on 2 May, penniless. No need to dwell on the details of the ordeal that awaited me there. It was the bottom point of my life. I was without money for weeks, often without food.

Neuritis laid me low; for days I could not walk. I thought it was the end of me. My plight had prompted me to make another attempt with Hitler. I wrote to Magda Goebbels, enclosing letters for her husband and for Hitler. Kind and gracious still, she sent me a kind reply. But nothing came of it, and now I was utterly desperate. My transit-visa had long since expired, and I could not afford to come into conflict with the French police.

Just when I was really at the very end of my hope, I managed to borrow enough money to buy a ticket for Quebec. And a kind Providence led me to Dr. P. Roucayeol, brilliant physician and generous man, who treated me gratis at the Hospital St. Louis and made me fit to undertake the ocean journey.

For almost a fortnight I had not been able to call for my mall. Two days before my boat sailed I went to my forwarding address. And there I found a letter.

Two thousand francs were enclosed. The message, so worded as to make it clear that it came from Roehm, said that the bearer had looked for me in Geneva, had followed me to Paris, and there had waited five days in vain. Obliged to return to Germany now, he urged me to get in touch with him in Basle.

Had I been wrong about the man in Geneva? No use speculating about that now-it was water under the bridge. But what should I do in this present dilemma? I had bought copies of the Voelkischer Beobachter and had not liked what I read there. A report of a speech delivered by Roehm at Goebbels' propaganda ministry led me to feel that he was, after all, making common cause with Goebbels. I was sickened by Rosenberg's flaying in glaring headlines 'the disgrace to civilization' of Austria's only concentration-camp, after he had heard from me the story of the disgrace of the Nazi camps. And there was a full-page article by Rosenberg on the occasion of Hitler's birthday whose mawkish praise had seemed to indicate that he had knuckled down completely. And my mind was set on return; my wife expected me on that boat; I had overstayed my transit-visa nearly a month; I was sick and exhausted. So I decided to sail. Having no idea then of the pressure Roehm must have been under, it merely seemed to me that he had proceeded in this matter with little foresight and attention to detail.

On 13 June I embarked at Cherbourg. It was the seventh anniversary of my marriage, but I faced the day with little hope of being able to save Mildred from the wreckage of my life. In the turmoil of my fight, she had gone neglected and unprovided for. Her last letter had held a mild warning: if I wanted to share the new life that I was facing with her, I would have to plan an existence that would offer her some security and peace. I knew that I could not ask Mildred to live with me in a mental strait-jacket I should have to wear at least until I had written the past from my chest.

Standing alone at the stem of the boat in the early dusk and gazing into the wake, I talked aloud to a man who could not hear.

Adolf Hitler, ever since I gave you my soul, there has not been a day or a night that I have not thought of Germany and you! Now that you have mutilated my whole being and made me an exile from the country I love, I pray for the power to put into words something that springs from my soul! Adolf Hitler - you fool! The energy and perseverance, the thought and will I have wasted in escaping from you, the efforts to integrate myself again that still lie ahead of me, could have moved a mountain for Germany and you!

The immigration officials at Quebec had never seen a German travelling on a Czech passavant, but finally let me pass when the American immigration-officer, after examining my re-entry permit, reassured his colleague: Canada would not be stuck with me, for the United States would let me in. But the delay nearly made me miss the boat-train Mildred was waiting for in Montreal. A wire reached me en route: she would meet me instead at the gate of the station in Toronto that night. But I hadn't money enough for the extra ticket to Toronto, and only a few minutes to change trains. Lost in despairing confusion, I stood beside my luggage in the Montreal station - and just then a Tokyo-bound Englishman, with whom I had exchanged a scant hundred words on the boat, walked past and waved me a friendly farewell. I ran up to him. There was no time to explain. Without a word of question he gave me what I asked for: five dollars and his card.

Mildred was at the gate in Toronto, but I felt so defeated I could not bear myself. In a few days I was on the road alone in the weather-beaten Ford that I no longer owned.

As I faced the self-torturings of frustration that I knew were ahead of me, I thought grimly of Ivy Lee and G.S. Viereck, who had finally succeeded me, and according to the newspapers, were now receiving many thousands of dollars for advice on the best manner and means of making Hitler more acceptable to the American people. I thought of my former Washington men: Dr. Leibbrandt, now chief of the Near-East division of Rosenberg's foreign bureau; Dr. Smetana, killed in Vienna in the motor-accident of King Alfonso of Spain. How would I end?

The roar, the smell and grime of New York assailed me on that I July like the menace of some huge monster. I drove straight to the 'Shelton,' parked the car, took a room, then came out and walked to the drug-store across the street, with a copy of the New York Times under my arm. Settling my tired limbs on a stool at the counter, I opened the paper and saw this:

HITLER CRUSHES REVOLT BY NAZI RADICALS
VON SCHLEICHER IS SLAIN, ROEHM A SUICIDE
Storm Troop Chiefs Die as Hitler and Goering Strike

I looked through tears and the staring eyes of the soda-fountain clerk into the bleakness of this rotten world.

XLII

THE BLOOD-PURGE

The bloody Saturday of 30 June 1934 will go down in history as the most unhappy chapter of Hitler's life. Developments leading up to the Blood-Purge are entangled in a hopeless snarl of lies, intrigues, and contradictions; it is still impossible to unravel the full truth, for dead men are silent. To one familiar with the external facts and the psychology of the persons involved, however, the background is sufficiently clear to allow a competent interpretation, not exact as to detail, but probably correct.

The precise historian who in some distant future seeks to analyze the purge is likely to have to deal entirely with opinions laid down for propaganda by Hitler's contemporary foes and by the admiring beneficiaries of his rights. The archives of the Gestapo or other agencies will be careful not to offer unfavourable documentary evidence. The chief protagonists undoubtedly have not confided compromising and incriminating data to paper. Hitler alone knows both sides of the story. History has not always succeeded in probing obscurity to the bottom, and perhaps will never sound this pit.

The interpretation of the Blood-Purge offered here is based on intimate knowledge of the natures of Hitler and his tools. It follows Dr. Otto Strasser's brilliant reconstruction in his Die Deutsche Bartholomaeusnacht[1] - but follows him only in part. Though the surviving Strasser is probably the best-informed commentator, he seems at times to shape matters to support his theory and to be guilty of obvious exaggerations.

In an earlier chapter, reference was made to Hitler's speech at Bad Reichenhall on 2 July 1933. The threats voiced on that occasion had not banished the spectre of the 'Second Revolution' that had hovered over the nation since March of that year. The general discontent and unrest had kept pace with the increasing economic difficulties and Germany's growing isolation. By the spring of 193'4, the negative, indeterminate aspect of the Nazi dictatorship was all too apparent. Now criticism was open and unrestrained, coming chiefly from the Conservative wing led by the economic reactionaries, and from the Radical wing led by the Nazi activists-those so-called 'National Bolshevists' who were weary of Hitler's middle course.

Hitler was following his characteristic policy of lurching along With a foot on each side. But it was obvious that if he did not soon crack down on the malcontents on both sides he would have to cope with either a second revolution or a reactionary

---

1 Reso Verlag, Zurich, 1935.

putsch. A greater man would have mastered the problem by superior statesmanship. Choosing the easiest way, he placed his reliance first on propaganda, then on terrorism-the indispensable weapons of the Hitler system. Goebbels knew how to brandish the first, Goering how to wield the second.

Hitler's eventual course was largely determined by the imminence of Hindenburg's death. The problem of succession was now acute. The man who wanted both the Presidency and the Chancellorship knew that the Reaktion had no intention of entrusting him with the supreme control of the Reich, including the high command of the army. Once more a forgiving fate offered Hider a chance to redeem himself, to attain his goal with the intellectual honesty of the strong. Again he chose another course.

The Fuehrer proceeded with his double game. In Roehm and Goebbels he had admirable instruments for goading the Radicals on and for holding the masses in line; Goering's job was to manipulate the reactionaries in his role of their house-servant. The Reaktion was not a unit, comprising as it did numerous groups and sub-groups, divided by political and economic interests, by personal ambitions and divergent viewpoints, in their attitude towards National Socialism. There were two main groups: the first, the Hindenburg faction, which included Papen, Neurath, and Blomberg, and was based on the landed aristocracy and the Reichswehr, represented the political side of the Reaktion; the second, the Gaering-Thyssen-Schacht group, guarding the interests of heavy industry and the banks, with the police and the Stahlhelm as instruments of power, stood for the capitalistic side.

The Hitler faction in the Reich embraced the middle classes, the farmers and the non-Marxian workers. The Party, the SA, and the SS were its instruments of power and were, in the main, revolutionary in spirit. If Hitler should choose to down the Reaktion by force, he could count on Rochm, Goebbels, Darre, Frick, Hess, Himmler, Ley, Rosenberg, and Schirach, his most prominent men with direct political power. Goering of course was in the reactionary camp, half by order, half of his own volition.

If, on the other hand, the Fuehrer chose to buy off the Reaktion, there was only one man he need fear - his chief of staff. Now that Gregor Strasser had been eliminated, Roehm was the sole independent revolutionary activist with a definite aim and definite power.

Hitler apparently was preparing himself for either eventuality. It is significant that at about this time he deprived Goering of his most powerful weapon-the Secret Police. On 20 April, Himmler, the leader of the SS, was made chief of the Gestapo. The man was Hitler's, body and soul. Only thirty-three years old, he now possessed formidable power second only to Roehm's.

The Fuehrer continued his strategy of luring Roehm out to the end of a limb. On 18 April, quite unnecessarily and of course to no avail, the chief of staff expounded the spirit of the SA and of the German Revolution in a bombastic address before the wrong audience and at the wrong place. He spoke before the diplomatic corps and the foreign Press at the propaganda ministry, in Goebbels' presence. Was it at his suggestion? In parading before the whole world the revolutionary significance of the SA, poor Roehm, straightforward and unimaginative, was thrusting his head farther into the noose.

The people had long believed that he had the Fuehrer's fullest backing, and he now became the focus of the aims and hopes of those Nazi activists who were striving for the Socialist fulfilment of the German revolution. But he also became the main target of the Reaktion.

Let us remember the dates. Roehm made his speech on 18 April. Himmler was appointed on 20 6 April. In early May. Goebbels opened his dykes for a new flood of propaganda against 'reactionaries and killjoys, alarmists and paltry critics.' The little agent provocateur was succeeding both in scaring the Reaktion and in throwing dust into Roehm's eyes. The SA chiefs blindness to his danger can be explained only by the supposition that he must again have fallen under the spell of Hitler's undoubted charm. Though it must be emphasized that Hitler definitely does not court popularity the Nazi colossus, physically unattractive as he: is, can nevertheless exert fascination, and a man of Roehm's peculiar nature perhaps could not escape from his magnetic orbit. Once more the captain, strong-willed though he was, fell for his Adolf, and played into the hands of his master against his own better judgment and original plan.

Roehm apparently advised reconciliation with Gregor Strasser. Through Rudolf Hess, Hitler opened secret negotiations with Gregor the Apostate, looking to his re-entry into the cabinet as Miniter of Economics. Significantly this was not to take place until the autumn-a point stressed by Dr. Otto Strasser.

It is unlikely that Hitler thought seriously for a single moment of taking Strasser back. He was negotiating with him for three reasons: to dupe Roehm, to make the Reaktion more tractable when he let it be known that something was afoot between him and Strasser, and to keep him as an ultima ratio. Obviously a potential Roehm-Strasser front with Hitler's blessing was a nightmare to the Reaktion. Nor was it relished by either Goering or Goebbels, and they redoubled their efforts.

Von Schleicher's reappearance on the Scene at this time did not simplify matters. His reconciliation with the Hindenburg circle suggested an opposing potential combination, for the General was ambitious and maybe been seeking revenge. He was invited to a meeting in Bad Nauheim on 16 May at which the commanding generals of the Reichswehr discussed the problem that would be created by Hindenburg's death. Apparently even then the generals were agreed with Blomberg on Hitler, who reputedly had already made his pact with the Reichswehr Minister on board the pocket-battleship Deutschland during a short sea trip after manoeuvres

On 11 April 1934.

It is alleged that on this occasion the generals also debated the plan of the Hindenburg circle for securing from the dying President a political testament which would name the ex-Crown Prince at his successor; he was to be a Regent, like Admiral Horthy in Hungary. The Regent would be entrusted with the direct command of the Reichswehr, and would immediately proclaim a state of siege which would automatically transfer the entire executive power from the Hitlerian civilian authorities to the reactionary military authorities. Though Hitler would remain as head of a new cabinet, government on the side by the Party and by the SA would be abolished. Hitler could not have relished the plan, and it was certainly opposed by Goering, Goebbels, and Roehm; by Goering, because he wanted Hitler to become President, with himself as Chancellor and semi-dictator; by Goebbels and Roehm because it would strip them of power.

The Reaktion was now united, however, in working for the liquidation of the SA, which they feared as the nucleus of a future 'People's Army.' That danger had to be averted at all costs, for it would deprive them of their chief instrument of power, the Reichswehr, and would provide the revolutionary wing of the Nazi Party with a tremendous increase of power and influence.

Though Goering was not popular with the Foreign Office, which loathed his incursions into foreign fields; or with the Reichswehr, which wanted his Air Force incorporated into the Reichswehr Ministry; or with Papen, who had not forgotten that he had been left in the impotent post of Vice-Chancellor when Goering had pushed him out of the powerful office of Reichskommissar for Prussia - nevertheless Hermann the Bully was now invaluable to the Reaktion because of his known hatred of both Strasser and Roehm. He had been Roehm's deadly enemy ever since the 'Beer Hall Putsch' in 1923.

While the front of the Reaktion with Papen, Neurath, Blomberg, Goering, Thyssen, and Schacht fought the battle of its life with the front of the Revolution headed by Roehm, with Gregor Strasser now looming in the background, Hitler still stood between the parties to strike with Himmler and the SS, but letting things drift.

Roehm was engaged in a duel with Seldte to bring about the liquidation of the Stahlhelm, the private army of the Reaktion. At first Hitler sided with his chief of staff, but withheld his approval when Roehm ordered its dissolution. The dispute ended in a compromise, with the Stahlhelm becoming an SA .reserve. Though Roehm seemed to have won the advantage, it was a Pyrrhic victory, for it had brought him into direct conflict with the Reichswehr, which was now convinced that his real ambition was to get the command of the army. As a matter of fact, he had sought the removal of the Stahlhelm with the sole purpose of clearing the field for the final battle he expected to wage with Hitler against the Reaktion.

Roehm's next step in the face of warning symptoms which should have put him on his guard is almost incomprehensible. If he had misgivings, his Fuehrer probably was still able to dispel them; no doubt he appealed to Roehm's sense of duty, harping on the old theme of 'higher interests,' pointing to the impending death of the 'Old Bull' which would settle everything. But now, for heaven's sake, let him keep quiet, for important decisions had to be made. There was the coming visit to Mussolini, and Schacht's efforts to obtain foreign loans. Hitler must have neglected to mention that Ribbentrop, his personal arms envoy, was already busy in Paris and Geneva offering reduction of the SA as an exchange for an increase in the Reichswehr, at that time still limited by the Versailles Treaty to 100,000 men.

At any rate, on 8 June the Voelkischer Beobachter printed an official report from Roehm's Press-bureau saying that the Reichsminister and chief of staff was suffering from 'a painful nervous disorder' and was taking a vacation of several weeks on the advice of his physicians; to forestall all misinterpretation, however, he declared that after his recovery he would continue to administer his office.

Evidently Roehm felt sure of his standing. Two days later the V.B. published his decree to the SA in preparation for its regular annual summer furlough, to begin 1 July. (This leave had not the significance generally ascribed to it, for in point of fact it had first been ordered by Roehm on 21 April, as announced by the V.B. on that date.) Scoffing now at rumours of the impending dissolution or reduction of the SA he thus challenged his opponents: "...If the enemies of the SA hope that after its leave the SA will not be recalled, or will be recalled only in part, they may enjoy this brief hope. They will receive their answer at such time and in such form as appears necessary. The SA is and remains Germany's destiny."

Hitler's visit to Venice on 14 and 15 June, though it may have given the harassed German people the satisfaction of seeing the Fuehrer and Il Duce together at last, could hardly have satisfied him. Instead of winning the Duce to his policy, he was obliged to agree to 'the full recognition of Austria's independence.' Mussolini must have been well advised by Papen and Neurath through the German ambassador in Rome, if the report is true that he offered amicable hints to his visitor that you make a revolution with one set of men but rule with another, and that certain Nazis, notably Roehm, were jeopardizing Hitler's reputation throughout the world.

Such hints from the only potential ally were bound to have some effect, for Germany's outlook was gloomy indeed. On 14 June, payments were suspended on the foreign debts of the Reich, including those imposed by the Young Plan. The financial-economic situation was further aggravated by the prospect of a poor harvest, by the growing domestic difficulties, by the disarmament crisis, and foreign isolation.

Back in Berlin again, Hitler continued to hurl defiance at external and internal enemies. On 17 June, in Gera, Goebbels denounced critics and reactionaries, and on the same day Papen made his famous speech before the students in Marburg,

THREE NAZIS IN MUFTI

Hitler (right) and Goering (left) are listening with heads bowed and eyes on the ground to Captain Ernst Roehm.

proclaiming the right to criticize the Nazis, attacking the totalitarian principle, the one-party system, the 'Second Revolution' and terrorism. At any rate he had taken pains to protect himself by sending advance copies to Blomberg and Hindenburg, and the old President in a telegram to his 'best comrade' had endorsed Papen's battle against national bolshevist elements within the Nazi regime. Goebbels struck back at once. The publication of Papen's address was suppressed, and his ghost-writer and friend, Dr. Edgar Jung, was arrested.

There is something somewhat remarkable in the spectacle offered by Goebbels on the very day on which he berated the 'absurd pigmies of the Reaktion,' ... 'the gentlemen in club-chairs.' Without batting an eye and in full view of an array of foreign correspondents, the little gnome chatted amiably at the same tea-table with the reactionary gentlemen-jockey. And a few days later, Papen in his turn harangued the women of the Saar in a eulogy of the Fuehrer. The whole duel may have been mere camouflage.

The Nazi onslaught against the Reaktion continued until the end of the month, and most of the prominent Party leaders delivered radical speeches throughout the Reich. Perhaps the best illustration of the sentiment then dominating excited Nazi souls was a cartoon printed in Goebbels' *Angriff*. It showed a top-hatted reactionary, whose creased features were those of Papen, stabbing a Storm Trooper in the back; the Trooper, turning, kicked him in the face.

Conflicts between the SA and the Stalhelm SA reserve became so violent that Hitler's own mouthpiece, the Voclkischer Beobachter, declared its continued existence intolerable, and SA leaders publicly demanded its dissolution. If this was a violation of Hitler's prerogative, Rosenberg, the editor-in-chief, was as guilty as Roehm. Moreover, the SA leaders were now under the temporary leadership of Roehm's representative, Obergruppenfuehrer Fritz Ritter von Krausser. Roehm, on furlough, was less responsible for this outburst than Hitler himself, the supreme commander of the SA. But undoubtedly the onus of blame came to rest on the absentee's sturdy shoulders.

And so, while the storm was at its height, Hitler had his creatures raise their voices in a song of moderation, a warning to trouble-makers on both sides not to interfere with the Fuehrer's will.

Goering, in a speech to the Prussian State Council on 19 June in Potsdam, said, "If the Fuehrer wishes a second revolution, then we will be on the streets tomorrow. If he does not wish it, then we will crush everybody who tries to make such a revolution against his will."

A remarkable 'warning' came from the pinched mouth of Rudolf Hess on 25 June. In a radio speech over a nation-wide hook-up, Hitler's deputy voiced the Chancellor's view, hitting directly both at the reactionaries and at the provocateurs who under the, guise of the 'Second Revolution' were aiming to start a rebellion against the National Socialist revolution. "Some day," said Hess, "Hitler might deem it necessary to drive developments ahead through revolutionary methods, but the revolution must be steered by him alone. Hitler is the great strategist of the Revolution; he knows the limits of what can be attained at a particular time, with the means at hand and under existing circumstances. He acts after close and ice-cold appraisal of the situation, often seeming only to serve the moment, yet always pursuing the ultimate aims of the Revolution ... Woe to him who breaks faith, and thinks to serve the Revolution through rebellion! Woe to him who clumsily tramples the Fuehrer's strategic plans in the hope of quicker results ! "

Such 'warnings' must have reached Roehm even in seclusion in Wiessee, not far from Munich. Probably he did not know of Hitler's interview on 25 June in the News Chronicle, in which the Fuehrer indicated that he might separate himself from old friends 'of the first hour,'- or of the report of a correspondent printed on the same date in the National Zeitung of Basle to the effect that preparations were being made for Hindenburg's death, that laws allowing Hitler to combine in himself the offices of Chancellor and President had been drafted, and that Hitler had decided to eliminate all 'national bolshevists' - an interesting piece of news for the City of London and Wall Street.

Two things, however, must have convinced Roehm of his impending fate. The first was Blomberg's leading article on the front page of the V. B. of 28 June: the

Reichswehr Minister declared that the army's role in the Third Reich was clear and unequivocal, that it acknowledged the new State and stood behind the new leadership. The second was the infamous exclusion of Roehm, an officer of the old army, the man on whose shoulders Hitler had risen to power, from the ranks of the 'National Union of German Officers.' It was a deadly insult, an irreparable blow to a Reichsminister and Hitler's chief of staff, and it could hardly have been dealt him without the consent of Hitler and the Reichswehr.

Whatever he may have thought, he must have known then that Hitler had outwitted him, 'the soldier who knew no compromise.' But he could scarcely have had an inkling of the end Hitler had in store for him when, in one of his last statements, Roehm said: "The Storm Troops are ready to die for the ideal of the swastika."

At any rate, a notice went out summoning all the SA leaders throughout the Reich to appear in Wiesse - Roehm's retreat - on 30 June for an important conference. Whether the call was sent on Roehm's or on Hitler's initiative will be discussed later.

Events moved swiftly toward the ignoble last act of the drama. The atmosphere was now sufficiently charged: the radicals feared a possible putsch on the part of the Reaktion, who in turn dreaded the outbreak of the 'Second Revolution.' Hitler was still keeping in the background.

On 28 June, Hitler flew with Goering to Essen, to attend the wedding of Staatsrat Terboven. Goering returned to Berlin on the 29th, and Goebbels joined the Fuehrer, who had embarked on a round of visits to labour-camps in the Rhineland 'in order not to warn the traitors, so that the plan to carry out a thorough purge could be laid down in all details.' This the little Doctor confided to his public in a radio-recital on 1 July.

In his apologia before the Reichstag, the Fuehrer later declared: "At one o'clock at night (the night of 29-30) I received two alarming despatches of the most urgent nature from Berlin and Munich … At two in the morning I flew to Munich. Minister-President Goering meanwhile had already received the order … immediately to take analogous measures in Berlin and Prussia in case of the action of purging."

It is history today that the Reichswehr had been under a state of alarm in the whole Reich since 25 June, and the SS since 28 June.

Hitler declared that he had decided "to go personally to a pre-arranged meeting of SA leaders in Wiessee," an admission that Roehm's last act - if Roehm's it was - had not been secretive and therefore not conspiratory. Hitler, as supreme leader of the SA, had the right to preside at any SA meeting, anywhere and at any time. Dr. Otto Strasser reports that he personally saw a telegram which the adjutant of an executed SA Gruppenfuehrer showed him. It ran: 'All Obergruppen and Gruppenfuehrer are ordered to appear in the staff-quarters of the chief of staff in Wiessee at 10 a.m. on 30 June. ADOLF HITLER.'

It is of course not impossible that Hitler convoked the meeting himself. It is more likely, however, that Roehm, now thoroughly alarmed at his exposed position, called this meeting to discuss his untenable situation with Hitler in the presence of the highest SA leaders. But it is incredible that Roehm was intending to put into effect at Wiessee the coup that Hitler accused the dead man of but never even attempted to prove. If he had really been preparing a putsch against Hitler's will or a complot against his life, the seasoned veteran certainly would not have waited completely helpless in a quiet little mountain retreat. Though no match for Hitler in political cunning, he was no novice. One thing, however, is obvious: if Hitler had refused to listen to what Roehm considered his legitimate demands, Wiessee would have been the prelude to the final showdown.

Reaching Munich at four in the morning of go June, Hitler was informed that the SA leaders residing there had already been either killed or arrested. He then set out for Wiessee, heavily guarded by SS men riding in armoured cars before and behind his cavalcade. With him were Dr. Goebbels, Major Buch, Wilhelm Brueckner-Roehm's former friend and confidant, now Hitler's adjutant - Julius Schaub, Sepp Dietrich, Christian Weber, and Emil Maurice. They arrived at the Gasthaus Heinzlbauer about six o'clock.

While his companions' stormed' the rooms of Heines and other SA leaders, Hitler pounded with the handle of his dog-whip on the door of Roehm's room. "Open the door!" he yelled.

Roehm's sleepy voice answered. "Yes, but who is it?"

"It's I-Hitler! Let me in!"

"What! You already? I thought you weren't coming before noon"-and Roehm opened the door. Hitler met him with a flood of abuse, and Roehm, coming to himself in anger, began to roar back at him. He was being handcuffed when the innkeeper, awakened by the uproar, appeared on the scene with a "Heil Hitler" on his trembling lips. " Na Ja, Gruess Gott!" said Roehm, and the Fuehrer asked that the disturbance be excused.

The cavalcade took the road back to Munich with Roehm and the SA leaders as prisoners. Whenever other SA leaders were encountered driving their cars toward Wiessee, Hitler arrested them. Still others were gathered in as they arrived at the railway station in Munich, coming from all parts of the Reich.

The death-caravan reached the Brown House, which had been occupied by the SS. Rudolf Hess was waiting there with everything in readiness, and Hitler had only to pass sentence, which he did looking rather seedy and shouting himself hoarse. The condemned men were transported to the old Stadelheim prison and there were shot by SS squads under the command of Major Buch.

Roehm was locked in a cell with a revolver-a last act of grace. The Press of the world reported his suicide. But he declined to do Hitler this favour, and on

THE 1935 NAZI PARTY DAY

Hitler, a miniscule figure on the tribune, addresses the SA and the SS in the Luitpold-Arena in Nuremberg. In the foreground are the assembled standards.

1 July, according to a laconic statement published in the Voelkischer Beobachter on the following day, he was killed. A leader of the SS shot Roehm in his cell, to be rewarded a few days later for his heroic deed by promotion to the post of 'Obergruppenfuehrer.'

Ernst Roehm had met his end in the very prison where he had been incarcerated eleven years earlier for his valiant efforts in support of Hitler in the 'Beer Hall Putsch.' He was sentenced to death, branded as traitor, and traduced in his grave as criminal and beast by the man who only a few months before had appointed him Reichsminister in his cabinet and had praised him for his imperishable services, thanking destiny for permitting him to number such men as Roehm among his friends and comrades-in-arms.

It is not my wish to make an entire martyr of Roehm. He was admittedly shaping plans which aimed to influence the trend of the Nazi revolution. But compared to others more fortunate, an honest revolutionary who always ranked the idea above the leader, and Germany highest of all. He was incapable of treason. Some day history will affirm that he deserved a better fate.

Men who were not SA leaders and not Nazis also met sudden death. Gustav von Kahr, the former minister-president of Bavaria, was now seventy-three. Eleven years earlier he had been chiefly responsible for the frustration of Hitler's 'Beer Hall Putsch.' He was dragged from bed in his nightshirt. Days later, his mutilated body was found in a swamp near Dachau, not far from Munich.

Meanwhile the chief hunter of the Reich was busy in Berlin. Most of Goering's quarry were killed in the former Kadettenanstalt Lichterfelde, then the barracks of the Hitler SS Leibstandarte.

The story goes that Karl Ernst, believing to the last that Hitler had also been betrayed, fell with ' Hell Hitler' on his lips. Hitler and Goering had been guests of honour at his wedding. If another story is to be credited, however, he must have foreseen a violent end. Apparently there exists a document, signed by him and deposited in a safe place for publication in case he should meet an unnatural death, which gives details of the actual Reichstag fire and raises grave accusations against prominent persons. It was first published, I believe, in 1934 by the Editions Du Carrefour, a semi-Communist publisher, in Paris. Text and tenor of the document appear genuine. .

At one-thirty o'clock on the afternoon of 30 June, five Gestapo officials called at Gregor Strasser's home. Strasser was at lunch with his family. They told him to come along; when he asked why, he was informed that he was suspected of treasonous activities and that his office at Schering-Kahlbaum was to be searched. When they arrived at the building, however, he was handed over to a waiting SS detachment. They drove with him into the Grunewald, a forest near Berlin, and there brutally beat him to death. That is one version; the other has it that he was taken to the basement of Gestapo headquarters and there was shot in the neck; when it was found that he still lived, he was killed by blows with gun-butts.

His widow tried in vain to get in touch with Hitler, Frick, and Goering, who had been in her house hundreds of times; Hitler was even the god-father of Gregor's twin sons. On 7 July she received an urn containing her husband's ashes. It bore the number 16 and the inscription: 'God with us! 'His death was kept a secret and was never officially admitted. Widow and relatives were forbidden to put an announcement of it in the Press.

Even Gregor Strasser's lawyer, Dr. Voss, was killed in his office when he refused to surrender documents entrusted to his care concerning Strasser's conflict with Hitler. Characteristically, Strasser had ignored a warning to deposit these papers in safe-keeping abroad - a fact which indicates that he had not I even thought of a coup against the State or against Hitler.

Obeleutnant Schulz, Strasser's right-hand man, was taken for a ride and thrown out on the road with the words: 'Now run, you swine!' And Schulz, fifteen times wounded, one of the very few men in the German army to become an officer for bravery under fire, ran for his life. Five bullets mowed him down, and he was left for dead, lying in his blood. Regaining consciousness, he dragged himself to the road, to be found hours later by a passing car. He was taken to safety, and later escaped into Switzerland.

Dr. Alexander Glaser, Strasser's former chief of staff, was shot at the door of his house in Munich and died in the Schwabing hospital. A fortnight after his family had buried his body, his brother was handed a tin of ashes and informed that they were Glaser's ashes. Here was Schlamperei in its grimmest manifestation!

Oberleutnant Rossbach, the famous Frei-Korps leader and Hitler's ally in bygone days, had parted company with him after the Fuehrer's return from Landsberg and had held aloof even after Hitler's rise to power, making no bones about his sentiments, especially for Goering, whom he utterly despised. Long afterwards, the bodies of the stiff-necked old fighter, his son, and his chauffeur, were found in a wood near Muchberg in Brandenburg.

Early in the afternoon of the bloody Saturday, four men of Goering's bodyguard stopped their car at the villa of General von Schleicher, former Chancellor of the Reich. They entered, and within a few minutes both Schleicher and his wife were dead.

As usual, two versions exist. One of them is Goering's. His statement to foreign newspapermen on 1 July declared that Schleicher had been killed because, finding himself faced with arrest, he had attempted 'a lightning assault on the men who had been ordered to arrest him.' That explanation would not have accounted for the murder of Schleicher's wife, and indeed Goering did not even bother to mention her.

The other version is embodied in a letter alleged to have been authored by Schleicher's old comrades-generals and staff officers of the Reichswehr - and to have been sent to Hindenburg under date of 18 July 1934. Demanding rehabilitation of Schleicher's honourable name and punishment of those guilty of the crime, the document related that a valet showed the four visitors to the reception-room; when the General and his wife entered, they were instantly shot down, without a word of warning. Disapproval was expressed of the attitude of Reichswehr Minister von Blomberg, whose responsibility it was, as representative of the army in the Government, to uphold the honour of the army, which was also the honour of the nation. The protest was doubtless occasioned by Blomberg's order to the army on 1 July, in which he had declared: 'With soldier-like resolution and characteristic courage, the Fuehrer himself has attacked and crushed the traitors and mutineers. The Wehrmacht, as bearer of arms for the entire people, aloof from inner political fights, will thank him with devotion and loyalty.'

Intriguer though Schleicher was, he was certainly no traitor to his country. Six months later, on 3 January 1935, at a meeting in Berlin of the leading officers of the German army, he was solemnly exonerated, and his death was lamented as a terrible mistake.

So much for the roll-call of blood. It has been concerned only with figures prominent in these pages. How many the unfortunates were will never be known. The official statements of Hitler, Goering, Goebbels, and Hess present a maze of contradictions. Hitler himself admitted only seventy-seven, but from all that has since leaked out it can be affirmed that from eight hundred to twelve hundred were put to death. Among them were a Pour Le Merite officer, officers who carried scars from the battle-fields of the great war, political 'suspects' and rivals, men who knew too much, and victims of purely personal revenge.

"Mutinies are broken according to iron laws which remain eternally the same," proclaimed the Fuehrer. "...In this hour I was responsible for the fate of the German nation, and therefore the supreme court of the German people, during these twenty-four hours, consisted of myself." He played furiously on the theme of his moral indignation at the utter corruptness and depravity of Roehm and his circle, which had imposed on him the duty of purging the Party and Germany of such rotten elements.

Hitler and Goebbels and Goering voiced their disgust over 'the shameless picture - Heines in bed with a homosexual youth.'

Not one of the Nazi chieftains had the courage to condemn the outrage. Without exception, Rosenberg included, Hitler's mamelukes sent their leader telegrams of undying gratitude and devotion. The only note of dissent was the Reichswehr's exoneration of Schleicher. No voice was raised in defence of the dead Nazis.

The nation remained amazingly calm. State and Party officials bowed before the 'inscrutable will' of the Fuehrer when a nation-wide broadcast publicized Hindenburg's telegrams of congratulation, thanking Hitler and Goering for crushing 'traitorous machinations' through 'resolute energy and courageous personal action,' and for 'rescuing the German people from grave danger.' In black on white, the newspapers printed Hitler's official amnesty, a decree passed by the Cabinet: 'The measures taken on 30 June and on 1 and 2 July 1934, for the suppression of acts of treason, are legalized as necessary measures for the defence of the State.'

The supreme court of the German people acquitted itself. There was satisfaction among the 'Haves' over the liquidation of the dreaded second revolution. On the whole, there was, for the time being at least, almost an atmosphere of gratification throughout the Reich. A revealing commentary on the force of 'the bonds of interests,' on the cowardice, forgetfulness, and philistinism of man, on his complex of envy and his indifference!

Time marches on! Great men must not be bothered with bagatelles. What is a little Blood-Purge beside the Bolshevik terror that has cost millions of lives? The world soon forgets. New headlines eclipse the old. It was time now to create some new ones, time to make the Anschluss an accomplished fact. But the Austrian adventure on 25 July ended in a terrible fiasco. The whole world held the Fuehrer responsible, at least in a sense for the murder of little Chancellor Dollfuss, friend of the Mussolini whose Popolo d'Italia now openly called the Nazis' assassins and pederasts.'

Yet Hitler's fabulous luck did not desert him. A week later he was saved by Hindenburg's timely death. The decease of the Field-Marshal was published by the German Press on 2 August, together with a law combining the functions of Chancellor and President and transferring the authority of the President to Adolf Hitler. A plebiscite was prescribed for 10 August: the German people could then decide for or against this new law. The Reichswehr was immediately sworn in to the new Commander-in-Chief.

Now all that remained undone was to utilize the husk of that 'fabulous reputation.' The Field-Marshal's funeral must furnish grandiose and solemn propaganda for the coming plebiscite. Even as he lay heavily in his flag-draped coffin on the gun-carriage drawn by six black horses, Hindenburg was exploited by 'the Bohemian Corporal.' Eulogized by his successor as the 'most venerable nobleman and soldier ... eternal patron and protector of the German Reich and the German nation,' the 'Old One' went to his final rest in the mammoth war-memorial at Tannenburg, birthplace of the Hindenburg legend.

"Departed General," said Hitler, "enter now into Valhalla."

A few days before the plebiscite, the German voters were acquainted with the 'Hindenburg-Testament,' which closed with the old Field-Marshal's approval of Hitler. And the German people endorsed the Reichsfuehrer with an overwhelming majority, affirming their trust in the man who had declared:

"I gladly assume responsibility for such mistakes as may be charged to me. They fall within the scope of human frailty. But I have never committed a deed or an act which I was convinced would not redound to the benefit of the German people. Ever since I first took my stand in the thick of this political battle, I have been actuated by only one motive-so help me God, only one thought: Germany!"

Two weeks later, at the annual Party Day in Nuremberg the opening ceremonies followed the established procedure. The guard of honour marched up and stood at present-arms. The Party banners on the stage formed great splotches offered around the Blood Flag of the Munich Putsch. Trumpets sounded assembly. Standing at Hitler's side, Victor Lutze, the new chief of staff of the SA, called the roll of the dead. The names were called two at a time, as if a company were mustering for duty. As each name rang out, the assembled guard answered with a loud shout of 'Here' in token that the souls of the two hundred and twenty-seven heroes fallen 'in the heroic battle of the SA in ten glorious years of fight' were present and carrying on. After each two names, trumpets sounded a fanfare of honour. When the last man had been raised from his grave, there was another brassy flourish, the standards were raised, and the massed band,; played the 'Horst Wessel' song.

But no one called the roll of the ghosts hovering over the stage. There were no trumpets for the names of Ernst Roehm, Gregor Strasser, and over five hundred SA men murdered in the brief space of thirty-six hours and now traduced in their graves.

XLIII

AN INVINCIBLE FORCE

itler, by Louis Bertrand,[1] shows how the element of time and the logic of facts, how power, pomp, and propaganda, can affect even the sceptical mind of a Frenchman. In this interesting study of the French-German problem, a member of the Academie Francaise, an honest patriot and fervent Catholic, strongly advocates a French-German entente. Another German defeat and the triumph of a French-Russian-Balkan coalition would lead, he says, to the complete Bolshevization of Europe.

Bertrand was a guest of honour at the 1935 Party Day in Nuremberg, which proclaimed: 'Adolf Hitler is Germany, Germany is Adolf Hitler.'

The Frenchman's impressions of Hitler and his show are a revelation of the power of mass-suggestion. Admiringly lie exclaims that in fifteen years-about the same time it had taken Bonaparte to place the imperial crown on his head-the little orphan from Braunau had become the unchallenged chief of a nation of sixty-five million people; had not only made a revolution but had restored to Germany her national pride, her faith in her destiny, and her military strength and prestige. He had torn to pieces treaties reducing her to a perpetual state of inferiority. He had re-established her liberty!

Scoffing at the des on-dits about Hitler's early end, Bertrand declares it dangerous to believe that Nazi Germany will soon collapse. France must realize that Hitler is here to stay. The obedient and disciplined Germany of today is a Germany more united, more centralized than ever before. Moralists may judge the man and his conduct, but France is concerned with politics, not with morals. France is interested not in Hitler as an individual, but in the work to which he has set his name, the great collective force he represents.

Describing the delirium of the frenzied crowds, Bertrand asserts that no hero ever received such adulation as this little man in the brown shirt, with the air of a worker; it was an adoration that was something more than mere popularity: it was religion. Hitler, in the eyes of his admirers, was a prophet, exalted as the Chosen of God. Though colossal, an the demonstrations escaped vulgarity, combining popular appeal, and great simplicity. The Frenchman depicts the throng of hundreds of thousands in the immense Zeppelin meadow, the invisible Wagnerian orchestra swelling into the March of the Nibelungen, the array of twenty thousand standards moving forward in rhythm with the triumphal music, dipping in one unanimous

1 Artheme Fayard & Cie, Paris, 1936.

salutation before the minuscule silhouette in the brown shirt, scarcely discernible high above the tribune-a bareheaded little man who has the audacity to assume the stupendous task of ruling a whole people; who salutes them now with arm outstretched in a sovereign gesture, but wears no crown, no white, gold-embroidered tunic of a Roman emperor, carries no Marshal's baton. In this Frenchman's view, it is Hitler's extreme simplicity which pleases, his total absence of pose, his air of comradeship, and the stern energy of his face, revealing both the chief and the man risen from the ranks. At first the Fuehrer appears quite ordinary, but the moment he mounts the platform or salutes his men, he is another person; 'caught by the Éclat of eyes centred on him,' he is transfigured. For the Germany which acclaims him he becomes Germany itself One no longer sees Hitler, but those sixty-five millions whose minds he has stirred to the joy of renascence.

"There we were, a few Frenchmen watching, our hearts oppressed, but nevertheless overwhelmed by the beauty of the spectacle. And we said to ourselves: 'Why don't we see this in France?'...These multitudes, this discipline-above all, this unanimity creating the effect of an invincible force! ..."

An invincible force? Perhaps it is. But whither is it tending?

It would be absurd for one absent from Germany for three years to predict specific developments-and prophecies are always apt to be coloured by wishful thinking. The Hitler-Nazi problem, with all that it involves, is so complex, the European chessboard changes so rapidly and by such devious moves, that it is difficult to foresee even a probable outcome. Moreover, reports from and about Nazi Germany, comments on current events or political speeches, on prevailing conditions or supposed symptoms, are often contradictory and misleading.

In all the Fascist states, particularly in Italy and Germany, individualistic capitalism is fast proceeding into collectives, by the road of state capitalism. This development is a serious blow to the economic royalists who backed the Fascist International without understanding the tremendous pressure of the problem of the 'Haves and Have-nots' on both individuals and nations. The newly legalized concept of property rights in Germany differs radically from the ideas of orthodox capitalism, though Marxian groups in particular persist in the erroneous contention that the Hider system is a phase of the reaction designed to enforce the stabilization of capitalism.

This fallacy is punctured in an article, 'The Destruction of German Capitalism,' written by 'V',[2] obviously a competent German intimately connected with German affairs.

For years, Fascist propaganda has offered Fascism as a safeguard against Communism, and Communism has exposed Fascism as its arch foe and antithesis. In fact, the world has never seen two supposedly hostile economic and social systems

---

2 *Foreign Affairs, July 1937.*

more alike in essentials, both of practice and ideology, than National Socialism and Communism ...

Whoever tries to arrive at a fair and well-balanced opinion of the Hitler system must keep in mind especially this: There is no legal limit to government or party interference in the routine life of business any more than there is a Habeas Corpus Act for the protection of civil liberties. This kind of totalitarianism, every day and everywhere, goes far beyond the written regulations.

According to this writer, everything planned by the Nazi Government is done in the interest of 'Wehrwirtschaft'-defence economy. This planned economy signifies complete State control of production, agriculture, and commerce; of exports, imports, and foreign markets; of prices, foreign exchange, credit, rates of interest, profits, capital investments, and merchandizing of all kinds. All the financial, indeed, all the vital resources of the nation, are reserved for the needs of the Government, the Reichsbank being the supreme control agency in all matters of finance. In fact, National Socialism has created a war-economy, subjecting the entire social and economic fabric to Government regulation.

In all fairness, it must be said that this system increases the security of the individual worker-provided-he does not violate Nazi rules-almost as much as it -restricts- his liberties. No doubt the workers also benefit by numerous social welfare provisions: social insurance, cheaper housing, cheaper food, and, in the event of need, first-aid from State or Nazi welfare organizations. In addition, most workers now get vacations with pay, and organized recreation provided by the 'Strength through joy' organization of the Labour Front-the largest leisure organisation in the world, with its own fleet of special vacation steamers and many other facilities affording cheap vacation trips inside and outside Germany.

'V' brings out another factor which' must be borne in mind if one is to understand the present status and attitude of the German bourgeoisie and proletariat:

...The economic and social policy of National Socialism does not include a single feature not conceited or practised in Germany in the past. The political philosophy and practice of National Socialism are exclusively the incarnation of familiar traits of German history. The German conception of capitalism was always essentially different from the Anglo-Saxon, because it was developed under an entirely different conception of state and government. . . . During the war a totalitarian regime was established for the first time. . . .

What National Socialism built up is war economy once more, but war economy on a Socialist ideological foundation. National Socialism is as genuine Socialism as it is genuine Nationalism. And this regime has inherited a full-fledged machinery from the improvised episode of democracy which struggled hopelessly for life from the hour of its birth in 1918. It was the democratic Republican, Government in Germany that was already in control of the banks, the railways, the power sources, the urban transit system, the municipal gas and water, vast housing developments, and large parts of heavy industries. How many German industrialists were still independent of the Government in 1932, before Hitler came into power? How many could afford to arouse the ire of a determined government, to challenge it by refusing co-operation? Hardly a handful.

And the workers? Should German workers, brought up in Marxist ideology, in the pursuance of collectivist ideals, trained to demand public ownership, should they oppose a totalitarian regime which promised to complete what their own men had left undone? Could they fight for individual liberties on economic and social grounds? Hitler had only to reap where his foes had sown. Capitalism is last where it is not built on liberalism and democracy. And liberalism and democracy are lost where they fail to convince the people of the necessity of capitalism as the only available economic safeguard of political, intellectual, and Spiritual freedom.

A somewhat opposing 'View is that of Otto D. Tolischus, Berlin correspondent of the New York Times, who claims in a recent article that Big Business is favoured by Nazi economics. Admitting the growing 'socialization of the national income,' he says:

German industry is undergoing a process of 'concentration' which tends to concentrate industrial control into a few mammoth concerns. But in this also lurks a menace, for it will make it all the easier for the Nazi regime to 'socialize' industry if it ever recalls the plank of that 'eternal programme,' which demands 'nationalization of all corporate enterprises (trusts).'

The class that has fared the worst so far is the great middle class-officials, small shopkeepers, and artisans--who were Hitler's first enthusiastic followers. Officials, unlike private employees, have had no improvement in their nominal earnings. The shop-keeper, who hoped to get rich from the elimination of Jewish competition has been forced to absorb the difference between increased wholesale prices and fixed retail prices, and small artisans are being crowded to the wall for lack of raw materials.

As the retailer's margin of profit is shrinking steadily ... there is a great dying-off of independent middle-class enterprise. But this is also in line with the Nazis' present policy. Both the commercial and the artisan classes are being combed out for the additional workers needed in industry and agriculture.

Tolischus poses a question:

What did the German people as individuals get out of their economic recovery? What is the national dividend? In the answer to this question lies a good part of the dissatisfaction smouldering behind the cheering and flag-waving front of the adherents of the regime, for there is a growing realization that, so far, at least, the main beneficiaries of the great national effort and all its strain and stress have been the State and the regime rather than the people.

Germany's economic recovery, her recapture of military power and prestige, which have restored her to the status of a Big Power mighty enough to demand a new division of the world to meet her needs and ambitions, is the 'German miracle' that impresses tourists and foreigners abroad. "And this miracle is all the more remarkable," says Tolischus, "because it was performed without foreign aid and even in the face of foreign opposition, making it appear that Germany actually pulled herself up by her bootstraps.

"But to the well-informed the 'miracle' is no miracle, because Germany's economic recovery is not based on natural economic processes or on a sound economic basis but on a boom wholly financed by the State."

Whether the Soviet and Nazi systems are alike, and to what extent, whether the Nazi war economy-the complete regimentation and militarization of every phase of German life-is genuine socialism, are questions which lie outside the scope of this book.

The writer may properly permit himself to observe, however, that the present Nazi-State-Socialism is not German Socialism. The entire Hitler system, with its Goebbels and its Goerings, is not German. The real German Nazi revolutionaries never intended that Germans should be degraded as serfs of an arbitrary Party dictatorship, surrendering body and soul to a single leader, and cringing in Asiatic servility before an un-German dictator.

Most of the practical application of the Nazi programme is an imitation of other systems, whereas the Nazi programme itself remains an unfinished product. Since about 1927, the Hitler Party as a whole has made little if any spiritual progress, and has systematically barred every spiritual development of the political concept in its own ranks, with the result that the vast majority have become a flock of bleating party-sheep.

With Gregor Strasser dead, Rosenberg is the only living Nazi who is an original thinker of importance, chiefly in the ethical and metaphysical fields. Hitler himself has contributed no new concepts to the complex of ideas called National Socialism. They were all in the air, many of them before Hitler was born. What he did was to translate those ideas into terms the masses could understand.

Of the three important dictatorships, that of the Soviets has been in power for twenty years, Mussolini's for fifteen years, Hider's for less than five. The Nazi regime has borrowed many administrative and propaganda devices from the Bolshevist and Fascist regimes, from the latter especially. Il Duce set the model for the administrative and propaganda technique of the Nazi dictatorship, yet in the most essential point, the technique of Revolution, Hitler refused to follow his master. He repeated Bonaparte's fundamental error on the eighteenth Brurmaire, the respect for ' legality.'

The corruption of our times and the mendacity of his opponents helped, of course, to make Hitler what" he is. But while he still strove for the highest aims, he himself became corrupted by his willingness to employ ignoble means. If Christianity must be reformed, if religion must be brought to the level of the scientific findings of to-day, if there is no room for the Christian Cross and the Swastika Cross in the same realm, then the struggle must be waged with honesty and truth. Christianity may be conquered only by elevating the moral plane of the people and not by lowering it.

True enough, cathedrals have been built with stolen money and forged documents, religions founded on falsifications and lies-but at a time when cinema and radio, headlines and telegraph did not exist to tell one side of the globe how the other was living and dying. It has yet to be demonstrated that the twentieth century will permit a Hitler, unique though he may be, to pass into history as the semi-divinity we now see exalted before the German people.

The fraud, the inner contradiction in Hitler, in the last analysis is the underlying conflict with which the whole Hitler system is diseased. It is this great deception, more than anything else, which has made Hitler vulnerable and has discredited his cause in the eyes of the world. History cannot and will not acquit him of guilt.

Just as it was once the tendency to under-rate Hitler the drummer, today there is a disposition to over-rate the dictator. Thus far, luck rather than genius has saved him from wrecking his ship. A series of events he could not foresee has played into his hands: the internal crisis in France and, at about the same time, Dollfuss's capital error of suppressing the anti-Nazi Socialist Party, a stupidity which would have dropped Austria like a ripe plum into Hitler's lap if he had waited instead of spoiling his chance by the clumsy coup d'etat in Vienna. His ghastliest mistakes were overshadowed by Hindenburg's timely death. Mussolini's war with Ethiopia forced both Italy and England to be friendly with Hitler, a situation which put him in an excellent trading position. The death of King George and the subsequent coronation muddle again tied England's hands and allowed him to gain time to re-arm and re-establish Germany's complete sovereignty. To all this luck, was added the unexpected degree of mediocrity and ineptitude displayed by certain statesmen and leaders of Capitalism, Christendom, and Jewry.

Germany's fundamental room-problem still remains The Problem. Nevertheless, Hitler's accomplishments are remarkable. Tremendous progress toward the fulfilment of the goal foreshadowed in Mein Kampf, a militant, regimented Reich dominant in Continental Europe and unchallenged in the world, is undeniable.

Yet his real achievement, the rehabilitation of Germany, is not the miracle of a mental giant, but an accomplishment any forceful leader could have effected with the superb clan of the movement he had behind him and the extraordinary power and authority Hitler has enjoyed from the beginning of his rule. And his rule was made easy by the fact that Germans were willing to renounce their civil liberty, suffer unbelievable hardships, and submit to a dictator at home rather than bow to a dictator from abroad.

Qui trop embrasse mal etreint! Germany is making a gigantic effort to prepare herself economically, militarily, and psychologically for perhaps the greatest war in history, but at the same time is fighting three powers: the Protestant Church, the Vatican, and Jewry. While Mussolini in wise limitation underpinned his new state, building a solid foundation stone upon stone, Hitler is attempting the impossible with inadequate means, refusing to hearken to a greater man who said: "Politics is the art of the possibilities."

'Du gleichst dem Geist, den du begreifst.' You resemble the spirit which you comprehend, said Goethe. In some ways, Hitler resembles his idol, Richard Wagner. The world has forgiven him his weaknesses. Hitler must prove that he also is a Titan before he can be forgiven. Posterity's final verdict will depend more on what he will do in the future than on what he has done in the past. Tempered and mellowed now by the maturity of age, the Fuehrer may still accomplish great things.

The world is suffering from an accumulation of crucial errors through centuries. We are living through the greatest crisis in history-a universal revolution which combines the elements of all previous crises. If ever an epoch needed truth, the courage to face undeniable facts, it is our own. And if ever a man had the unique opportunity to blazon out the truth, to create new standards and values, it was Hitler. Never in history had any great nation surrendered to its leader so completely as the German people to the Fuehrer; never In history did any great man-Mussolini and Stalin included-rule with so much emotional and physical power behind him. At a time when the whole world was craving for leadership, yearning for new values, Hitler failed. In disgracing himself he disgraced his cause, for these are times which need more than Beelzebub to drive out the Devil.

So long as man remains what he is, so long as he does not know how to live in wise harmony with the times and to adjust himself by peaceful change, he will have to endure bad or good dictatorships in periods of emergency, temporarily at least, until wholesome conditions are re-established. Mankind, like the individual man, to recover from the effects of stupid-or immoderate living must submit to a strict regimen, even though muscles and nerves protest against this dictatorial regimentation. The essential in both cases is to choose an honest and competent physician-dictator in order to regain health; then, grown a wiser man, to enjoy liberty again.

APPENDIX

THE PROGRAMME OF THE NATIONAL SOCIALIST GERMAN WORKERS' PARTY

(What follows is reprinted from the official English translation by E. T. S. Dugdale, published by Frz. Eher Nachf., Munich, 1932.)

THE 25 POINTS

The National Socialist German Workers' Party at a great mass meeting on 25 February 1920, in the Hofbräuhaus-Festsaal in Munich announced their Programme to the world.

In section 2 of the Constitution of our Party this Programme is declared to be inalterable.

THE PROGRAMME

The Programme of the German Workers' Party is limited' as to period. The leaders have no intention, once the aims announced in it have been achieved, of setting up fresh ones, merely in order to increase the discontent of the masses artificially, and so ensure the continued existence of the Party.

1. We demand the union of all Germans to form a Great Germany on the basis of the right of the self-determination enjoyed by nations.

2. We demand equality of rights for the German People in its dealings with other nations, and abolition of the Peace Treaties of Versailles and St. Germain.

3. We demand land and territory (colonies) for the nourishment of our people and for settling our superfluous population,

4. None but members of the nation may be citizens of the State. None but those of German blood, whatever their creed, may be members of the nation. No Jew, therefore, may be a member of the nation.

5. Anyone who is not a citizen of the State may live in Germany only as a guest and must be regarded as being subject to foreign laws.

6. The right of voting on the State's government and legislation is to be enjoyed by the citizen of the State alone. We demand therefore that all official appointments, of whatever kind, whether in the Reich, in the country, or in the smaller localities, shall be granted to citizens of the State alone.

We oppose the corrupting custom of Parliament of filling posts merely with a view to party considerations, and without reference to character or capability.

7. We demand that the State shall make it its first duty to promote the industry

and livelihood of Citizens of the State. If It IS not possible to nourish the entire population of the State, foreign nationals (non-citizens of the State) must be excluded from the Reich.

8. All non-German immigration must be prevented. We demand that all non-Germans, who entered Germany subsequent to 2 August 1914, shall be required forthwith to depart from the Reich.

9. All citizens of the State shall be equal as regards rights and duties.

10. It must be the first duty of each citizen of the State to work with his mind or with his body. The activities of the individual may not clash with the interests of the whole, but must proceed within the frame of the community and be for the general good.

We demand therefore :

11. Abolition of incomes unearned by work.

ABOLITION OF THE THRALDOM OF INTEREST

12. In view of the enormous sacrifice of life and property demanded of a nation by every war, personal enrichment due to a war must be regarded as a crime against the nation. We demand therefore ruthless confiscation of all war gains.

13. We demand nationalisation of all businesses which have been up to the present formed into companies (Trusts).

14. We demand that the profits from wholesale trade shall be shared out.

15. We demand extensive development of provision for old age.

16. We demand creation and maintenance of a healthy middle class, immediate communalisation of wholesale business premises, and their lease at a cheap rate to small traders, and that extreme consideration shall be shown to all small purveyors to the State, district authorities and smaller localities.

17. We demand land-reform suitable to our national requirements, passing of a law for confiscation without compensation of land for communal purposes; abolition of interest on land loans, and prevention of all speculation in land.[1]

18. We demand ruthless prosecution of those whose activities are injurious to the common interest. Sordid criminals against the nation, usurers, profiteers, etc., must be punished with death, whatever their creed or race.

19. We demand that the Roman Law, which serves the materialistic world order, shall be replaced by a legal system for all Germany.

1   *On 13 April 1928 Adolf Hitler made the following declaration:*

'It is necessary to reply to the false interpretation on the part of our opponents of Point 17 of the Programme of the N. S. D. A. P.

'Since the N. S. D. A. P. admits the principle of private property, it is obvious that the expression "confiscation without compensation" merely refers to possible legal powers to confiscate, if necessary, land illegally acquired, or not administered in accordance with national welfare. It is directed in accordance with national welfare. It is directed in the first instance against the Jewish companies which speculate in land.

(signed) ADOLF HITLER.
'Munich, 13 April, 1928.'

20. With the aim of opening to every capable and industrious German the possibility of higher education and of thus obtaining advancement, the State must consider a thorough reconstruction of our national system of education. The curriculum of all educational establishments must be brought into line with the requirements of practical life. Comprehension of the State idea (State sociology) must be the school objective, beginning with the first dawn of intelligence in the pupil. We demand development of the gifted children of poor parents, whatever their class or occupation, at the expense of the State.

21. The State must see to raising the standard of health in the nation by protecting mothers and infants, prohibiting child labour, increasing bodily efficiency by obligatory gymnastics and sport~ laid down by law, and by extensive support of clubs engaged in the bodily development of the young.

22. We demand abolition of a paid army and formation of a national army.

23. We demand legal warfare against conscious political lying and its dissemination in the Press. In order to facilitate creation of a German national Press we demand :

(a) that all editors of newspapers and their assistants, employing the German language, must be members of the nation;

(b) that special permission from the State shall be necessary before non-German newspapers may appear. These are not necessarily printed in the German language;

(c) that non-Germans shall be prohibited by law from participating financially in or influencing German newspapers, and that the penalty for contravention of the law shall be suppression of any such newspaper, and immediate deportation of the non-German concerned in it.

It must be forbidden to publish papers which do not conduce to the national welfare. We demand legal prosecution of all tendencies in art and literature of a kind likely to disintegrate our life as a nation, and the suppression of institutions which militate against the requirements above-mentioned.

24. We demand liberty for all religious denominations in the State, so far as they are not a danger to it and do not militate against the moral feelings of the German race.

The Party, as such, stands for positive Christianity, but does not bind itself in the matter of creed to any particular confession. It combats the Jewish-materialist spirit within us and without us, and is convinced that our nation can only achieve permanent health from within on the principle:

THE COMMON INTEREST BEFORE SELF

25. That all the foregoing may be realized we demand the creation of a strong central power of the State. Unquestioned authority of the politically centralized Parliament over the entire Reich and its organization; and formation of Chambers for classes and occupations for the purpose of carrying out the general laws promulgated by the Reich in the various States of the confederation.

The leaders of the Party swear to go straight forward - if necessary to sacrifice their lives - in securing fulfilment of the foregoing Points.

MUNICH, 24 February 1920.

A LETTER FROM MILDRED C. LUDECKE TO CHANCELLOR ADOLF HITLER

128 McLEAN AVE., H. P.,
DETROIT, MICHIGAN
15 January 1934.

Chancellor Adolf Hitler,

Berlin,

Germany

EXCELLENCY :

It is now three months since I have heard from my husband, Kurt Ludecke. I am sure that he would write if he were able, and I cannot persuade myself that he is not living, so I must conclude that for some reason his letters are withheld from me. Does this not seem unnecessarily cruel? Certainly the most autocratic state should respect the feelings of a husband for a wife, and I can think of no possible circumstances that would justify such a ruthless procedure.

Mr. Ludecke has written to me of his previous arrest, from which he was released after the personal intervention of Reichsminister Goering. He has also told me of his subsequent request for an inquiry to clear up the slanderous accusations his enemies made against him. .

It would seem to me that the privilege of defending himself against unjust accusations is one of the fundamental rights of man, without which a state becomes a hunting-ground for the ruthless and unscrupulous, who ruin men for their own personal gain or for their Own personal revenge. But apparently this right has been denied my husband. He has been shut off from his friends and even from his wife, while his enemies are left free to spread their slanderous lies about him. That his enemies should find it necessary to resort to such a desperate expedient as imprisonment to keep the truth from becoming known is, I should think, a - proof of his innocence.

There is nothing in Mr. Ludecke's life, I am sure, to justify such treatment as he has received at the hands of the National Socialists. He has been honourable in all his dealings, and if he can be accused of any sin, it is only that in serving the Cause he has neglected to build for our personal future. But of that sin, I, and not the German State, am the judge.

Apparently all sorts of rumours have been circulated about Mr. Ludecke in order to discredit him, but, as far as I know he has never been given a chance to face his accusers, and apparently no attempt has been made to verify or disprove these rumours. I cannot imagine what these lies could be, but it is very easy for you to discover that he has never come in conflict with the laws of this country. Police records are very carefully kept, and

565

you would be able to discover very quickly that he has never figured in them during his residence here. Moreover, you should know that, as an alien, he would have been deported at the end of his sentence if he had ever been convicted of any crime.

In the face of ridicule and discouragement, at the cost, often, of his means of livelihood, Mr. Ludecke has earnestly and successfully pleaded the National Socialist Cause wherever the opportunity arose. He has won thousands to the Cause, and has gained for it at least the tolerant sympathy of additional thousands. I do not believe a day ever passed but what he tried earnestly to convince someone. This constant, intelligent, sincere personal persuasion has won for the German Cause more staunch friends among the American people than any number of mass meetings could do.

Mr. Ludecke knows Americans and American psychology. He knows that the best means of gaining the sympathy of the American people is usually the least spectacular means. He has realized the magnitude of the task before him, and so has concentrated on the small, opinion-forming minority: writers, speakers, newspaper¬men and the like. You probably remember Mr. Ellery Walter, the American writer and lecturer, who first became interested in National Socialism through Mr. Ludecke. And there are hundreds like him. It is to the great advantage of the enemies of the National Socialist State that he has not been allowed to continue his publicity work in the United States.

Mr. Ludecke's task last spring was not an easy one. He had no active encouragement from Germany, and he was surrounded in this country by German officials hostile to the National Socialist Cause. You probably remember that it was due to his efforts that Consul Schwartz of New York was removed. Also, it must be a source of great relief to you that, also due to Mr. Ludecke's recommendations, the National Socialist Party in America had been dissolved before Herr Spanknoebl's fiasco in New York and his ignominious flight after a warrant had been issued for his arrest.

I might also remind you that, except for the few months in 1932-33 when Mr. Ludecke was the representative of the National Socialist Press in Washington, he has worked entirely without compensation and often to the detriment of his personal interests. Whereas your colleagues in Germany have not only secured from their political convictions a livelihood, but have also felt the thrill of working together with others for a great Cause and know the satisfaction of praise for work well done, Mr. Ludecke has lived in the greatest financial uncertainty has worked alone and unrecognized and has suffered the ridicule and dislike that always attend the prophet of a strange religion in a strange land.

I am not pleading for Mr. Ludecke's release as an act of mercy. I am demanding, as an act of justice, that he be allowed to face his accusers; that these slanderous rumours be brought out into the light of day and the truth be revealed. Then if this is done I am sure my husband will stand fully vindicated.

I beg of you to do this for the sake of justice and the honour of the German State.

Respectfully (signed)

MILDRED C. LUDECKE.

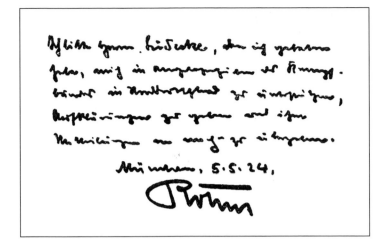

Roehm's carte de visite, dated Munich, May 5, 1924, authorizing the author to represent him in North Germany

Conclusive evidence that the author was Hitler's personal prisoner is this letter of 12 January 1935 signed by Reichsleiter Philip Bouhler, general secretary of the Party and chief of the Chancellery of the Fuehrer, and addressed to Ludwig Glaser, who was one of a committee which, after the author's escape from Germany, tried by direct appeal to Hitler to settle the Ludecke case in a way acceptable to both parties.

MUCH ESTEEMED HERR GLASER :

Your two letters of 15 and 21 December have been referred to me for duly qualified action by the chairman of the Highest Party Court (Major Buch). Unfortunately I received these papers only today. It is, therefore, especially because the Fuehrer is not at present in Berlin, a technical impossibility to settle this matter within the time limit prescribed by you. Please inform Herr Ludecke that I shall dispose of his case as quickly as possible. After examination of the proposals submitted, I shall let you know at once what decision is taken, and I can inform you that competent persons have already been occupied with this matter for some time.

You may rest assured that everything will be done here to settle this matter; I can only ask you to be patient beyond the proposed terminal date, in view of the time elapsed.

With German greetings and HEIL HITLER !

(Signed) P. H. BOUHLER.

Berlin W 8, den 12. Januar 1935.

Der Chef
der Kanzlei des Führers
der N.S.D.A.P.

Herrn
Ludwig Glaser,
445 East 84
New York N.Y.

Sehr geehrter Herr Glaser!

Durch den Vorsitzenden des Obersten Parteigerichts wurden mir Ihre beiden Schreiben vom 15. und 21.Dez. zur zuständigen Behandlung zugeleitet. Leider bin ich erst heute in den Besitz dieser Unterlagen gekommen. Es ist deshalb insbesondere, weil der Führer zur Zeit von Berlin abwesend ist, rein technisch unmöglich, die Angelegenheit zu dem von Ihnen vorgeschlagenen Zeitpunkt zu erledigen. Ich bitte Sie Herrn Lüdecke mitzuteilen, dass seine Angelegenheit nunmehr von mir so rasch als möglich bearbeitet werden wird. Ich werde Sie nach Prüfung der übermittelten Vorschläge von der getroffenen Entscheidung ehestens in Kenntnis setzen und darf Ihnen mitteilen, dass sich massgebende Stellen bereits seit einiger Zeit mit der Angelegenheit befassen.
Sie dürfen versichert sein, dass hier Alles getan wird, um die Angelegenheit zu bereinigen, nur muss ich Sie bitten, sich mit Rücksicht auf die vorgeschrittene Zeit noch über den vorgeschlagenen Termin hinaus zu gedulden.

Mit deutschem Gruss und Heil Hitler!

The certificate given the author by Kommandant Grutzeck of the Brandenburg concentration camp for presentation to the Kommandant at Oranienburg. It reads:

CERTIFICATE

The prisoner in protective custody Kurt Ludecke has been a member of the N.S.D.A.P. for many years, and has been so prostrated psychically and nervously by his incarceration that it has been necessary to transfer him to the hospital, where he has remained until today. It would be desirable if Ludecke could also be placed in the hospital in the concentration camp there.

(Signed) GRUTZECK.

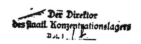

Der Direktor
des staatl. Konzentrationslagers
Nr. 1 . . . / . .

Brandenburg (Havel), den 29. 5. 34
Fernsprecher Nr. 1715
Postscheckkonto Berlin 129 078
Reichsbankgirokonto

B e s c h e i n i g u n g !
-.-.-.-.-.-.-.-.-.-.-.-.-.-.-.-.

Der Schutzhäftling   Kurt   L u e d e c k e   ist langjähriges
Mitglied der N.S.D.A.P. und ist durch die Inhaftierung seelich
und mit den Nerven so heruntergekommen, dass er in das Lazarett
eingeliefert werden musste, wo er sich bis heute noch befand.

Es wäre wünschenswert, wenn Luedecke auch im dortigen Konzentrati-
onslager im Lazarett übernommen wird.

Kommandant der Lagerwache

A letter from Raymond H. Geist, American Consul in Berlin, replying to the author's wife's inquiry for news of him, at a time when the Gestapo had cut him off from all communication with the outside world. It proves conclusively that he was a political 'prisoner for protective purposes.'

AMERICAN CONSULAR SERVICE

Berlin, Germany, January 3, 1934.

In reply refer to
  File No. 310/800
    RHG:HP

                Mrs. Kurt C.W. Luedecke,
                  128 McLean Avenue,
                    Detroit, Mich.

        Madam:

                The receipt is acknowledged of your letter of
        December 5, 1933, stating that you are an American
        citizen and that your husband is Mr. Kurt G.W.
        Luedecke. You state also that according to the
        information which you have received, he is
        interned at the concentration camp at Branden-
        burg on Havel. Upon the receipt of your letter
        I made inquiries of the chief of the State Secret
        Police and have received a letter, which in trans-
        lation reads as follows:

                "   In reply to your favor of the 16th
                inst. I have the honor to inform you that
                the writer Kurt Luedecke, born in Berlin
                on February 5, 1890, is at present in
                the State concentration camp in Branden-
                burg (Havel). I do not know that Mr.
                Luedecke has not written during the
                last two months. He is permitted to
                correspond in the same measure as all
                other "prisoners for protective purposes".

                It might be advisable in addressing further
        communications to your husband, to send them with
        a covering letter to the Chief of the State Secret
        Police, No. 8 Prinz Albrechtstrasse, Berlin, with
        the request that the letter be forwarded to your
        husband.

                        Very respectfully yours,

                        Raymond H. Geist,
                          American Consul.

570

MORE FROM THE SAME SERIES

Most books from 'The Third Reich from Original Sources' series are edited and endorsed by Emmy Award winning film maker and military historian Bob Carruthers, producer of Discovery Channel's Line of Fire and Weapons of War and BBC's Both Sides of the Line. Long experience and strong editorial control gives the military history enthusiast the ability to buy with confidence.

The series advisor is David McWhinnie, producer of the acclaimed Battlefield series for Discovery Channel. David and Bob have co-produced books and films with a wide variety of the UK's leading historians including Professor John Erickson and Dr David Chandler.

Where possible the books draw on rare primary sources to give the military enthusiast new insights into a fascinating subject.

For more information visit www.pen-and-sword.co.uk